Distributed Operating Systems
The Logical Design

Distributed Operating Systems
The Logical Design

Andrzej Goscinski

University College
The University of New South Wales
Australian Defence Force Academy

ADDISON-WESLEY
PUBLISHING
COMPANY

Sydney · Wokingham, England · Reading, Massachusetts
Menlo Park, California · New York · Don Mills, Ontario
Amsterdam · Bonn · Singapore · Tokyo
Madrid · San Juan

Cover designed by Jan Golembiewski, Australia
Typeset by Quaser Technology Pte. Ltd.
Printed in Singapore.

First printed 1991. Reprinted with corrections 1992 (twice).

National Library of Australia Cataloguing in Publication Data
Goscinski, Andrzej, 1944–
     Distributed operating systems.

     Bibliography.
     Includes index.
     ISBN 0 201 41704 9.

     1. Operating systems (Computers) 2. Electronic data processing – Distributed processing. I. Title.

     005.43

Library of Congress Cataloging-in-Publication Data
Gościński, Andrzej.
     Distributed operating systems: the logical design/Andrzej Goscinski.
        p.   cm.
     Includes bibliographical references and index.
     Undergraduate text.
     ISBN 0-201-41704-9
     1. Distributed operating systems (Computers) 2. System design. I. Title.
QA76.76.063G68 1991
004′.36–dc20   90–47725
                                                                      CIP

To Teresa, Agnieszka, Wojtek,
my mother Jadwiga, and the memory of my father Boleslaw

Preface

Overview

I identified the need for a book on distributed operating systems in the beginning of the 1980s when one of my Ph.D. students started her thesis on methods of resources naming in distributed systems. At the same time our team commenced a project on the design and development of an extension module for heterogeneous centralized operating systems to provide access to remote resources. There was no book or monograph which could be used as an in-depth introduction to network and distributed operating systems for a research student, to identify research and design issues of such systems, or to find guidelines for a designer. I found myself in a nearly identical situation six years later, in 1987, when trying to create an image of a distributed operating system to present research and design issues to postgraduate students and to members of my research and project team carrying out a project on the development of a research oriented distributed operating system. The situation was then much better because several experimental distributed operating systems had since been developed and the results of a number of projects had been reported. There was an excellent paper by A. Tanenbaum and R. van Renesse, many other papers by distinguished researchers working in the area of distributed operating systems, a couple of books summarizing projects carried out on the development of distributed operating systems, and one book on the design of such systems (we had the opportunity to use it in Australia at the end of 1987). Unfortunately, these papers and the majority of the books are devoted to a limited number of research and design issues and are oriented towards research specialists rather than postgraduate students. The creation of an overall image of distributed operating systems, the identification of all the research and design issues, and an exposition of the state of the art based on them, requires detailed study even for a person with a good knowledge of centralized operating systems and communication protocols. Moreover, preparation of lectures for postgraduate students is a complicated and time consuming task.

Motivated by these factors, and after completion of the first draft of my lecture notes on distributed operating systems and their problems, I decided to do research towards the preparation of a book on distributed operating systems.

Audience

This monograph has been developed chiefly for postgraduate students who are expected to have a good knowledge and understanding of centralized operating systems and communication protocols. I believe that the contents will also fulfill the requirements of lecturers teaching distributed systems, research workers involved in distributed systems and designers of distributed systems. In addition, it will assist the many undergraduate students who want to know a little more about distributed systems.

A person who wants to use this book needs a sound knowledge and understanding of centralized operating systems and communication protocols. There is no introduction to these two areas, because many excellent works are readily available.

Acknowledgements

I have been extremely fortunate in having the help of many people during the course of this project. I would like to emphasize very strongly that without their reading of drafts of this book, my research papers and reports which have been used in this book, and without their comments and the opportunity to discuss research and design issues of distributed operating systems, the preparation of this book would be impossible.

First of all, I would like to express my deep gratitude to George Gerrity for his thoughtful criticism, long discussions, and helpful suggestions which allowed me to produce this book in its current version. I would like also to thank Chris Lokan for his critical reading of the manuscript and helpful comments. I wish also to thank Andrew Lister for discussions and helpful suggestions. I also received helpful comments from Lawrie Brown, Geoff Collin, Jadwiga Indulska, Willma Nelowkin, Josef Pieprzyk, Andy Quaine, Aruna Seneviratne, Christopher Vance, and Brendan Williams.

The writing of this book could not have been realized without the support of my publishers, Andrew Semmens and Derek Hall. I also want to thank the anonymous reviewers who provided me with critical comments on the manuscript.

When carrying out this project I was influenced by the work of such researchers and their groups as David Cheriton, Raphael Finkel, Edward Lazowska, Barton Miller, Roger Needham, Gerald Popek, Richard Rashid, Andrew Tanenbaum, Douglas Terry, and Richard Watson. They indirectly helped me to form my image of distributed operating systems. My thanks to you.

I am indebted to Andy Quaine and Jennifer Seberry for creating a good research environment in distributed systems, and Geoff Wilson, Rector of the University College, for his support of my research.

Finally, I would like to thank Teresa for her unending patience while I carried out this project. Without her encouragement, support and understanding I would never have completed it. And my children: Agnieszka and Wojtek have always been my inspiration.

The publishers and I would like to thank the following companies for permission to reproduce material from published sources: Association for Computing Machinery, Inc., and Springer-Verlag Heidelberg.

Publishers acknowledgment

The publishers wish to thank the following for permission to reproduce figures and tables:

Chapter 2

Figure 2.8: Brownbridge D.R., *et al* The Newcastle Connection or UNIXes of the World Unite! In *Software—Practice and Experience*, **12** pp 1147–1162 © 1982 John Wiley & Sons, Ltd. Figure 2.5: Holler E. (1981). The National Software Works, Distributed Systems–Architecture and Implementation. *Lecture Notes in Computer Science No. 105*, Springer-Verlag.

Chapter 3

Figure 3.4: IEEE (1983). IEEE Project 802—Local Area Network Standard's Draft D. *IEEE.*

Chapter 4

Figure 4.10: Cheriton D.R. The V-Distributed System. *Communications of the ACM* **31**(3), 314–33 © 1988. Association for Computing Machinery, Inc., reprinted by permission. Figure 4.5: Nicol *et al* (1988). An Approach to Multiple Copy Update based on Immutability. In *Distributed Processing* (Barton M.H *et al* eds.), pp. 537-550, Elsevier, North-Holland.

Chapter 5

Figures 5.14 & 5.15: Bershad B. N., *et al* (1987). A Remote Procedure Call Facility for Interconnecting Heterogeneous Computer Systems. *IEEE Transactions of Software Engineering*, **SE-13**(8), pp. 880–94. Figure 5.17: Birrell A.D. and Neslon B.J. Implementing Remote Procedure Calls. *ACM Transactions on Computer Systems* **2**(1), 39–59 © 1984 Association for Computing Machinery, Inc., reprinted by permission. Figure 5.21: ISO-9804.3 (1989). *Information Processing Systems—Open Systems Interconnection—Service Definition for the Commitment, Concurrency and Recovery Service Element.* Standards Association of Australia. Figure 5.22: Larmouth J. (1986). Commitment, Concurrency and Recovery—ISO-CASE and IBM LU.62. In *Networking in Open Systems*, pp. 193–222, *Lecture Notes in Computer Science*, No. 248, Springer-Verlag. Figure 5.1: Rashid R.F. and Robertson G.G. (1981). Accent: A Communication Oriented Network Operating System Kernel. In *Proceedings of the Eight ACM Symposium on Operating Systems Principles* Pacific Grove, California, pp 64–75. Figure 5.24: Rashid R.F. (1986) Experienced with the Accent Network Operating System. In *Networking in Open Systems*, pp. 252–69, *Lecture Notes in Computer Science* No. 248, Springer-Verlag. Figure 5.11: Welch B.B. (1986). *The Sprite Remote Procedure Call System*, Report No. UCB/CSD 86/302, Computer Science Division, University of California, Berkeley.

Chapter 6

Figures 6.4 & 6.7: Bullis K. and Franta W. (1980) Implementation of Eventcounts in a Broadcast Network. *Computer Networks,* **4,** 57–69. Figure 6.20: Maekawa M. *et al. Operating Systems: Advanced Concepts.* Benjamin/ Cummings Publishing Co., Inc. Menlo Park, California. Figure 6.17: Raymond K. (1987). *Multiple Entries with Ricart and Agrawala's Distributed Mutual Exclusion Algorithm.* Technical Report 87/78 Department of Computer Science, the University of Queensland. Figures 6.3, 6.5 & 6.6: Reed D. P. and Kanodia R.K. Synchronization with Eventcounts and Sequencers. *Communications of the ACM,* **22**(2), 115–23 © 1979 Association for Computing Machinery, Inc., reprinted by permission. Figure 6.9: Ricart G. and Agrawala A.K. An Optimal Algorithm for Mutual Exclusion in Computer Networks. *Communications of the ACM,* **24**(1), 9–17 © 1981 Association for Computing Machinery, Inc., reprinted by permission.

Chapter 7

Figure 7.21: Cheriton D.R. (1986). Request-Response and Multicast Interprocess Communication in the V Kernel. Networking in Open Systems. *Lecture Notes in Computer Science No. 248,* 296–312, Springer-Verlag. Figure 7.12: Gligor V.D. and Lindsay B.G. (1979). Object Migration and Authentication. *IEEE Transactions on Software Engineering,* **SE-5**(6), 607–11. Figures 7.2 & 7.5: Hauzer B.M. A Model for Naming, Addressing and Routing. *ACM Transactions on Office Information Systems,* **4**(4), 293–311, © 1986 Association for Computing Machinery, Inc., reprinted by permission. Tables 7.1, 7.2 & Figures 7.24, 7.25, 7.26, 7.27 & 7.30: Terry D.B. (1985). *Distributed Name Servers: Naming and Caching in Large Distributed Computing Environments.* Palo Alto Research Center, CSL-85-1. Figures

7.8, 7.10 & 7.11: Watson R.W. (1981). Identifiers (Naming) in Distributing Systems. In *Distributed Systems—Architecutre and Implementation. An Advanced Course* (Lampson B.W., Paul M. and Siegert H.J., eds.) *Lecture Notes in Computer Science*, **105**, Springer-Verlag, pp. 191–210.

Chapter 8

Figures 8.10 & 8.12: Agrawal R. and Ezzat A.K. (1987) Location Independent Remote Execution in NEST, *IEEE Transactions on Software Engineering*, **SE-13**, No. 8. Figure 8.19: Artsy Y. and Finkel R. (1989) Designing a Process Migration Facility. The Charlotte Experience, *Computer*, **9** 47–56. Figure 8.11: Theimer M.M., Lantz K.A. and Cheriton D.R. Preemptable Remote Execution Facilities for the V-system. *Proceedings of the Tenth ACM Symposium on Operating Systems Principles*, Orcas Island, Washington pp. 2–12. © 1985 Association for Computing Machinery, Inc. reprinted by permission. Figures 8.5 & 8.8: Ousterhout J.K., *et al* (1988). The Sprite Network Operating System. *Computer* **21**(2), 23–36. Figures 8.14, 8.15, 8.16, 8.17 & 8.18: Powell M.L. and Miller, B.P. An Approach to Multiple Copy Update Based on Immutability, Bretton Woods, New Hampshire, pp. 110–9 © 1983 Association for Computing Machinery, Inc., reprinted by permission. Figure 8.20: Jul E *et al*. Fine-Grained Mobility in the Emerald System. *ACM Transactions on Computer System*, **6**(1), pp 109–33 © 1988 Association for Computing Machinery, Inc. reprinted by permission. Table 8.1: Bagrodia R. and Chandy K.M. A Micro-kernel for Distributed Applications. In *Proceedings of the 5th International Conference on Distributed Computing Systems*, Denver, Colorado, pp. 140–49.

Chapter 9

Figure 9.12: Casavant T.L. and Kuhl J.G. (1988). A taxonomy of Scheduling in General-Purpose Distributed Computing Systems. *IEEE Transactions on Software Engineering*, **SE-14**(2), 141–54. Figure 9.6: Dannenberg R.B. and Hibbard P.G. A Butler Process for Resource Sharing on Spice Machines. *ACM Transactions on Office Information Systems*, **3**(3), pp 234–52 © 1985 Association for Computing Machinery, Inc. reprinted by permission.

Chapter 10

Figures 10.12 & 10.15: Badal D.Z. The Distributed Deadlock Detection Algorithm. *ACM Transactions on Computer Systems*, **4**(4), 320–37 © 1986 Association for Computing Machinery, Inc., reprinted by permission. Figures 10.2, 10.3 & 10.4: Filali M. *et al*. *Safety of Task Migration in a Distributed Operating System Nucleus, Local Communication Systems: LAN and PBX*. Elsevier, North-Holland. Figure 10.7: Gray J.N. (1978). *Notes on Data Base Operating Systems, Operating Systems: An Advanced Course*, Springer-

Verlag. Figure 10.5: Knapp E. Deadlock Detection in Distributed Databases. *ACM Computing Surveys* **19**(4) 303–28. © 1987 Association for Computing Machinery, Inc., reprinted by permission. Figures 10.10 & 10.13: Menasce D.A. and Muntz R.R. Locking and Deadlock Detection in Distributed Data Bases. *IEEE Transactions on Software Engineering*, **SE-5**(3), 195–202.

Chapter 11

Figure 11.17: Ames S.R. *et al* (1983). Security Kernel Design and Implementation: An Introduction. *Computer*, **16**(7), 14–22. Figure 11.6: Denning D.E. A Lattice Model of Secure Information Flow. *Communications of the ACM*, **19**(5), 236–43 © Association for Computing Machinery, Inc., reprinted by permission. Figure 11.10: Gligor V.D. and Lindsay B.G. (1979). Object Migration and Authentication. *IEEE Transactions on Software Engineering*, **SE-5**(6), 607–11. Figures 11.4 & 11.5: Graham G.S. and Denning P.J. (1972) Protection: Principles and Practices. *Proceedings of the AFIPS Spring Joint Computer Conference*, **40**, 417–29. Figure 11.11: Mullender S.J. and Tanenbaum A.S. (1986). The Design of a Capability-Based Distributed Operating System. *The Computer Journal*, **29**(4), 289–99. Figure 11.18: Rushby J. and Randell B. (1983). A Distributed Secure System. *Computer*, **16**(7), 55–67.

Chapter 12

Tables 12.1 & 12.2: Buffenoir T. Security in the OSI Model. *Computer Standards & Interfaces*, 77145.50 © 1988 Elsevier Science Publishers, North-Holland.

Chapter 14

Figures 14.38, 14.40, 14.44 & 14.45: Accetta M. *et al* (1986). *Mach: A New Kernel Foundation for UNIX Development*. The Mach Group, School of Computer Science, Carnegie-Mellon University. Figure 14.30: Almes G.T., *et al* (1985). The Eden System: A Technical Review. *IEEE Transactions on Software Engineering*, **SE-11**, 43–59. Figure 14.17: Artsy Y. *et al* (1984) *Charlotte: Design and Implementation of a Distributed Kernel*. Report #554 Computer Science Department, University of Wisconsin-Madison. Figures 14.9, 14.10, 14.11, 14.13, 14.14, & 14.15: Berglund E.J. (1986) An Introduction to the V-System. *IEEE Micro*, 35–52. Figure 14.7: Cheriton D.R. (1986). Request-Response and Multicast Interprocess Communication in the V Kernel. Networking in Open Systems. *Lecture Notes in Computer Science No. 248*, 296–312. Springer-Verlag. Figure 14.28: Lazowska E.D. *et al*. The Architecture of the Eden System. *Proceedings of the Eight Symposium on Operating Systems Principles*, Pacific Grove, California, 148–49 ©

1981 Association of Computing Machinery, Inc., reprinted with permission. Figures 14.41 & 14.42: Mason W.A. (1987). Distributed Processing: The State of the Art. *Byte* 291–97. Figures 14.23: Mullender S.J. & Tannenbaum A.S. Protection and Resource Control in Distributed Operating Systems. *Computer Networks*, **8**, 421–32 © 1984 Elsevier Science Publishers, North-Holland. Figures 14.24 & 14.25: Mullender S.J. and Tanenbaum A.S. A Distributed File Service based on Optimistic Concurrency Control. *Proceedings of the 10th Symposium on Operating Systems Principles*, Orcas Islands, Washington, pp. 51–62 © 1985 Association for Computing Machinery, Inc., reprinted by permission. Figures 14.20 & 14.21: Mullender S.J. (1987) *Process Management in a Distributed Operating System*. Report CS-R8713, Centrum voor Wiskunde en Informatica, Amsterdam. Figures 14.31, 14.32, 14.33, 14.34 & 14.35: Popek G. and Walker B.J. (1985). *The LOCUS Distributed System Architecture*, Cambridge, Mass: The MIT Press. Figures 14.1, 14.2 & 14.3: Rashid R.F. and Robertson G.G. (1981). Accent: A Communication Oriented Network Operating System Kernel. In *Proceedings of the Eight Symposium on Operating Systems Principles*, Pacific Grove, California, 64–75. Figures 14.30 & 14.31: Mullender S.J., *Process Management in a Distributed Operating System*, Report CS-R8713, Centre for Mathematics and Computer Science © Stichting Mathematisch Centrum. Figures 14.18 & 14.19: Tanenbaum A.S. and van Renesse R. (1985). Distributed Operating Systems: *Computing Surveys*, **17**(4). Figures 14.46, 14.47 & 14.48: Young *et al.* (1987) *The Duality of Memory and Communication in the Implementation of a Multiprocessor Operating System*, CMU-CS-87–140. The MACH Group, School of Computer Science, Carnegie Mellon University.

Contents

1 Introduction

T he usefulness of computer systems, the scope and quality of services provided, and their user-friendliness depend very strongly on their operating systems. An operating system can be defined as that part of a computer which transforms lifeless hardware into a powerful and usable system. Operating systems are continually behind in the race with computer hardware to achieve the goal of meeting user expectations. There are many reasons for this situation, and an analysis of the history of operating systems and their current state of development makes it possible to identify the majority of them. Despite this, we can say that an operating system can improve the performance of hardware on which it runs or in the worst case, can hide all possibilities provided by that hardware.

To date, a large number of operating systems have been constructed for centralized computing systems, and detailed performance studies have been made on a number of them. Simulation models of the major functions exist, and their critical design parameters and architecture are well understood. A theory of centralized operating systems does exist and the methodology of operating system development (for a given application and defined requirements) is well known.

At present we are in the next stage of the development and use of computer systems. Research is being carried out both to increase the processing capacity of a single computer system, by using closely-coupled multiprocessors, and also to improve performance within the bounds of fixed and marginally increasing processing capacity. The latter is due to connections of computers spread over geographic distances and the development of distributed systems. This implies a need for specialized operating systems.

At the same time, the goal is to provide the user with a large virtual computing environment in which placement of data and locus of computation is handled automatically. As the user is interested in short response time, class of services provided, and the quality of these services work needs to be carried out in the area of distributed operating systems.

1.1 Motivation for distributed operating systems

Distributed systems are developed because of the enormous rate of technological change in microprocessor technology. **Distributed systems** is a term used to define a wide range of computer systems, from weakly-coupled systems such as wide area networks to strongly-coupled systems such as local area networks to very strongly-coupled systems such as multiprocessor systems. In this book we address local area networks and in some cases wide area networks which are those with high bandwidth.

Local area networks and fast wide area networks provide an opportunity to connect computers, in particular personal computers and workstations, and peripheral devices together. Personal computers and workstations have become a very attractive alternative to time sharing because:

(1) the construction based on microprocessors is very cheap and powerful;

(2) they can support very high data transfer rates between the processor and input/output devices;

(3) each has a dedicated function; and

(4) they provide a predictable response time to user requests.

The capabilities of personal computers and workstations are greatly enhanced when they are connected by a data communication network (a local area network, a fast wide area network) even though such a connection generates the problem of designing large systems composed of small processors. This problem is mainly solved at the software level of those systems.

Distributed systems developed on the basis of local area and fast wide area networks have advantages as well as disadvantages. The advantages of distributed systems developed on the basis of interconnecting personal computers, workstations, and computers by local area networks and fast wide area networks are:

(1) The whole system is more reliable and available than a time-sharing system – a few parts of the system can be inoperative without disturbing people using the other parts.

(2) It is possible to share a few expensive hardware resources such as printers, hard disks, plotters in a very effective way as well as sharing software resources.

(3) A network can have very considerable computing power, but its computing resources are distributed.

The disadvantages (problems) of distributed systems developed on the basis of local area networks and fast wide area networks are as follows:

(1) Security may dictate that some data cannot be transferred in whole or in part to any other machine, including the site of a requesting user; thus the user must use a remote processor to access data.

(2) The physical distribution of resources may not match the distribution of the demands for services. This implies that some resources may be idle while others are overloaded.

(3)   Even though a personal computer or a workstation may have significant computational capabilities, its power is less than that expected of a large mainframe computer.

All of these problems can be alleviated by **resource sharing**, which provides the answer to some of the problems generated by the nature of computer networks.

Sharing for information exchange

This type of sharing is related to the first of the disadvantages listed above, that is data security. In networks, there is no central trusted operating system. This implies that a specific owner of data must share a machine with users who need to access the data, and in order to protect specific data, the machine owner restricts what borrowers can do with the machine. Examples of this type of sharing are electronic mail programs, local databases, and appointment-making programs.

Sharing of load distribution

This type of sharing is a result of the problem connected with an imbalance of load on the network of machines. Sharing can be used to distribute the load more evenly. An examples of this type of sharing is a user running an interactive program and a background program. If there are idle machines available on the network, it may be advantageous to use the remote machine to execute the background process.

Sharing for computational parallelism

When computing resources in computer networks are distributed to obtain more processing power than is available at any given personal computer, some degree of sharing to run some processes in parallel is necessary. Examples of this type of sharing are image and signal processing, computer graphics, design-rule checkers for computer-aided design systems and simulation of physical systems.

An operating system of a distributed system developed on the basis of a local area network (and a fast wide area network) should cope with all the problems presented above. To do that effectively, such an operating system should be distributed. The place of an operating system in a distributed environment and its distribution are illustrated in Fig. 1.1.

Distributed operating systems have many aspects in common with centralized operating systems, but they also differ in many ways. A distributed operating system contains the same management elements

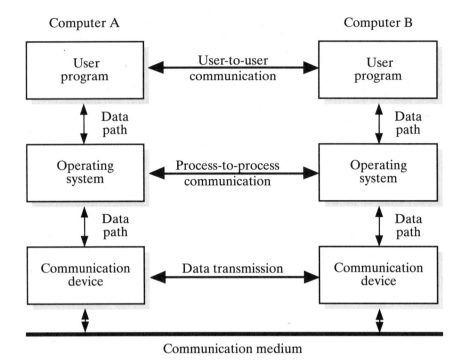

Fig. 1.1 The place of an operating system in a distributed environment.

as a centralized operating system: process (object) management, memory management, I/O management, communication management, device management and file management. The list of management elements defines also what a distributed operating system must do.

In a distributed system, the resources are dispersed in space and interconnected by a communications network. Moreover, the computing resources and the network are generally autonomous control entities. Thus, the primary goal of a distributed operating system is to control resource allocation, and then to integrate and control the computing resources and the communications network services into a single system. System resources should also be protected against accessing by unauthorized users. This provides services equivalent to those of a conventional centralized operating system. Moreover, a distributed operating system should provide the user with a virtual computer that serves as a convenient environment.

These goals should be achievable even in the presence of restrictions imposed by the designers and users of the system, and by the limitations of the component subsystems. These restrictions are usually: requirements for transparency and security, ability to function with subsystem failures, processing capacity, flexibility, simplicity, reliability and sometimes, a requirement to integrate heterogeneous subsystems. In the case of local area networks and fast wide area networks, the construction of an operating system fulfilling the requirements of the definition given above implies design and implementation problems not known in the area of centralized operating systems.

It should be pointed out that the distribution of resources, the lack of global state information, and transmission delays imply that the methods and techniques developed for centralized operating systems cannot be used in distributed operating systems. Even when centralized techniques fulfill the requirements for these systems, their implementation is usually too expensive.

1.2   A definition and functions of a distributed operating system

Taking all these requirements and comments into consideration we can present an informal definition of a distributed operating system.

A **distributed operating system** should:

(1)   control network resource allocation to allow their use in the most effective way;

(2)   provide the user with a convenient virtual computer that serves as a high-level programming environment;

(3)   hide the distribution of the resources;

(4)   provide mechanisms for protecting system resources against accessing by unauthorized users; and

(5)   provide secure communication.

A distributed operating system is one that looks to its user like an ordinary centralized operating system, but runs on multiple, independent central processing units where:

(1)   the use of multiple processors should be invisible (transparent) to the user (different levels of transparency will be discussed in Chapter 4); or

(2)   the user views the system as a virtual uniprocessor, not as a collection of distinct machines connected by a communication subsystem.

Any management (control) decisions should be made on the basis of adequate and up-to-date information. Lack of up-to-date information makes all management problems much harder and in many cases impossible. One of the most fundamental problems in distributed operating systems is the lack of global state information and up-to-date information.

Resource management issues such as processor scheduling, load balancing, deadlock avoidance or detection and recovery, interprocess communication and synchronization, naming (addressing) and protection, fault tolerance, secure communication, and the services to be provided, which create the background for management elements, should be solved having distribution in mind. It is well known from control theory that the development of distributed methods and algorithms is a very complex task.

Because of distribution of processing elements and other resources, one of the most important elements of distributed operating systems is communication between remote processes (processes in different sites) called here **remote interprocess communication**. Such high-performance communication is the most critical facility of the distributed system. It depends on interprocess communication primitives, and transport protocols that support these primitives. It is up to the transport layer protocol to bridge the gap between what the operating system offers to its users and what a communication subsystem actually provides.

The communication system should possess many special functions, such as process registration, and establishing, closing and manipulating paths between communicating processes. Moreover, this element should perform routing of messages, and provide for reliable transfer.

Two kinds of operating systems for local area networks can be distinguished: network operating systems and distributed operating systems. The most important factor used to differentiate network operating systems from distributed operating systems is transparency, that is, how aware the users are of the fact that multiple computers are being used. The definition of a distributed operating system presented in this section illustrates that this kind of system hides the existence and distribution of multiple computers. Users working with network operating systems are aware of where each of the resources used are located. The network operating system is built on a set of existing centralized (local) operating systems and handles the interfacing and coordination of remote operations and communications between these local operating systems. On the other hand, the distributed operating system is built from scratch on bare hardware, to control and optimize all operations and resources in a distributed system, not only those at the network communication level.

1.3 What issues are to be studied in the area of distributed operating systems? – The goal of this work

A theory of centralized operating systems does exist as does the methodology to develop an operating system for a given application and defined requirements.

In contrast, the study of distributed operating systems is in its infancy, and their design and construction is still an open problem. Indeed, only the critical problem areas have been identified, but there is little agreement among researchers about appropriate solutions.

A distributed operating system contains the same management components as an operating system for centralized systems: process management, memory management, resource management, and file management. The development of these components requires study of many research and design issues to find methods and algorithms which can be used to build these components. To identify these issues consider a distributed system in which a number of nodes (implemented by single- and/or multi-processor computers and workstations) are connected by a network. The entire distributed system is controlled and managed by a distributed operating system.

Each node of a distributed system supports a number of processes, which work on behalf of their users. All these processes communicate (interact) through message passing. This has resulted in the development of programming styles such as client-server model, remote procedure call, and a transaction model to reflect paradigms of process interaction. Messages can be send directly to another process or processes, or indirectly, to ports representing processes. Links can be used also by communicating processes. Performance of interprocess communication depends on communication primitives and the transport layer supporting these primitives. The transport protocol is provided with services by the lower communication layers.

Communicating (interacting) processes must be synchronized. Because of the lack of a common clock in a distributed system and because of communication delays, synchronization methods used in centralized systems cannot be used in distributed ones. This leads to the development of distributed synchronization algorithms. Three basic approaches are used for constructing such algorithms: time-based event ordering, token passing, and priority-based event ordering.

If a process wants to send a message to another process or processes (broadcast or multicast), the knowledge of names of communicating peers is necessary. Each object of a distributed operating system, that is, a process, a file, a printer, must have a name. Names used at a process level (unique computer-oriented identifiers, capabilities) are different from those used at a user level (character strings). Names can be managed in a centralized way as well as in a distributed fashion. In the latter case, the name space is collectively managed by a number of name servers. If a name space is distributed, this can lead to replication. Each name server should provide and support the following services: storing name information and database management, maintaining replications, name resolution, and name service operations. Name resolution in a distributed environment is the process of determining the authoritative name servers for a given named object.

Users of distributed systems want to be able to complete their computation tasks in the possible shortest time, use different computational environment such as special languages, special compilers, special processors most suitable for their application programs, and to use peripherals adequate to their applications. This generates some requirements for advanced process and resource management. Thus, there should be the possibility of running a process on a currently idle workstation (computer), or if there is no idle computer, on that which is lightly loaded, or on that computer which provides special compilers. Work load should be balanced to improve an average performance in a distributed system. Moreover, to achieve short response time, user files should be accessible on the closest file server. These files should also be replicated not only for performance reasons but also to achieve high reliability.

To fulfil such requirements, a distributed operating system should be equiped with some mechanisms and policy. The mechanisms should be such as to carry out operations on processes not only locally but also remotely (create, suspend, run, kill). Moreover, there should be a facility provided to support process migration from one computational environment to another, which is the best in a given sense.

Locating and accessing the 'best' remote resource are performed based on a given policy. Thus, the 'best' remote resources can be located and accessed directly through servers managing these as well as agents working on behalf of requesting processes. The latter can be seen as a fully distributed management method. Idle workstations can be found on random (worm approach), or using hierarchical or token mechanisms. Special methods and algorithms are necessary to balance the load in a distributed system. These algorithms should be global and dynamic. They should be also physically distributed.

In an environment in which processes compete for the same limited resources, deadlock can happen. Deadlock in a distributed system can cause expensive, time-dependent hangups or failures. Thus, there is the need for deadlock prevention, or deadlock detection and recovery. With distributed operating systems, deadlock detection is the main topic for consideration. Because of physical distribution, there are two kinds of deadlocks: resource deadlock and communication deadlock. Moreover, new models of a deadlock have been proposed and studied, these also allow for the development of different deadlock detection algorithms.

Users of the system store information on external storage, and share it among themselves as they share other system resources. Users also exchange information. However, if the system resources are to be shared by a number of mutually suspicious users, protection within the computer system is required. Moreover, if users, either eligible or noneligible (intruders), attack a communication system, the system requires provision of security mechanisms.

Protection mechanisms for distributed systems tend to be based on the use of capabilities, access control lists, or a lock/key mechanism. However, in some environments (mainly military), protection provided by these mechanisms is not enough, because they do not take into consideration the information content. If protection takes into consideration semantic aspects of information, information is classified and users are allocated some levels of clearance. This leads to different protection mechanisms in computer systems, based on for example, a lattice model or an information flow model.

Because of the value of information in transit between communicating processes, communication systems can be attacked passively or actively. To carry out communication operations securely some countermeasures utilizing cryptographic techniques must be provided. Two cryptosystems have been developed: symmetric and asymmetric. Because they use secret keys, some key management methods are necessary.

Users of a distributed system do not trust each other. They also assume that some non-eligible users will masquerade as eligible users. This leads to the need for user authentication. Such operations are provided through message authentication.

The most visible user object of any computer system is a file. User assessment of the quality of a distributed system is based on file services. They expect that file service will be fast and reliable. This implies that file service in a distributed system will use, but hide the main features: distribution, delay, and replication, to improve performance and high reliability. Thus, these features should be taken into consideration when implementing a file service.

The preceding presentation shows that the following research and design issues are of most interest:

(1) in the area of distributed processes and their management: remote interprocess communication, synchronization, naming, and process management; and

(2) in the area of resource management: resource allocation, detection of deadlocks, protection and security, and types of services to be provided.

On analysing the status of existing distributed operating systems, they are all seen to be experimental: in practice there is no commercial product available (currently only Mach is advertised as a commercial product). Moreover, these experimental systems were developed on the basis of quite different approaches. Many use the client-server model, although some have been built on the connection model. Communication in these systems is usually based either on some form of remote procedure call, or on an advanced form of message passing. The transaction approach has also been used. Relatively little research has been done on distributed naming, protection and resource management. To date, only straightforward name servers and process servers have been built. Considerable effort has been expended in developing different servers such as file server and print server, but much more needs to be done in the context of a total distributed operating system concept. The developers of these systems have given little explanation as to how they arrived at their design decisions, and consequently there has not been wide discussion on the merits of alternative design philosophies. Even if the explanations had been forthcoming, there is the problem of how to compare operating systems which have few methods and/or primitives in common, when the relative importance of these factors is unknown. This is further complicated by the fact that reported results contain very little quantitative data. Analytic and simulation methods can be used only to study the performance of some elements of such a complex entity as a distributed operating system. This is not enough to specify the best design approaches for a given application like office automation, factory automation or process control.

This situation leads to the conclusion that before determining the best design to adopt, a distributed operating system architect must know which methods and algorithms for a given management component can be used and why. To do so, the architect has to comparatively assess these methods in the context of a given component and the total structure of a distributed operating system. That task can be performed on the basis of a theory of distributed operating systems, or on the basis of work which leads to the development of such a theory. It must be emphasized that there has been very little of this research done.

This work is an attempt at a uniform attack on these problems. The main goal of the book is to identify and present research and design issues, together with methods and some algorithms specific for distributed operating systems. This is necessary to create a background for design and construction of such systems.

1.4 Organization and the contents

Having the basic definition and problems of distributed operating systems and the stated goal in mind, we can present and analyse the organization and the contents of this book. Its chapters may be grouped logically into three major parts. Chapters 2 through 4 form the first part. These chapters contain material which, I believe, should create a total image of distributed operating systems. Based on these chapters, a reader may identify an architecture of a distributed operating system, its components and functions. Communication protocols and their role are emphasized. Research and design issues and the main solutions of problems associated with them are presented and discussed. In general, the first part of the book presents the 'world' of distributed operating systems.

Chapter 2 presents an analysis of network operating systems and distributed operating systems. The location of remote interprocess communication in a hierarchical structure of an operating system is used to distinguish network operating systems from distributed operating systems and to show transparent access to remote resources.

The goal of Chapter 3 is the description of the environment of distributed operating systems, addressing in particular communication aspects. Distributed systems are introduced. Moreover, the following communication oriented topics are presented: protocols, the ISO/OSI Reference Model, the IEEE 802 LAN Model, and software for local area networks. In particular, general purpose transport protocols, special purpose transport protocols, and their suitability for supporting interprocess communication primitives are discussed.

Major problems, and research and design issues of distributed operating systems are identified and presented in Chapter 4. In particular, a communication model for distributed operating systems is given and, transparency and heterogeneity, with their importance and problems are described. Transactions for reliable computing, together with the multiple copy update problem are analysed. Architecture and components of distributed operating systems are introduced and differentiated from centralized operating systems. There is also an overview of research and design issues of components of distributed operating systems – those which are different from issues of operating systems for centralized computer systems because of their distributed nature. The following issues are introduced: remote interprocess communication, synchronization, addressing and naming, process management, resource management, deadlocks, protection, communication security and services provided.

Because this chapter also contains the current state of knowledge of research in components specific to distributed operating systems, some readers may stop their study at this stage. On the other hand, those readers who are interested in the details of current research in components specific to distributed operating systems and in implementation aspects should study the second part which includes Chapters 5 through 13.

Remote interprocess communication is discussed in Chapter 5. The following forms of interprocess communication are presented: message passing with one of its subforms – rendezvous, Remote Procedure Calls, and transactions. These forms are ordered according to an increasing level of abstraction and reflect how each form can be constructed from the preceding form. Primitives for interprocess communication between remote processes can be nonblocking or blocking, unreliable or reliable, buffered or unbuffered. Remote Procedure Call provides language-level mechanisms to support type-checked remote interfaces. Transactions, originally developed for database management systems, can be effectively used in the development of a remote interprocess communication facility for reliable systems. This chapter shows also the association of interprocess communication with memory management.

Chapter 6 contains a discussion of synchronization for distributed systems. First of all, event ordering in distributed systems is presented. With this background, centralized synchronization methods and algorithms are described. Distributed synchronization algorithms can be divided into three groups. To the first group belong those algorithms which use time based event-ordering. The second group contains those algorithms which are based on the token approach. The third group contains algorithms which use priority based event-ordering. Concurrency control in transaction processing is also included in this chapter.

Sending messages between processes, that is, objects supported by a distributed operating system, requires the operating system to know the names of these objects. The naming facility for distributed operating systems is introduced and described in Chapter 7. First, general aspects and goals of naming systems are presented. Based on this consideration, different names are introduced. Route and routing, and addresses and mapping are discussed. Unique computer identifiers are analysed. Following this, computer-oriented identifiers and protection are presented. Structural and functional components of a naming facility are discussed. Name distribution and resolution are considered for location-independent names. Two performance study approaches are discussed and some results are presented.

Process management is described in Chapter 8. The content of this chapter is closely associated with mechanisms which are necessary for implementing policy for resource (object) management. Concurrent execution of processes is introduced and then the concept of a distributed process is presented together with states of processes, shared address spaces and process scheduling. Remote operations on processes, such as process creation and termination, and port and link creation and destruction, are discussed. Remote execution of processes is discussed in detail. Migration of processes, in particular reasons for providing process migration, and basic problems of this operation are considered. Process migration mechanisms are discussed.

Mechanisms were introduced in Chapter 8 – however, policy, that is the problems of how to find an idle workstation, and when to migrate a process are dealt with in detail in Chapter 9, which discusses resource management and resource management policy. Problems connected with resource management in distributed systems are identified. Two classes of resource managers, a server-based resource manager, and an agent-based resource manager are discussed. Load sharing, known also as hunting for idle processor (workstation or computer), can be performed on the basis of many different organizations. Three of the most interesting are: processors organized in a logical hierarchy, processors organized in a logical ring and processors not organized in any special structure. Because system performance can be improved by providing not only load sharing, but also load balancing, there is a need for algorithms. Characterization of load balancing algorithms is given and a survey of selected load balancing algorithms is presented.

In a distributed system, as in a centralized one, there are a number of processes that compete for the same limited resources. If a process requests a resource which is not available at the requested time it enters a waiting state. This situation can result in deadlock. Deadlocks are discussed in Chapter 10. Two kinds of deadlocks are identified: resource deadlocks and communication deadlocks. Models of a deadlock and basic concepts for distributed deadlock detection algorithms are discussed. A survey of selected deadlock detection algorithms is given. The following algorithms are surveyed: Gray's algorithm, Menasce and Muntz's algorithm, Badal's algorithm, Mitchell and Merritt's algorithm, CHM algorithm, Natarajan's algorithm, and Bracha and Toueg's algorithm.

Protection in distributed operating systems is discussed in Chapter 11. Basic aspects of security and common violations in distributed systems are presented. They are followed by the discussion of access control approaches such as access matrix and flow models, and security kernel mechanisms. Implementation of these approaches is presented. In particular, the following implementation concepts of the access matrix are discussed: access control lists and capabilities, passing and revocating of access rights, and identifier protection. The possible ways of implementing information flow control and a distributed security kernel are presented.

Chapter 12 contains the discussion of communication security from the point of view of distributed operating systems. Basic problems of communication security are presented. Threats to interprocess communication security are discussed. Communication security measures and goals are analysed. The following measures are discussed: data encryption, key management, message authentication. Based on this discussion, security services and mechanisms are summarized. Finally, encryption protocols, in particular the placement of security services in the ISO/OSI Reference Model and primitive security functions, are discussed.

Chapter 13 contains a brief presentation of file service in a distributed operating system. Classifications of file servers are given and basic file and directory services are presented. The following services are discussed: disk (block) service, file service, directory service, and transaction service. Collaboration of file servers is considered. An analysis of selected file servers is presented. OSI file service is introduced.

Chapter 14, the third logical part of this book, presents several experimental distributed operating systems. These systems are based on different approaches. The following approaches for design and construction of distributed operating systems are presented: process-based approach, object-based approach, and UNIX-based approach. Next, the following distributed operating systems are surveyed: Accent, V, Charlotte, Amoeba, Eden, LOCUS, and Mach.

At this stage the two questions arise:

(1)   Do all these issues fit together?

(2)   Is it possible to see a distributed operating system through these issues discussed in several chapters?

The answer to both questions is yes. The relationship between the material covered in this text and the structure of a distributed operating system at every node of a distributed system is illustrated in Fig. 1.2.

1.5   Potential readers – how to use this text

I emphasized in the Preface that this monograph has been developed with the needs of postgraduate students in mind. This book does not contain material related to basic concepts of centralized operating systems or communication protocols, simply because there are many excellent books providing detailed coverage of these topics. Thus, students are expected to have a good knowledge and understanding of centralized operating systems, computer networks and communication protocols.

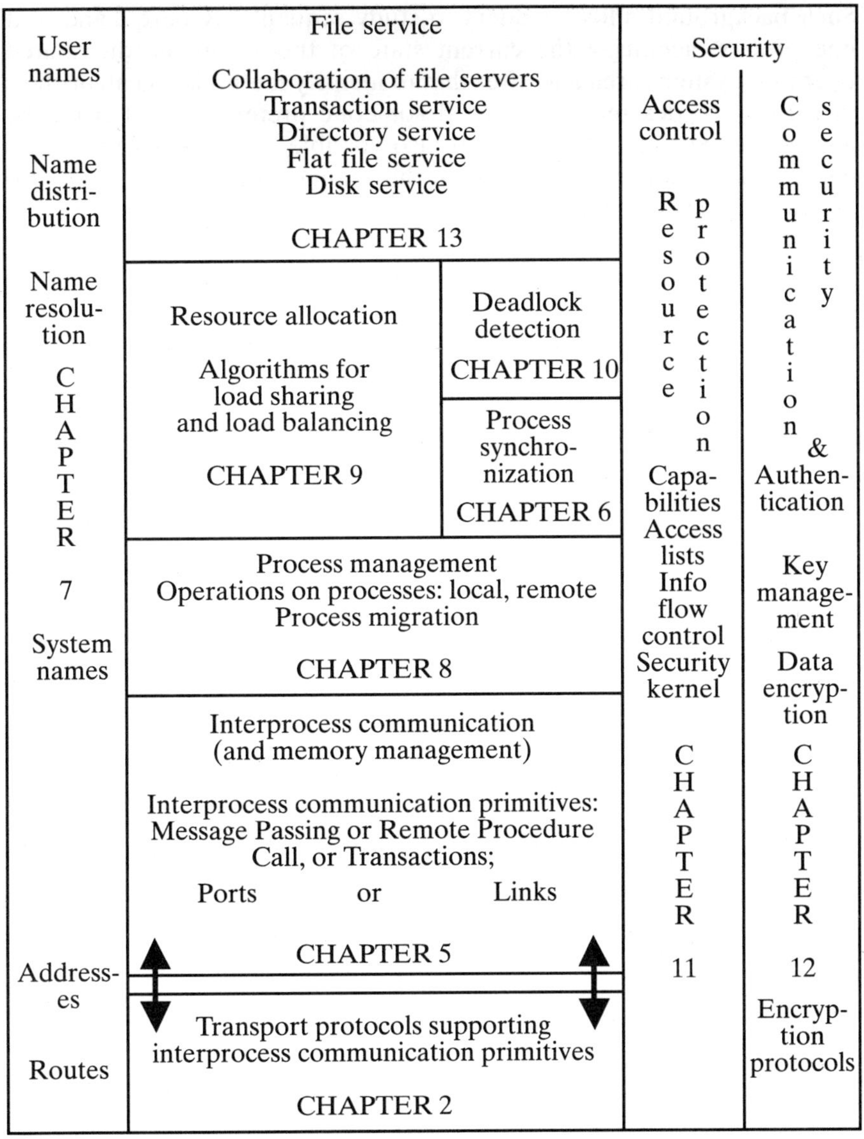

User names	File service	Security	
	Collaboration of file servers		C s
	Transaction service	Access	o e
	Directory service	control	m c
Name distri-bution	Flat file service		m u
	Disk service	R p	u r
		e r	n i
	CHAPTER 13	s o	i t
Name resolu-tion		o t	c y
	Resource allocation	Deadlock detection	u e	r a
			r c	t
C H A P T E R	Algorithms for load sharing and load balancing	CHAPTER 10	c t	i
			e i	o
		Process synchro-nization	o	n
	CHAPTER 9		n	&
		CHAPTER 6	Capa-bilities	Authen-tication
7	Process management Operations on processes: local, remote Process migration	Access lists Info flow control	Key manage-ment
System names	CHAPTER 8	Security kernel	Data encryp-tion
	Interprocess communication (and memory management)	C H A P T E R	C H A P T E R
	Interprocess communication primitives: Message Passing or Remote Procedure Call, or Transactions;		
	Ports or Links		
		11	12
Address-es	CHAPTER 5		
	Transport protocols supporting interprocess communication primitives		Encryp-tion protocols
Routes	CHAPTER 2		

Fig. 1.2 The relationship between the material covered in this text and the structure of a distributed operating system.

Although not small in terms of contents and number of pages, based on my experience, the complete text can be covered comfortably during two semesters. My suggestion is that persons who want to start their study of distributed operating systems should acquire basic knowledge based on the first part of the book, Chapter 1 through Chapter 4.

Such background allows readers to study sequentially part 2 and 3, if one prefers, acquiring the current state of the art in the distributed operating systems area and after that to identify methods and algorithms in existing or designed systems. If someone prefers to start from the analysis of existing systems, this is also possible. The first part provides enough material to use this book in this manner. Parts 2 and 3 can also be studied concurrently.

2 Network operating systems versus distributed operating systems

User processes
Local operating system
Network operating system
Communication module

Computer network

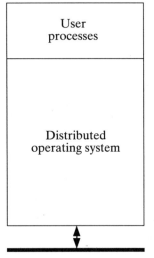

User processes
Distributed operating system

Computer network

Before starting a discussion of distributed operating systems, it is worth taking a brief look at network operating systems, as predecessors of distributed operating systems. Note that although the first network operating systems were developed nearly fifteen years ago, there are only a few attempts to characterize them in a general way. These include Tanenbaum and van Renesse (1985), Fortier (1986), and Watson and Fletcher (1980).

The goal of this chapter is to present the most important features of network operating systems, and based on this, to differentiate between network operating systems and distributed operating systems. To highlight the distinct features of network operating systems a short description of three different operating systems is presented.

2.1 Characterizing the distinction between network and distributed operating systems

2.1.1 Basic features of network operating systems

Two major factors started the development and implementation of network operating systems for local area networks and wide area networks are:

(1) a desire to improve computer performance within the bounds of the processor capacity, and

(2) a need for sharing resources.

Network operating systems were considered as a collection of operating systems of computers connected to a network incorporating modules to provide access to remote resources. Such a perception is simple and inexpensive when implemented but, in general, a user needs to know the location of a requested resource.

A network operating system has the following set of characteristics that distinguishes it from a distributed operating system (Tanenbaum and van Renesse 1985):

(1) Each computer has its private operating system, instead of running part of a global, system-wide operating system.

(2) Each user normally works on their own computer or on a designated computer; using a different computer invariably requires some kind of 'remote login', instead of having the operating system dynamically allocate processes to CPUs.

(3) Users are usually aware of where each of their files is stored and must move files between computers with explicit 'file transfer' commands, instead of having file placement managed by the operating system.

(4) The system has little or no fault tolerance; if one per cent of the personal computers crash, one per cent of the users are out of business, instead of everyone simply being able to continue normal work, albeit with one per cent worse performance.

The environment of a network operating system is illustrated in Fig. 2.1. The following modules structured hierarchically can be distinguished: communication, a network operating system, a local operating system, and user processes.

The communication module in the network operating system provides reliable delivery of messages between computers and computer facilities connected by a network.

The network operating system layer provides the following services: accepting requests for performing remote operations, determining the location of necessary resources, defining ways of initiation of these operations and returning services. It is necessary to emphasize at this stage that the network operating system links and coordinates remote actions and communication between local operating systems.

The local operating system is a traditional, centralized operating system. The only small difference between the local operating system and the traditional, centralized operating system is that it has to call the

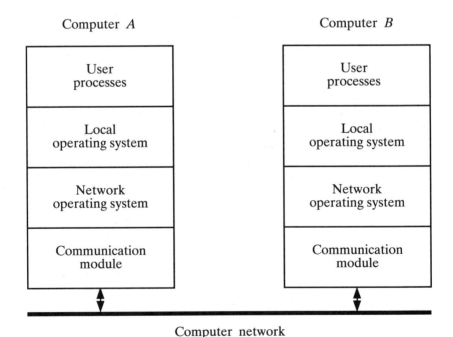

Computer A   Computer B

User processes	User processes
Local operating system	Local operating system
Network operating system	Network operating system
Communication module	Communication module

Computer network

Fig. 2.1 An environment of a network operating system.

network operating system when a request for performing an operation cannot be served locally. This means that the local operating system sees the network operating system as a normal, local server.

The fourth layer of the network operating system hierarchy is made up of the users.

2.1.2 Differences between network operating systems and distributed operating systems

Differences between network operating systems and distributed operating systems can be simply explained on the basis of analysis of the location (placement) of the interprocess communication module in a hierarchical structure of centralized operating systems, and its influence on services offered to the users of a distributed system.

To start this explanation it is useful to analyse centralized operating systems. The basic model of a centralized operating system and services offered to a user, if adequate resources are available, is illustrated in Fig. 2.2.

This model based on a hierarchical concept is very useful when analysing the influence of the location of an interprocess communication system, on the visibility of services provided to a user, in other words, resources offered to a user.

Assume that different resources are connected to a network as illustrated in Fig. 2.3. It has been assumed, to simplify our analysis, that at least one of each type of each class of resource is attached to the net-

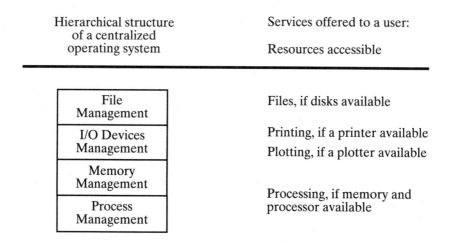

Fig. 2.2 The hierarchical structure of a centralized operating system and services offered to a user, if adequate resources are available.

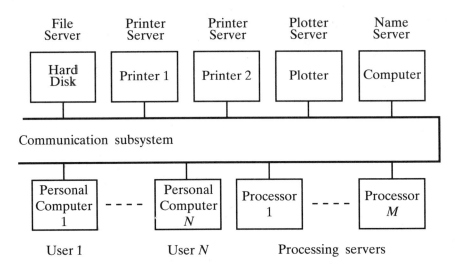

Fig. 2.3 Network based distributed system.

work. This means that a set of resources, similar to that in a centralized system, is available to users working on the network.

The location of the interprocess communication module (IPC) in a hierarchical structure of the operating system for a distributed system and the remote services offered to a user are as illustrated in Fig. 2.4.

It is seen that the lower the interprocess communication module is placed, the more transparent the network becomes. An analysis of Fig. 2.4(c) shows moreover, that only the structure of the operating system which contains the interprocess communication module as an integral part of the process management layer supplies services which fulfil the requirements of a distributed operating system, that is, only such a structure hides the resource location.

A typical network operating system is a collection of local, centralized operating systems along with a common printer, plotter, and file server, connected together by a network. The network operating system views the resources as being locally owned by computers. This implies that when users want to run a process remotely, they have to know a proper location and log onto the network. After this, users must associate their process with the remote process, and send a request to run that process on that chosen computer. The target local operating system will see that process as a newly created process. So, if any synchronization is required with any process from a source computer, this operation is the user responsibility and is only partially supported by the system.

Summarizing this, we can say that all operating system management functions; process management, I/O management, device manage-

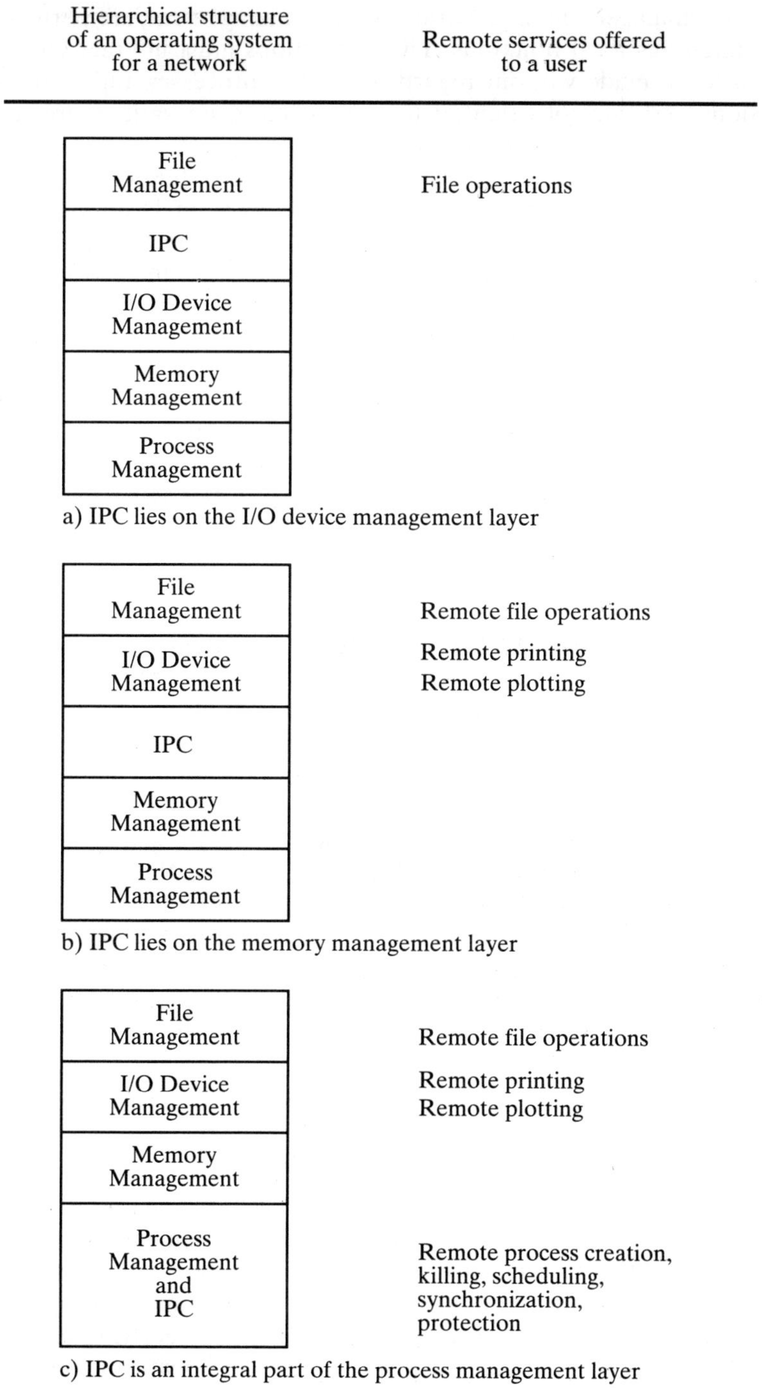

Hierarchical structure of an operating system for a network	Remote services offered to a user

File Management
IPC
I/O Device Management
Memory Management
Process Management

File operations

a) IPC lies on the I/O device management layer

File Management
I/O Device Management
IPC
Memory Management
Process Management

Remote file operations

Remote printing
Remote plotting

b) IPC lies on the memory management layer

File Management
I/O Device Management
Memory Management
Process Management and IPC

Remote file operations

Remote printing
Remote plotting

Remote process creation, killing, scheduling, synchronization, protection

c) IPC is an integral part of the process management layer

Fig. 2.4 Placement of IPC in a structure of an operating system.

ment, file management, in general resource management, are performed as autonomous local functions. These functions must interact but local decisions are made without regard to remote processes and resources. Decisions and control oriented towards remote operations are made only at the network communication level.

On the other hand, a distributed operating system is a single network-wide operating system viewed logically as a single operating system that exists for all the distributed computers (components). There are no individual operating systems of computers connected by a network. Users are not aware of where their files are stored; nor are they aware that their programs are executed by remote processors. The fault tolerance is very high. All decisions and control are (should be) performed globally; resources within the network are managed in a global fashion using global mechanisms rather than local mechanisms.

In summary, the major difference between these two concepts of operating systems is the way of seeing and managing local/global resources.

2.2 Network operating system concepts

Network operating systems can be constructed on the basis of local operating systems for computers connected by a network by building a module providing access to remote resources. Such a module is usually called an agent or a remote access system (RAS). Probably the first effort towards the development of a network operating system was undertaken in the middle of 1970; this is termed as the National Software Works (NSW) (Holler 1981). One simple example of such a network operating system for a heterogeneous network (different computers with different operating systems) is presented in Goscinski *et al.* (1983). Other well known network operating systems are extensions of UNIX (Blair *et al.* 1983, Brownbridge *et al.* 1982, Collinson 1982, Rowe and Birman 1982).

2.2.1 The National Software Works

The National Software Works (NSW) (Holler 1981) represents a very ambitious effort. The goal of this project was to design and implement a network operating system for a number of computers with heterogeneous CPU types, connected by the Arpanet network, and heterogeneous operating systems. It was assumed that changes to underlying operating systems should be restricted to a minimum, modifications to existing tools such as editors, file systems, high level language processors, debuggers and emulators had to be minimized, solutions had to allow easy integration of existing tools, and that operations should be performed in a transparent manner. The National Software Works was conceived as a distributed system in the sense that its components may be viewed as distributed processes cooperating to provide the National Software Works resources, and coordinated by the NSW monitor. Implementation was entirely at the application level.

Fig. 2.5 shows the National Software Works components and their interconnection. The communication component did not rely on existing higher layer communication protocols like Arpanet for file transfer and communication. A specific interprocess communication protocol, called MSG, was defined. MSG establishes the type of interprocess communication needed for the National Software Works in such a way that a variety of different computer networks may be used as target systems for implementation.

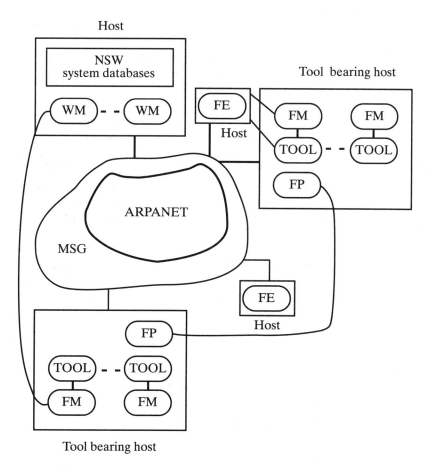

Fig. 2.5 NSW components and their interconnection {adapted from Holler, (1981)}.

A uniform mode of access to the National Software Works tools is provided by the system component known as the Front End (FE). One of its elementary functions is to interface various types of interactive terminals to the system via a virtual terminal protocol. This protocol causes all terminals to look alike to the other NSW components with respect to their communication characteristics and control functions. The Front End insulates the user from the peculiarities of different host operating systems.

All requests for NSW–specific resources (for example, file access) issued by tools operating on different computers must be taken care of by the NSW monitor, which is responsible for access control, accounting, and auditing. As a result, no tool may request any resource from the local host operating system directly. Tools requests are interpreted by a NSW component called Foreman (FM) and referred to the NSW monitor via MSG. Moreover, the Foreman must provide the tool with a link to the user via MSG to the Front End.

The heterogeneity of the underlying computer network implies that the output of one tool can be used as an input for another tool, involving the transfer of files between different hosts. This generates the need for transaction of data representations, reformatting, and file movement. The NSW component responsible for these operations is called the File Package (FP).

The National Software Works components are conceptually processes, which are distributed over the set of hosts connected by a network. The host which allows a user access must have a Front End. Each tool bearing host has a Foreman, each host providing for NSW file storage has a File Package. To allow for NSW component communication, each host in NSW has a MSG-server process. NSW component cooperation and allocation of NSW specific resources is controlled by the NSW monitor, called the Works Manager (WM). Works Manager is a network operating system.

It is the responsibility of MSG to provide for communication between the various NSW–system processes implementing Front End, Foreman, File Package (FP), and Works Manager, and to allocate and activate processes of an appropriate class (like File Package and Works Manager) to support a specific user initiated tool operation.

MSG supports the following types of communication:

(1)   Pattern 1 (infrequent, short element of interaction): Front End – Works Manager, tool/Foreman – Works Manager, Works Manager – File Package,

(2)   Pattern 2 (possibly frequent, longer elements of interaction with relationship between elements): Front End – tool/Foreman, tool/Foreman – tool/Foreman,

(3)   Pattern 3 (infrequent, very long elements of interconnection): File Package – File Package.

These types of communication are supported by providing two different modes of process addressing: generic addressing and specific addressing; and three different modes of communication: messages, logical connection and alarms. Generic addressing is always used to initiate pattern 1 communication, and is also used to specify a functional process class in cases where processes have not communicated before, or where the details of past communication are irrelevant. It is restricted to the message mode of communication. Specific addressing requires that the processes which want to communicate are familiar with each other in having communicated before, either directly or through intermediary processes.

The message mode is used for pattern 1 and some pattern 2 communications. The connection mode is provided by MSG mainly to support pattern 3 and such pattern 2 communications as file transfer and terminals-like communication. The alarm mode is supported by MSG to allow one process to alert another process to the occurrence of a specific event.

Although partial implementation of the NSW was achieved, it resulted in unacceptable performance so the project was terminated.

2.2.2 Simple network operating system

The goal of a project presented in Goscinski *et al.* (1983) was the development of a network operating system making possible an access to remote resources available on different computers running different operating systems. The solution proposed was based on a remote access system (RAS).

RAS is located on a communication subsystem providing a necessary subset of services defined by the four lowest layers of the ISO/OSI Reference Model. This system makes it possible for user processes to use remote resources by implementing remote operations called by these processes. The execution of remote operations requires that parts of a remote access system are in computers where the resources are located. These parts work on behalf of those processes requesting remote service by cooperating with their local operating systems. They receive requests, and work as any other local process requesting a service. After completion of requested operations, they check results of these operations, and send results to a requesting process.

For the operating system extensions discussed here it is assumed that in each computer in which there are remotely accessible resources and/or processes employing these resources, there resides a remote access system module. Each user process which uses the functions of remote access contains interface procedures linked with it, calls of which correspond to the execution of operations on remote resources. During their execution, interface procedures perform all actions necessary for cooperation with the rest of the remote access system. The return from a procedure takes place after the execution of all the actions connected with carrying out operations on a remote resource are over. Thus, the user is not conscious of the actions actually undertaken by a remote access system.

Apart from the interface procedure, execution of an operation indicated by the user by means of calling an appropriate procedure requires the use of:

(1)   a local module of the remote access system – local to the node where the user process resides,

(2)   a communication subsystem of the network,

(3)   a remote module of the remote access system – in the node in which a resource is localized,

(4)   local operating systems in computers of both nodes.

Fig. 2.6 illustrates the program interface between the components of the remote access system (RAS) engaged in executing a remote operation initiated by the user process which is in computer A on the resource which is available on computer B.

Access to a remote resource in computer A from computer B involves the same modules of the remote access system, with the roles reversed, and analogous interface procedure linked to the user process in computer B. However, since the operating systems of computer A and B are different, the operations defined on particular interfaces, identical at the logical level, may have a different manner of execution in components A and B and may engage their operating systems in a completely different way.

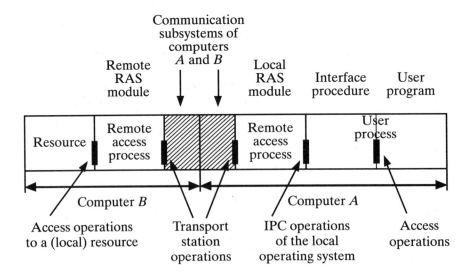

Fig. 2.6   Program interfaces between components of remote access system.

Fig. 2.7 illustrates the general cooperation scheme between remote access system (RAS) components. The aspect of the inner structure of the module of the remote access system was ignored; if the module consists of several processes, communication between them must be
established.

As a result of calling a remote access operation, the user process
turns over control to an interface procedure which formulates (1) the
request and transmits it to the local RAS module. After being accepted
(2), a request is sent on to an appropriate remote RAS module which
accepts it, registers it, and acknowledges (3) the readiness to perform
the service. The local RAS module transmits (4) the acknowledgement
supplemented with data which allow the interface procedure of a user
process to enter into a direct communication with the remote RAS
module. The interface procedure transmits (5) the input data connected
with an operation code. After having received it, the remote RAS module (processing module) starts to execute the operation on a resource
(6), and sends the acknowledgement (7) to the interface procedure.
When the operation has been completed (8), the acknowledgement of its

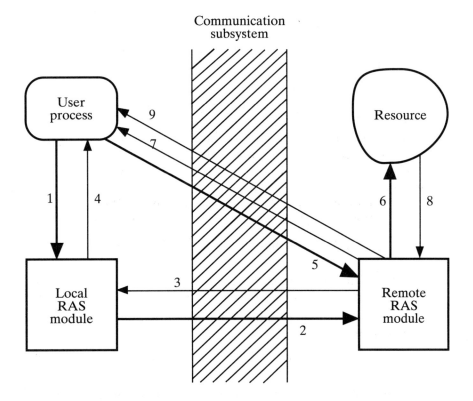

Fig. 2.7 Cooperation scheme between remote access system components.

execution and the result are transferred (9) to the interface procedure of a user process. The execution of the interface procedure ends by passing the result of the remote operation.

The scheme does not depend on the inner structure of a single RAS module; the structure varies depending on the type of operating system. Independently, however, of the services offered by an operating system in the range of operations on resources and interprocess communication, it is vital for each RAS module to:

(1) guarantee that the semantics of a remote access operation is identical with all other RAS modules; and

(2) establish cooperation with interface procedures and other RAS modules according to a homogeneous binding protocol.

The execution of an operation on a remote resource requires that the interface procedure for a given operation cooperates with RAS modules residing in nodes where there is a process and a resource. The principles of this operation are defined by a special protocol. As a basis for its construction two protocols were used:

(1) a protocol for communication in a network using a connection–oriented transport layer service; and

(2) a protocol for interprocess communication in a local operating system.

The latter, not standardized, was arbitrarily adopted at the level of user operations for sending and receiving a message. The operations are assumed to have blocked semantics; they indicate the destination process and identify the sender of the received message. Because of the variety of operations and connected requirements, a flexible cooperation protocol was constructed so that each remote access operation has a defined variant of protocol corresponding to it.

The following criteria were taken into consideration in choosing the final solution of the network operating system described above:

- minimization of the number of processes comprising a RAS module,

- minimization of the number of ports in the transport station, used by RAS modules and interface procedures,

- minimization of the memory requirements in requesting and serving computers,

- maximization of the number of user processes served concurrently,

- maximization of the system effectiveness, as measured by the average number of remote operations completed in a computer per unit of time.

2.3   The UNIX-based network operating systems

There is a strong tendency to develop an operating system for a distributed system based on the UNIX concept. In this work, one can distinguish two categories. The first is simply an extension of the centralized UNIX system to allow using remote resources. This category, which reflects network operating systems rather than distributed operating systems, contains these systems which are implemented at the user level. No kernel changes are required. The second is the construction, from scratch, of UNIX-like distributed operating systems. In this section we characterize the first category of systems.

Newcastle Connection (Brownbridge *et al*. 1982), called also by its authors UNIX United, was developed at the University of Newcastle Upon Tyne to connect loosely coupled UNIX systems. This system provides remote, transparent access to files, using what appears to the application to be the same system calls as used locally. The implementation is via extension to the language libraries of applications. Such a solution implies that local access is slowed down.

The UNIX United system is composed of a set of inter-linked standard UNIX systems. Each UNIX system has its own storage and peripheral devices, accredited set of users and system administrator. The naming structures (for files, devices, commands and directories) of each component UNIX system are joined together in UNIX United into a single naming structure. This implies that each user, on each UNIX system, can read or write any file, use any device, execute any command, or inspect any directory, regardless of the system to which it belongs.

The UNIX United system is provided by means of communication links, and the incorporation of an additional layer of software, called the Newcastle Connection, in each of the component UNIX systems (Fig. 2.8).

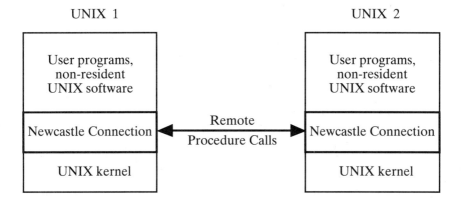

Fig. 2.8   The UNIX United system {adapted from Brownbridge *et al.* (1982)}.

The Newcastle Connection is located between the UNIX kernel and the rest of the operating system, that is the shell and the various command programs, and the user programs. From above, this layer is not distinguishable from the kernel. On the other side, from below, it appears to be a normal user process.

There are two main functions of the Newcastle Connection:

(1)   accepting system calls that have been directed to it from other systems,

(2)   filtering out system calls that have to be redirected to another UNIX.

Communication between the Connections is based on the use of a remote procedure call (RPC) protocol which is discussed in Chapter 5.

The characteristic feature is that local systems execute all system calls but calls to the file subsystem may access files on other machines. Remote access to files is based on the same system calls as used locally. These systems use one of two ways to identify remote files.

(1)   The first naming scheme is based on a special character inserted into a path name. The component name preceding the special character identifies a machine, and the remainder of the path name identifies a file on that machine.

(2)   The second naming scheme identifies remote files by adding a special prefix to inform a system that the file reference is remote; the second component name gives the remote machine name.

In the Newcastle Connection the kernel does not participate in determining that a file is remote. The C library functions that provide the kernel interface detect that a file access is remote and take the appropriate action.

The advantages of the Newcastle design are that:

(1)   processes can access remote files transparently, and

(2)   no changes need be made to the kernel.

There are several disadvantages of the Newcastle approach:

(1)   system performance may be degraded;

(2)   the library duplicates kernel functions and takes up more space;

(3)   because of the larger C library, each process takes up more memory even though it makes no remote reference;

(4)   local requests may execute more slowly because they take longer to get into the kernel, and remote request may also be slow be-

cause more processing is needed at user level to send requests across a network; and

(5)   larger processes take longer to start up in **exec** and may cause greater contention for memory, including a higher degree of paging and swapping on a system.

2.4   Summary

Network operating systems can be regarded as primitive forerunners of distributed operating systems. The major difference between these two classes of systems is that in the former system, if a remote resource is to be accessed, the user has to know its location. In general, the major difference manifests in the way of seeing and managing local and global resources.

Differences between network operating systems and distributed operating systems can be explained simply based on the analysis of the location of the interprocess communication facility in a hierarchical structure of an operating system. It is evident that the lower the interprocess communication facility is placed, the more transparent the network becomes, decisions may be performed globally, and resources are managed in a global fashion using global mechanisms rather than local mechanisms.

Network operating systems are extensions of local (centralized) operating systems making possible an access to remote resources available on different computers connected by a network.

Bibliography

Blair G.S., Mariani J.A. and Shephard W.D. (1982). A Practical Extension to UNIX for Interprocess Communication. *Software—Practice and Experience* **12**, 1147–62

Brownbridge D.R., Marshall L.F. and Randell B. (1982). The Newcastle Connection—Or UNIXes of the World Unite!. *Software—Practice and Experience,* **13**, 45–58

Collinson R.P.A. (1982). The Cambridge Ring and UNIX. *Software—Practice and Experience,* **12**, 583–94

Fortier P.J. (1986). *Design of Distributed Operating Systems. Concepts and Technology*, Intertext Publications, Inc., New York: McGraw-Hill

Franta W.R. and Chlamtac I. (1983). *Local Networks. Motivation, Technology and Performance*. Lexington Books

Goscinski A., Nogiec J. and Rakoczy W. (1983). *The Extension of Operating Systems to Provide Access to Network Resources*. Report No. 4, Institute of Computer Science, The University of Mining and Metallurgy, Krakow, Poland

Holler E. (1981). The National Software Works, Distributed Systems—Architecture and Implementation. *Lecture Notes in Computer Science No. 105*, Springer-Verlag

Rowe L.A. and Birman K.P. (1982). A Local Network Based on the UNIX Operating System. *IEEE Transactions on Software Engineering*, **SE–8**(2), 137–46

Tanenbaum A.S. and van Renesse R. (1985). Distributed Operating Systems. *Computing Survey,* **17**(4), 419–70

Watson R.W. and Fletcher J.G. (1980). An Architecture for Support of Network Operating System Services. *Computer Networks,* **4**

3 Communication issues of distributed computer systems

Computer 1	Computer 2	Computer 3		Computer N
System and user processes	System and user processes	System and user processes	• • •	System and user processes
Interprocess communication facility				
Transport protocols	Transport protocols	Transport protocols		Transport protocols
Network protocols	Network protocols	Network protocols		Network protocols
Data link protocols	Data link protocols	Data link protocols		Data link protocols
Physical protocols	Physical protocols	Physical protocols		Physical protocols
Communication medium				

C ommunication plays a key role in distributed operating systems by supporting interprocess communication primitives. Interprocess communication facility allows processes spread over a distributed computer system to communicate and access resources. Performance of a whole distributed computer system, in particular a distributed operating system, depends on this facility. Fast interprocess communication relies on efficient interprocess communication primitives and communication protocols, in particular a transport protocol which provides services to these primitives.

As mentioned in the previous chapter, a distributed operating system controls and manages a distributed computer system. Two questions arise:

(1)   What is a distributed computer system?

(2)   Why are distributed computer systems becoming so popular?

This chapter provides an introduction to distributed computer systems and answers these questions. It also presents major aspects of the ISO/OSI Reference Model, as a common basis for the development standards for system interconnection, and some elements of communication protocols. Because interprocess communication protocols are supported by a transport protocol, the Transport Layer of the ISO/OSI Reference Model is characterized. In particular services of this layer are discussed. Such a background is necessary for the analysis, design, and/or choice of a transport protocol that has to support communication between remote processes. Moreover, the knowledge of these problems is necessary to identify properly the location of several services in the process-to-process (end-to-end) communication architecture. We also briefly introduce local area networks, the IEEE 802 LAN Model, and other standards such as MAP and TOP. Finally, transport protocols are discussed. Two groups of the transport protocols are introduced: general purpose transport protocols and special purpose transport protocols. Their advantages and disadvantages are emphasized.

Knowledge of distributed computer systems, in particular local area networks, is important, not only because distributed operating systems run on these communication systems, but also because many techniques used in communication subsystem can also be used in distributed operating systems. Examples are:

(1)   distributed routing algorithms can be adopted to schedule processes on computers in a distributed computer system – 'there is a large degree of similarity between routing messages in subnet and scheduling processes on hosts of the distributed computer system' (Stankovic 1984);

(2) distributed synchronization algorithms can be developed on the basis of medium access protocols (Le Lann 1977, Chandy 1982, Goscinski 1989), and

(3) distributed processor allocation can be performed effectively when processors are organized in a logical ring, as will be discussed in Chapter 9.

3.1 Selected aspects of distributed computer systems

A distributed computer system can be defined as a collection of several autonomous computer systems (processors and data stores which support processes) connected by some form of a communication subsystem and logically integrated in varying degrees by a distributed operating system and/or distributed database system, in order to achieve an overall goal. The computers do not have a common shared memory and range from microcomputers to supercomputers, and from homogeneous systems to heterogeneous systems, in which heterogeneity can be found in the computer hardware, operating systems, and/or communication systems. The communication system connecting computers and computer facilities should be constructed in such a way that each computer should be able to send understandable messages to any other regardless of the make of internal design of the devices involved and without a knowledge of what other processes are on the net. A distributed system makes possible distributed computations, which means a set of processes, distributed among those computers, which must communicate to achieve some objective. Processes communicate by exchanging messages.

In summary, a distributed computer system must:

(1) be able to support an arbitrary (within limits) number of processes whose distribution should be transparent in many cases;

(2) provide an efficient communication facility based on message passing to allow processes to cooperate;

(3) be integrated into a single virtual computer system.

Distributed computer systems are subjects of research and are used because potentially they provide considerable advantages over traditional centralized systems. These advantages include:

(1) **Good performance** – due to multiple processors and an efficient communication subsystem, as well as avoiding contention and bottlenecks.

(2)   **A better adjustment to related applications** – computers can be spread among workers and the physical processes they control and manage. Users gain control over computing power.

(3)   **Availability** – due to placing data and applications close to the user.

(4)   **Good reliability and disaster protection** – achieved due to the possible redundancy of data and control. Geographic distribution is an essential aspect of disaster recovery and limits the scope of the disaster.

(5)   **Resource sharing** – a most important advantage achieved due to distributed operating system and support from a communication subsystem.

(6)   **Price** – in many cases many small computers and a communication subsystem are cheaper than one big mainframe. Savings can be also achieved by placing processors and data near the user.

(7)   **Extensibility and modular growth** – additional computer systems and computer facilities, such as external disks and printers can be added to an existing system without significant disruption of the system. For most existing and proposed applications, it is practically impossible to predict future demands for the system. That implies that modular growth of the hardware and software is a very attractive feature of the system.

The scope for research and applications of distributed computer systems is very wide and contains such major areas as networks, network operating systems, distributed operating systems, distributed databases, concurrent and distributed programming languages, and fault tolerant systems. There are also other areas – parallel architectures, computer supported cooperative work and problem solving in meetings, distributed simulation, and distributed debugging. This work is oriented towards distributed operating systems so discussion in this chapter is restricted to networks connecting autonomous computer systems and communication protocols.

Networks can be divided into two classes: local area networks (LANs) and wide area networks (WANs). These two classes of networks are different in many aspects. First of all, LANs usually interconnect computer systems located at short distances from each other (such as within a room, a building, or a plant site) using inexpensive transmission media. Devices to interface computer systems to the media are inexpensive and a physical connection is easy. Secondly, transmission rates are generally very high – usually greater than 1 Mbps. These two factors imply that communication delays and error rates are small in LANs. Thirdly, since computer systems connected by LANs usually belong to the same organization, sharing of resources is natural and achievable.

There is seldom a central controlling device. In general, LANs offer great potential and flexibility for applications requiring resources at many nodes. On the other hand, WANs are characterized by their large geographic span, low transmission rates, higher error rates, and complex management systems.

The communication system (local area network, wide area network) connecting computers and computer facilities must be constructed in such a way that users should be able to exchange understandable messages regardless of the internal design of the devices involved or knowledge of other processors. That is possible by adhering to communication standards. To carry out discussion in this area it is necessary to introduce the concept of a protocol.

3.2 Protocols

Communication among objects in a network requires a definition of rules, called protocols, to govern the manner in which communication is allowed to take place. We say that a protocol is a formal set of rules and conventions governing the format and relative timing of message exchanges between two or more communicating processes (users). To design a protocol, it is necessary to:

(1)   build the basic scenario – this requires the simultaneous definition of the basic messages and the basic sequence of these messages,

(2)   introduce procedures for error recoveries – this gives rise to additional messages and increases the list of acceptable sequences.

Protocols are developed to satisfy qualitative and quantitative requirements for process interconnections. Qualitative requirements for protocols include the functionality to be provided by the protocol, flexibility (to accommodate new users and features), deadlock avoidance, synchronization mechanisms, error detection and recovery, buffer overflow avoidance, message sequencing assurance, duplicate message detection and recovery, priority mechanisms, accounting mechanisms, security mechanisms, message delivery guarantees, data code/format transformation, and compatibility of features of computer equipment, operating system, and communication network. Quantitative requirements for protocols include throughput, delay and cost.

Communication between processes requires interworking. Interworking demands that users agree to observe the same rules in order that they may understand data and be able to cooperate to perform some tasks. Interworking requirements can be divided or layered into processing-oriented functions and communication-oriented functions. This implies that protocols can be divided into high-level protocols, con-

Computer *A*   Computer *B*

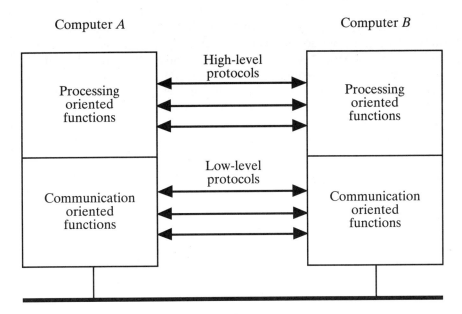

Communication medium

Fig. 3.1   Interworking in networks.

cerned with the ability of two systems to exchange information and to understand it, and low-level protocols, concerned with the use of the physical data transmission network (see Fig. 3.1).

The design, implementation, 'clean' operation and ease of modification of protocols dictate the need to organize them into a series of layers in such a way that a protocol of a higher layer uses services provided by a protocol of a lower layer. The communication at the lowest layer is transmission of physical signals. The communication used by higher layers is a virtual communication. The service of the highest layer protocol is exported to a user. The number of layers, the name of each layer, and the function of each layer differ from network to network. The interface that exists between each pair of adjacent layers defines which primitive operations and services the lower layer offers to the upper one. Usually, the set of layers and protocols is called the network architecture.

3.3   The ISO/OSI Reference Model

To interconnect systems that have different architectures provided by different suppliers, and to be able to exchange understandable messages, it is necessary to define formats and protocols. From the beginning of the communication network development, many of them were developed hierarchically, as a series of layers, but in practice, each of these networks has its own set of layers. The ISO Open Systems Interconnection Reference Model is an international standards activity which deals with communication problems in networks. Since this model can be effectively used as a basic model for interprocess communication in distributed computer systems, we will characterize it at a required level of detail.

The purposes of the Open Systems Interconnection Reference Model of the International Organization for Standardization are (ISO 1981):

(1)   to provide a common basis for the coordination of the development of standards for the purpose of systems interconnection, while allowing existing standards to be placed into perspective within the overall Reference Model,

(2)   to identify areas for developing or improving standards,

(3)   to provide a common reference for maintaining consistency of all related standards,

(4)   interconnection of systems of different vendors.

The previous section notes that for different reasons protocols are divided into layers. It may be difficult to prove that any particular layering is the best possible solution. There are general principles which can be applied to the question of where a boundary should be placed, and how many boundaries should be required. Based on such principles, ISO proposed the seven-layer Reference Model (ISO 1981). According to the Model, protocols interface directly with protocols in adjacent layers and through lower level protocols, and interface indirectly with peer protocols (protocols operating on the same layer).

The architecture of the ISO/OSI Reference Model is illustrated in Fig. 3.2. The description of the ISO/OSI RM seven layers which follows has been developed from such works as ISO (1981), Tanenbaum (1981a), Tanenbaum (1981b) and Aschenbrenner (1986).

(1)   **The Application Layer** – protocols of this layer directly serve the end communication user by providing the distributed information service (exchange of meaningful information) appropriate to an application, to its management and to system management. This layer provides identification of intended communication users (for example, by name, by address, by definite description) and identification of subjects to be communicated. Many different types of subjects are relevant to the OSI RM: text processing, banking, airline reservations, agreement on resources, terminal to computer transaction processing, real-time process control programs. Communication utilities are: network file transfer, virtual terminal, terminal to terminal, and network control.

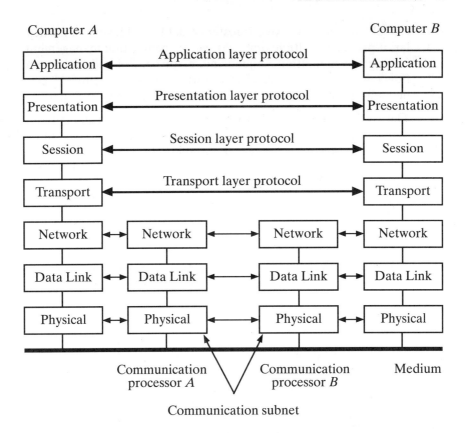

Fig. 3.2 The seven-layer ISO/OSI Reference Model.

(2) **The Presentation Layer** – the purpose of this layer is to represent information to communicating application layers in a way that preserves meaning while resolving syntax differences. In particular this layer provides the following services: data transfer, protocol encryption/decryption, selection of the user data syntax, protocol conversion, data format conversion and database management.

(3) **The Session Layer** – provides the means necessary for cooperating presentation layers to organize and synchronize their dialog and manage their data exchange. In particular, this layer provides session connection establishment and release, synchronization, multiplexing, priority management, resource (buffer) management, exception reporting and communication services.

(4) **The Transport Layer** – provides transparent transfer of data between session layers (entities). The transport layer relieves transport users from any concern with the detailed way in which

reliable and cost effective transfer of data is achieved. In particular, it provides multiplexing, addressing, connection management, message segmentation, sequencing, error control and end-to-end flow control. Three types of transport services are identified: connection-oriented, transaction-oriented and broadcast-oriented.

(5) **The Network Layer** – provides the means to establish, maintain, and terminate network connections between systems containing communicating application entities, and the functional and procedural means of exchanging information between two transport entities over network connections. In particular, this layer provides addressing, message forwarding/lifetime control, routing, congestion control and flow control.

(6) **The Data Link Layer** – provides the functional and procedural means to activate, maintain, and deactivate one or more data link connections among network layers. In particular, it provides access control (local area networks), framing, addressing, sequencing/windowing, error detection/correction, link management, and node-to-node flow control. It provides two types of services: connection-oriented and connectionless.

(7) **The Physical Layer** – provides mechanical, electrical, functional and procedural characteristics to activate and maintain physical connections for transparent bit transmission between data link entities. In particular, it provides transmit and receive information specifications, bit synchronization and media dependent signals.

The lowest three layers are communication-oriented. They have a weak influence on higher level services provided. However, there is the problem of whether connectionless or connection-oriented services should be used in these areas to achieve the best performance with minimal overhead.

Each layer of the network architecture performs some function on the information, called encapsulation. At the sending end, each layer attaches a header (and sometimes a trailer): at the receiving end this header (and trailer if any) is removed by a peer protocol. Names and data units exchanged at the several layers are as follows: user data – Application Layer, encrypted user data – Presentation Layer, message – Session and Transport Layers, packet – Network Layer, frame – Data Link Layer, bit stream – Physical Layer.

This model can be used to connect computers with different operating systems, character codes, and ways of viewing the world, and to create a general vision of communication problems in computer networks.

The ISO/OSI Reference Model was conceived as a model for computer networking primarily in the point-to-point or packet switching environment. Moreover, ISO has concentrated much of its effort in computer communications on the open system interconnection environment.

Protocols based on the ISO/OSI Reference Model, called also **general-purpose protocols**, can support a wide range of applications. It is an advantage that they be general and able to support a wide range of distributed applications. On the other hand as a result of the following features, each layer represents an added overhead. Each layer has its own protocol, which may generate additional messages. Secondly, each layer has to construct appropriate headers on the sending side and analyse them on the receiving side. Thirdly, each layer must usually communicate with its neighbors, resulting in a decrease in the overall system performance. This implies that the use of general-purpose protocols for local area networks should be very carefully analysed.

Three approaches are suggested to be used to deal with these problems:

(1) Simplification of the communication architecture by reducing the number of layers (Tanenbaum and van Renesse 1985, Svobodova 1986). This approach is discussed in detail in Chapter 4 and a simplified architecture is proposed.

(2) Simplification by restricting services provided by several layers, on the basis of some important features of local area networks (Cheriton 1986). This approach is analysed in Section 3.5.

(3) Improving implementation strategies and techniques for general layered communication architectures. This approach was suggested in Svobodova (1986), Watson and Mamrak (1987). This approach is also analysed in Section 3.5.

Moreover, when applying ISO/OSI Reference Model concepts to the local area networks, some modifications are required. There are the following differences between the ISO/OSI Model of WANs and a LANs concept:

(1) In the ISO/OSI Model, a sender and receiver of a block of information will first of all enter into an agreement about exchanging information, whereas in LANs blocks of information may be delivered to a destination from a number of different sources within a short time interval.

(2) The exchange according to the ISO/OSI Reference Model is generally one-to-one and/or one-to-many. In LANs, the exchange is generally many-to-many.

(3) The ISO/OSI Reference Model is often said to be 'connection-oriented'. LANs require a 'connectionless' service.

This implies that it makes sense to build a modified reference model which is particularly suited to local area networks, but which uses as much as possible of the ISO/OSI Reference Model. Such a model will be introduced in Chapter 4.

As emphasized earlier two aspects are critical when one wants to achieve effective and efficient interprocess communication:

(1)   type of service that is connectionless or connection-oriented provided in lower layer (in particular in the data link layer and in the transport layer); and

(2)   the transport layer and services provided by a protocol of this layer. Now, we present more details on these two topics.

3.3.1 Connectionless versus connection-oriented services

One of the most critical design problems in the communication protocols is the type of the service provided by the network layer to the transport layer (Tanenbaum 1981*a*). This problem can be extended to the case of local area networks by adding the question of the type of the service provided by the data link layer to the transport layer (through the network layer if there is one). Finally it is possible to ask what type of service should be provided by the transport layer. The latter problem will be addressed in the following sections. Here, we discuss the former problem.

There are two dominant types of services: connection-oriented service (also called virtual circuit service) and connectionless service (also called datagram service). The analysis of these two services follows the presentation in ISO (1981), Tanenbaum (1981), Meister *et al.* (1985*a*, *b*):

(1)   In the communications system based on the connectionless protocol, each data unit (message) is passed to the layer that provides the service, which tries to deliver it as an isolated unit. There is no assumed relation between successive data units transmitted.

(2)   Data unit delivery based on the connection-oriented protocol is through an established earlier logical channel. So, this protocol has three distinct phases: connection establishment, data transfer and connection release. The logical channel between communicating entities is represented by a record containing data-transfer parameters and channel-state information. Parameters are set up as a result of a negotiation process between the communicating entities. These parameters specify the quality of service, addressing, formatting, sequencing and flow of data units, and are used to control data transfer.

The connection can be released by both of the communication entities, either after successful data delivery or at any stage of the transfer. For the latter case, the cause of the interruption has to be presented to the second party.

Both of these types of services have their advantages and disadvantages. The major advantage of the connectionless service is that the protocol is simple, data delivery is fast and there is no connection management (establishment, release) overhead. However, the delivery of data units is unreliable. Errors have to be handled explicitly by the host and there is no end-to-end flow control. Moreover, destination addresses are required in every packet and data units/messages are not necessarily delivered in the order they were sent. Moreover, because each packet is self-identifying, the headers are usually longer than the headers in connection-oriented protocols, and this leads to a greater transmission overhead.

On the other hand, the connection-oriented protocol provides reliable service. Error handling is done by lower layer protocols and is transparent to the host. End-to-end flow control is also provided by the subset and messages are delivered in the order in which they were sent. Moreover, a destination address is needed only during the logical channel establishment, but because of the overhead created by the establishment and release operations, this service is less efficient.

As mentioned earlier, the importance of design, that is whether connectionless or connection-oriented protocol should be provided in several layers (data link, network, transport) is emphasized in many works. However, there have been very few projects carried out to present quantitative results. The most interesting results were obtained by a team from IBM Zurich Research Laboratory (Meister *et al*, 1985*a*, 1985*b*). They considered the data link layer and transport link layer and analysed the influence of the type of service provided to the connection-oriented transport based layer by the data link layer. It was shown that in the absence of packet losses, the use of a connection-oriented protocol at the link layer may reduce throughput for file transfer by as much as 50 per cent. The authors emphasized also that careful implementation of a connection-oriented protocol combined with acknowledgement accumulation reduces the overhead significantly.

The type of service that be provided in the transport layer is a problem which is addressed in Section 3.3.3.

3.3.2   Classes of the Transport Layer Protocols

Following the ISO/OSI Reference Model (ISO 1981) the transport layer exists to provide the transport service, that is, transparent transfer of data between processes (the transport users – session or application entities), relieving them from any concern with the detailed way in which reliable and cost effective transfer of data is achieved. Reliable transfer means that data units are delivered error-free, in sequence, with no loss or duplication. These transport services are provided in association with the underlying services provided by the supporting layers.

The transport layer protocol is very important and the most complex of all communication protocols. That is because it provides for high quality end-to-end service, deals with a range of communication services and shields applications from the details of underlying communication services. The following discussion of standardization of the Transport Layer is based on Knightson (1983), OSI (1983b), Stallings (1985a).

The complexity of a transport protocol depends on the nature of the underlying service. The ISO developed two standards for the transport layer:

(1)   Connectionless Transport Protocol (OSI 1983a), which is unreliable and may discard, duplicate or reorder messages,

(2)   Connection-oriented Transport Protocol (OSI 1983b).

Here we characterize the latter protocol. This protocol supports connection establishment, data transfer, and connection release functions. Moreover, depending on the class of protocol, it can support flow control, multiplexing and demultiplexing, concatenation and separation, segmenting and reassembling, splitting and recombining.

Classes of transport service have been associated with errors which can happen in the communication system. An error is defined as a lost or duplicated network packet. No damage is done in the system if the error is detected and corrected transparently to the transport entity by the network service. If the error is detected and cannot be recovered, but is signalled to the transport entity, this event is known as a signalled failure. Errors detected but not corrected and not signalled to the transport entity are called residual errors.

Based on this, three types of network service used in specifying transport protocol standards have been defined by the ISO:

(1)   **Type A** – Network connections with acceptable residual error rate and acceptable rate of signalled failures.

(2)   **Type B** – Network connections with acceptable residual error rate but unacceptable rate of signalled failures.

(3)   **Type C** – Network connections with residual error rate not acceptable to the transport service user.

The differences among underlying network services have been taken into consideration in defining classes of transport protocols. There are five classes of protocols, differing in levels of error detection and recovery:

(1) **Class 0: Simple Class** – It provides the simplest kind of transport connection. Only functions for connection establishment, data transfer with segmenting, and error reporting are available. No functions are provided for disconnection (the lifetime depends upon the lifetime of the network connection), flow control, multiplexing, explicit ordering or error control.

(2) **Class 1: Basic Error Recovery Class** – It provides basic error recovery from network-signalled errors, disconnection, and flow control. It is possible to determine which data messages were lost.

(3) **Class 2: Multiplexing Class** – It is assumed that network service is highly reliable. The enhancement to Class 0 is the ability to multiplex connections onto a single network connection. Moreover, it provides in addition to Class 0 the following functions: flow control, exchange of user data during connection establishment, explicit disconnection. No functions are provided for error detection or error recovery.

(4) **Class 3: Error Recovery Class** – It is the union of Class 1 and 2 capabilities, in that it provides error recovery and multiplexing.

(5) **Class 4: Error Detection and Recovery Class** – It provides error detection and recovery based on the assumption that the underlying network service is unreliable. This protocol has to deal with the loss and misordering of messages. The main differences from Class 3 are the addition of time-out mechanisms and resultant extra procedures, and a checksum mechanism.

According to the ISO, the transport service specification is the same for all classes.

The type of network services require by each of the five classes of transport protocol is as follows:

(1)   Class 0 – Type A
(2)   Class 1 – Type B
(3)   Class 2 – Type A
(4)   Class 3 – Type B
(5)   Class 4 – Type C

End-to-end transport protocols is an active area of research and development. Such major bodies as the National Bureau of Standards (U.S.A) and the U.S. Department of Defence have been active participants in the development of the ISO standards. NBS decided that only Class 2 and Class 4 will experience significant demand in the United States. DoD initiated study to replace the Transmission Control Protocol (TCP) by the ISO Class 4 Transport Protocol. These protocols provide approximately the same set of user services, but the user interfaces are different. All this means that general purpose transport protocols, in particular the ISO Class 4 Transport Protocol, are becoming more and more popular.

However, research and development in the area of end-to-end transport protocols does not go only in the direction of general purpose protocols. In particular, for local area networks and distributed operating systems, projects on the design and implementation of special purpose protocols have been carried out. Whether general purpose or special purpose protocols should be used to support interprocess communication primitives is an open problem. Some analysis and arguments are presented in 3.5.4.

3.3.3 Services and mechanisms of the Transport Layer Protocols

Services and mechanisms necessary to implement transport protocols can be divided into four groups: connection management, error handling, flow control and message size. The presentation of these services and mechanisms which follows is based on Watson and Mamrak (1987). When the mechanisms are implemented in general purpose protocols they can be a source of a big computation overhead. The problem is to determine how big this overhead is and how it can be reduced. Section 3.6 deals with these problems.

Connection management mechanisms
Connection management is involved mainly in:

(1)   dealing with such end-to-end issues as allocating, synchronizing and deallocating state (primarily identifiers needed for error and flow control), and

(2)   negotiating modes of operation and needed resources.

Reliable connection management can be achieved using combinations of the following two mechanisms:

(1)   **Message exchange** (handshaking) – this mechanism is used in most existing general purpose transport protocols. It is based on exchange of connection opening and closing packets. This packet exchange overhead makes the handshaking mechanism expensive.

(2)   **Timer** – In this connection management approach, the concept of a transaction rather than connection is in use. Moreover, the mechanism is based on explicit or implicit assumptions about bounds of certain time intervals. According to this approach the

receiver keeps state (for example, sequence numbers or connection identifiers) until all old duplicate requests have died. The sender keeps state until it can receive an acknowledgement if sent. Depending on the details of the protocol, the sender keeps it possibly long enough to guarantee it will generate acceptable sequence numbers (or other identifiers). The problem with this approach is the determination of appropriate timer intervals.

Error control mechanisms

Transferred messages can be damaged, lost, duplicated, and missequenced. A transport protocol must deal with the errors which are implied by these events. The following mechanisms can be used to control these errors:

(1) **Checksums** – This mechanism can be used for detecting damaged messages (packets). Damaged messages are discarded. Recovery in the case of damaged messages is performed through the use of acknowledgements and retransmissions.

(2) **Explicit acknowledgements** – This mechanism is in use to prevent message loss. It has some problems. The first is related to acknowledging responses. Because responses can be lost, duplicate requests will be generated. To deal with these problems, a connection-management mechanism is required. Another loss recovery problem is related to determining the appropriate timeout for retransmission.

(3) **Implicit acknowledgements** – The goal of this application-level mechanism is also to prevent data loss.

(4) **Sequence numbers and/or other identifiers** – This mechanism is used to prevent duplication and missequencing. Duplicate messages result mainly from retransmissions, whereas missequencing is a result of transport level loss and retransmissions.

Flow control

Flow controls include *a priori* or negotiated agreements, special messages, or state piggybacked on acknowledgements. The following mechanisms can be provided to perform flow-control:

(1) explicit sliding window;

(2) implicit sliding window (for example, one outstanding request/ response at a time);

(3) assumptions about relative sender and receiver transmission rates, with discard on overflow; and

(4) transmission rate.

Message size

The size of a message in general can differ from the size supported by the communication protocol(s). This implies the need for segmentation. If a message is transmitted in segments, errors and flow control problems can occur. It is known that the overall cost of dealing with message segmentation/reassembly and intra-message error and flow control is insignificant.

3.3.4 Features of the DARPA Protocol Suite: TCP/IP, UDP

Computers connected to the DARPA Internet share a set of communication protocols which are commonly called the DARPA protocol suite or Transmission Control Protocol/Internet Protocol (TCP/IP). In the DARPA protocol suite, there is also User Datagram Protocol (UDP).

Transmission Control Protocol (TCP/IP)

The development of TCP/IP goes back to 1974 as an result of an order from the U.S. Department of Defence. This protocol has been widely implemented. Since TCP is in use in many local area networks and is used in some experimental distributed operating systems to support interprocess communication primitives, we present some of its features here. The aim of the TCP/IP protocols is to define the universal identification of computers, and specify also a common routing mechanism that sends packets toward their destination on the internet. A knowledge of this protocol is important because it aids in understanding research directed towards the development of highly efficient transport protocols.

As mentioned earlier, TCP and ISO Class 4 provide the same services, but their user interfaces differ. A presentation of a conversion between the TCP and ISO Class 4 Transport Protocol is given in Groenbaek (1986). TCP is a connection-oriented transport protocol. It uses end-to-end mechanisms to ensure reliable ordered delivery of data over a logical connection. These goals are achieved by using the following constructs: flow control, positive acknowledgements with timeout and retransmission, and sequence numbers. There is a connection establishment procedure called the 'three-way handshake', and significant state information is kept. The total address is the concatenation of the network, host, protocol and port fields. This protocol uses end-to-end flow control using windows on a per-logical-connection basis. The TCP acknowledgements are not directly available to the user.

The main function of the Internet Protocol (IP) is that of network routing. Note that this function is essentially the same as the internet sublayer of the ISO network layer. The basic operations performed by IP are the construction of the internet datagram and selecting a route.

User Datagram Protocol (UDP)

The User Datagram Protocol provides the mechanism which is used by a sender to distinguish among multiple receipients on a single computer. It provides unreliable delivery; acknowledgements are not used to confirm message delivery, and messages may arrive out of order. This means that messages can be lost, duplicated or arrive out of order.

Note that to transfer a UDP message from one computer to another, it is necessary to use the underlying Internet Protocol (IP). This is the result of division responsibilities among layers of network protocols.

3.4 Local area networks

According to Cheriton (1983), 'a local network can be viewed as an extended backplane when it connects a cluster of the workstations and server machines managed by a distributed operating system'.

Stallings (1984) defines a local area network as 'a communication network that provides interconnection of a variety of data communicating devices within a small area'. It is necessary to emphasize that it is a communication network, not a computer network. This means that the network software required to connect computers to form a network is not included in this system. We can say, referring to the ISO/OSI RM, that local area networks are formed by a communication medium, and blocks that implement functions and services defined by the two lowest layers of this Model, with some restrictions and requirements imposed on these elements.

These restrictions and requirements are as follows. A communication medium should be single but shareable, to decrease costs and allow a network to be privately owned rather than to be a public or commercially available utility. The low costs of computers and communications and relatively high costs of peripherals such as disk drives and printers allows utilization of the latter through a local area network. Transmission rates should be high to allow fast exchange data between computers (0.1–100 Mbps). This requirement imposes a restriction on a geographic area on which connected computers are spread (0.1–50 km). Error rates should be low (10^{-8}–10^{-12}) to decrease communication overheads.

The nature of a local area network is determined by its topology and transmission medium. This determines the type of data that may be transmitted, and the speed and efficiency of communications. There are three common topologies: star, ring and bus. Knowledge of a topology is important when developing a distributed operating system because some topologies can support some operations in a very natural way whereas others require some special solutions. An example is interprocess communication when sending messages to more than one process (multicasting or broadcasting). This operation is easily implemented in local networks with a bus structured communication medium and requires some special solutions in ring-structured local area networks.

Transmission media and signalling techniques also have an influence, although indirect, on a distributed operating system, and in particular, on the performance of such a system (or response time). Some communication media and signalling techniques allow high-speed transmission rates (coaxial cable using digital or single-channel analog signalling techniques, or optical fibre cable using an analog signalling technique), while others (for example, twisted pair wire) are typically used for low-speed transmissions.

In all local area networks, all devices must share the network transmission capacity. Any communication between two processes requires some means of controlling access to the communication medium. There are a number of access protocols commonly used. They can be linked with two major transmission media topologies – bus and ring – and they are as follows:

(1)   Broadcast bus-sharing techniques; including such conceptually basic techniques as:

    (a)   Aloha technique (Abramson 1973);

    (b)   Reservation technique: time slots, polling, token passing;

    (c)   Contention technique: carrier sense multiple access (CSMA), persistent CSMA, carrier sense multiple access with collision detection (CSMA/CD) (Metcalfe and Boggs 1976), carrier sense multiple access with collision avoidance (CSMA/CA) and collision free-protocols (bit-map protocol, BRAP, MLMA).

    Only some of them have been standardized and/or used in real networks (token passing – IEEE Std 802.4, and CSMA/CD – Ethernet and IEEE Std 802.3). Some of them, in particular collision free-protocols (bit-map protocol, BRAP) can be used effectively in distributed operating systems (Goscinski 1989).

(2)   Ring-access techniques; with such basic conceptually techniques as:

    (a)   Slotted ring (Pierce 1972),

    (b)   Register or buffer insertion (Hafner *et al.* 1974),

    (c)   Token passing (Farmer and Newhall 1969).

    And again, only some of them have been standardized and/or have been used in real networks (token ring – IEEE Std 802.5; Apollo token ring, and slotted ring – Cambridge Ring).

There are two transmission (signalling) techniques used for bus local area networks: baseband – which uses digital signalling with the entire spectrum of the medium used by the signal; and broadband – which uses analog signalling in the radio frequency range with the spectrum of the medium divided into channels carrying analog signals or modulated digital data (Stallings 1984).

After considering the main features and advantages of local area networks there are still some problems to be solved to such networks efficiently:

Efficiency It is difficult to achieve data transfer rates close to the bit communication rate of most local area networks with current protocols and interfaces (also presented in Goscinski and Nickolas [1987]). The main reason for this is processing overhead (in wide-area networks, physical communication facility is critical). This implies that protocols for local area networks should be designed in such a way as to minimize processing overhead. Cheriton (1983) emphasizes that this can be achieved by exploiting the low error rate and low delay of local area networks. Cheriton emphasizes that the choice of a protocol and its implementation should be carefully tuned to achieve high data transfer rates.

Reliability Because of very high bit transmission communication rates, one computer can flood one or more others with packets. Another similar failure, called broadblasting, happens when one computer broadcasts packets very rapidly. If these packets are sent faster than they can be processed, and packets are handled at the kernel interrupt level, computers are disabled.

Security In all networks based on broadcast sharing techniques, each computer connected to a medium can read any unencrypted data. On the other hand, encryption can add some overhead. Another problem arises in systems where location of resources is based on broadcasting inquiry messages. Another node which listens can intentionally or unintentionally play the role of a requested resource (an example is a file server).

Network protocols should provide facilities for dealing with these problems. The general-purpose protocols do not provide such facilities.

3.4.1 IEEE 802 Local Area Network Reference Model

Effective communication requires agreement on a number of technical points, such as the communication medium and certain protocols and conventions, in order that information be exchanged. Is it possible to use the ISO/Open Systems Interconnection Reference Model for local area networks? The answer is yes, but not directly.

It was said earlier that the ISO/OSI RM is oriented towards wide area networks rather than local area networks. But the need for standardization for local area networks is at least as strong as for wide area networks. The first important event in terms of local area networks standardization was the joint project and production by the Digital, Intel and Xerox Corporations of a specification for commercial Ethernet. However, the most significant project was carried out by the IEEE. It was called IEEE 802 LAN (IEEE 1983).

The overall objective of the IEEE 802 LAN standard is to promote compatibility between equipment made by different manufacturers such that data communication can take place between equipment with the minimum effort on the part of the users or the builders of the system. It is assumed that the whole set of protocols, interfaces and services should correspond as far as possible with the architecture set out in the ISO/OSI RM. The committee carried out work in three areas: media, data link together with media access control, and high-level interface.

The ISO/OSI RM has been used in the development of the IEEE 802 LAN standard for the following reasons:

(1)   The Model provides a common vehicle for understanding and communicating the various components and interrelationships of the LAN standard.

(2)   The Model provides a convenient scale with which to measure the generality (the openness) of the LAN standard.

(3)   The Model provides a convenient framework to aid in the development and enhancement of the LAN standard.

(4)   Because higher level protocols are outside the scope of the IEEE 802 LAN standard, the high-level interface committee treats the five upper layers of the OSI Reference Model as a background and modifies them, taking into account the particular requirements of local area networks.

The IEEE 802 LAN standard is concerned with the two lowest layers of the ISO/OSI RM. It points out the most important feature of the local area networks, that is, that the physical medium is a resource shared by all nodes connected to it. A new layer – the Media Access Control Layer (MAC) – has been created. This layer includes functions associated with both the Physical and Data Link layers of the ISO/OSI RM. The relationship between the IEEE 802 LAN Model and the ISO/OSI RM is illustrated in Fig. 3.3.

The IEEE 802 LAN is a set of standards for local area networks. The relationship among these standards is illustrated in Fig. 3.4.

The standards define a single logical link control protocol and four types of media and media access technologies each appropriate for particular applications:

- IEEE Standard 802.2 – a common logical link control protocol, intended to be used in conjunction with each of the four media access standards,

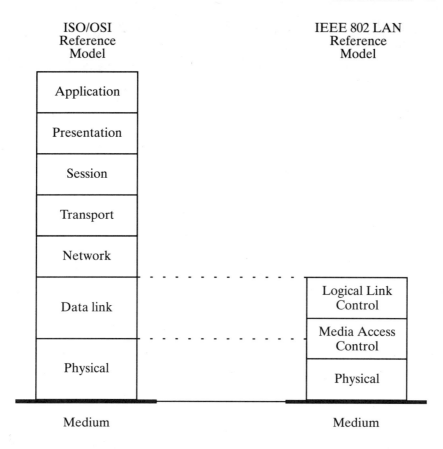

Fig. 3.3 The relationship between the ISO/OSI RM and the IEEE 802 LAN Model.

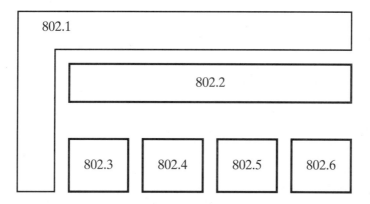

Fig. 3.4 The relationship among the IEEE 802 family of standards {adapted from IEEE (1983)}.

- IEEE Standard 802.3 – a bus utilizing CSMA/CD as the access method,

- IEEE Standard 802.4 – a bus utilizing token passing as the access method,

- IEEE Standard 802.5 – a ring utilizing token passing as the access method,

- IEEE Standard 802.6 – a metropolitan area network.

A document, IEEE Standard 802.1, describes the relationship among these standards and the ISO/OSI RM in more detail. It also contains an explanation of the relation of the IEEE 802 Standards to higher layer protocols, and a discussion of internetworking and networking management issues.

The general structure used by the IEEE in defining the standards is given in Fig. 3.5. The functions of the various layers and their most important features are as follows:

Network Layer   In a local area network it is concerned with providing a media- and access mechanism-independent interface to the upper layers in the architecture of the attached devices. Its other function is to decide on the route of the packets of data (especially relevant where the device concerned is a gateway, a multiplexer, or a message or packet switch). The IEEE Committee has not included specifications for higher layer protocols for the LAN model. However, the four highest layers of the ISO/OSI RM are being suggested.

Multi-link Sub-layer   It is an optional part of the Data Link Control Layer and its applies to devices which support more than one link protocol, such as a switch or a gateway.

Data Link Control Sub-layer   It is the part of the Data Link Control Layer which provides the usual data link layer protocol functions of framing, addressing and formatting. It is in a form independent of the access mechanism, topology, and physical medium in use.

The Layer provides two types of services:

(1)   The Type 1 or Connectionless service, which allows the exchange of data units without the requirement for establishing a logical link. Frames are not acknowledged in this layer and no error recovery or flow control are provided.

(2)   The Type 2 or Connection-oriented service, which requires the establishment of a logical link between two communicating entities (logical ports of the higher layer) prior to exchanging the user data. As a result, frames are delivered in sequence. Both error recovery and flow control are provided.

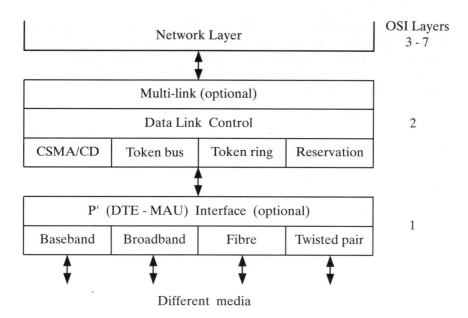

Network Layer	OSI Layers 3 - 7

Multi-link (optional)	
Data Link Control	2

CSMA/CD	Token bus	Token ring	Reservation

P' (DTE - MAU) Interface (optional)	1

Baseband	Broadband	Fibre	Twisted pair

Different media

Fig. 3.5 The general structure of the IEEE standards; DTE – Data Terminal Equipment, MAU – Medium Access Unit.

Section 3.3 discussed which of these two types of services should be used to support distributed operating systems. The importance of this problem has been emphasized a number of times, but has not been studied extensively except in the context of file transfer in local area networks (Meister *et al.* 1985*b*). Arguments of simplicity and the corresponding lower overhead can be used to support connectionless protocols. However, such reasons as packet loss, compatibility issues (between the link layer software providing connectionless service and higher layer software which cannot guarantee reliable delivery), and the possibility of connecting local area networks to wide area networks (concomitant higher error rates) can be used as an argument to support connection-oriented protocols.

Packets may be addressed either to individual uniquely-defined entities/stations (direct addressing), or to selected group of entities (multicast), or to all entities (broadcast). Broadcast and multicast addressing is very important for distributed operating systems.

Media Access Control Methods The Media Access Control protocol depends on the application and topology. The following access methods were standardized: Carrier-Sense Multiple Access with Collision Detection (CSMA/CD), Bus-Token Passing and Ring-Token Passing. Each has its advantages and disadvantages, and each is important for particular applications.

P′ Interface to the Medium Access Unit   It is a device responsible for transmitting and receiving frames of data on the medium. It (generally) consists of two parts: a transceiver/coupler/modem, and a cable tap. This sub-layer is optional, only being needed when the transceiver is not integrated into the Data Terminal Equipment (DTE).

P Interface   Maybe with the following specified media: baseband, broadband, fibre optics, and twisted pair.

The IEEE 802 LAN Model is general enough to be used in applications such as data processing, factory automation, process control, office automation, energy management, distributed computation, computer supported cooperative work and problem solving in meetings, distributed programming language, and teleconferencing.

3.4.2   MAP and TOP

Unfortunately, as we said earlier, the IEEE 802 LAN Model does not contain a higher layer protocol specification. However, two projects have been carried out which not only address the communication-oriented part of the network, but also higher layer protocols. The architectures of the standards developed as a result of these projects, Manufacturing Automation Protocol (MAP), and Technical and Office Protocols (TOP), have been defined by the selection of specific ISO standards for each layer of the OSI seven-layer model. The implementation of services and standards is defined by the selection of options from the specific ISO standard. The lower layers of MAP and TOP are compatible with the IEEE 802 LAN standard. Here we characterize these two standards briefly, mainly to identify their transport protocols.

We recall that CSMA/CD and token bus are suited for different applications: CSMA/CD is suitable for an office environment, whereas token passing is more suitable for a factory environment. Moreover, the majority of local area networks installed today which use these media access techniques are baseband. However, in recent years, broadband capabilities have become more attractive for manufacturers as well as for users.

The objective of MAP (developed by General Motors Corporation) was to define a local network and associated communication protocols for programmable controllers, robots, and terminals within a plant (factory). Because a plant local area network might have a small number of stations with frequent signalling, a small delay per station is less crucial than guaranteeing it has a chance to transmit before a proceeding station gets to send a second message. This implies that the token passing is more appropriate in MAP. Thus, the MAP specification has been written for the IEEE 802.4 broadband token passing network.

On the other hand, an office network might have many stations, but on average requests are relatively infrequent. Moreover, not all network requests are generated at the same time. This implies the use of the CSMA/CD protocol in TOP (the IEEE 802.3 baseband network).

The MAP network architecture and its TOP counterpart are based on the ISO/OSI RM. MAP as well as TOP have identical structures in the higher layers. In particular both use IEEE 802.2 logical-link control standard, that is, the Type 1 connectionless protocol. Moreover, it has been decided that the MAP and TOP will include the ISO Class 4 Transport Protocol.

Note that the commonality of both implementations allows interconnection between MAP and TOP networks.

3.5 General-purpose versus special-purpose transport protocols

Interprocess communication is a critical facility for distributed systems, and in particular, for distributed operating systems. Its performance depends on two major factors: interprocess communication primitives, and the transport protocol which supports these primitives. This implies that process-to-process transport protocols continue to be an important and active area of research and development. The work in this area involves:

(1)   the design and implementation of special-purpose protocols; and

(2)   a re-examination of the design and implementation of general-purpose protocols (Svobodova 1986, Watson and Mamrak 1987). The problem of which of these protocols is better and why is still open. There is no agreement between researchers on this subject.

There are two important issues. The first is that general-purpose transport protocols as well as special-purpose transport protocols must deal with the following issues:

(1)   deciding what abstractions are being communicated (that is, message, packets, byte streams),

(2)   identifying the communicating parties,

(3)   detecting and recovering from possible errors,

(4)   managing resources such as buffers,

(5)   synchronizing the communicating parties,

(6)   protecting the information against unauthorized reading or identification.

The second issue is that mechanisms available for implementing transport protocols are largely independent of the wide range of communication primitives and associated semantics.

The goal of this section is the presentation of pros and cons for both types of transport protocols and some suggestions according to their applications. Some elements of the design and implementation of transport protocols are presented. Some transport protocols are also given. This section mainly follows the considerations presented in Svobodova (1986), Watson and Mamrak (1987), Cheriton (1983) and (1986), Lantz et al. (1985) and Saltzer et al. (1984).

3.5.1 Special-purpose transport protocols

The transport protocol described in Section 3.3 is the most complex and probably the most important protocol. If it is standardized, manufacturers are encouraged to implement it to achieve greater market penetration, and users do not have to consider proposals from different vendors. So, standardization of the transport protocol is widely accepted. However, existing standardized transport protocols do not fulfil all the requirements of distributed operating systems and local area networks, because of performance requirements and the complexity of these protocols. The standard transport protocols have to be very general to be able to support different applications and as a result of this they are complex. Moreover, general-purpose protocols are based on the connection-oriented approach because they have been developed for session-type communication as used in wide area networks. Such protocols and their generality implies a considerable computation overhead, which cannot be accepted for transaction type communication in systems connected by high-speed local area networks or in wide-area networks with fibre optic channels. It is emphasized very strongly that because of very low error rates, many parts of the general-purpose transport protocols are not useful and can be removed. Cheriton (1986) argues that general-purpose protocols are not well suited for high-speed networks, because they do not provide facilities to support effective sharing of resources, multicasting and utilization of clusters of computers for real-time applications such as process control, collaboration and problem solving in meetings.

As a result of the drawbacks of the general-purpose transport protocols, in many distributed systems based on local area networks there is a tendency to use the simplest protocols possible (Birrell and Nelson 1984, Cheriton 1986, Lee et al. 1986), the so-called special-purpose protocols.

Special-purpose transport protocols which are used in local area networks and in networks controlled by distributed operating systems are as simple as possible. The simplifications have been achieved on the basis of many assumptions, some of which have been presented in the previous sections.

One major simplification has been achieved through the minimization of a connection mode. This can be achieved in three different ways:

(1)   Use a connectionless protocol whenever possible.

(2)   The second method is to use a 'lightweight connection' protocol (Svobodova 1986). A lightweight connection protocol, like the connectionless protocol does not have explicit separate connection establishment and connection release phases. The connection is established by the server after receiving the first request, each subsequent request from the user being treated as logically connected to the previous, until some indication of the end of data transfer or failure. This closes the connection.

(3)   The established connection is maintained for the time needed to satisfy a request.

Another simplification can be achieved by reducing packet exchange overhead by minimizing the number of packets required for connection management and acknowledgement. Such a reduction of packet exchanges is a result of:

(1)   assumptions about network error characteristics; and

(2)   a combination of the connection management mechanisms, that is, packet exchange, timer and unique connection identifications presented in Section 3.5.

Section 3.5 emphasized that packet handling in the case of packet loss is expensive. This argument is also in use to simplify transport protocols. That is achieved by reducing the number of required acknowledgements by using the receipt of an application level response to provide the acknowledgement of the corresponding request. Another simplication can be achieved in the area of services provided for acknowledging responses. Assuming that there is no packet duplication or missequencing and that only a single outstanding request is allowed at a time, receipt of the next request, if it follows soon enough, is treated as an acknowledgement of the last response.

Simplification of a general-purpose protocol can be also achieved by indicating whether or not the transport layer acknowledgement and retransmission mechanism needs to be used for a given buffer or message (Cheriton 1986). However, such flexibility requires additional higher level mechanisms and complexity for effective use (Watson and Mamrak 1987).

Another assumption used in the development of special-purpose protocols is that missequencing cannot occur because of the use of a single request/response interaction. As a result, connection management and packet acceptance handling can be simplified.

A number of special-purpose transport protocols have been developed for distributed operating systems or for local area networks (Birrell and Nelson 1984, Cheriton 1986, Lee *et al.* 1986, Fry 1987) using many of the simplifications presented above. One of these, VMTP, has very high performance. Another protocol, specially developed to support remote procedure calls, is presented in Chapter 5.

3.5.2 Characteristic features of VMTP

The Versatile Message Transaction Protocol (VMTP) is a transport protocol which is optimised for request response behavior between a client and one or more server processes (Cheriton 1986, Cheriton and Williamson 1987).

This protocol does not use explicit connection establishment or release. It is based on a transaction concept which consists of a request packet and a response packet. The latter acknowledges the request. If a client does not receive a response to its request within a defined timeout period, it retransmits a request with a control bit indicating a need for an immediate acknowledgement. This operation is repeated a number of times. If a response is not received, a client concludes that the server has failed. Usually a response is acknowledged by the next request or by a timeout after the response has been sent. The server can explicitly request an acknowledgement. There are special packets which are used to check the existence of a server or client process; to identify the other entity (current transaction identifier); and to redirect a request from one server to another.

VMTP provides multi-packet requests and responses for transmission of messages longer than a network packet. It allows the transfer of a short user datum in a packet header. One part of the VMTP protocol is the blast protocol, which belongs to the class of bulk data transfer protocols. This protocol supports multicast, datagram, forwarding, streaming, security and priority. VMTP provides simple and efficient selective retransmissions using a delivery mask to indicate packets to retransmit. It uses rate-based flow control within packet groups.

Cheriton (1988) emphasized that 'although VMTP was designed to support efficient V network IPC, it is largely independent of V and suitable for more general use'. It was proposed as a candidate for a standard protocol in the context of the DoD internet.

3.5.3 Improving efficiency of general-purpose transport protocols

Watson and Mamrak (1987) argue in their paper 'that general-purpose protocols can be effective in a wide range of distributed applications because:

- many of the mechanisms used in special-purpose protocols can also be used in general-purpose protocol designs and implementations;

- special-purpose designs have hidden costs; and

- very special operating system environments, overall system loads, application response times, and interaction patterns are required before general-purpose protocols are the main system performance bottlenecks'.

It has been emphasized by these authors that general-purpose transport protocols can be made as efficient as special-purpose ones by a new synthesis of improved protocol mechanisms and supplementation techniques.

The services and mechanisms provided by general-purpose transport protocols have been presented in Section 3.3.3, so the next step is to concentrate on implementation strategies for gaining high computation efficiency. The importance of the implementation over the design of the transport protocol has been emphasized in Svobodova (1986) and Watson and Mamrak (1987). The following areas of implementation optimization can be taken into consideration:

(1) Layered architecture, noting that avoiding a layered design as a requirement for a correspondingly layered implementation can improve the performance. This approach is addressed in more detail in Chapter 4.

(2) Pushing implementations of general-purpose protocols into the operating system kernel or even into the microcode.

(3) Explicit support for lightweight tasking in the kernel.

(4) Support data transfer directly from user memory space to the network hardware and vice versa.

3.5.4 General-purpose or special-purpose transport protocols

Both groups of transport protocols discussed above have advantages and disadvantages. The general-purpose protocols have such advantages as portability across environments, applications independence, support for environmental evolution, and only a single protocol needs to be maintained for a broad range of network and application environments. The main disadvantage of this group of transport protocols is that their performance can be somewhat less efficient than that of special-purpose protocols.

The main advantages of special-purpose protocols are their more efficient execution and low delay. They have also disadvantages, such as close connection to particular network or application architectures, which decreases portability; potentially introducing complexity due to special-case mechanisms; and of failing to guard adequately against error cases. Analysis of the general-purpose and special-purpose transport protocols shows that at this stage it is hard to say definitely which type of protocol should be used to support interprocess communication primitives. Many factors should be taken into consideration when designing or choosing a transport protocol. Moreover, problems of transport protocols and their performance require further study.

3.6 Summary

Distributed systems are becoming more and more popular because they can provide services faster, more reliably, and give results which are not achievable on a centralized personal computational environment. In order to gain this, a distributed operating system must be equipped with a communication facility. Fast interprocess communication is the most fundamental facility of a distributed operating system, and depends on efficient interprocess communication primitives and a suitable transport protocol which provides services to these primitives.

A transport protocol is part of a communication system. Such a system must be developed based on a proper communication model. The ISO/OSI Reference Model is recognized as the best model.

One of the most critical design problems in the area of the comunication protocols, in particular the transport protocol, is the type of the service provided to the higher layer, in the latter case, to interprocess communication primitives. There are two dominant types of services: connectionless and connection-oriented. These services together with types of classes of transport protocols are basic elements of the transport protocol standardization. As well as these general-purpose transport protocols there are also special-purpose ones.

The services and mechanisms necessary to implement transport protocols can be divided into the following groups: connection management, error handling, flow control and message size.

A distributed operating system controls and manages distributed computer systems whose backbone is a local area network. Several medium access control mechanisms are used. They are closely associated with network topologies. The two major topologies are bus and ring. The following major mechanisms were developed: token passing and CSMA for the bus topology, token passing for the ring topology.

Effective communication within local area networks requires agreement on a number of technical points. They are summarized by the standard called IEEE 802 LAN, the development of which was based on the ISO/OSI Reference Model. This standard does not address higher layer protocols, however, there are two standards: MAP and TOP which use the IEEE 802 LAN standard at the lowest layers, and contain higher layer protocols.

The research and development of the transport protocols for distributed operating systems involves: the design and implementation of special purpose protocols, and a re-examination of the design and implementation of general-purpose protocols. Both groups have advantages and disadvantages. At this stage of their research and development it is hard to say definitely which type of protocol should be used to support interprocess communication primitives.

Bibliography

Abramson N. and Kuo F. (eds) (1973). *The ALOHA System Computer-Communication Networks*, Englewood Cliffs: Prentice-Hall

Aschenbrenner J.R. (1986). Open Systems Interconnection. *IBM Systems Journal*, **25**(3/4), 369–79

Birrell A.D. and Nelson B.J. (1984). Implementing Remote Procedure Calls. *ACM Transactions on Computer Systems* **2**(1), 39–59

Chandy K.M. (1982). *A Mutual Exclusion Algorithm for Distributed Systems*. Technical Report University of Texas

Cheriton D.R. (1983). Local Networking and Internetworking in the V-System. Proceedings of the Eighth Data Communications Symposium. *Computer Communication Review*, **13**(4), 9–16

Cheriton D.R. (1986). VMTP: A Transport Protocol for the Next Generation of Communication Systems. Communications Architectures and Protocols. Stowe, Vermont, August 5–7, *Computer Communications Review*, **16**(3), 406–14

Cheriton D.R. (1988). The V Distributed System. *Communications of the ACM* **31**(3), 314–33

Cheriton D.R. and Williamson C.L. (1987). *Network Measurement of the VMTP Request-Response Protocol in the V Distributed System*. Report No. STAN–CS–87–1145, Department of Computer Science, Stanford University

Cheriton D.R. and Zwaenepoel W. (1983). The Distributed V Operating System and Its Performance for Diskless Workstations. In *Proceedings of the Ninth ACM Symposium on Operating Systems Principle* 128–40

Farmer W.D. and Newhall E.E. (1969). An Experimental Distributed Switching System to Handle Bursy Computer Traffic. In *Proceedings of the ACM Symposium on Problems in the Optimization of Data Communications* ACM, New York

Fry M.R. (1987). The Transport Layer in a Microcomputer Network. *The Australian Computer Journal*, **19**(2), 56–62

Goscinski A. (1989). Synchronization Algorithm for Processes with Dynamic Priorities in Computer Networks with Node Failures. *Information Processing Letters*, **32**(3), 129–136

Goscinski A. and Nickolas P. (1987). A Performance Study of a File Server System on the AppleTalk Personal Network. *Computers in Industry*, **8**(4), 283–91

Groenbaek I. (1986). Conversion Between the TCP and ISO Transport Protocols as a Method of Achieving Interoperability Between Data Communication Systems. *IEEE Journal on Selected Areas in Communications*, **SAC–4**(2), 288–96

Hafner E.R., Nenadal Z. and Tschanz M. (1974). A Digital Loop Communications System. *IEEE Transactions on Communications*

Hedrick C.L. (1989). Introduction to the Internet Protocols. *AUUGN*, **10**(1), 66–96

IEEE (1983). IEEE Project 802—Local Area Network Standards' Draft D. *IEEE*

Iggulden D. (1989). After OSI: Open Distributed Processing. *Telecommunications* **23**(4), 38–45

ISO (1981). Data Processing—Open Systems Interconnection—Basic Reference Model. *ISO*

Knightson K. (1983). The Transport Layer Standarization. *Proceedings of the IEEE*, **71**(12), 1394–6

Lantz K.A., Nowicki W.I. and Theimer M.M. (1985) An Emirical Study of Distributed Application Performance. *IEEE Transactions on Software Engineering*, **11**(10), 1162–74

Lee D., Chon K. and Chung C. (1986). A Reliable Datagram Transport Protocol on Local Area Networks, Communications Architectures and Protocols, Stowe, Vermont, August 5–7. *Computer Communications Review* **16**(3), 320–7

Le Lann G. (1977). Distributed Systems—Toward a Formal Approach. *Proceedings of the IFIP Congress 77*, 155–60

MAP (1984). General Motors' Manufacturing Automation Protocol: A Communications Network for Open Systems Interconnection, Version 2.1. *General Motors Corporation, Manufacturing Engineering and Development, Advanced Product and Manufacturing Engineering Staff (APMES), APMES A/MD—39*, GM Technical Center, Warren, MI 48090–9040

Meister B., Janson P. and Svobodova L. (1985). Connection-Oriented versus Connectionless Protocols: A Performance Study. *IEEE Transactions on Computers,* C–34, No. 12, 1164–73

Meister B., Janson P. and Svobodova L. (1985). File Transfer in Local Area Networks: A Performance Study. *The 5th International Conference on Distributed Computing Systems.* Denver, Colorado, 338–49

Metcalfe R.M. and Boggs D.R. (1976). Ethernet: Distributed Packet Switching for Local Computer Networks. *Communication of the ACM,* **19**(7), 395–404

Nowicki B. (1989). Transport Issues in the Network File System. *Computer Communication Review,* **19**(2), 16–20

OSI (1983). OSI—Transport Service Definition. *ISO Draft Int. Stand. 8072*

OSI (1983). OSI—Connection Oriented Transport Protocol Specification. *ISO Draft Int. Stand. 8073*

Pierce J.R. (1972). Network for Block Switches of Data. *Bell Systems Technical Journal*, **51**(6)

Postel J.B. (1980). Internetwork Protocol Approaches. *IEEE Transactions on Communications*, COM–28, No. 4, 604–61

Saltzer J.H., Reed D.P. and Clark D.D. (1984). End-To-End Arguments in System Design. *ACM Transactions on Computer Systems*, **2**(4), 277–88

Stallings W. (1984). Local Networks. *Computing Surveys*, **16**(1), 3–41

Stallings (1985). Can We Talk. *Datamation*, 101–6

Stallings W. (1985). *Local Networks. An Introduction.* Macmillan Publishing Company–Collier Macmillan Publishers

Stallings W. (1988). *Data and Computer Communications.* Second Edition. Macmillan Publishing Company

Stankovic J.A. (1984). A Perspective on Distributed Computer Systems. *IEEE Transactions on Computers*, C–33, No. 12, 1102–15

Stewart N. (1988). Computer Communications for Industrial Automation: The MAP Protocols. *Computer Communications*, **11**(5), 262–6

Svobodova (1986). Communication Support for Distributed Processing: Design and Implementation Issues Networking in Open Systems. In *Lecture Notes in Computer Science*, 248, (Miller G. and Blanc R.P. eds,) Springer-Verlag

Tanenbaum A.S. (1981). Network Protocols. *ACM Computing Surveys,* **13**(4), 453–89

Tanenbaum A.S. (1981). *Computer Networks.* Prentice Hall International Inc.

Tanenbaum A.S. and van Renesse R. (1985). Distributed Operating Systems. *Computing Surveys,* **17**(4), 419–70

TOP (1985). *Technical and Office Protocols Specification*, Version 1.0, Second Printing, The Boeing Company

Watson R.W. and Mamrak S.A. (1987). Gaining Efficiency in Transport Services Appropriate Design and Implementation Choices. *ACM Transactions on Computer Systems,* **5**(2), 97–120

4 Research and design issues of distributed operating systems

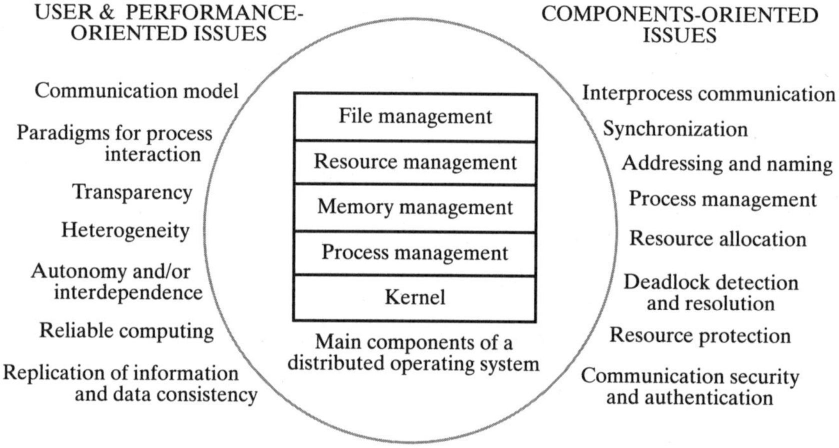

USER & PERFORMANCE-ORIENTED ISSUES
Communication model
Paradigms for process interaction
Transparency
Heterogeneity
Autonomy and/or interdependence
Reliable computing
Replication of information and data consistency
File management
Resource management
Memory management
Process management
Kernel
Main components of a distributed operating system
COMPONENTS-ORIENTED ISSUES
Interprocess communication
Synchronization
Addressing and naming
Process management
Resource allocation
Deadlock detection and resolution
Resource protection
Communication security and authentication

The Introduction introduced basic research and design issues associated with software components of a distributed operating system, and showed that they are relevant to a general logical model of such a system. However, these issues, though basic for designing distributed operating systems, should be discussed in terms of fundamental features of these system, such as for example transparency. A need for this feature was emphasized in Chapter 2. The question arises: what are these research and design issues? This chapter attempts to answer this question.

There are two goals of this chapter. The first is the identification and discussion of major problems and issues in distributed operating systems; the second is the presentation of the relationship between components' issues of a distributed operating system and the creation of a framework model of a distributed operating system. The following chapters will study details of this model and fill up its basic blocks.

To achieve the first goal, eight major issues important from the research point of view as well as in the development and applications of distributed operating systems have been identified. The first is a communication model for a distributed operating system which is necessary to create a framework for message passing. The second issue discussed is paradigms for process interaction in a distributed computing environment. The third issue is transparency: various degrees of network transparency and problems connected with it are presented. The next issue is heterogeneity: Is it desired or not? The fifth design issue deals with autonomy and/or interdependence – a distributed operating system provides autonomy for different reasons: to achieve policy freedom, provide robustness and increase security. Is it possible to achieve them without interdependence?

Issue six, of growing importance, is reliable distributed computing; in particular, transactions for reliable distributed computing. Before the presentation of transaction applications in distributed operating systems, basic terms of reliability are presented. Transactions and atomic actions are treated as basic concepts for recovery. Finally, transactions in programming systems are discussed. The seventh issue is replication of information in distributed systems and data consistency. In particular, the multiple copy update problem and their solutions are presented.

The eighth issue, oriented also towards the second goal of this chapter, is related to the state of knowledge in components specific for distributed operating systems. These components strive to provide services to the users. Two main groups of components are characterized. The first is oriented towards distributed processes and their management, and contains such topics as interprocess communication, synchronization, naming, and process management. The second group is oriented towards resource management and addresses such topics as resource allocation, deadlocks, protection, communication security and authentication, and services. All these components will be discussed in detail in following chapters. The last issue discussed in this chapter is how these components are realized in a distributed system. Two models (mechanisms) for the distributed operating system design are identified: the process model and the object model.

4.1 Introduction

After many years of research and experiments, and as a result of the development of several experimental and commercial operating systems, we know how to build an operating system for a centralized computer system. On the other hand, although significant progress has been made in the development in distributed operating systems during the last decade, they are still in an early phase of development, with many unanswered questions and relatively little agreement among workers in the field about how things should be done. There are three reasons for this situation. First, there is the problem of obtaining a full understanding of distributed applications. The second reason is that information about all objects of a distributed computer system is not located in one place as in a centralized operating system. It is well known from control theory that control and management of distributed systems is a very complex problem. The last reason is that in distributed systems there is no common time reference. Each computer component of a distributed system has its own notion of time. There is no global ordering of events.

Because of the resource distribution and lack of information about all objects of a distributed computer system located in one place, methods and algorithms developed for centralized operating systems cannot be used for distributed operating systems. Moreover, operating systems, in particular distributed operating systems, are very complex units. However, this complexity is not of interest to users of computers controlled by these systems. They are interested in their performance, services provided and a simple interface.

Research and development of distributed operating systems started with the introduction of local area networks, and developed from a belief that their appealing properties – such as support for resource sharing, extensibility, redundancy and high degree of physical coupling – can improve access, efficiency and cost of utilization of computer facilities. Many attempts have been made to develop distributed operating systems which reflect the benefits of local area networks. In particular, research in this area has been directed towards achieving the following properties:

(1) **Resource sharing** – The distributed operating system should provide the mechanism for sharing resources among various nodes of

a local area network. Moreover, the location of these resources should be transparent to the user.

(2) **Extensibility** – It would be beneficial if the distributed operating system allows the addition of new nodes to a network (either statically or dynamically) and hence new services.

(3) **Availability** – The distributed operating system should be constructed, if possible, in such a way that it survives the loss of components.

The development of a distributed operating system should be carried out on the basis of 'good' models of distributed computing. Such models can be oriented towards various elements of distributed computer systems.

4.2 Communication model for distributed operating systems

A distributed operating system, being a global systemwide operating system, can be illustrated as in Fig. 4.1. This figure shows that there are two very important parts of a system, the existence of which is a result of a distribution of personal computers, resources and their connection by a network. These are:

(1) A communication subsystem which links all personal computers and servers, and provides an effective communication service;

(2) Interprocess communication (IPC) which allows remote processes to exchange messages.

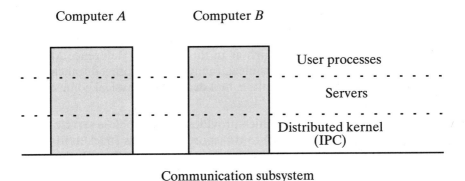

Fig. 4.1 Structure of a distributed operating system.

Computers forming a network-based distributed system normally do not share main memory. This implies that communication via shared memory techniques used in centralized operating systems, such as semaphores and monitors, is not applicable. Message passing in different forms must be used.

Thus, a message passing system is one of the most important parts of a distributed operating system. The next step is to find a suitable model (framework) for message passing systems.

The ISO/OSI Reference Model, a widely discussed framework for message passing systems, was introduced in Chapter 3. Analysis of this model generates the question: is this model directly applicable for distributed operating systems? Unfortunately, the answer to the question is no.

This can be explained in the following way. The ISO/OSI Reference Model is based, on the layer structure. This means that information is passed down through all layers on the sending computer and back up through all layers on the receiving computer. Since each layer adds overhead to a data transmission, whether or not that overhead is required, such a model is usually not efficient in a distributed computer system based on a local area network.

This observation leads to the conclusion that distributed operating systems should be developed using a simpler model and on the basis of a functional hierarchy.

Such a model can be developed by analogy with programs which use a functional hierarchy. In a functional hierarchy, a program at one level may directly call any visible operation of a lower level. No information flows through any intermediate level. A significant advantage of functional levels over information-transferring layers is efficiency: a program that does not use a given function will experience no overhead from that function's presence in the system.

An analysis of distributed operating systems designed to date shows that processes in a local computer network can effectively communicate using a five level functional model. These levels are:

(1) **The physical level** – which as in the ISO/OSI Reference Model, provides electrical, mechanical, functional and procedural characteristics to activate, maintain, and deactivate physical connections for bit transmission.

(2) **The datagram level** – which provides connectionless services (delivery is not guaranteed) to transport datagrams (packets) from a source process to a destination process, and deals with the location of services.

(3) **The transport level** – which deals with reliable transport of messages (requests and replies) between client and server; it is sometimes called the **transaction level** because we refer to a request–

reply pair as a transaction. A distinct trend is observed towards connectionless interprocess communication services; this means that message-based systems (using requests and replies to transport datagrams reliably) are proposed rather than connection-based systems.

(4) **The binding level** – which deals with the location of resources of the same type (for example, file servers) and establishing logical communication paths between processes.

(5) **The user level** – which deals with the semantics of the requests and replies to make transmitted information understandable to users.

The user (computation process, production process controller or programmer) sees the transport level interface only, since the lowest three levels are implemented by the hardware and kernel. This observation generates the need for an analysis of relationships between processes, resources, and data in a distributed environment.

4.3 Paradigms for process interaction in a distributed computing environment

There are four basic paradigms for process interaction in a distributed computing environment: the client–server model, the integrated model, the pipe model and a remote procedure call.

4.3.1 Client–server model

The majority of distributed systems adhere to a process model in which control is distributed among the various processes in the system. There is a trend towards building operating systems in such a way that a large part of the operating system code is moved up to higher layers (this means in practice that this part is removed from the operating system), leaving a minimal kernel. This implies that most of the operating system functions are implemented in user processes. Processes are generally classified as either clients or servers (in some cases a server may also be a client).

An analysis of a communication model for distributed operating systems and functions of the transport level shows, that at the highest level, messages are sent between clients and servers. To request a service, a user process (known as a client process) sends the request to a server process, which then does the work and sends back a response. Because of the restricted number of servers (implied by a restricted number of resources on which these servers were implemented), clients compete for these servers (Fig. 4.2). Different existing and designed distributed operating systems provide different services to users using servers.

Following Svobodova (1984) we can define a server in the following way. A **server** is a subsystem that provides a particular type of **service** to *a priori* unknown clients. At this stage, it is useful to distinguish between a service and a server. A **service** is a software entity running on one or more machines. A **server** is the service software running on a single machine. The clients of a server normally run on separate machines, although in some special cases a client might share hardware with the server. The client–server model in distributed systems is illustrated in Fig. 4.3.

Several experimental distributed operating systems have been developed on the basis of the client–server model, for example, Eden (Lazowska *et al.* 1981), V Kernel (Cheriton and Zwaenepoel 1983), Amoeba (Tanenbaum and van Renesse 1985), the Cambridge Distributed System (Needham and Herbert 1982). The most important feature of these systems is that their control model is the same, that is, control is functionally distributed among the various servers in the system. Control of individual resources is centralized in a server. Usually, servers are allocated to individual computers connected to a network.

There are three major problems of the client–server model:

(1)   The first is due to the fact that the control of individual resources is centralized in a single server. This means that if the node sup-

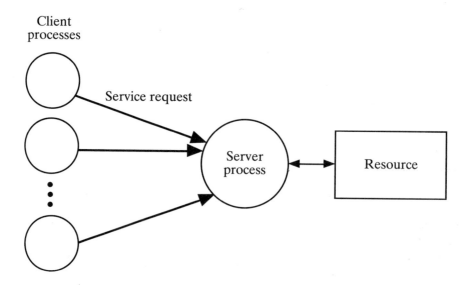

Fig. 4.2   Illustration of the client–server model.

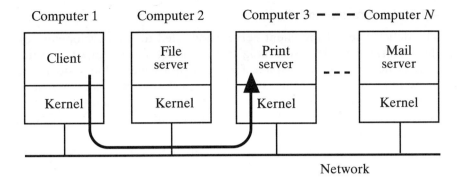

Fig. 4.3 The client–server model in a distributed system.

porting a server fails, then that element of control fails. Such a solution is not tolerable if a control function of a server is critical to the operation of the system (for example, a name server or a file server). Thus, the reliability/availability of an operation depending on multiple servers is a product of the reliability of all computers and devices and of communication lines.

(2) The second problem is that each single server is a potential bottleneck. The problem is exacerbated as more nodes with potential clients are added to the system.

(3) To improve the performance of a client–server based system, multiple implementations of similar functions can be used. However, this increases total costs of a distributed system. Such costs can be reduced when a local cache of information is provided for at least some server functions.

Different solutions to these problems have been proposed. For the Cambridge Distributed System Craft (1983) developed a resource manager with increased reliability. His simpler solution was based on one server. The second, more advanced solution, allows several resource managers. Each of these servers maintains a complete copy of the necessary state information, and can independently service requests. The existence of more than one identical server generates new problems connected with the consistency of their state information. Other solutions were proposed by Raymond and Lister (1982), who proposed some modifications of the basic client–server model to increase servers availability and extensibility; and Danenberg (1982), who proposed a distributed solution to a client–server model based on an agent concept. It is necessary to decide which control model is better, centralized or decentralized? Resource management is discussed in detail in Chapter 9.

4.3.2 Integrated model

The deficiencies of the client–server model led to the development of the integrated model. According to this model, each computer's software is designed as a complete facility with a general file system and name interpretation mechanisms. This implies that each computer in a distributed system would run the same software. Configuration of the system in this case is easy. LOCUS (Walker *et al.* 1983) has been developed based on the integrated model.

Note that a distributed system that has been developed based on the integrated model can be easily made to look like a client–server based system if suitable configuration flexibility has been provided.

4.3.3 Pipe model

The pipe model is based on the concept of a process. A pipe is a communication facility which allows transfer of data between processes based on a first-in-first-out (FIFO) strategy. Pipes also allow synchronization of process execution.

Traditionally, pipes are implemented using the file system for data storage. Communication through pipes is special because it allows processes to exchange messages even though they do not know what processes are on the other end of the pipe.

The most distinct feature of a pipe is that it allows a process to send bulk data to a remote node. To carry out such an operation, a pipe is used as a remote procedure. However, a pipe call does not block the caller and does not return a result. The former implies that a pipe call implicitly starts concurrent activity of a remote process.

There are two kinds of pipes: named and unnamed. They are nearly identical. The difference is in the way that a process initially access them.

In UNIX, the **open** system call is used by processes for named pipes, and the **pipe** system call to create an unnamed pipe. After completing these operations, processes use the same file-oriented system calls to manipulate pipes. Note that only related processes, descendants of a process that issued the **pipe** call, can share access to unnamed pipes (Fig. 4.4). Unrelated processes cannot communicate via unnamed pipes.

The restricted possibility of sharing access to a pipe is a drawback of unnamed pipes. On the other hand, named pipes allow unrelated processes to communicate. However, they cannot generally be used across a network, nor it is possible to multiplex a named pipe to provide private channels for pairs of communicating processes.

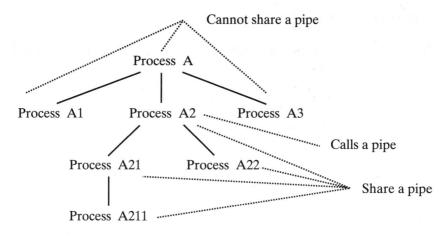

Fig. 4.4 Sharing access to an unnamed pipe.

4.3.4 Remote procedure call model

The remote procedure call model is discussed in detail in the next chapter. Its basic concepts are introduced here to complete this section on paradigms for process interaction.

Communication models based on remote procedure calls allow a process to call a procedure at a remote computer. This operation is performed in the same manner in which a local procedure is called. A remote procedure call blocks the caller until the call is complete and a reply has been received.

When a call is made, a request message is sent to a remote computer where a desired procedure resides, a process is created to execute this procedure, and after this process completes, a reply message is sent to the calling process.

4.4 Transparency

A distributed operating system ensures that users view a distributed system as a virtual uniprocessor, not as a collection of distinct machines connected by a communication subsystem, and they do not see any differences between local and remote resources – they are transparent to users.

On the other hand, the development and maintenance of software for distributed systems is far more difficult and expensive than centralized system software. That is because:

(1) the way of accessing remote resources is different from local resource access;

(2) the possible number of errors in distributed systems is greater than in centralized systems; and

(3) the transmission delay is such that it influences operations in distributed systems.

To solve these software problems it is necessary to analyse the means of interconnections of system at the various software levels. The major result of this work is the concept of making the network invisible to most users and/or applications.

Network invisibility is usually referred to as network transparency. Network transparency refers to the ability of a distributed system to hide machine boundaries from people and application programs, that is, all resources are accessed in the same manner, independent of their location.

Network transparency is valuable and achievable in the local area network environment. Local area network transparency has been demonstrated in a number of systems, such as the V-system (Cheriton 1988) and LOCUS (Popek and Walker 1985). On the other hand, access to remote resources (objects) in wide area networks is not transparent, mainly because of very low transmission rates. This can create some problems, in particular in systems where local area networks are connected by a wide area network. In such an environment, users have transparent access to resources belonging to one local area network, but nontransparent access to resources stored at other site. Moreover, processes have to interact in a nontransparent way.

Following Kreissing (in Svobodova 1985), Popek and Walker (1985), and Gray (1987) it is possible to identify various degrees of network transparency that can be required to achieve a distributed operating system:

(1) **Access transparency** – where a process has the same type of access mechanism for both local and remote resources.

(2) **Location transparency** – where the location of a resource is invisible to the access method.

(3) **Name transparency** – where the meaning of a name, that is, the object with which it is associated, is not dependent on the node in the network from which it is issued.

(4) **Control transparency** – where all information describing a system has identical appearance to a user or application.

(5)   **Data transparency** – which provides the ability to transparently access remote data.

(6)   **Execution transparency** – which allows load balancing, moving programs and data, interprocess communication between processes on different processors.

(7)   **Performance transparency** – which means that users should not experience excessive performance degradation on remote access.

There are also the following additional advantages which could be achieved when providing network transparency:

(1)   easier software development;

(2)   support for incremental changes;

(3)   potential for increased reliability; and

(4)   simpler user model of a distributed system – the user sees resources and operations to be performed on these resources, and does not see their location.

Three levels at which transparency can be provided within a distributed system can be taken into consideration:

(1)   **The programming language level** – some researchers proposed some form of a remote procedure call as a central approach to transparency.

(2)   **The distributed database level** – such a system is responsible for keeping track of where the data is and the user sees what appears to be a system-wide transparent database.

(3)   **The operating system level**.

There is no agreement between researchers on the need for full transparency, the possibility of its achievement, and its value. According to Popek, Walker, and Sheltzer (Popek and Walker [1985] and Sheltzer and Popek [1986]) full transparency is feasible and highly desirable, in particular in collections of local area networks connected by a wide area network. They argue that the wide area network transparency can be achieved when the systems at either end of the wide area network are similar, and the network has links comparable in quality to the Arpanet. Sheltzer and Popek also emphasize that 'remote access can be provided with precisely the same interface as local access'. However, the requirements presented by them are in many cases difficult to fulfil.

In contrast, Cheriton (in Svobodova [1985]) argues that full transparency is not achievable, or even desirable.

This statement will be supported in the context of the transparency degrees presented above. Access transparency should be solved in such a way that syntax and semantics of system calls used to access the resources is separated from resource location control. This implies that access mechanisms for local resources should not be fully identical to access mechanisms for remote resources, because that generates a large overhead. So, access mechanisms for local resources should provide efficiency comparable to that in centralized operating systems.

An exception must be made also, of course with great care, in the case of location transparency. In some circumstances, the user should be provided with a mechanism which allows identification of the location of a resource or server and allows a service to be requested in that location.

Data transparency is connected strongly with distributed databases. Distributed databases have the drawbacks of poor manageability, poor modularity and poor message performance, which means that data transparency is a capability which cannot be recommended. The requester–server model of data access is recommended instead.

The need for complete network transparency is questionable in a heterogeneous environment. This is because a user should be aware of the different capabilities of the connected computers and devices. Heterogeneity will be discussed in the next section.

The reader can find more details on this topic, and an explanation of why the operating system level is preferable to provide transparency, in Popek and Walker (1985).

4.5   Heterogeneity

At the workshop on 'Operating Systems in Computer Networks', Cheriton raised 'the most controversial issue' asking 'Why homogeneity?' The problem is whether 'there is a need for complete network transparency, particular in a heterogeneous environment, or should the user be aware of the different capabilities of the connected systems' (in Svobodova [1985]).

There is hardware and software heterogeneity. In particular:

(1)   Computer hardware heterogeneity, caused by differences between instruction sets, incompatibilities in data representations, and configuration incompatibilities. Hardware heterogeneity, with the exception of data representation incompatibilites, can be easily handled.

(2)   Network heterogeneity, caused by differences between transmission media, signalling techniques, computer-media interfaces, lower-layer protocols (for example, data link layer protocol).

(3)   Operating system heterogeneity, which generates many serious problems.

These heterogeneities arise for many reasons. First, some computer systems are better suited to some applications because of such factors as the compilers, processing capacity. Second, some computer systems provide services which are not available on other computer systems. There could be also a need for local autonomy or some optimization desires.

In general we can say that heterogeneity in distributed systems is the major problem because it restricts the efficient and effective utilization of resources. The problem can be solved by providing, for example:

- Coherence (coherence defined as enforcing high-level uniformity in software while permitting implementation on diverse hardware) which was suggested in Balkovich *et al.* (1985); Morris *et al.* (1986), and coherence supported by the client-server model.

- So-called 'loose integration through shared network services' supported by two facilities: remote procedure call and naming, proposed in Notkin *et al.* (1986).

- Transparent operating system bridges, presented by Gray in Mullender (1987).

In general, the heterogeneity issue is a very important but still open problem, which requires a global solution. This is mainly because distributed systems become more sophisticated to fulfil user requirements.

4.6 Autonomy and interdependence

Why autonomy and interdependence are design issues of distributed operating systems is a question which can be partly answered by looking at two different kinds of distributed systems.

To the first kind belong those systems that consist of autonomous computers which trade resources with one another, but keep local control over them. These systems suffer from some basic drawbacks such as redundancy of functions, problems of heterogeneity, and poor resource sharing performance.

In other distributed systems, computers depend on networked services, such as filing and authentication. These systems also have some disadvantages, which are generated by dependency:

(1) computers are vulnerable to failure of networked services – they cannot work stand-alone;

(2) they are globally controlled to achieve the required level of homogeneity;

(3) global control makes it difficult to identify sources of authority and responsibility; and

(4)   mutually suspicious users want to protect private resources from invasion and misuse.

It is worth noting that one of the main reasons for having autonomous systems is security requirements. Moreover, a lack of autonomy leads to a bureaucratic system. It is well known that no system under central control management could work correctly, probably could not work at all. On the other hand, some degree of interdependence is necessary to allow different systems to communicate and to achieve a good overall system performance.

The solution to this autonomy/interdependence problem is difficult because research in this area is at an early stage. The architects of existing distributed operating systems did not address these two issues directly. However, some practical solutions can be identified when analysing such research and design issues as naming, resource management, in particular load sharing and load balancing, protection, security and different global servers.

A distributed operating system provides autonomy for the following reasons:

(1)   to provide policy freedom, by giving a user a choice of where, how, and when to compute;

(2)   to provide robustness: a system remains operational despite temporary failures of resources; and

(3)   to control cooperation between mutually suspicious users and to make a distributed system working correctly in the face of different attacks.

Interdependence, as was mentioned above, is necessary. However, a high degree of interdependence is not desired. Thus, to minimize interdependence, the following methods are proposed (Needham and Herbert 1989):

(1)   services which are not needed should not be used;

(2)   to avoid a communication overhead use a workstation on which a requested service can be provided locally; and

(3)   resources (physical, logical) should be replicated if a service which utilizes it is crucial.

4.7   Transactions for reliable distributed computing

Distributed computer systems are potentially very reliable. This is because of the possibility of providing redundant resources on different nodes. Moreover, the redundancy and autonomy permit failures to be masked or localized. However, the distribution of redundant resources also generates some serious problems, such as the lack of global state information, the possibility of partial failure, and the performing of many operations in parallel. These problems imply that it is difficult to maintain data consistency. To overcome these problems atomic transactions were invented.

Another aspect of distributed computer systems is that a single communication cannot always be used to provide interaction between two processes (for example, withdrawal from a bank account). The total interaction may be a sequence of communications and computations. In this case the concept of a transaction is a convenient means of representing the totality of communication and computation.

Transactions were originally developed for database management systems, to aid in maintaining arbitrary application-dependent **consistency constraints** on stored data. The transaction approach and mechanisms simplify the construction of reliable systems. Transactions should provide uniform support for invoking and synchronizing operations on shared data objects, assurance of the serializability of transactions with one another, and atomic behaviour and recovery in the face of network and nodal failures. It is desirable from the user and program point of view that the transaction facilities be entirely transparent.

Most of the research carried out in the development of transaction mechanisms relates specifically to database systems. The techniques resulting from this research cannot be used directly in distributed operating systems because of the lack of flexibility and efficiency needed in the latter systems. Therefore the transaction model must be extended to meet distributed programming requirements.

Before presenting the application of transactions in distributed operating systems, the basic terms relating to reliability and the database approach to transactions will be discussed. Such a background will help the reader to pick up the essentials of this research and design issue.

4.7.1 Basic terms of reliability

The basic terms of reliability in distributed computer systems are presented on the basis of the survey carried out by Randell, Lee, and Treleaven (1978) and used by Kohler (1981). They state that:

> 'The **reliability** of a system is taken to be a measure with which the system conforms to some authoritative specification of its behaviour.
>
> When the behaviour deviates from that which is specified for it, this is called a **failure**. A failure is thus an event, with the

reliability of the system being inversely related to the frequency of such events.

We term an internal state of a system an **erroneous state** when the state is such that there exist circumstances (within the specification of the use of the system) in which further processing, by the normal algorithms of the system, will lead to a failure which we do not attribute to a subsequent fault. ... The term **error** is used to designate that part of the state which is incorrect.

A **fault** is the mechanical or algorithmic cause of an error, while a **potential fault** is a mechanical or algorithmic construction within a system such that (under some circumstances within the specification of the system) the construction will cause the system to assume an erroneous state.

The significance of the distinction between faults and errors may be seen by considering the repair of a database system. Repair of a fault may consist of the replacement of a failing program (or hardware) component by a correctly functioning one. Repair of an error requires that the information in the database be changed from its currently erroneous state to one which will permit the correct operation of the system. In most systems, recovery from errors is required, but repair of faults which cause these errors, although very desirable, is not necessarily essential for continued operation.'

The following sections present basic concepts and emphasize these software structuring techniques, for example, transactions and atomic actions, which can be used to achieve error recovery in the distributed system.

4.7.2 Transactions

Transactions, which originate from the field of contract law have the following properties: consistency – they must obey the law; atomicity – they either happen entirely or they do not happen; and durability – once committed (a transaction **commit** means **successful completion**) they cannot be cancelled.

In the area of computer science, in particular in the database literature, the notion of **transaction** was introduced to define consistency among multiple users of a common database. Lampson (1981) defines a transaction as a sequence of read and write commands sent by a client to a file system. It is important to notice that the write commands may depend on the results of previous read commands in the same transaction.

In general, the term **transaction** describes a sequence of operations on one or more database objects that transforms a current consistent state of the system into a new consistent state. Not all system states are consistent and therefore some changes are not allowed to occur. The assertions about the allowable changes in the system are called the **consistency constraints** of the system.

The processing of transactions can be seen as making changes to the database. It can happen that before all changes have been made, the consistency constraints may not be satisfied. This implies that other transactions wanting to perform operations on the objects involved in the currently running transaction, must wait until a consistent state is achieved. If more than one transaction is processed in the system, each of them when considered alone can preserve consistency. However, all of them together have two properties, temporary inconsistency and conflict.

Note that because temporary inconsistency is inherent in all sequential computations, consistency requirements cannot generally be enforced before the end of a transaction. On the other hand, conflict can and must be avoided to achieve consistency. This can be achieved in two different ways. The first is by running transactions serially. This, however, reduces the performance of the system. The second way allows the maximal concurrent processing of transactions by scheduling. Such concurrency implies the interleaved ordering of the operations of a set of concurrently running transactions. A schedule giving each transaction a consistent view of the state is known as a **consistent schedule**.

A sufficient condition for a schedule to be consistent is that the effect of running the schedule is equivalent to the effect of running transactions serially. This condition is called **serializability**. A consistent schedule satisfying the serializability condition is called a **serializable schedule**. Finally, for transactions to be serializable they must appear to be indivisible with respect to other concurrently running transactions.

The requirements and properties of database systems presented above have led Spector and Schwarz (1983) to the following definition of a transaction:

A **transaction** is an arbitrary collection of operations bracketed by two markers – BeginTransaction and EndTransaction – and having the following special properties:

- **Failure atomicity** – either all or none of a transaction's operations are performed.

- **Permanence** – if a transaction completes successfully, the results of its operations will never subsequently be lost.

- **Serializability** – if several transactions execute concurrently, they affect the database as if they were executed serially in some order.

- An incomplete transaction cannot reveal results to other transactions, in order to prevent **cascading aborts** (the **transaction abort** action cancels all actions performed by this transaction) if the incomplete transaction must subsequently be undone.

This definition introduces the next property of a transaction: atomicity.

4.7.3 Atomic actions and recovery

An atomic action is considered as generalization of the concept of transaction. Kohler (1981) presents the four equivalent properties of atomic actions. The first three have been invented by Lomet (1977) and the fourth by Randell (1979).

(1) An action is atomic if the process (processes) performing it is (are) not aware of the existence of any other active processes, and no other process is aware of the activity of the process (processes) during the time the process is (processes are) performing the action.

(2) An action is atomic if the process (processes) performing it does (do) not communicate with other processes while the action is being performed.

(3) An action is atomic if the process (processes) performing it can detect no state changes except those performed by itself (themselves) and if it does (they do) not reveal its (their) state changes until the action is complete.

(4) Actions are atomic if they can be considered, so far as other processes are concerned, to be indivisable and instantaneous, such that the effects on the system are as if they were interleaved as opposed to concurrent.

Since high-level atomic actions can be built from lower level atomic actions, 'atomicity' must be viewed as relative rather than absolute.

Simultaneous accesses to data objects require some special techniques to deal with temporarily inconsistent states. Locking is one possibility. A transaction or atomic action may lock objects to ensure their inaccessibility while in a temporarily inconsistent state. Because transactions can potentially modify any objects they access, they have to fulfil some conditions. Transactions must be well-formed and two-phase in order to guarantee consistency.

We say that a transaction is well formed if the following conditions are fulfilled. The first is that a transaction locks an object before accessing it. The second, it does not lock an object which is already locked. The last is that, before it completes, it unlocks each object it locked.

A transaction is two-phase if no object is unlocked before all objects are locked.

These two properties are important for synchronization and recovery.

Atomic actions are associated with the design of fault-tolerant systems because they provide a conceptual framework for error detection and recovery. The definition of an atomic action shows that if a failure occurs which prevents the successful completion of an atomic action, then the state of all objects that the atomic action has modified must either be restored to their state prior to the atomic action or advanced to the next update state.

Since an atomic action is considered as a generalization of the concept of a transaction, the recovery problem can be expressed equivalently using transaction terms. Thus the recovery problem for a transaction system means:

(1) Returning the system to the last consistent state, that is, when a transaction aborts, all the effects of the transaction must be undone and the system comes back to the state it was in at the time the transaction started. Randell calls this **backward error recovery** (Randell 1979); or

(2) Advancing the system to the next consistent state when a failure occurs, that is, when a failure occurs after the final commit but before the transaction has finished executing, the recovery mechanism must ensure that all operations of the transactions are completed. This is called **forward error recovery** (Taylor 1986). Thus, to perform forward error recovery it is necessary to gather enough information at commit time to complete execution and make all required updates.

Atomic transactions are recoverable if:

(1) initial states of the objects modified by the action can be reconstructed; and

(2) objects modified by the action are not made available to other actions before the action has completed.

The former condition can be satisfied by the use of either the technique of **logging** or **shadows**, and the second by the use of a synchronization mechanism. Such a mechanism prevents access to the modified objects during the action.

As was previously mentioned, to perform forward error recovery it is necessary to gather enough information at commit time to complete execution and make all required updates. Also to perform backward error recovery information gathering is necessary to return data objects to their original state. This information is maintained in the form of a log.

The use of shadow objects is an alternative to logging. Operations within transactions are executed on shadow objects. Shadow objects are invisible outside the transaction until commit time, when they become visible. A transaction could be atomic if all its shadow objects become visible at the same time. This is achievable by using a two-phase commit protocol.

4.7.4   Transactions for programming systems

Transactions are widely used in database management systems to maintain consistency and to implement reliability at a high level in the system. It is interesting that these concepts are also applicable to distributed systems, in particular to distributed operating systems (Spector and Schwarz 1983, Walker *et al.* 1983).

However, the transaction model has to be modified to cope with the requirements of a distributed programming environment. These additional requirements include the following features:

(1)   **Nested transactions** – transactions whose success or failure depends on subtransactions which may themselves be nested. Nested transactions can be used to improve the reliability of conventional transaction systems by allowing sub-transactions to restart after failures without aborting the parent transaction. Note that nested transactions cause difficulties for conventional synchronization mechanisms, because of the higher degree of concurrency and because they can be long term transactions.

(2)   **Long term transactions** – transactions can cause problems in distributed programming environments because they are frequently required to be active for long periods of time. Hence objects used by these transactions are not accessible for long periods of time. This, of course, can limit concurrency and hence the performance of the system.

(3)   **Operations on user defined abstract data types** – while concurrency in nested and long term transactions may be reduced, it may also be increased by making use of semantic information about

the type of object and the operation to be performed, for example, the use of read and write locks. Semantic information can also be used to permit concurrent access to data types whose behaviour under certain types of operation does not lead to inconsistency, for example, the insertion of a new key into a directory service.

Moreover, the following two requirements are listed: provision for operations on devices; the need for version control to maintain object histories and configuration control; and the use of objects with larger granularity than database objects.

4.8 Maintaining consistency – Multiple copy update problem

Reliability is one of the important aspects of computer science. Reliability is improved in a natural way in distributed systems through multiple copies of processors, I/O devices, and other facilities. Reliability of distributed systems can also be improved by increasing the availability of data stored in the system. This implies that data is stored redundantly at different sites of the system. This approach is used broadly in databases. It is required also in distributed operating systems. Typical examples of subsystems of a distributed operating system which implement this approach are name servers and file servers.

It is obvious that at any time, all copies of replicated information should be identical. However, the problem of keeping all data items mutually consistent is a difficult one. In the literature this problem is known as the **multiple copy update**. Several solutions to this problem have been proposed and this section discusses the most representative one. A reader who wants to know more should study this problem and its solutions in Bernstein (1985), Gifford (1979), Holler (1981), and Nicol *et al.* (1986).

4.8.1 Replication of data

Replication of data is used in databases as well as distributed operating systems. Redundancy in databases may take various forms:

(1) **Fully redundant** – in this case only replicas (or copies) of the complete database are distributed.

(2) **Partially redundant** – in this case the database is partitioned with certain partitions being stored as distributed replicas.

Distributed operating systems, such as those presented in Blair *et al.* (1986) and Walker *et al.* (1983) also feature the replication of data (for example, files) on different storage devices. In both cases, replication increases reliability and improves performance of the total system, because the closer location of data reduces communication overhead.

Replication of data generates two very important problems: owner's rights, of no interest here, and maintaining consistency, that is, solving the multiple copy update problem. It is necessary to maintain internal consistency associated with concurrency control as well as mutual consistency in a system that replicates data. Replicas in a system are mutually consistent if they are identical. However, not all replicas are accessible (are mutually consistent) when access to one of them is required. This implies the need to relax the mutual consistency constraints. It is only required that all replicas must converge in the same state, after all access activities cease.

Here, we are interested only in solutions to the multiple copy update problem in the context of distributed operating systems. Therefore we are concerned with transactions which access single (replicated) data items.

4.8.2 Classification of solutions

The general structure of this section follows the examination presented in Nicol *et al.* (1986). The authors classified solutions to the multiple copy update problem as illustrated in Fig. 4.5.

Solutions to the multiple copy update problem can be voting or non-voting. Voting solutions are results of negotiations between sites to reach agreement on control decisions. On the other hand, non-voting solutions are not the result of any negotiations. The solution is worked out by one site which is in control at a given time.

4.8.3 Non-voting solutions

Two classes of non-voting solutions are shown in Fig. 4.5. The first is based on primary sites and the second is based on token-passing.

The primary site approach

The primary site approach is based on the concept of centralization. Among all controller processes located in all sites, there is one which is in charge of making all sequencing and synchronization decisions for all transactions requested by other controllers. This is a very simple approach, because detecting and resolving transaction conflict centrally can be made very easy. The drawback of this approach is low reliability. If the node of the controller in charge fails, the total system crashes. The reliability of this centralized solution can be improved by assigning priorities to each controller. If the highest priority controller is not operational, then the next highest priority controller assumes control.

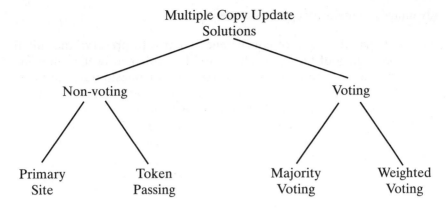

Fig. 4.5 A classification of multiple copy update solutions {adapted from Nicol *et al.* (1988)}.

The token passing approach

A process which holds a unique control message, called a token, is in charge of making all sequencing and synchronization decisions. At a given time only one controller is in charge, and practically there is a centralized way of desision making. The token is passed from one controller to the next one according to the order defined by a virtual ring. This approach has some advantages as well as disadvantages. Detailed discussion of token passing in the context of synchronization is presented in Chapter 6.

Both of these non-voting solutions to the multiple copy update problems are non-democratic. Solutions that are based on equal authority of all controllers should be preferred. This leads to voting algorithms.

4.8.4 Voting solutions

Voting solutions are results of negotiations (by voting) of all sites to reach a global agreement about the ordering of transactions to be performed in the distributed system. This means that control is decentralized. All sites are not required to participate in decision making. Fig. 4.5 shows two classes of voting solutions; those based on majority voting, and those based on weighted voting.

Majority voting

According to the majority voting approach to the multiple copy update problem, a site, on which a transaction updating a given replicated data is to be performed, must obtain the consent of at least a majority of sites storing a copy of this data. If the site does not obtain a majority of votes, the transaction is not allowed to proceed until some later time. The advantages of majority consensus are:

(1)   It forms the basis of concurrency control to preserve the initial consistency of the data. This could be explained in the following way. In the case where some transactions request potentially conflicting access to the same replicated data item, majority consensus guarantees that there is at least one common voting site which will be involved in deciding on ordering of these transactions. This site is able to detect and prevent conflicting transactions from simultaneous processing.

(2)   It maintains mutual consistency in the system, because the majority of data copies are guaranteed to converge to the same value. This is because for the transactions which access the replicated data item, majority voting guarantees that at least one of the replicas being accessed has been recently updated. This implies that copies with old values will be updated.

Two interesting majority voting algorithms have been presented by Thomas (1979) and Bernstein (1985). While these general multiple copy update algorithms are acceptable in distributed database environments, they cannot be used in distributed operating systems for performance reasons. The most important feature of Thomas's algorithm is its complexity, in particular, the complexity of the voting rule. Bernstein's algorithm has computational overheads and communication overheads, so performance of the algorithm suffers.

Weighted voting
Reasearch towards performance improvement of algorithms for multiple copy update problems has been carried out at the Carnegie–Mellon University. The result of this research is the new algorithm for the maintenance of replicated files, known as the weighted voting algorithm, proposed by Gifford (1979).

The weighted voting algorithm can be characterized informally in the following way:

(1)   Each copy (replica) of a data item (file) is assigned some number of votes.

(2)   To perform a read operation on a data item, a transaction must collect a read quorum of r votes. To perform a write operation on a data item, a transaction must gather a write quorum of w votes to write to the data item. The values r and w must be such that $r + w$ is greater than the total number of votes allocated to that data item. This ensures that there is non-null intersection between every read quorum and every write quorum. Satisfying this constraint guarantees that the replica with the most recent value of

the data item will be contained in the subset of replicas participating in every transaction.

(3)   As a result of (2), any read quorum that is gathered is guaranteed to have a current copy.

(4)   Version numbers make it possible to determine which copies are current.

The weighted voting algorithm has the following properties:

(1)   It guarantees serial consistency of transactions. This means that it appears to each transaction that it alone is running. A user is provided with the most current version of a data item.

(2)   It continues to operate correctly with inaccessible copies.

(3)   It does not insist that a majority of the data item's replicas are updated.

(4)   It permits the system administrator to tune the system's performance and availability characteristics on a per replicated data item basis by manipulating r, w, and the voting structure of a replicated data item (file).

(5)   Better performance may be achieved by giving certain replicas a heavier weighting; moreover, when high availability is required on a given replicated data item, then the total number of votes for that data item should be evenly distributed among the data item's replicas.

The flexibility offered by weighted voting algorithms is very important in the distributed operating system environment, where different applications have different requirements. These requirements can be expressed by giving 'good' weights.

4.9   Overview of distributed operating system components

The next group of research and design issues is associated with the components of distributed operating systems. Before discussing these components, we analyse the structure of distributed operating systems and the kernel/server pool-based approach.

4.9.1   Structure of a distributed operating system

The primary goal of a distributed operating system is to integrate the computing resources and services connected by a communication network into one system. This goal should be achieved in the presence of some restrictions imposed by users or computer systems, such as transparency, failure conditions, security, and sometimes heterogeneity. To create such a virtual computer, a distributed operating system has to make management decisions oriented towards all resources and all the nodes on the network.

A distributed operating system should be constructed on top of the bare machine. This allows it to see from its level all resources without interference from any part of an old centralized operating system. The resources are globally owned and globally managed. Global mechanisms should be used to access resources. However, a distributed operating system must manage, as a centralized operating system, the processing cycles, the memory allocation and operations, the devices, the input and output operations, and the communications among all these facilities. The major difference between these facilities developed for a centralized operating system and a distributed operating system is that the decisions in the former one are elaborated based on total and accurate knowledge of the state of a system. A distributed operating system does not have up-to-date, consistent knowledge about the state of a distributed system. There is no common clock, delivery of messages is delayed, and messages could even be lost.

However, despite all these problems, a user should be able to see a distributed system as a virtual centralized system. Nearly the same services should be offered to a user. Thus the structure of a distributed system, from a user viewpoint, is as illustrated in Fig. 4.6.

In this context, the question is what is a general view of a distributed operating system structure? To perform all the functions presented in Chapter 1, a distributed operating system must contain the same management components as an operating system for a centralized computer system. These components are as follows: process management, memory

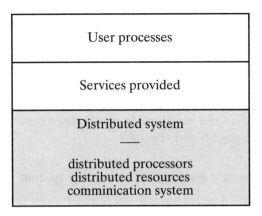

Fig. 4.6   Distributed system from user's viewpoint.

management, resource management, in particular I/O management and device management, and file management. The components are structured as illustrated in Fig. 4.7.

However, because of the distribution of objects (resources), and global mechanisms to be used to access these resources, these components possess some special features. Thus it is necessary to discuss these components individually, to create a proper image of an architecture of a distributed operating system. Moreover, this discussion allows identification of research and design issues, and finds methods and algorithms which can be used to build these components properly.

4.9.2 Kernel/server pool-based approach

The introduction and development of kernels for operating systems was the result of two major factors:

- the growth of operating systems implied a need for segmenting this software in a rational fashion; and

- a desire for secure operating systems – those that could assure that the access to data stored within was controlled and protected in an uncircumventable way.

These factors are even more important in the case of distributed systems.

The result of these efforts is a concept of a small and as simple as practical nucleus which provides necessary primitive functions, and

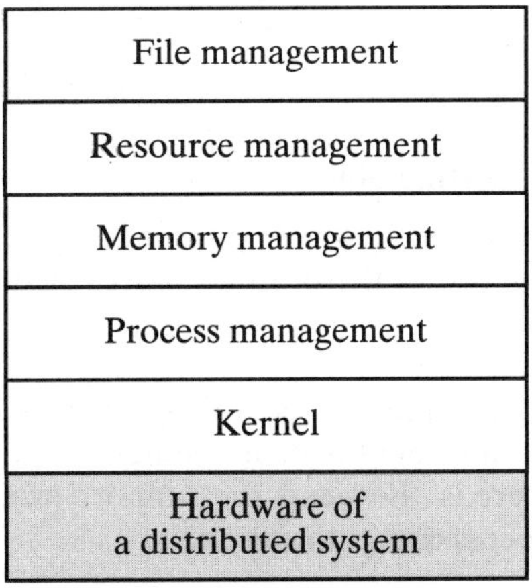

| File management |
| Resource management |
| Memory management |
| Process management |
| Kernel |
| Hardware of a distributed system |

Fig. 4.7 A general structure of a distributed operating system.

is wholly responsible for the security of the operating system, including whatever was built on the top of that nucleus. One of the goals of these efforts was to minimize the size and the complexity of the resulting nucleus, based on the belief that to do so would greatly increase the likelihood that the resulting software would be correctly implemented.

The following design constraints affect kernel architecure, and must be specified before it will be possible to develop appropriate kernel specifications (Popek and Kline 1978):

Security policy
The particular security policy has a great influence on the amount of mechanism that must be included in a kernel. One goal is reliable data security – assuring that it is possible for users only to access data to which they are specifically entitled.

Data security policy can be subdivided on a number of criteria:

(1)   What are the objects that are protected? An operating system kernel may support processes, files, messages and/or message channels, records, etc.

(2)   What is the object grain – the size of the object protected?

(3)   What are the rules governing the alteration of system data that records the security policy – centralized or distributed?

System functions
The functions and services to be supported by a kernel have an impact on the design and implementation of it.

The following elements are taken into consideration at this stage:

(1)   Possibilities of creating and destroying objects of all types supported by a kernel or only certain cases.

(2)   Type extensibility – is it possible for user programs to create new objects and have these new objects protected in a similar fashion to previously existing objects?

(3)   The convenience with which operating system software can be constructed on top of the primitives provided by a kernel.

Hardware effects
The hardware on which a kernel is built influences its size, complexity, overall architecture, and details of implementation. In the case of distributed systems, there is the need for support processor coordination and remote interprocess communication.

Performance
A number of design principles guide the design of a kernel.

Overall system architecture

Overall system architecture is associated with the question of the relationship of the kernel to the rest of the operating system. The possibilities are that:

(1)   The kernel is essentially part of a user process (even sharing the process address space).

(2)   The kernel is separated from all other software.

Resource pools

One of the most effective ways to reduce the size and complexity of an operating system kernel is to remove, as far as possible, all of the resource management functions for a particular type of resource and relegate those functions to untrusted code.

There are three aspects to resource handling in operating systems that are subject to removal from a kernel:

(1)   **Type integrity**

(a)   The most extreme action possible is to remove the entire resource as well as all of its supporting software from a kernel. As a result, the kernel does not provide protection of these resources as such. User software is responsible for the type integrity of these resources. This strategy implies that the single pool of resources usually maintained for all processes by the operating system is broken up into a number of smaller subpools, each managed independently.

(b)   As a result, the kernel is simplified but separate subpools are generally more poorly utilized.

(2)   **Resource management policy**

(a)   In those cases where it is not possible to completely exclude support of a resource type from the kernel, it may be possible to remove the management of the resource, but leave that portion of the software responsible for the integrity of the resource objects. This means that the mechanisms which actually operate on the resource are part of the kernel, but the policy software which decides which operation should be performed, and under what circumstances, is untrusted, and part of the user processes.

(3)   **Naming**

(a)   A considerable part of an operating system is devoted to managing the names of resources in addition to the management of the resources themselves.

(b)   The more of this name management that can be removed from the kernel, the simpler the resulting kernel software.

Heterogeneity in distributed computer systems is potentially the major factor restricting effective resource utilization. Because distributed computer systems can be built on the basis of different computer networks, there is a large degree of heterogeneity.

The generally accepted approach to heterogeneity is to use the kernel/service model as the method for providing coherence. Based on this approach, the distributed operating system is essentially used as a tool to minimize the system-provided mechanism to increase security, flexibility, efficiency, transparency and simplicity. As such, the minimum requirement for each computer is the use of a homogeneous kernel which provides services that support the use of remote services given the large degree of service design heterogeneity. The software for one node of a heterogeneous distributed computer system is illustrated in Fig. 4.8.

A kernel should be designed and developed so as to minimize system-provided mechanisms. By providing a homogeneous distributed operating system kernel two of the problems of heterogeneity are solved:

- machine independence is achieved to a large degree; and
- network transparency is provided.

The kernel provides a secure homogeneous base on which to build services, creating great flexibility when deciding on the service's implementation.

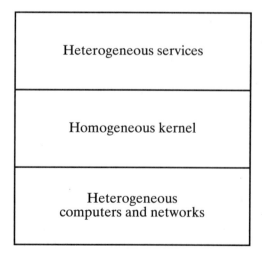

Fig. 4.8 Kernel/service pool approach to heterogeneity.

4.9.3 Kernel

All of the management components identified in Section 4.9.1 must be supported by a distributed operating system. The interface between management components of an operating system and the hardware of a computer system is called a kernel.

A kernel is a part of an operating system which allows each processor to operate. In the case of a distributed system, there is also another function of the kernel. It is responsible for communication among connected computers; in particular it communicates with its peer kernels. In distributed operating systems a kernel is replicated in all computers, creating (together with a communication facility) a distributed computer system, as illustrated in Fig. 4.9.

The size of a kernel is one of the major decision issues. It depends on the functions performed within it and services offered to components lying on it. Both large kernels and small kernels have their advantages and disadvantages. A large kernel offers more services than a small one. Services are provided more efficiently than in the case where they are offered outside the kernel. However, putting many services into a kernel reduces the overall flexibility and configurability of the resulting operating system. In the case of a small kernel, the majority of services are put into management components, in particular into separate servers. Usually, each server has its own address space and can be programmed separately. Each server can be easily replaced. The small kernel requires less programming. Thus, the major advantage of a small kernel is its simplicity. The problem with a small kernel is that servers have to use some form of interprocess communication to communicate with each other.

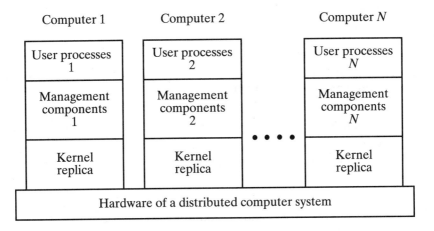

Fig. 4.9 Replicated kernel in a distributed operating system.

At the minimum, an operating system kernel is a basic set of primitive operations and processes from which the reminder of the system may be constructed, and contains two parts. The first part depends on the hardware of a computer (processor), and the second part affects the actual control and operation of this processor. Such a simple kernel

(1)   stores basic information about processes and resources;

(2)   manages the queues used for states of execution (running, ready, suspended, waiting); and

(3)   performs kernel operations, such as handling interrupts triggered by various system events, and carrying out basic interprocess communication.

On the other hand, an operating system kernel, as well as providing the functions listed above, may perform such operations as process and memory management, name management, interprocess communication, and device management. We noted earlier the advantages and disadvantages of such big kernels.

There is, however, one solution which links advantages of the above two approaches. It has been proposed for the V distributed system (Cheriton 1984, 1988). The V kernel is built of two parts. The first consists of (i) a system which performs the functions of the above described small kernel, and (ii) code that handles the communications. The second part is a set of the following kernel servers (service modules): time, process, memory, communication and device management. Both parts of the V kernel are replicated in each computer of a distributed system to handle local processes, memory and devices. A server is invoked by a user process using the standard interprocess communication facility, as if the server executed outside the kernel as a process (Fig. 4.10).

Cheriton emphasizes that such replication of servers in each kernel and their interfacing to these servers through the interprocess communication facility has a number of advantages:

(1)   Local operations are fast because they are served by local servers;

(2)   A client process can access the kernel servers as the other servers. In both cases the same interprocess communication facility is used;

(3)   The use of the interprocess communication primitives to access these servers avoids adding additional kernel traps beyond those required by the interprocess communication primitives.

(4)   Since the servers and the interprocess communication are separated, the interprocess communication facility may be tuned sepa-

Computer *A*   Computer *B*

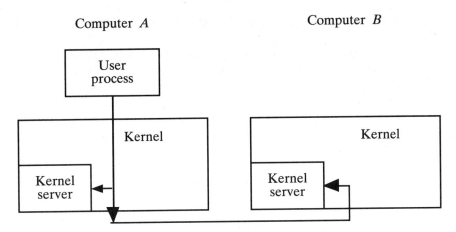

Fig. 4.10 Invocation of a kernel server {adapted from Cheriton (1988)}.

rately from other services to improve the performance of the total system.

(5) Since the invocation mechanism is general, the kernel can be extended by adding additional kernel servers.

4.9.4 Process management

Process management in a centralized operating system deals with policies and mechanisms for sharing a processor among a number of user processes. This can be achieved by providing the capability to create, name, run, block, schedule, synchronize, interrupt and kill processes. Moreover, a priority may be associated with a process and this information may be used when performing operations on processes.

The goal of global process management is to provide policies and mechanisms for sharing processing resources spread around a network among all processes. To achieve this goal in the best possible way it is necessary to provide policies and mechanisms to perform local and remote operations on processes (create, name, rename, delete, run, etc.), to synchronize processes, and to manage their states. Thus, a distributed operating system has all the same mechanisms as a centralized operating system.

However, these mechanisms have to be extended to deal with distribution of resources, and distribution of information about states of these resources and states of other processes using these resources or requesting them. Moreover, these mechanisms have to provide the distributed control and synchronization of all processes that are communicating or requesting resources. These two functions are performed based on incomplete and inaccurate state information. There is the lack of information consistency. Despite all these problems, the mechanisms should work such that a distributed computer system works as a unified system.

In a distributed system, as in a centralized one, processes have to be described to the system to perform mangement, that is, every process is represented by a data structure containing its basic state, identification, its creator, priority, etc. These data structures are referred to as **process control blocks** or **process descriptors**. All of them represent the state of an operating system. However, in the case of a distributed operating system, the state is distributed among all connected computers.

Every process, in a centralized system as well as in a distributed one, exists in many different states associated with its levels of completion. However, in a distributed system, a process being in different states may be located in different computers (nodes). This is illustrated in Fig. 4.11.

It is important to perform process management operations, such as create, delete, run, schedule, synchronize, not only locally, but also remotely. This is one of the basic design issues of process management in distributed operating systems.

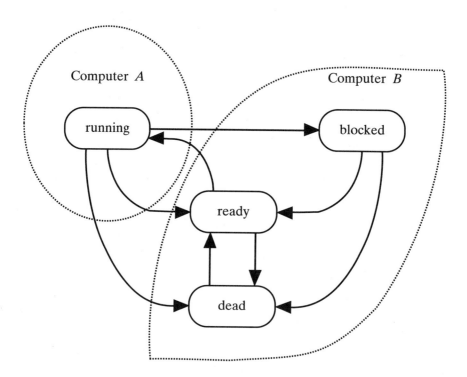

Fig. 4.11   State transition diagram – process states located in different computers.

4.9.5 Memory management

Memory is a critical resource of a computer system. It influences computer performance very strongly. The goal of this component is the management of available memory resources, that is, keeping the memory loaded with that data from external memory which is most likely to be accessed over a given, fixed period of time. Memory management, in centralized computer systems as well as in distributed ones, is carried out through performing the following functions: allocation, deallocation, access, sharing memory resources among processes, and protecting information. The difference between memory management in centralized systems and in distributed systems is that in the latter case this function should be performed from a global view. Memory management in distributed systems is mainly concerned with providing storage for process and data migration.

Even though problems of memory management such as allocation, access and control of memory resources, are functions of global process scheduling and allocation, only a small part of this task has a global character, and it can be associated with interprocess communication (some primitives for interprocess communication can be oriented towards memory management). Moreover, it can be seen as a part of the more general problem of resource management. For this reason, this component is not discussed in detail here.

4.9.6 Resource management – I/O management and device management

I/O and device management services have been developed to provide a fair resource sharing among all processes and to remove the user from dependencies on peripheral devices. Moreover, I/O and device management allows I/O and devices to be seen in the logical sense, acceptable to a programmer. The architecture of I/O and device management is a hierarchical one, and contains three major levels.

The highest level, I/O control and management, interfaces the logical file system and the device interfaces of channels and buffers. This level accepts commands such as open, close, create, read, from the file system and determines the proper action to perform the requested operation. Control functions of this level are performed through the use of the channel controller and buffer controller which link physical devices and logical devices. They form the second level of the I/O and device management architecture. The third, lowest level is the device management. This level controls and transfers physical blocks from the device to the control unit.

Device management is concerned with device allocation, device control and device status. Device allocation is concerned with how to allocate a device to a process. To carry out this operation, the system has to know a device and its state. Thus, as a process, every resource (device) is represented by a data structure containing its state, identification, type and creator.

It can be seen from the definition of a distributed operating system that the goal of resource management is to control local and remote resource allocation, as in centralized systems, while having in mind total system performance. To perform local and remote resource allocation, this component of the distributed operating system must keep a global accounting of resources and their current states. This information can be distributed over some or all nodes of a network, or can be centralized.

When a client process issues a request for a service in a distributed environment, this request has to be processed by a resource manager in global terms which take into account the state of all resources of a given type and all other requests for the same service. It is possible to imagine a distributed system where there is only one resource manager, providing centralized resource management services, or where there are more than one. In the former case, a manager must maintain a database containing information about all resources. In the latter case, resource management is performed in a distributed way. Information about resources can be distributed and replicated, implying data consistency problems. These two cases are illustrated in Fig. 4.12.

In the case of distributed management, a client process can send a service request directly to the chosen resource manager (client processes 2 and N) or it can broadcast such a request (client process 1). In the latter case more than one manager is involved in processing this request. The solution to problems of this type is presented in Chapter 9.

Each resource is controlled by a server process (sometimes called a guardian, or administrator). Such a server accepts requests for service on its resource, processes these requests, provides service to a requesting process, and returns results. A server process may be responsible for one (single resource server) or more resources (multiple resource server). This is illustrated in Fig. 4.13. In general terms, a multiple resource server works as a scheduler which controls optimal sharing of M resources among K requesters.

One special device, a network interface, and its management should be mentioned here. The major goal of network management is to support interprocess communication primitives by providing message transfer mechanisms. It allocates network ports to communicating processes, transmits messages with a requested quality of service, and controls the flow of messages. All these network management services are provided by communication protocols which are discussed in Chapter 2.

In general, the resource management globally controls the use of resources, and supports services of a distributed operating system.

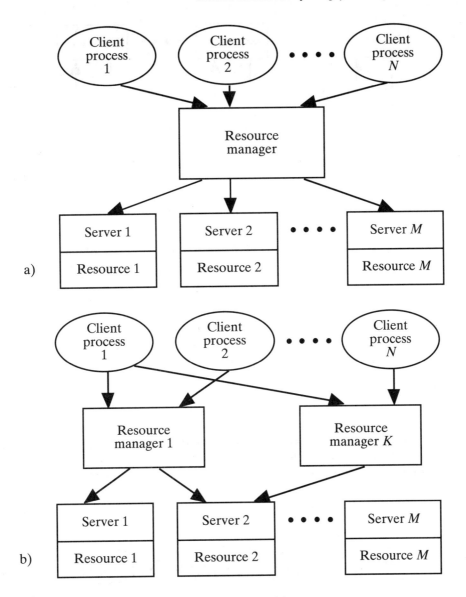

Fig. 4.12 Centralized (a) and distributed (b) resource management.

4.9.7 File management

A user sees a computer systems through files, which represent a collection of information organized according to user requirements. Files hide a physical storage and allow the user to see programs and data from a logical point of view. Files are known and managed by their logical names. A file management facility must allow a user to create, change,

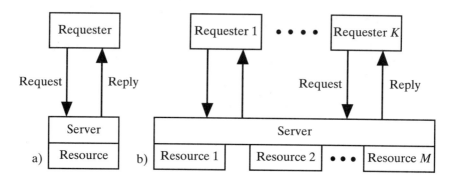

Fig. 4.13 Single resource server (a) and multiple resource server (b).

rename or delete, files. The file manager has to keep track of where files are stored, how they are used. Moreover, the file management facility must control access to files and protect them.

In the case of distributed systems, the goal of the distributed file management system is not only translation of files from the logical level to the physical, and manipulation of files at the physical level, but also the creation of a single, logical file system from a collection of local files, physically distributed over the network, while hiding this distribution. To achieve this goal, the file manager has to provide transparent mechanisms to perform all necessary operations on these distributed files. In many cases file management systems are part of a distributed database management system.

File management is particularly important in distributed computer systems because of the tendency to connect cheap, diskless personal computers and workstations, and to share expensive peripherals such as hard disks and printers. Such a configuration is illustrated in Fig. 4.14. Thus, file services are provided by file server(s).

4.10 Overview of research and design issues of distributed operating system components

The development of a distributed operating system and its proper components, in particular, systems implementing mechanisms and management systems, requires study of many basic research and design issues to find methods and algorithms which can be used to build these components. The following research and design issues are of most interest:

Distributed processes and their management, in particular
Interprocess communication which allows processes to cooperate and compete and is closely associated with synchronization, since some forms of communication require synchronization.

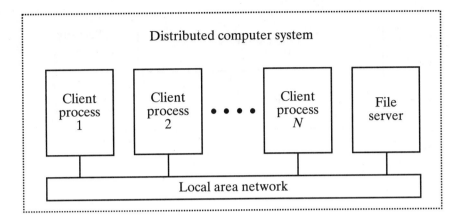

Fig. 4.14 File server in a distributed environment.

Synchronization which is the satisfaction of constraints on the inter-leaving of the actions of different processes. Communication and synchronization influence the correct cooperation of processes.

Naming facility which facilitates sharing in a distributed environment by allowing objects to be named unambiguously.

Process management which deals with the operating system's mechanisms and policies for sharing processing resources spread around a network among all processes, in particular to perform local and remote operations on processes.

Resource management

Resource allocation which is mainly involved in processor allocation and distributed scheduling (load balancing), and peripheral resource allocation.

Deadlock detection which deals with a permanent blocking of a set of distributed processes which either compete for resources or communicate with each other.

Protection and security which controls access to the resources, who can perform which operation and on what object, and protects communication subsystem.

Services provided which deals with subsystems responsible for providing particular services to client processes.

The relationship between these issues is illustrated in Fig. 4.15. These issues form a complete set which allows logical designing of a distributed operating system.

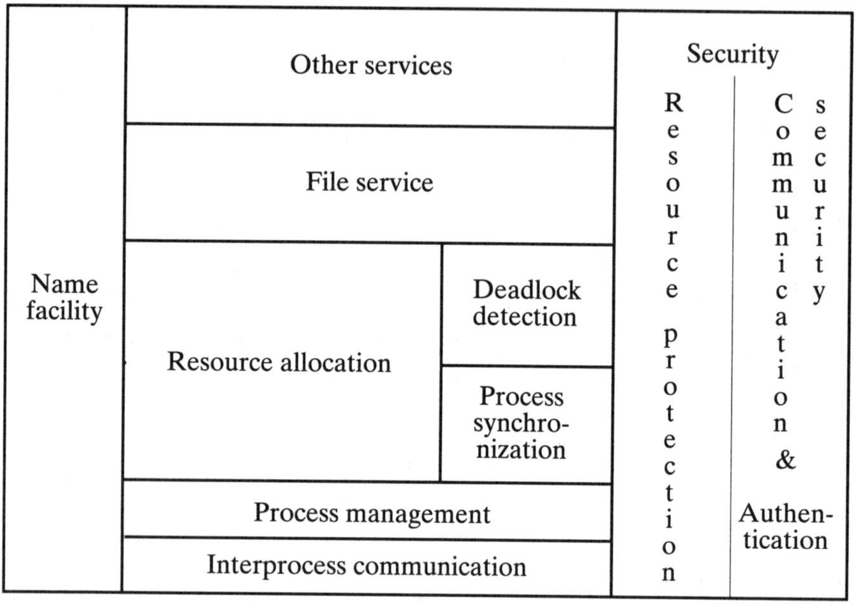

Name facility	Other services		Resource protection	Security
	File service			Communication security &
	Resource allocation	Deadlock detection		
		Process synchro-nization		
	Process management			Authen-tication
	Interprocess communication			

Fig. 4.15 The relationship between the research and design issues and the structure of a distributed operating system.

4.10.1 Remote interprocess communication

High performance interprocess communication is the most crucial facility of a distributed system because of the necessity of providing fast exchange of data. Fast data exchange can be achieved by using both proper interprocess communication primitives and a suitable and efficient transport protocol supporting these primitives. The latter topic is discussed in Chapter 3.

The following three forms of remote interprocess communication can be used for developing primitives:

(1)   message passing and advanced message passing (Silberschatz 1979, Gentleman 1981, Cheriton 1984);

(2)   Remote Procedure Call (RPC) (Birrell and Nelson 1984); and

(3)   transactions (Spector and Schwarz 1983).

The three forms were developed on different basic concepts.

Message passing between remote processes is connected with a client–server model and is a natural extension of interprocess communication for centralized systems. Primitives for remote interprocess communication can be:

- nonblocking, if its execution never delays its invoker; or blocking otherwise;

- buffered, when messages are buffered between the time they are sent and received; or unbuffered (sometimes called rendezvous);
- unreliable, when no guarantee of data delivery is provided; or reliable, when data are delivered, and messages are not duplicated or delivered out of order.

The sender and receiver have to be synchronized. The synchronization between them is defined by the semantics of the send operation.

Messages can be sent using single datagrams or multidatagrams. Communication can be between processes or ports. Links used for communication are a simplex link, defined as one-way communication path (Powell and Miller 1983, Miller *et al*. 1987) and a duplex link, defined as two-way communication path (Finkel *et al*. 1983).

Message passing suffers from some drawbacks. An improvement can be achieved by moving towards strong typing, that is by providing language-level mechanisms to support type-checked remote interfaces. The Remote Procedure Call (RPC) is an interprocess communication form which has such features. The very general term RPC means a type-checked mechanism that permits a language-level call on one computer to be automatically turned into a corresponding language-level call on another computer. RPC supports communication between one client and one server (Birell and Nelson 1984) as well as between many clients and many servers. The latter was introduced in the Sprite Network Operating System (Ousterhoust *et al*. 1988). Because some systems do not deal with distributed language-level primitives, the term RPC is used just to describe the transfer protocol.

Transactions were originally developed for database management systems, but can effectively be used in the development of a remote interprocess communication system. The transaction approach simplifies the construction of reliable systems. In distributed systems based on the transaction model, messages are exchanged between sockets, which are logical addressable entities in nodes of a network.

None of these forms is visible to a user, but each generates a different overhead measured in terms of message transmission delay and memory occupation. The simplicity of a communication system is also very important. Not much work has been carried out in the area of quantitative comparison between these communication forms.

4.10.2 Synchronization

The term synchronization, except for its use to express the cooperation between a sender and receiver, refers to the solution of either of two distinct but related problems:

(1) specification and control of the joint activity of cooperating processes; or

(2)   serialization of concurrent access to shared objects by multiple processes.

To share resources, concurrent processes must be synchronized. Because in distributed systems there is no common memory or clock, there is the problem in determining which of two events occurred first. This problem was successfully attacked by Lamport (1978) who introduced the happened-before relation. Based on this relation problems can be analysed and different synchronization methods can be developed.

Synchronization in distributed systems can be done using centralized or distributed mechanisms. Among centralized synchronization algorithms, the most interesting are: an algorithm using a unique clock, an algorithm based on a central process, an algorithm based on eventcounts and an algorithm with a static sequencer.

Analysis of the literature on distributed synchronization algorithms shows that a theoretical background has been well established. The following are the main approaches used to construct distributed synchronization algorithms:

(1)   Lamport's event-ordering approach. The most important feature of algorithms based on this approach is the use of timestamps to order all requests from processes that wish to enter the critical section. The most representative algorithms of this group are Lamport's algorithm (Lamport 1978), Ricart and Agrawala's algorithm (Ricart and Agrawala 1981), and Suzuki and Kasami's algorithm (Suzuki and Kasami 1985).

(2)   Token passing approach. The idea of this approach is to provide for a unique message having a specific format called the token, that circulates among the processes according to the order defined by a virtual ring as in the Le Lann algorithm (Le Lann 1978). In the Chandy algorithm (Chandy 1982) the token need not be passed if no process wishes to enter the critical section – such an approach reduces transmission overhead at the interprocess communication level. In algorithms developed on the basis of the event-ordering approach, there is an assumption that the communication delay is unpredictable. Token approach makes prediction possible.

(3)   Priority based event-ordering. Because of many problems associated with time stamped event-ordering algorithms (generated by the lack of a common clock), it has been suggested (Goscinski 1989a,b) that events be ordered on the basis of priorities of the processes rather than on times when they happen. For real-time systems and systems using priorities for scheduling, a priority-based approach is more natural and improves the performance of the total system.

All these algorithms allow only one process (node) to be in the critical section. Raymond (1987) developed an algorithm, which is an extension to the Ricart and Agrawala algorithm, for the case when K identical resources must be shared between N processes. The algorithm enables up to K nodes to be within the critical section simultaneously.

4.10.3 Addressing and naming

Sending messages between processes, and in general objects supported by a distributed operating system requires the operating system to know the names of the objects to be accessed. To access an object it is necessary to know what a process wants to access (name), where this object is (address) and how to get there (route).

The naming system should be efficient in that the delay and the number of messages that have to be exchanged to initialize and map names before messages are sent to perform the desired function must be minimized. Moreover, the system should support at least two levels of names: one convenient for people, called a user name, and one convenient for computers, called an internal name or a system name.

Names are characterized by three attributes: structure – flat, partitioned, and descriptive names; time – static and dynamic names; and number – group and individual names. Communication becomes effective if a name can be mapped into the corresponding route. This mapping is called routing. An address can be treated as an intermediate form between the name and the route. It is oriented to computer processing and used to generate a route.

An internal name can be of two types:

(1)   unique-computer identifiers – they are large integers or bit strings; they should be so large that at a given time the same identifier does not refer to two different objects; and

(2)   structured names – contain more than one component, some of which indicate the location of the named object.

Capabilities can also be used for naming purposes. A capability is a trusted object identifier specifying a unique object and containing additional redundancy for protection.

Components in a naming facility can be classified according to two aspects: structure and function. There are two structural components in a naming facility: name servers, which can be centralized or distributed; and agents, which maintain a detailed knowledge of the name space and of existing name servers. Communication, database management and name management are functional components of a naming facility.

A name space must be managed in a decentralized way. Thus, the goal is to develop an architecture for a distributed name service that allows authority for parts of the name space to be divided among the various organizations participating in the distributed computing system environment. A name server participating in distributed name management should provide and support storing name information and database management, maintaining replications, name resolution, and name service operations.

When carrying out distributed name service operations, name resolution is performed first and is one of the most important operations. It requires the name service to determine the authoritative name servers for every named object. The next step is locating the authoritative name servers. In the third step, database operations on name attributes are performed.

The following structures of naming facility exist for distributed operating systems: centralized, replicated, decentralized, distributed system and hierarchical. All have advantages and disadvantages. The influence of these systems on the performance of a total distributed operating system has not been studied fully.

4.10.4 Process management

One of the most important design issues in distributed operating systems is the separation between mechanism and policy. The main separation is reflected by two components: process management and resource management.

The process management system interacts with a memory management system and interprocess communication system to provide the execution environment for processes. The goal of process management in distributed operating systems is to provide mechanisms, but few policies, for sharing processing resources spread around a network among all processes.

Distributed operating systems should support local as well as remote operations on processes. In an ideal case all operations on remote processes should be transparent to the user. The following operations should be supported remotely: create, destroy, suspend, resume, and run processes, allocate/create port, and deallocate/destroy port. The major problem in remote execution of a process is selection of an execution site. Note that this is a policy problem and should be solved by the resource management system.

Another important part of process management is process migration, which is crucial for distributed scheduling (load balancing). A process migration task (policy) is needed to define when to migrate which process where. Many policies have been proposed and studied. This is also a policy aspect and is considered below under resource allocation. When a decision 'when to migrate a process to where' has been made, migration is performed by the kernels of those computers which are involved in that operation.

There are only a few systems which provide services supporting process migration. The oldest and least sophisticated solution was proposed by Powell and Miller (1983). The most characteristic features of this solution are that the process allocation is controlled by a source computer and that there is a remaining process on a source computer which links all processes communicating with a migrated process. Solutions proposed in Theimer *et al.* (1985), Artsy *et al.* (1986) do not have these weaknesses.

4.10.5 Resource allocation

Management is:

(1)   planning and organizing the provision of resources, where resources may be located, and their availability;

(2)   the control of the use of, and access to, resources according to allocation, optimization, and authentication rules; and

(3)   the task of ensuring that resources remain accessible and that they function correctly.

The principles underlying the management of resources apply whether systems are centralized or distributed. However, approaches, methods, and algorithms of resource management in distributed computer systems are different from those in centralized computer systems.

In the area of resource management there are two important subareas: resource allocation, and processor allocation and scheduling. Resource allocation can be managed by server-based resource managers or agent-based resource managers. In systems based on the former approach, all resources can be managed by centralized resource managers or by decentralized resource managers. In the case of management based on an agent approach, it is necessary to have two agents located on two different computers because agents control access to resources of remote computers, and provide protection.

In the distributed computing environment, it can happen that some computers are idle and/or lightly loaded while others are heavily loaded. This leads to the possibility of improving the performance of the distributed system by migrating jobs from the heavily loaded computers to the idle or lightly loaded computers. The problem is how to find an idle workstation and when to migrate a process. Solutions to this problem can be achieved through load sharing and load balancing.

Load sharing, known also as processor allocation or hunting for an idle processor, can be performed on the basis of many different organizations imposed on a set of available processors. Four of the most interesting are:

(1)   processors are organized in a logical hierarchy (Wittie and van Tilborg 1980);

(2)   processors are organized in a logical ring (Goscinski 1989c);

(3)   processors are not organized in any special structure (Shoch and Hupp 1982); and

(4)   the Condor scheduling system.

Load balancing (distributed scheduling) algorithms can be divided into two groups:

(1)   **task placement algorithms** – algorithms which find the optimal location for all processes before they start execution (static load balancing); and

(2)   **dynamic load balancing** (associated with process migration algorithms) – algorithms which allow processes to migrate to remote computers once they have begun execution.

From the point of view of distributed operating systems dynamic load balancing is of most concern. Load balancing algorithms are based on different concepts. They can use information about processes exchanged by pairs of computers, or maintained by processors in the form of load vectors, in which case performance is improved locally. They can use a bidding approach, which enables performance to improve globally; or a stochastic learning automation, which improves the performance with the precision of the heuristic method in use; or a Bayesian decision theory.

4.10.6   Deadlock detection and resolution

Deadlock is a state of permanent blocking of a set of processes which either compete for resources or communicate with each other. There are many algorithms developed for deadlock detection, avoidance and prevention in centralized operating systems. Because distributed systems do not have global memory and message transmission delays are nonnegligible, centralized techniques for solving deadlock problems are too expensive.

Many algorithms for solving resource deadlock problems by determining the global states of distributed systems have been developed. According to Gligor and Shattuck (1980) many of the published algorithms are incorrect and impractical. Chandy and Lamport (1985) stated that a reason for this 'may be that the relationship among local process states, global system states, and points in a distributed computation are not well understood'.

Broadly speaking, there are two kinds of deadlocks in distributed systems:

(1)   **Resource deadlocks** – the traditional deadlock, which has mostly been studied in the context of distributed databases; and

(2) **Communication deadlocks** – deadlock among a set of processes which communicate directly. This occurs when all these processes are idle waiting for messages from other processes in order to start execution, but there are no messages in transit between them.

This division is not precise enough to develop a deadlock detection algorithm for a distributed operating system as special features of applications should be taken into consideration. One feature is a kind of a resource request. Wait-For-Graph, One-Resource, AND, OR, AND-OR, $\binom{n}{k}$, and unrestricted are models developed for a resource request. These models led to the development of some distributed deadlock detection algorithms.

There are four classes of distributed deadlock detection algorithms, based on the following approaches: path-pushing, edge-pushing, diffusion computations, and global state detection.

4.10.7 Protection and security

The relationship between protection and security in distributed systems needs to be understood. Computer security can be divided into three areas:

(1) External security, concerned with physical access to a computer system. This is an organizational problem and not of interest here.

(2) Interface security, dealing with identification of users on the basis of authentication methods.

(3) Internal security:

(a) protection of objects in a computer system,

(b) communication security,

(c) file security which deals with safeguarding of stored information.

Protection is the control of access to the resources, that is, controlling who can perform which operation and on which object. A number of approaches used to provide protection are based on access control models.

Access control models can be implemented as discretionary access control systems or non-discretionary access control systems. The access control models are as follows:

(1) The access matrix model which is a generalized description of an operating system protection mechanism. This model does not consider information semantics. It can be implemented using access control lists or/and capabilities;

(2) The lattice security model, which is an extension to the access matrix model to include information classifications, user clearance and rules concerning the classifications. It can be implemented using Bell and LaPadula's approach;

(3) Information flow models, in which the focus is on flow of information from one object to another rather than on individual accesses to objects. It is also based on the lattice security concept. It can be implemented using clearance capabilities; and

(4) A security kernel mechanism, which is based on the concept of a reference monitor.

A distributed system gives rise to the additional need to protect the communication subsystem because it can be regarded as open to line tapping, and the reading of data. This is becoming more and more important because more sensitive information is transmitted over communication channels. In order to secure information, some mechanisms have to be developed to protect data access and transfer.

Two groups of potential interprocess security violations were identified by Voydock and Kent (1983):

(1) Passive attacks when messages passing on a network are observed without interference. The following threats are possible in this area:

(a) release of message contents,

(b) traffic analysis.

(2) Active attacks when there is interference with messages passing on a network. The following threats are possible in this area:

(a) message stream modification,

(b) denial of message service,

(c) spurious connection initiation.

Cryptography is a technique for protecting the communication system against such malicious attempts. The transferred data can be protected using encryption. Two different types of encryption are in use, symmetric encryption and public-key encryption. In both systems messages can be transferred securely if a sender and receiver are provided with matching keys. This generates the problem of key management. One of the most important aspects of key management is key distribution. There are specific schemes for key distribution in symmetric and asymmetric cryptosystems.

Another security aspect is generated by the fact that users exchanging messages do not trust each other. They also can assume that some non-eligible users will masquerade as eligible users. This leads to the need for user/message authentication. Cryptographic techniques are also used for authenticating messages.

4.10.8 Services provided

Management of shared resources is an important service that should be provided by a trusted authority (this problem was partially highlighted in Section 4.8.6). Such a trusted authority is the total distributed operating system, and in particular a server implemented in one of the computers connected by a network.

The following servers are of major importance in distributed operating systems: file server, name server, resource manager, boot server, directory server, print server, time server and authentication server.

4.11 Models of distributed operating system design

The previous section presented components of a distributed operating system to show what such a system must do, and discussed research and design issues which provide methods and algorithms to develop these components. The problem is how these components are to be realized in a distributed operating system. This section deals with design models used to implement these components.

Distributed operating systems can be developed on the basis of one of the two following models: the process model or the object model. The major difference between these two models is in mechanisms by which the notions of functional entity and synchronization are implemented. Note that at the level of policy these two models are equivalent, that is, processes in the process model can be mapped into object in the object model. There is full logical equivalence. The systems developed on the basis of these two models are different at the level of mechanisms.

4.11.1 Process model

The process model is based on a process and a message. All actions in the system are performed by processes. This implies that management systems (process management, memory management, I/O management, file management) are constructed as sets of processes which provide services to the system. Processes cooperate and interact by passing messages. The process-oriented model is characterized by facilities or mechanisms provided to perform operations on processes (for example, to create a process, delete, allocate) and to exchange messages between processes (for example, for defining message ports, addresses).

4.11.2 Object model

'The object model is both a concept and a tool' (Jones 1978). This means that this model provides guidelines for characterizing the abstract entities in terms in which we think. We perceive the world around us as a variety of objects.

The basic part of the object model is an object. We define an object informally as a collection comprising of a data structure and a set of operations defined on this data structure. The object is an abstract data type that hides any internal details. This level of abstraction requires that objects communicate via communication primitives (for example, send, wait) implemented on the basis of messages. Synchronization and control are performed via management and allocation of capabilities. Operations to the system developed on the basis of this model are provided by objects.

A precise definition of an object has its roots in programming systems. In traditional programming systems, data and procedures are separate entities. A programmer is responsible for two tasks: applying active procedures to passive structures, and ensuring that the procedure will work correctly on the data types to which it is applied. On the other hand, programming systems supporting objects do not view an object as passive data, but as the combination of its private state and the operations that manipulate it.

In the object model emphasis is placed on characterizing the components of the physical or abstract system to be modeled by a programmed system. These components are modelled by objects. There exist invariant properties that characterize an object and its behaviour. The object model dictates that these invariant properties are preserved by a set of operations that are the only means by which an object can be directly manipulated. To alter a state of the object, an appropriate operation must be invoked. This means that the set of operations for an object collectively defines its behaviour.

The major problem with object based systems is their poor execution time performance, which is due to the inefficient implementation of access to objects.

4.12 Summary

There are a number of issues which should be taken into consideration when a distributed operating system is designed. The first is a communication model for a distributed operating system. The ISO/OSI Reference Model can only be treated as a basic framework for message passing systems. It requires passing information down and up through all layers on the sending and receiving computers, respectively, and it is too complicated to be applicable for distributed operating systems. A functional hierarchy based model should be used.

Paradigms for process interaction in a distributed computing environment are the second research and design issue. The following basic paradigms are identified: the client–server model, the integrated model, the pipe model and a remote procedure call.

A distributed operating system ensures that users view a distributed system as a virtual uniprocessor, not as a collection of distinct machines connected by a communication system. Moreover, users do not see any difference between local and remote resources – geographic distribution is not visible. These invisibility is possible due to network transparency. Various degrees of network transparency can be required in a distributed operating system: access, location, name, control, data, execution and performance.

Transparency is closely associated with homogeneity. However, some applications and external circumstances (for example, administrative, managerial) generate the need for heterogeneity. This issue generates process, name and resource management problems.

Transparency and heterogeneity are closely associated with the next issue, autonomy and interdependency, which is of a double nature. Users want a distributed operating system to provide autonomy to achieve policy freedom, robustness, and security. On the other hand, interdependence allows autonomous computer systems to communicate, decreases overall costs of distributed systems, makes efficient utilization of resources possible, and improves performance.

In order to achieve reliable distributed computing, transactions and atomic actions were proposed. Reliability is also greatly improved by providing redundant resources on different nodes. However, resources generate some serious problems, such as the lack of the global state information, and the possibility of partial failures. They imply difficulties in maintaining data consistency. Multiple copy update can be carried out based on two solutions: nonvoting, using either prime sites or token passing approaches, or voting, using either majority voting or weighted voting approaches.

A distributed operating system contains the same management components as an operating system for centralized systems, that is, process management, memory management, resource management, and file management. The development of these components requires study of many research and design issues to find methods and algorithms which can be used to build these components. The following issues of distributed operating system components are the most important: interprocess communication, synchronization of remote processes, object naming, process management, resource allocation, deadlock detection, resource protection and security, and services provided.

The problem arises of how the components are to be realized in a distributed operating system. There are two basic implementation models: the process model, which is based on the elements of a process and a message, and the object model, which is based on the concept of an object.

Bibliography

Artsy Y., Chang H.-Y. and Finkel R. (1986). *Process Migrate in Charlotte*. Computer Science Technical Report No. 655, University of Wisconsin–Madison

Balkovich E., Lerman S. and Permelee R.P. (1985). Computing in Higher Education: The Athena Experience. *Communication of the ACM*, **28**(11), 1214–24

Berstein A. (1985). A Loosely Coupled Distributed System for Reliable Storing Data. *IEEE Transactions on Software Engineering*, **SE–11**(5), 446–54

Birrell A.D. and Nelson G.J. (1984). Implementing Remote Procedure Calls. *ACM Transactions on Computer Systems*, **2**(1), 39–59

Blair G.S., Nicol J.R. and Yip C.K. (1986). *A Functional Model of Distributed Computing*. CS–DC–1–86, Department of Computing, University of Lancaster

Chandy K.M. (1982). *A Mutual Exclusion Algorithm for Distributed Systems*. Technical Report University of Texas

Chandy K.M. and Lamport L. (1985). Distributed Snapshots: Determining Global States of Distributed Systems. *ACM Transactions on Computer Systems*, **3**(1), 63–75

Cheriton D.R. (1984). The V Kernel: A Software Base for Distributed Systems. *IEEE Software*, 19–42

Cheriton D.R. (1988). The V Distributed System. *Communications of the ACM*, **31**(3), 314–33

Cheriton D. R. and Zwaenepoel W. (1983). The Distributed V Kernel and its Performance for Diskless Workstations. In *Proceedings of the Ninth ACM Symposium on Operating Systems Principles* Bretton Woods, New Hampshire, 129–40

Craft D.H. (1983). Resource Management in a Decentralized System. In *Proceedings of the Ninth ACM Symposium on Operating Systems Principles*, Bretton Woods, New Hampshire, 11–9

Dannenberg R.B. (1982). Resource Sharing in a Network of Personal Computers. *Ph.D. Thesis*, Department of Computer Science, Carnegie–Mellon University

Finkel R., Solomon M., DeWitt A. and Landweber L. (1983). *The Charlotte Distributed Operating System*. Department of Computer Science Technical Report No. 502, University of Wisconsin–Madison

Gentleman W.M. (1981). Message Passing Between Sequential Processes: the Reply Primitive and the Administrator Concept. *Software—Practice and Experience*, **11**, 435–66

Gifford D.K. (1979). Weighted Voting for Replicated Data. In *Proceedings of the Seventh Symposium on Operating Systems Principles,* 150–162

Gligor V.D. and Shattuck S.H. (1980). On Deadlock Detection in Distributed Systems. *IEEE Transactions on Software Engineering,* **SE–6**(5), 435–40

Goscinski A. (1990). Two Algorithms for Mutual Exclusion in Real-time Distributed Computer Systems. *The Journal of Parallel and Distributed Computing,* **9**, 77–82

Goscinski A. (1989). A Synchronization Algorithm for Processes with Priorities in Computer Networks with Node Failures. *Information Processing Letters,* **32**(3), 129–36

Gray J. (1978). Notes on Data Base Operating Systems, Operating Systems—An Advanced Course. *Lecture Notes in Computer Science,* (60), 393–481

Gray J. (1987). Transparency in Its Place. *UNIX Review,* 42–50

Holler E. (1981). Multiple Copy Update, Distributed Systems—Architecture and Implementation. *Lecture Notes in Computer Science,* (105), 284–303, Springer-Verlag

Jones ˙A.K. (1978). The Object Model: The Conceptual Tool for Structuring Software, in Operating Systems—An Advanced Course. *Lecture Notes in Computer Science,* pp. 8–16, Springer-Verlag

Kohler W.H. (1981). A Survey of Techniques for Synchronization and Recovery in Decentralized Computer Systems. *ACM Computing Surveys,* **13**(2), 149–83

Lamport L. (1978). Time, Clocks and the Ordering of Events in a Distributed System. *Communications of the ACM,* **21**(7), 558–65

Lampson B.W. (1981). Atomic Transactions, Distributed Systems—Architecture and Implementation. *Lecture Notes in Computer Science,* (105), pp. 246–265, Springer-Verlag

Lazowska E.D., Levy H.M., Almes G.T., Fisher M.J., Fowler R.J. and Vestal S.C. (1981). The Architecture of the Eden System. In *Proceedings of the Eighth Symposium on Operating Systems Principles,* Pacific Grove, California, pp. 148–159

Le Lann G. (1977). Distributed Systems—Towards the Formal Approach, In *Proceedings of the IFIP Congress,* Toronto, North-Holland Publishing Company, pp. 155–160

Lomet D.B. (1977). Process Structuring, Synchronization, and Recovery Using Atomic Actions. *SIGPLAN Notices,* **12**(3), 128–37

Miller B.P., Presotto D.L. and Powell M.L. (1987). DEMOS/MP: The Development of a Distributed Operating System. *Software—Practice and Experience,* **17**(4), 277–90

Moris J.H., Satyanarayanan M., Conner M.H., Howard J.H., Rosenthal D.S.H. and Smith F.D. (1986). Andrew: A Distributed Personal Computing Environment. *Communication of the ACM,* **29**(3), 184–201

Mullender S. (1987). Report on the Second European SIGOPS Workshop 'Making Distributed Systems Work'. *Operating Systems Review,* **21**(1), 49–84

Needham R. and Herbert A. (1982). *The Cambridge Distributed Computing System.* Addison-Wesley

Needham R. and Herbert A. (1989). Report on the Third European Workshop Autonomy or Interdependence in Distributed Systems. *Operating Systems Review,* **23**(2), 3–19

Nicol J.R., Blair G.S. and Shepherd W.D. (1988). An Approach to the Multiple Copy Update based on Immutability. In *Distributed Processing* (Barton M.H. *et al.* eds.), pp. 537–550, Elsevier, North-Holland

Notkin D., Hutchison N., Sanislo J. and Schwartz M. (1986). Report on the ACM SIGOPS Workshop on Accomodating Heterogeneity. *Operating Systems Review,* **20**(2), 9–24

Ousterhout J.K., Scelza D.A. and Sindhu P.S. (1980). Medusa: Experiment in Distributed Operating System Structure. *Communications of the ACM,* **23**(2), 92–105

Popek G.J. and Kline C.S. (1978). Issues in Kernel Design, Operating Systems. An Advanced Course, *Lecture Notes in Computer Science, No. 60*

Popek G. and Walker B.J. (1985). *The LOCUS Distributed System Architecture.* Cambridge: The MIT Press

Powell M.L. and Miller B.P. (1983). Process Migration in DEMOS/MP. In *Proceedings of the Ninth Symposium on Operating Systems Principles,* Bretton Woods, New Hampshire, pp. 110–119

Randell B. (1979). Reliable Computing Systems, Operating Systems: An Advanced Course. *Lecture Notes in Computer Science,* 282–391, Springer-Verlag

Randell B., Lee P.A. and Treleaven P.C. (1978). Reliability Issues in Computing System Design. *ACM Computing Surveys,* **10**(2), 123–65

Raymond K. (1987). *Multiple Entries with Ricart and Agrawala's Distributed Mutual Exclusion Algorithm.* Technical Report 87/78 Department of Computer Science, The University of Queensland

Raymond K. and Lister A. (1982). STREAMS: An Implementation of Distributed Mailboxes. In *Proceedings of the Australian Computer Science Conference* **ACSC–6**, 173–81

Ricart G. and Agrawala A.K. (1981). An Optimal Algorithm for Mutual Exclusion in Computer Networks. *Communications of the ACM,* **24**(1), 9–17

Sheltzer A.B. and Popek G.J. (1986). Internet Locus: Extending Transparency to an Internet Environment. *IEEE Transactions on Software Engineering* **SE–12**(11), 1067–75

Shoch J.F. and Hupp J.A. (1982). The Worm Programs—Early Experience with a Distributed Computing. *Communications of the ACM,* **25**(3), 172–80

Silberschatz A. (1979). Communication and Synchronization in Distributed Systems. *IEEE Transactions on Software Engineering,* **SE–5**(6), 542–6

Spector A.Z. and Schwarz P.M. (1983). Transactions: A Construct for Reliable Distributed Computing. *Operating Systems Review,* **17**(2), 18–35

Suzuki I. and Kasami T. (1985). A Distributed Mutual Exclusion Algorithm. *ACM Transactions on Computer Systems,* **3**(4)

Svobodova L. (1984). File Servers for Network-Based Distributed Systems. *Computing Surveys,* **16**(4), 353–98

Svobodova L. (1985). Workshop on Operating Systems in Computer Networks. *Workshop Summary, Operating Systems Review,* **19**(2), 6–39, Ruschlikon, Switzerland

Tanenbaum A.S. and van Renesse R. (1985). Distributed Operating Systems. *Computing Surveys,* **17**(4), 419–70

Taylor D.J. (1986). Concurrency and Forward Recovery in Atomic Transactions. *IEEE Transactions on Software Engineering,* **SE–12**(1), pp. 69–78

Theimer M.M., Lantz K.A. and Cheriton D.R. (1985). Pre-emptable Remote· Execution Facilities for the V-system. In *Proceedings of the Tenth ACM Symposium on Operating Systems Principles* Orcas Island, Washington, pp. 2–12

Thomas R.H. (1979). A Majority Consensus Approach to Concurrency Control for Multiple Copy Databases. *ACM Transaction on Database Systems,* **4**(2), 180–209

Voydock V.L. and Kent S.T. (1983). Security Mechanisms in High-Level Network Protocols. *Computing Surveys,* **15**(2), 135–71

Walker B., Popek G., English R., Kline C. and Thiel G. (1983). The LOCUS Distributed Operating System. In *Proceedings of the Ninth ACM Symposium on Operating Systems Principles,* Bretton Woods, New Hampshire, pp. 49–70

5 Interprocess communication

User names	File service				Security		
	Collaboration of file servers Transaction service Directory service Flat file service Disk service				Access control	C o m m u n i c a t i o n	s e c u r i t y
Name distri-bution	Resource allocation	Deadlock detection	R e s o u r c e	p r o t e c t i o n			
Name resolu-tion	Algorithms for load sharing and load balancing	Process synchro-nization					&
					Capa-bilities	Authen-tication	
System names	Process management Operations on processes: local, remote Process migration				Access lists	Key manage-ment	
Ports	Interprocess communication (and memory management) Interprocess communication primitives: Message Passing or Remote Procedure Call, or Transactions; Links or Ports				Info flow control	Data encryp-tion	
					Security kernel		
Address-es	↕ ↕						
Routes	Transport protocols supporting interprocess communication primitives					Encryp-tion protocols	

5.1   Introduction

A distributed operating system should encompass all the computers in the network – encompassing is a necessary condition to have a distributed processing system. In a distributed environment, cooperating processes communicate by sending messages. Communication between processes on different computers can be given the same format as communication between processes on a single computer.

A good interprocess communication facility is important because of the need to provide access to resources distributed over a local area network (in some cases over local and wide area networks) in a uniform manner independent of language, network location, or in some cases, host operating systems. To achieve this goal, the interprocess communication facility must provide policies and mechanisms to effect local and remote communication between consenting processes, and between processes and resources.

High-performance communication is the most critical facility in a distributed computer system. The performance of such a system depends on fast interprocess communication which is composed of two parts: interprocess communication primitives, and a transport protocol that supports these primitives. Different transport protocols were discussed in Chapter 2.

Since computers in distributed computer systems do not share memory, communication via shared memory is not applicable. Interprocess communication can only be performed by exchanging messages.

Different sets of primitives can be used in remote interprocess communication. However, the three most common are based on:

(1)   message passing;

(2)   remote procedure call (RPC); or

(3)   transactions.

They are ordered here according to increasing level of abstraction; each form can be constructed from the preceding form.

These three forms of interprocess communication are based on different basic concepts. Message passing between remote processes is associated with a client–server model and is an extension of interprocess communication for centralized systems. The flow of information is **unidirectional** from the client (sender) to the server (receiver). However, in advanced message passing, such as rendezvous, information flow is **bidirectional**, that is, a return message is provided in response to the initial request.

Message passing is a completely untyped solution. One way of simplifying the encoding and decoding of transmitted arguments is to define conventional transmission representations for common language types and require all network interfaces to be defined in terms of these types. These solutions have some disadvantages. Improvement can be achieved by moving towards strong typing, which provides language-level mechanisms to support type-checked remote interfaces.

The first step in this direction was done by introducing guardians (Liskov 79). Liskov suggested that remote interprocess communication should be based on passing typed messages between program modules termed **guardians**. Guardians are intended to be the units of distribution within a multi-computer system and can be seen as autonomous servers. The guardians' semantics was no-wait-send similar to conventional datagrams.

An alternative approach is based on the fundamental linguistic concept known as the procedure call. The very general term **remote procedure call** means a type-checked mechanism that permits a language-level call on one computer to be automatically turned into a corresponding language-level call on another computer. This mechanism requires a transport protocol to support the transmission of its arguments and results. It is important to note that the term remote procedure call is sometimes used to describe just this low level transfer protocol. Remote procedure call primitives provide bidirectional flow of information.

Transactions were originally developed for database management systems, to aid in maintaining arbitrary application-dependent **consistency constraints** on stored data. The transaction approach and mechanisms simplify the construction of reliable systems. They should provide uniform support for invoking and synchronizing operations on shared data objects, assurance of serializability of transactions with one another, and atomic behavior and recovery in the face of network and nodal failures. It is desirable, from the user and program point of view, that the transaction facilities are entirely transparent.

Message passing and remote procedure call are in wide use today, but distributed operating system support for transactions has not yet been fully recognized. We can also say that whereas the semantics of the remote procedure call are well known, message-based communication, because of its variety, is not so well understood. The syntax and semantics of the remote procedure call are a function of the language being used. The choice of precise syntax and semantics for message passing communication is a more difficult task because there are no fully accepted standards.

The following topics are discussed in this chapter. For message passing: communication primitives, semantics of these primitives, ports and links, alternatives for passing data, interprocess communication schemes, and messages. For RPC: primitives and their semantics, RPCs for many clients and many servers, client–server binding, remote procedure calls in heterogeneous environment, and special communication protocols for RPC. For transactions: basic primitives, their semantics, sockets, basic concepts of commitment, concurrency and recovery (CCR), their simple protocol, recovery procedures in the CCR exchanges, and two-phase commit.

5.2 Message passing – message oriented communication

One of the first reported operating systems based on message passing was developed by Brinch Hansen (1970). This system was followed by DEMOS (Baskett *et al.* 1977) and Thoth (Cheriton *et al.* 1979). In the late 1970s, message passing was adopted for distributed computer systems.

Message oriented communication is defined as a form of communication in which the user is explicitly aware of the message used in communication and the mechanisms used to deliver and receive messages. A message could be viewed as a collection of typed data objects, which is constructed by a process, that can be manipulated (in accordance with its type), and which is delivered to its final destination.

5.2.1 Messages

We can say that a message is a typed collection of data objects consisting of a fixed size header and a variable (sometimes constant) length body, which can be managed by a process, and delivered to its destination. A type associated with a message provides structural information on how the message should be identified. A message can be of any size and may contain either data or typed pointers to data outside the contiguous portion of the message. The contents of a message are determined by the sending process. On the other hand, some parts of the header containing system-related information may be supplied by the system.

Two examples of simple message formats are illustrated in Fig. 5.1 (Rashid and Robertson 1981). Part (a) of this figure shows a simple message header with data whereas part (b) presents a simple message header with a pointer.

One of the most important problems associated with messages is what structure, if any, should be imposed upon messages. This problem was analysed by Rashid (Rashid and Robertson 1981). Based on his work we can say that ideally a message should be considered as a collection of program objects, the structure of which is preserved by transmission from one process address space to another. This goal is very difficult to attain.

Messages may be completely unstructured or structured. The use of unstructured messages which are then interpreted as needed by user processes has problems. That is because some parts of messages (for

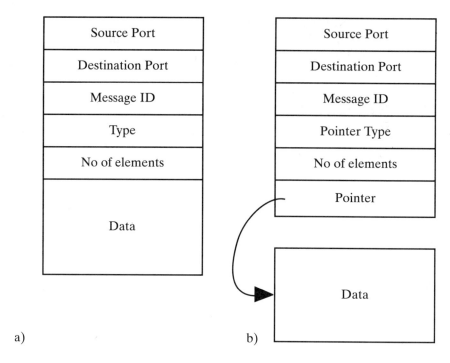

Fig. 5.1 Simple message formats; (a) simple message header with data, (b) simple message header with pointer {adapted from Rashid (1981)}.

example, source port names) must be interpreted by the distributed operating system (kernel) because they must be translated to be meaningful to another process. Moreover, in heterogeneous networks, only typed information allows the transparent transfer of data items such as integers, reals or strings. Structured messages are also favored for efficiency reasons. Most information transferred between processes is structured in that it represents data items of different types. The use of unstructured messages for such data can be expensive because the encapsulation and decapsulation of structured messages into unstructured linear forms adds a layer of overhead which increases the cost of communication.

5.2.2 Basic message passing primitives

Message oriented communication is very closely connected with the client–server model presented in Chapter 4, where one process, a client (or sender), sends a message (a request) to another process, called server (or receiver), and then waits either for a reply message, or continues running. There are two issues in the area of message passing based communication:

(1)   what is the set of communication primitives, and

(2)   what are their semantics.

A message is sent and received by executing primitives shown in List 5.1.

---

send expression_list **to** destination_identifier
   the message contains the values of the expressions in expression_list at the time **send** is executed. The user can control a destination of a message with destination_identifier (one destination or many destinations).

receive variable_list **from** source_identifier
   variable_list is a list of variables. The user can control where the message came from with source_identifier.

List 5.1   Basic message passing primitives.

The simplest form of the communication primitives: **send** and **receive** given in List 5.1, and the behaviour of the two processes involved in communication, are illustrated in Fig. 5.2.

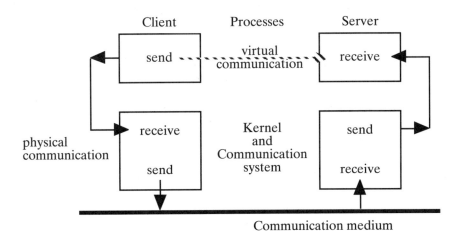

Fig. 5.2   Connection between the client and server communicating using **send** and **receive** primitives.

Fig. 5.2 shows that

<table>
<tr><td align="center">CLIENT PROCESS
issues
send(server, message)</td><td align="center">SERVER PROCESS
issues
receive(process id, buffer)</td></tr>
</table>

where:

(1)   the client process has to specify in the primitive the destination address (server) and the message; and

(2)   the server process specifies from whom a message is desired, and provides a buffer to store an incoming message.

No initial setup is required and no connection is established; hence no disconnection is required. Of course, when the server process sends any message to the client process, they have to use these two primitives also; the server sends a message by executing primitive **send** and the client receives it by executing primitive **receive**.

Sometimes, a primitive allows a guarded and/or selective receiving of messages. The guarded receive primitive is presented in List 5.2. This means that a receive primitive can be preceded by a guard or boolean condition.

---

receive variable_list **from** source_identifier **when** B
     permits only receipt of messages if B is true.

List 5.2   The guarded **receive** primitive.

Moreover, the receiving process can name the set of message sources from which it is prepared to accept a message. This is expressed by the set of primitives given in List 5.3.

---

select
     receive variable_list **from** source_id1
     or receive variable_list **from** source_id2
     or receive variable_list **from** source_id3
end

List 5.3   Selective **receive**.

Execution of a given receive statement is associated with availability of a message. In the case when more than one message is available, the choice of which message is received is usually non-deterministic. However, an order can be imposed on these statements given in List 5.3.

There are several points that should be discussed at this stage. All of them are connected with a problem stated as follows: What semantics ought these primitives to have? Liskov (1979) identified the following communication primitives:

(1)   **The no-wait send** – the process sending a message waits only until the message has been composed.

(2)   **The synchronization send** – the process sending the message waits until the message has been received by the destination process. This communication requires the sender and the receiver to synchronize to exchange messages.

(3)   **The remote invocation send** – the sending process waits for a response from the receiving process that the command has been carried out.

These semantics do not explain all details and are too general. This is because a set of message passing primitives must provide for identifying the processes involved in a communication, for moving data between them, for synchronizing their actions, and providing reliable transfer of data. The semantics should be easy to understand, efficient to implement, and not error prone.

A larger set of primitives than Liskov's will be considered here; one partially associated with some primitives for the transport layer supporting the interprocess communication facility. Such a presentation creates a good window into the interprocess communication facility. The following alternatives are presented:

- blocking versus nonblocking primitives,
- buffered versus unbuffered primitives,
- reliable versus unreliable primitives (with the at-least-once or exactly once semantics used to implement recovery mechanisms),
- fixed-size or variable-size messages; multidatagram messages,
- direct or indirect communication; ports,
- passing data by value or by reference,
- address mapping.

5.2.3 Blocking versus nonblocking primitives

One of the most important properties of message passing primitives concerns whether their execution could cause delay. Blocking and nonblocking primitives are distinguished. We say that a primitive has nonblocking semantics if its execution never delays its invoker; otherwise a primitive is said to be blocking. In the former case, a message must be buffered.

With nonblocking primitives:

(1) **send** returns control to the user program as soon as the message has been queued for subsequent transmission or a copy made (these alternatives are determined by the method of cooperation between the network interface and the processor);

(2) when a message has been transmitted (or copied to a safe place for subsequent transmission), the program is interrupted to inform it that the buffer may be reused;

(3) the corresponding **receive** primitive signals a willingness to receive a message and provides a buffer into which the message may be placed; and

(4) when a message arrives, the program is informed by interrupt.

The advantage of nonblocking primitives is that they provide maximum flexibility. Moreover, these primitives are useful for real-time applications. For example, a process which controls a temperature does not wait for confirmation that a control message has been received by the destination process, because the next message will be sent after a time period determined by dynamic characteristics of a controlled object. The same can be observed in the case of a process gathering information (for example, pressure) and sending it to another process which maintains these data and uses them for controlling purposes.

The disadvantages of nonblocking primitives are that they:

(1) may require buffering to prevent access or change to message contents before or during transmission, or while it is waiting to be received. Buffering may occur on source or destination sites. If a buffer is full, a process must be blocked, which contradicts the original definition of this primitive;

(2) make programming tricky and difficult (nonreproducible, timing dependent programs are painful to write and awful to debug).

Blocking primitives provide a simple way to combine the data transfer with the synchronization function. If the **send** primitive has blocked semantics, the sender is blocked until the receiver actually receives the message. On the other hand, the receiver is also suspended until the sender has executed the **send** request. This results in synchronization of the sending and receiving processes.

With blocking primitives:

(1)   for unreliable blocking, **send** does not return control to the user until the message has been sent; the program may modify the buffer;

(2)   for reliable blocking **send** does not return control to the user until the message has been sent and an acknowledgment received; the program may modify the buffer;

(3)   **receive** does not return control until a message has been placed in the buffer; and

(4)   blocking and unblocking primitives do not conflict.

There are three forms of **receive** primitive. The blocking **receive** is the most common, since the receiving process often has nothing else to do while awaiting receipt of a message. There are also a nonblocking **receive** primitive, and a primitive for checking whether a message is available to receive. As a result, a process can receive all messages and then select one to process. **send** and **receive** primitives with blocking semantics are illustrated in Fig. 5.3.

The problem with blocking primitives is that they inhibit parallelism – a process blocked in **send** or **receive** cannot do any useful work – and do not enable a process to be blocked waiting for more than one kind of event.

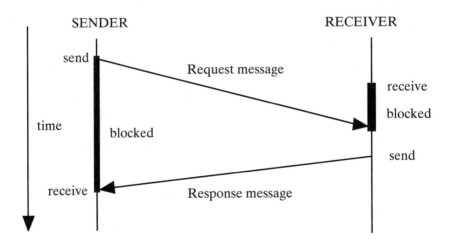

Fig. 5.3   **send** and **receive** primitives with blocking semantics.

5.2.4   Unbuffered versus buffered primitives – local and remote rendezvous

In some message based communication systems, messages are buffered between the time they are sent and received. If a buffer is full when a **send** is executed, there are two possible solutions: the **send** may delay until there is a space in the buffer for the message, or the **send** might return a code to the invoker (sender), indicating that, because there is no space in the buffer, that is, the buffer is full, the message could not be sent. The situation for **receive** is similar. Execution of **receive**, when no message that satisfies the source designator is available for receipt, might either cause a delay or terminate with a code, signifying that no message was available.

Consider two extremes: a buffer with unbounded capacity and one with no buffering. If the buffer has unbounded capacity, then a process is never delayed when executing a **send**. Systems based on this approach are called systems with asynchronous message passing or systems with no-wait send. The most important feature of asynchronous message passing is that it allows a sender to get arbitrarily far ahead of a receiver. Consequently, when a message is received it contains information about the sender's state that may no longer be valid. If the system has no buffering, execution of **send** is always delayed until a corresponding **receive** is executed. Then the message is transferred and both proceed.

When the buffer has finite bounds, we deal with buffered message passing. In this case the sender is allowed to get ahead of the receiver, but not arbitrarily far ahead. In buffered message passing based systems:

(1)   The sender is allowed to have multiple **sends** outstanding on the basis of a buffering mechanism (usually in the operating system kernel).

(2)   In the most often used approach, the user is provided with a system call **create buffer**, which creates a kernel buffer, sometimes called a **mailbox** or **port**, of a size specified by the user.

(3)   This solution implies that the sender sends a message to a receiver's port, where it is buffered until requested by the receiver.

Buffered message passing systems are characterized by the following features:

(1)   They are more complex than unbuffered message passing based systems, since they require creation, destruction, and management of the buffers.

(2)   They generate protection problems.

(3)   They cause catastrophic event problems, when a process owning ports dies or is killed.

In a system with no buffering strategy, processes must be synchronized for a message transfer to take place. This synchronization is called **rendezvous**. Because this strategy is important, we will consider it more deeply. It can be explained simply based on the presentation of a local rendezvous and its extension to a remote one (Gammage and Casey 1985) and (Gammage *et al.* 1987).

Local rendezvous

Local rendezvous is used for bidirectional communication between two processes in the same program executing in the same address space. A rendezvous occurs as a consequence of one process invoking an entry declared in the interface of a second process, and the second process executing an accept statement enabling a call on that entry.

The entry may have both input and output parameters. The input parameters are passed by value from the sender (invoker) to the receiver (invoked process) when the rendezvous begins, and the output parameters are passed back to the sender from the receiver when the rendezvous ends. Fig. 5.4 shows the sequence of events during a local rendezvous.

If the accept is issued before the rendezvous call from the sender, the receiver is suspended. When the rendezvous call occurs, the input parameters are copied from the sender to the receiver, the sender is suspended, and the receiver executes the code of the entry procedure. When the entry procedure completes execution, the output parameters are copied from the receiver to the sender, which resumes execution from the point that it made the rendezvous call.

If the rendezvous is invoked before the accept has been issued, the sender is suspended as before. If, when the accept is issued, there is more than one acceptable invocation waiting, the one that has been waiting longest will be accepted; the receiver continues running, executing the code of the entry procedure.

Remote rendezvous

Remote rendezvous is a uniform extension of the local rendezvous. The semantics of the remote rendezvous are, as far as possible, identical to the semantics of the local rendezvous. This form of communication also provides for bidirectional information flow, and is essential for programming client–server paradigms. The client is synchronized with the server.

To invoke a remote rendezvous, a process must have both:

(1)   Visibility to the interface of the remote process. The interface is provided by copying the interface definition of the receiver (target process) into the text of any program that wishes to invoke it; and

(2)   The remote process_id for it; The remote process_id consists of the process_id of the target process and the identity of the node in which it is executing.

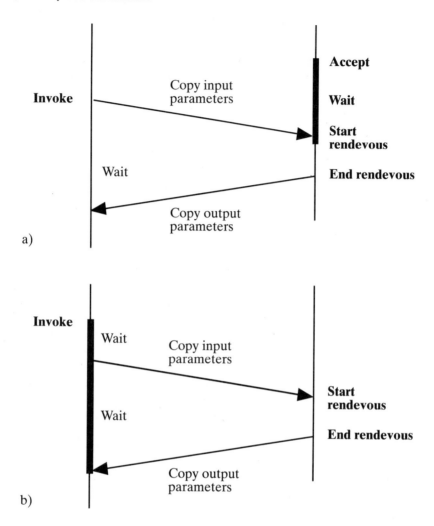

Fig. 5.4 Rendezvous events sequence: (a) accepter first, (b) invoker first.

The remote rendezvous is invoked in exactly the same way as a local rendezvous. The parameters are transmitted as data packets over a network.

(1) If a receiver has not yet executed a **receive** primitive, and a sender has a message to be sent, it is blocked until **receive** is completed. At that time a message is copied from sender to receiver.

(2) A message can be copied to a sender internal buffer. A problem occurs, if before a **receive** is executed, the sender does want to do more **sends**.

Fig. 5.5 illustrates the simple four-packet protocol used to implement remote rendezvous between nodes. It provides secure delivery service and has good characteristics under load. It is possible to use a three packet protocol which also provides a secure delivery service, but it does not have good characteristics under load.

For a remote rendezvous to take place, a process must obtain the remote process_id of the process with which it wishes to communicate.

(1)   The remote process_id may be obtained from the name server. An instance of the name server can be created on each node of a system and given a special, well-known process_id.

(2)   A process that is prepared to be invoked remotely can register itself with the name server on its node, supplying its process_id and a unique text string name.

(3)   Another process can obtain the remote process_id of this process by presenting the same text string to the name server on its node.

(4)   All the name server processes communicate, using remote rendezvous, to exchange the names and process_ids of registered processes so that they may be invoked from any program on any node.

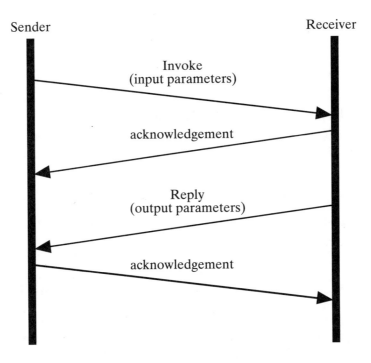

Fig. 5.5   Remote rendezvous protocol.

(5) Remote process_ids may also be exchanged between processes as parameters of a rendezvous. A program therefore only needs to register one process with the name server, and the registered process can then hand out the process_id of other processes of the program.

When the interface declaration and the remote process_id are available, a remote rendezvous is invoked. After that it proceeds in the same way as a local rendezvous.

There are two checks associated with a remote rendezvous. The first is performed by the compiler – it checks a remote rendezvous invocation against the copy of the interface to catch inconsistencies between usage and the declaration in the copy of the process interface. Catching inconsistencies between the copy and the actual server process that is invoked is the main task of the second checking. Inconsistencies of this type are mismatches in entry names or in parameters of entries. This problem is solved based on the concept of run-time **loose coupling** of the client and server. According to this concept, when a remote rendezvous is invoked, the symbolic name of the desired entry is used to locate the entry. This ensures a proper match of entry names. After that, potential inconsistencies between the formal parameters expected by an entry and the actual parameters passed in a remote rendezvous are checked.

The concept of loose coupling is a simple and effective technique for ensuring that type mismatches are detected, usually at compile time, and if not, at run-time.

5.2.5 Unreliable versus reliable primitives

Different catastrophic events, such as a node crash or a communication system failure can happen in a local area network. These can cause either:

(1) a requesting message being lost in the network, or

(2) a response message being lost or delayed in transit, or

(3) the responding node 'dying' or becoming unreachable.

Moreover, messages can be duplicated, or delivered out of order. The primitives discussed above cannot cope with these problems. These are so-called unreliable primitives.

The unreliable primitive **send** merely puts a message on the network only. No guarantee of delivery is provided and no automatic re-transmission is carried out by the operating system when a message is lost.

Dealing with failure problems requires providing reliable primitives. In a reliable interprocess communication, the **send** primitive handles lost messages using internal retransmissions, and acknowledgements on the basis of time-outs. This implies that when **send** terminates, the process is sure that the message was received and acknowledged.

The question arises of whether reliability should be dealt with at such high level. Should recovery mechanisms be provided either by a transport protocol and/or lower level protocols? These problems were attacked in Saltzer *et al.* (1984) where the authors proposed design principles that help guide placement of functions among modules of a distributed computer system. One of these principles, called **end-to-end argument**, suggests that 'functions placed at a low level of a system may be redundant or of little value when compared with the cost of providing them at that low level'. This allows us to state that a suggestion of the placement of recovery mechanisms at a process level is sound.

Reliable and unreliable **receive** differ in that the former automatically sends acknowledgement confirming message reception, whereas the latter does not. Two way communication requires the utilization of these simple message passing primitives in a symmetrical way. If the client requested any data, the server sends reply message (responses) using the **send** primitive. For this reason the client has to set the **receive** primitive up to receive any messsage from the server. Reliable and unreliable primitives are contrasted in Fig. 5.6.

Two types of semantics are defined, depending on what the receiver does if it receives multiple copies of a message. It might repeat its processing of the message, even if only one execution was actually desired. Since in this case the reliable primitives do their best to ensure that the request is executed at least once as illustrated in Fig. 5.7a, we call this type – communication with at-least-once semantics.

In many cases, repeated execution of a request could destroy the consistency of information, so it is desirable to have primitives which ensure that a request is executed once and only once. A primitive with exactly-once semantics makes sure that only one execution of the receiver's operation is performed. It is the most desired semantics, but difficult to implement.

Exactly-once primitives can be implemented on the basis of a request list maintained by the responding end of the system (Fig. 5.7b). In this case, each time a request message is received, the server checks whether a message_id is on the request list. If yes, this means that this request has been retransmitted and a response message is lost. The previously computed result is sent in a new response message. Otherwise, a message_id is placed on the request list, the requested task is performed, a result is associated with a message_id entry, and a response message is sent out.

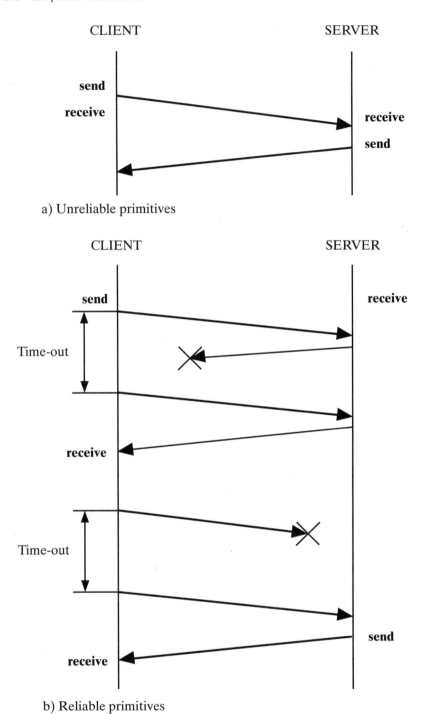

a) Unreliable primitives

b) Reliable primitives

Fig. 5.6 Unreliable versus reliable primitives in simple message passing system.

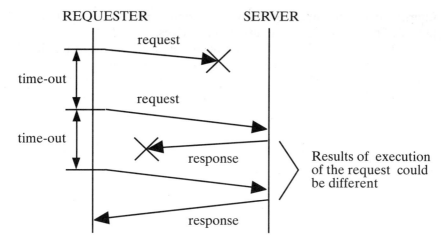

a) At-least-once recovery mechanism

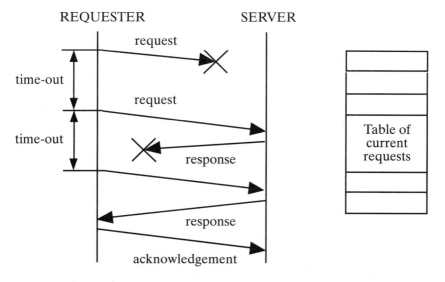

b) Exactly-once recovery mechanism

Fig. 5.7 Recovery mechanisms.

5.2.6 Structured forms of message passing based communication

High-performance communication is the most critical facility of distributed systems. It depends, among other things, on the performance of interprocess communication primitives. One way of achieving fast interprocess communication is by using simple primitives. That can be provided by imposing a structure on primitives.

A structured form of communication using message passing is achieved by distinguishing requests and replies (more precisely, through request-response behaviour of operations), and providing for bidirectional information flow. This means that the client sends a request message and waits for a reply. The set of primitives is given in List 5.4.

---

send

> sends requests and gets replies; it combines a previous client's **send** to the server with a **receive** to get the server's reply.

get_request

> is done by the receivers (servers) to acquire messages containing work for them to do.

send_reply

> the receiver (server) uses this primitive to send a reply after completing the work.

List 5.4   A structured form of message passing primitives.

These primitives were used in the V-system (Cheriton 1984) and CONIC (Kramer *et al.* 1983) to implement interprocess communication.

It should be emphasized that different semantics can be linked with these primitives. The result of the **send** and **receive** combination in the structured form of the **send** primitive is one operation performed by the interprocess communication system. This implies that rescheduling overhead is reduced, buffering is simplified (because request data can be left in a client's buffer, and the response data can be stored directly in this buffer), and the transport-level protocol is simplified, because error handling as well as flow control exploit the response to acknowledge a request and authorize a new request (Cheriton 1988*a*).

When the requesting process is blocked when waiting for a reply, it can happen that it is blocked indefinitely. This can occur because of a communication failure, failure of a destination computer, or simply because the server process does not exist any longer or it is too busy to compute a response in a reasonable time. This requires provision of a mechanism to allow the requesting process to withdraw from the commitment to wait for the response.

There are different solutions to the problem of whether a server can receive more than one request message? In CONIC, each request should be given a response before the next is received. The V-system does not support such reordering.

5.2.7 Direct and indirect communication – links and ports

The next issue in message based communication is where messages go. Message communication between processes uses one of two techniques: the sender designates either a fixed destination process or a fixed location for receipt of a message. The former technique is called direct communication in that it uses direct names; the latter is called indirect communication.

Symmetric addressing

In direct communication, each process that wants to send or receive a message must explicitly name the recipient or sender of the communication. In this case, the **send** and **receive** primitives are defined as shown in List 5.5.

---

send(P, message)
    send a message to process P.

receive(Q, message)
    receive a message from process Q.

List 5.5   Primitives for direct communication.

A communication link in this scheme has the following properties:

(1)   A link is established automatically between every pair of processes that want to communicate. The processes need only know each other's identity to communicate.

(2)   A link is associated with exactly two processes.

(3)   Between each pair of communicating processes, there exists exactly one link.

(4)   The link is bidirectional.

This scheme exhibits a symmetry in addressing, that is, both the sender and the receiver have to name one another in order to communicate.

Asymmetric addressing

A variant of this scheme employs asymmetry in addressing: only the sender names the recipient, whereas the recipient is not required to name the sender. In this case, the **send** and **receive** primitives are defined as shown in List 5.6.

---

send(P, message)
   send a message to process P.

receive(id, message)
   receive a message from any process; id is set to the name of the process with whom communication has taken place.

   List 5.6   Primitives with asymmetric addressing.

Direct communication is easy to implement and to use. It enables a process to control the times at which it receives messages from each other process. The disadvantage of the symmetric and asymmetric schemes is the limited modularity of the resulting process definition. Changing the name of the process may necessitate the examination of all other process definition. All references to the old process must be found, in order to modify them to the new name. This is not desirable from the point of view of separate compilation. Moreover, the **receive** in a server should allow receipt of a message from any sender (client) to provide a service to whatever client process calls it.

   Direct communication (naming) does not allow more than one client. That is because, at the very least, a **receive** would be required for each requester. The server process cannot reasonably anticipate the names of all potential clients. Similarly, direct naming does not make it possible to send one request to more than one identical server. This implies the need for a more sophisticated technique. One such technique is based on links, another is known as indirect communication and is based on mailboxes.

Links

The idea of using links for interprocess communication was introduced by the DEMOS operating system (Baskett *et al.* 1977), and is successfully adopted in two experimental distributed operating systems, DEMOS/MP (Powell and Miller 1983, Miller *et al.* 1987), and Charlotte (Artsy *et al.* 1987).

   A link is defined as a one-way (simplex) communication channel to a user process, system process, or kernel. A link is a protected object and can be used as a naming mechanism for resources controlled by a centralized resource manager. To use a link as a communication facility, each process has a table of links associated with it. Each entry of this table contains a communication path available to the process. So, the table identifies all communication paths which interface the process with the remainder of the system. A process can generate a new link or destroy a link.

A link defined as a one-way communication path reflects an asymmetry in the client–server relationship. This implies that only the sender of a message has to keep state information, but if it wants to request a service, it has to have a link for that service. The server must hold a link to a client only for the period of time from the moment of message generation until a response is sent. This implies that a response link must be created for each request to a server.

Links can be efficiently used for supporting process migration because:

(1)   links can be considered as global addresses to processes, and links are the only mechanisms needed to locate a process; and

(2)   link data areas provide potential optimization for both local and remote large data transfers.

Unfortunately, one-way (simplex) links have several shortcomings:

Dangling links   This happens when a process dies. In this case all links for that process become invalid.

Link management overhead   Responses require new link creation. Many such links are used once and discarded.

Migration   A process has to be left in the source computer whenever a process migrates (this problem will be discussed in detail in the chapter oriented towards process management).

To avoid these problems, two-way (duplex) links were invented (Artsy *et al.* 1987). Different semantics can be associated with two-way links: buffered or unbuffered, blocked and unblocked. These semantics generate some problems. Using buffered messages, since no operating system can supply unlimited intermediate buffers, buffer management problems have to be solved very carefully to prevent (complex) deadlocks or, at least, to detect them. If communication requests do not block the requester, a process may post **send** and **receive** requests on many links without waiting for any to finish. This allows the server to communicate with clients without fear of being blocked. On the other hand, this solution requires some identification of completion of these operations and some decisions about these operations and the links involved.

For this case of links, the **send** and **receive** primitives are defined as shown in List 5.7.

---

send(link, buffer)
sends a message from a buffer along the indicated transmission link.

receive(link, buffer)
receives a message on the indicated transmission link and places it in the buffer.

List 5.7   Link oriented communication primitives.

There is one very important feature of two-way links. The end of a link held by a process can be transferred to another process. Because the link can be represented by a number which is an index into a table held by a kernel, this moving operation can be simply performed by enclosing it in a message. The operation is transparent to the holder of the other end of the link. This implies that while a link end is moving, the holder of the other end can still call **send** and **receive** requests.

The **send** primitive for this case has the form presented in List 5.8. And again, different semantics can be connected with this operation.

---

send(link, buffer, link_end)
sends an end of a link, link_end, on the indicated transmission link and places it into the buffer.

List 5.8   The **send** primitive which allows to send an end of a link.

In summary, a link is an example of a connection-oriented communication system, similar to virtual circuits. Links have advantages and disadvantages. The advantage is that message delivery through a link is reliable and sequenced. On the other hand, the overhead for setting up and closing a link is substantial. Moreover, link-based systems do not recognize the fact that many client–server interactions use only a single request. This implies that the overhead is particularly undesirable and that these interactions are better handled by a transaction-oriented mechanism.

Ports

The second technique is known as indirect communication and is based on global names, sometimes called mailboxes (Andrews and Schneider 1983). A mailbox can appear as the destination designator in any **send** primitive, and as the source designator in any **receive** primitive. This implies that messages sent to a given mailbox can be received by any process that executes a **receive** naming that mailbox. Indirect communication based on a mailbox is well suited for programming client–server models. Gelernter and Berstein (1982) showed that implementing mailbox can be quite costly without a specialized communication network, because when a message is sent, it must be relayed to all nodes where a **receive** could be performed on the destination mailbox. In the next step, after a message has been received, all these nodes must be notified that the message is no longer available for receipt.

A special case of mailboxes which do not suffer these deficiencies was introduced by Balzer (1971). They are called ports and can be abstractly viewed as a protected kernel object into which mesages may be placed by processes and from which messages can be removed, that is, the messages are sent to and received from ports. Processes may have ownership, send, and receive rights on a port. Each port has a unique identification that distinguishes it.

A process may communicate with other process by a number of different ports. The primitive which allows a message to be received on a given port is shown in List 5.9.

---

receive(B, message)
˙receive a message from port B.

List 5.9   The **receive** primitive to communicate through a port.

In this scheme, a communication path has the following properties:

(1)   it may be associated with more than two processes;

(2)   there may be a number of different paths between each pair of communicating processes, each corresponding to one port;

(3)   it may be either unidirectional or bidirectional.

Logically associated with each port is a FIFO queue of finite length. Messages which have been sent to this port but which have not yet been removed from it by a process reside on this queue. Messages may be added to this queue by any process which can refer to the port via a local name (for example, capability). A port should be declared. A port declaration serves to define a queuing point for messages, that is, the interface between the sender and receiver. A process which wants to remove a message from a port must have receive rights. Usually, only one process may have receive access to a port at a time.

Messages to a port are normally queued in FIFO order but an emergency message can be sent to a port and receive special treatment with regard to queuing.

A port can be owned either by a process or by an operating system. If a port is owned by a process, the port is attached to or defined as a part of the process. This solution implies that:

(1)   It is possible to distinguish in a simple way between an owner, who can only receive a message through this port, and a user who can only send message to the port.

(2)   When a process that owns a port terminates, the port disappears. This implies that any process that subsequently sends a message to this port must be notified that the port no longer exists (a form of exception handling).

(3)   There are two possible ways to designate the owners and users of a port:

(a)   a process that is allowed to declare variables of type **port** is its owner,

(b)   declare a shared port and then externally declare the identity of the owner.

A port can be created by a process which owns that port. The process also has a receive access to that port. If a single process both owns and has receive access to a port, this process may destroy it. This possibility is provided in Accent (Rashid and Robertson 1981). The problem is what can happen to a port when its owner dies. If this process has receive access to that port, the best solution to this problem is automatic destruction of the port. Otherwise, an emergency message is sent to the process which has access right to it. If the process which is not the owner but has access right to a port dies, then the emergency message is sent to the owner.

Ownership of a port can be passed in a message from one process to another. Receive access to a port may be also passed in a message. In this case the **send** primitive is defined as in List 5.10.

---

send(A, port)
    send port to port A.

List 5.10   **send** primitive with passing port's ownership.

An operating system can also own a port and when this occurs, it provides a mechanism that allows a process to:

(1)   create a new port (the process is its owner by default),

(2)   send and receive messages through the port,

(3)   destroy a port.

A finite length of the message queues attached to ports is used to prevent a sender from queuing more messages to a receiver than can be absorbed by the system, and as a means for controlling the flow of data between processes of mismatched processing speed. Some implementations can allow the processes owning a port to specify the maximum number of messages which can be queued for that port at any time. In the case of Accent, the following three things can happen when a process attempts to send a message to a full port:

(1)   The process is suspended until the message can be placed in the queue. This option is likely to be used by a user process when communicating with a server process. In this situation the user process does not care if it is suspended for some time while waiting for a message to be delivered to the server.

(2)   The process is notified of an error condition (after a short suspension for up to a specific period of time waiting for the message to be sent). This option is to be used when a process does not care whether a particular message is sent to a destination, but is using the message only to wake up a dormant partner.

(3)   The message is accepted and the kernel sends a message to the sending process when the message can actually be placed in the queue. This option is likely to be used by a server process when dealing with a client process. The server cannot afford to be suspended waiting on a user to clear its queue.

5.2.8 Getting data from a process

There are two alternatives for passing data from one process to another

(1)   processes pass data by value through the exchange of messages; or

(2)   processes pass data by reference.

By-value message systems require that message data be physically copied. If the semantics of communication primitives allow the sender to be suspended until the message has been received, only one copy operation is necessary. Asynchronous message semantics often require that all message data be copied twice: once into a kernel buffer and again into the address space of the receiving process. Data copying costs can dominate the performance of by-value message systems. Moreover, by-value message systems often limit the maximum size of a message, forcing large data transfers to be performed in several message operations.

Passing data by-reference requires sharing of memory. Processes may share access to either specific memory areas or entire address spaces. As a result, messages are used only for synchronization and to transfer small amounts of data, such as pointers to shared memory. The main advantage of passing data by-reference is that it is cheap; large messages need not be copied more than once. The disadvantages of this method are that the programming task becomes more difficult, and it requires a combination of virtual memory management and interprocess communication.

Linking both approaches, passing data by-value and passing data by-reference, can be the most effective solution. The integration of virtual memory management and interprocess communication to improve the efficiency of passing data between processes has been implemented in Accent (Fitzgerald and Rashid 1986), the V-system (Cheriton 1984, 1988a), and Mach (Accetta *et al.* 1986).

5.2.9 Interprocess communication schemes

A sender must specify a particular receiver to be a destination of a message. The performance of a communication system which is very important for highly parallel distributed computations requires a number of communication schemes that should be provided by interprocess communication primitives.

A common scheme of message based interprocess communication is one-to-one (denoted sometimes 1 : 1). A single sending process sends a message to a single receiving process, and usually gets a response back. It is also possible that the sender does not expect any respond. Thus, response handling in one-to-one (unicast) communication is simple.

In many distributed applications the need for one-to-many communication or **broadcasting** becomes apparent. This type of communication may be needed for notifying an exceptional condition to many interested parties. Also, rather than locating and requesting service from one specific resource manager, the client process may wish to request service from any manager of a given type of resource. One-to-many communication can be implemented using multiple one-to-one messages, but such a solution is not satisfactory, in particular in the following three cases (Cheriton and Zwaenepoel 1984):

(1) First, the identity of all the desired receivers of a message may not be known.

(2) Second, in the case of very large number of receipients, the cost of sending separate one-to-one messages can be very expensive and

can cause time delays (in particular, when a hardware communication subsystem provides broadcast).

(3)   Third, some forms of one-to-many communication do not need the full reliability provided by primitives supporting one-to-one communication.

It is very important that most distributed systems based on local area networks provide efficient broadcast communication. (A very good example of such a local area network is Ethernet.) Thus, the implementation of one-to-many communication at interprocess communication level is very natural. When implementing one-to-many communication it is necessary to remember that it should be provided as an integral, and transparent part of regular, one-to-one communication. Such a solution avoids redundant code in the distributed operating system (usually kernel). Moreover, one-to-many communication should be efficient in terms of delay, network bandwidth and processor usage. These features are particularly important for parallel distributed computations.

In some applications there is the need for **multicasting** which allows a subset of the virtual network to receive messages of the same type. Note, there are a growing number of applications which require some type of multicast communication: systems supporting remote and concurrent meetings, commit protocols, and control of production processes. This type of communication is often denoted $1 : K$, where $K < N$, and N is a number of processes involved in transfer of messages.

For example, many-to-one communication is a scheme used in a situation where there is one client and many identical servers. In this case the client, being a receiver of a message from the server must provide a set of sources from which it accepts a message.

The last communication scheme considered here is many-to-many communication. In practice, simultaneous communication between multiple clients and replicated servers is resolved into many-to-one communication (one client and many identical servers), via a shared port or a dedicated interface process, followed by one-to-one communication.

In the last two communication schemes there is the problem of response handling. This is because the process sending a request can receive responses from any number of destination processes (servers). This leads to the following broadcast/multicast response handling taxonomy:

(1)   **No response** – The sender is not expecting any responses, destination processes are not expected to respond. An example of this type of application is a time-signal generator.

(2)   **Single response** – The sender expects a response from any of the destination processes. An example of a system which uses this category is a system with a number of identical file servers.

(3)   **Many responses** – The sender expects responses from more than one destination.

(4)   **All responses** – The sender expects responses from all destination processes. A two-phase commit protocol is an example of an all responses category.

In the V-system (Cheriton 1984, 1988*a*), a process can request one of three response types from the kernel: no response; single response where the first response received by the process' kernel is returned to the process, all subsequent responses are discarded by the kernel; and many responses where each response received is queued by the kernel.

5.2.10 Multidatagram responses

The final consideration with respect to messages sent is whether they are fixed-sized or variable-sized.

   Sending messages of a fixed-size can be characterized by the following two features:

(1)   the physical implementation is straightforward; and

(2)   the task of programming is more difficult.

On the other hand, messages of a variable-size:

(1)   require more complex physical implementation; and

(2)   the programming is simple.

Consider a communication system in which messages sent are of a fixed-size. They must be delivered reliably. In many cases a message to be transmitted is longer than the maximum size of a packet (datagram, if they have the same length). Reliable delivery of messages results in one response/acknowledgement packet for each request packet. This leads to a communication overhead. To improve communication performance, a number of acknowledgement packets should be reduced. This implies that a long message should be divided and sent as a multipacket (multidatagram) message.

   Usually, requests messages (the **send** primitive) are restricted to one packet such as a request to read a disk block or a page of file. Because response messages can be much longer and might not fit in a single packet they are allowed to be constructed of several packets (such a primitive is useful, when the requester requests a file to be sent). In this case only a group of packets is confirmed by an acknowledgement message. Of course a separate request message must be sent for each group of packets. All packets of a group of course bear a sequential relationship to one another. In general, when the requesting node receives all the response packets of all groups, that is, all multipacket responses, the operation is complete and the response is delivered as a single logical entity to the process. However, this is only true when a response message is not too long and does not require very long buffers. Otherwise, each multipacket response is delivered as a single logical entity to the process.

Before sending a request for a multi-packet response, the requester has to set aside enough buffer space to receive all expected packets in a group. The number of buffers allocated (equal to the number of packets in a group) is indicated by a bit map (sequence number), which is one of the fields of the request packet.

Recovery mechanisms in a multi-packet based system are more complicated than in the case of a one request message – one acknowledgement based system. If some datagrams are lost during the transfer, there are three basic mechanisms to handle it:

(1)   If the receiver detects a loss of a packet, it does not send an acknowledgement message. This results in a timeout of the sender, which retransmits the whole group of packets. These retransmissions generate a communication overhead.

(2)   If the receiver detects a loss of a packet, it ignores the following packets and sends an acknowledgement message containing the sequence number of the last received packet. The sender retransmits the following packets. This method is a little better than the previous one, but is more difficult to implement.

(3)   If the receiver detects a loss of a packet, it receives the following packets and leaves space for the lost packet(s). It uses a bitmap to remember the position of the lost packet(s) in the group. After receiving the last packet in the group or a packet with end_of_message flag, it sends an acknowledgement message containing the bitmap. The sender only retransmits packets indicated in the bitmap. This mechanism is most complicated but very efficient.

The system handling lost datagrams by using the bit-map is illustrated in Fig. 5.8.

Communication primitives used in this case should support both at-least-once and exactly-once modes as user-elected options. In the case of primitives with at-least-once semantics, the system handles timeouts and retransmissions of requests but does not attempt to prevent duplicate requests from being passed to the request receiver (server). In this case, if request actions are not idempotent, it is up to the responding process to filter duplicates. A request is idempotent if repeat execution of it is the same as executing it once.

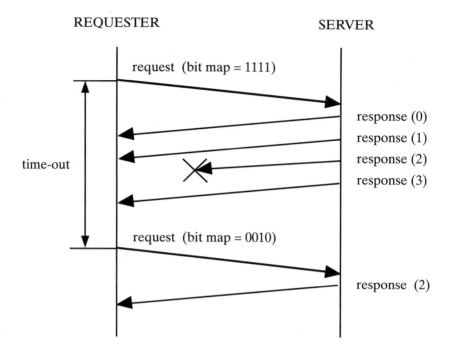

Fig. 5.8 Multidatagram response.

5.2.11 Exception conditions

Distributed computer systems are more reliable and robust than central-ized ones because of loose coupling between components and provision of redundant hardware and software. On the other hand, distributed systems based on local area networks are more error prone than central-ized ones. When a failure occurs some exception handling facilities must be provided. At this stage we will consider some problems associated with process termination, lost messages and scrambled messages.

In the case of process termination two situations must be con-sidered: either a sender or receiver terminates before a message is processed.

(1) If receiver terminates, some messages sent will never be received (the sender sent a message to the receiver that has terminated). In the automatic-buffering scheme, no harm is done; the sender continues with its execution. If the sender needs to know that its message has been processed by the receiver, the acknowledge approach has to be used. In the no-buffering case, the sender will block forever. This implies that the operating system may either terminate the sender, or notify it that the receiver has terminated.

(2) Processes can wait for messages that will never be sent (the receiver waits for a message from a sender that has terminated). In this case the receiver process will be blocked forever, if no action is taken. The system may either terminate the receiver or notify it that sender has terminated.

Let us assume now that a message from the sending process to a receiver becomes lost. The question arises: who is responsible for solving this problem? There are three basic methods for dealing with this event and with scrambled messages.

(1) The operating system is responsible for detecting this event and for resending the message.

(2) The sending process is responsible for detecting this event and for retransmitting the message, if it so wants.

(3) The operating system is responsible for detecting this event; it then notifies the sending process that the message has been lost. The sending process can proceed as it wants.

The solution discussed in detail earlier is based on **timeout**. Note that there are some arguments against the use of the timeout mechanism: the extra syntax can clutter a program and hide a normal execution, and time can be considered as a poorly defined quantity which, in addition, is an implementation-dependent one.

In general, deciding of what should be done when a failure is detected is difficult. However, the following elements can be taken into consideration when designing an interprocess communication facility:

- actions are very application-dependent;

- non-critical exceptions can be ignored; others can lead to abortion of a component of a distributed system;

- in other cases, retrying the operation is a reasonable solution;

- in the cases in which a failure causes partial execution of operation and results in side-effects, a transaction/atomic action approach should be used. Note that this element leads in a natural way to using transactions in distributed operating systems.

5.3 Remote Procedure Calls

The client–server model for process interaction requires two messages to be exchanged. As seen in Chapter 4, this type of relationship is better served by a traditional procedure call mechanism (a mechanism for transfer of control and data within a program running on a single computer), where waiting for the result is implicit in calling for the service. Because the traditional procedure call mechanism is not suited for distributed systems, the **remote procedure call** was developed to provide this kind of higher level synchronization over a network.

5.3.1 Features

Remote procedure call is a linguistic approach based on a fundamental concept known as the procedure call. The idea of **remote procedure calls** (RPC) is very simple and is based on the observation that the model **a client sends request, and then blocks until a remote server sends a response (reply)** looks very similar to a well-known and well-understood mechanism referred to as a procedure call.

Thus, the goal of remote procedure call is to allow distributed programs to be written in the same style as conventional programs for centralized computer systems. One of the main advantages of this communication approach is that the programmer need not be aware that the call invokes a local or a remote procedure (or a process).

The difference between procedure calls and remote procedure calls is implied by the fact that the caller (client) and called procedure are in separate processes, usually running on separate computers. Thus:

(1)   they are prone to the failures of computers as well as communication systems,

(2)   they do not share the same address space; and

(3)   they have separate lifetimes.

The very general term remote procedure call means a type-checked mechanism that permits a language-level call on one computer to be automatically turned into a corresponding language-level call on another computer. This mechanism requires a transport protocol to support the transmission of its arguments and results. It is important to note that the term Remote Procedure Call is sometimes used to describe just this low level transfer protocol.

Message passing systems and their more advanced mutations (such as structured forms of message passing, systems with multigram responses, systems providing reliable primitives) provide services rarely extending above the Transport Layer of the ISO/OSI Reference Model. Functions provided by the Presentation Layer are generally encapsulated in application programs. The RPC facility is responsible for mapping the language's calls and high level typing system into the facilities provided by the network Transport Layer.

Although message passing and remote calling are analogous, message-based systems and remote procedure call-based systems differ in the relationship between communicating processes. Processes in message-based systems act as partners whereas processes in remote procedure call-based systems use a master-slave relationship.

There is also another difference. Whereas in message passing all required values must be explicitly assigned into the fields of a message before transmission, the remote procedure call provides marshalling of the parameters for message transmission, that is, the list of parameters is collected together by the system to form a message.

The remote procedure call is sent by a caller (client process) in the form of the call (request) message to the remote process – callee. The callee (server process) executes the procedure and sends back a result (response) message. In the message exchange illustrated in Fig. 5.9, it is obvious that the remote procedure call provides for bidirectional information flow.

The semantics of remote procedure calls is analogous to local procedure calls:

(1)   the caller is suspended when waiting for results,

(2)   the caller can pass arguments to the remote procedure,

(3)   the called procedure can return results.

However, since the caller's and callee's processes are on different computers (with disjoint address spaces) the remote procedure has no access to data and variables of the caller's environment.

The first and most complete description of the RPC concept was presented by Birrell and Nelson (1984). RPC is available on Xerox workstation products, Xerox research systems (Birrell and Nelson 1984), the Eden system (Almes *et al.* 1985), the CMU Spice system (Jones *et al.* 1985), the Sun Microsystems version of UNIX (Sun 1985), and the research system built at HP Laboratories (Gibbons 1987).

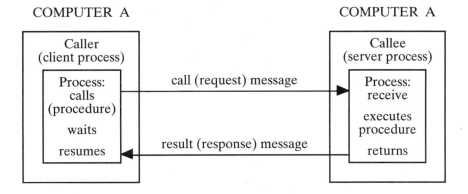

Fig. 5.9   A remote procedure call.

5.3.2 Major issues

Properties and primitives are major issues of a remote procedure call mechanism.

Properties

A remote procedure call mechanism should exhibit the following six properties (Nelson 1981, LeBlanc 1982 and Hamilton 1984):

Uniform call semantics   a transparent remote procedure call implementation must maintain the same semantics as that used for local procedure calls. Otherwise, remote and local procedures must be coded differently.

 This property is based on a definition of transparency. Nelson (1981) presented the following definition: 'Two programming languages mechanisms are transparent if they have identical syntax and semantics. In particular, a transparent language-level RPC mechanism is one in which local procedures and remote procedures are (effectively) indistinguishable to the programmer'. However, total transparency cannot be achieved between local and remote calls, mainly because of failures and message delays.

 Liskov and Scheifler (1982) argue that although the remote procedure call system should hide low-level details of message passing from the user, failures and long delays should not be hidden from the caller.

Type checking   the level of static type checking applied to local procedure calls applies equally to remote procedure calls. A remote procedure call is treated by the compiler exactly as a local procedure call.

Full parameter functionality   all basic data types should be allowed as parameters to a remote procedure call. Primitive types, structured types and user defined types must be considered.

Concurrency control and exception handling   these are not the fundamental aspects of the remote procedure call, but the programming language that supports RPC should provide these services.

Distributed binding   a programming language which uses RPC must have some means of compiling, binding, and loading distributed programs onto the network.

Orphan computations   this issue regards the reliability of an RPC mechanism, in particular a recovery from a remote procedure call that fails.

 Two major techniques have been used to deal with orphans:

(1)   Extermination; to find and abort orphan computations that result from a crash;

(2) Expiration; to determine when a computation (likely to be orphan) has existed beyond its expected lifetime. The computation is automatically aborted after lifetime expires. This technique is analogous to timeout.

Other desirable but nonessential properties of a RPC mechanism, such as good performance, atomic transactions, respect for autonomy, type translation, and remote debugging, are considered in (LeBlanc 1982).

Primitives

When remote procedure calls are used a client interacts with a server by means of a call statement as shown in List 5.11.

---

call service(value_args; result_args)
> where service is really the name of a communication channel defined comprising both source and destination designators. If direct communication is used, service designates the server process; if indirect communication – port is used, service might designate the kind of service requested.

List 5.11   call statement.

A remote **call** is executed in the following way: the value arguments are sent to the server and the calling process delays until both the service has been completed and the results have been returned and assigned to the result arguments.

Andrews and Schneider (1983) identified two basic approaches to specifying the server side of RPC:

(i) The remote procedure is a declaration (like a procedure in a sequential language) with the form shown in List 5.12.

---

remote procedure service(**in** value_parameters; **out**
> result_parameters)
> body
> **end**

List 5.12   Procedure-type specification of an RPC server.

Such a procedure declaration is implemented as a process. This process, the server, awaits receipt of a message containing value arguments from some calling process, assigns them to the value parameters, executes a body, and then returns a response message containing the values of the result parameters. It is important to notice that the synchronization resulting from the implicit **send** and **receive** occurs, even if there are no value or result parameters.

(ii)   The remote procedure is a statement with the form shown in List 5.13.

---

accept service(**in** value_parameters; **out**
    result_parameters) —> body

List 5.13   Rendezvous-type specification of an RPC server.

This statement can be placed anywhere any other statement can be placed. Execution of this statement delays the server until a message resulting from a **call** to the service has arrived. Then the body is executed, using the values of the value parameters and any other variables accessible in the scope of the statement. Upon termination a response message, which contains the values of the result parameters, is sent to the caller. When **accept** is used to specify the server, the remote procedure call is called a rendezvous. This is because the caller and the callee 'meet' for the duration of the execution of the body of the **accept** statement and then go their separate ways. We restrict our considerations here to the first approach.

5.3.3   A simple model of RPC

The general concept of the RPC can be characterized on the basis of the following simple model (Birrell and Nelson 1984).
When a remote procedure is invoked:

(1)   the calling environment is suspended;

(2)   the parameters are passed across the network to the environment where the procedure is to execute and they are copied into the procedure environment; and

(3)   the desired procedure is executed there.

When a procedure finishes and produces results:

(4)   the results are passed back to the calling environment and assigned to the result arguments, where execution resumes as if returning from a single-computer call.

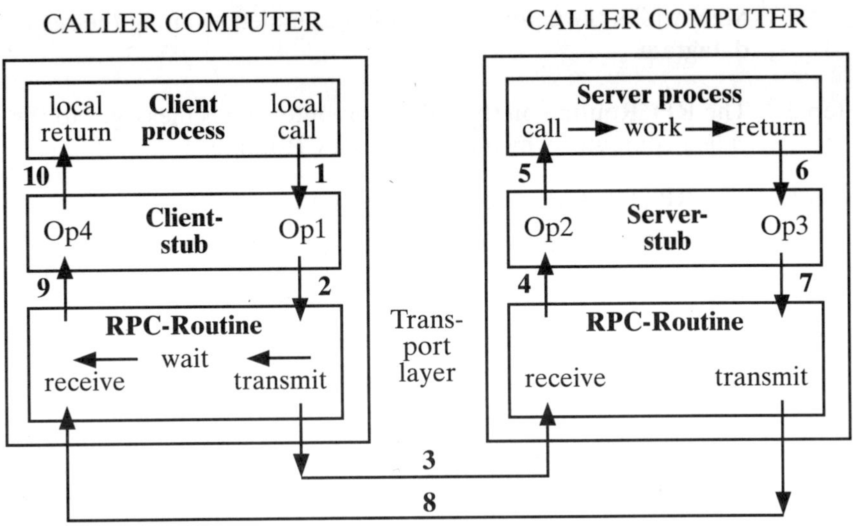

CALLER COMPUTER   CALLER COMPUTER

Fig. 5.10 The components of the system, and their interaction for a simple RPC. Op1 – marshal parameters, generate RPC id, set timer to reply; Op2 – unmarshal parameters, note RPC id; Op3 – marshal results, set timer for ACK of reply; Op4 – unmarshal results, send ACK.

A possible program structure proposed by Birrell and Nelson (1984) to use for remote procedure calls is presented in Fig. 5.10.

This structure uses the approach of **stubs**. One interesting feature of the stub approach is that it does not require any changes to the compiler of the language in which the calling program is written. It has also the side effect that remote procedure calls are indistinguishable from local calls despite the fact that they have different call semantics.

Fig. 5.10 shows the relationship between the following five elements involved in a remote procedure call – the client, the client-stub, the RPC communication package (called also RPCRoutine), the server-stub, the server. Moreover, this figure shows the relationship between the several elements of the program.

The interactions of the elements of the system are as follows:

Step 1   When the client wishes to make a remote call, it makes a normal local call which invokes a corresponding procedure in the user-stub. The stub procedure is linked within the client process' address space.

Step 2   At this stage the client-stub is responsible for two main tasks:

(i)   placing a specification of the target procedure and the arguments into one or more messages, and

(ii)   asking the RPCRoutine (the transport layer) to transmit these reliably to the callee.

Meanwhile, the calling process is suspended awaiting the result datagram.

Step 3   The RPCRoutine on the caller computer sends messages to the callee computer which also runs RPCRoutine.

Step 4   The RPCRoutine in the callee computer:
        (i)   receives these messages, and
        (ii)   passes them to the server-stub.

Step 5   The server-stub performs two tasks:
        (i)   unpacks the received messages; and
        (ii)   makes a normal call to invoke the appropriate procedure in the server; parameters are passed in the standard way.

Step 6   When the call in the server completes, it returns to the server-stub and the results are passed back to the suspended stub in the standard way.

Step 7   The server-stub is now responsible for two main tasks:
        (i)   placing results into one or more messages, and
        (ii)   asking the RPCRoutine to transmit them reliably to the caller computer.

Step 8   The RPCRoutine transmits the message(s) to the caller computer.

Step 9   The RPCRoutine in the caller computer:
        (i)   receives these messages, and
        (ii)   passes them to the client-stub.

Step 10   The client-stub:
        (i)   unpacks results, and
        (ii)   returns them to the user and assigns to the result arguments.

While the calling environment is suspended, other processes on that computer may (possibly) still execute (depending on the parallelism of that environment and the RPC implementation). The only procedures that know that the call is remote are the stubs.

     RPCRoutine is responsible for retransmissions, acknowledgements, datagram routing, and protection. RPCRoutine based communication could be developed on the basis of message passing.

The remote procedure call can be seen as a refinement of the reliable, blocking, structured **send, get_request,** and **send_response** primitives. It has the following advantages:

(1)   It has clean and simple semantics – this makes it easier to build distributed computations, and to get them right.

(2)   It is an efficient remote inter-process communication form – procedure calls seem simple enough for the communication to be quite rapid.

(3)   It is a general approach – in single-computer communications, procedures are the most important mechanism for communication between parts of an algorithm.

Thus the RPC mechanism can be used to provide an interprocess communication facility between a single client process and a single server process. Such a mechanism can be extended to a system of many clients and many servers. One extension was presented in Welch (1986); this extension is described in the next section.

The RPC facility can be used in homogeneous as well as heterogeneous computer systems. The possibilities of using RPC in heterogeneous computer systems, and implementation problems, were studied in a number of projects. The most representative results were obtained while carrying out MIT's Project Athena (Balkovich *et al.* 1985) and CMU's ITC Project (Morris *et al.* 1986). These projects seek to accommodate heterogeneity through coherence, that is, enforcing high-level uniformity in software while permitting implementation on diverse hardware. The authors of LOCUS seek to construct transparent operating system 'bridges' between heterogeneous systems (Sheltzer and Popek 1986). Another very interesting approach is presented in the HCS Project (Bershad *et al.* 1987). Authors of this project accepted as a promise that heterogeneity is necessary and desirable in a research computing environment. This project is characterized in Section 5.3.8.

5.3.4 RPC for many clients and many servers

The basic RPC mechanism has been extended in the Sprite Network Operating System (Ousterhout *et al.* 1988). The basic RPC mechanism of Sprite is a kernel-to-kernel RPC facility similar to the one described in the previous section.

There are two possible extensions. The first is one that supports RPC-type communication between many clients and many servers. The second supports concurrency within each host computer, that is, client host and server host. As a result:

(1)   a client kernel can provide services to more than one process, making a remote procedure call at the same time, and

(2)   a server kernel can service many clients at one time.

The basic concepts of these extensions are presented here following Welch (1986).

Both extensions can be implemented based on the idea of client channels which connect client processes to a server process, and are used to serialize the RPCs from various client processes. The server process keeps information about the client channels used by client processes; it does not have to know about the processes themselves. There are few client channels in each client computer. Therefore processes compete for them. A process can use a channel if it is free. A server computer has some number of server processes. As a result it can handle RPC requests from more than one client at one time. One example of the extended RPC communication is illustrated in Fig. 5.11.

Because the number of different server processes on one computer is limited, they are multiplexed between the client channels that use the server. The server kernel assigns a server process to a particular client channel for a series of remote procedure calls. The server process is released after receiving an acknowledgement from a client channel ending the series of RPCs. Matching a message from a client channel to the correct server process is based on the ID of the server process that was used to service the last request.

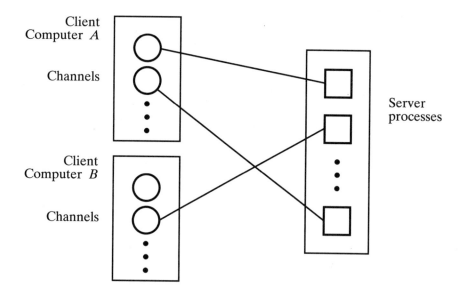

Fig. 5.11   Client channels and server processes in distinct computers {adapted from Welch (1986)}.

Another extension to the RPC facility adds the possibility of broadcasting an RPC request. This is closely associated to the problem of the client-server binding. This extension is described in Section 5.3.6.

To achieve high availability in a distributed system where computers have independent failure modes, the concepts of a **troupe** and **replicated procedure call** were introduced (Cooper 1985). A troupe is a set of replicas of a module executing on several computers. Individual members of a troupe do not communicate among themselves because they are unaware of one another's existence. However, troupes can communicate with each other. The extension of the basic remote procedure call for communicating troupes is a replicated procedure call.

The replicated procedure call provides, like Sprite's mechanism, many-to-many communication, but its semantics is different. The semantics of the replicated procedure call is exactly-once execution at all troupe members, that is, when a client troupe makes a call to a server troupe, each process of the server troupe performs the requested procedure exactly once, and each process in the client troupe receives all the results (Fig. 5.12).

To achieve replication transparency, troupe members must behave deterministically, that is, two replicas in the same state must execute the same procedure in the same order, produce the same side effects, and return the same results.

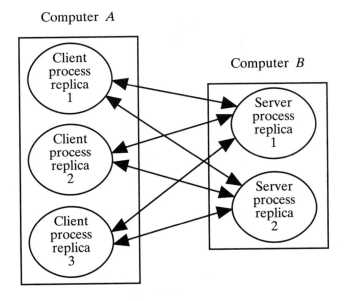

Fig. 5.12 Replicated procedure call.

5.3.5 Parameters and results in RPCs

One of the most important problems of remote procedure calls is parameter passing and the representation of parameters and results in messages.

Parameters can be passed by value or by reference. Passing value parameters over the network is easy: the stub copies parameters into a message and transmits it. Passing reference parameters (pointers) over a network is more complicated.

A unique, systemwide pointer is needed for each object so that it can be remotely accessed. For large objects such as files, some kind of capability mechanism could be set up using capabilities as pointers, but for small objects such as integers or booleans the overhead involved in creating a capability and sending it is too large, so that is highly undesirable.

The representation of parameters and results in messages is natural for homogeneous systems. The representation is complicated in heterogeneous systems.

5.3.6 Marshalling parameters and results

Remote procedure calls require the transfer of language-level data structures between two computers involved in the call. This is generally performed by packing the data into a network buffer on one computer and unpacking it at the other site. This operation is called marshalling.

More precisely, marshalling is a process performed both when sending the call as well as when sending the result, in which three actions can be distinguished:

(1) taking the parameters to be passed to the remote procedure and results of executing the procedure;

(2) assembling these two into a form suitable for transmission among computers involved in the remote procedure call; and

(3) disassembling them on arrival.

The marshalling process must reflect the data structures of the language. Primitive types, structured types, and user defined types must be considered. In the majority of cases, marshalling procedures for scalar data types and procedures to marshal structured types built from the scalar ones are provided as a part of the RPC software. According to Nelson, the compiler should always generate in-line marshalling code for every remote call. This permits more efficient marshalling than interpretive schemes but can lead to unacceptably large amounts of code. However, some systems allow the programmer to define marshalling procedures for types that include pointers (Bacon and Hamilton 1987).

5.3.7 Exception handling

The parameters exported to a remote procedure might contain errors or be inconsistent. If the callee (server process) cannot resolve them, this should be reported to the caller (client process). Thus, a relevant service must be provided. This service is called **exception handling**. Exception handling mechanisms are language dependent. However, there is the need for a method to distinguish unsuccessful calls from successful calls. Thus, the caller has to test every return value and, when failure is reported, it must request more information about this failure.

There are different solutions to the exception handling problem. Some languages such as CLU (Liskov *et al.* 1981) provide language constructs for exception handling based on the concept that the expected result of a procedure is either a result or an exception. Such an exception consists of its name and possibly some results. Mesa, which is used in Cedar (Birrell and Nelson 1984), provides exception handling based on facilities for notifying exceptions. In this case, the remote procedure can pass the exception in a response message. When the caller receives such a message, the exception handling procedure is called.

5.3.8 Implementing a callee and caller

The two processes involved in a remote procedure call have separate lifetimes. There are two conceptually different implementations of the process that executes the remote call.

(1)   The callee's process exists before the call and runs continuously. This is a typical server type implementation. Thus this process listens for call (request) messages, executes the appropriate procedure, and sends back result (response) messages. Such a server may be called by any number of remote processes. Call are executed sequentially. There could be one or more servers.

(2)   A process which executes a remote procedure is created for each caller or for each procedure call. Thus, multiple calls result in the creation of processes to handle each call. All processes may execute in parallel. After completion of a requested procedure, the process is killed.

5.3.9 Client–server binding

Usually, RPC hides all details of locating servers (callees) from clients (callers). (Mayflower's RPC was developed with different philosophy in mind, in that RPC does not hide from the programmer that certain processing is remote [Bacon and Hamilton 1987].) However, in a system with more than one server, for example a file server and a print server, the knowledge of location of clients files or a special type of a printer is important. This implies the need for a mechanism to bind a client and a server, in particular, to bind an RPC stub to the right server and remote procedure.

Birrell and Nelson (1984) identified two aspects of binding:

(1) the way the client specifies what he wants to be bound to which – the problem of naming;

(2) the ways of determination by the requester (caller) of the computer address of the server (callee), and the specification of the procedure to be invoked – the problem of addressing.

These two problems are discussed in Chapter 7. However, some elements of the problems, very closely related to RPC, are discussed in this section.

In a distributed system there are two different forms of cooperation between clients and servers. The first form assumes that a client requests a temporary service. Another situation is generated by a client which wants to arrange for a number of calls to be directed to a particular serving process. These imply a need for a run-time mechanism for establishing long term bindings between this client and a server.

The first aspect of binding, naming, was solved in Birrell and Nelson (1984) in terms of interface names. In their proposal, which was implemented in the Cedar/Mesa system, individual procedures are identified by entry point number within interface. Interface names are user created.

There are two possible ways to locate a server for a client. The first solution uses broadcast or multicast messages to locate a defined process or server. The first response is given to the client process and all subsequent responses are discarded. Usually, there is not any retry if there is no response after the timeout period. That is because all computers have to be involved in broadcast processing which is expensive. The second solution is based on a name server concept.

In the case of requests for a temporary service, the problem can be solved using broadcast and multicast (to more than one) messages to locate a process or a server. In the case of solution based on a name server that is not enough, because the process wants to call the located server during a time horizon. This means that a special binding table should be created and all established long term binding objects, that is, a client name and a server name (address), should be registered. The RPC run-time procedure for performing remote calls expects to be provided a binding object as one of its arguments. This procedure directs the call to the binding address received. It should be possible to add new binding objects to the table, remove binding objects from the binding table (which in practice means breaking a binding), and update the binding table. In systems with name server(s), broadcasting is replaced by the operation of sending requests to a name server requesting a location of a given server and sending a response with an address of this server.

A binding system based on a name server is illustrated in Fig. 5.13.

A server registers with the name server by sending its name, network address and unique identifier (Steps 1 and 2). When the client process makes the first call (Step 3), its stub sends a query message containing a server name 4 to the name server (Step 4). In response, the name server sends the network address and unique identifier of a called server (Step 5).

In summary, binding can be performed in two different ways:

(1) statically – through the third party such as name server; clients and servers are user processes (Birrell and Nelson 1984); and

(2) dynamically – this binding is between a client channel and a server process, and is controlled by the server which can allocate its server process to active channels (Welch 1986).

It is important to know when binding can take place. The construction and use of an RPC-based distributed application can be divided into three phases: compile time, link time and call time (Bershad *et al.* 1987).

Compile time
- The client and server modules are programmed as if they were intended to be linked together.

- A description of the interface implemented by the server is produced. It yields two stubs: client and server. The client stub, which

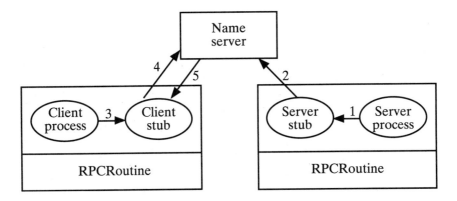

Fig. 5.13 Name server based binding system.

looks to the client like a server, is linked with the client. The server stub, which looks to the server like a client, is linked with the server.

- The stubs shield the client and server from the details of binding and transport.

- Ideally the stubs are produced mechanically from the definition of the interface, by a stub generator.

Link time

- A server makes its availability known by exporting (or registering) itself through the RPC routine support mechanism.

- A client binds itself to a specific server by making an import call to this mechanism.

- Calls can take place, once the binding process has been completed.

- It is expected that binding will be performed less frequently than calling.

Call time

- In providing procedure call semantics at the OSI Presentation Layer, the stubs employ some underlying Transport Layer protocol to transmit arguments and results reliably between clients and servers.

- Different Transport Layer protocols can be used. One of them, known as the packet exchange protocol (Birrell and Nelson 1984), will be presented further.

- The RPC facility should include some control information in each transport packet to track the state of a call.

5.3.10 Message sending schemes

In systems based on remote procedure calls communication between processes is performed on the basis of a master–slave model. So far, there has been discussion about invocation of one process only, one to many, and RPC between many clients and many servers. However, such a scheme may not be the most efficient in some applications which require message broadcasting or multicasting (these problems were discussed in detail in Section 5.2.9). Broadcast and multicast messages in the wider context of remote procedure calls will now be considered. An interesting presentation of this topic has been given by LeBlanc (1982) and we will use it as the basis for our analysis.

The first problem in extending a one-to-one communication scheme to a broadcast one is connected with declaration of broadcast ports. These are provided by extending the notion of a local port to that of a network port, where network ports are queuing points within each computer (processor) for broadcast messages.

Secondly, broadcast port calls should be similar to local port calls. The difference is in the number of destination computers and the number of reply values expected, which in turn effect the manipulation of reply values and the choice of checkpoints.

The third problem is associated with broadcast responses. A broadcast port that specifies a return value expects one from each computer. Therefore, a broadcast port with a return value of type T actually returns an array of type T as a result. The index type of the array is an enumeration type containing the names of all computers (processor modules in the program). This implies that the value returned by computer i may be referenced using an array subscript notation with index i.

The next problem is associated with broadcast completion semantics. The points at which broadcast can be said to have completed are the same as for local port calls. The difference is that many different computers may have to arrive at that point before completion.

Multicast messages share nearly identical problems with broadcast messages. The difference is implied by the fact that multicasting is the sending of messages to a subset of the virtual network. As a result, the semantics of the network port should be such as to support this capability.

5.3.11 Remote Procedure Calls in heterogeneous environment

Discussion in the previous section shows that there are the following five components of an RPC facility:

(1) compile time support, including the programming language, the interface description language, the stub generator, and the structure of stubs;

(2) the binding protocol;

(3) the transport protocol;

(4) the control protocol; and

(5) the data representation protocol.

The last three protocols are employed at call-time.

It is evident that RPC facilities for existing and designed systems make significantly different choices in each of these five areas. This implies that development of a remote procedure call facility for interconnecting heterogeneous computer systems is a complex problem.

An interesting solution to this problem was presented by Bershad and his co-workers in Bershad *et al.* (1987). In their system they carefully specified clean interfaces between all five of the RPC components. As a result, a client (or server) of their remote procedure call facility (called HRPC facility – Heterogeneous Remote Procedure Call facility) and its associated stub can view each of the remaining components as a 'black box'. These black boxes can be mixed and matched. The set of protocols to be used is determined dynamically at bind time – long after a client (or server) has been written, a stub has been generated, and the two have been linked. We remember that in RPC facilities for homogeneous computer systems, all decisions regarding the various components and their implementations are made at the time the RPC facility is designed.

An example of an implementation on three different computer systems of a server that, when called, replies with a list of the users logged in to the computer on which it resides, is illustrated in Fig. 5.14.

The reason for clearly defined procedural interfaces is that it was required that an HRPC stub and any component of control protocol, data representation, and transport protocol components be able to function together. The interaction between these components is illustrated in Fig. 5.15. The directions of the arrows indicate the direction of calls during the call portion of an RPC (as opposed to the return portion).

It must be noted that the basic remote procedure call developed by Birrell and Nelson is not fully adequate for interprocess communication in a network of heterogeneous systems with resource sharing. This point was raised in Gifford *et al.* (1985) and Eberle and Schmutz (1986). This is because such types of parameters as procedure parameters and linked structures are not supported. Moreover, existing remote procedure call systems have no means of supporting abstract objects as data types which can be passed to procedures as a parameter or returned by procedures as results. An example of this would be an open file.

One solution to this problem was proposed in Alpine (Brown *et al.* 1985), where object package was implemented on top of the RPC. The reader interested in other solutions should refer to Eberle and Schmutz (1986).

5.3.12 Remote Procedure Call semantics

Because the caller and callee are separate processes which run on separate computers, they are prone to failures of themselves, their computers or the communication system. The possible failure events and recovery mechanisms have been discussed in detail in the section dealing with semantics of message passing. Here, since the semantics of a RPC call in the above mentioned terms is very similar to the semantics of message passing, we emphasize only the major aspects of an RPC call.

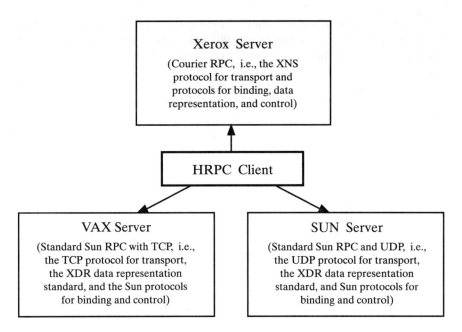

Fig. 5.14 HRPC emulation of multiple RPC facilities {adapted from Bershad *et al.* (1987)}.

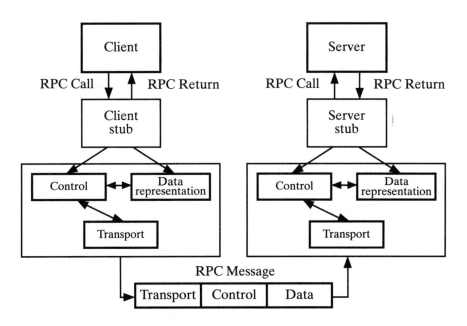

Fig. 5.15 Interaction among call-time components in HRPC {adapted from Bershad *et al.* (1987)}.

The remote procedure may not complete successfully, that is, the result message is not returned to the caller as a response to its call message, because the four events may occur. These events form the basis for design of RPC semantics:

(1) the call message is lost;

(2) the result (response) message is lost;

(3) the callee computer crashes and is restarted; and

(4) the caller computer crashes and is restarted.

Three different semantics of RPC and their mechanisms can be identified to deal with problems generated by these four events:

(1) **maybe** call semantics – timeouts are used to prevent caller waiting indefinitely for a response message.

(2) **at-least-once** call semantics – the mechanism usually includes timeouts and a call retransmission procedure. The caller tries to call the remote procedure until it gets a response or can tell that the callee has failed.

(3) **exactly-once** call semantics – in the case of **at-least-once** call semantics it can happen that the call can be received by the callee more than once, because of responses lost. This can have the wrong effect. To avoid this the callee sends each time (when retransmitting) as its response the result of the first execution of the called procedure. Thus, the mechanisms for these semantics include, in addition to those used in **at-least-once** call semantics (that is, timeouts, retransmissions), call identifications and the callee's table of current calls. This table is used to store the calls received first time and procedure execution results for these calls.

5.3.13 Special communication protocols for RPCs – simple calls and complicated calls

The call semantics of remote procedure call systems should not be tied to any communication protocol implementation. RPC Routines can thus be developed on the basis of different protocols to transport their messages. To the first group of these protocols belong reliable byte stream protocols, such as TCP. The Sun RPC can use this protocol. The second group of protocols is formed by unreliable datagram protocols, for example UDP. This protocol can also support the Sun RPC. Systems developed on the basis of remote procedure calls use different communication primitives (such as primitives described in Section 5.2), which can be considered as background for RPC-type interprocess communication. We will describe here the communication protocol proposed by Birrell and Nelson (1984) and adopted also for the Sprite system (Ousterhout *et al.* 1988). We present this protocol here, because it has been specifically designed to support RPC.

According to the proposed protocol, to obtain a reliable exchange of requests and responses this protocol uses only two network packets per RPC. In practice, this reflects the fundamental need of RPC for communication – the result of a call is an acknowledgement. Birrell and Nelson proposed two types of remote procedure calls for homogeneous computer systems (some of their elements can be used in heterogeneous computer systems): simple calls and complicated calls. The presentation of their network protocol in the case of these two calls follows the original description (Birrell and Nelson 1984) and a report on the Sprite's RPC (Welch 1986).

Simple calls are used in the situation where:

- all the arguments as well as all the results will fit in a single packet buffer;
- frequent calls are made.

The per call communication should be particularly efficient. Complicated calls are used in the situation where the conditions for simple calls are not fulfilled.

Simple calls

To make a call, the caller process sends a **call packet** containing:

- a call identifier,
- data specifying a desired procedure, and
- the arguments.

When the callee computer receives this packet, the appropriate procedure is invoked.

When a procedure returns, a result packet containing:

- the same call identifier,
- the results,

is sent back to the caller.

The packets transmitted during a set of simple calls are presented in Fig. 5.16.

The computer that transmits a packet is responsible for retransmitting it until an acknowledgement is received, in order to compensate for lost packets. However, this RPC network protocol uses implicit acknowledgement which eliminates explicit acknowledgement messages. This implies that the result of a call is sufficient acknowledgement that

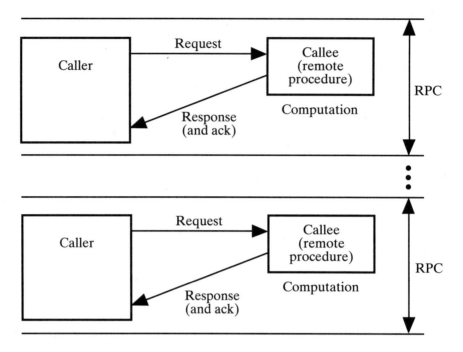

Fig. 5.16   The packets transmitted during a set of simple calls.

the call packet was received, and that a call packet is sufficient to acknowledge the result packet of the previous call made by that process. So, in a situation where a duration of a call and the interval between calls are each less than the transmission interval, only two packets per call are transmitted (one in each direction).

However, this scheme requires a guard against lost messages. Such a guard has been developed on the basis of a timeout technique, and requires a client process to re-transmit its request message if it does not receive the response message before a timeout period elapses. This request indicates that an explicit acknowledgement message for the request is expected. There are three possible cases when the network layer receives a retransmitted request:

(1)   The original request is lost. In this case, the retransmitted request is treated as the original one.

(2)   Neither a request message nor an acknowledgement message were lost, but the called procedure is still executing. In this case the explicit acknowledgement message is returned by the transport layer.

(3)   The called procedure has completed but the response message was lost. Because this recovery protocol is based on exactly-once

recovery mechanism, the called procedure does not execute again. The result of the original computation is retransmitted.

Complicated calls

Complicated calls are in use in two cases:

(1)   in situations where there are long duration calls or large gaps between calls; and

(2)   if the arguments (and/or results) are too large to fit in a single packet – in this situation they are sent in multiple packets.

In situations where there are long duration calls or large gaps between calls, there are two strategies for retransmissions and acknowledgements.

The first strategy for retransmissions and acknowledgements follows these steps:

(1)   The transmitter of a packet is responsible for retransmitting a packet until it is acknowledged;

(2)   When the caller is satisfied with its acknowledgements, its starts waiting for the result process;

(3)   While waiting, the caller periodically sends a **probe** packet to the callee computer, which the callee is expected to acknowledge. This allows the caller to notice if the callee has crashed or if there is some serious communication failure, and to notify a user of an exception.

The second strategy for retransmissions and acknowledgements requires that the recipient of a packet has to spontaneously generate an acknowledgement if he does not generate the next packet significantly sooner than the expected retransmission interval. This would save the retransmissions of a packet when dealing with long duration calls and large gaps between calls.

For the case when the arguments (and/or results) are too large to fit in a single packet two alternative solutions are possible. The first is to use several RPCs such that each transfer an amount that fits in one network packet. This solution is inefficient, because each RPC has a fixed amount of overhead. The second solution requires an extension to the network protocol that allows more data to be transmitted in a single RPC.

The latter solution requires the division of a large data block (request and/or response) into fragments. In this case the system behaves in the following way.

(1)   The request and/or response (arguments and/or results) are sent in multiple packets with each one but the last requesting explicit

acknowledgement. Avoiding acknowledgements of individual fragments improves the performance.

(2) To eliminate duplication, the fragments – the multiple data packets within a call – each have a call-relative sequence number. Duplicate fragments that arrive because of retransmissions can be discarded without having to copy them into their destination buffers.

In the case of lost fragments two solutions can be implemented:

(1) The entire message is retransmitted. This is a very simple solution but very inefficient. It degrades the performance of the overall interprocess communication system. Moreover, if the receiver is a slower computer, this strategy may not work. This is because the fragments are sent out with almost no delay between them, and a slower receiver may always drop the last fragments of a message.

(2) Only missing fragments are retransmitted. This strategy improves the performance of the overall interprocess communication system, and it works in the case of transmitting to a slower receiver. Of course, the protocol is more complicated.

The packet sequences for complicated calls are illustrated in Fig. 5.17.

5.3.14 Message passing versus Remote Procedure Calls

A comparison of the two interprocess communication facilities is needed to decide which is better, if any, and whether there are any suggestions for when, and for what systems, these facilities should be used.

The syntax and semantics of the remote procedure call are functions of the programming language being used. On the other hand, choosing a precise syntax and semantics for message passing is more difficult than for RPC because there are no standards for messages. Moreover, neglecting language aspects of RPC and because of the variety of message passing semantics, these two facilities can look very similar. Examples of message passing systems that look like RPC are message passing for the V-system (which in Cheriton [1988a] is called now the remote procedure call system) and message passing for Amoeba (Tanenbaum and van Renesse 1985).

Note that from the client process point of view, remote procedure calls are very similar to remote rendezvous. This is because both involve a blocked call with parameter passing in both directions. However, the differences between these two communication systems manifest in the implementation of the mechanisms on top of the transport layer and in the usage pattern.

CALLER COMPUTER   CALLEE COMPUTER

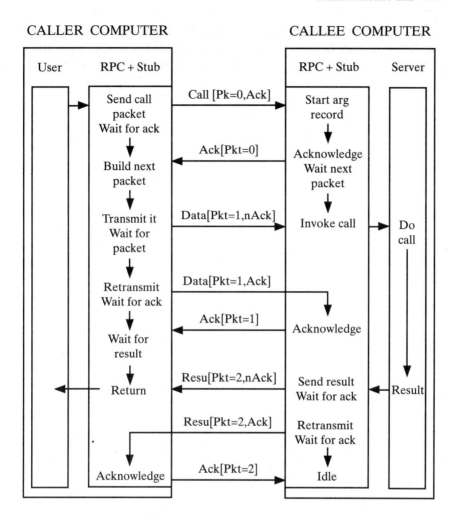

Fig. 5.17 A complicated call (Ack means please Ack, nAck means do not Ack). The call duration is long enough to require retransmission of the last argument packet requesting an acknowledgement, and the result packet is retransmitted requesting an acknowledgement because no subsequent call arrived {adapted from Birrell and Nelson (1984)}.

Comparing the remote procedure call and message passing, the former has the important advantage that the interface of a remote service can be easily documented as a set of procedures with certain parameter and result types. Moreover, from the interface specification, it is possible to automatically generate code that hides all of the details of messages from a programmer. Note that a simplified structure that hides messages reduces the range of communication options available to the applications programmer.

On the other hand, a message passing model provides flexibility not found in remote procedure call systems. However, this flexibility is at the cost of difficulty in the preparation of precisely documented behaviour of a message passing interface.

The problem is when these facilities should be used. Cheriton (1988a) emphasized that the message passing approach appears preferable when serialization of request handling is required. The RPC approach appears preferable when there are significant performance benefits to current request handling. It was pointed out in Ousterhout *et al.* (1988) that RPC is particularly efficient for request-response transactions. This form was expected to be the most common form of interaction between kernels in Sprite.

Interprocess communication is a distributed operating system facility whose performance has been extensively studied, in contrast to other facilities or issues. Unfortunately, these studies have been carried out mainly for one particular system (Cheriton 1988a, Rashid 1986, Welch 1986). This implies that it is very hard to say which form of interprocess communication offers the best performance.

There is one work which contains a comparison between the RPC primitives' implementation in the StarMod system and the message passing send/receive primitives of Charlotte (LeBlanc 1982). Both systems have been developed on the same network of PDP 11/23s. It should be emphasized that the Charlotte implementation was then at an early stage of development and the performance results were preliminary. The send primitive of Charlotte was nonblocking, in that the sender might continue execution once the message had been buffered. Both implementations used for supporting communication had an almost identical version of a stop-and-wait protocol.

The comparison of the time required to send a message from one user process to another remote process in Charlotte, and RPC port call implementation in StarMod shows that the former is significantly more expensive. The following factors contribute to the difference in performance:

(1)   The underlying protocol in Charlotte is a layered protocol that tends to introduce considerable overhead.

(2)   Charlotte was written in C whereas StarMod was constructed using Modula. The quality of the code produced by the various compilers could be a factor in the performance comparison.

(3)   The structures of the kernels are different. The StarMod kernel was constructed for the type of communication supported by StarMod and was designed for high performance. The StarMod kernel was constructed using Modula-like processes. The Charlotte kernel is a layered structure that explicitly reflects interprocess and

intermachine communication. Charlotte contains a single system process and interrupt handlers. Charlotte is based on dynamic communication links that require run-time processing.

Note that both type-safe remote interprocess message passing and type-safe remote procedure call appear potentially useful tools for building distributed systems. These two alternatives are clearly duals in the same way that message passing operating systems and monitor based operating systems are duals.

5.4 Communication for transactions in distributed operating systems

Distributed computer systems potentially are very reliable because of the possibility of providing redundant resources on different nodes. However, the distribution of redundant resources also generates some serious problems, such as the lack of global state information, the possibility of partial failure and the performance of many operations in parallel. These problems imply some difficulty in maintaining data consistency. To maintain the consistency of data, distributed atomic transactions (presented in Chapter 4) have been invented.

Another aspect of distributed computer systems is that a single communication cannot always be used to provide interaction between two processes. The total interaction may be a sequence of communications and computations. In this case the concept of a transaction is a very convenient representation of the totality of communication and computation in distributed systems.

Distributed transaction processing can be defined as the execution of transactions on data stored in multiple partitioned and replicated databases on various network nodes (Spector 1986). Because distributed transaction processing provides applications with access to shared data that are stored with high data integrity and availability, it must be supported by an efficient **distributed transaction facility**. Spector and his coworkers (Spector *et al.* 1985) define this facility as a distributed collection of components that supports standard abstractions such as processes and interprocess communication as well as the execution of transactions and the implementation of objects on which operations can be performed.

One of the most important parts of the distributed transaction facility is a communication system. Such a system should be very efficient, firstly because frequent transmissions are needed to maintain many data replicas, and secondly because short response times are required by transaction clients. A communication system should of course provide conventional communication services such as datagram, file transfer and data streaming. Moreover, applications with access to shared data that are stored on several nodes require more unusual facilities to support data replication, atomic commitment, a coherent system-wide notion of time, and authenticated protected data access. Of course, these higher level abstractions are supported by conventional services. The conventional services can be developed on the basis of classical message passing primitives and remote procedure call and supporting transport protocols issues discussed in previous sections. This section concentrates on communication issues of the unusual facilities necessary to support data replication and atomic commitment, etc.

5.4.1 Basic communication primitives for transactions

In the area of computer science, in particular in the database literature, the definition of a transaction is as follows: a **transaction** is an arbitrary collection of operations bracketed by two markers: BeginTransaction and EndTransaction, and having the following special properties: failure atomicity, permanence, serializability, and that an incomplete transaction cannot reveal results to other transactions.

In distributed operating systems, the definition of a transaction is very similar: a **transaction** is an interaction, consisting of a **request** (equivalent to BeginTransaction) and a **response** (equivalent to EndTransaction), such that a requesting process requests a responding process to perform a given function and to report to the requester. This is illustrated in Fig. 5.18.

The following primitives supporting the transaction based communication model can be used in a distributed operating system. The message is sent, received, and results are sent to the requesting process by executing the primitives **sendTReq**, **getTReq**, and **respT** respectively. These primitives are described in List 5.14.

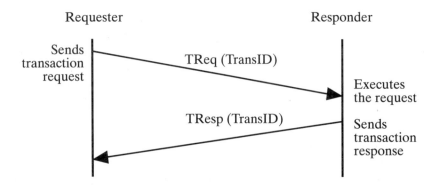

Fig. 5.18 Transaction (ID – transaction ID).

---

sendTReq(header, value_args; result_args)
> where header designates the names of a sender, and a receiver, the kind of service requested, transactionID, and other information relevant to reliability, message structure, etc., value_args are value arguments of the sender, and result_args are result arguments.

getTReq(source_designator, variable_list)
> where source_designator gives the programmer control over where the message came from. Receipt of a message causes assignment of the values from value_args and some from header in the message to the variables in variable_list.

respT(header, results)
> where header designates the names of a sender, and a receiver, transactionID, and other information relevant to the request. The results results are assigned to the result arguments result_args.

List 5.14   Primitives supporting transaction based communication.

The transaction must be performed in the face of various situations inherent in the loosely-coupled nature of networks, for example,

- Transaction request (TReq) is lost in the network,
- Transaction response (TResp) is lost or delayed in transit,
- The responding end 'dies' or becomes unreachable from the requesting end.

Different recovery mechanisms at the requesting end must be activated when the requesting end does not receive the transaction response and must conclude that the transaction was not completed. These consist of timeout, and an automatic retry mechanism. Transaction ID (TID) is used to prevent duplicate requests from being passed to the transaction responder.

There are transaction protocols semantics which ensure transaction execution:

(1)   **exactly-once** – used if the request is not idempotent; serious damage could result from repeated execution of the request.

(2)   **at-least-once** – used if the request is essentially idempotent, for example, repeated execution of a request is the same as executing it once.

These protocols were discussed in detail in the section oriented towards message passing.

5.4.2 Sockets

In distributed systems based on a transaction model, messages are exchanged between sockets (sources and destination of messages).

Sockets are logical addressable entities in nodes of a network, identified by socket numbers, which should be unique within a given node. This implies that an unambiguous identifier for any socket on a single network can be provided by the socket number concatenated with the node identifier. If a distributed system consists of a number of local area networks, then the internet address of a socket consists of socket number, the node ID (of the node in which the socket is located) and the network number (of the network on which the node is located).

Sockets are owned by socket clients (typically processes or functions implemented in software in a node). This is illustrated in Fig. 5.19. Socket clients provide code that is said to be the socket's listener (the code that receives messages addressed to that socket). A socket's listeners should be registered; information about them is maintained in a data structure called a socket table. Sockets can be seen as ports in message based and procedure calls models.

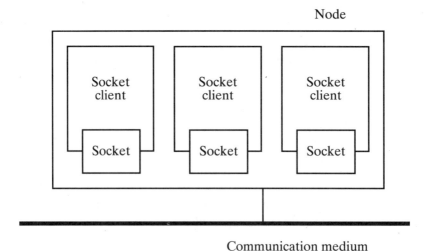

Fig. 5.19   Sockets and socket clients.

There are two types of sockets:

(1) Well-known sockets reserved for use by well-known socket clients (for example, a file server's request receiver socket, a name service socket).

(2) Dynamically assigned sockets; assigned dynamically by a system upon a request from a client.

This implies that there should be primitives to open a well-known socket as well as a dynamically created socket and to close a given socket. Moreover, the socket listener should provide a mechanism for sending and reception of messages.

The basic transaction primitives of List 5.15, together with sockets, form the background for higher level transaction communication. Transaction oriented higher level communication should support the following three fundamental operations: Commitment, Concurrency and Recovery (CCR). The next section presents these three control operations and emphasizes their communication aspects.

5.4.3 Commitment, Concurrency and Recovery – basic concepts

It was shown in Chapter 4 that there is a strong interaction between the three basic issues of transaction processing, that is, commitment, concurrency control, and recovery. They provide the basis for the term CCR (Commitment, Concurrency, and Recovery). The following presentation of the CCR is based on Larmouth (1986), ISO–9804.3 (1989) and ISO–9805.3 (1989).

CCR is designed to ensure successful coordination and completion of activities distributed across several open systems (which together form a heterogeneous distributed system), taking into account the possibility of network failures and system crashes. It is important that Commitment, Concurrency, and Recovery is a single set of procedures; separation of the three features is not meaningful.

This chapter mainly deals with communication aspects of distributed operating systems, so it is useful to present another informal definition of CCR that emphasizes communication aspects. Thus, CCR can be seen as coordinating the synchronization of communications activity across several connections, or alternatively, CCR may be regarded as coordinating the information processing at the nodes linked by the connections.

There are some areas where use of CCR, or some CCR-like handshake is desirable:

(1) No-loss, no-duplication transfer of an object (originally 'material') from system A to system B, without requiring an indefinite retention of knowledge about completed transfers or the intervention of a user on crashes;

(2)   Updates to two different systems by a third party, where it is essential for neither or both updates to occur before other users access the affected information;

(3)   Any remote operation where guarantees are required of precisely one performance of the operation, without requiring an indefinite retention of knowledge of completed operations or the intervention of a user on crashes.

Moreover, the CCR mechanisms are useful (according to some essential):

(1)   whenever more than two entities (parties) communicate, and

(2)   in the two party case if application-independent recovery is required.

5.4.4   A simple protocol for Commitment, Concurrency and Recovery

A simple protocol for CCR is illustrated in Fig. 5.18. According to this protocol, a requester (initiator) requests (TReq[**TransID**]) an action and a responder either performs the requested action and sends an acknowledgement or refuses to do it and provides an appropriate diagnostic (TResp[**TransID**]).

There are two serious flaws in the simple protocol. They arise from:

(1)   crashes, and

(2)   the need for a requester to work simultaneously with several responders (for example, to debit one bank account and credit another).

In the distributed systems two types of end-system crashes can happen. The first is caused by a network failure. In this situation, interprocess communication primitives and communication protocols supporting them provide recovery. These problems have been discussed in Chapter 3 and in previous sections of this chapter. The second type of a crash can be caused by a failure or by a crash of one or both of the communicating parties, either the requester or the responder. In this situation, interprocess communication primitives and communication protocols do not provide any recovery services. The most important thing is that the requester does not know

(1)   whether the action request was lost (Fig. 5.20a), or

(2)   whether the action was performed but the acknowledgement message lost (Fig. 5.20b), or

(3)   whether the action was refused but the diagnostic was lost (Fig. 5.20c).

Different recovery mechanisms at the requesting end must be activated when the requesting end does not receive the transaction response and must conclude that the transaction was not completed. The simplest recovery puts transaction identifier (TID) on the request. The requester retries the action with the same identifier, and the responder, according to the **exactly-once** recovery protocol, detects the duplicate request and performs necessary operations. However, the problem is for how long the identifier and the transaction result have to be remembered. Ac-

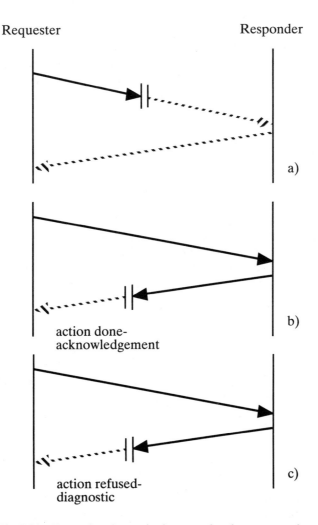

Fig. 5.20   Exceptional cases in the case of end-system crashes.

cording to one simple protocol, 'until a request with a different identifier comes from the same requester'. This protocol works well if there is only one single activity between the two transaction entities. However, if there are multiple simultaneous activities between the two entities then the responder has to hold the information indefinitely.

The question is what is the practical meaning of the term 'indefinitely'? It is possible to say that it is a period which is long compared with the expected recovery time of a requester. However, the assessment of this time is the complicated task.

It may also be possible to use application-specific mechanisms to determine whether an action has occurred or not. This becomes arbitrarily complex if, before communication can be resumed between requester and responder, some other requesters generate actions at the responder (this is associated with concurrency aspects).

The second flaw in the simple protocol is exemplified by the master–slave system, in which the master initiates changes on at least two other systems, slaves, such that for consistent operation, either both changes must occur simultaneously (that is before other users access the resource) or neither must occur. Mending these two flaws in the simple protocol requires extra handshakes, (communication exchanges). The CCR exchanges are discussed in the next section.

5.4.5 The CCR exchanges

The master CCR service and protocol exchanges messages with the slave CCR in the form of two-way communications. These master–slave communications form part of some tree of activity. Such a CCR tree of activity is an atomic action, all the changes required by the action occur, or none of them occur – the action is rolled-back by the master. An example of a CCR activity tree is illustrated in Fig. 5.21.

The most important element of the CCR tree is a protocol (and corresponding local actions) between a master and a slave. Each master should, when exchanging messages, retain control with slaves at all times. An interaction between a master and a slave form a basic handshake. These can be analysed on the basis of events which occur on any one communication.

The events which occur on any one communication between a master and a slave are:

(1) The start of an atomic action. The master issues a **C–begin** primitive with an atomic action identifier in order to mark the start.

(2) Application-specific exchanges occur, defining the action. During this phase, any data used for the action has concurrency controls, which are associated with the atomic action identifier, applied.

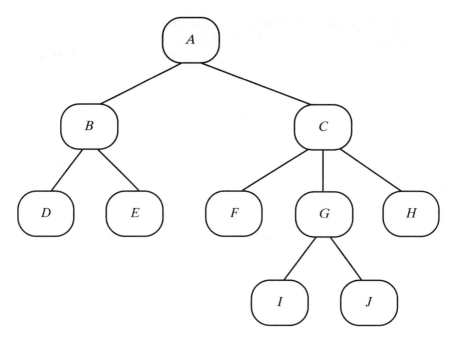

Fig. 5.21 A CCR activity tree: Masters: *A, B, C, G*; Slaves: *B, C, D, E, F, G, H, I, J* {adapted from ISO–9804.3 (1989)}.

(3) The master

(a) explicitly, with a **C–prepare** primitive, or

(b) implicitly, by an application-specific exchange, indicates that the intended action is complete and that it wishes to know whether the slave is prepared to commit.

(4) The slave

(a) offers commitment with a **C–ready** primitive, or

(b) refuses it with a **C–refuse** and a diagnostic, either now or at any earlier time.

From this point on, the slave is required to ensure that both commitment to the action and rollback (release of resources in the initial state) continue to be possible. This is achieved by applying concurrency controls to all affected resources.

(5) The master orders

(a) commitment by a **C–commit** primitive, or

(b) rollback (restoration of the initial state of resources) by a **C–rollback** primitive.

(6)   The **C–commit** or **C–rollback** is a confirmed service, the response/
       confirm providing an acknowledgement by the slave to the master
       that all concurrency controls have been released, and the slave
       has 'forgotten' the action. When this is received, the master can
       also 'forget' the action. It can reuse the atomic action identifier in
       a subsequent action. It is necessary to emphasize the critical na-
       ture of the final message in specifying the end of the master's
       responsibility.

These events form a basic CCR handshake, and are illustrated in Fig.
5.22.

       The basic protocol can be extended by introducing the concept of
heuristic commitment or rollback, which is vital for operation in the real
world.

       Heuristic commitment (rollback) permits a slave who was offered
commitment, and who consequently loses communication with its master or crashes, to decide unilaterally either to commit (heuristic commit-

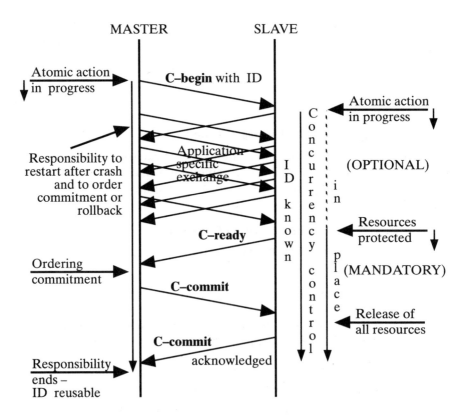

Fig. 5.22 Basic CCR handshake {adapted from Larmouth (1986)}.

ment) or to rollback (heuristic rollback) if the master fails to restart soon enough (Larmouth 1986). This definition emphasizes a heuristic aspect, that is, the slave must guess whether:

- the master is more likely to order commitment than rollback, and

- whether guessing wrong does more damage in the commitment or the rollback case.

A heuristic decision is needed because of the undesirability of applying concurrency controls to a resource for an indefinite period, in particular when locking is used. Larmouth says that in general, the need for heuristic action will depend on the demands of other users to access the resource and the importance of meeting those demands.

However, when making this decision it is necessary to remember the disadvantage of a heuristic decision. The whole CCR service fails if the guess is wrong, because the atomic nature of the action is lost, distributed resources can be left in an inconsistent state, and loss or duplication of actions can arise.

5.4.6 Recovery procedures in the CCR exchanges

Recall that reliability and recovery are major reasons for introducing the transaction and atomic action approach to distributed operating systems. Thus, one can expect some comments on recovery procedures in the basic CCR handshake exchange.

In the basic handshake, issuing a **C−begin** with the atomic action ID implies that a conforming master is required to complete the atomic action with a rollback or commit. This is necessary to ensure release of resources by the slave. Thus, if any of the two parties crashes the master tries to restart the atomic action. This operation is performed using a **C−restart** primitive with a parameter which is the atomic action ID.

Fig. 5.22 shows that if the crash occurs prior to receipt of the **C−begin** or after issue of the **C−commit** (or **C−rollback**) acknowledgement, the ID would be unknown. However, the question arises whether the master can distinguish these two cases. The answer is 'yes' because the master records its decision to commit. At this point the update is essential to the correctness of the protocol. At the slave site, resources will normally be protected as they are used in the action. The protection is recorded to guard against crashes and this operation is recorded when **C−ready** is issued.

Finally, Larmouth emphasizes that the CCR specification ensures that its requirements are the minimum necessary number of disk updates to ensure fully reliable operation of CCR, no matter when crashes occur.

5.4.7 The CCR protocol

In this section we finally discuss the CCR service primitives and their parameters which form the basis for the CCR exchange. They are presented in List 5.15.

C–begin

marks the start of an atomic action. It is issued by a master. It does not require acknowledgement. These are the parameters for this primitive:

- atomic action identifier – an application-entity-title that unambiguously identifies the master, and a suffix that is a character string unambiguously identifying the action among all current actions with the same master;
- branch identifier – an application–entity–title that unambiguously identifies the sub-master, and a suffix that is a character string unambiguously identifying this branch of the atomic action tree among all branches of the same atomic actions with the same sub-master;
- atomic action timer – (optional or advisory) a signed integer value, say N, that warns the slave that the master intends to rollback the atomic action if it is not completed in T (for example, 2^N) seconds;
- heuristic timer – (optional) if present, specifies the time the slave is required to wait after offering commitment before it is permitted to perform heuristic commitment or rollback. The value of it could be 'indefinite' or in seconds, obtained like the atomic action timer. The heuristic timer is **permissive**. This means that heuristic commitment is not required to occur after its expiry;
- heuristic-decision – (optional) if present, constrains any heuristic decision to be the one it specifies (that is, either COMMIT or ROLLBACK);
- user data – carries information of a user process.

C–prepare

indicates that the intended action is complete and that it wishes to know whether the slave is prepared to commit. It is issued by a master. As with **C–begin**, it does not require acknowledgement. There is only one parameter for this primitive:

- user data – carries information of a user process.

C–ready

is issued by a slave which offers the commitment. This message is not acknowledged. There is only one parameter for this primitive:

- user data – carries information of a user process.

C–refuse

is issued by a slave which refuses the commitment. It also provides a diagnostic. This message, like **C–ready**, is not acknowledged. There is only one parameter for this primitive:

- user data – carries structured diagnostic information.

C–commit

this primitive orders commitment.

C–rollback

this primitive orders rollback, that is, restoration of the initial state of resources. Both of these primitives are issued by a master and have to be acknowledged.

- these primitives do not carry parameters.

C–restart

this primitive is issued by a master following a crash to restart the atomic action. This primitive could be also issued by a slave, but only if communication has not failed. In both cases the primitive requires an acknowledgement. These are the parameters for this primitive:

- atomic action identifier – the same as for **C–begin**.
- branch identifier – the same as for **C–begin**.
- restart timer – (optional) the same form as the atomic action timer. The master intends to break the association (and attempt the restart later) if a response is not received within the stated time.
- resumption point – if the master has not issued (prior to the crash) a **C–commit** or **C–rollback** it is ACTION, otherwise it is COMMIT or ROLLBACK respectively.
- user data.

The **C–restart** response and confirm carries only one parameter:

- resumption point – this parameter could be one of the following:

  DONE – indicates either (i) that the **C–begin** was not received or a ROLLBACK or **C–commit** response has been issued (atomic action ID unknown), or (ii) that the **C–restart** ordered COMMIT or ROLLBACK and commitment or rollback, respectively, has occurred (either now or by an earlier heuristic).

  RETRYLATER – indicates that restart is not possible at this time.

  REFUSED – indicates that the slave has previously issued a **C–refuse** for this atomic action.

  COMMITTED – indicates that ROLLBACK had been ordered, but that a previous commitment decision had been taken.

  ROLLEDBACK – indicates that COMMIT had been ordered, but that a previous rollback decision had been taken.

  Following the COMMIT (ROLLBACK) response, the master issues **C–commit (C–rollback)**. This final handshake message is necessary to ensure that the master has received notification of the incorrect heuristic decision before the slave forgets the atomic action.

  MIXED – indicates that heuristics have occurred. Following this response, the master issues either **C–committ** or **C–rollback** to commit or rollback any remaining resources.

  ACTION – following this response, the atomic action is restarted, either from the begining or from an application-specific check point, or from a CCR global checkpoint.

List 5.15 CCR service primitives and their parameters.

5.4.8 Two-phase commit

The discussion of communication in distributed operating systems based on transactions and atomic actions is concluded by presentation of a general algorithm for two-phase commit. It is a basic technique to implement atomic actions, and it is applicable to almost any multiprocess (multiparty) operation.

Suppose, there is a master process and N slave processes. The two-phase commit algorithm is illustrated in Fig. 5.23. This algorithm evidently shows two phases. In the first phase, the master process sends requests to the N slaves asking for some operations. Every slave checks whether it can carry out its request. If it can, it stores the request and initial state of the relevant object, locks this object (no other request from other master processes may interfere), and sends a message confirming the ability to do the requested work. Otherwise, it sends a message refusing to carry out the requested work.

```
MASTER                              SLAVE_i (i = 1, . . , N)
C–begin; {atomic action}
   send(request_1};
   send(request_2};

   . . .
   send(request_i);                 receive(request_i);

   . . .
   send(request_N);
   C–prepare; {Prepare to Commit}
                                    C–prepare;
                                    if action can be performed
                                       then begin
                                          lock object;
                                          store an initial state;
                                          store the request;
                                          C–ready    {the i-th slave is
                                                      able to do it work}
                                       end
                                       else
                                          C–refuse;
if all slaves sent C–ready
   then C–commit {commit the action}
   else C–rollback; {abort the action}
wait for response
                                    if C–commit
                                    then begin
                                       do work;
                                       unlock object
                                    end
                                    send response;
```

Fig. 5.23 Two-phase commit algorithm.

The second phase starts when all responses from the slaves have arrived. At this time, the master checks whether all the slaves can carry out their requested tasks. If they can, the master informs them to perform these tasks. Otherwise, that is, when one or more slaves refuses to carry out a requested operation, the master aborts the action. All slaves are requested to unlock their object and restore its initial state. Thus, no work is done and no object is changed.

There is one reliability problem – a slave can crash after receiving a request and before carrying out its work. We recall, a slave can recover when it comes back up. This is done by using stored initial state and request.

5.5 Interprocess communication and memory management

Chapter 4 emphasized that memory management in distributed operating systems is strongly associated with resource management, in particular computational resource management. We said also, that memory in distributed systems is managed locally. A global view of memory management only takes place when space available is checked against memory requirements of a process to be migrated to a remote computer. Such migration may be desirable for several reasons: balancing the load across the processors in a distributed system, the local computer does not provide sufficient power, requested hardware or software resources are not accessible remotely, providing reliability or a variety of other reasons. These problems are discussed in detail in Chapters 8 and 9. In general, in the existing or designed distributed operating systems memory management has a very loose connection with other management or supporting facilities, in particular with interprocess communication.

However, there are distributed operating systems in which interprocess communication and memory management are integrated. Accent (Rashid and Robertson [1981], Rashid [1986, 1987], Zayas [1988], Mach (Young *et al.* 1987), and the V-system are the best systems in which interprocess communication, virtual memory, and file storage facilities are closely integrated, and operating symbiotically. This integration is such that it preserves the logical structure of interprocess communication while providing performance advantages over previous communication based systems.

Note that an integration of virtual memory with interprocess communication allows one process to manage the virtual address space of another. This can be done either:

- by allocating virtual memory from the Accent's kernel and sending it to another process, or

- by explicitly managing page faults.

As a result, a kernel-transparent mechanism for cross-network paging is provided.

The following presentation of integration of interprocess communication and memory management follows Rashid and Robertson (1981), Rashid (1986, 1987), and Young *et al.* (1987).

5.5.1 Virtual memory and files in Accent

The Accent distributed operating system maintains a virtual memory table for each user process and for the operating system kernel. The virtual address space of an Accent process is flat and linearly addressable. The design of the virtual memory for Accent was influenced by the following assumptions:

(1) process maps had to be compact, easy to manipulate, and to support sparse use of a process address space;

(2) the number of contiguously mapped regions of the address space would be reasonably small; and

(3) large amounts of memory would frequently be passed copy-on-write in messages.

A segment is the basic unit of virtual memory allocation and secondary storage management. There are two kinds of segments: temporary and permanent.

Temporary segments are allocated by processes as required for their memory needs. When all processes which have access to these segments are terminated, temporary segments are released.

Permanent segments are allocated by sending messages to a special port normally supplied only to special processes and do not disappear. However, they can be destroyed by explicit message. The file system of Accent is formed of the storage contained in permanent segments.

5.5.2 Transmission of large amounts of data

In Accent, data is never shared between communicating processes. This implies that message communication over a network has precisely the same semantics as local message communication. However, there are some differences between transmission of typical amounts of data and transmission of large amounts of data. In the former case, data copying to move information from one process to another is used. The latter is based on memory mapping techniques. Though these differences are of implementation nature rather than semantics, they have a very strong influence on system performance.

In a typical message exchange in Accent, double copy semantics is in use. This means that:

- when transmitting, messages are logically copied from a process' address space into a kernel message data structure, and

- when receiving, messages are logically copied from the kernel to a process' address space.

The semantics in this case means that all data sent in a message are logically copied from one address space to another. In general, this copying is time consuming, in particular when large amounts of data are transferred.

Thus, optimization for transmission of large amounts of data should be provided. Rashid and Robertson emphasize that double copy semantics does not imply the need for copying the data twice. This statement can be used to optimize the method used in a typical message exchange.

Such optimization can be provided by the Accent's kernel by mapping the sent data copy-on-write in both the sending and receiving processes. Let us assume that a process sends a message pointing to pages in its virtual memory and either releases the memory or simply never changes it. In this case double copy semantics is preserved by marking the pages referenced in the message as copy-on-write. It does not actually copy them into the operating system's address space. No copy of data need be performed on the receiving computer, if the receiver is not interested in data placement or desires to place it in its memory on the same page boundaries. Transmission of large amounts of data based on memory mapping techniques is illustrated in Fig. 5.24.

The transfer of large amounts of data is performed in the following way. When a message is transferred by process A to a local port, that part of the sender's address space which contains the message is not copied but marked copy-on-write. The meaning of this is that any page referenced for writing will be copied and the copy placed instead into A's virtual memory table. The copy-on-write data then resides in the address space of the kernel until process B receives the message. After that the data is removed from the address space of the kernel.

On reception into an area of the receiver's virtual memory, pages referred to in the incoming message are mapped again rather than copied. The kernel of the destination computer determines where in the address space of the newly received message the data is placed. As a result of this, the kernel minimizes memory mapping overhead.

Sender   Receiver

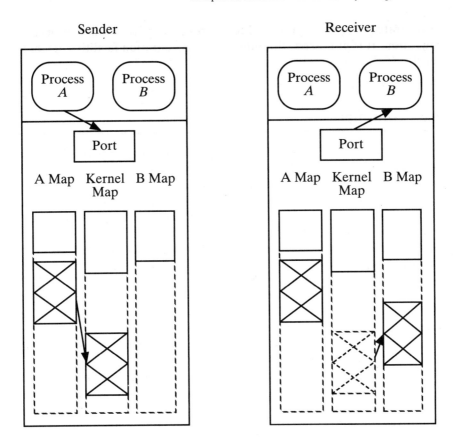

Fig. 5.24 Memory mapping operations during message transfer {adapted from Rashid (1986)}.

5.5.3 The advantages of the integration of interprocess communication and virtual memory

There are three major advantages of integrating interprocess communication and virtual memory. The first is associated with the use of virtual memory by interprocess communication, which represents a functionally transparent optimization. This optimization can increase the speed of communication between processes by reducing the number of copies made when exchanging data between processes.

The second advantage of the Accent approach is that it allows one to consider virtual memory as a resource provided by a process. The third advantage of integrating interprocess communication and virtual memory is that a copy-on-write technique aids in the construction of another strategy, referenced to as copy-on-reference. The copy-on-reference strategy has been proposed to improve the performance of process migration. It is discussed with other process migration facilities in Chapter 8.

5.6 Summary

A distributed operating system encompasses all the computers in a network and leads to a distributed computing system. In such a system, because of the lack of commonly shared memory, processes communicate by sending messages. This implies that high performance interprocess communication is the most crucial facility of a distributed system, because of the necessity of providing fast exchange of data. Fast data exchange can be achieved by using both proper interprocess communication primitives and a suitable and efficient transport protocol which supports these primitives.

The following three forms of remote interprocess communication can be used for developing primitives: message passing and advanced message passing, remote procedure call (RPC), and transactions. Each form can be constructed from the preceding form. These three forms were developed on different basic concepts.

Message passing is a natural extension of interprocess communication for centralized systems. Its basic primitives provide for unidirectional communication from the client process to the server process. Primitives for remote interprocess communication can be:

- nonblocking, if its execution never delays its invoker, or blocking otherwise,

- buffered, when messages are buffered between the time they are sent and received, or unbuffered (sometimes called rendezvous, if some synchronization conditions are fulfilled).

- unreliable, when no guarantee of data delivery is provided, or reliable, when data are delivered and messages are not duplicated or delivered out of order.

Structured form primitives and rendezvous provide for bidirectional information flow.

The sender and receiver have to be synchronized. The synchronization between them is defined by the semantics of the send operation.

Messages can be sent using single datagrams or multi-datagrams. In the latter case special recovery mechanisms must be provided to achieve reliable delivery of messages. Processes communicate by sending messages directly to other processes or ports. Links are also used for communication – either a simplex link, defined as one-way communication path, or a duplex link, defined as two-way communication path. Because links are an example of a connection-oriented communication system, they have its advantages and disadvantages.

When sending a message, a sender process must specify a particular receiving process, a group of receivers, or can direct a message to all processes. In the last two cases there are some categories of response handling. The sender can expect no response, a single response, many responses, or responses from all destination processes.

Message passing suffers from some drawbacks. An improvement can be achieved by moving towards strong typing, that is by providing language-level mechanisms to support type-checked remote interfaces. The remote procedure call is an interprocess communication form which has such features. The very general term RPC means a type-checked mechanism that permits a language-level call on one computer to be automatically turned into a corresponding language-level call on another computer. This results in writing distributed programs in the same style as conventional programs for centralized computers – the application programmer need not be aware that the call invokes a local or remote procedure.

RPC supports communication between one client and one server as well between many clients and many servers. Because some systems do not deal with distributed language-level primitives, the term RPC is used just to describe the transfer protocol.

Remote procedure calls require the transfer of language-level data structures between two remote processes. For this purpose RPC provides marshalling of parameters for message transmission, that is, the list of parameters is gathered together by the system to form a message.

Usually, RPC hides all details of locating servers from clients. This implies the need for a mechanism for binding a client and a server, in particular to bind an RPC stub to the right server and remote procedure.

Distributed systems are very reliable and robust. This is because of the possibility of providing redundant resources on different nodes. A single communication cannot always be used to provide interaction between two processes because the total interaction is a sequence of communications and computations. In this case the concept of a transaction is very convenient. The transaction approach also simplifies the construction of reliable systems. In distributed systems based on the transaction model, messages are exchanged between sockets, which are logical addressable entities in nodes of a network.

To achieve successful interaction, coordination and completion of activities distributed across a distributed computing system, the concept known as Commitment, Concurrency, and Recovery (CCR) is proposed. From an interprocess communication point of view, CCR may be regarded as coordinating the information processing at all computers linked by the connections.

None of these forms is visible to a user, but each of them generates a different overhead measured in terms of message transmission delay and memory occupation. The simplicity of a communication system is also very important. Not much work has been carried out in the area of quantitative comparison between these communication forms.

The performance of a whole distributed computing system can be improved if the interprocess communication facility is closely integrated with memory management, and if they operate symbiotically. This integration should be such as to preserve the logical structure of interprocess communication while providing performance advantages over classic solutions of communication based systems.

Bibliography

Accetta M., Baron R., Golub D., Rashid R., Tevanian A. and Young M. (1986). *Mach: A New Kernel Foundation for UNIX Development.* Computer Science Department, Carnegie–Mellon University

Almes G.T., Black A.P., Lazowska E.D. and Noe J.D. (1985). The Eden System: A Technical Review. *IEEE Transactions on Software Engineering,* **SE–11**(1), pp. 43–59

Andrews G.R. and Schneider F.B. (1983). Concepts and Notations for Concurrent Programming. *Computing Surveys,* **15**(1), 3–43

Artsy Y., Chang H.-Y. and Finkel R. (1987). Interprocess Communication in Charlotte. *IEEE Software,* pp. 22–28

Bacon J.M. and Hamilton K.G. (1987). *Distributed Computing with RPC: The Cambridge Approach.* Technical Report No. 117 Computer Laboratory, University of Cambridge

Balkovich E., Lerman S. and Parmelee R.P. (1985). Computing in Higher Education: The Athena Experience. *Communications of the ACM,* **28**(11), pp. 1214–1224

Balzer R.M. (1971). PORTS—A Method for Dynamic Interprogram Communication and Job Control. In *Proc. AFIPS Spring Joint Conference,* Atlantic City, N.J., pp. 485–489

Baskett F., Haward J.H. and Montagne J.T. (1977). Task Communication in DEMOS. In *Proceedings of the Sixth ACM Symposium on Operating Systems Principles,* New York: ACM Press, 23–31

Bershad B.N., Ching D.T., Lazowska E.D., Sanislo E.D. and Schwartz M. (1987). A Remote Procedure Call Facility for Interconnecting Heterogeneous Computer Systems. *IEEE Transactions on Software Engineering,* **SE–13**(8), pp. 880–894

Birrell A.D. and Nelson B.J. (1984). Implementing Remote Procedure Calls. *ACM Transactions on Computer Systems,* **2**(1), pp. 39–59

Brinch Hansen P. (1970). The Nucleus of a Multiprogramming System. *Communications of the ACM,* **13**(4), 238–41

Brown M.R., Kolling K.N. and Taft E.A. (1985). The Alpine File System. *ACM Transactions on Computer Systems,* **3**(4), 261–93

Cheriton D.R. (1984). An Experiment Using Registers for Fast Message-Based Interprocess Communication. *Operating Systems Review,* **18**(4), 12–20

Cheriton D.R. (1988*a*). The V Distributed System. *Communications of the ACM,* **31**(3), 314–33

Cheriton D.R., Malcolm M.A., Melen L.S. and Sager G.R. (1979) Thoth. A Portable Real-Time Operating System. *Communications of the ACM,* **22**(1), 105–15

Cheriton D.R. and Zwaenepoel W. (1984). *One-to-Many Interprocess Communication in the V-System.* Report No. STAN–CS–84–1011, Department of Computer Science, Stanford University

Cooper E.C. (1985). Replicated Distributed Programs. In *Proceedings of the Tenth ACM Symposium on Operating Systems Principles,* Orcas Island, Washington. *Operating Systems Review,* **19**(5), 63–78

Eberle H.M. and Schmutz H. (1986). Network Operating System Kernels for Heterogeneous Environments. In *Networking in Open Systems, Lecture Notes in Computer Science, No. 248,* pp. 270–295, Springer-Verlag

Fitzgerald R. and Rashid R.F. (1986). The Integration of Virtual Memory Management and Interprocess Communication in Accent. *ACM Transactions on Computer Systems,* **4**(2), 147–77

Gammage N. and Casey L. (1985). XMS: A Rendezvous-Based Distributed System Software Architecture. *IEEE Software,* **2**(3), 9–19

Gammage N.D., Kamel R.F. and Casey L. (1987). Remote Rendezvous. *Software—Practice and Experience,* **17**(10), 741–55

Gelernter D. and Berstein A.J. (1982). Distributed Communication via Global Buffer. In *Proceedings of the Symposium on Principles of Distributed Computing,* Ottawa, pp. 10–18

Gibbons P.B. (1987). A Stub Generator for Multi-language RPC in Heterogeneous Environment. *IEEE Transactions on Software Engineering,* **SE–13**(1), pp. 77–87

Gifford D.K., Baldwin R.W., Berlin S.T. and Lucasson J.M. (1985). An Architecture for Large Scale Information Systems. In *Proceedings of the Tenth ACM Symposium on Operating Systems Principles,* Orcas Island, Washington, pp. 161–170

ISO–9804.3 (1989). *Information Processing Systems—Open Systems Interconnection—Service Definition for the Commitment, Concurrency and Recovery Service Element.* Standards Association of Australia

ISO–9805.3 (1989). *Information Processing Systems—Open Systems Interconnection—Protocol Specification for the Commitment, Concurrency and Recovery Service Element.* Standards Association of Australia

Hamilton K.G. (1984). A Remote Procedure Call System. *Ph.D. Thesis,* Technical Report No. 70, Computer Laboratory, University of Cambridge

Jones M.B., Rashid R.F. and Thompson M.R. (1985). Matchmaker: An Interface Specification Language for Distributed Processing. In *Proceedings of the 12th ACM Symposium on Principles of Programming Languages,* pp. 225–235

Kramer J., Magee J. and Sloman M. and Lister A. (1983). CONIC: An Integrated Approach to Distributed Systems. *IEE Proceedings, Part E, Computer Control,* **130**(1), 1–10

Larmouth J. (1986). Commitment, Concurrency, and Recovery—ISO–CASE and IBM LU.62. In *Networking in Open Systems,* pp. 193–222, *Lecture Notes in Computer Science, No. 248,* Springer-Verlag

LeBlanc T.J. (1982). The Design and Performance of High-Level Language Primitives for Distributed Programming. *Ph.D. Thesis,* Computer Science Technical Report #492, Computer Science Department, University of Wisconsin–Madison

Liskov B. (1979). Primitives for Distributed Computing. In *Proceedings of the 7th ACM Symposium on Operating System Principles,* Pacific Grove, California, pp. 33–43

Liskov B., Schaffer C., Scheifler R. and Snyder A. (1981). *CLU Reference Manual. Lecture Notes in Computer Science, No. 114,* Springer-Verlag

Liskov B. and Scheifler R.W. (1982). Guardians and Actions: Linguistic Support for Robust, Distributed Programs. *ACM Transactions on Programming Languages and Systems,* **5**(3), 381–404

Miller B.P., Presotto D.L. and Powell M.L. (1987). DEMOS/MP: The Development of a Distributed Operating System. *Software—Practice and Experience,* **17**(4), 277–90

Morris J.H., Satyanarayanan M., Conner M.H., Howard J.H., Rosenthal D.S.H and Smith F.D. (1986). Andrew: A Distributed Personal Computing Environment. *Communication of the ACM,* **29**(3), 184–201

Nelson B.J. (1981). Remote Procedure Call. *Ph.D. Thesis,* CMU Report CMU–CS–81–119

Ousterhout J.K., Cherensen A.R., Douglis F., Nelson M.N. and Welch B.B. (1988). The Sprite Network Operating System. *Computer,* **21**(2), 23–36

Powell M.L. and Miller B.P. (1983). Process Migration in DEMOS/MP. In *Proceedings of the Ninth Symposium on Operating Systems Principles,* Bretton Woods N.H., pp. 110–119

Rashid R.F. (1981). Interprocess communication facility for UNIX. In *Local Networks for Computer Communications* (West A. and Janson P., eds.), pp. 319–54. North-Holland

Rashid R.F. (1986). Experiences with the Accent Network Operating System. In *Networking in Open Systems,* pp. 252–269, *Lecture Notes in Computer Science, No. 248,* Springer-Verlag

Rashid R.F. (1987). *From RIG to Accent to Mach: The Evolution of a Network Operating System.* Computer Science Department, Carnegie–Mellon University

Rashid R.F. and Robertson G. (1981). Accent: A Communication Oriented Network Operating System Kernel. In *Proceedings of the Eighth Symposium on Operating Systems Principles,* Pacific Grove, California, pp. 164–175

Saltzer J.H., Reed D.P. and Clark D.D. (1984). End-To-End Arguments in System Design. *ACM Transactions on Computer Systems,* **2**(4), 277–88

Sheltzer A.B. and Popek G.J. (1981). Internet Locus: Extending Transparency to an Internet Environment. *IEEE Transactions on Software Engineering,* **SE–12**(11), pp. 1067–1075

Spector A.Z. (1986). Communication Support in Operating Systems for Distributed Transactions. In *Networking in Open Systems,* pp. 313–324, *Lecture Notes in Computer Science, No. 248,* Springer-Verlag

Spector A.Z., Daniels D., Duchamp D., Eppinger J.L. and Pausch R. (1985). Distributed Transactions for Reliable Systems. In *Proceedings of the Tenth ACM Symposium on Operating Systems Principles,* Orcas Island, Washington, pp. 127–146

Sun (1985). *Remote Procedure Call Protocol Specification*. Sun Microsystems, Inc.

Tanenbaum A.S. and van Renesse R. (1985). Distributed Operating Systems. *Computing Surveys,* **17**(4), 419–70

Welch B.B. (1986). *The Sprite Remote Procedure Call System*. Report No. UCB/CSD 86/302 Computer Science Division (EECS), University of California

Young M., Tevanian A., Rashid R., Golub D., Eppinger J. Chew J., Bolosky W., Black D. and Baron R. (1987). The Duality of Memory and Communication in the Implementation of a Multiprocessor Operating System. In *Proceedings of the Eleventh ACM Symposium on Operating Systems Principles*, Austin, Texas, *Operating Systems Review*, **21**(5), 63–76

Zayas E.R. (1987). Attacking the Process Migration Bottleneck. In *Proceedings of the Eleventh ACM Symposium on Operating Systems Principles,* Austin, Texas, pp. 8–11

6 Synchronization

			Security		
User names	File service		Access control	C o m m u n i c a t i o n & Authentication	s e c u r i t y
	Collaboration of file servers Transaction service Directory service Flat file service Disk service		R e s o u r c e	p r o t e c t i o n	
Name distribution	Resource allocation	Deadlock detection			
Name resolution	Algorithms for load sharing and load balancing	Process synchro-nization	Capa-bilities		
System names	Process management Operations on processes: local, remote Process migration		Access lists	Key manage-ment	
Ports	Interprocess communication (and memory management) Interprocess communication primitives: Message Passing or Remote Procedure Call, or Transactions; Links or Ports		Info flow control Security kernel	Data encryp-tion	
Address-es Routes	Transport protocols supporting interprocess communication primitives			Encryp-tion protocols	

A distributed operating system should allocate resources to allow their effective utilization; should ensure good performance, data consistency, lack of deadlock, and secure operations; and should provide the user with a convenient virtual computer that serves as a high-level programming environment. In order to achieve this, some management decisions must be made. As we have seen, in distributed systems decision making is not straightforward because the state information is distributed among different computers, and is out of date due to communication delays. In general, a global view of the distributed system is not possible. Thus, a distributed operating system should provide partial and consistent views for all cooperating and competing processes. Such partial and consistent views of the system can be provided by synchronization mechanisms.

The term synchronization is used to refer to three distinct but related problems:

(1) synchronization between the sender and receiver of a message;

(2) specification and control of the joint activity of cooperating processes;

(3) serialization of concurrent access to shared objects by multiple processes. This is the major problem when one instance of a resource is to be shared among N processes – it is the classical operating system problem. This problem is also known in database literature where it is referred to as concurrency control.

It was emphasized in Chapter 5 that both communication and synchronization are necessary to achieve correct cooperation among processes. It was observed that these two concepts are closely associated since some forms of communication require prior synchronization. Two processes communicating by messages have to be synchronized. The synchronization between the sender and receiver has been defined by the semantics of the send operation. In this chapter it will be shown that synchronization in distributed computer systems cannot be achieved without communication.

Competing and cooperating processes must be able to inform one another that they have completed a certain action. We can say that **synchronization** is a general term for any constraint on the temporal ordering of operations. Another definition, more relevant to this chapter, can be presented on the basis of an analysis of events that can happen in a system of distributed processes. These processes are considered to proceed in discrete steps. Each step produces an event which can be local to the process and imperceptible to other processes. For this model, we can use the following definition: **synchronization** is a temporal ordering of the set of events produced by the concurrent processes in time.

It is always possible to determine the order of events in a centralized or multiprocessor (tightly coupled) system because there is a single shareable memory and a clock. On the other hand, in distributed systems based on local area networks, there is no common memory or common clock. Processes communicate via message passing. The message communication delay is not negligible compared to the time between events in a single process. Messages may be lost and may be retransmitted. This implies that it is sometimes impossible to determine which of two events signalled by different processes occurred first.

Because of resource distribution, lack of global information and transmission delays, synchronization methods and algorithms developed for centralized systems cannot be used in distributed operating systems.

This chapter presents synchronization problems and algorithms suitable for distributed systems. First of all, event ordering in distributed systems is presented. Based on this background, two groups of synchronization mechanisms, centralized and distributed, are discussed. In the set of centralized mechanisms, the following methods/algorithms are discussed: physical clock, central process, eventcounts and static sequencer.

The main approaches used to construct distributed synchronization algorithms for allocation and mutual exclusion are:

(1) Lamport's time-based event-ordering approach. The most important feature of algorithms based on this approach is the use of timestamps to order all requests from processes that wish to enter the critical section. Here, the following algorithms are discussed: multiple physical and logical clocks, Lamport's algorithm, Ricard and Agrawala's, and Suzuki and Kasami's algorithms.

(2) Token passing approach. The idea of this approach is to provide for a unique message having a special format, called a token, that circulates among the processes according to the order defined by a virtual ring. Le Lann's and Chandy's algorithms are discussed.

(3) Priority based event-ordering. Algorithms in this group order events on the basis of priorities of the processes rather than on times when they happen. This results in the elimination of problems associated with timestamps event-ordering. Special synchronization algorithms for real-time systems and for processes with different priorities are discussed (Goscinski 1989, 1990).

An extension to Ricart and Agrawala's algorithm is presented which enables up to K nodes (processes) to be within a critical section simultaneously.

Another goal of this chapter is the discussion of concurrency control in transaction processing. Many approaches have been proposed to solve these problems. The three main approaches are discussed here: locking, optimistic concurrency control and timestamps.

6.1 Event ordering in distributed systems

In distributed systems it is sometimes impossible to determine which of two events occurred first because global time (clock) is not freely available. If a global time (clock) is required it must be provided explicitly. It is necessary to remember that we can provide such a global time (clock) only within certain margins of error.

Our considerations on ordering of events in distributed systems without using physical clocks are based on the **happened-before** relation, which is delivered from the law of causality (Lamport 1978). The definition of the happened-before relation on a set of events, denoted by '$\rightarrow$', is as follows:

The relation '$\rightarrow$' on the set of events of a system is the smallest relation satisfying the following three conditions:

(1)   If a and b are events in the same process, and a was executed before b, then $a \rightarrow b$.

(2)   If a is the event of sending a message by one process and b is the event of receiving that message by another process, then $a \rightarrow b$.

(3)   If $a \rightarrow b$ and $b \rightarrow c$ then $a \rightarrow c$.

Two distinct events a and b are said to be **concurrent** if $a \rightarrow b$ and $b \rightarrow a$.

Since an event cannot happen before itself, that is, $a \rightarrow a$, the $\rightarrow$ relation is an irreflexive partial ordering on the set of events.

To relate this to distributed systems, consider a set of processes that communicate by sending messages. Assume that sending or receiving a message is an event in a process. Processes can have only their local clocks but in general they are not perfectly accurate. Without a global clock, determination of the order in which events happened must be based on message passing. However, there is a transmission delay, which we assume (Lamport 1978, Verjus 1983) is:

- greater than the time which separates two observable events of the same process, and

- variable, depending on the moment under consideration, with a potentially significant range of values, and variable among differing send-receive pairs of nodes.

Also, messages may be lost.

For example, Fig. 6.1 shows message transmission between four concurrent processes. Some of the happened-before relations in Fig. 6.1 are:

$$p1 \rightarrow q2$$
$$q1 \rightarrow p3$$
$$q1 \rightarrow s3 \quad (\text{since } q1 \rightarrow s1 \text{ and } s1 \rightarrow s3)$$

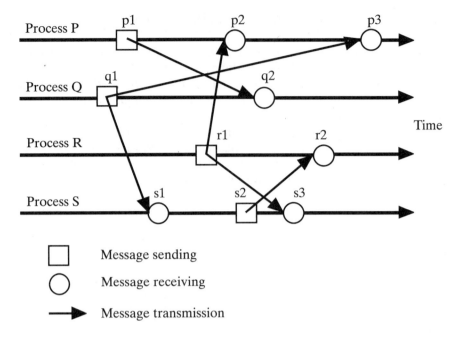

Fig. 6.1 Relative time for four concurrent distributed processes.

It is apparent that:

- At any given time, a process executing in one node can have only approximate knowledge of the state of any other process in another node.
- Even in the case when for any two nodes i and j, the order in which i sends messages to j is identical to the order in which j receives them from i, any two observable events in the system can be perceived as occurring in a different order by different nodes.

In summary:

- The relation **happened before** is therefore only a partial ordering of the events in distributed systems.
- Without an adequate tool which can guarantee a consistent ordering among the nodes, it will be difficult to reconstruct the true and legal trace of events in the distributed system.

To determine that an event a happened before an event b, global time must be available, and we need either:

- a common clock, or

- a set of perfectly synchronized clocks.

Since distributed systems have no such clocks, global time is not freely available and the happened-before relation has to be defined without the use of physical clocks. This implies that global time can be provided only within certain margins of error.

An alternative to global time is Lamport's **logical time**, provided by his logical clock algorithm. Using Lamport's approach we can see a clock as a way of assigning a number to an event, where the number is thought of as the relative time at which the event occurred. In other words his algorithm assigns to every event in the distributed system a **timestamp**. Formally, a clock C_i for each process P_i is a function which assigns a number $C_i<a>$ to any event a in that process. The entire system of clocks is represented by a function C which assigns to any event b the number $C<b>$, where $C<b> = C_j<b>$ if b is an event in process P_j.

Based on this, the **global ordering** requirement can be defined: for every pair of events a and b, if $a \rightarrow b$ then the timestamp of a is less than the timestamp of b.

However, the problem is how to enforce the global ordering requirement. A solution to this problem can be found by thinking of the above clocks C_i as logical rather than physical clocks. This means we define within each process P_i a **logical clock**, LC_j. The logical clock can be implemented as a simple counter which is incremented between any two successive events executed within a process.

Since the logical clock has a monotonically increasing value, it assigns a unique number to every event,

if $a \rightarrow b$ in process P_i then $LC_j(a) < LC_j(b)$

The timestamp for an event is the value of the logical clock for that event.

This scheme ensures that for any two events in the same process the global ordering requirement is met.

The result of this discussion is that on the basis of different times available in distributed systems two different synchronizing units (processes) could be implemented either central or distributed.

6.2 Synchronization in distributed systems

The problem now is how to determine a particular ordering on any given set of events in a distributed system. This is the purpose of synchronization mechanisms. We define synchronization to be a way of enforcing a partial or a total ordering on any set of events.

There are two approaches to solve synchronization problems, which induce the existence of two groups of synchronization mechanisms: centralized and distributed. Since the performance of a function such as process scheduling, data access control, may be controlled by a synchronizing unit, this can lead to either centralized or distributed control of a function.

Every synchronization mechanism which is based on the existence of a central synchronizing unit will be called centralized. The central synchronizing unit must have a unique name known to all processes that need to synchronize with each other, and at any time, any of these processes may access this unit. The term synchronizing unit is used to refer to objects such as semaphores, processes and interlocks. The following centralized mechanisms can be distinguished:

- unique physical clock,
- central process,
- eventcount; although an eventcount may be implemented on several physical components (physically distributed), it still constitutes a unique unit to be used as such, as for example, by processes which read the eventcount,
- static sequencer.

Synchronization mechanisms which are not based on a centralized synchronizing unit will be said to be distributed. They include:

- multiple physical clocks,
- multiple logical clocks,
- pair-wise shared variables,
- circulating token,
- circulating sequencer.

Some synchronization mechanisms are based on the concept of mutual exclusion, that is, a mechanism that induces a total time ordering on the execution of pieces of code in a system of concurrent processes. These mechanisms can use different techniques such as a central process (coordinator) or, token, to initiate mutual exclusion. Other mechanisms to be discussed do not use a concept of mutual exclusion – instead they are based on observing the sequencing of significant events in the course of an asynchronous computation. The following objects belong to this class of synchronization mechanisms: eventcount – it is a communication path for signalling and observing the progress of concurrent computations; and sequencer – it assigns an order to events occurring in the system (Reed and Kanodia 1979). Some mechanisms link several of these concepts to synchronize processes.

6.3 Centralized synchronization mechanisms

The essential aspects of centralized synchronization mechanisms will now be presented. In a centralized mechanism, one node is designated as a control node. Its task is to control access to shared objects. This means that only the central node is allowed to make a decision. Moreover, this node must store information about all processes requesting resources. This presentation of centralized synchronization mechanisms follows Reed and Kanodia (1979), Bullis and Franta (1980), Le Lann (1983), Maekawa *et al.* (1987).

6.3.1 Physical clock

The idea of the physical clock mechanism is to build a unique physical time frame within a distributed system by providing for a single clock (as in centralized systems). Processes may use the physical timestamps either delivered by or read from the central clock to express some ordering on the set of actions they initiate.

The advantage of this mechanism is simplicity. There are, however, many drawbacks:

(1) correct timestamping relies entirely on the possibility of receiving correctly at all times the current value displayed by the clock;

(2) transmission errors become an impediment to a desired ordering taking place;

(3) an accurate *a priori* knowledge or *a posteriori* estimation of inter-process message transmission delays is required; and

(4) the degree of accuracy depends on the constraints placed on the system.

6.3.2 Central process

This concurrency control mechanism relies on a central process which receives all requests from processes to be synchronized. Synchronization is achieved via the mutual exclusion performed by this central process. When this central process (coordinator) fails, one of the processes in the system is chosen to coordinate the entry to the critical section.

A mechanism which requires three messages per critical section entry is as follows:

(1) each process that wants to invoke mutual exclusion sends a **request** message to the coordinator;

(2)   when the coordinator receives a request message, it checks to see whether some other process is in its critical section; if not, it immediately sends back a **reply** message; otherwise, the request is queued;

(3)   when a process receives a reply from the coordinator, it can proceed to enter its critical section;

(4)   after exiting its critical section, the process sends a **release** message to the coordinator;

(5)   when the coordinator receives a release, it removes one of the request messages from the queue (according to a given scheduling algorithm) and sends a reply message to that process.

This synchronization mechanism has some advantages as well as disadvantages. The advantages are:

(1)   the mechanism ensures mutual exclusion,

(2)   if the scheduling algorithm is fair (FIFO) no starvation can occur.

The disadvantages are:

(1)   it requires three messages per critical section entry,

(2)   if the coordinator fails, then a new process must take its place and perform the following steps:

    (a)   detection of a failure,

    (b)   election of a unique new coordinator,

    (c)   reconstruction of a request queue,

(3)   unconstrained delay.

6.3.3   Eventcounts – Reed and Kanodia's implementation

An eventcount is an abstract object which allows processes to control the ordering of events directly, rather than using mutual exclusion. A more formal definition is as follows. An eventcount (Reed and Kanodia 1979) is an object which keeps a count of the number of events in a particular class (for example, actions) that have occurred so far in the execution of the system, in other words it is a non-decreasing integer, whose initial value is zero.

This presentation of eventcounts will compare two implementations: one by Reed and Kanodia (Reed and Kanodia 1979), and one by Bullis and Franta (Bullis and Franta 1980). Reed and Kanodia's implementation of eventcounts is presented first.

Three primitives defined on an eventcount are presented in List 6.1.

advance(E)

increases the integer value of E by 1. This primitive is to signal the occurrence of an event associated with a particular eventcount. A process that executes **advance** operations on an eventcount E is referred to as a signaler of that eventcount. The value of the eventcount, set initially to zero, equals the number of advance operations that have been performed on it.

The value of an eventcount can be observed by a process in one of two ways. It can either read the value directly or it can block itself until an eventcount reaches a specific value v.

read(E)

returns the 'current' value of E. The value returned by **read**(E) counts all of the **advance** operations that precede the execution. It may or may not count **advance** operations in progress during the **read**. So, it is a lower bound on the current value of E after the **read**, and an upper bound on the value of E before the **read**.

await(E, v)

suspends the calling process until the value of the eventcount E is at least v (this variable must not change while the process is suspended). This primitive is useful when a process does not wish to execute until some event has happened.

List 6.1   Primitives defined on an eventcount.

One important objective is to allow for concurrent execution of these primitives on the same eventcount, without using mutual exclusion as an underlying mechanism (as for example with hardware interlock).

The following example illustrates the possibility of using eventcounts to solve a simple synchronization problem. It is desired that statement *A* be completed before statement *B* is started. The program fragment that satisfies this requirement (that is, implements precedence) is illustrated in Fig. 6.2.

The definitions in List 6.1 are adequate in a system with processes communicating through shared memory. They are not adequate in distributed systems because there may be a communication delay between the time an **advance** operation is finished and the time that another processor can determine that an **advance** has occurred.

PROCESS A'	PROCESS B'
$A;$	**await**(E, 1)
advance(E);	$B;$

Fig. 6.2   A possibility of using eventcounts in synchronization.

Because of this inadequacy for distributed systems, Reed and Kanodia modified slightly Lamport's definition of time in a distributed system (presented in Section 6.1). This modification allows definition of eventcounts in a precise way.

To be consistent with Lamport's work, we have to say that the execution of **advance, read**, and **await** primitives constitute events. Time ordering of events in the system can be defined by a partial-order relation on events, denoted by → (read 'precedes'), which can be any relation that satisfies the following axioms:

C1.   If a and b are events in the same process, and a is executed before b, then $a \rightarrow b$.

C2.   If a is transmission of a message by one process and b is the receipt of that message, then $a \rightarrow b$.

C3.   If $a \rightarrow b$ and $c \rightarrow d$, then $a \rightarrow d$ or $c \rightarrow b$.

C4.   For all events a, $a \rightarrow a$ does not hold. (C3 and C4 imply the transitivity of →)

As in Lamport's model, two processes a and b are called concurrent, if neither $a \rightarrow b$ or $b \rightarrow a$ holds.

For notational convenience Reed and Kanodia introduced another relation, denoted ⇒ (read 'precedes or is concurrent'). This relation is defined in terms of relation → in the following way: $a \Rightarrow b$ if and only if not $b \rightarrow a$. There is the useful property: if $a \rightarrow b$, and $c \rightarrow d$, and $b \Rightarrow c$, then $a \rightarrow d$.

Based on these relations Reed and Kanodia specified the timing relationships of the eventcount **advance, read**, and **await** primitives. There is the possibility that these operations on the same eventcount may be concurrent.

C5.   If W_E is the execution of an **await** operation of the form **await**(E, t), then there are at least t members of the set $\{A_E | A_E$ is the execution of **advance**(E) and $A_E \Rightarrow W_E\}$.

C6.   If R_E is the execution of a **read** operation of the form $v := $ **read**(E), then there are at most v members of the set $\{A_E | A_E$ is the execution of **advance**(E) and $A_E \rightarrow R_E\}$ and there are at least v members of the set $\{A_E | A_E$ is the execution of **advance**(E) and $A_E \Rightarrow R_E\}$.

The next example shows eventcounts used for the synchronization of processes in the single producer – single consumer system. Processes use a shared *N*-cell ring buffer. It is desired that no buffer's contents be consumed before it is produced, and that the limitation of *N* buffers be observed. There are two eventcounts used to synchronize the producer and consumer, IN and OUT, initially set to zero, and synchronized as follows:

- the consumer does not read the *i*-th value from the buffer until it has been stored by the producer, and

- the producer does not store the $(i + N)$-th value into the buffer until the *i*-th value has been read by the consumer.

The program fragment is shown in Fig. 6.3.

In the paper by Reed and Kanodia one can find a correctness proof for the synchronization of the producer and consumer using eventcounts. It is necessary to emphasize that the synchronization of the producer and consumer is obtained because the eventcount primitives maintain a relative ordering on events, rather than by mutual exclusion. The problem which arises at this time is: 'What happens when an eventcount overflows?' The answer is that if it is implemented properly it will never overflow.

```
procedure producer;
  begin
    integer i;
    for i := 1 step 1 do
    begin
      await(OUT, i − N);              {wait for an empty buffer}
      produce(buf[i mod N]);
      advance(IN);
    end;
  end;

procedure consumer;
  begin
    integer i;
    for i := 1 step 1 do
    begin
      await(IN, i);                   {wait for something to consume}
      consume(buf[i mod N];
      advance(OUT);
    end;
  end;
```

Fig. 6.3 Eventcounts in the producer-consumer system {adapted from Reed and Kanodia (1979)}.

Reed and Kanodia presented one possible implementation of eventcounts in a distributed system. One fact is important in this implementation – the sum of any finite set of eventcounts has all the properties of an eventcount. Using this fact it is possible to construct general eventcounts using eventcounts that are each **advance**d by only one process.

Other assumptions are:

(1) only one process in the entire system is considered to be doing **read**s or **await**s, although the extension to several processes is simple;

(2) each node has facilities for local eventcounts, multiple processes, and communication with the other nodes; and

(3) local eventcounts are eventcounts that are manipulated only by processes on a given node.

Moreover, the following terms are used. The process that **advance**s the eventcount is called the signaller. The process that **read**s the eventcount is called the observer. They reside respectively on the signaller node and the observer node. Each node has its own copy of an eventcount E.

Whenever the signaller node's copy is **advance**d, a message is sent to the observer node causing a process there to **advance** that copy. Thus **await**s performed on the observer's copy function correctly. The implementation of the **read** primitive consists of three steps:

(1) The observer sends a request for the value of E to the node, along with a sequence number; this sequence number is incremented with each **read**;

(2) A process at a signaller node sends back the value of its copy of E, along with the sequence number;

(3) When the observer receives the reply containing the correct sequence number, it returns the reply's value of E as the value of the **read**.

An example (the so called secure readers-writers problem) of using access permission on eventcounts to control the transmission of information is discussed in Section 6.3.6.

6.3.4   Bullis and Franta's implementation of eventcounts

The implementation of eventcounts by Reed and Kanodia in a distributed environment is based on an assumption that in the system communication degradation or failures can happen, but nodes are not subject to failures.

An implementation of eventcounts in a broadcast network in which nodes can fail has been given in Bullis and Franta (1980). Networks considered in their work, in addition to the above-mentioned broadcast capabilities, have the following properties:

(1) Communications are reliable, that is, messages are not lost, garbled or duplicated.

(2) Nodes may fail, that is, at any time all processes residing on a node may stop running. This implies that all information at the node is lost.

(3) Failure of a node can be identified by others if a process on a node does not respond to some messages.

The goal of the Bullis and Franta implementation was:

- to ensure robustness with respect to node failure, that is, a system should continue to perform its function, possibly in a degraded manner; and

- to permit the return of a repaired node into the system during network operation.

Achieving this goal required some modifications to the primitives proposed by Reed and Kanodia. These modifications are presented in List 6.2.

Bullis and Franta replaced the **read** primitive with primitives that return lower bounds on the value of an eventcount rather than its exact value. Two primitives were introduced, **lread**, meaning 'local read', and **rread**, meaning 'remote read'. These primitives are shown in List 6.3.

Bullis and Franta adapted Reed and Kanodia's axioms, presented in the previous section, to govern their primitives. These axioms are as follows.

C1. If a and b are events in the same process, and a is executed before b, then $a \rightarrow b$.

C2. If a is a transmission of a message by one process and b is the receipt of that message, then $a \rightarrow b$.

C3. If $W\{E\}$ is the completion of an operation **await**(E, v), then there are at least v members of the set $S = \{A\{E\}|A\{E\}$ is the completion of **advance**(E) executed at any node and $A\{E\} \rightarrow W\{E\}\}$.

C4. (a) If $R\{E\}$ is the completion of an operation $v := $ **lread**(E), then there are at least v members of the set $S = \{A\{E\}|$ $A\{E\}$ is the completion of **advance**(E) executed at any node and $A\{E\} \rightarrow R\{E\}\}$.

(b) If $R\{E\}$ is the start of an operation $v := $ **lread**(E) at node n, then there are at most v members of the set $S = $

advance

the Reed and Kanodia implementation is not robust because the current value of an eventcount, E, exists only at one node. The value is lost when a node fails. To achieve robustness it was proposed that each node have a copy of every eventcount. This implies the need for broadcasting an advance of an eventcount, and that this broadcast message is received by each node to maintain consistency.

await

the Reed and Kanodia **await** primitive is also not robust, since a process executing it will wait forever, if necessary, for E to attain the value v. This problem can be solved by adding a third parameter to this primitive, which specifies the maximum waiting time. As a result the new primitive has the following form

await(E, v, timelimit).

Its semantics is as follows:

wait for either E ≥ v or a timeout;
if E ≥ v
    then return 0
    else return −1

read

in Bullis and Franta's implementation an eventcount consists of several copies which do not in general have the same value. This implies that it is impossible to define the value of an eventcount. As a result, Reed and Kanodia's **read** primitive cannot be implemented, because it relies on the concept of an eventcount having a unique value that can be read.

List 6.2   Modifications to primitives.

$\{A\{E\}|A\{E\}$ is either the completion of **advance**(E) executed at node n or the receipt of an '**advance**(E)' message at node n, and $A\{E\} \rightarrow R\{E\}\}$.

C5.   (a)   If $R\{E\}$ is the completion of an operation $v := $ **rread**(E, n), then there are at least v members of the set $S = $

lread(E)

> returns the value of the local copy of E. Because it does not involve communication with remote nodes, there is no robustness problem to be considered.

rread(E, n)

> returns with the requested value, if node n responds to a message requesting its value of E.

> returns the value -1, if node n does not respond within some fixed time interval. If a process running on node i executes v := **rread**(E, i), it is equivalent to v := **lread**(E).

List 6.3 New primitives introduced by Bullis and Franta.

$\{A\{E\}|A\{E\}$ is either the completion of **advance**(E) executed at node n or the receipt of an '**advance**(E)' message at node n, and $A\{E\} \rightarrow R\{E\}\}$.

(b) If $R\{E\}$ is the start of an operation $v := $ **rread**(E, n) at node n, then there are at most v members of the set $S = \{A\{E\}|A\{E\}$ is either the completion of **advance**(E) executed at node n or the receipt of an '**advance**(E)' message at node n, and $A\{E\} \rightarrow R\{E\}\}$.

C6. If $a \rightarrow b$ and $b \rightarrow c$, then $a \rightarrow c$.

Bullis and Franta presented a solution of the secure readers–writers problem, using their proposed primitives. Their solution together with a solution of this problem by Reed and Kanodia is presented in Section 6.3.6.

6.3.5 Static sequencer

Some synchronization problems require arbitration, that is, a decision based on which of several events happens first. According to Reed and Kanodia (1979), arbitration consists of deciding on ordering between events that may otherwise be unordered, and returning enough information so that the system can make a decision based on the order.

To see a real problem of this type consider sharing a printer by a set of processes (Bullis and Franta 1980). Requests to use the printer arrive at unpredictable times. The problem is to give each process mutually exclusive access to the printer, and a process must be granted use of the printer within a finite time after making a request. Eventcounts cannot be used to solve this problem because they do not have an ability to discriminate between two events that happen in an uncontrolled order. To solve this synchronization problem **sequencers** are introduced.

A sequencer is a non-decreasing integer with initial value zero. Only one primitive operation on a sequencer is defined. It is shown in List 6.4.

---

ticket(S)
>   returns the correct value of sequencer S and then increments the value of S by one.

>   **List 6.4**   A primitive operation on a sequencer.

Fig. 6.4 shows how to use sequencers in sharing a printer.

Unlike eventcounts, sequencers require a separate mutual exclusion mechanism for ensuring that the **ticket** primitive is atomic (indivisible). The activation of two **ticket** primitives by any two producers cannot be concurrent. The formal definition of a sequencer in terms of the partial ordering relation → is as follows:

C1.   If T and T' are events corresponding to **ticket** operation on the same sequencer S, then either $T \rightarrow T'$ or $T' \rightarrow T$.

C2.   If T is an execution of $t :=$ **ticket**(S), then the value assigned to t is the number of elements of the set $\{X|X$ is execution of a **ticket** operation on S and $X \rightarrow T\}$.

Now consider the use of a sequencer in a producer–consumer problem solved using eventcounts. Sequencers need to be used in this problem because we assume that there are multiple producers, and we want the

```
begin
   integer myturn;
   forever do
   begin
      myturn := ticket(S);
      await(C, myturn);
      'printing';
      advance(C);
      'non-printing activities';
   end;
end;
```

Fig. 6.4   Using sequencers in sharing a printer {adapted from Bullis and Franta (1980)}.

deposit operations to be mutually exclusive, but we are unwilling to place *a priori* sequence constraints on the several producers. In this example a sequencer T is used by each producer to obtain a ticket for depositing its message into the buffer. Each producer which has a ticket must wait for a completion of all operations by producers that obtained prior tickets. Each producer executes the program shown in Fig. 6.5. The consumer process executes the same program as in Fig. 6.3).

This program works by using the total ordering among the **ticket**(T) operations to totally order the stores into the buffer array. The **await**(IN, t) operation does not terminate until the **advance**(IN) operation of the producer that got the value $t - 1$ from its **ticket** operation is executed. Moreover, this **advance**(IN) operation enables the consumer process to read the value just stored; this implies that reading of cell t **mod** N can be concurrent to storing into cell $(t + 1)$ **mod** N.

There are two problems with static sequencers that need to be looked at carefully:

(1)   how do corresponding synchronization mechanisms survive the failure of the sequencer? and

(2)   how is mutual exclusion achieved?

6.3.6   Implementation of eventcounts and sequencers

In this section we present an example, so called the secure readers–writers problem, using access permission on eventcounts to control the transmission of information. All processes belonging to two groups, readers and writers, share access to the same database. The writer processes modify a database which is read by the reader processes. There are some requirements. First, each write operation should be performed

```
procedure producer;
   begin
      integer t:
      do forever
      begin
         comment synchronize with producers;
         t := ticket(T);
         await(IN, t);
         comment synchronize with consumer;
         await(OUT, t – N + 1);          {wait for an empty buffer)
         produce(buf[t + 1) mod N]);
         advance(IN);
      end;
   end;
```

Fig. 6.5   Sequencers in the producer-consumer problem {adapted from Reed and Kanodia (1979)}.

in such a way that a database stays in a consistent state. Second, the writers have to read and update the database to fulfil the first requirement, and should be able to communicate with all other writers. Third, the readers cannot use the database or any synchronization mechanism to affect or communicate with another reader or any of the writers.

First of all, look at the algorithm developed by Reed and Kanodia (1979). The readers have permission only to read from the database, and have only observer permission to any eventcount associated with the database. This condition guarantees the security requirement, by forbidding readers to use **advance** and **ticket** operations. The sequencer T is used to provide mutual exclusion for the writers and eventcounts E_1 and E_2 to inform the readers of when the database is being updated.

The program fragment shown in Fig. 6.6 solves the problem.

Bullis and Franta assumed that a writer can die. If a writer is found to have died while modifying the database, the database may be inconsistent and must be specially fixed. A solution of the secure readers–writers problem with the above assumption has been developed, based on Bullis and Franta's algorithm (Bullis and Franta 1980), and is given in Fig. 6.7.

This algorithm shows that the robustness of the eventcount implementation can be achieved by replacing the original **read** primitive proposed by Reed and Kanodia by the **lread** and **rread** primitives. Eventcounts and sequencers can be used successfully in a distributed environment.

```
procedure writer();
    comment when E₁ > E₂, the database is being written
    begin
        integer i;
        advance(E₁);
        i := ticket(T):
        await(E2, i);
        'read and update database';
        advance( E₂);
    end;

procedure reader();
    begin
        integer j;
abort:        j := read(E₁);
        await(E₂, j);
        'read database';
        advance(E2);
    end;
```

Fig. 6.6 Reed and Kanodia's algorithm {adapted from Reed and Kanodia (1979)}.

```
procedure writer();
    comment when E₁ > E₂, the database is being written
    begin
        integer i;
        advance(E₁);
        t := ticket(T);
        c := lread(E2);
        for i := c step 1 until t do
        begin
            j : await(E₂, i, timelimit);
            if j = −1 then return('error');
            comment a writer died in its critical region
        end;
        'read and update database';
        advance(E₂);
    end;

procedure reader();
    begin
    retry:
        s1 := lread(E₁)
        error := await(E₂, s1, timelimit);
        comment a timeout means that a writer died in its critical region
        if error<> −1 then
            comment a writer did not die; the database is intact
            'read database';
        s2 := max(rread(E₁, 1), . . . , rread(E₁, N));
        if s2 <> −1 and error <> −1 then
            comment if s2 = −1 then all nodes containing writers have failed;
                            the database must be assumed unusable
            if s1 = s2 then return
                        else
                            begin
                            comment the database may have been updated
                                    during the read
                                'try again';
                                go to retry;
                            end
        else
            comment the database is inconsistent
            'abort the read';
            return('error');
    end;
```

Fig. 6.7 Bullis and Franta's algorithm {adapted from Bullis and Franta's (1980)}.

In summary, centralized mechanisms adopted to distributed systems do not fulfil requirements of this class of systems. That is because of reliability – they may not be available for a reason of a crash of a unique clock or the central synchronization entity, and because of their poor performance implied, for example, by a bottleneck created by the central entity.

6.4 Distributed synchronization algorithms using time-based event ordering

The distribution of decision making across the entire system implies that synchronization problems are much more complicated. The problem is how to extend a partial ordering to a somewhat arbitrary total ordering and how to use it in synchronization problems. The first solution was proposed by Lamport (Lamport 1978), who used his event-ordering scheme to totally order all the requests to critical sections, serving processes in FIFO order.

Lamport introduced two clocks:

- multiple physical clocks,
- multiple logical clocks,

which are used to build synchronization mechanisms.

6.4.1 Multiple physical clocks

The objective is to obtain a unique physical time frame within the system so that consistent schedules may be derived from a total chronological ordering of events (actions) occurring in the system. Using one physical clock in a distributed system is infeasible, mainly because of transmission delay. Let us assume now that each node has its own physical clock. When several clocks are used, it is not enough for the clocks individually to run at approximately the same rate. They must be synchronized, so that the relative drifting of any two clocks is kept smaller than a sufficiently small constant. Since two different clocks will never run at exactly the same rate, they will tend to drift further and further apart.

Lamport (1978) presented the following solution to this problem by introducing some conditions, rules, and an algorithm. The first condition should be fulfilled by a physical clock C_i to be a true physical clock: this clock must run at approximately the correct rate.

C1. There exists a constant $k \ll 1$ such that for all i: $|dC_i/dt - 1| < k$ where $C_i(t)$ is a continuous, differentiable function of t and dC_i/dt represents the rate at which the clock is running at time t.

Moreover, all clocks must be synchronized so that $C_i(t) \approx C_j(t)$ for all i, j, and t. This is expressed by the following condition:

C2.   There exists a sufficiently small constant ε so that for all i, j:
$|C_i(t) - C_j(t)| < \varepsilon$.

Two clocks never run at the same rate. This implies the need for an algorithm to ensure that condition C2 always holds. To develop such an algorithm let us assume that a process P_i sends a message m at physical time t. This message is received by a process P_j at time t'. The transmission delay of the message m is given by $\delta_m = t' - t$. The receiving process does not know this delay. It knows only the minimum delay $\mu_m \geq 0$. Clearly $\mu_m \leq \delta_m$. The difference between these delays is called the unpredictable delay, $\rho_m = \delta_m - \mu_m$.

Based on these definitions it is possible to present rules for the physical clocks.

R1.   For each i, if P_i does not receive a message at physical time t, then C_i is differentiable at t and $dC_i(t)/dt > 0$.

R2.   (a)   If P_i sends a message m at physical time t, then m contains a timestamp $T_m = C_i(t)$.

   (b)   Upon receiving a message m at time t', process P_j sets $C_j(t')$ equal to the maximum $(C_j(t' - 0), T_m + \mu_m)$.

Note that a process needs only to know its own clock reading and the timestamps of messages it receives.

We will show now that the algorithm presented above can be used to satisfy condition C2. First let us assume that the system is modelled by a strongly connected graph of processes. Arcs in this system represent communication lines over which messages can be sent directly between processes. The diameter of this directed graph is the smallest number d, such that for any pair of processes P_a, P_b, there is a path from P_a to P_b having at most d arcs. We say that a message is sent over an arc from process P_i to process P_j every τ seconds, if for any t, P_i sends at least one message to P_j between physical times t and $t + \tau$. Every process is provided with a clock. Every τ seconds a synchronization (sync) message is sent over every arc. A sync message contains a physical timestamp T. Upon receiving a sync message, if needed, a process should set forward its local clock to be later than the timestamp value contained in the incoming message. It is assumed that both a lower bound u and an upper bound $u + z$ are known for interprocess message transmission delays. Let k be the intrinsic accuracy of each clock (for example, $k < 10\text{E-}6$) and ε the allowed drifting of any two clocks. If $\varepsilon/(1 - k) \leq u$ and $\varepsilon \ll \tau$ then it is possible to compute the approximate value of ε which is $d(2k\tau + z)$.

Depending on the requirements as regards clocks' relative drifting and the validity of the assumptions as regards transmission delay boundaries, one may decide:

(1) either to take the risk of missing some sync messages from time to time, because of some excessively large message transmission delays, thus achieving what could be called probabilistic synchronization, or

(2) not to take this risk. Then, if the upper bound chosen for message transmission delays has to be rather large, one should evaluate the consequences as regards performance. The key parameter here is the ratio z/u .

6.4.2 Multiple logical clocks

This presentation of multiple logical clocks follows Lamport's work (Lamport 1978). An abstract point of view of an introduction of clocks into the system is as follows: a clock is just a way of assigning a number to an event, where the number is thought of as the time at which the event occur. Precisely, a clock C_i for each process P_i is a function which assigns a number $C_i\{a\}$ to any event (action) a initiated locally in that process. The entire system of clocks is represented by the function C which assigns to any event b the number $C\{b\}$, where $C\{b\} = C_j\{b\}$ if b is an event in process P_j. At this time, no assumption about the relation of the number $C_i\{a\}$ to a physical time is made, so it is possible to think of the clocks C_i as logical rather than physical clocks. They may be implemented by counters with no actual timing mechanism.

One of the most important things now is what it means for such a system of clocks to be correct. Such a definition cannot be based on physical clocks, as discussed in Section 6.3.1. A definition must be based on events and the order in which they occur. This condition is as follows:

Clock Condition: For $\forall a, b$: if $a \rightarrow b$ then $C\{a\} < C\{b\}$

The definition of the relation $\rightarrow$ implies that the *Clock Condition* is satisfied if the following two conditions hold:

C1. If a and b are events in process P_i, and a comes before b, then $C_i\{a\} < C_i\{b\}$

C2. If a is the sending of a message by process P_i, and b is the receipt of that message by process P_j, then $C_i\{a\} < C_j\{b\}$

To guarantee that the system of clocks satisfies the *Clock Condition*, it is necessary to insure that it satisfies conditions C1 and C2. To satisfy C1, the processes need only obey the following implementation rule:

IR1. Each process P_i increments C_i between any two successive events.

Now we will consider the next condition, C2. The problem is that these logical clocks will be quickly drifting out of alignment. This implies that the clocks have to be synchronized, that is, consistency among these distributed clocks has to be maintained. This implies that to satisfy C2, it is required that each message m be stamped with a **timestamp** T_m which equals the sender logical clock at which the message was sent. Upon receiving a message timestamped T_m, a process compares its time with the attached to the message clock value, T_m, and it must advance its clock to be later than T_m, according to the following implementation rule:

IR2. (a) If event a is the sending of a message m by process P_i, then the message m contains a timestamp $T_m = C_i\{a\}$.

(b) Upon receiving a message m, process P_j sets C_j greater than or equal to its present value and greater than T_m (Fig. 6.8).

C1 and C2 guarantee a correct system of logical clocks. A system of clocks satisfying the *Clock Condition* can be used to place a total ordering on the set of all system events. But, we simply order the events by the times at which they occur. So, we use any arbitrary total ordering (represented by "⟨ ") of the processes.

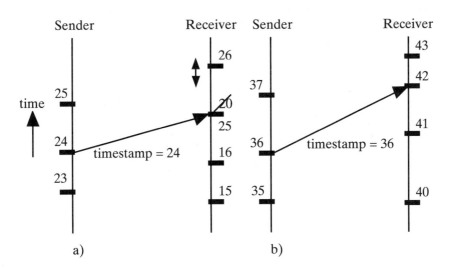

Fig. 6.8 Lamport's logical time; (a) clock in the sender running fast – clock in the receiver advanced, (b) clock in the sender running slow – no action required.

More precisely, we define a relation $\Rightarrow$ as follows:

If a is an event in process P_i and b is an event in process P_j, then $a \Rightarrow b$ if and only if either

(i) $C_i\{a\} < C_j\{b\}$ or
(ii) $C_i\{a\} = C_j\{b\}$ and $P_i \langle P_j$.

This defines the total ordering. Moreover, the *Clock Condition* implies that, if $a \rightarrow b$ then $a \Rightarrow b$. In other words the relation $\Rightarrow$ is a way of completing the 'happened-before' partial ordering to a total ordering.

The synchronization mechanism defined by rules IR1 and IR2 and the total ordering $\Rightarrow$ allow for the building of consistent scheduling actions. We should remember that the ordering implied by the $\Rightarrow$ relation is not unique and it may not be equivalent to a chronological ordering. This is why it may be necessary to implement such a system of logical clocks on a system of several physical clocks.

As we have seen, there is the problem of clock drifting, which implies the need for distributed clock synchronization. Synchronization algorithms are not presented here; the reader can refer to Lundelius and Lynch (1984), Lamport and Melliar-Smith (1984), Srikanth and Teueg (1987), and Gusella and Zatti (1989). Note that it is difficult to compare the various clock synchronization algorithms, because they require different methods of reading clocks and each clock generates a different error.

The total order of events can be very useful in implementing a distributed system. The use of Lamport's total ordering of events was presented by Lamport to solve the mutual exclusion problem (Lamport 1978). Lamport's algorithm is presented in the next section.

6.4.3 Lamport's algorithm

The first algorithm for mutual exclusion in computer networks whose nodes communicate only by messages and do not share memory was proposed by Lamport (Lamport 1978). According to Lamport, a system consists of a set of N processes which share a single resource. Because only one process can use this resource at time, these processes must be synchronized. The goal is to develop an algorithm for granting the resource which satisfies the following conditions:

(1)   a process holding the resource must release it before it can be granted to another process,

(2)   different requests for the resource must be granted in the order in which they are made,

(3)   if every process which is granted the resource eventually releases it, then every request is eventually granted.

To solve the problem, the following simplifying set of assumptions are made:

(1)   for any two processes P_i and P_j, the messages sent from P_i to P_j are received in the same order as they are sent,

(2)   every message is eventually received,

(3)   a process can send messages directly to every other process.

Notice that assumptions (1) and (2) can be neglected by introducing message numbers and a message acknowledgement protocol.

In our distributed system each process maintains its own **request queue** which is never seen by any other process. Let us assume that the request queues initially contain the single message $T_0 : P_0$ **requests resource**, where P_0 is the process initially granted the resource and T_0 is less than the initial value of any clock.

The algorithm for solving the mutual exclusion problem is as follows (for convenience the actions defined by each rule are assumed to form a single event):

(1)   Process P_i sends the message $T_m : P_i$ **requests resource** to every other process, and puts that message on its request queue; T_m is the timestamp of the message.

(2)   When process P_j receives the message $T_m : P_i$ **requests resource**, it places it on its request queue and sends a (timestamped) acknowledgement message to P_i.

(3)   Process P_i is granted the resource when the following two conditions are satisfied:

(i)   There is a $T_m : P_i$ **requests resource** message in its request queue which is ordered before any other request in its queue by the relation $\Rightarrow$. (To define the relation $\Rightarrow$ for messages, a message is identified with the event of sending it.)

(ii)   Process P_i has received a message from every other process timestamped later than T_m.

The conditions (i) and (ii) are tested locally by P_i.

(4)   To release the resource, process P_i removes any $T_m : P_i$ **requests resource** message from its request queue and sends a timestamped P_i **releases resource** message to every other process.

(5)   When process P_j receives the P_i **releases resource** message, it removes any $T_m : P_i$ **requests resource** message from its request queue.

The algorithm presented is a distributed algorithm – there is no central synchronizing process or central storage. Each process independently performs this algorithm, which requires $3*(N-1)$ messages per critical section entry, where N is the number of processes.

The most important feature of this approach is the requirement for a process to know the location of a resource it wants to access.

6.4.4 Ricart and Agrawala's algorithm

Ricart and Agrawala (Ricart and Agrawala 1981) proposed a distributed algorithm which also provides mutual exclusion in computer networks. This algorithm is also based on Lamport's event-ordering approach, but requires only $2*(N-1)$ messages, where N is the number of processes. We will present a more detailed description of this algorithm, because it can be treated as a model for many other algorithms for mutual exclusion in distributed systems. The most important features of this algorithm are that it is symmetrical, exhibits fully distributed control, and is insensitive to the relative speeds of nodes and communication links.

A node wanting to invoke mutual exclusion sends a **request** message to all other nodes. A message contains a sequence number and the node identifier, which are used to define a priority order among requests. A node, upon receipt of the **request** message, either

(1)   sends a **reply** message immediately, if it is not requesting or if the sender has priority greater than its own priority, or

(2)   sends a **reply** message after it leaves its own critical section, that is, response is delayed.

This means that a node can enter its critical section after all nodes have been notified by sending a **request** message to them and receiving a **reply** message from all of them. This requires $N-1$ **request** messages and $N-1$ **response** messages giving a total of $2(N-1)$ messages per critical section entry. The sequence numbers and node numbers form a virtual ordering among requesting nodes, based on a FIFO discipline.

When 'priority' aspects are considered, the problem is what should be done in the case when two or more nodes wish to enter the critical section at the same time. Ricart and Agrawala proposed to solve this problem in the following way. Each **request** message has a sequence number, which is a number of attempts to enter the critical section. A decision rule is based on these sequence numbers, as follows.

Let us assume that node i wishes to enter the critical section. The sequence number associated with this node is S_i.

(1)   If this node/process, i, receives a **request** from node j with sequence number S_j, such that $S_j < S_i$, then node i sends the **response** message immediately.

(2)   If $S_i < S_j$, then node i defers the **response** message, to enter the critical section before node j. The **response** message is sent to node j after exiting the critical section.

(3)   If $S_j = S_i$, then the node identity is taken into consideration.

Each node of a network has its own copy of an algorithm, which can be executed concurrently with other copies. To run an algorithm, the node has to know the number N of nodes in the system and its identity **me**. (The algorithm presentation follows descriptions given in Ricart and Agrawala [1981], Raymond [1987]).
        The variables of each node are as follows:

- Our_Sequence_Number : integer := 0;
        {the sequence number of a current attempt to enter the critical region}

- Highest_Sequence_Number : integer := 0;
        {the largest sequence number seen in any **request** message}

- Outstanding_Reply_Count : integer;
        {the number of **response** messages still to be received before the node may enter the critical section}

- Requesting_Critical_Section : boolean := false;
        {true when a node is wishing to enter the critical section or is in the critical section}

- Reply_Deferred : array[1 ... N] of boolean := false;
        {Reply_Deferred[i] is true when a response to node i has been deferred until this node exits the critical section}

The code of the algorithm has four parts identified by events which can happen in the system, as illustrated in Fig. 6.9.
        Ricart and Agrawala proved that their algorithm guarantees mutual exclusion, that deadlock is impossible, and that freedom from starvation is ensured. There are mechanisms to handle node insertion, removal, and failures. However, handling these events is connected with solving two problems:

(1)   each process/node has to know the identity of all other nodes, and

(2)   if one of the processes fails, then the algorithm does not work.

Because of the first drawback, node insertion requires that each process builds a database containing the names of all other processes. To overcome the second problem it is necessary to monitor the state of all processes. If one process fails, others are notified. As a result of this, they will not send request messages to the failed process.

```
procedure node_wishes_to_enter_the_critical_section;
begin
    Requesting_Critical_Section := true;
    Our_Sequence_Number := Highest_Sequence_Number + 1;
    Outstanding_Reply_Count := N − 1;
    for i := 1    to N do
                 if i ≠ me then send request(Our_Sequence_Number) to i
end;
```

```
procedure node_receives_request(Sᵢ)_from_i;
begin
    Highest_Sequence_Number := max(Highest_Sequence_Number, Sᵢ);
    if Requesting_Critical_Section and (Our_Critical_Section, me) < (Sᵢ, i)
    then Reply_Deferred[i] := true
    else send response to i
end;
```

```
procedure node_receives_response_from_i;
begin
    Outstanding_Reply_Count := Outstanding_Reply_Count − 1;
    if Outstanding_Reply_Count = 0
    then enter Critical section
end;
```

```
procedure node_exits_critical_section;
begin
    Requesting_Critical_Section := false;
    for i := 1 to N do
        if Reply_Deferred[i]
        then    begin
                    send response to i;
                    Reply_Deferred[i] := false
                end
end;
```

Fig. 6.9   Ricart and Agrawala's algorithm {adapted from Ricart and Agrawala (1981)}.

As mentioned earlier, Ricart and Agrawala's algorithm requires $2*(N-1)$ message exchanges for each mutual exclusion invocation. The authors claimed that this number is optimal 'in the sense that no symmetrical, distributed algorithm can use fewer messages if requests are processed by each node concurrently'. Carvalho and Roucairol (1983) have shown that this is not totally true, since it does not include the assumption that the requests are managed in the first-in-first-out order based on the use of timestamps. They proposed an algorithm which fulfils exactly the same requirements as Ricart and Agrawala's algorithm. The basic idea of their concept is as follows. Node i does not send a **request** message to node j if it received a **response** message from node j more recently than i has sent a **response** to node j. This decision may be made based on the assumption that node j cannot be in the critical section, since no request message from j has been received by i after receiving the last **response** message.

6.4.5 Suzuki and Kasami's algorithm

Independently of the work reported in Ricart and Agrawala (1981) Suzuki and Kasami (Suzuki and Kasami 1985) developed a similar distributed, symmetrical mutual exclusion algorithm. The basic concept of their algorithm is to transfer a privilege for entering the critical sections by using a single **privilege** message. The privilege message has the form **privilege**(Q, LN), where Q is a queue of requesting nodes and LN is an array of size N, such that, LN[j] is the sequence number of the most recently granted request by node j. A request message of node j has the form **request**(j, n), where j is the node identifier and n ($n = 1, 2, \ldots$) is a sequence number indicating that node j is now requesting its $(n + 1)$-st critical section invocation. To record the largest sequence number ever received from each of the other nodes, a node has an array RN of size N, which is updated in the following way. If **request**(j, n) is received by node i, then node i updates RN by RN[j] := max(RN[j], n). Critical sections are granted in a FIFO manner.

When node i finishes executing its critical section, the array LN, containing the last **privilege** message received by node i, is updated by LN[i] := RN[i], to indicate that the current request of node i has been granted. Next, all node identifiers j (node j is requesting), such that RN[j] := LN[j] + 1 are appended to Q, provided that j is not already in Q. After completion of this update, if Q is not empty then **privilege**(tail(Q), LN) is sent to the node found at the front of Q, otherwise, node i retains the privilege until a requesting node is found by arrivals of **request** messages.

It is possible to prove that based on Suzuki and Kasami's algorithm, mutual exclusion is obtained. This algorithm is deadlock free and starvation free. It requires $2*(N - 1)$ message exchanges for each mutual exclusion invocation. This number is optimal if nodes act independently and concurrently.

6.4.6 Utilization of pair-wise shared variables

A synchronization mechanism may take advantage of the fact that all requesting processes may be totally ordered. Such an ordering may be used to view these processes as being organized on a chain or as a loop. This logical order does not imply any particular physical topology.

A synchronization mechanism based on the concept of a logical ring has been presented in Dijkstra (1974). In his concept, possession of a control privilege may be inferred by every process from the observation of a variable shared with one of its two neighbours.

Algorithms are presented in Le Lann (1983) whereby a system being provided with any number of control privileges at initialization time reaches a stabilized state where there is only one such privilege in existence. The type of synchronization achieved by this mechanism is mutual exclusion.

6.5 Distributed synchronization algorithms using token passing

In Chapter 2 we emphasized that knowledge of local area networks is important not only because they are the principal systems on which distributed operating systems run, but also because they operate on the basis of techniques which can be adopted to mechanisms and algorithms for distributed operating systems. In local area networks one single resource which has to be serially shared is a communication medium. Serial sharing of a communication medium can be enforced, among other techniques, by using a token approach. Le Lann (1977) proposed an interesting method of providing mutual exclusion even on the basis of the token approach. The idea of this approach is to provide for a unique message having a specific format, called the (control) token, that circulates among the processes in the system.

At any time only the process which possesses the token can enter the critical section. Since there is only a single token in the system, only one process can be in the critical section at a time. There are two possible systems based on the token approach:

(1) a ring structured system,

(2) a non-ring structured system.

6.5.1 Ring structured systems

In a ring structured system the processes are **logically** organized in a ring structure and the token circulates permanently on the virtual ring of the processes. The token when sent by a process comes back to it after passing every other process once. This means that all processes are fairly served. This organization does not impose any restrictions on the topology of the physical communication network.

Virtual rings are usually set up statically. They can be changed only when a new process is inserted or a process dies. Static setting means that each process i, $i = 1, 2, \ldots, N$, where N is the number of processes, has to know an address of its logical successor, $succ_i$, or an address of its logical predecessor, $from_i$. In our considerations we use the former technique.

A process i, after receiving the token carrying the identity of the addressee, addr, checks whether it is addressed to it. If yes, that is, addr = i, it sets the addr field of the token to $succ_i$, proceeds performing a given task, and after completing the task, sends the token on. If the token is not addressed to this process, that is, addr $\neq i$, then it sends on the token immediately to the next process (addressee or a next process defined by a routing function R_i). Formally, this can be expressed by the algorithm given in Fig. 6.10.

Rings could be also set up dynamically. Examples of algorithms for dynamic ring construction can be found in Awerbuch (1985), and Helary and Raynal (1987).

Mutual exclusion can be implemented by passing the token around the logical (virtual) ring. When a process receives the token:

(1) if it wants to enter its critical section, it keeps the token, and it enters the critical section,

(2) if it does not want to enter its critical section, it passes the token to its virtual neighbour.

After the process exits its critical section, it passes the token around again, that is, to its virtual neighbour. This process is illustrated in Fig. 6.11.

The advantages and disadvantages of the mutual exclusion algorithm based on the token approach have been inherited from the token approach. The advantages of this algorithm are:

• only one process can be in its critical section, since there is only a single token,

• if the ring is unidirectional, no process can be starved,

• it requires $N-1$ messages (token passing messages) to enter the critical section,

```
{process i upon reception of the token(addr) from process j}
do
    if addr = i then
                    begin
                        'perform a task';
                        addr := succ_i
                    end
        k := R_i;
        send token(addr) to process k
end
```

Fig. 6.10 Process behaviour after reception of the token.

```
{process i upon reception of the token (addr) from process j}
var
    wish_enter : Boolean;
do
    wish_enter := true;
    if addr = i then
                    begin
                        if wish_enter then 'critical section';
                        wish_enter := false;
                        addr :=succ_i
                    end
        k := R_i;
        send token(addr) to process k
end
```

Fig. 6.11   Mutual exclusion algorithm based on the token approach.

- each process wishing to enter the critical section will receive the token within a finite time, because of the token circulation time.

Problems associated with this algorithm are:

- a process or a portion of the communication system can either fail or come up; this implies that the virtual ring should be able to re-configure itself;

- there is the possibility that more than one token can circulate in the system; it is necessary to guarantee that at any time, there is one and only one token on the virtual ring; this implies a need of an election algorithm.

There are a number of different protocols for election and for recon-struction of a logical ring, for example, Le Lann (1978), Garcia-Molina (1982). One such protocol, described in Le Lann (1983), is presented here.

Let us assume that each process has a timer. This timer is reset upon reception of a control token (CT) or any other token. Tokens on the ring circulate on the basis of a FIFO discipline.

The protocol proposed, which is an example of a distributed mechanism, is as follows:

(1) Whenever a timer awakes, the corresponding process generates an election token (ET) which contains the process name. The timer is set again. We say that the process has entered an election phase.

(2)   Whenever a candidate receives the CT before its own ET is back, it should cancel the election phase and removes its ET when back.

(3)   Whenever a candidate i receives an ET, it should record the name of the originating producer in the list of candidate names $S(i)$, where i is a process name.

(4)   Whenever a candidate receives its own ET, it removes it from the ring, resets its timer and runs algorithm A.

Algorithm A: if $i = \min S(i)$ then generate a new CT; set timer.

We will show now that with algorithm A no new CT is generated in the case when the CT is not lost and only one new CT is generated in the case when the CT is lost. To do that we have to have the state transition table of a process i on the ring (Table 6.1).

The following events are distinguished:

0   awakening of the timer
1   reception of the control token
2   reception of the election token, the identity of which is smaller than i
3   reception of the election token, the identity of which is greater than i
4   reception of the election token i (after a complete revolution on the ring)

The states of the system are as follows:

a idle, token timer is set
b election token timer is set and $i = \min S(i)$
a^* generation of the new CT and immediate switching to state a

Le Lann introduced the following notation:

$I(CT, x)$ instant of CT reception by process x

Table 6.1   Process state transition table.

External events State (i)	0	1	2	3	4
a	b	a	a	a	a
b	b	a	a	b	a^*

$I(t(x), y)$ instant of reception of election token x by process y
$I(x, 0)$ instant of generation of an election token by process x
$I(x, x)$ instant of occurrence of event 4
$\sim k$ non-occurrence of event k

Let us assume now that two processes generate 'simultaneously' a new CT and let us show that this situation is impossible. Assume for example that identity$(x) <$ identity(y). Process y will generate a new CT if and only if state(y) at $I(y, y)$ is b; this implies ~ 1 and ~ 2 between $I(y, 0)$ and $I(y, y)$. Identically, assuming that x will generate a new CT implies that ~ 1 between $I(x, 0)$ and $I(x, x)$ as $x < y$. It is easy to show that a subset of these conditions leads to a contradiction. ~ 2 between $I(y, 0)$ and $I(y, y) <=> I(i(x), y) > I(y, y)$ for process y. ~ 1 between $I(x, 0)$ and $I(x, x) <=> I(CT, x) > I(x, x)$ with the CT received by x being generated by y. This constraint and the FIFO hypothesis imply that, for producer y, we have $I(i(x), y) < I(y, y)$.

Finally, we can say that a new CT cannot be generated by two different processes during one token revolution on the ring. The new CT is generated in a finite time delay whose upper bound value can be computed, if we can assess transition and processing delays. Any failure occurring during an election phase will not make the duration of this phase longer.

6.5.2 Non-ring structured systems

In non-ring structured systems there is no logical structure imposed on the processes in a system. A process holding the token can pass it to any of the processes in the system. Moreover, the token need not be passed if no process wishes to enter the critical section. A good example of this approach was presented by Chandy (1982).

The algorithm developed by Chandy ensures that each process requesting entry to its critical section will receive the token within a finite time of requesting entry.

There are N processes in the system indexed from 1 to N. Associated with a token is a vector $T = (T_1, T_2, \ldots, T_N)$, where T_i is the number of times process p_i has entered its critical section.

The system based on the Chandy's algorithm works in the following way:

(1)   When a process p_i wants to enter its critical section for the m_i-th time it sends the message **request**(p_i, m_i) to all the other processes and then waits until it receives the token.

(2)   When a process p_i receives the token, it sets $T_i := m_i$ in the token vector T, and enters its critical section.

(3) After process p_i exits its critical section, it examines the incoming request queue;

   (a) if the queue is empty, it continues with its normal execution until it receives a request message from some other process,

   (b) if the queue is not empty, process p_i removes the first request, say (p_j, m_j) from the queue (FIFO), and

   (c) if $m_j > T_j$ then p_i sends the token to p_j, otherwise its discards this request because it is an old request that has already been satisfied, removes the next request and it proceeds as above;

   (d) this continues until the queue is either empty or the token is sent out to another process.

6.5.3 Circulating sequencer

Another method based on a circulating privilege is known as a circulating sequencer (Le Lann 1983). A circulating sequencer is a sequencer which circulates permanently on a virtual ring, via the control token mechanism.

One way to achieve distributed mutual exclusion among processes which share a sequencer is as follows. Upon receiving the token, the process may activate a number of **Ticket** primitives and then send the token to its successor on the ring.

Mechanisms based on a circulating sequencer can be explained on the basis of the following example presented in Le Lann (1983).

Let p be a process and n be the number of actions which are pending when p receives the token. The strategy may be to allow p to acquire exactly n consecutive tickets. In some cases, the necessity for an action to wait until the token is back before being ticketed may be judged unacceptable. Le Lann presented different algorithms which allow for anticipated selection of tickets. Depending on the strategy adopted for selecting tickets, consumer processes may use the total ordering inferred from ticket numbers either for avoiding inconsistent schedules or for detecting the occurrence of possibly inconsistent schedules and taking the appropriate decision.

6.6 Distributed synchronization algorithms using priority-based event ordering

Real-time systems are real concurrent systems, which generate new problems for the design of distributed operating systems. One of these is the synchronization of processes.

Distributed synchronization algorithms using time-based event ordering are not fully suited to use in real-time distributed systems. Firstly, the algorithms suffer from several problems, due mainly to the lack of a common clock. Secondly, processes that run in real-time environment have priorities attached to them, and are served in an order determined by those priorities; event times are not important. Thus, it has been suggested that events be ordered on the basis of the priorities of the processes, rather than on times when they happen (Goscinski 1990). A priority-based approach is more natural, and improves the performance of the total system.

In the most representative papers on algorithms for mutual exclusion in computer networks, Ricart and Agrawala (1981), and Suzuki and Kasami (1985), there is an assumption that transmission times may vary and that communication delay is unpredictable. The performance of such systems is adversely affected. Here, we show that it is possible to develop a priority-based algorithm for the case where there is an upper boundary on transmission delay.

Two algorithms were developed (Goscinski 1990) to handle mutual exclusion in computer networks in which processes communicate only by messages and do not share memory. The computer network functions either:

- in an environment requiring priorities, or
- in real-time (also called hard real-time) environment where processes must meet their deadlines.

The following assumptions about the communication network are made:

- it is an error-free fully reliable network, and
- messages may not be delivered in the order sent.

The algorithms are based on:

- requests broadcasted to all the other processes in the system by a process that wishes to enter the critical section, and
- the token passing service approach, but the token need not be passed if no process wishes to enter the critical section. Possession of the token entitles its holder to enter the critical section.

These algorithms are fully distributed, and insensitive to the relative speeds of node computers and communication links. They use only N messages between node computers, where N is the number of nodes (processes). The algorithms are optimal in the sense that a symmetrical, distributed algorithm cannot use fewer messages if requests are processed by each node computer concurrently. They ensure that each process requesting entry to its critical section will receive the token within a finite time of requesting entry. Moreover, critical sections, according to such algorithms as those presented in Chandy (1982), Lamport (1978), Le Lann (1977), Ricart and Agrawala (1981), Suzuki and Kasami (1985), are granted in a first-in-first-served manner. In the algorithms proposed here the queue of requests to enter the critical section is maintained in priority order.

6.6.1 Algorithms for fully reliable networks

The two algorithms developed share the same concept. One is suitable for an environment requiring priorities, and the other can be used in a real-time environment. In the system, each node of the computer network executes an identical algorithm, appropriate to the environment. These two algorithms differ in the way they reflect the features of environments as well as the methods used to ensure freedom from starvation. The general description of the algorithm is common to both variants. However, their important features and specific differences will be pointed out.

In the presentation we use a notation based on an abstract definition of a queue (Hille 1988). The following operations are used: Head – returns the head of a queue; Delete – deletes the head of a queue; IsNew – tests whether a queue is empty; Append – concatenates two queues; Merge – merges two priority queues; Add – inserts an item to a queue.

Basic concepts

Suppose there are N processes located in N nodes of the network indexed from 1 to N. Each process i is characterized: in the case of a system with priorities (called here the P-system) by its priority $p(i)$, or in the case of a real-time system (called here the RT-system) by remaining time $T(i)$ to run the process.

In the P-system, associated with the token is a priority queue $P = (i_1, i_2, \ldots, i_m)$, where i_j indicates a process which wants to enter its critical section, $i_1, i_2, \ldots, i_m$ is a permutation of the sequence of numbers 1, 2, ..., m, such that, $m \leq N$, and defined by relation $\rangle$ in the following way: $i_k \rangle i_t$ if and only if for each $k < t$, $p(i_k) > p(i_t)$.

In the RT-system, associated with the token is a priority queue $P = ((i_1, T(i_1)), (i_2, T(i_2)), \ldots, (i_m, T(i_m)))$, where i_j indicates a process which wants to enter its critical section, $i_1, i_2, \ldots, i_m$ is a permutation of a sequence of numbers 1, 2, ..., m, such that, $m \leq N$, and defined by relation $\rangle\rangle$ in the following way: $i_k \rangle\rangle i_t$ if and only if for each $k < t$ their remaining times satisfy the condition $T(i_k) < T(i_t)$.

For both cases, if two processes have the same priority or remaining times, the process with the smaller value of index i is placed first.

When a process i wants to enter its critical section it sends the message **request**(i, $p(i)$) (in the case of a P-system) or **request**(i, $T(i)$) (in the case of the RT-system) to all other processes in the system. It is kept waiting until it receives the token.

When the process j holding the token is in its critical section, other processes wanting to enter their critical sections can send request messages. An incoming priority request queue Q is formed in the node computer running process j. All processes in this queue are ordered according to relation $\rangle$, or relation $\rangle\rangle$ (defined above). If two processes have the same value of priority, the process with a smaller value of index i is placed first.

A process j holding the token, after exiting the critical section, examines the incoming request queue Q and the queue P received with the token, if any. In the case of the RT-system, the clock routine must perform decrementing operations on appropriate fields of the queue P and requesting queue Q elements, that is, $T(i)$, to maintain real-time consistency.

(1)   If the queue P is empty and the queue Q is empty, the process continues with its normal execution until it receives a request message from some other process.

(2)   If the queue P is not empty and the queue Q is empty, process j deletes the process with the highest priority.

(3)   If the queue P is empty and the queue Q is not empty, process j deletes (from the priority queue Q the process with the highest priority, and creates the new queue P by appending (P-system), or merging (RT-system) the queue P and the queue Q.

(4)   If the queue P is not empty and the queue Q is not empty, process j deletes from the priority queue Q the process with the highest priority, and creates the new queue P by appending (P-system) or merging (RT-system) the original queue P and the modified queue Q.

(5)   The process finally sends the token with the new queue P to the first process recorded in the queue P.

The algorithms

Fig. 6.12 shows the algorithm for the system with priorities, the P-system. The structure of the algorithm for a real-time system, RT-system, is identical to the structure of this algorithm. Moreover, the algorithm for RT-system can be easily obtained from the algorithm given in Fig. 6.12 by replacing all instances of function Append with instances of function Merge. Notes to several lines of the Algorithm indicate where this may be done.

```
const       I : Integer; {the identifier of a given node}
var             j : Integer;
            P, Q : queue of integers;
            IsNew(P), IsNew(Q) : Boolean; {to test whether a queue is empty}
            Requesting : Boolean;
            HaveToken : Boolean;

procedure wants_to_enter;
begin
   Requesting := true;
   if not HaveToken
   then begin
            for all j in {1, 2, . . . , N} \ {I} do
               Send request(I, p) to node j;
            Wait until token is received;
            HaveToken := true
         end;

   Critical Section;

   if IsNew(P) and IsNew(Q)
   then Wait until request is received
   else  begin
            if not IsNew(P) and IsNew(Q)
            then begin
                   Delete(P):
                   HaveToken := false;
                   Send token, Token(Tail(P)), to Head(P)
                 end
            else  if IsNew(P) and not IsNew(Q)
                  then begin
                         Delete(Q);
                         Append(P, Q) --> P;          {Merge(P,Q) --> P}
                         HaveToken := false;
                         Send token, Token(P), to Head(P)
                       end
                  else  begin
                         Delete(P);
                         HaveToken := false;
                         Append(P, Q) --> P;          {Merge(P, Q) --> P}
                         Send token, Token(P), to Head(P)
                       end
            Requesting := false
         end;
end;
```

Fig. 6.12 Synchronization algorithm for fully reliable networks.

```
procedure request_arrives;
begin
   if not HaveToken
   then for j = {1, 2, . . . , N} \ {l} do
           discard request(i, P)
   else begin
           Delete(P);
           for j = {1, 2, . . . , N} \ {l} do
               Add(j, Q) --> Q;                    {insert an additional request}
               Append(P, Q) -->  P;                {Merger (P, Q) --> P}
               Send token, Token(P), to Head(P)
       end
end;
```

Fig. 6.12 (cont.)

Procedure wants_to_enter is called when a node attempts to enter the critical section and procedure request_arrives is executed when a request message arrives. In both cases the same algorithm is executed by each node.

6.6.2 Assertions

In this section we present the most important features of the algorithms. We demonstrate that using these algorithms, mutual exclusion is achieved, deadlock is impossible, and freedom from starvation is ensured. Moreover, we present an analysis of message traffic and in particular an assessment of the upper bound of delay.

Mutual exclusion

We consider mutual exclusion to be achieved if no pair of processes located in different nodes are ever simultaneously in their critical sections. This implies that if process i_i is executing in its critical section then no other process can be executing in its critical section.

Assertion

Mutual exclusion is achieved.

Proof

Only one process can be in its critical section at a time, since there is only a single token.

Deadlock

Distributed processes are deadlocked if no process is in its critical section, and no requesting process can ever proceed to its own critical section.

Assertion
Deadlock is impossible.

Proof (by contradiction)
Suppose that two processes are deadlocked. This means that two distributed processes are in their critical sections and wait for each other. This means that two nodes hold tokens. This contradicts the token passing approach, which asserts that there is one and only one token in the system.

Starvation
Starvation occurs when one process must wait indefinitely to enter its critical section while other processes are entering and exiting their own critical sections.

Assertion
Freedom from starvation is ensured.

Proof
This assertion must be proved for both systems separately, because of different approaches to the construction of the queue P in the case when neither the original queue P nor the requesting queue Q is empty.

(1)   Because:

    (a)   there is a finite number of distributed processes (N) ordered according to the priority values,

    (b)   processes creating original queue P (received with the token) have greater priority than processes from the requesting queue (ordered and attached to the original sequence), and

    (c)   processes are served in the priority order,

    (d)   the time of waiting for entering a critical section is finite, and starvation is impossible.

(2)   Because:

    (a)   all processes are ordered according to the decreasing values of the remaining times to run,

    (b)   the remaining times are finite, and

    (c)   remaining time decrementing operations on appropriate fields of the queue P and requesting queue Q elements, that is, $T(i)$, are performed,

    (d)   a time of waiting for entering a critical section is finite, and again, starvation is impossible.

Message traffic

Each algorithm requires one broadcast message **request** sent by a process wanting to enter its critical section, and one message to pass the token, to make it possible to enter the critical section. The process in the node holding the token does not need to send a request message to itself. Since the network has N processes distributed among N nodes, N messages have to be transmitted.

The worst case delay involved in granting the critical section resource is the period of time beginning with the requesting node asking for the critical section and ending when that node enters its critical section for the process with the longest remaining time. This delay can be assessed in the following way. Let τ_{tp} be the time of passing the token from one node to another (the time of transfering the request message has approximately the same value) and τ_{cs} be the length (in time) of the critical section. The process with the longest remaining time occupies the $(N-1)$th position in the ordered sequence. Assuming that the time, denoted by ε, spent by procedures of an operating system to perform operations such as inserting processes in the priority request queue Q, merging two priority queues, and remaining time decrementing operations, is much smaller than the time of token passing, that is, $\varepsilon \ll \tau_{tp}$, then the worst case delay δ is expressed by the formula:

$$\delta \le \tau_{tp} + (N-1)(\tau_{tp} + \tau_{cs}) + \varepsilon$$

and this means that the upper bound can be assessed. This value depends greatly on the length (in time) of the critical section. It is likely that when critical sections include exchange of messages between producers and consumers, this time could be very long. This is a problem for all synchronization algorithms.

6.6.3 Problems of real networks

Two different types of events or failures can happen in realistic networks:

(1) token oriented failures, such as loss of the token, or the occurrence of more than one token; and

(2) network node oriented failures, such as insertion of new nodes, removal of nodes, and node failure (it is obvious that events of this type can cause token oriented failures).

It is also possible that:

(3) transport communication protocols supporting these synchronization algorithms may work unreliably.

Token oriented failures

Protocols providing for failure detection and recovery have to be provided to deal with these failures.

Loss of the token If all processes wanting to enter their critical sections sent their request messages and did not receive the token during the time $\delta + 2\varepsilon$, they can assume that the token is lost. An appropriate action should be performed. If the token is lost, an election is called and the elected process generates a new token (Le Lann 1978, Le Lann 1983, Garcia-Molina 1982). All processes which want to enter their critical sections have to send request messages again to reconstruct queue P. There are other algorithms to solve these problems.

Existence of more than one token If more than one token is detected, the processes (located in two nodes) have to make an agreement to destroy one of the tokens they hold. At this, if any two processes are deadlocked (both of them are in their critical sections), recovery from this deadlock will be done.

Node oriented events

Insertion of new nodes New processes located in new nodes may be added to the group participating in the mutual exclusion algorithm – this operation can be accommodated because the algorithms do not use and maintain any logical ring. The only requirement is a unique name for the new process to be added. This problem is solved by an identification system. Of course, the delay time will increase with each insertion, and this can cause a problem in a boundary case (real-time requirements).

If the node was previously operational in the group (for example, it failed and is now restoring), it should treat itself as a brand new process, sending its request message if it wants to enter its critical section. If before failure this process held the token, it should destroy this token and its associated queue P, to avoid the existence of two tokens in the system.

Removal of nodes A node wishing to leave the group may do so if it presently does not hold the token by notifying all other nodes of its action. This is necessary to remove it from the queue P. The node holding the token must send an acknowledgement message (after removing the node).

Node failure It can happen that the node or process in the node fails and will not behave as expected. The node failure can occur in two different situations: First, when the node holds the token, and second, when it sends a request message wanting to enter its critical section and is recorded in the queue P. Because these algorithms do not provide any detection algorithm before the occurrence of special events (for example, long delays of holding the token), both cases are treated uniformly. To prevent this situation from negating the proposed mutual exclusion algorithms, a time-out recovery mechanism may be used.

Unreliable transport communication protocol

In distributed operating systems, interprocess communication can be supported by an unreliable transport protocol. Unreliable communication means that messages (packets) can be lost, and message delivery is not guaranteed.

In the next sections we show that the algorithms may be extended to deal with all of the network problems just discussed.

6.6.4 The synchronization algorithm for unreliable networks

As in the previous case, the computer network functions in an environment requiring dynamically changing priorities based on the remaining time to run a process. The following assumptions about the communication network have been made:

(1) nodes can fail,

(2) nodes can be removed or added,

(3) messages may be lost or may not be delivered in the order sent, and

(4) interprocess communication is supported by unreliable transport protocols.

The problem is to design a distributed algorithm which will handle mutual exclusion such that at any time:

(1) at most one process (node) can proceed in its critical section,

(2) critical sections are granted in a priority manner,

(3) events are ordered based on their priorities (importance) rather than on times of their occurrence,

(4) it provides a recovery from node failures,

(5) it allows insertion and removal nodes with minimal overhead and without any additional messages, and

(6) each process may enter its critical section during a finite time period.

Moreover, the algorithm has to have a mechanism to deal with unreliable communication systems.

The proposed failure-tolerant algorithm is an extension of the algorithms discussed in Section 6.6.1. This algorithm is based on:

(1) requests broadcast to all the other processes in the system by a process which wishes to enter the critical section; and

(2)   the token passing service approach, but the token need not be passed if no process has to enter the critical section.

This algorithm is also symmetrical and fully distributed, and is insensitive to the relative speeds of node computers and communication links. It has been shown in Section 6.6.2 that in the case of fully reliable networks, that is, without node failures and with reliable message delivery, the subset of this algorithm uses only N messages between node computers, where N is the number of nodes (processes). Here, we show that in the case of node failures, the algorithm uses $(N + 1)$ messages. This allows one to believe that this algorithm is optimal. The optimality is understood in the sense that a symmetrical, distributed algorithm cannot use fewer messages if requests are processed by each process concurrently, if processes act independently, or if nodes fail.

This algorithm ensures that each process requesting entry into its critical section will receive the token within a finite time. Because the algorithm has been designed to be used in real-time environments, it has the mechanism to handle the loss of the token and the existence of more than one token. Moreover, this algorithm allows easy node insertion and removal. The algorithm works well with unreliable communication protocols.

Basic concepts

Once again consider N processes located in N nodes of the network indexed from 1 to N. Each process i_j, $j = 1, \ldots, N$, is characterized by priority $p(i_j)$ which dynamically changes with time, which can be the remaining time to run a process (also called waiting time). Associated with the token is a priority queue $P = (i_1, i_2, \ldots, i_m)$, where i_j indicates a process which wants to enter its critical section. $i_1, i_2, \ldots, i_m$ is a permutation of the sequence of numbers $1, 2, \ldots, m$, such that, $m \le N$, and defined by relation '$\rangle$' in the following way: $i_k \rangle i_h$ iff for each $k < h$, $p(i_k) > p(i_h)$. If two processes, i_k and i_h, have the same priority $p(i_k) = p(i_h)$, then the process with the smaller index value is placed first.

A process i_j wanting to enter its critical section broadcasts the message **request**(i_j, $p(i_j)$) to all other processes in the system. Each of those requesting processes is kept waiting until it receives the token. When the process i_j holding the token is in the critical section, other processes wanting to enter the critical section can send request messages. An incoming priority request queue Q is formed in the node computer running process i_j. All processes in this queue are ordered according to the relation $\rangle$ (defined above).

A timeout recovery mechanism is needed so that token-oriented or node-oriented failures do not prevent mutual exclusion being achieved.

To implement such a mechanism, each process i_j sending the token to another process, say i_1 (how to choose such a process is presented in the next paragraph), starts its timeout clock. If process i_j did not receive from process i_1 an acknowledgement message **ack**(j) before time-out, then it assumes that process i_1 failed and sends the token with modi-fied queue P to the next node, say i_2. If all processes which sent their request messages do not receive the token during the token-rotation time, they can assume that the token is lost. The appropriate action should be undertaken (see Section 6.5.1).

A process i_j holding the token, after exiting its critical section, ex-amines the incoming request queue Q and the queue P received with the token, if any. The clock routine must perform decrementing opera-tions on appropriate fields of the queue P and requesting queue Q items to maintain real-time consistency. It is necessary to remember that in the queue P, the process with the highest priority, Head(P), is an ad-dress of a node to which an acknowledgement message must be sent. There are the following cases of a system behaviour:

(1)   If queue P is empty and queue Q is empty, the process continues with its normal execution, and waits until it receives a request message from some other process.

(2)   If queue P is not empty and queue Q is empty, the process i_j sends the token to node i_2, Head(Tail(P)), and sets a timeout. If during timeout the process does not receive an acknowledge-ment, it deletes request i_2 from the queue and sends the token to the next process in the queue, that is, to the process with the highest priority. This is repeated until the process receives an ac-knowledgement.

(3)   If queue Q is not empty, whether or not queue P is empty, the process i_j creates the new queue P by merging queues P and Q. The operations described in (2) are then performed.

In summary, the proposed recovery mechanism requires: (i) sending the token and acknowledgement message, and (ii) performing operations on the queue P and the requesting queue Q by two 'neighbour' (predeces-sor, successor) processes/nodes.

The basic algorithm
The basic algorithm (Fig. 6.13), for a distributed operating system with reliable transport protocols, is executed by each node. Procedure wants_to_enter is called when a node attempts to enter the critical section and procedure request_arrives is executed when a request message arrives. In both cases the same algorithm is executed by each node.

The proposed algorithm requires one message **request** sent by a process wanting to enter its critical section and one message to pass the token, to make it possible to enter the critical section. Moreover, it requires one acknowledgement message **ack** to confirm a token recep-tion. The process in the node holding the token does not need to send a

```
const    I : Integer; {the identifier of a given node}
var      j : Integer;
         Timeout : Integer;
         P, Q : queue of integers;
         p : Real;
         IsNew(P), IsNew(Q) : Boolean; {to test whether a queue is empty}
         Requesting : Boolean;
         HaveToken, HaveAck : Boolean;

procedure send_token;
begin
   HaveToken := false;
   Send token, Token(P), to Head(Tail(P));
   Set Timeout;
   repeat
      if Timeout ≤ 0
      then   begin
                   Delete(Tail(P));
                   Send token, Token(P), to Head(Tail(P));
                   Set Timeout
             end
      until HaveAck;
   Clear buffer with queue P
end;

procedure wants_to_enter;
begin
   Requesting := true;
   if not HaveToken
   then begin
                   for all j in {1, 2, . . . , N} \ {I} do
                      Send request(I, p) to node j;
                   Wait until token is received;
                   HaveToken := true;
                   Send acknowledgement, Ack(Head(P));
                   Delete(P)
             end;

   Critical Section;

   if IsNew(P) and IsNew(Q)
   then Wait until request is received
   else begin
                   if not IsNew(P) and IsNew(Q)
                   then send_token
```

Fig. 6.13 Fault-tolerant distributed synchronization algorithm for systems with a reliable communication protocol.

```
                    else  if IsNew(P) and not IsNew(Q)
                          then begin
                                   Merge(P, Q) --> P;
                                   send_token
                          else begin
                                   Delete(P);
                                   Merge(P, Q) --> P;
                                   send_token
                               end
                       Requesting := false
                   end;
       end;


       procedure request_arrives;
       begin
          if not HaveToken
          then  for j = {1, 2, . . . , N} \ {I} do
                    Discard request(j, P)
          else begin
                   for j = {1, 2, . . . , N) \ {I} do
                       Add(j, Q) --> Q; {insert an additional request}
                       Merge(P, Q) --> P;
                       send_token
               end
       end;
```

Fig. 6.13 (cont.)

request message to itself. Since the network has N processes distributed among N nodes, $(N + 1)$ messages have to be transmitted to maintain a reliable distributed synchronization based on mutual exclusion.

6.6.5 Recovery from node insertion and removal

Insertion of new nodes

New processes located in new nodes may be added to a group participating in the mutual exclusion algorithm, because the algorithms do not use and maintain any logical ring. The only requirement is a unique name for the new process to be added. This problem can be solved by a naming system. Of course, the delay time will increase with each additional insertion, and this can cause a problem in a boundary case (real-time requirements). If the node was previously operational in the group (that is, it failed and is now restoring), it should treat itself as a brand new process, sending its request message if it wants to enter its critical section. If before failure this process held the token, it should destroy this token and its associated queue P, to avoid the existence of two tokens in the system.

Removal of nodes

A node wishing to leave the group may do so if it presently does not hold the token by broadcasting information about its action. This operation is necessary to remove the process from the queue P or from request queue Q. In practice it would be enough to send this information to a process holding the token. Since this algorithm is fully distributed, it is not known which process is holding the token at a given time. So broadcasting is necessary. The node holding the token must send an acknowledgement message confirming completion of the removing operation.

6.6.6 The algorithm for an unreliable communication protocol

The algorithm described in Section 6.6.4 can be also used in distributed operating systems, in which interprocess communication is supported by an unreliable transport protocol. Unreliable communication means that messages (packets) can be lost, and message delivery is not guaranteed. On the other hand, using unreliable communication protocols implies that to achieve reliable message passing some mechanisms have to be provided in the synchronization algorithm.

In the case of the proposed algorithm, an unreliable transport protocol can cause the loss of either a request or the token. Because the basic algorithm has a mechanism built in to deal with the loss of the token, we only consider the former problem here. The loss of a request requires its retransmission. This generates two problems. First, when is a node (process) allowed to retransmit its request? Second, what should the node holding the token do after receiving a retransmitted request when an original request has been received, and how does it recognize that it was a retransmitted request?

The former problem can be simply solved on the basis of timeout, the value of which should be set to at least the value of the worst case delay. The solving of the latter problem requires adding to a request from the i_i-th node an additional field containing a request id, r_id, and the retransmission id, ret_id, (the original request has retransmission id equals 0), that is, **request**(i_i, p(i_i), r_id(i_i), ret_id(i_i)). The node holding the token, before inserting a new request in queue Q, checks id of this request, r_id(i), against ids of requests in P or Q queues sent by the same node, r_id($k \in P \cup Q$), and if it finds such a request, it compares its retransmission id, ret_id(i_i), with retransmission id of stored requests, r_id($k \in P \cup Q$). If retransmission id of a new request is greater than that of a stored request, then it rejects the new request, otherwise it records the request. Of course, a request is inserted if it has not been previously recorded. The relevant part of procedure wants_to_enter is presented in Fig. 6.14.

The modified version of procedure request_arrives is shown in Fig. 6.15.

```
procedure wants_to_enter;
begin
    Requesting := true;
    if not HaveToken                                    {modification starts}
    then begin
        repeat
            for all j in {1, 2, . . . , N} \ {I} do
                    Send request(I, p, r_id, ret_id) to node j;
            Set up req_timeout;
            Wait until token is received;
        until HaveToken;
        HaveToken := true;      {modification ends}
        Send acknowledgement, Ack(Head(P));
        Delete(P)
    end
end;
```

Fig. 6.14   Retransmission of a request.

6.6.7   Properties of the algorithm

The proposed algorithm possesses a number of properties. Some of these are that it guarantees that mutual exclusion is achieved, deadlock is impossible, and freedom from starvation is ensured. Because these as-

```
procedure request_arrives;
begin
    if not HaveToken
    then for all j in {1, 2, . . . , N} \ {I} do
            Discard request(j, p, r_id, ret_id)
    else  for all j in {1, 2, . . . , N} \ {I} do
        begin
            if (request(j, p, r_id, ret_id) is not either in P or Q) or
                ((request(j, p, r_id, ret_id) is in P or Q) and (r_id(j) ≠ r_id(k∈ P∪Q))
            then begin
                    add(j, Q) --> Q;
                    Merge(P, Q) --> P;
                    send_token
            end
            else if ((r_id(j) = r_id(K∈ P∪Q)) and (ret_id(j)  ret_id(k ∈ P∪Q))
                    then Discard request(j, p, r_id, ret_id)
        end
end;
```

Fig. 6.15   Procedure request-arrives for a distributed operating system with unreliable communication protocol.

sertions can be proved using the same methods as in Section 6.6.2 we do not present detailed proofs here.

Only the ability of the algorithm to recover in the case of either the loss of the token or existence of more than one token is presented here.

Recovery in the case of loss of the token

If all processes wanting to enter their critical sections sent their request messages and did not receive the token during the time $\delta + 2\varepsilon$, they can assume that the token is lost. If time of holding the token is longer than token rotation time, then the process that holds the token can broadcast periodically a special message to avoid starting a procedure for recovery from loss of the token. However, if the token is lost an election is called and the elected process generates a new token (Garcia-Molina 1982, Le Lann 1977, Silberschatz and Peterson 1988). After that a process which holds the new token must open a request period. All processes which want to enter their critical sections have to send request messages again to reconstruct queue P.

Recovery in the case of existence of more than one token

Any synchronization algorithm should be constructed in such a way as to exclude the possibility of entering the critical section by two processes simultaneously, because, if such an event happens, unpredictable catastrophic events could occur.

The original token based synchronization algorithm (Le Lann 1978) does not have any mechanism to detect the existence of two tokens. For the proposed algorithm a mechanism to detect the existence of the second token can be easily built in. The mechanism uses data previously presented. The algorithm should be modified to reflect the following idea. A node, after receiving the token, looks in queue P for a request with its name, priority, request id, and retransmission id. If it finds such a request which is neither a Head(P) nor Head(Tail(P)), it can suspect that something happened and that the token received is the second token. This follows from the earlier mechanism which implies that the first item in queue P is its sender and the second item is the receiver of the (original) token. The node sends a query message 'where is the token?'. If a response does come during query_timeout, that confirms the node's expectation that it is the second token – this token is then destroyed. Otherwise, the token received is treated as the valid token. However, because something extraordinary has happened a request period should be opened. The modified version of procedure wants_to_enter presented in Fig. 6.13 is shown in Fig. 6.16.

The algorithm proposed requires one message **request** sent by a process wanting to enter its critical section and one token message passing, which makes it possible to enter the critical section. Moreover, it requires one acknowledgement message to confirm a token reception.

```
procedure wants_to_enter;
begin
   Requesting := true;
   if not HaveToken
   then begin
            for all j in {1, 2, . . . , N} \ {I} do
                Send request(I, p) to node j;
            Wait until token is received;
            HaveToken := true;
            HaveQueryResp := true;
            for all j in P = (3, . . . , k} do
            begin
               if I = j and r_id(I) = r_id(j) and ret_id(I) = ret_id(j)
               then {it could be the second token}
                  begin
                     Send query 'where is the token?';
                     Set up query_timeout;
                     if (query_timeout ≤ 0 and not HaveQueryResp)
                     then
                        Open a request period
                     else
                        Destroy the token
                  end
            end;
            Send acknowledgement, Ack(Head(P));
            Delete(P)
         end;

   Critical Section;

   if IsNew(P) and IsNew(Q)
   then Wait until request is received
   else begin
            if not IsNew(P) and IsNew(Q)
            then send-token
            else if IsNew(P) and not IsNew(Q)
                 then begin
                    Merge(P, Q) --> P;
                    send_token
                 end
                 else begin
                    Delete(P);
                    Merge(P, Q) --> P;
                    send-token
                 end
            Requesting := false
         end;
end;
```

Fig. 6.16   Detection of the second token.

The process in the node holding the token does not need to send the request message to itself. Since the network has N processes distributed among N nodes, $(N + 1)$ messages have to be transmitted to maintain a reliable distributed synchronization based on mutual exclusion.

6.7 Mutual exclusion algorithm for sharing K identical resources

All the above presented algorithms allow only one process (node) to be in its critical section. The problem arises when there are K identical resources in a system and they have to be shared between N processes. Raymond (1987) developed an algorithm, which is an extension to Ricart and Agrawala's algorithm, which enables up to K nodes to be within the critical section simultaneously.

The algorithm is based on the principle that a process is permitted to enter the critical section if no more than $K - 1$ out of $N - 1$ other processes are running in the critical section at this time. This means that $(N - 1) - (K - 1)$ must not be in the critical section. A process which sent a **request** message to $N - 1$ processes, because it wishes to enter the critical section, may proceed if it receives $N - K$ **response** messages.

Raymond's algorithm shares the same concepts as Ricart and Agrawala's algorithm. The major difference is the circumstances in which **response** messages arrive. In the latter, **response** messages arrive when a node is waiting to enter the critical section. In Raymond's algorithm $N - K$ **response** messages arrive when a node is waiting; the remaining $K - 1$ messages arrive when this process is executing in the critical section, and/or after leaving the critical section, and/or when waiting to enter the critical section. **response** messages should be distinguished somehow; this can be solved by each process maintaining a count of the number of outstanding **response** messages still to come from each other process.

In Ricart and Agrawala's algorithm the array Reply_Deferred was of type boolean, because a process could defer at most one **response** to another node. It is possible in Raymond's algorithm that a process may have to defer many **response** messages to another process. That required the array Reply_Deferred to be declared as of type integer. Moreover, in Raymond's algorithm it was necessary to distinguish between attempting to enter the critical section and executing the critical section.

The variables of each process (node) are as follows:

- Our_Sequence_Number : integer := 0;
  {the sequence number of a current attempt to enter the critical region}

- Highest_Sequence_Number : integer := 0;
    {the largest sequence number seen in any **request** message}
- Outstanding_Reply_Count : array[1 . . . N] of integer := 0;
    {the number of **response** messages still to be received before the node may enter the critical section}
- Requesting_Critical_Section : boolean := false;
    {true when a node is wishing to enter the critical section or is in the critical section}
- Executing_Critical_Section : boolean := false;
    {true when a node is executing the critical section}
- Reply_Deferred : array[1 . . . N] of integer := 0;
    {Reply_Deferred [i] is the number of **response** messages to node i that have been deferred until this node exits the critical section}

The code of the algorithm has the following four parts identified by events which can happen in the system (Fig. 6.17).

Raymond proved that her algorithm preserves many properties of Ricart and Agrawala's algorithm. It guarantees mutual exclusion, deadlock is impossible, and it ensures freedom from starvation. It requires $2(N-1)$ messages per entry to the critical section.

```
procedure node_wishes_to_enter_the_critical_section;
begin
    Requesting_Critical_Section := true;
    Our_Sequence_Number := Highest_Sequence_Number + 1;
    for i := 1 to N do
            if i ≠ me then
                        begin
                            send request(Our_Sequence_Number) to i;
                            Outstanding_Reply_Count[i] := Outstanding_Reply_Count[i] + 1;
                        end
end;

procedure node_receives_request(Sᵢ)_from_i;
begin
    Highest_Sequence_Number := max(Highest_Sequence_Number, Sᵢ);
    if Executing_Critical_Section or
        Requesting_Critical_Section and (Our_Sequence_Number, me) < (Sᵢ, i)
    then    Reply_Deferred[i] := Reply_Deffered[i] + 1
    else    send response(1) to i
end;
```

Fig. 6.17 Raymond's algorithm {adapted from Raymond (1987)}.

```
procedure node_receives_response(Count)_from_i;
begin
   Outstanding_Reply_Count[i] := Outstanding_Reply_Count[i] – Count;
   if Requesting_Critical_Section and Not_In_CS() ≥ N – K
   then
      begin
         Requesting_Critical_Section := false;
         Executing_Critical_Section := true;
         enter Critical section
      end
end;
```

```
where Not_In_CS() is defined as:
   Cnt := 0;
   for i := 1 to N do
            if i ≠ me and Outstanding_Reply_Count[i] = 0
            then
                 Cnt := Cnt + 1;
   Return (Cnt)
```

```
procedure node_exits_critical_section;
begin
   Executing_Critical_Section := false;
   for i := 1 to N do
      if Reply_Deffered[i] ≠ 0
      then    begin
                 send response(Reply_Deferred[i]) to i;
                 Reply_Deferred[i] := 0
              end
end;
```

Fig. 6.17 (cont.)

6.8 Concurrency control in transaction processing

Chapter 4 emphasized the need for reliable computing and noted that it can be achieved:

- by developing distributed operating systems based on the transaction concept, and
- by using multiple copies of objects and properly solving the multiple copy update problem.

Because of this we have been involved in the discussion of such basic issues as recovery, transactions, atomic actions, and multiple copy update algorithms. In Chapter 5 we discussed reliable communication, in particular message exchange in the case of a possible crash of one of the communicating entities. Recall that concurrency is closely associated with communication. Concurrency is also an intrinsic part of the Commitment, Concurrency, and Recovery (CCR) approach discussed earlier. At the beginning of this chapter we said that concurrency control generally considers the problem from either an operating system perspective (physical and logical resources) or from a database transaction processing perspective. Previously we discussed concurrency in distributed operating systems. Here we will consider those aspects of the concurrency control in database processing which are closely associated with distributed operating systems.

6.8.1 Concurrency control mechanism requirements

Kohler (1981) says that if a system has not failed, all concurrency control mechanisms must ensure that:

(1)   consistency of objects is preserved, and

(2)   each atomic action is completed in finite time.

He notes also that good concurrency control mechanisms for distributed computer systems should:

(1)   be resilient to node and communication network failure,

(2)   permit parallelism to the extent necessary to satisfy system performance requirements,

(3)   incur modest computational and storage overhead,

(4)   perform satisfactorily in a network environment that has significant communication delay, and

(5)   place few constraints on the structure of the atomic actions.

Many approaches have been used or proposed to solve the concurrency control problem in transaction processing systems. They can be divided into six categories: locking, optimistic concurrency control, timestamps, circulating permit and tickets, conflicting analysis, and reservations. Since conflicting analysis and reservations are based on timestamps we will not consider these approaches. A reader interested in them can use such sources as Bernstein *et al.* (1980) and (Kohler 1981). We can see that some of them (circulating permit and tickets) are in use in distributed operating system and have been described in previous sections. Here, we discuss locking, optimistic concurrency control and timestamps.

6.8.2 Locking

The most common synchronization technique is locking (Gray 1979). It is a facility which regulates access to shared resources. In the simplest form each object has a unique lock. A transaction or atomic action may lock objects to ensure their inaccessibility during a temporarily inconsistent state, that is, to achieve mutual exclusion. This implies that other transactions or atomic actions that attempt to access (lock) such locked objects either wait, abort or preempt the existing transaction. When two or more transactions are waiting, they may be deadlocked. An object, locked and modified by an aborted or preempted transaction, can be unlocked after its state is restored to the state it was prior to the transaction's beginning.

To achieve transaction synchronization with locking schemes, all transactions must be well-formed and two-phase. These two conditions guarantee that consistency can be achieved in the environment where each transaction can potentially modify any accessed object. A transaction is well-formed if it:

- locks an object before accessing it,
- does not lock an object which is already locked, and
- before it completes, unlocks each object it locked.

A transaction is two-phase if it does not lock any objects after the first unlock operation has been performed. Thus, the first phase is used to lock all the required objects. The first unlock operation signals the end of the first phase. The second phase is used to release all the locks obtained in the first phase.

Well-formed, two-phase transactions are illustrated in Fig. 6.18, which shows explicit **lock, unlock, read, write** operations on three objects A, B, and C. This figure is a modification of Kohler's Fig. 3 (Kohler 1981).

A global concurrency control mechanism based on local locking can be implemented in a distributed system in the following way. Let us assume that there are two distinguished nodes of a distributed computer system, N_1 and N_2. Objects A and B used in Fig. 6.18 are located on node N_1 and object C is located on node N_2. Each node has a local lock manager which controls the locks with objects located on that site. Objects must be locked before they are accessed by transactions. Thus, transaction T_1 must communicate with the local lock manager at node N_1 to request and obtain locks on objects A and B. On the other hand, transaction T_2 must request and obtain the lock on object B from the remote lock manager at node N_1, and the local lock manager at node N_2 to request and obtain locks on object C. This sequence of events is illustrated in Fig. 6.19.

A transaction receives exclusive access to the object after a lock manager grants a lock to it. Such access is assigned until the lock is released by an **unlock** operation. A transaction can start operations (read, write) on objects without any interference from other transactions after receiving all required locks. We can expect that each transaction will complete in some finite but not necessarily bounded time, and release all locks that it holds.

Transaction T₁

begin
    lock object A (e.g., account A)
    read object A (e.g., account A obtaining A_Balance)
    lock object B (e.g., account B)
    read object B (e.g., account B obtaining B_Balance)
    write object A (e.g., A_Balance – $100 to account A)
    unlock object A (e.g., account A)
    write object B (e.g., B_Balance + $100 to account B)
    unlock object B (e.g., account B)
end

Transaction T₂

begin
    lock object B (e.g., account B)
    read object B (e.g., account B obtaining B_Balance)
    lock object C (e.g., account C)
    read object C (e.g., account B obtaining C_Balance)
    write object B (e.g., B_Balance – $80 to account B)
    unlock object B (e.g., account B)
    write object C (e.g., C_Balance + $80 to account C)
    unlock object C (e.g., account C)
end

Fig. 6.18   Well-formed, two-phase transactions.

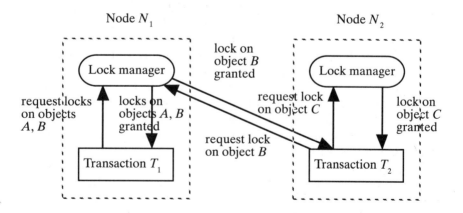

Fig. 6.19 A global concurrency control mechanism based on local locking in a distributed system.

6.8.3   Optimistic concurrency control

A number of inherent disadvantages of locking have been identified by Kung and Robinson (1981):

(1)   Maintenance of locks generates an overhead that does not exist in systems that do not support concurrent access to shared resources. Even read-only transactions use locking in order to guarantee that the data being read is not modified by other transactions at the same time. Locking may be used only in the worst case.

(2)   The use of locks can lead to deadlock, which as we will show in Chapter 10 requires some special methods for resolution. Since deadlock prevention reduces concurrency, other methods must be used, for example, deadlock detection.

(3)   Locks can be released only at the end of the transaction. This implies that even if a transaction is aborted locks cannot be released immediately. This may significantly reduce the potential for concurrency.

Kung and Robinson proposed an alternative approach to the serialization of transactions that does not have these disadvantages. Their approach is based on the observation that, in most applications, the likelihood of two transactions accessing the same object is low. Because of this assumption the approach is called **optimistic**.

As a result of this **optimism** a transaction is allowed to proceed as though there is no possibility of conflict with other transactions. This process is performed until the client completes its task and issues a **Close-Transaction** request. Until this event, which terminates the first phase of a transaction, read requests are performed immediately, but write requests are recorded in a tentative form, which is invisible to other transactions. Two sets are kept of data items accessed within a transaction: **a read set** which contains items read by the transaction and **a write set** containing the items written, created, or deleted by the transaction.

The **CloseTransaction** request starts the second phase of the transaction. Within the second phase, the transaction is validated. The goal of this process, which is based on the notion of serial equivalence, is to determine whether or not the write operations should be made permanent. If the validation is successful, the write operations are recorded in the relevant files, **CloseTransaction** delivers **Commit**, and the transaction completes successfully. Otherwise, the transaction is aborted and **CloseTransaction** delivers **Abort**.

To perfom the validation, the read and the write sets of the transaction are compared with the write sets of all the other concurrent transactions that reached the end of the first phase before it. If any element of the write sets of these checked transactions refers to the same data item as an element of the read or write sets of the validated transaction, the validation fails. The reader interested in detailed description of the validation process should refer to Kung and Robinson (1981).

One distinctive feature of optimistic concurrency control is that old versions of files corresponding to currently committed transactions are stored by the server. This is not necessary with either locking or timestamping.

6.8.4 Timestamps – basic timestamp ordering algorithm

A concurrency mechanism based on timestamps assigns a unique **timestamp**, that is, a unique number, to a transaction, and all conflicting actions are processed in timestamp order. In many cases, a timestamp is chosen as a function of the time of day. In a distributed computer system where each computer has its unique identifier, a timestamp can be generated by concatenating the local time and the local identifier. Since all transactions have unique timestamps, timestamp ordering is deadlock-free. Thus timestamps can be used to avoid deadlock in systems which lock objects, or as a substitute for locks altogether.

In the basic (ignoring two-phase commit) timestamp ordering algorithm, each transaction T is supervised by a single **transaction manager** (TM), which is in complete charge of overseeing the distributed computation. At the transaction–transaction manager interface the operations presented in List 6.5 are defined.

---

read(E)
  returns the value of entity E, which is realized as one or more data objects.

write(E, value)
  sets entity E to the specified value.

begin and **end**
  are used to bracket a transaction execution.

List 6.5 Operations of the transaction–transaction manager interface.

Object managers (OM) perform actions on their respective objects in response to requests from the transaction managers. This two level abstraction implies that more than one object manager may work for a single transaction manager.

Suppose now that transaction manager TM attaches a unique timestamp to a new transaction T. Moreover, transaction manager TM assigns the timestamp to all actions issued to object managers (OMs) on the behalf of the transaction. Each object manager (OM) has a **time-stamp ordering scheduler** that schedules local actions according to their timestamp ordering.

The steps of the timestamp ordering algorithm are as follows:

(1)   For every object O, the scheduler at an OM records the largest timestamp of all completed **read_object** actions (denoted TS_R) and all completed **write_object** actions (denoted TS_W).

(2)   For a **read_object** request, the scheduler compares the timestamp TS with TS_W. If $TS < TS_W$, the scheduler rejects the action and the TM aborts the issuing transaction. Otherwise, the scheduler places the action in a strict FIFO queue for pending actions on object O and sets TS_R to max (TS_R, TS).

(3)   For a **write_object** request timestamp TS, the scheduler compares timestamp TS with the maximum of TS_R and TS_W. The scheduler rejects the action if TS is smaller; otherwise, it places the action in the queue and sets TS_W to TS.

(4)   When a transaction is aborted, it is assigned a new and larger timestamp by its TM and is restarted.

The basic timestamp ordering is illustrated in Fig. 6.20, in which the values of TS_R and TS_W reflect the completion of processing of the actions by the scheduler.

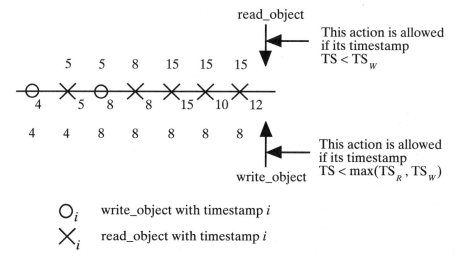

Fig. 6.20   Basic timestamp ordering {adapted from Maekawa *et al.* (1987)}.

The basic timestamp ordering approach has the following three drawbacks:

(1) **cyclic restart** – when an endless sequence of restarts of at least two transactions is possible;

(2) **unnecessary restart** – when the actual execution sequence is in the reverse order to timestamp; and

(3) **infinite restart** – a starvation-related problem; infinite wait can occur if an older transaction, each time it restarts, finds it has to wait for a younger conflicting transaction.

6.8.5 Timestamp ordering algorithm with two-phase commit

The timestamp approach to synchronization can be extended by incorporating two-phase commit. Two-phase commit is implemented by introducing a **prewrite** action which must be requested by transaction manager TM prior to the subsequent **write_object** action. Both actions must be assigned with the same timestamp. The effect of the **prewrite** operation is similar to setting a write-lock on object O for the duration of the two-phase commit. Thus, once a **prewrite** with timestamp TS has been accepted by the scheduler, it must not reject any **read_object** (or **write_object**) with timestamp greater than TS until the **write_object** is output. This rule is implemented by buffering **read_objects**, **write_objects**, **prewrites**.

The basic timestamp ordering with two-phase commit uses the variables presented in List 6.6 (Maekawa *et al.* 1987).

TS_R
　the maximum timestamp of any **read_object** that has been processed

TS_W
　the maximum timestamp of any **write_object** that has been processed

$\min(TS_R)$
　the minimum timestamp of any buffered **read_object**

$\min(TS_W)$
　the minimum timestamp of any buffered **write_object**

$\min(TS_P)$
　the minimum timestamp of any buffered **prewrite**

List 6.6　Variables used in basic timestamp ordering with two-phase commit.

It is based on the following assumptions. Each **read_object, write_object, prewrite** action is an indivisible operation with respect to the local scheduler. All timestamps and the above defined variables are initialized to zero, and $\min(TS_R)$, $\min(TS_W)$, and $\min(TS_P)$ retain their values when the corresponding buffers become empty.

The basic timestamp ordering with two-phase commit is as follows.

(1) A **read_object** with timestamp TS is

  (a) Rejected if $TS < TS_W$

  (b) Output to be performed by the object manager if $TS_W = \min(TS_P)$ (prewrite phase)

  (c) Output if $TS_W < \min(TS_P)$ (write phase) and $TS = \min(TS_P)$

  (d) Buffered if $TS_W < \min(TS_P)$ and $TS > \min(TS_P)$

(2) A **prewrite** with timestamp TS is rejected if $TS < \max(TS_R, TS_W)$. Otherwise, it is buffered.

(3) A **write_object** is never rejected provided that the corresponding **prewrite** has been accepted. The request is buffered if its timestamp $TS > \min(TS_P)$. Otherwise, it is output. When the **write_object** request is output, the corresponding **prewrite** is deleted from the buffer. If this causes $\min(TS_P)$ to increase, the buffered **read_objects** and **write_objects** are retested to see whether any of them can be output.

It should be noted that, although this algorithm is constructed for an individual object, a transaction actually has a series of **prewrites**, one for each object to be updated, prior to committing.

Some techniques to improve the basic approach have been developed. We will not discuss them here. The reader interested in them is advised to use Bernstein *et al.* (1980).

6.9 Evaluation criteria for synchronization methods

Because synchronization mechanisms do not have identical properties, the problem is: 'Which synchronization mechanism should be chosen for a given system?'

There are a number of criteria useful for evaluation synchronization mechanisms (Le Lann 1983):

Response time and throughput Any mechanism should take full advantage of the parallel (distributed) nature of the system, resulting in high throughput and short response time.

Resiliency Any synchronization mechanism should survive failures. There is a need for a precise measurement of such a property which would express the number of simultaneous failures a system with a given mechanism may survive; this is the notion of resiliency.

Overhead   The cost of a given mechanism must be carefully evaluated, in particular the overhead as regards:

- traffic measured in number and size of additional messages,
- processing when handling additional messages, and
- storage for synchronization information.

Convergence and fairness   The mechanism must be developed in such a way that starvation will be avoided and processes are provided with equal rights.

Extensibility   The mechanism should allow for dynamic system reduction (resiliency) and dynamic system extension. The latter means that the mechanism must cope with added nodes and newly-created processes.

Determinacy   A mechanism may be designed so that it always achieves some necessary synchronization – it is a deterministic mechanism. A mechanism is said to be probabilistic if it achieves some necessary synchronization only most of the time.

Recovery   Determine how much help may be provided by a synchronization mechanism as regards error recovery? In particular determine:

- how easy is it for non-failed elements to be kept in a consistent state when a failure or a succession of failures occurs,
- how easy and how fast is it for repaired elements to reach a state known to be consistent with the global system state.

Connectivity   Find out the relative costs of mechanisms that require that processes be fully logically connected and mechanisms where processes know only about their neighbours.

Initialization   How easy is to initialize a system and to let any process know when it is allowed to produce or to consume items?

Utilization   Is there any constraint brought by a given mechanism as regards utilization?

Understandability/simplicity   Formal correctness proofs will be easier to give if a mechanism is simple. Simplicity is desired at the following stages: implementation, specification, debugging, maintaining, and modifying software.

In general, the performance of synchronization mechanisms for distributed systems depends on very efficient communication. This points out again the importance of remote interprocess communication and its primitives.

6.10 Summary

In distributed systems in order to achieve efficient resource utilization, good performance, data consistency, lack of deadlock, and to provide the user with a high-level programming environment, management decisions must be made. Because in distributed systems the state information is distributed in space and time, only partial but consistent views of the system can be provided to processes. To achieve this, synchronization mechanisms are used.

The term synchronization expresses the cooperation between communicating processes, in particular the sender and receiver, and refers:

- to specification and control of the joint activity of cooperating processes, or serialization of concurrent access to shared objects by multiple processes, and

- deals with concurrency control in transaction processing.

Synchronization methods and algorithms developed for centralized systems cannot be used in distributed operating systems because of resource distribution, lack of global state information and communication delays. This implies the need for new methods and algorithms addressing features of distributed systems.

To share resources, concurrent processes must be synchronized. Because in distributed systems there is no common memory or clock, there is the problem in determining which of two events occurred first. This problem was successfully attacked by Lamport, who introduced the happened-before relation. Based on this relation problems can be analysed and different synchronization methods can be developed. In some computational environments, for example, real-time systems, events should be ordered on the basis of priorities of the processes rather than on times when they happen. In these cases, the happened-before relation is not useful and other methods must be used.

Synchronization algorithms in distributed systems are based on centralized or distributed mechanisms. In a centralized mechanism, one node is designated as a central node, which controls access to shared objects. Among centralized synchronization algorithms, the most interesting are: an algorithm using a unique clock, an algorithm based on a central process, an algorithm based on eventcounts and an algorithm with a static sequencer.

A search of the literature on distributed synchronization algorithms shows that a theoretical background has been well established. The following are the main approaches used to construct distributed synchronization algorithms for allocation and mutual exclusion:

(1)   **Lamport's event-ordering approach** – This approach uses timestamps to order all requests from processes that wish to enter the

critical section. The most representative algorithms of this group are Lamport's; Ricart and Agrawala's; and Suzuki and Kasami's.

(2)   **Token passing approach** – The token approach makes prediction possible. It provides for a unique message having a specific format, called the token, that circulates among the processes according to the order defined by a virtual ring. In Chandy's algorithm (Chandy 1982) the token need not be passed if no process wishes to enter the critical section; such an approach reduces transmission overhead at the interprocess communication level. In algorithms developed on the basis of the event-ordering approach, there is an assumption that the communication delay is unpredictable.

(3)   **Priority-based event-ordering** – Because of problems associated with timestamps event-ordering algorithms (generated by the lack of a common clock), it has been suggested that events be ordered on the basis of priorities of the processes rather than on times when they happen. The most representative algorithms of this group are Goscinski's algorithms. For real-time systems and systems using priorities for scheduling, a priority-based approach is more natural and improves the performance of the total system.

These algorithms allow only one process (node) to be in the critical section. Raymond developed an algorithm, which is an extension to the Ricart and Agrawala algorithm for the case when K identical resources must be shared between N processes. The algorithm enables up to K nodes to be within the critical section simultaneously.

Reliable computing requires distributed operating systems to be developed based on the transaction concept. In such systems, all concurrency control mechanisms must ensure that:

- consistency of objects is preserved, and
- each atomic action is completed in finite time.

Many approaches have been used or proposed to solve the concurrency control problem in transaction-based systems. The following three can be treated as the basic ones: locking, optimistic concurrency, and timestamps.

Bibliography

Awerbach B. (1985). A New Distributed Depth-First-Search Algorithm. *Information Processing Letters,* **20**(3), 147–50

Bernstein P.A., Shipman D.W. and Rothnie J.B.Jr. (1980). Concurrency Control in a System for Distributed Databases (SDD–1). *ACM Transactions on Database Systems,* **5**(1), 18–25

Bullis K. and Franta W. (1980). Implementation of Eventcounts in a Broadcast Network. *Computer Networks,* **4**, 57–69

Carvalho O.S.F. and Roucairol G. (1983). On Mutual Exclusion in Computer Networks. *Communications of the ACM,* **26**(2), 146–7

Chandy K.M. (1982). *A Mutual Exclusion Algorithm for Distributed Systems.* Technical Report. University of Texas

Coulouris G.F. and Dollimore J. (1988). *Distributed Systems. Concepts and Design.* Addison-Wesley Pub. Co.

Dijkstra E.W. (1974). Self-stabilizing Systems in Spite of Distributed Control. *Communications of the ACM,* **19**(11), 643–4

Garcia-Molina H. (1982). Elections in a Distributed Computing System. *IEEE Transactions on Computers,* **C–31**(1), 48–59

Goscinski A. (1990). Two Algorithms for Mutual Exclusion in Real-time Distributed Computer Systems. *The Journal of Parallel and Distributed Computing,* **9**, 77–82

Goscinski A. (1989). A Synchronization Algorithm for Processes with Dynamic Priorities in Computer Networks with Node Failures. *Information Processing Letters,* **32**, 129–36

Gray J.N. (1978). Notes on Data Base Operating Systems, Operating Systems. An Advanced Course. *Lecture Notes in Computer Science,* (50), 393–481, Springer-Verlag

Gusella R. and Zatti S. (1989). The Accuracy of the Clock Synchronization Achieved by TEMPO in Berkeley UNIX 4.3BSD. *IEEE Transactions on Software Engineering,* **15**(7), 847–53

Helary J.-M. and Raynal M. (1987). Depth-First Traversal and Virtual Ring Construction in Distributed Systems. *Rapports de Recherche,* (704), Institut National de Recherche en Informatique et an Automatique

Hille R.F. (1988). *Data Abstraction and Program Development.* Prentice-Hall Int.

Kohler W.H. (1981). A Survey of Techniques for Synchronization and Recovery in Decentralized Computer Systems. *Computing Surveys,* **13**(2), 149–83

Kung H.T. and Robinson J.T. (1981). Optimistic Methods for Concurrency Control. *ACM Transactions on Database Systems,* **6**(2), 213–26

Lamport L. (1978). Time, Clocks and the Ordering of Events in a Distributed System. *Communications of the ACM,* **21**(7), 558–65

Lamport L. and Melliar-Smith P.M. (1984). Byzantine Clock Synchronization. In *Proceedings of the 3rd ACM Annual Symposium on Principles of Distributed Computing,* Vancouver, pp. 68–74

Le Lann G. (1977). Distributed Systems – Towards a Formal Approach. In *Proc. IFIP Congress,* Toronto, North-Holland Publishing Company, pp. 155–160

Le Lann G. (1978). Algorithms for Distributed Data Sharing Systems which use Tickets. In *Proc. 3rd Berkeley Workshop*

Le Lann G. (1983). Synchronization, in Local Area Networks: An Advanced Course (Hutchison, D. Maraiani, J. and Shepherd, D., eds.) *Lecture Notes in Computer Science,* (184), Springer-Verlag, pp. 361–395

Lundelius J. and Lynch N. (1984). A New Fault-Tolerant Algorithm for Clock Synchronization. In *Proceedings of the 3rd ACM Annual Symposium on Principles of Distributed Computing,* Vancouver, pp. 75–88

Maekawa M., Oldehoeft A.E. and Oldehoeft R.R. (1987). *Operating Systems. Advanced Concepts,* The Benjamin/Cummings Publishing Co., Inc.

Raymond K. (1987). *Multiple Entries with Ricart and Agrawala's Distributed Mutual Exclusion Algorithm.* Technical Report 87/78 Department of Computer Science, The University of Queensland

Reed D.P. and Kanodia R.K. (1979). Synchronization with Eventcounts and Sequencers. *Communications of the ACM,* **22**(2), 115–23

Ricart G. and Agrawala A.K. (1981). An Optimal Algorithm for Mutual Exclusion in Computer Networks. *Communications of the ACM,* **24**(1), 9–17

Silberschatz A. and Peterson J.L. (1988). *Operating Systems Concepts.* Addison-Wesley Pub. Co.

Srikanth T.K. and Teueg S. (1987). Optimal Clock Synchronization. *Journal of ACM,* **34**(3), 626–45

Suzuki I. and Kasami T. (1985). A Distributed Mutual Exclusion Algorithm. *ACM Transactions on Computer Systems,* **3**(4), 344–9

Verjus J.-P. Synchronization in Distributed Systems: An Informal Introduction. In *Distributed Computing Systems,* pp. 3–22, Academic Press

7 Naming facility

	File service	Security	
User names			
	Collaboration of file servers	Access control	C s
	Transaction service		o e
	Directory service		m c
	Flat file service		m u
	Disk service	R p	u r
Name distri-bution		e r	n i
		s o	i t
	Resource allocation	Deadlock detection	o t c y
			u e a
			r c t
			c t i
Name resolu-tion	Algorithms for load sharing and load balancing	Process synchro-nization	e i o
			o n
			n
		Capa-bilities	& Authen-tication
System names	Process management Operations on processes: local, remote Process migration	Access lists	Key manage-ment
Ports	Interprocess communication (and memory management)	Info flow control	Data encryp-tion
	Interprocess communication primitives: Message Passing or Remote Procedure Call, or Transactions;	Security kernel	
	Links or Ports		
Address-es	⇕		
			Encryp-tion protocols
Routes	Transport protocols supporting interprocess communication primitives		

S ending messages between objects (such as processes, mailboxes, nodes, I/O devices, files, directories) supported by an operating system requires the presentation to the operating system of the names (identifiers) of objects for which access is desired. Objects should be referenced in such a way as to preserve location transparency. The term **object** will be used here to refer to any entity in a distributed system that deserves a name. Some of these objects are active, such as processes, while others are passive, and hence have to be managed by active objects. This implies a need for a good naming facility.

By a naming facility or naming service we mean a facility which enables clients to name objects (since names are bound to objects), that is, assign character-string names to objects, and subsequently to use these names to refer to those objects; to provide information about those objects; to locate objects given only their names; and to discover how to access those objects. This implies that a naming facility affects the following:

- sharing, relocation, inclusion, and replication of resources/objects, and

- distributed operating system and application view of resource/object access.

Taking these aspects into consideration, a naming facility should encompass desirable properties, like uniqueness, which are acceptable to the users. To facilitate sharing, naming conventions need to be established which provide a standard nomenclature for object naming. Names should be of a form that can be freely passed around an internet. However, there are currently some difficulties in interconnecting existing distributed environments due to the incompatible naming facilities in use. Moreover, in many existing computer systems, separate naming conventions are used for different types of objects (for example, file names typically differ from names of other objects). One can argue that, in distributed systems, there is a need for a uniform naming convention to identify the many available objects. On the other hand, specialized naming facilities can exist within a global naming facility to locate more specific facilities.

In the previous chapters we emphasized the importance of the client-server model of distributed computing in describing relationships between active objects. If we look at the naming facility from this point of view, the name service is a 'master' service, a central point for other servers and their clients. This is because the name server enables other services to be identified and accessed in a uniform way. Thus users need only know how to access the 'well-known' name service in order to gain access indirectly to all other services. The naming facility is thus one of the most important components in distributed operating systems.

The development of a naming facility for a centralized system is a complex task. For a distributed computer system the problem is compounded due to the distribution of objects among all the computers in the distributed system. Thus, it should be emphasized that a naming facility for a distributed system must take into consideration not only naming aspects of individual computers but also the requirements for the specification of names for computer networks.

A naming facility for a distributed operating system is discussed in this chapter, using a hierarchy of identifiers. The following identifiers and mapping between them are discussed: user names, system names, and ports, which identify objects within a computer system; and names, routes, and addresses, which are used to name communicating objects and entities. However, some important questions arise:

(1)   What structure for a naming facility is the best? In detail, where should context be maintained and the mapping performed between different levels of identifiers?

(2)   What type of identifiers are required at each level of the distributed system architecture?

(3)   How to deal with heterogeneity?

To answer these questions, we introduce the general term of a **name**, and characterize different names in the context of three attributes: structure, time and number.

This is followed by a presentation of **routes** and different routing algorithms. The concept of an **address**, which is associated with object (entity) location in a distributed system, is introduced. These concepts are summarized by a discussion of the architecture of names, addresses and routes in the ISO/OSI Reference Model.

Because user names cannot be effectively used at the computer level, system names must be used. Two types of such names are discussed: unstructured and structured. Capabilities, which are used for both identification and protection, are discussed. Finally, mapping of system names onto ports is presented.

In the next main part of this chapter, user names are discussed. Different string names are presented taking into account name parts. Structural components of a naming facility such as name servers and agents are considered. This is followed by a discussion of the two main functional components of a naming facility: database management, and name management, which allows a name to be resolved. Using these two components, name distribution and distributed name service operations are introduced and discussed. In particular, name resolution for attributed names is presented.

The chapter concludes with an analysis of two models to study performance of a name facility structures. Some results are given.

7.1 General aspects of the naming facility

Names have been widely used in centralized computer systems as a convenient way of referring to shared resources. In distributed systems, there are more resources than in centralized ones and also these resources are spread over a network(s) connecting all processing and peripheral devices. A naming facility for a distributed system should thus be involved not only in computer resources but also in communication resources.

7.1.1 Names/identifiers in distributed systems

A **name** (**identifier**) is a string of symbols (bits or characters) that identifies an object. As seen from a computer system's internal point of view, digital identifiers (binary numbers) are the most suitable means for designating or referring to an object. On the other hand, human users cannot cope efficiently with binary numbers and prefer human-readable text strings to identify objects supported by an operating system. This implies two classes of names within the computer system: **user names**, and **system names**. In many cases, as we have seen in Chapter 5, it is necessary to consider a third class of identification in distributed systems, **ports**. This requirement arises when messages are not sent directly to processes.

In distributed systems, presenting (using) a name for communication purposes is not enough. Because communicating processes execute on different computers, the knowledge of their current location is necessary. This leads to the problem of naming in communication systems.

There are three basic terms in this area: a **name**, an **address**, and a **route**. The meaning of these terms can be explained using the following intuitive definitions (Shoch 1978):

(1) The **name** of an object (for example, resource, server) specifies **what** a process seeks (what it wants to access).

(2) An **address** specifies **where** this object is.

(3) A **route** specifies **how to get there**.

Each of these identifiers represents a tighter binding of information:

(1) Names are mapped onto addresses. This mapping is necessarily application-specific, since the syntax and semantics of names depend entirely on what types of entities are being named and also on what use is being made of them; and

(2) Addresses are mapped onto routes.

Because Shoch's definitions can be misleading and leave a lot of room for interpretation, alternate definitions of the terms **name** and **address** can be used. These definitions are the result of an analysis of communication networks and the binding among such network entities as services, nodes, ports of a network and paths. Thus, an object's **address** is the **name of the object it is bound to.**

The most important difference between these two sets of definitions is that the former complies with the computer approach to naming: names are chosen by users, whereas addresses refer directly to objects and are assigned by the system. The latter associates properly a named object with its location.

We thus have a hierarchy of naming terms, identifiers, in both a computer system and a communication system, as illustrated in Fig. 7.1. (Another logical approach to the name hierarchy, in particular to names, addresses, and routes, will be presented in Section 7.6.2.)

A designer of a distributed operating system is mainly involved in computer system resources, but because there should not be any

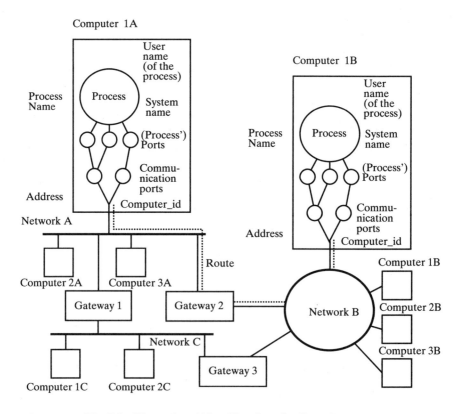

Fig. 7.1 Hierarchy of identifiers in a distributed system.

distinction between local and remote objects (resources), communication-oriented naming must be considered. Note that the general concept of a **name**, as a part of a communication identification system, covers all three identifiers used for naming of computer objects.

Fig. 7.1 shows clearly that when dealing with naming facility there are two basic problems:

(1) choosing names/identifiers and their structures for all objects; and

(2) mapping between different levels of identifiers.

Before discussing the problems that must be addressed in a naming facility, we should say what is expected from a naming facility and state its goals.

7.1.2 Characterization of a naming facility

What is expected from a naming convention, and how should identifiers be characterized? There are at least four basic principles that a naming convention should satisfy:

(1) **Generality** – A naming convention must be in a position to name a variety of entities in different applications as well as different environments.

(2) **Multiple definitions of the same entity** – Because an entity can be known by different names in different environments, the naming convention should allow the feature of multiple names and leave the problem of resolution to some address translation mechanisms.

(3) **Distributability** – It is likely that the naming convention will manifest itself, in some form, as a directory, to aid the name validation and address translation. The database of names may be fragmented amongst the network hosts, possibly based on geographical, organizational, or user load requirements.

(4) **User-friendliness** – The user should be in a position to infer the entity's name from the knowledge he possesses. The naming convention should not allow any scope for the wrong interpretation of the names.

Some general characteristics of names and a naming facility are as follows:

(1) Identifiers are used for a wide variety of purposes, such as referencing, locating, scheduling, resource management, error control, synchronization, protection, and sharing of objects (resources).

(2) Identifiers (names; user and system names, and ports; addresses; and routes) exist in different forms at all levels of a distributed

system architecture. This implies a need for the mapping of higher-level identifiers to lower-level identifiers, and finally to identifiers of specific locations. The number of these levels can change from system to system.

(3)   A naming facility, a communication system, synchronization mechanisms (algorithms), a resource management system, error control, and protection systems often interact. It is necessary to be aware of how design decisions in one of these areas can affect those in other areas.

(4)   Identifiers appear in different forms (convenient for people or computers). Some identifiers are unique within a global context for the whole system (internet), others are unique only within a local context (single network).

(5)   There are many possible ways to designate the object(s) desired:

(a)   by an explicit name or address (object x or object at x),

(b)   by content (object(s) with value(s) y or values > expression),

(c)   by source (all 'my' files),

(d)   broadcast identifier (all objects of a class),

(e)   group identifier (all participants in subject V),

(f)   by route (the object found by following path Z),

(g)   by relationship to a given identifier (all previous sequence numbers), etc.

7.1.3   Goals of a naming facility

The most important goals of a naming facility are as follows:

(1)   The naming facility should be seen as a global space of identified objects rather than a space of identified host computers containing locally identified objects. The naming facility should be independent of the physical connectivity or topology of the system or the current location of the named object. This implies that the facility should support three types of identifiers: names, addresses, and routes. These identifiers should be efficiently mapped.

(2)   The naming facility should support at least two levels of identifiers to identify objects within a computer system, one convenient for people and one convenient for computers. Moreover, the mechanisms for these two levels should be cleanly separated. However, an efficient mapping between these levels must be provided.

(3)   Unique identifiers need to be generated in a distributed fashion. To support this goal, structured identifiers are required. A central unique identifier generator introduces efficiency and reliability issues that do not occur in systems with identifiers generated in a distributed manner. However, it also generates some problems associated with reliability and communication traffic.

(4)   The naming facility should be efficient in the sense that the delay, and the number of messages exchanged to initialize and map identifiers before the specified messages are sent, should be minimized. The naming facility should support transaction and session oriented services equally efficiently.

(5)   For performance reasons (load balancing, load sharing), objects must be moveable. Thus, the naming facility should support relocation of objects. This implies the need for dynamic binding of at least two levels of identifiers, names and addresses.

(6)   Names and addresses should use not only one-to-one mapping, but also a one-to-many mapping $(1 : N)$, for example, one name at a user level may be dynamically bound to more than one server address at a computer level.

(7)   The naming facility should support the use of multiple copies of the same object, which may be necessary to improve reliability, robustness and performance. A user should not be aware that multiple copies of an object are in use.

(8)   The naming facility should allow multiple local user-defined identifiers for the same object, that is, there may be unique global identifiers for objects and at least one level of local identifiers. This implies the need for a mechanism to bind local and global identifiers.

(9)   The naming facility should allow many different objects to share the same identifier (process teams), and should support broadcast and group addressing (multicast). This requires at least two levels of identifiers and one-to-many mapping.

(10)   The number of independent naming facilities needed across the whole distributed system based on a connection of networks, that is, internet, should be minimized.

In summary, developing a distributed naming facility and choosing the naming conventions involves a tradeoff between performance, ease of name assignment, object mobility, availability of naming information, individual autonomy, storage space requirement, and the cost of maintaining data consistency.

We need to discuss identifiers in the context of both computer systems and communication systems. We will discuss the latter first. As we have seen, Shoch proposed some communication-oriented identifiers and gave their definitions. Although they are simple and intuitive, they are not satisfactory. Now, we will have a closer look at them.

7.1.4 Shoch's definitions

Shoch's definitions of names, addresses and routes are not satisfactory for the following reasons:

(1) The definition of an address may raise ambiguities with regard to its interpretation. Two examples exemplify this:

(a) Groups or teams are used very often in distributed systems. All members of each group have the same name. However, a group address cannot really indicate where the group is. This is because members of a group may be spread over many locations. Moreover, other members may be added to a group, and some members may be removed from a group. This implies that locations of the members can change; a name is still the same, whereas an address changes.

(b) Some objects have absolute addresses (for example, an Ethernet address). However, an absolute address (like an Ethernet address) does not indicate the location of the entity. This is because there is deliberately neither an internal structure in such an address, nor rules to interpret their values.

(2) The Shoch definitions do not introduce a fourth concept that is a key point for naming and addressing problems: the concept of mapping. We have indicated earlier that there must be efficient mapping of identifiers belonging to different levels. Names and routes are the quintessential concept, because if it is known how to derive a route from a name, or, in other words, how to map a name into a route, the communication problem is solved.

Addresses can serve as a bridge between names and routes (ISO 1981, Danthine 1982, Tanenbaum 1981, Hauzeur 1986), that is, names are usually statically bounded to the objects they denote and routes may change with changes of network configuration and topology. Moreover, addresses decompose the global mapping function into two steps: mapping names into addresses and then addresses into routes.

Now we will examine more closely these three fundamental concepts in distributed systems: names, routes and addresses. Note that the following discussion of names also relates to computer object identifiers.

7.2 Names

The name is a fundamental concept in communication, and is a convenient way of referring to computer objects such as processes and resources. Higher-level names can be used to provide for multiple copies, and to support object relocation. Basic concepts and features of names have been studied and summarized by a number of researchers and standardization bodies. Among them are Terry (1985), Hauzeur (1986), and ISO (1984). In the following discussion we will use some of their results.

A **name** is an linguistic object that singles out a particular object (entity) from among a collection of objects. According to the ISO, the correspondence between names and objects (entities) is the relation of **denoting**. A name denotes or identifies the object to which it is bound. It should be noted that a name is not always a human-readable string.

To help to remember the locations or addresses of a distributed computer system's objects, higher-level naming contexts are required: to meet the needs of the human users for their own local, mnemonic names; and to assist them in organizing, relating, and sharing objects.

However, names need to be independent of network location in order to allow an object to migrate to a new location in the distributed system without changing its name, and hence without requiring changes in references to the named object by other objects.

Names may be characterized by source properties. A name that refers to at most one object is **unambiguous**. This means that the same name cannot be used by different clients of the naming facility to refer to different objects. Ambiguity implies a one-to-many relationship between names and objects. A name is **unique** if it represents the only name for its referrant. Thus, several **non-unique** names may identify the same object. In this case, one name is treated as a preferred name. The others are called **aliases** or **nicknames**. Non-uniqueness implies a many-to-one binding.

A name may be **global** (absolute or relative). It is global if it is interpreted in a consistent manner by all clients and all services, regardless of their location in the distributed system, or of any other factors. A name is relative when it is interpreted according to some state information.

Names may be characterized by structure, time, and number.

7.2.1 Name structure

Naming objects requires some syntactic representation of names as well as their semantic interpretation. The set of names complying with a given naming convention is called the **name space** or **name domain**.

The following names could be distinguished on the basis of their structure: a **primitive** or **flat** name, a **partitioned** name, and a **descriptive** name.

A **primitive** or **flat** name in a specific domain is a name which does not have internal structure but identifies unambiguously a particular object, out of the set of objects composing that domain.

A **partitioned** name is commonly structured as a series of primitive names identifying, respectively, a domain, a subdomain, a sub-sub-domain, and so on, followed by a primitive name identifying the object inside that sub-sub- . . . -domain. Syntactically, the primitive names in a partitioned name space (usually alphanumeric labels) are delimited by a special separation token, such as '@', '%','/','.' or '!'. For example, $A@B@C$ consists of three labels, 'A', 'B' and 'C'. A partitioned name has components, composed of one or more labels and the embedded separation characters; for example, the name $A@B@C$ contains the following components: A, B, C, $A@B$, $B@C$, $A@B@C$. Note that hierarchical names belong to the class of partitioned names. If the partitioned names are used in a distributed system, the users are allowed to use abbreviations. Abbreviations are short forms for names that may be used as substitutes for the complete names. They are used by users rather than the long names but they are not treated as a fully qualified name. For this reason abbreviations are not generally recognized by the naming facility. Thus, before being presented to the naming facility they are converted to fully qualified names.

Names are always associated with some context. A context can be defined as the environment in which a name is valid. In a distributed computer system, contexts represent a partitioning of the name space (domain), often along natural geographical or organizational boundaries. As the result of this approach, a name may occur in more than one context, and contexts may be nested. Thus, for example the login name 'ang' may exist within the context of both domains 'pyr0' and 'pyr1'.

A context based name is composed of components. A component may denote a context in which other parts of the name exist. It is called an explicit context because it is explicitly represented in the structure of the name. For example, in the name $A@B@C$, $B@C$ is a name existing explicitly in the context of A.

There is also an implicit context. A context that is not an explicit part of a name is called an implicit context. Note that relative naming conventions involve interpreting a name according to some implicit context. In this case absolute naming conventions may be attained if implicit contexts are universal. Domains are arranged in a strictly nested structure and must not overlap.

A **descriptive** name is a list of attributes that are true for exactly one object (for example, a personal name, and password). A partitioned name is a particular form of descriptive name that has a rigid structure (a rigid set of attributes). With descriptive names, domains can be arranged in any manner, and names may not be unique for the same object.

This naming convention reflects the fact that the information maintained about a named object by the naming facility consists of a set of **attributes** for that object. An object's attribute has both a type and a value, where the type indicates the format and meaning of the value field. For instance, a list of attributes that is true for exactly one object is as follows, 'Personal Name = A. Goscinski, Organizational Unit = Department of Computer Science, Organization = University of New South Wales, Place = Canberra, Country = Australia.' In this example, the value is a primitive name. Note that in this case the conjunction of several attributes produces the unique result, although each individual attribute may not give a unique result.

It is important to notice that organizations using a naming facility supporting descriptive names, agree on the structure and semantics associated with object attributes. In particular, the format of attribute values is important in a heterogeneous environment.

An attribute can be constructed for a list of names. Names that have such attributes are called **group names**. They are used in mail distribution lists and access control lists.

7.2.2 Time and names

Time can also be used to differentiate names. In this case names can be divided into two groups, static and dynamic names. A **static** name is a name that permanently denotes the same object. A **dynamic** name is a name that is assigned to an object for only a limited period of time, short compared to the lifetime of the object. Such names are of little interest in practice – humans cannot handle them.

7.2.3 Number and names

If a **Number** is used to identify and locate objects, names can be divided into two classes, group (team) and individual names. A **group (team)** name is a name which denotes a defined set of objects. An **individual** or **specific** name denotes a single entity.

Each of the name types absolute, partitioned, or descriptive, could be a global name if its domain totally covers the distributed computer system and is valid for a long period of time. If a distributed computer system is a connection of several networks, the global name is not restricted to one of these, but it covers all networks.

A global static flat name is often used and is called an **absolute name** (Hauzeur 1986). Such a name has some advantages:

- flat naming suits users very well; and

- static naming is independent of the communication support; objects keep the same name when they change locations.

The importance of the last property is implied by the fact that changing the name would require changing not only source mapping tables, but also user programs, documentation, scribbled notes, advertising copies, etc.

In summary it is possible to present the distributed computer system (the network) as a network of resources rather than a network of computers.

In the next two sections we discuss routes and addresses. Since communications is one of the fundamental elements of distributed systems, in this discussion we will try to emphasize the communications aspects of these issues. Naming of computer objects will be presented in Section 7.8.

7.3   Routes and routing

The route is the second fundamental concept in communication. When dealing with communication between processes, we are involved in end-to-end communication between a source and a destination. A route is a **list of names** representing the path from source to destination. It was mentioned earlier that addresses are names. In this case a list of addresses is only a particular form of a route. This is the most usual form of route.

Communication becomes effective if a name can be mapped into its corresponding route. The mapping function is called routing and is implemented on the basis of routing algorithms. Some desirable properties in routing algorithms are: correctness, simplicity, robustness, stability, fairness, and optimality (Tanenbaum 1981). Robustness implies that the routing algorithm must be able to cope with changes in topology and traffic in a distributed computer system. This should be done without the unscheduled termination of processes and rebooting after crashes of some elements of the system. Fairness and optimality can sometimes be contradictory goals. Thus, it is necessary to find tradeoffs between them.

There are four attributes of routing which may be used as a basis for classifying routing algorithms. These are: the place where the routing decision is made, the place where the routing function is performed, the time constant of the information upon which the routing function is based, and the control mechanism for adaptive routing. Because routing is discussed in many books on computer networks, the following presentation is brief.

7.3.1   Where routing decisions are made

There are three possible ways to control routing:

(1)   **Source routing** – The entire decision is determined at the source process. This means that the mapping of the destination name into a list of names is performed by a source entity.

(2)   **Hop-by-hop routing** – Only the next portion of the route is determined at each step. Thus a list of names is not required at the source.

(3)   **Broadcast routing** – Each packet is broadcast through a network and every object receives it, but only the one that recognizes its name (or address) picks up the packet from the network. This type of routing might be used for example in load balancing (distributed scheduling); a process wants to find out which other processors are willing and able to run another process.

7.3.2   Static and adaptive routing

The time constant of the information upon which the routing function is based generates two classes of routing:

(1)   **Static** (called also **fixed**, or **deterministic**) routing – in which routing tables do not change for very long periods of time and,

(2)   **Adaptive** (or **dynamic**) routing – in which the routing information is constantly updated.

Static routing algorithms are the simplest and are the most widely used. The disadvantage of these algorithms is that they do not adapt to changes made to the topology of the distributed system, or to traffic changes. Static routing tables are designed on the basis of mean traffic conditions. The performance of a system with these algorithms can be good if topology and traffic do not change too much.

Adaptive routing algorithms, however, adapt to traffic changes on the basis of measurements or estimates of the current traffic and topology. Decisions can be made either centrally, locally in isolation, or in a distributed manner.

7.3.3   Centralized and distributed routing

The place where the routing function is performed determines whether the routing function is **centralized**, **partially distributed**, or **distributed**. Centralized routing is very similar to static routing. They differ in the way the routing tables are constructed. Whereas static routing tables are computed in advance and used for long periods of time, centralized routing tables are constructed periodically based on information gathered from other nodes.

The main advantages of centralized routing are that the routes are globally optimal and that the nodes are not involved in routing computations. However, there are also some drawbacks. If the traffic changes often, then new tables need to be constructed frequently. If the distributed computing system is large, table computations can be very time consuming. Moreover, centralized routing is not reliable, since table construction is performed in a single node. Further problems are associated with distributing the tables to the various nodes.

Because of these shortcomings, decentralized routing algorithms have been developed. There are two groups of such algorithms. To the first group belong those algorithms which use only local information, in which nodes do not exchange routing information with their neighbours. These algorithms are called distributed (or partially distributed) algorithms.

To the second group belong those algorithms which exchange routing information. Routing information can be updated in an **isolated** manner by trying various routes and observing performance, or on the basis of a **centralized** approach when a few objects are responsible for promulgating the updated information. The update process may be **distributed** among all objects mutually exchanging the routing table updates.

A graphical summary of these considerations is illustrated in Fig. 7.2.

7.4   Addresses and mapping

This section deals with addresses which are associated with the location of objects, and some communications aspects of mapping.

7.4.1   Addresses

An address can be treated as an intermediate form between a name and a route, as illustrated in Fig. 7.3.

Based on this figure one can propose the following general definition of an address. An address is an intermediate form between the name and the route, which is associated with the location of named objects, oriented towards computer processing, and which is used to generate the route.

This general definition can be extended, leading to a definition based on the fact that objects which want to participate in a communications process are linked to a communications object through which they

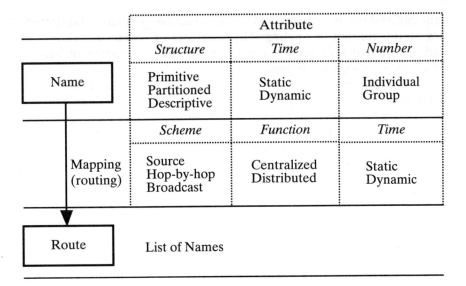

Fig. 7.2 Names, routes and routing {adapted from Hauzeur (1986)}.

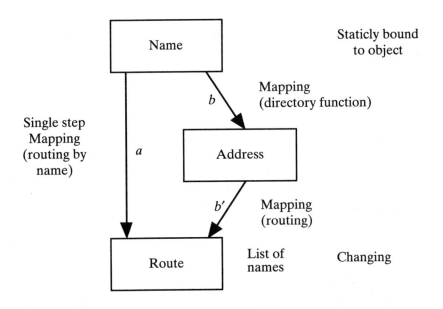

Fig. 7.3 A name, address and a route {adapted from Hauzeur (1986)}.

can send and receive messages. This construction-oriented definition relies on the concept of binding: The addresses of objects are chosen in such a way that they are the names of the communications objects to which these objects are bound.

A distinction can be drawn between names and addresses. The main difference between pure names (which are not addresses) of objects and addresses is that an address is attached to a communication object but not to an entity. The name directly denotes the entity; the address refers to the entity through binding.

It is important that addresses, because they are names, can be classified as names and that the same three attributes (structure, time and number) are applicable to them.

Thus, an address can be flat or partitioned. A partitioned address is a hierarchical one if it is constructed over the lower layer address. An address can also be descriptive. For example, an internet address proposed by Xerox, called XNS address, of the form <net_number, host_number, socket_number>, where socket_number is an internet service access point, is a mix of partitioned (a pair <host_number, socket_number>) and descriptive structures, which is brought by the net_number.

An address may be static or dynamic, and also may refer either to an individual entity, or to a number of entities formed in a group (team).

The concepts of naming, addressing and routing can also be considered in the context of the remote interprocess communication. Two of the services offered by the (remote) interprocess communication are:

(1)   to provide a global identifier space of unique process names, and

(2)   to provide whatever mechanism is required to route information from one address to another.

7.4.2 Mapping

Fig. 7.3 shows that mapping a name into a route can be done in two different ways:

(1)   The name is directly mapped into a route. This mapping is performed using mapping function a, and is called routing by name.

(2)   The name is mapped into an address by mapping function b (a directory function), and the address is mapped into a route by mapping function b' (a routing function). This double mapping is called routing on the basis of addresses.

Routing by name is used less often than address-based routing. An example of the former is broadcast routing by name. In this case each network entity stores port-identifiers, created and owned by a named process. Thus, this identifier corresponds directly to an object. A sender network entity, after receiving a request to send a message to a process, broadcasts a packet whose destination field contains a process port-identifier. This implies that only this network entity will receive the message which stores this port-identifier.

Each of the mapping functions in address-based routing may be distributed among several communication entities. Usually, the routing function is performed in a distributed way by ISO network layer algorithms on areas such as intermediate nodes and gateways. The directory function is usually performed by name servers. Name servers will be discussed in the following sections.

7.4.3 Names, addresses and routes in the ISO/OSI Model

The meaning and some implementation aspects of names, addresses, and routes in terms of the ISO/OSI Reference Model need to be identified.

As we saw in Chapter 3, the ISO/OSI Reference Model is a hierarchical, seven layer architecture. Each layer is composed of communication entities. Each entity is identified by a static name (originally called a **title**), regardless of its location. This name may have a flat or partitioned structure. The name is unique within the name domain. The layers themselves are name domains.

Two entities in adjacent layers are associated by a **service access point** (SAP). An (N) address identifies a particular (N) service access point. Thus, the (N) address of the $(N + 1)$ entity is the name of the (N)SAP it is bound to. This means that the address is attached to the SAP and not to the entity. Entities, their names, SAPs, and their addresses are illustrated in Fig. 7.4.

Although the name, address, and route concepts may apply to any layer of the Model, as Fig. 7.4 shows, strictly defined functions of each layer restrict this possibility. This results in the practical model illustrated in Fig. 7.5.

Fig. 7.5 shows that a name is used at the User Process. Because in the Transport Layer and layers above it end-to-end protocols are used, the route is simply the destination entity (process) address and the routing function is straightforward. The Application, Presentation and Session addresses are equal to the Transport address.

In the case of the distributed system based on a single local area network, Layer 3 does not exist. This implies that Data Link address is equal to the Transport address, and some routing functions may take place in the Data Link Layer.

Network addresses are used when a distributed system is constructed from a number of local area networks. A route is determined by a sequence of gateway (bridge) (G) addresses. Naturally, if local area networks are connected to wide area networks, subnet dependent layer is present in the architecture. A route is determined based on addresses of gateways and intermediate nodes within a wide area network.

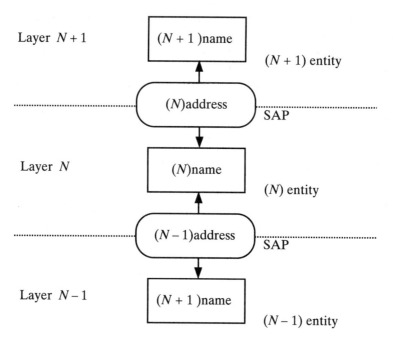

Fig. 7.4   Entities and their names, SAPs, and their addresses in the ISO/OSI Model.

7.5   System names

In the previous section we considered several aspects of communication-oriented identification (naming) in distributed systems. We introduced and discussed three identifiers: names of communicating and/or accessed objects, addresses associated with communication entities, which allow us to locate these objects, and routes which allow us to reach destination objects using addresses.

As we have seen, process names used by users differ from names used within a computer system (so-called internal names or system names). Moreover, in many cases, messages are not sent directly to processes, but to their ports; these ports can be seen as low level names. We need to discuss the relationship between these different names in a computer system. The scope of this discussion is shown in Fig. 7.6.

Ports were discussed in Chapter 5, because these objects are used for communication purposes, so this chapter will only present mapping from system names onto ports. The mapping of addresses, in particular transport addresses (discussed in Section 7.4.3), onto process ports is straightforward and will not be examined here.

We will start the discussion of computer-oriented identifiers from system names. The very general requirement is that it must be possible

DESTINATION

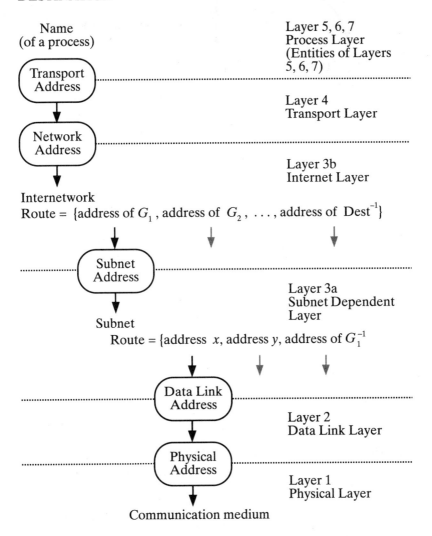

Fig. 7.5 Naming and addressing architecture in the ISO/OSI Model: G – gateway {adapted from Hauzeur (1986)}.

at some level of the naming facility to create a foundation which uniquely identifies every object in the global distributed system (Watson 1981). On this foundation it is possible to build higher level identification constructs, that is, user names, to support the goals presented in Section 7.1.3.

The system name in a distributed system can be of two different types: unique computer-oriented identifiers, or protection-oriented

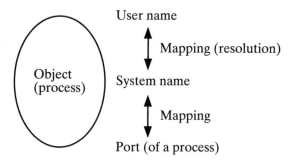

Fig. 7.6 Object identifiers within a computer system.

names. Unique computer-oriented identifiers can be seen as large integers or bit strings. However, some other information can be incorporated within them. The most distinctive feature of unique computer-oriented identifiers is that they are so large that at a given time the same unique computer-oriented identifier does not refer to two different objects. These identifiers are unstructured. There could be also structured identifiers. Structured identifiers contain more than one component, some of which indicate (or can help to indicate) the location of the named object. These components may also indicate the route to the object.

The second group of system names are capabilities, which are identifiers which intrinsically confer some rights over the referenced object. Capabilities are discussed in Section 7.6.

7.5.1 Unique computer-oriented identifiers

Unique computer-oriented identifiers have been widely used in distributed file systems. Pilot (Redell *et al.* 1980) uses 64 bit long identifiers to name files. These identifiers are guaranteed to be unique in both space and time. There is no fear of conflict if removable volumes are migrated between computers. Unique computer-oriented identifiers are mapped to physical disk addresses using a B-tree.

Another system which uses unique computer-oriented identifiers is the distributed file system (DFS) (Sturgis *et al.* 1980). A simple locating service is provided in this system to help find the server which maintains a file, given only its unique computer-oriented identifier. A B-tree is used also to map the identifiers to physical disk addresses.

A special system-generated unique computer-oriented identifier, called File Identifier (FI), is used in the Felix File Server (Fridrich and Older 1981). It is a universal access capability for the file it names.

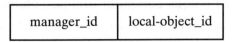

Fig. 7.7   The V object identifier.

Discussion of other systems using unique computer-oriented identifiers as internal names may be found in Leach *et al.* (1982).

In the V-system, objects are referenced using structured object identifiers. Object identifiers, structured as shown in Fig. 7.7, are used to identify open files, address spaces, and contexts or directories.

Process identifiers are different from these identifiers, but they are also structured. They are unique within a context of a local network. On the SUN workstation, the first field – the high-order 16 bits – stores a logical host identifier, while the second field is used to store a locally unique identifier. Note that the V identifiers are location independent.

There are the following reasons for choosing unstructured unique computer-oriented identifiers as system names:

(1)   **Location independence** – which allows the separation of the internal name of an object from its location in the distributed system. This enables objects to be moved without having to find and alter all references to them.

(2)   **Absolute names** – do not require any relocation when objects migrate.

(3)   **Uniformity** – allows the naming of all objects uniformly.

(4)   **Construction of composite objects** – allows the construction of composite objects, that is, objects which refer to other objects.

(5)   **Typed objects** – allow for typing of objects.

Moreover, there are some other advantages of unstructured unique computer-oriented identifiers. Because they are short, they can be easily hashed, stored, and passed in interprocess messages. These identifiers are also hard to guess. This implies that there are certain protection aspects to them. Since they are also unique, it is possible to use them as transaction IDs.

However, there are some problems, the most basic of which is the creation of a global unique identifier. Guaranteeing the uniqueness of these computer-oriented identifiers is another, very closely associated problem. Other problems are locating an object given its identifier, naming different versions of an object, replication of objects, and lost objects.

7.5.2 Creation of unique computer-oriented identifiers

There are three well-known strategies for creating a global identifier space.

Hierarchical concatenation   According to this strategy, it is necessary to create a unique identifier for each identification domain (usually a host computer), then to concatenate to the unique identifier for the domain the identifiers used within this domain. This scheme has two disadvantages:

- the form and length of identifiers used within heterogeneous domains may vary so widely that it may be awkward or inefficient for applications to be prepared to deal with them; and

- host computer boundaries are explicitly visible.

Uniform approach   According to this strategy, it is necessary to develop a standard, uniform global identifier form and space for all resources, and some way to partition these global identifiers. The binding of local identifiers to global identifiers can be permanent or temporary. This mechanism immediately introduces a level of indirection, with some desirable advantages:

- local identifiers can be chosen as most appropriate for their local language or operating system environment;

- several local identifiers can be mapped to the same global identifier or vice versa; and

- the global identifier can be reassigned if objects are relocated.

Concatenation   According to this strategy, it is necessary to concatenate the node ID of the generating node with a reading from its real time clock.

A scheme for the creation of a uniform, unique, computer-oriented, global, identifier space was presented in Watson (1981). It is interesting from the naming facility point of view as well as from the protection one. Here, we will follow Watson's discussion. A model is developed based on entities called **object-identifiers**. This model has the following properties (which do not restrict a general approach to distributed operating systems) which should be reflected in the naming facility:

(1)   processes are the fundamental communicating objects;

(2)   all objects or resources are managed by server processes; and

(3)   resources are created, manipulated and destroyed by client processes sending request messages to server processes and in turn receiving replies.

The standard form for object-identifiers is envisioned as a special data type. Object-identifiers can be unstructured or structured, although for their generation to be distributed a structured form is required. If object-identifiers have a structure with two components **server-identifier**, **unique-local-identifier**, then a server is allowed to generate object-identifiers for the objects it serves.

The next problem, which results from the discussion presented above, is how can each of these identifier components be obtained?

Obtaining the unique-local-identifier

Every object type is represented at the interface by an abstract data structure. A server responsible for an object implements this structure as some real data structure. Thus, a particular object exists as an instance of one of these real data structures located at a particular place. This object, in the general heterogeneous case, will have a **local-implementation-identifier** unique within the local domain of the server, reflecting a local programming environment.

The server is responsible for:

- creating unique local-identifiers according to the standard form, and

- binding them to its local-implementation-identifiers.

These operations are illustrated in Fig. 7.8.

An object may have several copies. In this case, each instance has a unique local-implementation-identifier (one part of it can be a copy number) within the context of its server and location. When an object is

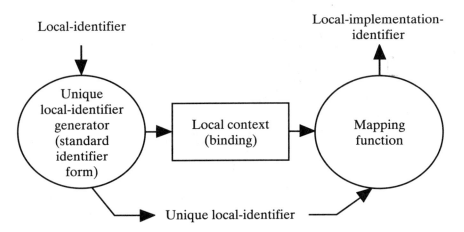

Fig. 7.8 Generating and mapping unique local-identifiers from/to local-implementation-identifiers {adapted from Watson (1981)}.

relocated it gets a new local-implementation-identifier, and its implementation representation can change to reflect the existence of more than one copy. However, in either of the two cases – multiple copies of an object, or a relocated object – the object can still have the same object-identifier if the same server is involved. If the object can be relocated across servers, then additional constraints are imposed on identifier form and binding.

Obtaining the server-identifier

The remote interprocess communication system has to have identifiers for all processes in order to perform its message delivery service. In some systems this identifier is an address. In other systems it is a port. It is bound to an object by some mapping operation. (Other terms used to name this identifier – a **mailbox**, or a **socket** – were discussed in Chapter 5.)

It is useful for processes to have more than one port, to enable parallel error and flow controlled conversation between two or more processes, the partitioning of services, or for other purposes (Fig. 7.9).

It is also useful to associate one identifier with several physical processes (process local-implementation-identifiers) so that services can be relocated, or so generic services may be created in which any one of several processes may provide the same logically equivalent service. This is illustrated in Fig. 7.10.

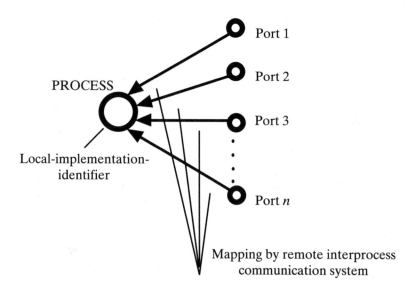

Fig. 7.9 A process with multiple ports.

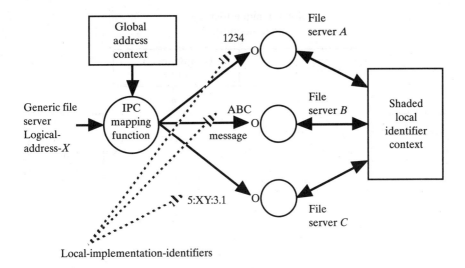

Fig. 7.10 Generic file servers, IPC mapping routes address X to one instance (ABC) {adapted from Watson (1981)}.

The interprocess communications system has to map this name to a specific server. This mapping can take place at the origin of a specific hierarchical address space or be distributed. These possibilities have been discussed in Section 7.5.

The system maps ports (there is a one-to-one mapping between addresses and ports) to routes. Given originating and destination ports and a message, one of the IPC system services is to find a path or **route** from the originating port to the destination port along which to move the message. The last step in the routing maps a port to a process's local-implementation-identifier.

Some additional aspects should be noted:

(1) Processes obtain their ports from a process manager.

(2) A process manager either obtains addresses from the IPC service if they are unstructured, or it may construct them if they are structured according to known rules.

(3) Process managers have to form addresses according to global system rules.

(4) A process manager binds ports to process local-implementation-identifiers by setting routing tables as appropriate. If a service is relocated, the process manager can rebind the port to a new process local-implementation-identifier and make appropriate changes to other routing tables.

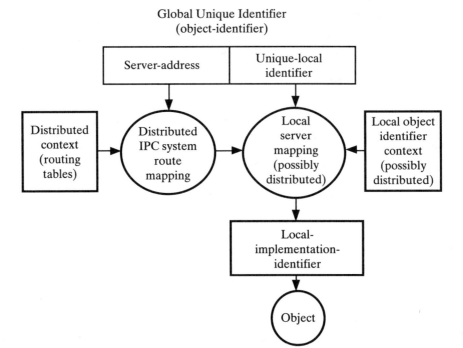

Fig. 7.11   Mapping of unique global name (object-identifier) {adapted from Watson (1981)}.

It seems reasonable to use a port of a server as the server-identifier in the object-identifiers needed for its objects. Complete object-identifier mapping is presented in Fig. 7.11.

It should be emphasized that a naming scheme which results in **address (port)**, **unique local-identifier** either provides or supports many of the identification goals presented earlier. Moreover, it should be remembered that processes have in effect two forms of identifiers associated with them:

(1)   object-identifiers used as parameters in requests for services applied to them (the address/port) part being the address of the process manager); and

(2)   addresses used to send them messages in regard to services performed by them.

An important need in all naming facilities, whether global or local, is to be able to create unique identifiers in the face of crashes that can cause loss of identifier generator state information.

7.5.3 Locating objects

Locating objects is the second problem, which was addressed partially in the previous section. Binding is a way of locating objects which, in general terms, can be seen as the identification of the location of the server (service) and of the path between the object (for example, a named process) and that server (another named object). To send a message to a server one must consider two bindings:

(1)   Find a network address to which that service is connected and operates.

(2)   Find a route from the named process requesting the service to that service address.

The network address can be identified on the basis of two distinct approaches:

(1)   by sending a broadcast message: such a message is picked up by a server which sends to the requester a response containing its service address;

(2)   by sending a directed message to a name server which sends in response a packet containing the address of the required service.

Other aspects of object location will be presented in the section on name resolution (Section 7.12).

7.5.4 Replication

Some problems with unique computer-oriented identifiers are associated with particular object types: for example, objects which are files. For reliability reasons, it is desirable to have some files stored redundantly on more than one node. This generates so-called replicated objects. Some basic properties of replicated objects were discussed in Chapter 4.

A replicated object can be **immutable** or **mutable**. It is known that immutable objects do not create any special problems from the naming point of view. All replicas of the immutable object can have the same unique computer-oriented identifier, and a kernel can easily support this object. Any copy found by the kernel can be used, because all copies are immutable and identical – there is only one logical object with a given identifier.

Discussion about mutable objects in Chapter 4 emphasized that all copies of an object should be maintained in such a way that all clients see them in a consistent state. This is an example of the multiple copy update problem. Analysis of its solution shows its complexity. Because of this, management of these copies should be performed outside the kernel. A user should not be aware of the replication of an object, because internally they could be in different states. This implies that the user should be able to refer to the replicated object via one unique computer-oriented identifier. It is the responsibility of the naming facility to map a unique computer-oriented identifier presented by a client into the unique computer-oriented identifier of the mutable object.

7.5.5   Object version and lost objects

There are two other problems with unique computer-oriented identifiers for files: object version and lost objects. A user of an object such as a file may not be interested in a particular instance, but in its latest version. In this case the fundamental problem arises that the same unique identifier cannot name two different objects, even if they are just two different versions. This problem is similar to the problems with mutable objects addressed above.

A lost object is defined as one which exists, but for which no reference exists, and is thus inaccessible. The problem is that such a lost object still takes up disk space: physically it still exists but its entry is lost.

The reader can find more about a proposed solution to the object version problem and possible recovery solutions in Leach *et al.* (1982).

7.6   Capabilities – naming and protection

There are two basic object (resource) access mechanisms – capability-based and access list-based control. One of these two protection methods, capability-based, is closely associated with naming, in particular with system names. Capabilities, introduced by Dennis and Van Horn (1966), are unforgeable tickets specifying one or more permission modes, which allow their holders to access a named object. A capability can be used to protect the object it references. Thus, using naming terms, a capability is

(1)   a trusted identifier (object-identifier) which specifies a unique object, and

(2)   an identifier which contains additional information redundancy for protection.

Capabilities can be used to name objects, protect them and define operations that may be performed on these objects. Capabilities have the following properties:

(1)   · Possession of a capability gives a client an authority to access the relevant object.

(2)   They allow objects to be shared – all clients (processes) which have capabilities to a given object, can share this object. However, several capabilities for the same object may confer different rights to each holder, whereas the same capability held by different holders conveys the same right.

(3)   Capabilities must be unforgeable and be protected from disclosure. A protection system which allows a user to produce a capability is not useful.

There are three categories of design and implementation of capabilities: tagged, partitioned and sparse. Here we will characterize each of these categories. A tag is a string of a few bits added to each memory cell, codifying the type of the object stored in that cell. For instance, it enables a distinction to be made between data and capability. Because tagging is a technique which is computer-architecture-oriented rather than name-oriented (Corsini *et al.* 1984, Lopriore 1984), it will not be discussed any further.

Partitioned implementation means that capabilities are stored in special segments separately from data. The goal of such segregation is to preserve the integrity of the capabilities. These segments, or objects, can only be accessed by the system. The segregation has some disadvantages (Jones 1980): it is necessary to provide a segregated space, and it can cause an undesirable proliferation of objects. Again, partitioning is a technique which is computer-architecture-oriented rather than distributed system name-oriented.

Note that partitioning has another very distinct feature: it deals with kernels of operating systems. Because of physical distribution, there are problems with protecting objects. This implies that a partitioning-based approach is not acceptable in distributed operating systems.

An analysis of the third approach to implementing capabilities, which is based on sparseness, shows that it can be used not only to protect objects in distributed systems, but also to name them. This is because the sparseness approach does not require capabilities to be distinguished from data either by separation or tagging – capabilities are bit strings of a defined length. They are simply values which can be recorded in any medium in or out of the computer system.

There is a second reason for using the sparseness approach in distributed operating systems. In a centralized system with a protected operating system kernel, capabilities can be stored in the kernel. However, in distributed systems, the kernels of user computers cannot be trusted. This implies the need for another protection mechanism. A mechanism which provides a trusted solution in distributed systems can be constructed on the basis of the sparseness of some object identifier (or capability) space. Several sparse capability systems have been proposed. Here, we will present the most representative sparseness-based systems.

7.6.1 Encrypted signature capabilities

Encrypted signature capabilities were invented by Gligor and Lindsay (1979) when carrying out a project on object migration and authentication. The goal of that research project was the development of a mechanism which allows the type manager to recognize and authenticate its objects when they are returned to the control of the manager. One of the objects which has to be migrated is a capability.

A valid capability is composed of two strings, an object-identifier and some rights information. This valid capability is extended by adding a signature string which is computed from the contents of the main part, that is, a valid capability (Fig. 7.12). This extension provides sparseness of a capability. Sparseness is understood in the following way. The three strings, object identifier, rights information, signature, are sparse in the sense that of all strings of the appropriate length, only these strings whose signature field agrees with the valid capability can be valid.

Because a user can deduce the signature function from the three basic strings, all of them are encrypted using a kernel key (the kernel has an access to an encrypting/decrypting algorithm or hardware). This encrypted, signed capability may be stored in unprotected memory. The revalidation of the capability requires the kernel to decrypt the bits from memory using a secret key. This operation must be performed before checking the signature. The authors of this proposal emphasize that the DES encryption system is quite resistant to attempts to deduce the key. The reader can find more about encryption systems in the chapter on protection and security in distributed operating systems (Chapter 12).

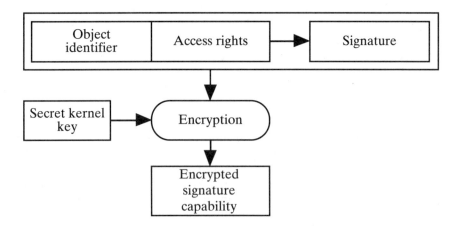

Fig. 7.12 Encrypted signature capability {adapted from Gligor and Lindsay (1979)}.

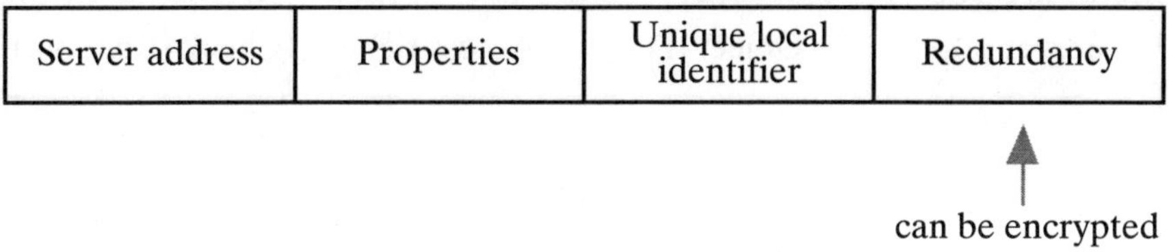

Server address	Properties	Unique local identifier	Redundancy

can be encrypted

Fig. 7.13   Lawrence Livermore National Laboratory's capability.

7.6.2   LLNL's capabilities

Watson (1981) presents the object-identifier for the system designed at the Lawrence Livermore National Laboratory. It is a capability of the form shown in Fig. 7.13. In this case, a capability is used to protect unique local-identifier and server address.

The capability consists of the following four fields:

(1)   **Server address** – the address of the server that manages the resource. A process can use this address in one of the capabilities in a request message to determine where to send the request.

(2)   **Properties** – a set of standard bits and fields that indicate to a client process the resource type, access mode, resource lifetime or security level. It is state information included in the capability to reduce messages to the server.

(3)   **Unique local-identifier** – used by the server to identify and locate the specific resource named, and possibly for other server-dependent purposes.

(4)   **Redundancy** – guards (if present) the unique local-identifier part of the capability against forgery. Encryption can be used for this purpose.

In the LLNL system, the unique local-identifier has been made sparse. This implies that without knowledge of this name a process cannot access the resource named. To achieve uniqueness of names, the unique local-identifier can be generated (long identifiers) or built using two or more levels of storage or more than one storage device (shorter identifiers but increased complexity). In the next section we will see that the Amoeba's capability and LLNL's capability share some conceptual similarities.

7.6.3   Amoeba's capabilities

The Amoeba distributed operating system is an object-oriented system, which uses an encrypted sparse capability to protect message

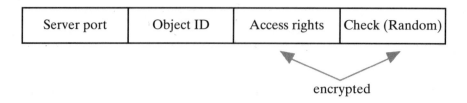

Fig. 7.14 Amoeba's capability.

ports (Tanenbaum and Mullender 1984) and (Tanenbaum and van Renesse 1985). The capability consists of four fields, as illustrated in Fig. 7.14.

(1) **Server port** – is the put-port of the server that manages the object.

(2) **Object _id** – is an object number meaningful only to the server managing the object. This means that every different server could have an object with the same object _id, and it would be a different object. Moreover, there would be no relationship between all the objects.

(3) **Access rights** – is an access rights field which contains 1 bit for each permitted operation on the named object.

(4) **Random** – is a random number for protecting the capability from forgery. This field is checked by the server which maintains for each object it holds a valid pair <access rights, random>. **Random** field makes the capability sparse.

In the Amoeba distributed operating system, the server port name has been made sparse; port names are chosen randomly. This implies that if a process does not know a port name, it cannot access the service behind the port. The ports are stored in directory servers. Clients can encrypt ports for added protection before passing them to the directory service. Thus, a client requesting a service has to give the name of the service, and this name is used to look up the ports for that service.

This explanation shows that a capability is a globally unique name and is ordinary data. Because knowledge of the capability conveys rights over the object, a capability must be protected from theft and disclosure.

Mullender and Tanenbaum (1984) propose two methods for storing capabilities. First, capabilities can be kept in a user's private directory, which is part of the tree directory structure of the directory service. Second, if a user does not divulge the capability for his private directory, he can keep everything in it secret.

How is a capability created? When a server receives a user request asking for creation of an object, it picks an available slot in its internal tables, puts the information about the new object there, and picks a new random number. This number is used exclusively for this object. Next, the server builds a capability of the form <its port, the object number, the rights, the random number>. Initially, all rights are present. Finally, the last two fields are encrypted; a random number is used as a key.

When a process wants to perform an operation on this object, it must send to the server a message containing the object's capability. The server uses the non-encrypted (plaintext) object number to find the relevant internal table entry to extract the random number. This number is used as a key to decrypt the rights and check fields. If the decrypted random (known) number is correct, the rights field is believed. This allows the server to check whether the requested operation is permitted. Note that there is no checking of user identity. If this is required, some authentication procedures must be used. User (message) authentication is discussed in Chapter 12.

7.6.4 Password capabilities

In Anderson *et al.* (1986), password capabilities were introduced for a tightly coupled multiprocessor. A password capability is defined as any string (128 bit value) that identifies some extant object and can be used to gain some access to it. Such a capability is built of two parts: a unique object identifier and a password, as illustrated in Fig. 7.15.

The integrity of a password capability depends on the password. The authors proposed a very long (64 bit) password, which makes it very difficult to guess. Because pseudo-random generators are of finite complexity and the output can be predicted, a hardware device is used as a source of unpredictable numbers.

The object identifier for files comprises two fields:

(1)   a volume identifier which indicates a unique logical volume on which the object resides; and

(2)   a serial number, as illustrated in Fig. 7.16.

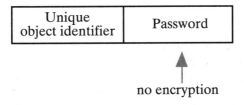

no encryption

Fig. 7.15 Password capability.

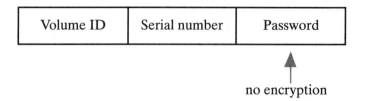

Fig. 7.16 Password capability for files.

A volume's identifier is unique and is retained by the volume for its lifetime. All valid capabilities for all objects residing on the volume are stored in a protected table, called a catalogue. To designate a particular object in a volume, the serial number of the capability is used. The validation of password capabilities is performed by table lookup in the designated catalogue using the serial number as well as a random number.

Anderson and the co-workers claim that password capabilities have some advantages over encrypted capability schemes.

- Since there is no encryption, there is no need to keep a secret key.

- In a system based on password capabilities, when capabilities are validated, the process is one of lookup and matching. On the other hand, in systems with encrypted capabilities the following operations have to be performed: lookup, decryption and matching.

- If someone does manage to procure a password capability, there is no way to manipulate the access rights. This implies that capabilities cannot be used to determine the value of any other capability to the object.

However, password capabilities also have disadvantages. The first is that sharing is very difficult. All that happens is that instead of one key, a system has as many keys as users. Thus, one password may be a strong restriction. The situation may be alleviated by using multiple passwords.

7.6.5 Conditional capabilities

A conditional capability, which is a generalization of a conventional capability, has been introduced by Ekanadham and Bernstein (1979) for a system which is capable of maintaining protected items. A protected item is an object which can only be modified by the system kernel, although it may be stored anywhere in the system. One such protected item is a conditional capability, which is informally defined as an ordi-

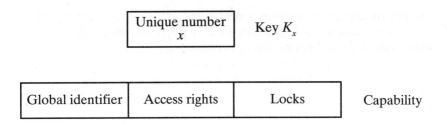

Fig. 7.17   Protected items.

nary capability associated with a set of conditions. Another protected item is a condition key which is used to check conditions. These two items are illustrated in Fig. 7.17 and defined in the following way.

A conditional capability is a protected item containing:

(1) **Global identifier** – which gives information leading to the address of an object;

(2) **Access rights** – the set of access bits that determine which operations are allowed on this object via capability; and

(3) **Locks** – a set of unique numbers generated by the system (conditions).

A condition key is a protected item which contains a unique number generated by the system. Thus, when a conditional capability is referenced during an access, the protection system must determine whether all conditions associated with its use are satisfied. The conditions are represented as locks on the capability. The lock is used to guarantee that the capability is exercised only when the condition is true. We say that a condition on a capability is satisfied if a corresponding key can be presented along with the capability. This means that in order to exercise a capability with a lock L_x a matching key K_x must be presented. Thus the action of checking conditions is an operation of matching between locks and keys (a lock and key have to have the same unique number).

7.7   Mapping a system name onto a low level name

Low level names are at the level where the communication end points of server processes are named. Low level names are associated with the type of communication, which can be indirect or direct. This implies that low level names in distributed systems which are based on indirect communication are different from names in systems using direct communication. As we have seen, in the former case ports are used, whereas in the latter unique identifiers of server processes are used.

The question is how a system name is mapped onto a low level name: this mapping depends on the type of communication (the type of a low level name). We will answer this question using two experimental distributed operating systems: Amoeba, which uses indirect communication and ports, and V, which uses direct communication. Consequently, these two systems use two different types of system names.

7.7.1   Mapping in Amoeba

Messages in Amoeba are sent to ports. These ports do not indicate the process structure of the server(s) behind them. Moreover, a port, presumably merely an unstructured number, gives no indication of its location. As we have seen, ports are protected by sparseness; capabilities passed to it are protected by both sparseness and encryption. This implies that knowledge of a port is taken to impart the right to send to it.

An Amoeba port is illustrated in Fig. 7.18. A port has two numbers: the put port number is a one-way encrypted copy of a get port number. Thus, only the server can receive from the port.

The mapping from capability (system name) onto port (low level name) is performed using extraction, as is shown in Fig. 7.19.

Put = Encrypt (Get)

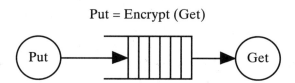

Fig. 7.18   An Amoeba port.

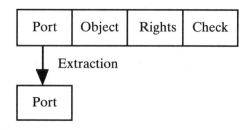

Fig. 7.19   Extraction of a port from an Amoeba capability.

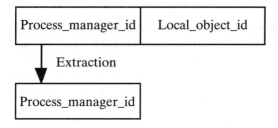

Fig. 7.20 Extraction of a manager's process_id from a V-system object (system) name.

7.7.2 Mapping in the V-system

The V-system uses structured unique identifiers, which are location independent. They are numbers which are designed not to be reused within some reasonable period of time.

The mapping from a V object system name onto its manager's process_id uses direct extraction, as illustrated in Fig. 7.20.

The kernel caches a mapping of a manager's process_id onto process location (address). Note that interprocess communication traffic is protected in the same sense that a message is directed toward a process_id, and only that process will receive the message.

7.8 User names

As we have seen, system names are digital identifiers of a fixed length, and of known and compact form, in order to make system calls using them efficient. Because users cannot cope efficiently with binary numbers, textual/character string names are used at the user level. The user names are mapped onto system names.

A character string name may have a number of parts:

(1) syntactic (hierarchical);
(2) specified attributes (explicit);
(3) implicit attributes (environment).

Note that parts (1) and (2) need not both be specified. Alternatively, part (1) can be looked at as being merely a particular attribute, and is subsumed in part (2). Another alternative is to allow all attributes to have hierarchical values.

In the following subsections we will characterize user names used in some representative distributed operating systems or distributed systems.

LOCUS

LOCUS object names at the user level look like names in a single, centralized UNIX environment (Walker *et al.* 1983). This means that virtually all objects appear with globally unique names in a single, uniform hierarchical name space. Each object is known by its path name in a tree. The path name does not contain any location-oriented string. This implies that an object can be easily moved or even executed from different sites. To avoid long path names, users can set their **working directories**.

Profile

Profile is an attribute-based (descriptive) naming service which is used to identify users and organizations (Peterson 1988, and Bowman *et al.* 1989). In this service, clients identify objects with a set of attributes or properties that describe the object. The set of attributes which are used by a client to describe an object is called an **attribute-based name**. The attribute-based naming paradigm is supported by a name server. This name server maintains a database of attributes for each of the collection of objects, and computes the set of objects described by the attributes, when it is given an attribute-based name.

The attribute-based naming paradigm is powerful enough

- to identify users and organizations; and

- to identify computational resources and conventional naming systems that map names onto addresses.

The V-system

The V naming facility is based on a three level model, structured as character-string names, object identifiers and entity identifiers. The highest level of the naming facility assigns character-string names to objects. To have each object manager implement names for its own set of objects (for example, each file server implements its own directory system), character-string names are interpreted in some context. The result is that each server manages its own context, and character-string names are partitioned by type using prefixing. However, a single name space is used by all servers of all types. The naming facility is syntactic and names are maintained by the object servers, not by a separate service. This leads to a hierarchical system with names similar to UNIX. Every object server belongs to the same process group which handles the top level of the name space. Caching of <prefix> → <server> mapping is done by the client process, not the kernel.

User names must be mapped onto system names. This operation, in general, is very complicated, and many problems associated with it remain unsolved. However, two aspects must be addressed when dealing with this mapping: structural components and functional components in a naming facility. Some of the problems associated with these components were studied in (Oppen and Dalal 1983, Terry 1985, Lantz *et al.* 1985, and Cheriton and Mann 1986, 1989).

7.9   Structural components of a naming facility

Components in a naming facility can be classified according to two aspects: structure and function. The former implies building a naming facility on the basis of active entities called name servers. A name server provides an instance of the name service which enables clients to name objects (for example, resources) and share information about these objects. This can be provided by a single name server, or in general, in cooperation with other name servers. These servers allow for and provide the sharing of the responsibility of name space management. Clients can request services directly or through name agents.

The second classification aspect, function, allows us to distinguish the following three components: communication, database management and name management. They are necessary to store data reliably, to communicate among servers, to communicate between servers and clients or their agents, and to query and modify a distributed (or centralized) name service database. Functional components are discussed in Section 7.10.

7.9.1   Name servers

Name service can be provided in a centralized or distributed manner. A name server can be centralized if a single server manages the complete name service database. The CSNET Name Server (Solomon *et al.* 1982) is an example of a server organized in a centralized fashion.

A name service can be also distributed. In this case, several name servers collectively manage the name space and support the basic set of operations. However, only control and data are decentralized. The function of the name service is not partitioned among servers. The problem is how to distribute control and data.

For example, in the V-system (Cheriton and Mann 1986), host names and other user-oriented names are implemented logically as a global directory. This directory provides uniform global interpretation of the names. The directory is implemented using a decentralized approach, where each server implements the portion of the global naming for the objects it implements (Fig. 7.21). Other possibilities will be discussed later.

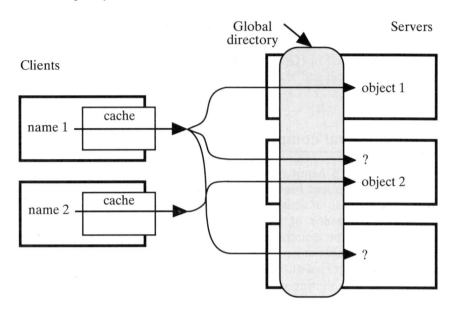

Fig. 7.21   The V distributed naming directory {adapted from Cheriton (1986)}.

Here it is necessary to emphasize another issue; whether the name service should be located in a dedicated computer (or computers), or run on user workstations with other services and clients. Some services run on dedicated computers, for example, the CSNET Name Server uses one computer, and the Grapevine system (Birrell *et al.* 1982) runs on a set of dedicated computers. On the other hand the Cronus Distributed Operating System, for availability reasons, requires a name server on every computer. In the V-System, several object-specific name servers may reside on a workstation.

7.9.2 Agents

The location of name servers should be transparent to clients of the name service. The clients want to be unaware of the distribution of the name service. Transparency can be achieved through name agents which act between name servers and their clients.

The name agents are present in many name services, but under various names. For instance, the following names are used: 'Grapevine User' in the Grapevine system (Birrell 1983), 'user interfaces' in the COSIE Name Server, 'resolvers' in the DARPA Internet Domain naming facility, 'name server agent programs' in the CSNET Name Server (Solomon *et al.* 1982), and 'stub clearinghouses' resident in every client of the Clearinghouse system (Oppen and Dalal 1983).

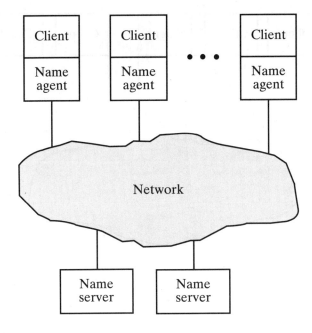

Fig. 7.22   Individual name agents.

The functions which may be performed by name agents are:

- speaking the proper communication protocol,
- maintaining a detailed knowledge of the name space and of existing name servers.

Dannenberg (1982) suggests also using name agents to negotiate for resource availability and compatibility once a resource manager is located through the name service.

There are two organizations of name agents, a single name agent (Fig. 7.22) and a shared name agent (Fig. 7.23).

A single name agent works on behalf of only one name service client. It is a private agent. This requires that the agent be structured as a set of subroutines that are linked into the client program. A shared agent implemented among clients may be seen as a part of an operating system kernel with system calls to invoke name service operations, or as a separate process accessed via interprocess communication primitives.

7.10   Functional components of a naming facility

There are three functional components of a naming facility: communication, database management and name management. We will be involved

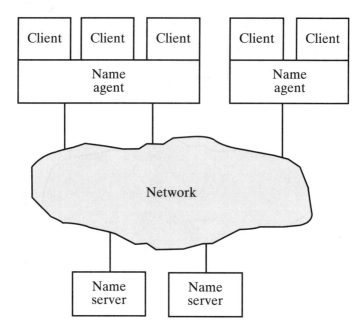

Fig. 7.23 Shared name agents.

mainly in name management. Communication and database management are characterized briefly for completeness.

7.10.1 Communication

A naming facility may be distributed among nodes of a distributed system. In such an environment communication takes place among the name servers and the name agents/clients, and between servers.

There are three styles of communication for the server/agent and server/server protocol:

(1) self-contained datagrams for exchanging data (the DARPA Internet uses datagrams to invoke name service operations);

(2) establishing virtual circuits to transmit byte-streams (Grapevine); and

(3) employing remote procedure calls to invoke remote operations as in local sites.

Different protocols may be desired for different modes of communication taking place among name servers and agents. However, the protocol used to support name service should be consistent with the communication primitives and protocols of a given distributed operating system.

7.10.2 Database management

A name service database is necessary to store and manage objects' attributes. In general, databases that occur in the design of operating systems and distributed systems are small or medium-sized. A simple and efficient technique for implementing such sort of databases is described in Birrell *et al.* (1987). To make this technique feasible, the authors took advantage of the existence of very large virtual memories, and quite large real memories. The database is maintained as a strongly typed data structure in virtual memory, record updates are performed incrementally on disk in a log. Checkpoints of the entire database are made occasionally. Recovery from crashes is provided by restoring the database from an old checkpoint then replaying the log. The major limitation on the applicability of this design concerns availability.

In other operating systems, if they are simple almost all databases are stored as ordinary text files (for example, UNIX-like systems). If they are large scale ones, the databases are implemented by *ad hoc* schemes, which involve a custom designed data representation in a disk file, and specialized code for accessing and modifying the data.

Only one system, COSIE Name Server, uses a general-purpose database management system to store name information. This is probably due to the reputation that general database management systems have of being slow and because database query languages are too complex.

There are two very important problems in database name management: reliability and consistency of the stored name data. To solve the former issue, database transactions can be used to implement atomic name service operations (Kohler 1981, Lampson 1981). Reliable data storage may not always be necessary. This was supported by the architecture and functions of the COSIE Name Server.

The latter problem is more serious. It is very closely associated with the reliability of a distributed system. In a naming facility with frequent updates, name servers should have access to consistent copies of replicated data. The task of ensuring that all copies of a name (object's attributes) are kept consistent is a difficult problem. In the literature, this problem is known as the 'multiple copy update' problem. This problem was considered in Chapter 4 as one of the basic research and design issues of distributed operating systems.

Since general algorithms for maintaining consistent copies of replicated data assume no knowledge of the data being managed, researchers involved in distributed operating systems have based their work on Gifford's weighted voting (Gifford 1979) within which performance has been improved using properties of name directories (Daniels and Spector 1983). The improvement has been achieved by introducing higher concurrency by dynamically partitioning the set of names stored in a directory, and maintaining a version number for each partition.

In new naming facilities many algorithms for replicated data are constructed on the assumption that data storage sites are able to communicate with each other. In local area networks communication can take place almost without restriction. On the other hand, in dialup networks servers may only be able to exchange data at limited times.

7.10.3   Name management

There are two major tasks of name management, **name distribution** and **name resolution**. The former deals with the assignment of authority for managing the name space to various name servers; the latter with locating the attributes of a specific object given its name. These two functions are influenced by the name structure.

Name distribution and structures of naming service are discussed in detail in the next section. Here we highlight the relationship between name service and name structure in some existing systems.

Some name servers utilize centralized name service. An example of a system with a centralized name service is the early DARPA Domain Name System (Mockapetris and Dunlap 1988, Cerf and Cain 1983). On the other hand, some systems, such as the Pup name service (Boggs 1983) and DDLCN (Lin *et al.* 1982) are based on fully-replicated name service information in all servers.

The replication of name service information implies that name resolution is unnecessary, since any name server can respond to any lookup request. The problem, however, is with maintaining consistency of information in all servers.

The name service database can also be partitioned and distributed. The database can be partitioned differently. There are also varied forms of distribution. The basic problem in distributed name management is how to find a proper name server. This problem can be solved using broadcasts or searches of name servers to find information.

The name service database can be distributed such that each name server manages only local objects (Deschizeaux *et al.* 1979, Friedrich and Eser 1983, Janson *et al.* 1983). To reference a local object it is necessary to access the local name server. Resolution of names for remote objects requires broadcast.

The name space can also be partitioned into regions. Each regional directory maintains name-to-address mapping for all objects belonging to its region. Also each node (computer) maintains its local names. To resolve a name it is necessary to perform the following steps:

(1)   access the local name server;

(2)   if its requested name is not found, then a regional server is approached;

(3)   if it is not able to resolve the name, then a request is broadcast to all other regional name servers.

Name management might be of different forms depending on the name structure. Location-dependent names, of the form 'local-name@machine', are very useful if one wants to avoid broadcast but permit distributed data (Curtis and Wittie 1984). In this case an object network location is incorporated into its name. Local name servers manage local objects. The disadvantage of location-dependent names is that it is very difficult to move objects.

The Grapevine system (Birrell *et al*. 1982) use **location-independent names**, called also **domain names** or **organizationally-partitioned names**. This implies that an object's name is only indirectly associated with the server or servers that maintain information about the object. In the Grapevine system, registers are maintained of all objects; the register set partitions the registered data. Registers can be replicated in several servers; a given server can manage more than one register. Object names explicitly contain the register in which the object resides. One register, which is replicated in every registration server, enables any server to determine which servers contain the database entry for a particular register. In this system, name resolution requires two steps:

(1) discovery of the authority for the name register, and

(2) contact with one of them.

It is also possible that each catalogue manager maintains information about all locally stored objects and all objects that were created locally. Such a management system can be developed based on so-called **authority-dependent names**, of the form 'object-name@object-site', where the 'object-site' is the birthsite of the object. This solution allows objects to migrate to other sites, but the birthsite remains the authority for the object. Moreover, the birthsite must track the movements of an object to resolve a name.

Authority-dependent names are also used in the V-System (Cheriton and Mann 1984). However, these names are managed in a different way: each server for a class of objects manages the names for these objects. All names are prefixed by the server identifier and are of the form 'server.object name'. This allows a uniform interpretation of object names. Thus, to resolve a name it is necessary

(1) to contact a 'context prefix name' which shows where to forward the resolution request, and

(2) to send a request to the indicated server.

A distributed operating system such as LOCUS (Popek *et al*. 1981) supports **tree-structured object names**. These names are also used in the Domain Naming System. In these systems, names are partitioned into 'zones'; in LOCUS 'file groups' correspond to zones. It maintains a network wide 'mount' table for resolving names. A zone can be specified by the domain name of its root and the names of its endpoints. In the

Domain Naming System, zones represent the administrative divisions within the name space. Name resolution is started at the root and traversing is performed down the branches of the tree. The resolution migrates from server to server with the delegation of authority until all labels of the name have been resolved.

The name services presented above distribute names to authoritative name servers on the basis of the syntactic characteristics of the names. A division of the name space based on syntax has two major drawbacks. First, it generally fails to satisfy the desires for strong administrative control. Second, it restricts graceful growth. In this context it is necessary to emphasize the following:

(1)   In systems based on location-dependent and authority-dependent names, an object's authority is directly represented in its name. This implies that changing the authority requires changing the object's name, which is very expensive and hence (normally) prohibited.

(2)   In systems based on location-independent names, authority is assigned using zones. To determine the object's authority, it is necessary to define a zone to which an object's name belongs, based on the syntactic characteristics of the name.

There are other reasons for looking for more efficient name services. In many large distributed systems, users may require that not all name servers can be authoritative for all objects and that the authority be divided among servers according to administrative areas. The organizations which share a common name space desire flexibility in configuring the distributed naming facility, in other words, flexibility in choosing the authorities for an object. For this reason, **structure-free name distribution** was proposed (Terry 1985). A structure-free name distribution is one that places no restrictions on the administrative control over parts of a name space. The information maintained about a named object consists of a set of attributes for the object. Structure-free name distribution can be considered as a scheme in which each object belongs to its own zone. A name service based on this approach permits maximum flexibility in the administrative assignment of authority. Moreover, it simplifies name management because name servers need not agree on what zones make up the name space.

7.11   Name distribution

Suppose the name space in a distributed system is collectively managed by a set of name servers, which support a basic set of operations. It

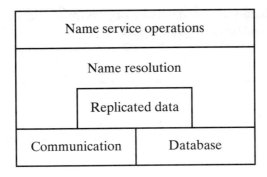

Fig. 7.24   Layers in a name server {adapted from Terry (1985)}.

is required that a name space be managed in a decentralized way. The goal is to develop an architecture for a distributed name service that allows authority for parts of the name space to be divided among the various organizations participating in the distributed computing system environment.

A name server should provide and support the following services: communication, storing name information and database management, maintaining replications, name resolution and name service operations. These services can be organized in functional layers, as illustrated in Fig. 7.24.

Now, we will characterize the layers of the architecture presented above for a distributed name service. Because we discussed communication aspects in detail in Chapters 3 and 5, we will not discuss the communication layer further. The only requirement we emphasize is the necessity of reliable delivery of messages. This implies the need for the use of a remote procedure call mechanism or reliable primitives for message passing.

7.11.1   Information support – database and replication

Information about all objects is stored in the name service database, which is distributed and replicated among the name servers. Each name server uses a database management system to store a set of **attribute tuples**. An attribute tuple consists of an object's name along with an attribute type and value. Attribute tuples are maintained in special **database objects**. It is possible for a given attribute to be managed by more than one server, but a solution in which all attributes of an object are managed together is much simpler. The name servers that store data for a particular object, and manage that data reliably, are called the **naming authorities** or **authoritative name servers** for that object.

The operations on database objects provided by the database management systems are given in List 7.1.

Query
> this operation retrieves the attribute tuple with a given name and type from the specified database object.

AddTuple
> this operation inserts the given tuple into the database object.

DeleteTuple
> this operation removes the given tuple from the database object.

ModifyTuple
> this operation performs an atomic update to a database attribute tuple: It looks for a tuple whose name and type matches the parameter tuple and replaces its value.

Enumerate
> this operation allows the contents of a database object to be retrieved a tuple at a time. A parameter indicating the next tuple to return may be given as NIL to start the enumeration.

List 7.1   Operations on database objects.

Because of the sensitivity of database objects, they have to be protected. Not all users are allowed to perform such operations as **AddTuple**, **DeleteTuple**, or **ModifyTuple**. This implies that the database management system must enforce the right to change existing attributes or add new attributes to an object.

The reliability of a distributed system can be improved by replicating information about an object's names among name servers. In this case, an object with several authoritative name servers has its attributes replicated among those servers. Such replication requires the participation of several computers in name service operations in order to read and update replicated database tuples. As we have seen in Chapter 4, replicas can be maintained using different multiple copy update algorithms, preferably using Gifford's weighted voting algorithm (Gifford 1979).

7.11.2   Distributed operations

There is a set of distributed name service operations on the attributes of a named object. These operations consist of several steps (Terry 1985).

Name resolution

The first step is determining the authoritative name servers for the named object. Name resolution in a distributed environment requires the name service to determine the authoritative name servers for every named object. This can be accomplished by maintaining **configuration data**. Such configuration data contains a list of the authoritative name servers for every object and is stored in the name server database as attribute tuples of the special type **authority**. They are attributes of an object but they are used solely by the name service. Authority attributes comprise the configuration database used for name resolution. Thus, name resolution requires a single database query. There is a space problem with replicating the configuration database in every node. It is necessary to reduce the amount of storage required to add new name servers or named objects to the environment. This topic is addressed in the next section.

Locating the authoritative name servers

Since name servers are objects, they can be placed on any node in a network. This implies the need for locating them before they can be accessed. Because of this, the main attribute of a name server has to be its address. Locating the authoritative name servers for a named object requires performing two steps:

(1)   Getting the internet address of the authoritative servers; a client or an agent working on behalf of a client only needs to locate a single name server, because name servers should be able to locate each other easily.

(2)   Selecting the authorities necessary to perform the database operation; this operation could be performed using a database of server addresses stored at every server. In this case, the location of a name server for a named object is a database query. However, the name server address can be obtained by means other than the name service; this can require the broadcast of an inquiry message over a distributed system.

Accessing the appropriate attribute tuples

After completing the location operation and selecting the authority name server for a named object, it is possible to perform database operations. Accessing the appropriate attribute tuples involves two steps:

(1)   performing the appropriate database operation at the computer on which the selected server runs;

(2)   returning the result, if any, to the calling client.

7.12   Name resolution

Name resolution in a distributed environment is the process of determining the authoritative name servers for a given, named object. Depending on the structural features of a name space, name resolution methods can be classified into two categories: structure-oriented name space, and structure-free name space. Thus, there are two groups of name resolution mechanisms:

(1)   structure-oriented name resolution, which locates the set of authoritative servers for a named object based on the structure of the name space, and

(2)   structure-free name resolution which locates the set of authoritative servers for a given object without relying on the structure of the name space.

Recall that name services supporting structure-oriented name spaces distribute names to authoritative servers based on the syntactic characteristics of the names. We have seen that the syntactic distribution of the name space generally does not satisfy the desire for strong administrative control and graceful growth. Moreover, name services supporting location-dependent and authority-dependent names as well as location-independent names suffer from some drawbacks, as discussed in the previous section. On the other hand, structure-free name distribution permits maximum flexibility in the administrative assignment of authority and simplifies name management. Thus, we present structure-free name distribution as a model solution. This decision moves us towards structure-free name resolution.

Name resolution can be considered as two conceptual topics, name resolution models and name resolution mechanisms. Here, we consider both.

7.12.1   Name resolution model

Section 7.11.2 introduces a simple model of name resolution accomplished by maintaining configuration data which contains a list of the authoritative name servers for every object and is stored in the name server database. Thus, all names can be resolved in one step; requiring only a single database query. However, there is a serious space problem with replicating the database in every node.

This implies that the configuration database has to be distributed to decrease the size of the databases stored on name server's nodes. As a result, no server has complete knowledge of the configuration. This leads to the basic problem of locating the authority attribute tuple for a named object. Name servers have to communicate among themselves to determine the authoritative servers.

Context objects and clustering

The problem is how to decompose the configuration database to be distributed among the name servers. To resolve a name, several interactions between servers may be required before the authoritative server(s) is located. Thus, the decomposition should be such that the number of interactions is minimized, so that communication overhead is decreased and the resolution process speeded up.

Such a solution can be found using the idea of **context**. Contexts represent indivisible units for storage and replication of configuration database tuples. In terms of the configuration database, a context is an object which contains a configuration. Each context is a named object which can be maintained by any collection of name servers. However, contexts are also different from other objects registered with the name service. They are actually managed by the name service and are basic to their functioning.

The name space can be partitioned into contexts by using clustering conditions. A clustering condition is defined as an expression which, when applied to a name returns TRUE or FALSE, depending on whether the given name exists in a particular cluster. It is important that any procedure which behaves in this way can serve as a clustering condition.

There are three basic clustering methods which can be used in distributed name resolution: algorithmic, syntactic, and attribute clustering (Terry 1985). Names are clustered algorithmically according to the value that results from applying a function to them. Syntactic clustering is performed through pattern matching. Names are grouped according to attributes they possess. The reader can find more about these clustering methods and clustering conditions in the last part of this section.

Context bindings and name resolution chains

When a configuration database is too large to be stored by each server, it is necessary to partition it into various contexts. As a result, information about a named object is not freely available. Name resolution is no longer a simple database query. Thus, to resolve a given name, the queried server must first look in a local context for an authority attribute for the named object. If the authority cannot be determined by the server locally, it is necessary to use additional configuration data. This requires a redirection of the resolution query to another context located in different servers.

Name resolution is based on clustering conditions and **context bindings** (Terry 1985). A context binding is an attribute, called context_binding', used for name resolution, whose value gives a new name to be resolved in a new context. Thus, the simple algorithm for resolving names is as follows. Let us assume that a given name must be resolved in some context. This context is searched for either

- an authorities attribute for the named object, that is, a name server applies a series of clustering conditions to the name until one of them is satisfied, or

- a context binding containing a clustering condition that returns TRUE when applied to the name.

In the second case, the name is resolved in the new context specified by the context binding attribute. In general, resolving a name is a process of binding names within contexts, that is, traversing a **resolution chain** of 'context_binding' attribute tuples, until the authoritative name servers for the name objects are discovered, that is, an 'authorities' attribute is encountered.

To start a resolution chain an initial context must be chosen. The initial context must contain authority attributes or context bindings for all names in the name space. Note that

- global names result if and only if the initial context is a global one, that is, all names share a common initial context; and

- relative names arise if the initial context is not a global one, but is relative to the particular server presented with the resolution request or to some other implicit context.

Applying the name resolution model to existing naming conventions
In this subsection we will say more about cluster conditions and demonstrate the possibility of applying the name resolution model presented above to describe some existing naming conventions (Terry 1985).

Algorithmic clustering Names are clustered algorithmically according to the value that results from applying a function to them. The clustering condition has a form as follows 'f[name] = value'. This method allows names, which must be unambiguous, to be resolved independent of their structure. Because a hash function maps cluster keys into buckets, hashing can be successfully used to cluster names algorithmically. For instance, let us assume that there is a function that maps a name into a real number in the range (0, 1]. Clustering a name space through this hashing function is illustrated in Fig. 7.25. The most important feature reflected by this figure is that partitions do not correspond to the structure of the names.

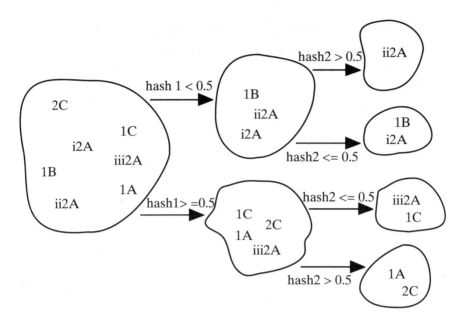

Fig. 7.25   Clustering a name space through hashing {adapted from Terry (1985)}.

Syntactic clustering   Syntactic clustering is performed using pattern matching techniques, where **patterns** are templates against which a name may be compared. They range from names that may contain wildcards to regular expressions. Thus, the clustering condition, when it is applied to a name, returns TRUE if the name matches a pattern.

Note that syntactic clustering allows names to be resolved in a manner similar to their structure, as is done by virtually all name management systems. This means that simple matching suffices as a clustering technique. Moreover, existing naming conventions can be characterized by the types of clustering used. There are some particular approaches that can be classified according to the name structure's effect on name resolution.

In the case of authority-dependent names, such as 'subname.server', these names indicate explicitly the authorities over parts of the name space. No configuration data is required by this scheme. Because the name shows the physical storage location of information for it, the name space is called **physically partitioned**.

In the case of organizationally partitioned name space (organizationally partitioned names), name management is flexible because the organizational authority for assigning names is explicitly recognized. However, the organizational authority is decoupled from the authoritative name servers for those names. This implies that the database partitions correspond to organization rather than name servers. The form of these names is 'subname.org'. This implies that:

- the initial context contains a context binding tuple for each organization; and

- each organization maintains a context object containing authority attributes for all named objects within that organization.

An organization's name serves as a convenient name for its context.

Hierarchical names consisting of more than two parts are used in many systems. Very often, these names reflect the organizational structure. In the case of these names, the contexts at the lowest level of the hierarchy contain the authority attribute tuples while higher levels contain context bindings. The context bindings reflect the delegation of authority for managing parts of the name space. Note that the amount of configuration data that must be stored in context objects at the various levels of the hierarchy is proportional to the degree of branching of the name space tree. The syntactic clustering of the sample hierarchical name space shown in Fig. 7.26 is illustrated in Fig. 7.27. Here, names are initially clustered according to their last characters.

Fig. 7.27 shows that name management mechanisms resolve names a label at a time. However, syntactic clustering conditions are not restricted to matching a single additional label in each step. This leads to variable syntactic clustering in which a variable number of labels can be matched.

Attribute clustering   This clustering method results from a study of attribute-based naming conventions. The grouping of names in this case is based on attributes these names possess. The group can be formed of all names which have the same attribute type/value pair 'AttributeType = AttributeValue'. For instance, all names with attribute type and value such as 'Organization = University College' belong to the same cluster.

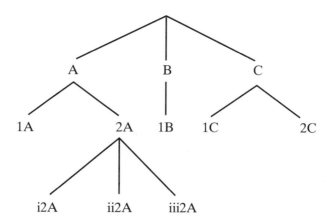

Fig. 7.26   Sample hierarchical name space {adapted from Terry (1985)}.

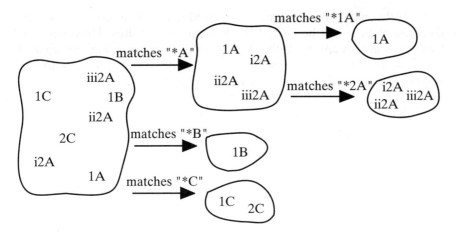

Fig. 7.27 Syntactic clustering of a hierarchical name space {adapted from Terry (1985)}.

7.12.2 Name resolution mechanism

We recall that resolving a name is a process of successfully binding names within contexts until the authoritative name servers for the name objects are discovered. Contexts form the database configuration database, and are stored and replicated on various name servers. The contents of context objects reflect the policy for resolving names according to a particular naming convention. On the other hand, the mechanics of name resolution is independent of the given naming convention. There are two major problems associated with a name resolution mechanism: locating context objects, and styles of name resolution. Different styles are implied by the different forms of interaction between servers and name agents cooperating in name resolution.

Locating context objects

Names are always resolved in some context. Thus, the question is how to determine the authoritative servers for the particular context. Since contexts are also objects, they can be distributed and replicated on different name servers. Moreover, there can be any number of these name servers. This implies that locating a context involves resolving its name. However, the location of the context is triggered by the resolution of a name in the first place. Thus, we observe an infinite recursion. This situation of recursive name resolution can be alleviated if some special techniques are utilized for locating certain contexts. One technique is based on the so-called **metacontext**. This means that there is a special context which contains the authoritative name servers for all other named contexts. Thus, to locate a given context it is necessary to bind that context name in the metacontext.

If the metacontext is small compared to the complete name server database then it can be stored at all name server sites. However, this solution is not acceptable if the distributed system has a large number of contexts. In this case, the name servers only store references to the servers that store the metacontext, while the remote metacontext contains the actual authorities attributes for all contexts. This can be improved by distribution of the context configuration database in the same way as in the decentralization of the configuration data for other objects.

Styles of name resolution

Names may be cooperatively resolved by servers and agents in the three different ways: recursively, iteratively and transitively. Three styles of resolution are illustrated in Fig. 7.28.

In a system implementing **recursive** name resolution, the resolution activity migrates from server to server so that names are resolved in a new context. The migration process is carried out until an authoritative server is determined. The responsibility for performing the name service operation rests with the initial name server that received the operation request. The name agent (or client) is not aware of the existence of multiple servers. There is one very important feature of recursive name resolution. Whereas the name agent has little work to do, name servers may be involved in processing several requests at the same time. The situation can be critical if the ratio between name agents and name servers is very high.

In a system based on **iterative** name resolution, an agent calls each server while retaining control over the resolution process. Name servers do not call each other directly. Each name server does its best to resolve a given name locally. Thus, a name server after receiving a request from a name agent, starts a resolution process. If the name has been completely resolved the result is returned. If the name server cannot continue the activity it returns to the calling agent the current state with the address of a server that the name agent should contact next. To continue the name resolution, the name agent calls another name server. The name agent is responsible for presenting the current resolution state and an operation request to the indicated name server to continue the resolution process where it left off.

In a system with **transitive** name resolution, a name server that is not able to continue the resolution activity passes the activity to a server that can continue name resolution. This resolution style has features of both previously presented mechanisms. Name agents are not involved in a name resolution activity, as in the recursive mechanism. A name server gives up its responsibility for performing name resolution action when it cannot resolve a name locally, as in the iterative mechanism. The (authoritative) name server which successfully completes the operation returns the result to the name agent.

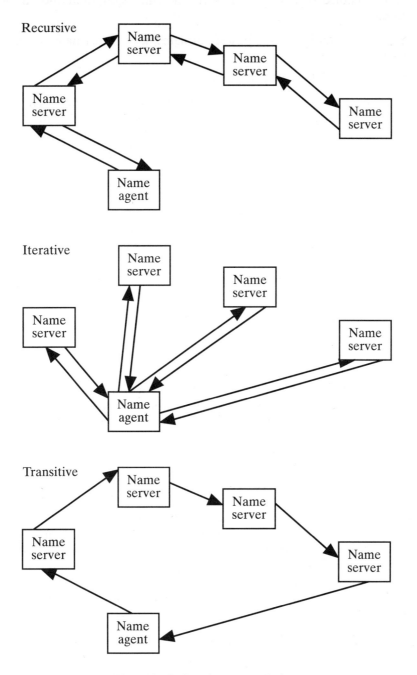

Fig. 7.28   Styles of name resolution.

The choice of a particular style of name resolution should be based on

- the relative processing powers of name servers and name agents, and

- the semantics of the communication protocols used.

Comparison of the communication requirements of the name resolution styles shows that the iterative approach requires the name agent to do more work. This could be repaid because a name agent can play a more intelligent role in the name resolution activity. All mechanisms require approximately the same amount of computation from the name servers. The only major difference is that in the systems supporting the iterative mechanism the servers do not communicate between each other. Moreover, because each name server in the recursive name resolution can be forced to pass a request to another server, it should be able to start another job when waiting for a response. This requires the name server to be multiprogrammed.

The transitive approach requires the fewest number of messages. However, as can be seen in Fig. 7.28, a sender does not receive any acknowledgement messages once an operation is passed on. This implies that the transitive name resolution should be used in systems with reliable communication. On the other hand, recursive and iterative approaches can be efficiently supported by remote procedure call based communication systems, because they use a 'call-response' model.

Attributed naming facilities are becoming more and more popular. Examples of such facilities are Univers (Bowman *et al.* 1989), Profile (Peterson 1988), and RHODOS Naming Facility (Vance and Goscinski 1989).

7.13 Terry's model to study performance

Sending messages between processes and objects supported by an operating system requires the presentation to the operating system of the names of the objects the processes want to access. The problem is how to locate named objects. This is directly connected to the management of the name space and the structures of the naming facility.

As we have seen, name servers act as distributed binding agents that bind an object's name to some of its properties, including the object's location. Some name servers can store information about the particular objects. Such name servers are called the naming authorities or authoritative name servers for that objects. The problem is how to distribute name servers, that is, which of the structures of a naming facility is the best.

Different criteria can be taken into consideration when developing the naming facility for distributed computer systems. At the stage of analysis of the structure of naming facility, we will use the most important of those criteria, namely performance. This criterion is important for a distributed environment because there is usually a number of inter-connected networks (the same is true in the case of one local area network connecting a large number of personal computers and/or workstations, and different servers), which implies that the cost of communication between clients and name servers is the major bottleneck in locating remote resources. In this case, the performance of name server queries is dominated by the number of name servers that must be accessed and the cost of accessing those name servers.

The factors which affect the efficiency with which the name space can be managed and the cost of retrieving name server information are:

(1)   the clients' patterns of reference to name server information;

(2)   the choice of authoritative name servers for parts of the name space;

(3)   the placement of name servers throughout the internet;

(4)   the amount of replication of name server information;

(5)   the number of name servers that are currently operational; and

(6)   the performance of each individual name server.

All these factors, except the last, were considered by Terry (1984) when developing a model to make performance comparisons of different naming facility structures.

7.13.1   A model to study performance of name facility structures

The model developed by Terry (Terry 1984) to study performance of different structures of the naming facility is as follows. The name server database is distributed among N servers, $NS_1, \ldots, NS_N$. At any time only some of them are available because of some failures; F is the current number of name servers whose data is inaccessible.

Clients of those name servers may be specific programs, hosts or networks, and are denoted $1, \ldots, U$. Clients are distinguished by their location, and by the particular objects they reference. A name server client needs only to know the location of a single name server, presumably the closest one. Name server queries are made in an iterative way. If one name server cannot answer the query, it returns the location of another, more knowledgeable colleague.

The name server database is strictly partitioned into K fragments, which often reflect partitions in the name space, $db_1, \ldots, db_K$, which in turn correspond to indivisible units of storage. Each name server has authority over some subset of the database partitions. Although it is admissible, no single name server stores the complete database. The set S_k

contains those name servers that store partition db_k. S_k, for $k = 1, \ldots, K$, is a subset of $\{NS_1, \ldots, NS_N\}$.

Each client has a set of objects (resources) that it regularly references. For client u, a reference mix is represented by $r_{u1}, \ldots, r_{uK}$, where r_{uk} is the percentage of name server accesses performed by client u to the database partition db_k.

The costs which were distinguished in the model are as follows.

- d_i denotes the cost of executing a query at NS_i. This cost depends on such factors as the overall size of the database maintained by NS_i, and the kind of database facilities employed. It is assumed to be fixed over time.

- c_{ui} is the cost of communicating with NS_i from client u. It depends on the site at which the client is executing. This cost depends on such factors as the number of gateways traversed, and the speed of transmission lines.

- C_{ui} specifies the complete cost of accessing the name server, NS_i, remotely from client u, and is expressed by the following formula:
  $C_{ui} = d_i + c_{ui}$.

The cost of retrieving the name server information about a set of named resources depends on client location relative to various name servers and the client's reference mix and can be expressed by the formula:

$$E(L_u) = \sum_{k=1}^{K} r_{uk} L_{uk} \tag{7.1}$$

where L_{uk} represents the total cost of querying the information in database partition d_k, including the cost of locating the desired data. Because we are interested in the cost of retrieving an individual object's name server entry, we will ignore the client's access patterns in $E(L_u)$, concentrating only on L_{uk}.

7.13.2 Structures of the naming facility

The following basic structures of naming facility for the distributed operating systems have been identified by Terry (1984) and Indulska and Goscinski (1989):

(1) a centralized naming facility,

(2) a replicated naming facility,

(3) a decentralized naming facility,

(4) a distributed naming facility,

(5) a hierarchical naming facility.

Some of these structures and their modifications are illustrated in Fig. 7.29.

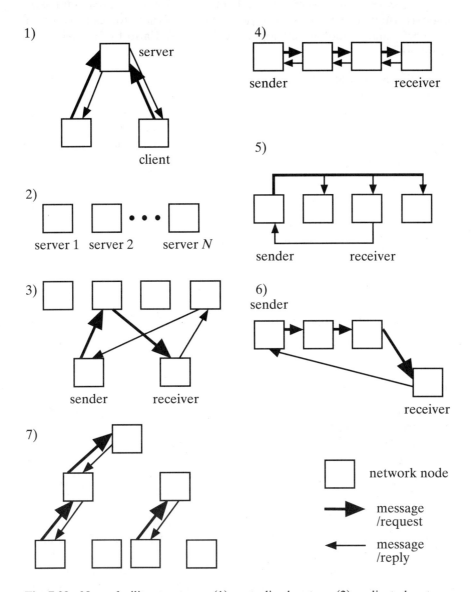

Fig. 7.29 Name facility structures. (1) centralized system, (2) replicated system, (3) decentralized system with division into object types, (4) fully distributed system – local resources known in each node, (5) fully distributed system – local resources known in each node and broadcast message passing to resource servers in each node, (6) distributed system – resource address determined by a hashing function which is defined over the set of resource identifiers, (7) hierarchical.

Now, we will describe these naming facility structures emphasizing performance evaluation. The presentation of these topics is based on the performance model developed by Terry, and also by Indulska and Goscinski.

·Centralized naming facilities

A centralized naming facility is implemented using a single name server, which maintains a table or database providing the necessary name-to-address mappings. This system manages a flat name space where names are character strings exhibiting no structure. The name server's database is built up by registering services, processes, ports (mailboxes) and other relevant details that want to be publicly known. File directories can be regarded as a special case of name service. In this case, S_k = NS. The name server contains the complete set of information about all named objects in the distributed environment. The retrieval cost is simply $L_k = C$, where C specifies the maximum cost of accessing name server NS remotely by the farthest client u.

The advantage of this naming structure is its simplicity, and the avoidance of any inconsistency problems which have been identified in some systems with more than one server. The disadvantages are low reliability of the whole distributed system, and large traffic overhead and long delays in accessing the server and before starting a required service-oriented transmission.

Replicated naming systems

A replicated naming facility manages a flat name space also. Each computer node (site) of the distributed system maintains a copy of the database providing the necessary name-to-address mappings for the whole system. In this case, $S_k = \{NS_1, \ldots, NS_N\}$. Because each name server contains a complete set of information about all named objects (resources) of the distributed system, any client can query the physically-closest name server, denoted here NS_{main}. This implies that the retrieval cost is simply $L_k = C_{main}$.

This system has the following advantages: it is very fast, it has no binding-oriented operation delays, the number of binding-oriented messages is zero, and it has high reliability. The problems are maintaining consistency between copies, name actualization problems (if a process dies, or a service becomes unavailable) and large memory requirements of each node.

Name database entry oriented decentralized systems

A name database entry oriented decentralized system also manages a flat name space, but each name server entry is stored at some arbitrary site. In this case, $S_k = \{NS_j\}$. Such a solution for a naming facility structure implies that the storage and consistency problems, mentioned in the previous approach, are avoided. This is the main advantage of this structure. The drawback of this system is locating the desired data, because it may necessitate querying each name server. On average, half of the name servers must be accessed to retrieve the object's information. Assuming that the name servers are queried in numerical order, the retrieval cost are as follows:

$$L_k = \sum_{j=1}^{K} C_j \qquad (7.2)$$

This system is costly in terms of name server lookups.

A simple modification of the above system is the **distributed naming facility**. In this system each computer node (site) maintains a database providing the necessary name-address mapping for its own local objects (processes, ports, services, resources). This system requires broadcasting on the network the name of a requested object.

None of the systems just described is very practical for large distributed systems. The situation can be improved by adding structure to an object's name. This structure should reflect the management authority for the name.

Decentralized naming systems

A decentralized naming facility is implemented using a number of name servers working in strictly defined domains. The structure is added to an object's (resource's) name to reflect the management authority for the name. The following naming convention can be used:

(1) **proper_name@name_server**, where **name_server** identifies the name server that is responsible for managing information about the object, and

(2) **proper_name** unambiguously identifies the object in the context of the naming authority.

If the name servers are unambiguously named then the complete name **proper_name@name_server** is globally unambiguous. Effective management of such a name space following this naming convention requires that each name server knows the location of other name servers.

There are different approaches to decentralize a name space:

(1) geographic (physical) partitioning: if the system is composed of multiple local area networks connected by bridges and gateways, it is natural to have one name server for each network; and

(2) organizational (functional) partitioning: the partition of the whole system in domains can be done on the basis of organizations.

In **physically partitioned naming systems** one-to-one mapping exists between database partitions and name servers, that is, $K = N$ and $S_k = \{NS_k\}$. Such a structure requires two accesses to obtain the information about a given object (resource): one to locate the naming authority and one to access the data. Only one access is necessary when the desired naming information is stored in the primary name server, $\mathrm{NS_{main}}$. The cost of lookup is expressed by the formula:

$$L_k = \begin{cases} C_{main} + C_k & \text{if } k \neq main \\ C_{main} & \text{if } k = main \end{cases} \tag{7.3}$$

In **organizationally partitioned naming systems** the database partitions correspond to organizations rather than name servers. Each name server can be the authority for some subset of the organizations. In this case names take the form **proper_name@organization** in which the authority for assigning names is explicitly recognized. In this case the name service can be easily reconfigured because the assignment of object names is independent of the assignment of the responsibility for maintaining information about the objects.

Let us consider the lookup costs. Suppose, for the moment, that each organization's data is managed by a single name server as with a physically partitioned name space, $S_k = \{NS_k\}$. In order to efficiently access information about a given object, each name server should know which name server has responsibility for each organization. Based on this structure, name server queries can be processed in two steps as in physically-partitioned naming systems. The lookup cost is expressed as follows:

$$L_k = C_{main} + C_k \tag{7.4}$$

Two database retrievals are always required since a name server cannot determine whether or not it is the authority for the desired data without consulting the local database. If the primary name server can retrieve and return the name server entry directly upon discovering that it is the storage site for the desired data, then

$$L_k = C_{main} + d_{main} \qquad \text{if } S_k = \{NS_{main}\} \tag{7.5}$$

One of the most important advantages of an organizationally-partitioned name space is the ease with which replicated naming information can be accommodated. This means that the name server database can be partially redundant. From the management point of view, supporting replication requires that the lookup algorithm described above be extended in such a way as to recognize several authoritative name servers for each organization rather than a single responsible one. As a result, each name server should know the complete set of authoritative name servers for each organization, S_k. An example of a system based on this approach is the Grapevine system (Birrell *et al.* 1982). The name server lookup cost becomes

$$L_k = \begin{cases} C_{\text{main}} + C_{\text{mink}} & \text{if mink} \neq \text{main} \\ C_{\text{main}} + d_{\text{main}} & \text{if mink} = \text{main} \end{cases} \tag{7.6}$$

This formula was developed on the assumption that the closest authoritative name server can be determined with negligible cost. The cost for a system with replicated data should be less than the cost for a system with organizationally-partitioned name space since the name server accessed by various clients, NS_{mink}, can differ from client to client, whereas in the previous case each client is forced to access the same name server.

The influence of the replication of data can be illustrated by one very simple example. Let R be number of copies, $R \leq N$, distributed uniformly, that is, R authoritative name servers are chosen at random for each database partition. Assume that the name servers are ordered such that $C_i \leq C_j$ for $i < j$ and $NS_i = NS_{\text{main}}$. This assumption does not imply any loss of generality. For such a system, the expected lookup cost can be expressed as follows:

$$\begin{aligned} L_{\text{uniform}} &= C_{\text{main}} + \text{Prob}(\text{main} = \text{maink})d_{\text{main}} + \sum_{i=2}^{N} \text{Prob}(i = \text{mink})C_i \\ &= C_{\text{main}} + Rd_{\text{main}} / N + \sum_{i=2}^{N} \binom{N-i}{R-i} / \binom{N}{R} * C_i \end{aligned} \tag{7.7}$$

The influence of replication in this formula is manifested by R.

Hierarchical naming systems

A hierarchical naming facility is an extension of the previous system by extending two-part structured names to hierarchical names consisting of more than two parts. There are two basic approaches: fixed number of layers, or an arbitrary hierarchy. With hierarchical name space management, the complete name server configuration data (S_k for all k) need not be stored at every name server. It is sufficient that each name server store only enough information to locate the authoritative name servers for the top level of the hierarchy. The top level name servers should know the authoritative name servers for the name space subtrees directly under their administrative control. An analysis of hierarchical naming structures can be performed by recursively applying the techniques for two-part names. Consider a system using the names of the form **local_name:domain:organization**, that is, a hierarchy with three levels. The lookup cost formulas can be applied in this case in two steps

$$L_k = (C_{\text{min}} + C_{\text{min\_org}}) + C_{\text{mink}} \tag{7.8}$$

The analysis for hierarchies of more than three levels is a straightforward extension.

7.13.3 Performance study

Terry (Terry 1984) presents two interesting results of a performance study for the network (the Grapevine system) illustrated in Fig. 7.30. The circles represent 3 Mbps Ethernet local area networks, numbered from 1 to 12, and the lines represent long distance links with data rates of either 56 kbps or 9.6 kbps. The rectangles represent the various name servers, labeled from A to Q.

The performance of a distributed system is influenced by the location of the name servers. This influence is through the database objects

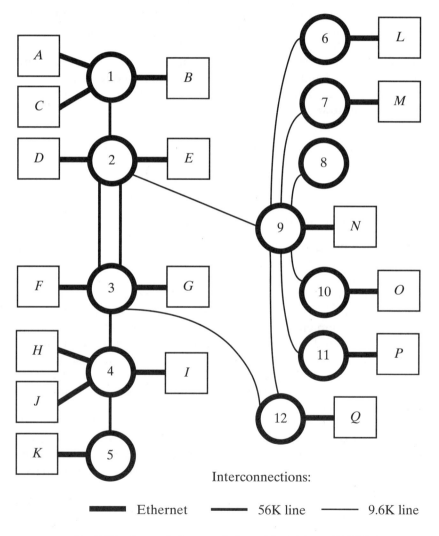

Fig. 7.30 A sample internet {adapted from Terry (1985)}.

Table 7.1 Communication costs.

from network	to server								
	A	B	C	D	E	F	G	H	I
1	1	1	1	56	56	111	111	166	166
2	56	56	56	1	1	56	56	111	111
3	111	111	111	56	56	1	1	56	56
4	166	166	166	111	111	56	56	1	1
5	479	479	479	424	424	369	369	314	314
6	682	682	682	627	627	682	682	737	737
7	682	682	682	627	627	682	682	737	737
8	682	682	682	627	682	682	682	737	737
9	369	369	369	314	314	369	369	424	424
10	682	682	682	627	627	682	682	737	737
11	682	682	682	627	627	682	682	737	737
12	424	424	424	369	369	314	314	369	369

from network	to server							
	J	K	L	M	N	O	P	Q
1	166	479	682	682	369	682	682	424
2	111	424	627	627	314	627	627	369
3	56	369	682	682	369	682	682	314
4	1	314	737	737	424	737	737	369
5	314	1	1050	1050	737	1050	1050	682
6	737	1050	1	627	314	627	627	627
7	737	1050	627	1	314	627	627	627
8	737	1050	627	627	314	627	627	627
9	424	737	314	314	1	314	314	314
10	737	1050	627	627	314	1	1	627
11	737	1050	627	627	314	627	627	1

that are assigned to the particular name servers and the cost of communicating with these servers.

Table 7.1 shows the costs of communicating between a client on each network and each name server, assuming that the communication cost is proportional to the data transmission rate of the communication medium.

Thus, assuming that communication costs are normalized so that communication over a local Ethernet costs one unit, say T, transmission over a 56K and 9.6K lines cost 54T and 312K, respectively. The cost of communication may differ by several orders of magnitude. Fortunately, the performance may be improved by replication.

Table 7.2   Effects of replication on lookup costs.

client's network	replication factor R					
	1	2	3	4	5	6
1	297.35	145.99	84.83	56.72	41.53	32.15
2	261.76	124.96	74.40	53.69	43.39	36.94
3	271.47	125.76	74.24	53.63	43.38	36.94
4	300.59	142.34	82.65	55.96	41.34	32.12
5	576.76	398.65	323.48	281.71	251.52	226.25
6	645.18	548.70	448.14	435.57	387.66	343.13
7	645.18	548.70	488.14	435.57	387.66	343.13
8	976.59	896.22	849.47	808.41	769.71	732.08
9	369.00	307.04	278.71	256.05	235.77	216.55
10	645.18	548.70	488.14	435.57	387.66	343.13
11	645.18	548.70	488.14	435.57	387.66	343.13
12	439.41	347.85	302.26	271.68	246.62	223.93
avg.	506.14	390.30	355.21	298.34	268.66	242.46
$\Delta\%$	–	–22.89	–14.11	–11.00	–9.95	–9.75

The effects of replication on lookup costs are presented in Table 7.2. These results have been compiled using the estimates of communication costs given in Table 7.1 along with Equation 7.7. Terry assumes that the copies are uniformly distributed. The cost decreases with the number of replicas. This is due entirely to reducing the amount of communication between clients and very remote name servers.

7.14   Simulation study of naming facility performance

In a simulation model developed by Indulska and Goscinski (1989), a distributed operating system is presented as a set of functionally-connected servers. In comparison with models of a centralized operating system, the model contains processes serving new types of operating system resources, that is, messages and data structures describing the location of objects (resources) (Goscinski and Indulska 1984). The model simulates the mapping of requests for access to objects directed to the operating system by its environment into servers. The structure of the simulated operating system makes it possible to present servers at various levels of abstraction. It enables the simulation model to be modified by changing any server and the connections between servers.

7.14.1   The simulation model

The design of a simulation model to study the effectiveness of different name facility structures requires the definition of:

(1)   the set of events controlling the distributed operating system, and

(2)   a suitable set of servers.

Events controlling a distributed operating system
A distributed operating system is controlled by a set Z of events in a local computer network. A given event in Z is associated with a network node. An event is for service according to a defined method of serving the events which arrive at the same time. This choice is made by the interrupt system of the associated node computer. The set of events of the i-th node depends on the architecture of the node computer. The elements of this set belong to classes distinguished in the set Z by the type of interrupt. All other internal and external events are divided (on the basis of their sources and their stochastic characteristics) into the following classes:

Z_1 random external interrupts from the environment of the distributed operating system, (for example, from equipment controlled by the system in a process-control environment, or from operator intervention). These interrupts activate user (application) processes (process activation requests),

Z_2 interrupts generated by the network interface (signalling message arrival),

Z_3 clock interrupts activating cyclic processes,

Z_4 I/O interrupts (disk, printer),

Z_5 interrupts generated by system calls (from processes of the distributed operating system and user processes controlling the environment of the distributed operating system),

Z_6 requests for a process relocation (introduced in the simulation tool to study the effectiveness of addressing methods in the case of dynamic changes of the location of resources).

In the set Z of events there are classes of events characterized by random characteristics which do not depend on the distributed operating system (Z_1, Z_3, Z_6). In the model, it is assumed that from the point of view of servicing these events, the operation is equivalent to servicing a queue with losses. Such an approach is justified by noting that in a given node, only one process activated by a given event can be run, and the number of stored process activation requests is restricted. On the other hand, the service of other types of events is equivalent to servicing a queue without losses. The events leave the system after completion of service.

Server processes

In this model, two classes of processes are distinguished in the set R: processes managing physical resources and processes managing logical resources. In the set R the following classes of server processes are distinguished:

R_1 the class of message-passing servers in node computers,

R_2 the class of scheduling servers,

R_3 the class of process dispatchers,

R_4 the class of message-passing servers in network interfaces,

R_5 the class of name servers managing data structures describing the location of resources in the network,

R_6 the class of servers managing the I/O devices of a node computer,

R_7 the class of servers managing clocks of node computers,

R_8 the class of servers connecting external events with processes of the distributed operating system and processes of the environment of the distributed operating system (a change of the state of processes activated by external events).

Processes belonging to classes R_1–R_8 run the interrupt service. In each node there are processes belonging to classes R_1–R_5 (Fig. 7.31); the presence of processes belonging to other classes depends on the node resources. A server of the class R_1 serves a request for message passing which is issued by processes (event Z_5) or receives messages coming from the network (event Z_2). The process R_1 checks if the destination process is local or not. If not, it passes the message on to an addressing process (the functions of which vary according to the chosen naming facility structures) and then sends it into the network. In case a message is to be directed to a local destination process it is sent there by the process R_1. If a message is to be delivered to a user process, the process changes its state into 'ready' if it was awaiting the message, or the message waits in the message queue until it is received. If a message is to be delivered to a server process (for example, it contains a I/O request), the process R_1 passes the request on to the queue of the appropriate server process. After each operation in a server process is completed, the message with the result is sent to the request sender by the process R_1 (the addressing process being used again). A server of the class R_5 provides an address to a remote message. The address is defined by a name resolution system, in particular a simple addressing function.

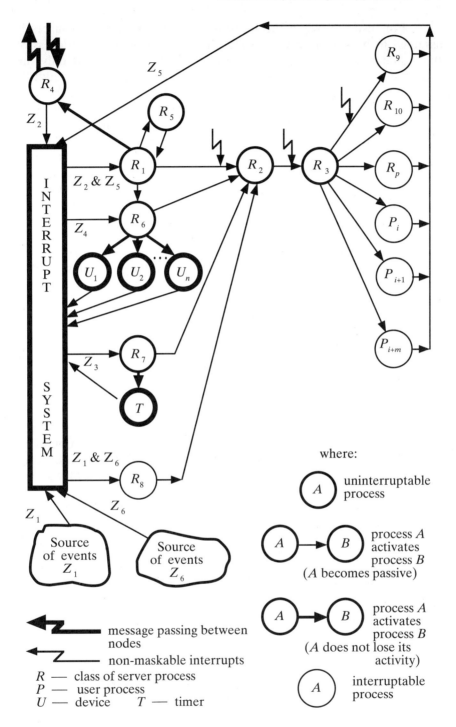

Fig. 7.31 A model of interactions of server processes in the *i*-th node.

For instance, when the location of all the network resources is assumed to be known in each node, the server R_5 gives the address of the resource owner node to the message. If we assume that only the local resources are known in each node, the process R_5 gives the address of the neighbouring node to the message, or, alternatively, the message is broadcast, another possibility. The study goal implies that definitions of servers of class R_5 can be different. Each variant is equivalent to one resource addressing method.

Moreover, in the model of an operating system of a network node there can exist processes of classes R_9–R_p, $p > 9$, treated here as user processes in the environment of the operating system (interruptable). Servers of these classes manage logical resources such as files (an access to a file) and local procedures (a remote call to a local procedure). Servers of class R_9 are used to serve requests for process relocation and to implement different protocols for process relocation from node to node. The diversity of these protocols depends on naming facility structures. These protocols contain three important parts: (1) protocols for process relocation, (2) operations on name database, and (3) synchronization of these operations. By defining processes of class R_9, it becomes possible to study the effectiveness of different addressing methods in the presence of dynamic relocation of network resources. Processes of classes R_{10}–R_p do not have visibly-defined operations at the level of abstraction employed for the description of user processes requests.

Processes of classes R_1–R_8 service the interrupts in a network node. This set of service processes models the kernel of a distributed operating system. Functional connections between servers belonging to classes R_2, R_3, R_6, R_7, R_8 are the image of connections used in centralized operating systems. The service of interrupts in the tool was extended by adding servers of classes R_1, R_4, R_5 managing message passing in the network. The connections between processes R_1–R_8 in one network node are illustrated in Fig. 7.31.

7.14.2 Modelling service requests in a distributed operating system environment

The set of events generated by the environment of a distributed operating system can be divided into three groups (based on the statistical characteristics of the request arrival times):

(1)   events in which the probability distribution of request arrival times is independent of the distributed operating system (hardware errors, events signalling requests from the computer system environment);

(2)   deterministic events; and

(3) events in which the probability distribution of request arrival times is dependent on some strategy used in the distributed operating system such as a scheduling algorithm.

The model of the requests makes use of the division given above and it contains:

(1) sources of requests of independent events (Z_1, Z_6),

(2) sources of requests determined by the execution time of an operation (Z_2, Z_3, Z_4),

(3) a static model of user processes which includes declarations of dependent events: system calls (Z_5).

The assumption that communication and synchronization are performed by message passing implies that there are two classes of events:

(1) a request for message passing between processes,

(2) a request for performing an operation on a resource (for example, I/O operation, a call of a process to perform a procedure) by the operating system.

Requests by the distributed operating system environment can be treated as requests for interprocess communication between processes in the environment and server processes (independent of the implementation of the distributed operating system). A request for communication can be blocked or unblocked depending on whether or not the requesting process is suspended. Declarations of events in a user processes can be modelled by message passing primitives:

> **send_message**(receiver, parameters)
> **receive_message**(sender, parameters)

The allocation of user processes to network nodes defines the set of requests in the i-th node. This model of process requests presented here is the basic one needed for generating events of class Z_5. The times of arrivals of the events Z_2, Z_4 are calculated in the simulation tool. For instance, the completion of an I/O operation causes the results to be sent in a message – the next operation being taken from a server queue. The completion of an operation is an event of class Z_4. The independent events Z_1, Z_6 are described in the simulation tool by a probability distribution.

7.14.3 Simulation studies

Representation of objects in the distributed operating system environment

The modules of the environment in the simulation tool are data structures containing models of user processes. The processes are characterized by the following set of attributes: the address and priority of the process, the activating event (clock interrupt Z_3 or event Z_1 or a (random) message from another process), the sequence of events modelling the process, the process status word – set up during the simulation, the process state (ready, running, suspended) – set up during the simulation. The constant attributes of a process (address, priority, event) are generated using a uniform distribution of the given attribute. The number of user processes is a decision variable of the simulation tool.

Events Z_5 modelled in a process are described by the following attributes:

- the type of the event (receive, send, end)
- the receiver or sender of messages generated by the event
- the identifier of the message (computed parameter)
- the relative time for an instance of the next event (required processor time between two communication primitives)
- the time required to perform an operation on a resource (an operation performed by a receiver server process)
- the current time of an instance of the event (set up during a simulation)
- the priority of the event (the priority of a message).

We assumed that these attributes have a uniform distribution.

All simulated events are described by the following parameters:

- The events Z_1, Z_6 the probability of occurrence of the event, the distribution of arrival times of events, the time of occurrence of the next event (computed value). It was assumed that random events Z_1 and Z_6 have a Poisson distribution with event rates c_1 and c_2 (c_1, c_2 – decision variable of the simulation tool).

- Event Z_2 the priority of a message, the identifier of the receiver, the identifier of the sender.

- Event Z_3 the time of occurrence of the next event (computed value)

- Event Z_4 the address of the receiver of an operation result, the time of occurrence of the next event (computed value).

- Event Z_5 the attributes of events Z_5 are characterized in the model of the environment.

Performance indices

One of the most important problems of a simulation study is the choice of the performance indices. There is a dearth of measured performance indices for operating systems. Moreover, performance indices used and presented in the literature do not have uniform definitions. This implies that operating systems can be properly assessed only for several classes of applications. In Indulska and Goscinski (1989) the following performance indices were taken into consideration:

E1 the mean time to respond to an event (minimize);

U the utilization of processors – the relative time spent in the state 'user' (maximize);

S the relative time spent by processors in the state 'system' (minimize).

Simulation experiments

The following naming facility structures have been studied:

1 Centralized addressing

2 Replicated

3 Centralized addressing in resource classes

4 Local addresses known in each node

5 Local addresses known in each node; broadcast message passing to resource servers in each node

6 Resource addresses determined by a hashing function defined over the set of resource identifiers. When addressing is static, the resource address is in accord with the actual resource location in the network; when the resource is relocated, the access to it is realized by searching the network.

A good deal of research was carried out in order to determine the influence of the selected values of decision parameters on the performance comparisons of naming facilities structures. All the decision variables were examined and the most characteristic results are discussed below. Fig. 7.32 gives the results of examining the average response time to an event for the six naming facilities structures, when there are different transmission rates from 0.5 to 10 Mbps.

In this case the best results are obtained for two methods: 4 – local addresses known in each node and 6 – resource addresses determined by a hashing function defined over the set of resource identifiers, and the worst ones for method 2 – centralized addressing. The influence of transmission rate on the mean response time is small. During the

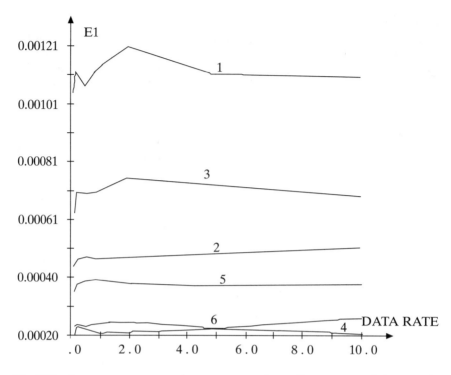

Fig. 7.32 An average response time to an event depending on transmission speed.

investigation it was found that the relation between the index U of different addressing methods is largely independent of the transmission rate of the network.

Fig. 7.33 presents the index U for the study of the specially important decision variable (w_{i4}) that is the mean time to access one element of the data structure describing the location of an object (the values of X coordinates are given in milliseconds). The study has not shown a great influence of the changes in the values of decision variables on the performance relations of addressing methods.

Fig. 7.34 shows how the response time to an event depends on the number of network nodes when the set of user processes is fixed. The greater the number of network nodes, the greater the number of processes being executed at the same time. Thus, the number of requests for access to resources increases. It lengthens the response times in the case of central resource addressing, since requests for addressing are served by one process.

Fig. 7.35, however, presents a relative increase of the index S when we use the addressing method which is based on information about local node objects.

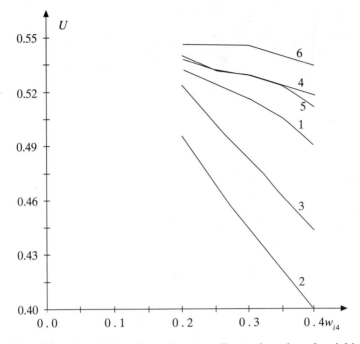

Fig. 7.33 The value of index U varying according to the value of variable w_{i4}.

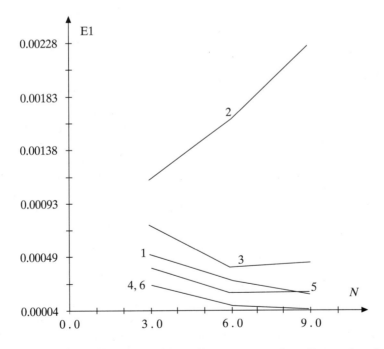

Fig. 7.34 An average response time depending on the number of network nodes.

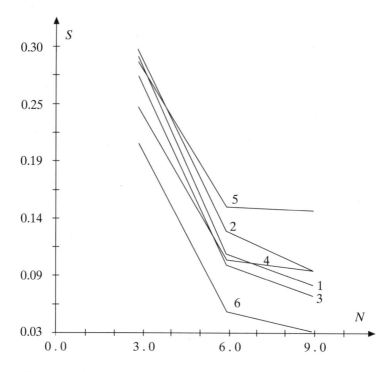

Fig. 7.35 The value of index S depending on the number of network nodes.

7.15 Summary

Processes need to refer to objects of a distributed system, and this should be done in such a way as to preserve location transparency. This requires all objects to be named and managed by a naming facility.

A naming facility enables clients to name objects, in particular, assign character-string names to objects, and subsequently to use these names to refer to those objects; to provide information about those objects; to locate objects given only their names; and to discover how to access those objects.

To perform these operations, a naming facility should encompass desirable properties which are acceptable to the users. To facilitate sharing, naming conventions need to be established which provide a standard nomenclature for object naming. Names should be of a form that can be freely passed around an internet. However, there are currently some difficulties in interconnecting existing distributed environments due to the incompatible naming facilities in use. Moreover, in many existing computer systems, separate naming conventions are used for different types of objects (for example, file names typically differ from names of other objects). This implies the need for a uniform naming convention to identify the many available objects. On the other hand, specialized naming facilities can exist within a global naming facility to locate more specific facilities.

The name service is a central point for other servers and their clients. This is because the name server enables other services to be identified and accessed in a uniform way. Thus, users need only to know how to access the 'well-known' name service in order to gain access indirectly to all other services. For all of the above-mentioned reasons, the naming facility is one of the most important components in distributed operating systems.

The development of a naming facility for a distributed system is a more complex task than for a centralized system, due to the distribution of objects among all the computers in the distributed system. Thus, a naming facility for a distributed system must take into consideration not only naming aspects of computers but also the requirements for the specification of names for computer networks.

A naming facility for a distributed operating system must be designed to deal with a hierarchy of identifiers. The following identifiers and mapping between them can be identified: names, in particular, **user names** – human readable text strings; **system names** – binary numbers used to designate or refer to objects; and **ports** – objects used to allow processes to communicate indirectly; all these three identifiers identify objects within a computer system. In addition, there are **routes** – a list of names representing the path from source to destination; and **addresses** (also names) – used to name communicating objects and entities and to associate with object (entity) location in a distributed system.

In general, names are characterized in the context of three attributes: structure, time and number.

System (internal) names are in use because user names cannot be effectively used at the computer level. Two types of such names have been developed: unstructured and structured. Structured names may have a field which indicates (may help to indicate) the location of an object. Capabilities, also structured names, are used for both identification and protection.

In those distributed operating systems where processes communicate indirectly, system names are mapped onto ports. Usually, this is performed by simple extraction of data from one field of a system name.

Users of a distributed system use text strings to name objects. In a user name one can distinguish different parts: syntactic, specified attributes and implicit attributes. These parts have an influence on mapping (resolution) user names onto system names, and functions performed by a naming facility.

When dealing with a naming facility at this level two types of components must be considered: structural and functional. There are two basic structural components of a naming facility: name server(s) – instances of a naming service, and agents – which act between name servers and their clients. Name service can be provided in a centralized or distributed manner.

There are two main functional components of a naming facility: database management, used to store name information, and name management; both of them are used to resolve a name. There are two major tasks of name management: name distribution, which deals with the assignment of authority for managing the name space to various name servers; and name resolution, which deals with locating the attributes of a specific object given its name.

Bibliography

Anderson M., Pose R.D. and Wallace C.S. (1986). A Password Capability System. *The Computer Journal,* **29**(1), 1–8

Birrell A.D. (1983). The Grapevine Interface. In *Grapevine: Two Papers and Report,* Xerox Palo Alto Research Center. Technical Report CSL–83–12

Birrell A., Levin R., Needham R.M. and Schroeder M.D. (1982). Grapevine: An Exercise in Distributed Computing. *Communications of the ACM,* **25**(4), 260–74

Birrell A., Jones M.B. and Wobber E.P. (1987). A Simple and Efficient Implementation for Small Databases. In *Proceedings of the Eleventh ACM Symposium on Operating Systems Principles,* 8–11 November, Austin, Texas, pp. 149–154

Boggs D.R. (1983). Internet Broadcasting. *Ph.D. Thesis,* Stanford University— Technical Report CSL–83–3 Palo Alto Research Center

Bowman M., Peterson L.L. and Yeatts A. (1989). *Univers: An Attribute-Based Name Server* TR 89–10, Department of Computer Science, University of Arizona

Cerf V.G. and Cain E. (1983). The DoD Internet Architecture Model. *Computer Networks,* **7**(5), 307–18

Cheriton D.R. (1986). Request-response and multicast interprocess communication in the V Kernel networking in open systems. *Lecture Notes in Computer Science No. 248,* pp. 296–312. New York: Springer-Verlag

Cheriton D.R. and Mann T.P. (1984). Uniform Access to Distributed Name Interpretation in the V-System. In *Proceedings of the 4th International Conference on Distributed Computing Systems,* San Francisco, California

Cheriton D.R. and Mann T.P. (1986). *A Decentralized Naming Facility.* Computer Science Department, Stanford University

Cheriton D.R. and Mann T.P. (1988). Decentralizing a Global Naming Service for Improved Performance and Fault Tolerance. *ACM Transactions on Computer Systems,* **7**(2), 147–83

Corsini P., Frosini G. and Lopriore L. (1984). The Implementation of Abstract Objects in a Capability Based Addressing Architecture. *The Computer Journal,* **27**(2), 127–34

Curtis R. and Wittie L. (1984). Global Naming in Distributed Systems. *IEEE Software*, pp. 76–80

Daniels D. and Spector A.Z. (1983). An Algorithm for Replicate Directories. In *Proceedings of the Second ACM Symposium on Principles of Distributed Computing*, Montreal

Dannenberg R.B. (1982). Resource Sharing in a Network of Personal Computers. *Ph.D. Thesis*, Department of Computer Science, Carnegie–Mellon University

Danthine A. (1982). Network Interconnection. In *Proceedings of IFIP/WG6.4 Symposium on Local Computer Networks* (Ravasio P.C., Hopkins G. and Naffah N. eds.), North-Holland Publishing Company, IFIP, pp. 289–308

Dennis J.B. and Van Horn E.C. (1966). Programming Semantics for Multiprogrammed Computers. *Communications of the ACM*, **9**(3), 143–55

Deschizeaux P., Griesner R. and Ladet P. (1979). A Real-Time Operating System for Microcomputer Network. *Sococo '79*, Prague

Ekanadham K. and Bernstein A.J. (1979). Conditional Capabilities. *IEEE Transactions on Software Engineering*, **SE–5**(5), 458–64

Fridrich M. and Older W. (1981). The FELIX File Server. In *Proceedings of the Eighth Symposium on Operating Systems Principles*, pp. 37–44

Friedrich G.R. and Eser F.W. (1983). Management Units and Interprocess Communication in DINOS. *Simens Forsch—and Entwicklung Ber.*, **Bd 12**(1), 21–7

Gifford D.K. (1979). Weighted Voting for Replicated Data. In *Proceedings of the Seventh Symposium on Operating Systems Principles*, pp. 150–162

Gligor V.D. and Lindsay B.G. (1979). Object Migration and Authentication. *IEEE Transactions on Software Engineering*, **SE–5**(6), 607–11

Hauzeur B.M. (1986). A Model for Naming, Addressing, and Routing. *ACM Transactions on Office Information Systems*, **4**(4), 293–311

Indulska J. and Goscinski A. (1989). A Simulation Study of Resources Addressing Methods for a Distributed Operating System. *Angewandte Informatik*, (6), 244–54

ISO (1981). Data Processing—Open Systems Interconnection—Basic Reference Model. *Computer Networks*, **5**, 81–118

ISO (1984). OSI Directory Concepts and Directory Access Service. Second Draft, *ISO*

Jansen P.A., Bux W. and Mumprecht E. (1983). Addressing and Naming in Local-Area Inter-Networks, IBM Zurich Research Laboratory. In *Proceedings of the Workshop on Ring Technology Local Area Networks*, Kent, U.K.

Jones A.K. (1980). Capability Architecture Revisited. *Operating Systems Review*, **14**(3), 33–5

Kohler W.H. (1981). A Survey of Techniques for Synchronization and Recovery in Decentralized Computer Systems. *Computing Surveys*, **13**(2), 149–83

Lampson B.W. (1981). Atomic Transactions in Distributed Systems—Architecture and Implementation (Lampson B.W., Paul M. and Siegert H.J., eds.) *Lecture Notes in Computer Science, No. 105*, Springer-Verlag

Lantz K.A., Edighoffer J.L. and Hitson B.L. (1986). Towards a Universal Directory Service. *Operating Systems Review*, **20**(2), 43–53

Leach P.J., Stumpf B.L., Hamilton J.A. and Levine P.H. (1982). UIDs as Internal Names in a Distributed File System. In *Proceedings of the Symposium on Principles of Distributed Computing,* Ottawa, pp. 34–41

Lin M.T., Tsoy D.P. and Lian R.C. (1982). *Design of a Network Operating System for the Distributed Double-Loop Computer Network (ODLCN), Local Computer Networks,* North-Holland Co., IFIP

Lopriore L. (1984). Capability Based Tagged Architectures. *IEEE Transactions on Computers,* **C–33**(9), 786–803

Mockapetris P.V. and Dunlap K.J. (1988). Development of the Domain Name System. In *Proceedings of the SIGCOMM '88 SYMPOSIUM on Communications Architectures & Protocols,* Stanford California, pp. 123–133

Oppen D.C. and Dalal Y.K. (1983). The Clearinghouse: A Decentralized Agent for Locating Named Objects in a Distributed Environment. *ACM Transactions on Office Information Systems,* **1**(3), 230–53

Peterson L.L. (1988). The Profile Naming Service. *ACM Transactions on Computer Systems,* **6**(4), 341–64

Popek G., Walker B., Chow J., Edwards D., Kline C., Rudisin G. and Thiel G. (1981). LOCUS: A Network Transparent, High Reliability Distributed System. In *Proceedings of the Eighth Symposium on Operating Systems Principles,* 14–16 December Pacific Grove, California, pp. 169–177

Redell D.D., Dalal Y.K., Horsly T.R., Lauer H.C., Lynch W.C., McJones P.R., Murray H.G. and Purcell S.C. (1980). Pilot: an Operating System for a Personal Computer. *Communications of the ACM,* **23**(2), 81–91

Shoch J.F. (1978). Internetwork Naming, Addressing, and Routing. In *Proceedings of the 17th IEEE Computer Society International Conference 4 (COMPCON)* pp. 72–79

Solomon M., Landweber L.H. and Neuhengen D. (1982). The CSNET Name Server. *Computer Networks,* **6**(3), 161–72

Sturgis H., Mitchell J. and Israel J. (1980). Issues in the Design and Use of a Distributed File System. *Operating Systems Review,* **14**(3), 55–69

Tanenbaum A.S. (1981). *Computer Networks.* Prentice-Hall

Tanenbaum A.S. and Mullender S.J. (1984). *The Design of a Capability-Based Distributed Operating System.* Rapport nr. IR–88 Subfaculteit Wiskunde en Informatica Vrije Universiteit, Amsterdam

Tanenbaum A.S. and van Renesse R. (1985). Distributed Operating Systems. *Computing Surveys,* **17**(4), 419–70

Terry D.B. (1984). An Analysis of Naming Conventions for Distributed Computer Systems. SIGCOMM'84 Tutorials & Symposium on Communications Architectures and Protocols. Montreal, Quebec, June 6–8, *Computer Communications Review,* **14**(2)

Terry D.B. (1985). *Distributed Name Servers: Naming and Caching in Large Distributed Computing Environments.* Palo Alto Research Center, CSL–85–1

Vance C.J.S. and Goscinski A. (1989). *The Logical Design of a Naming Facility for RODOS.* Technical Report CS89/15, Department of Computer Science, University College, The University of New South Wales

Walker B., Popek G., English R., Kline C. and Thiel G. (1983). The LOCUS Distributed Operating System. *Operating Systems Review,* **17**(5), 49–70

Watson R.W. (1981). Identifiers (Naming) in Distributed Systems. In *Distributed Systems—Architecture and Implementation. An Advanced Course* (Lampson B.W., Paul M. and Siegert H.J., eds.) *Lecture Notes in Computer Science, No. 105,* Springer-Verlag, pp. 191–210

8 Process management

User names	File service		Security	
	Collaboration of file servers Transaction service Directory service Flat file service Disk service	Access control	C o m m u n i c a t i o n	s e c u r i t y
Name distri-bution	Resource allocation	Deadlock detection	R e s o u r c e	p r o t e c t i o n
Name resolu-tion	Algorithms for load sharing and load balancing	Process synchro-nization		
			Capa-bilities	& Authen-tication
System names	Process management Operations on processes: local, remote Process migration		Access lists	Key manage-ment
Ports	Interprocess communication (and memory management) Interprocess communication primitives: Message Passing or Remote Procedure Call, or Transactions; Links or Ports		Info flow control	Data encryp-tion
Address-es			Security kernel	
Routes	Transport protocols supporting interprocess communication primitives			Encryp-tion protocols

We have considered three topics that relate to distributed process: remote interprocess communication, synchronization, and addressing and naming. The fourth and last topic, process management, is the subject of this chapter. The process management system interacts with a memory management system and interprocess communication system to provide the execution environment for processes. Thus, these four topics are the basis for designing the kernel of a distributed operating system.

Process management of a centralized operating system deals with mechanisms and policies for sharing a processor among a number of user processes. This is achieved by providing the capability to perform operations on processes, such as create, name, run, block, schedule, synchronize, interrupt or kill. Moreover, a priority may be associated with a process and this information may be used when performing operations on processes. Note that except for scheduling, all other operations are concerned with implementation of process management in that they address mechanism aspects.

The goal of process management in distributed operating systems is to share processing resources, spread around a network, among all processes. To achieve this goal in the best possible way it is necessary to provide mechanisms, and some policy, to perform operations on processes (create, name, rename, delete, run) locally and remotely; to synchronize processes; and to manage their states.

These mechanisms have to be extended from those in centralized operating systems to deal with distribution of resources, and distribution of information about states of these resources and states of other processes using or requesting them. Moreover, these mechanisms have to provide the distributed control and synchronization of all processes communicating as well as requesting resources.

Concurrency in distributed systems may be achieved in a very natural way due to the physical distribution of processing resources. Some problems must be overcome: management functions are performed based on incomplete and inaccurate state information. There is a lack of information consistency. Messages, which are used to communicate between processes, are delayed and also may be lost. Despite all these problems, the mechanisms should work such that a distributed computer system works as a unified system.

To improve response time, share and/or balance a work load, and to share resources, new operations are needed: remote execution of a process and process migration.

When and where to execute a process remotely, or migrate a process, and how to deal with process scheduling, are questions of policy. Separation of policy from mechanism is an important principle in this book. Thus, all policy questions associated with remote execution and process migration are addressed in the next chapter. Here, only the association between mechanism and policy is presented; we concentrate on mechanisms.

The solutions of the earliest problems faced in designing concurrent systems, that is, providing notations and mechanisms for parallel execution, and process management are based on the process concept. We do not have to review here the concept of a process, a state of a process, or a definition of concurrency. The reader can find an excellent presentation of these elements in Peterson and Silberschatz (1985). However, we think that it would be good to emphasize the most important features of distributed processes.

There are two topics of process management which should be taken into consideration when discussing distributed operating systems. The first is connected with concurrency in distributed systems, in particular with primitives that allow dynamic creation and termination of concurrent and distributed processes. The second, closely connected with the first, concerns remote operations which can be performed on processes. These two topics are discussed in Section 8.1.

In Section 8.2 distributed processes are discussed. In particular, lightweight and mediumweight processes, and process scheduling are presented. Section 8.3 deals with remote operations on processes: creation and termination, and port and link creation and destruction.

Remote execution is discussed in Section 8.4. Some topics discussed are models of remote execution, selection of remote site and implementation of remote execution. Remote execution in the V-system and NEST are used as examples.

Section 8.5 deals with process migration, which is one of the basic mechanisms of distributed operating systems. The following topics are discussed: basic problems of process migration, handling message delivery, design decisions and process migration mechanisms. To demonstrate that the cost of process migration depends on interprocess communication facilities and the size of a computation context, process migration mechanisms in DEMOS/MP, Charlotte, and in the V-system are discussed.

To demonstrate the further ways of improving process migration performance, two distinct approaches are given: one based on the copy-on-reference mechanisms, and the second oriented toward moving objects. The possibility of process migration in a heterogeneous environment is also mentioned.

8.1 Concurrent execution of processes

Process management deals with processes and operations on processes. To carry out operations on processes such as create, delete, run, schedule and synchronize, locally and remotely, it is necessary to provide a notation to specify concurrent execution. In this section we discuss some representative constructs which allow the expression of concurrent execution.

There are two basic groups of primitive constructs that allow the creation and termination of concurrent processes: low level constructs and higher-level language constructs. Each of these constructs can be used to specify computations having either a static number of processes or, together with process-creation mechanisms, a dynamic number of processes.

8.1.1 Low level constructs

Fork and **join** primitives are the first low level language constructs for specifying concurrency that allow dynamic creation and termination of concurrent processes. They were introduced by Convay (1963) and Dennis and Horn (1966). When a **fork** instruction is executed by a process, a second new process, a child process, is created. This process will execute concurrently with its creator, often called the parent process.

To synchronize with completion of a child process, the parent process can execute a **join** primitive. Thus, a **join** operation combines the execution of two processes into one process. **Join** has been specified in several ways (see Andrews and Schneider 1983, and Peterson and Silberschatz 1985).

Andrews and Schneider assume that only the parent process may execute a **join**. In this case the parent waits for the child process or children processes to terminate before the parent may proceed. Thus, we observe a synchronization with completion of the invoked routine. Executing **join** delays the invoking routine until the designated invoked routine has terminated. The use of **fork** and **join** based on Andrews and Schneider's specification is presented in Fig. 8.1.

```
program P1;              program P2;
.......                     .......
.......                     .......
.......                     .......
fork P2;                    .......
.......                     .......
join P2;              end
.......                     .......
.......                     .......
```

Fig. 8.1 The use of **form** and **join** as specified by Andrews and Schneider.

```
computation P1;              computation P2;
   .......                      .......
   .......                      .......
   .......                      .......
fork P2;                        .......
   .......                      .......
join P2;                        .......
                                .......
                             join P1
```

Fig. 8.2 The use of **form** and **join** according to the Peterson and Silberschatz specification.

According to Peterson and Silberschatz, each of the two computations, which may execute with different speeds, must request to be joined with the other. In this case, if two processes both execute a **join**, the process that executes the **join** first is terminated, while the second computation is allowed to continue. In the case where three processes are to be joined, the first two to execute the **join** are terminated, whereas the third is allowed to continue. The use of **fork** and **join** based on Peterson and Silberschatz specification is presented in Fig. 8.2.

The **fork** and **join** primitives have great expressive power for writing concurrent programs. They have been widely used in many systems. However, this construct has one very important disadvantage: the **fork** instruction can be used in an undisciplined manner, thus producing unstructured code. That is because this primitive is similar to the **go-to** statement.

8.1.2 Higher-level language constructs

The **cobegin** and **coend** statement is a construct which provides a structured way of denoting concurrent execution of processes and a structured way to dynamically create and terminate processes (Dijkstra 1968, Wegner and Smolka 1983). This statement has the following form

cobegin P_1; P_2; . . . ; P_N **coend**

When a **cobegin** primitive is executed, two or more processes are created. These processes will proceed concurrently. All processes terminate together when all reached the execution of the **coend** statement.

The **cobegin** and **coend** construct is not as powerful as **fork** and **join**. It provides only a very weak form of synchronization that is only sufficient if the processes do not cooperate or share variables. However, it is sufficient for specifying most concurrent computations.

8.1.3 Distributed programming language primitives

Modern concurrent programming languages use both the **fork/join** primitive or **cobegin/coend** primitives to implement concurrency. Note that, in general, routines that may be executed concurrently are explicitly declared as processes.

Distributed Processes (Brinch Hansen 1978) and SR (Andrews 1981) use system declarations equivalent to a **cobegin** that spawns a fixed number of processes that will not grow or diminish during execution. This implies static systems of processes. Argus (Liskov and Scheifler 1983) includes the **cobegin** primitive explicitly. In Concurrent Pascal, invocation of a process by a call spawns a process, **fork** primitive, which terminates when its sequential execution terminates.

In the literature, one can find a variety of program structures that have been proposed to model concurrently executing processes and to construct distributed programs. For example, CSP is based on parallel processes (Hoare 1978), DP is based on distributed processes (Brinch Hansen 1978), ADA is based on tasks and packages (Gehani 1983), (Burns *et al.* 1987), and CMAY is based on entities and messages (Bagrodia and Chandy 1985). A summary of the primitives provided by these four distributed programming languages is given in Table 8.1,

Table 8.1 Comparison of CSP, DP, ADA, and CMAY.

	CSP	DP	ADA	CMAY
System configuration	distributed or centralized	distributed	distributed or centralized	distributed or centralized
Process representation	parallel processes	distributed processes	tasks	entities
Process creation	dynamic	static	dynamic	dynamic
Process termination	automatic		explicit, uncontrolled	explicit, autonomous
Process variables	restricted	No	Yes	Yes
Communication primitives	rendezvous	remote procedure call	remote procedure call via rendezvous	buffered message passing
Synchronization primitives	rendezvous and input guards	guarded region conditional delay	rendezvous and input guards	conditional receives
Recursion	No	No	Yes	No

adapted from Bagrodia and Chandy (1985). We will not discuss them further in this book. A reader may find more about distributed programming languages and their primitives in the literature.

8.2 Distributed processes

The concept of a **sequential process** has been introduced to cope with the highly nondeterministic nature of a computation environment. A sequential process is a program in execution. In other words it is the activity which results from the execution of a program with its data by a sequential processor. Such an execution must progress in a sequential fashion. A process needs certain resources such as processor, memory, files and I/O devices to accomplish its task. These resources are given to the process when it is created and/or when it requests them.

Processes within a computer system do not act in isolation. Some important reasons to run processes concurrently are sharing physical and logical resources and computation speedup. We say that **processes are concurrent** if their execution overlaps in time. Concurrent processes can be executed either by allowing them to share one or more processors; referred to as **multiprogramming**, or by running each process on its own processor; physical concurrency. In the later case, if the processors share a common memory, the approach is referred to as **multiprocessing**. When processors are connected by a network (local or wide) we are dealing with **distributed processing**.

8.2.1 Description and states of processes

In a distributed system, as in a centralized one, processes have to be described to the managing system. Every process is represented by a data structure containing its basic state, identification, its creator, priority, address space and stack. (The address space is the area of memory to which a process has direct access. The stack is the local memory area which is located in the process workspace.) These data structures are referred to as **process control blocks** or **process descriptors**. All of them together represent the state of a system. However, in the case of a distributed operating system, process control blocks are distributed among all connected computers.

Moreover, every process, in a centralized system as well as in a distributed one, may exist in many different states – ready, running, waiting or suspended. However, in a distributed system, a process being in different states may be located in different computers (nodes). Such a possibility is illustrated in Fig. 4.8. Thus, a **distributed process** is one that can migrate to execute on a remote node, and whose process control block and states are distributed among computers (nodes) of a distributed computer system.

Performing a task defined by a user (such as a programmer or a production process control system) in a computer system requires executing one or more concurrent processes that communicate with each other. In a distributed system either all processes of a single task may be running on one computer (physical node), or they can be spread among several computers. The latter means that processes are migrated from a source computer to another computer, more suitable at given time because it is idle or lightly loaded. The main reason for this is load balancing, and/or the requirement for reducing the computation time of the given process. This results in the possibility of different mappings of tasks and their processes (seen as logical nodes of a distributed system) onto computers (physical nodes). Figs. 8.3(a) and 8.3(b) illustrate examples of mapping of tasks and their processes onto computers in distributed systems without migration and with migration, respectively.

In these figures dotted lines show mappings of tasks and processes onto computers, and left-right arrows indicate communications paths between several processes. Computer 3 shown in Fig. 8.3(a) is idle, while Computers 1 and 4 seem to be overloaded.

To improve performance, as illustrated in Fig. 8.3(b), task T_2, with its processes P_{21} and P_{22}, was migrated to Computer 3; also task T_5 (with its process P_{53}) was moved to Computer 3 in order to reduce traffic implied by exchange messages between processes P_{53} and P_{22}. Process P_{13} migrated to Computer 2 in order to decrease the load of Computer 1.

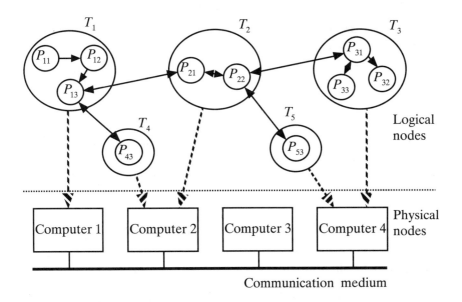

Fig. 8.3(a) Example of mapping of tasks and their processes onto computers in a distributed system without migration; T_i – task, P_{ij} – process.

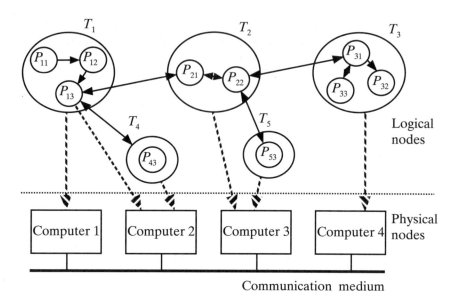

Fig. 8.3(b) Example of mapping of tasks and their processes onto computers in a distributed system with migration; task T_2 (processes P_{21} and P_{22}) migrated to Computer 3; process P_{13} migrated also to Computer 2, and task T_5 migrated to Computer 3.

Distributed processes can be based on either

(1)   a **static process model** – in which all processes are created when a task program is initiated, or

(2)   a **dynamic process model** – which allows an arbitrary number of processes to be created and destroyed during the lifetime of a task.

These two models are associated with different types of environment. For example, the static model is used in the production process control environment, for which a static number of processes are created and they never terminate. The dynamic process model is applicable for example in university and research environments.

8.2.2   Lightweight, heavyweight and mediumweight processes

There are three possible types of processes supported by distributed operating systems: lightweight, heavyweight and mediumweight processes. They are illustrated in Fig. 8.4.

The division of processes into these three types, as shown in the figure, is based on the degree of shared memory; processes under distributed operating systems may or may not share memory.

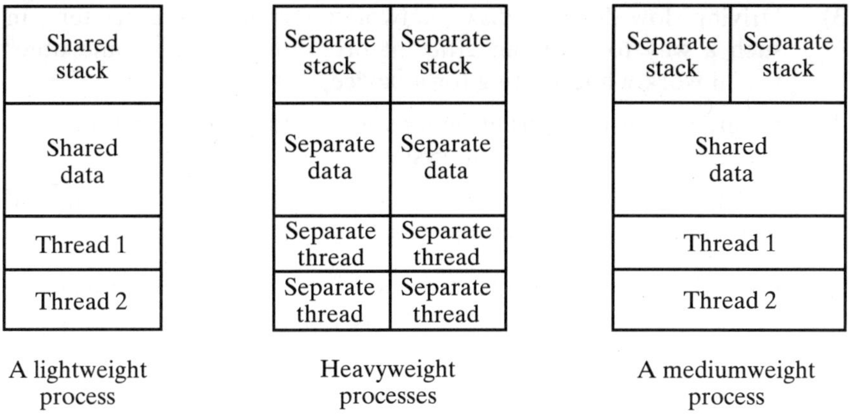

Shared stack		Separate stack	Separate stack		Separate stack	Separate stack
Shared data		Separate data	Separate data		Shared data	
Thread 1		Separate thread	Separate thread		Thread 1	
Thread 2		Separate thread	Separate thread		Thread 2	

A lightweight process	Heavyweight processes	A mediumweight process

Fig. 8.4 Three possible types of processes.

Before we discuss these three types we have to introduce the concept of a thread. A **thread** is a piece of executable code which has access to data and stack. It is not necessarily a process because it may not have a separate entry in a process control block. Sharing data space provides efficient communication between threads. However, sharing the same stack gives little interthread protection.

A **lightweight process** is one which contains more than one thread in it; all of them use the same text, data and stack (sometimes these processes are called threads). Lightweight processes execute in a common memory partition on a uniprocessor or on a single shared memory multiprocessor. This means that the computer's addressing hardware is configured in such a way as to permit the processes (threads) to read and write the same memory locations.

Lightweight means that process (thread) creation, existence, killing and synchronization primitives are so cheap compared with adequate primitives of heavyweight processes, that the programmer will use them for all concurrency needs. This results in the cheap utilization of the processors.

Major reasons for providing memory sharing among user processes are:

(1) Reduction of the overheads of interprocess communication and process-to-process transitions. This is crucial not only in distributed systems but also in multiprocessors. In the latter systems, communication performance is the most important factor. Shared memory provides the fastest possible communication;

(2) Development of a server(s) which can handle clients' requests in parallel, instead of either serializing them or creating one server process per client;

(3)   Driving slow devices (disks, networks, terminals and printers) in such a way to allow an efficient program of doing some other useful work while waiting for a device;

(4)   Programming concurrent actions expected by human users (for example, a modern window system);

(5)   A set of processes in a shared address space is the most natural way to program many applications.

A **heavyweight process** is a standard one which does not share memory with other processes; there is only one thread in this process. All heavyweight processes run in separate address space, and have separate entry in a process control block.

A **mediumweight process** is a compromise between lightweight and heavyweight process types. There are several threads of control, however each has its own stack. It results in better interthread protection than between threads in lightweight processes, while still allowing efficient communication. Each thread is considered as a separate process.

Different distributed operating systems support different types of processes. The Charlotte distributed operating system is an example of a system that does not permit memory sharing among processes – it supports only heavyweight processes. There are few distributed operating systems that support more than one type of processes. In the V-system, heavyweight and mediumweight processes coexist. The mediumweight processes belong to a team; all processes with the same address space are said to be on the same team. Data sharing is done through message passing. However, shared memory can be implemented through servers which manage bounded buffers (Cheriton 1984, Berglund 1986). The team concept is used also in the PEACE operating system (Schroder 1987), where a team specifies a common execution domain for a certain group of lightweight processes. All processes of a team share the same access rights onto PEACE objects (for example, a file, device, address space, team, process).

In Mach, an individual flow of control within a task, which is an execution environment of the basic unit of resource, is called a thread. A thread running within a task would then be a process. It is typical to have few tasks but many threads within those tasks. This implies that optimization can be concentrated on thread creation and destruction rather than on the optimization of task creation and destruction. Mach permits both copy-on-write and read/write sharing of memory between tasks where a task is the basic unit of resource allocation including a paged address space and protected access to system resources) (Rashid *et al.* 1987). The former is typically the result of large message transfer. The latter can be created by allocating a memory region and setting its inheritance attribute. As a result, each created child task shares the memory of its parent according to its inheritance value.

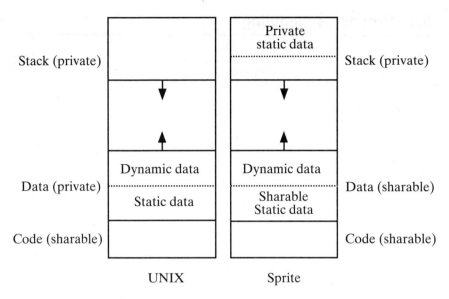

Fig. 8.5 The organization of virtual memory in traditional UNIX and Sprite {adapted from Ousterhout *et al.* (1988)}.

A very simple form of memory sharing is provided by Sprite (Ousterhout *et al.* 1988). When a process creates a new process (by invoking the Proc_Fork kernel call) it may request that the child process share the parent's data segment. The stack segment which contains procedure invocation records and private process data is not shared – it is private to each process. This sharing is based on the 'all-or-nothing' idea that a process cannot share part of its data segment with one process and part of it with another process. Sprite's memory sharing is illustrated in Fig. 8.5.

In this figure one can see the organization of virtual memory in traditional UNIX and Sprite. In UNIX, processes may share code, but not data and stack. In Sprite, the data segment may be shared between processes. This includes statically allocated and dynamic data. Private data may be stored at the top of the stack segment.

The distributed operating systems that support lightweight or mediumweight processes offer similar facilities, but they differ in basic concepts and details. Nevertheless, it is possible to distinguish the following commonly used mechanisms: lightweight or mediumweight process creation, mutual exclusion, waiting for events, and getting out of an unwanted long-term wait.

The reader interested in the design of the lightweight and mediumweight process facility can refer to (Cheriton 1984, 1988, Rashid *et al.* 1987 and Birrell 1989).

8.3 Process scheduling

Though process scheduling is associated with policy, here we introduce basic concepts associated with this operation. This will help a reader to understand the need for performing operations such as remote execution and migration on remote processes.

In operating systems there is a close association between processes and resources. For clarity of presentation and study, it is good to discuss these two research and design issues separately. It is, however, useful to emphasize this association where it is most visible and natural in the area of process scheduling.

A processor is a special resource and requires separate treatment, because processes waiting for it are not logically blocked – they are in the special state 'ready'. Thus, the problem is how to allocate ready processes to an available processor. This task is usually divided into two parts. The first is referred to as process scheduling. It implements decision-making policies that determine the order in which ready processes may share a processor. This part is known as a scheduler. The second part is performed by a process dispatcher, which removes the process determined by the scheduler from the ready queue, changes its status, and loads the processor state. Because the latter part is performed locally and it does not have any special implication for a distributing operating system, we will not discuss it here any further.

A distributed scheduling policy can be divided into two components:

(1) A local scheduling discipline which determines how a processor (at a single node) is allocated among its resident processes; and

(2) A load distributing strategy which distributes the overall distributed system workload among the processors at different nodes through process migration.

Different scheduling algorithms may be used to determine locally the order in which active processes should compete for the use of a processor. For example, the Charlotte distributed operating system uses round-robin scheduling (Finkel *et al.* 1983), whereas the V-system uses priority scheduling (Cheriton 1984). The Accent's scheduling system provides time slice scheduling with sixteen priority levels. To enable time-critical processes to meet their demands, pre-emption is provided. Also ageing is provided to support some degree of fairness in scheduling (Rashid and Robertson 1981). However, local scheduling does not guarantee the best performance from an individual process point of view as well as a global system.

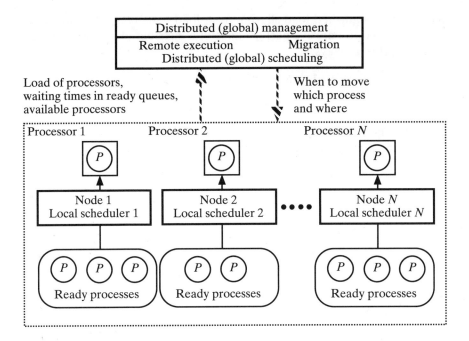

Fig. 8.6 Local and distributed scheduling in a distributed system.

Local scheduling is not sufficient; processes should be scheduled globally. Algorithms which are used for this purpose are usually called load sharing and load balancing algorithms, and the whole operations are called load sharing and load balancing, respectively. A two level management system providing local as well as global scheduling is illustrated in Fig. 8.6.

The reader can easily perceive that in distributed operating systems, process and resource management are very closely connected to local and distributed scheduling. There are two basic problems associated with distributed management, in particular, with the determination of the order in which processes should compete for the use of distributed processor:

(1)   Performing remote operations on processes. The system should be able to create, destroy (terminate), suspend, migrate a process, to share or balance a load. This process management problem is oriented towards mechanisms, and is discussed in the following sections of this chapter.

(2)   Distributed resource management – how to manage resource allocation and provide load balance. This problem is oriented towards policy, and is discussed in the next chapter.

We have distinguished load sharing from load balancing. They are each strategies used to improve performance of a distributed system, but they work in different ways:

(1) The goal of load sharing algorithms is to assure that no computer (processor) is idle while some processors are overloaded, and processes wait for service.

(2) The goal of load balancing algorithms is to equalize the workload among processors at different nodes.

Note that both load sharing and load balancing use process migration.

8.4 Remote operations on processes

In centralized operating systems, a set of primitive kernel operations is defined to implement the high level concept of a process. These primitives are used to maintain the state of an operating system. Usually, the following primitive operations are defined on processes: create a new process, destroy (terminate) a process, suspend a process, resume a process change its status to ready and set a new priority for the process.

Distributed operating systems should support local as well as remote operations on processes. In the ideal case all operations on remote processes should be transparent to the user. Transparent support for remote processes requires primitives and facilities to create a process, destroy a process, suspend a process, resume a process, allocate/create a port, deallocate/destroy a port, run a process on a remote computer and migrate a process. We now discuss the most important of these facilities.

8.4.1 Process creation on a remote computer

A model solution of process creation in distributed operating systems is used in the V-system (Cheriton 1984). This process is performed in the same way locally and remotely; due to the IPC facilities, remote operations work 'for free'. A (remote) process is created by the **CreateProcess** library stub routine, which formats and sends a requesting message to the kernel server on the (remote) machine executing that process. Processes can be created dynamically. When a process is created, it is assigned a unique process identification (PID) that is subsequently used to specify that process. A newly created process is in the state **awaiting reply** from its parent. This is to allow a parent to pass initial data to start its child's execution.

Process creation is done by some create operation (such as **fork** in UNIX). Several possible implementations exist:

(1)   Execution – concurrent versus sequential.

(a)   The parent continues to execute concurrently with its children. This possibility is adopted in the fork/join constructs.

(b)   The parent waits until all its children have terminated. This possibility is adopted in the concurrent statements.

(2)   Sharing – all versus partial.

(a)   The children share only a subset of their parent's variables. This approach is adopted in the UNIX operating system in the following way:

When process P_i creates a new process P_j, this new process has an independent memory image of P_i, including access permission to all open files of P_i. The variables accessible to P_i cannot be accessed by P_j since P_i and P_j have independent memory images. This implies that in UNIX, P_i and P_j can only communicate by the use of shared files. The UNIX **fork** operation is illustrated in Fig. 8.7.

The UNIX **fork** call is used to create processes remotely in the LOCUS distributed operating system. This is done in a manner as easy as creating the process locally. A creation (execution) site can be specified by a calling process or dynamically selected. No rebinding is needed and the mechanism is entirely transparent.

(b)   The parent and children share all variables in common. This approach is adopted in both the fork/join constructs and in the concurrent statements.

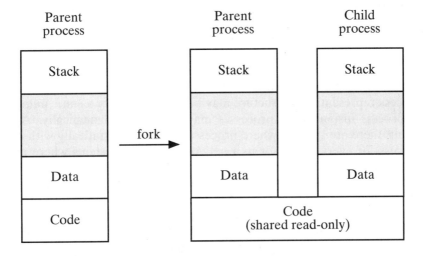

Fig. 8.7   The UNIX **fork** operation.

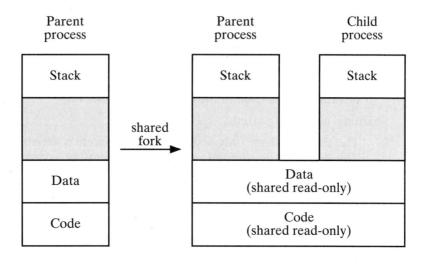

Fig. 8.8   The Sprite shared **fork** operation {adapted from Ousterhout *et al.* (1988)}.

The UNIX **fork** primitive may be extended. The Sprite network operating system creates a new process by invoking the Proc_fork kernel call. It may request a traditional, UNIX **fork** or it may request that the new process share the parent's data segment (Fig. 8.8).

Another problem associated with creation of a process is port allocation. A process may be created with a data port which it owns and a service port which is owned by a system. These ports are used to communicate with the system. The problem is how a process can start communication with other processes. A parent process which creates a process may give this child process a set of ports – they can then be used immediately. Another solution is to give a child process ports to communicate with the system only. This implies that such a process has to demand that ports be created when it needs to communicate with other processes.

Notice that, depending on the nature of intended applications, the process representation structure may be used to specify a static number of process instances, or processes may be created dynamically. As a result, there are systems where processes are created statically with one process for every processor in a network, and also systems where processes are created dynamically, but with a fixed upper bound on the number of processes that can be created.

One very important aspect of process creation is the allocation of processes among available processors. There are two approaches. In the first, the distributed program configuration is controlled by the system (language or operating system). The system allocates all processes and may cause and control migration of these processes. As a result, the mapping of processes onto the network is completely transparent to the user. The advantage of this approach is transparency; the disadvantage is the need for a sophisticated distributed operating system. In the second approach, the programmer creates the processes on specific processors. In this case the distributed operating system is much simpler, but the programmer must be involved in all allocation decisions.

8.4.2 Termination of processes remotely

Processes in some systems may exist forever. No process termination mechanisms are then required.

In other applications, processes may need to be terminated. Several different process termination mechanisms exist. In some systems, a process terminates automatically when the command list has been executed (CSP). Another possibility is that a process can cause the termination of another process by issuing the command **kill** id, where id is the name of the process to be terminated. The **kill** operation can usually only be invoked by the parent of the process to be terminated. The parent may terminate the execution of one of its children for a variety of reasons, for example, the child has exceeded its usage of some of the resources it has been allocated, or the task assigned to the child is no longer required.

In some systems, the abort statement may be used to terminate any process. Moreover, there are systems in which a process terminates itself by executing a termination statement (CMAY [Bagrodia and Chandy 1985]). In such a system a process cannot be terminated by another process.

In the V-system, a process can be dynamically destroyed by the sending of a message to the kernel server process executing on a computer on which the particular process runs. When a process is destroyed, it stops executing, its PID becomes invalid, all processes blocked on it become unblocked, and all its children are also destroyed.

8.4.3 Port and link creation and destruction

In many systems interprocess communication is based upon the notion of passing messages between ports. A port can be created:

- when a process is created, or
- when a process demands it.

Usually, only the creator of a port has the ability to receive messages on that port. Send-rights can be passed on by the creator to any number of processes with which it wishes to communicate. Receive-rights can be but are usually not passed on.

A parent process which creates a child process may give the child process sets of input and output ports which the child may utilize immediately: these ports are useful for providing a new process access to other processes in the network.

In some cases, a process can be created with two ports: a data port which is owned by this process, and a service port which is owned by an operating system. The latter is used for communication of this process with the operating system.

A port can exist:

- as long as a process is alive – when a process is destroyed all ports it possesses are destroyed, or

- until it is destroyed by an owner process – this operation can be performed by a process at nearly any time.

We recall that in some distributed operating systems (Roscoe [Solomon and Finkel 1979], Charlotte [Finkel *et al.* 1983], DEMOS/MP [Miller *et al.* 1986]) the link concept is used for communication, naming, and protection. For example, a Charlotte link is a connection between two processes, each of which has a capability to one end of the link. A process that wishes to communicate with another process has to have a link. A new link is created as a result of the **MakeLink** kernel call. Link identifiers (two ends) are assigned by the kernel when the link is formed.

A process may give its end of a link away by enclosing it in a message addressed to another process. A receiver of this message gets a new link (to which it arbitrarily assigns a link identifier). A process at the other end of a link is not aware that the second end has moved.

A process may destroy a link in which it is no longer interested. This operation is performed by submitting a **LinkDestroy** request to the kernel, even if communication operations are pending on that link. The process is blocked until the kernel completes its work.

8.5 Remote execution

Remote execution and migration of processes are two load sharing and load balancing concepts that allow a user of his/her own workstation to offload processes onto idle or lightly loaded workstations in a distributed computer system. A remote execution facility permits processes to be created on remote workstations, but does not allow the processes to be moved once initiated. A process migration facility permits an initialized process to be moved to another computer and executed there.

The flow of execution of a remotely executing process and of a migrating process are illustrated in Fig. 8.9, (a) and (b), respectively. In this section we discuss the remote execution of processes. The second facility is discussed in the following section.

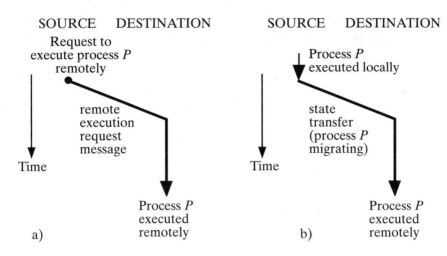

Fig. 8.9 Flow of execution: (a) of a remotely executing process, (b) of a migrating process.

A load sharing load and load balancing policy can be divided into three parts:

(1)   The **transfer policy** – to determine whether to execute a process locally or remotely;

(2)   The **selection policy** – to determine which process should be transferred;

(3)   The **location policy** – to determine to which computer (node) a selected process should be transferred.

A load sharing and load balancing mechanism provide facilities to implement a policy.

Remote execution in homogeneous and heterogeneous environments
One of the most important issues in remote execution is the ease with which remote resources can be made available to users (processes working on their behalf). In this context it is necessary to consider homogeneous and heterogeneous environments and resources.

Homogeneous environments   In this case, the only problems of a remote execution facility are migration of a state from the source computer to the destination computer, and which tools should be provided to aid remote execution.

Tools can be provided at three different levels:

(1)   The programming level where the possible tools are remote procedure calls and shared memory paradigms;

(2)   The command level where remote system utilities such as Berkely UNIX remote file copy and remote shell execution can be used to provide distributed file access. Such access can be transparent, as in LOCUS (Walker *et al.* 1983) and Eden (Almes *et al.* 1985);

(3)   Remote execution systems such as Butler (Dannenberg 1982), remote execution facility in the V-system, and NEST (Agrawal and Ezzat 1987). These systems are based on different models; they will be discussed in the following sections.

Heterogeneous environments   Remote execution is both more desirable and more difficult to provide in these environments. It is more desirable because of the variety of computation and peripheral resources which can be used by users to do their different tasks. On the other hand, the variety of resources requires a remote execution facility which can accommodate the different environments and also deal with the problems of any homogeneous environment. This results in both translation and migration of the state, respectively.

The following problems are generated by heterogeneity:

(1)   Object naming because in some large distributed systems it is impossible to assume the existence of a global name space. This problem can be attacked by using attributed names (see Chapter 7), and/or a naming system proposed in Cheriton and Mann (1989);

(2)   How to describe a service to execute, a problem which is implied by differences in syntax and semantics in command lines among systems;

(3)   Binary translation of data as it moves from one architecture to another. See Section 8.5.10.

The possibility of creation of new network services utilizing existing applications is presented in Bershad and Levy (1988).

Remote execution requirements
There are three very important requirements imposed on remote process execution.

(1)   There should be a mechanism for propagating information on the availability of idle (or lightly loaded) workstations, or for identifying such workstations in a distributed system.

This is very closely associated with the resource management system, and will be discussed in detail in the next chapter. Here we present only the necessary information to create a complete image of remote process execution.

(2)   Pre-emption. The owner of a workstation suffers degraded performance when someone else's process executes remotely on the

workstation. Remote use of a workstation must be able to be stopped when the owner of that workstation claims it.

(3) Remote execution should be performed just as easily as running the process locally. This means that the execution of a process should be location-independent.

In other words, remote execution should be pre-emptable and transparent, where the term pre-emptable means here that a remotely-executed program can be migrated elsewhere on demand. Transparency will be discussed now in more detail, because it is a basis for location independent remote execution.

8.5.1 Models of location-independent remote execution

The development of remote execution facilities is based on a model of location-independent remote execution. Different models use different definitions of transparency. There are two main definitions of transparent execution. According to the first, remote execution is considered to be transparent if programs need not be written with special provisions for executing remotely. The second definition is oriented towards network-transparent remote execution, which depends on the network transparency of interprocess communication primitives and the use of global naming.

The first definition was used by Agrawal and Ezzat (1987) for the development of location-independent remote execution in NEST – a UNIX-like distributed operating system. This model provides location-independence of process execution by preserving the process view of the file system, parent-child relationships, process groups, and process signalling within a logical machine boundary. The logical machine has been defined as a collection of processes, both local and remote, that belong to a physical machine. This logical machine is illustrated in Fig. 8.10.

There are two main parts to this model: the client machine from which a process for remote execution is initiated, and the server machine on which the task is executed. In the NEST system, the authors wanted to preserve all UNIX system capabilities transparently within the logical machine. That was the main goal of their project. One of the features of their system, which distinguishes it from other systems, is the autonomy of each workstation, that is, each workstation has its own separate root directory.

Other features of NEST are that:

- a remote process must use the file system that existed on the originating computer,
- a remote process must be able to send/receive all standard UNIX system signals to/from any process within the logical computer,
- the process groups must be preserved within the logical machine,

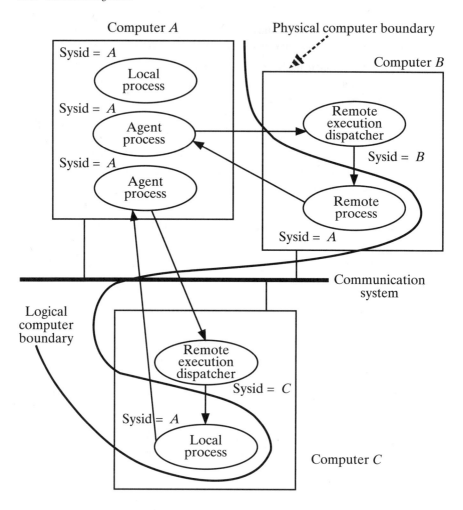

Fig. 8.10   Logical computer model {adapted from Agrawal and Ezzat (1987)}.

- the parent-child tree-based relation must be preserved within the logical machine, and

- a remote process must be able to access its remote controlling terminal transparently.

A remote execution facility based on the second transparency model was developed for the V-system (Theimer *et al.* 1985). This facility allows a user to offload programs onto idle workstations. Only those programs that do not require low-level access to the hardware devices of the machine from which they originated can be executed remotely.

Based on this model, programs should be provided with a network-transparent execution environment. This guarantees that remote execution is the same as execution on the local machine. In the V-system there are also logical hosts, defined as groups of V address spaces and their associated processes. An execution environment includes the names, operations and data with which the program can interact during execution.

8.5.2   Selection of an execution site

A computer for the remote execution of a process can be selected on the basis of two different approaches. The first is based on propagating information about the available (idle) computer servers and/or requests for a server by a client. The second approach, requiring a more sophisticated distributed operating systems, is based on information provided by the resource management systems, in particular resource managers. In this case it is the responsibility of a resource manager (processor manager) to find a computer for remote execution and perform all necessary operations. Here, we discuss the first approach. The second approach is considered in the next chapter.

The selection of an execution computer based on the first approach can be performed on the basis of information stored by each workstation in a locally maintained database. Such a database contains

- data on servers in which this workstation is interested, and
- data on clients to which it may lend resources.

Two operations on this database should be possible: adding to the server pool, and withdrawing from the pool:

Adding a workstation to the server pool is performed using the following algorithm:

- When a server decides to make itself available, it broadcasts a message to all the clients or multicasts a message to those which are in its database.
- All clients register the availability of a given server.
- If a client does not hear the advertisement message (a client computer is down), this message is ignored. The server pretends that the client has heard the message and registers the client in the database.

Withdrawing a workstation from the pool is performed using the following algorithm:

- When a server decides to withdraw itself from the pool, it broadcasts a message to all the clients or multicasts to those to which an advertisement was earlier issued.

- A client node, after receiving the withdrawal message, removes the server from its available servers list.

- If a client does not hear the withdraw message (a client computer is down), this message is ignored. The server pretends that the client has heard the message and updates its database.

A client wanting to execute a process remotely must select an execution computer. Performing this operation depends on the state of the client. If the client was active and had registered all advertisement messages, it can make a selection on the basis of the content of its database of servers in which it is interested. The decision depends on a selection strategy (for example, FIFO, a computer with the smallest load). If a client's computer was down when servers advertised their availability, it must collect information about available servers. After gathering the information, it can select a server. This gathering can be performed in the following way:

(1) A client that comes up sends a request message to all servers or multicasts only to those which are known to it (they are stored in its server database), asking for their availability status (inquiry request).

(2) All servers currently down do not hear this message.

(3) A currently unavailable server sends a negative acknowledgement message.

(4) An available server that receives an inquiry request message checks its clients' database. It responds positively if an advertisement was sent earlier to that client. Otherwise, it sends a negative acknowledgement.

(5) After receiving positive acknowledgements, the client updates its database of servers.

8.5.3 Implementation of remote execution

If an execution operation is to occur remotely, then the execution site is selected and the process is effectively moved at that time. In the new location it is necessary to initialize the new process's environment correctly. No rebinding or any other action should be needed.

It is hard to present a general approach to building the new process's environment, because the operations are very closely associated with the architecture and process creation primitives of a particular computer system. We will present two different implementations of remote execution: remote execution in the V-system (Theimer *et al.* 1985) and remote execution in NEST (Agrawal and Ezzat 1987).

Remote execution in the V-system

A remote execution of a V program is initiated by typing at the command interpreter level:

<program><arguments>@<machine-name>

to execute the specified program on a defined computer,

or   <program><arguments>@*

to execute the specified program on any randomly chosen computer. A standard library routine provides a similar facility that can be invoked by any program. The problem is what should be done to execute a program remotely.

Remote execution is very similar to local execution. There are two stages of a local execution of a process in the V-system: initialization and execution. Initialization of a local execution requires sending a request to the local program manager to create a new address space and load a specified program image file into this address space.

The program manager performs the following operations or actions. It uses the kernel server to set up the address space and create an initial process. This initial process waits for a reply from its creator. Next, it turns over control of the newly created process to the requester by forwarding the newly created process to it. After completing these operations, the requester initializes the new program space with program arguments, default I/O, and 'environment variables'. Finally, it starts execution of a program by replying to its initial process. Communication between programs during creation is illustrated in Fig. 8.11.

Initialization of a remote execution requires sending a query to the specified remote program manager requesting a response with an amount of processor and memory resources available. The V-system uses the process group mechanism, which allows a message to be sent to a group of processes. As a result, one or several responses are received. In the latter case, a client selects the program manager that responded first, since that is generally the least loaded host. Finally, a request is sent to that program manager to create a new address space and load a specified program image file into this address space.

Programs are provided in the V-system with a network-transparent execution environment. This feature, and the assumption that programs do not directly access hardware devices, implies that remote program execution appears the same as a local program execution. That is manifested in the following:

(1)   The program address space is initialized the same as when the program is executed locally.

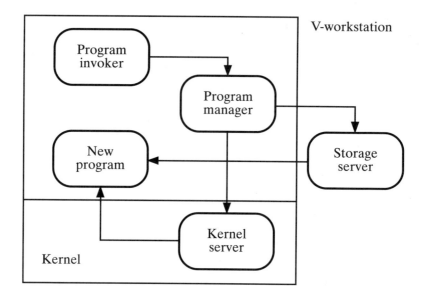

Fig. 8.11   Communication during program creation {adapted from Theimer *et al.* (1985)}.

(2)   All references by the program outside its address space are performed using network-transparent primitives and globally unique identifiers.

(3)   The kernel server and program manager provide identical services for remotely executing programs as the local kernel server and program manager provide for locally executing programs.

The authors of the V-system conclude that transparent pre-emptable remote execution of programs is feasible.

Remote execution in NEST

In NEST, remote execution of an operation, for example, background execution, standard I/O redirection, formally the 'command string', can be performed by using the command

    rexec [-s server-name] 'command string'

The target computer server is specified by server-name. A group of computer names can be specified also. In this case the system automatically selects a computer for the execution of the command string according to some optimization criteria. Such criteria as random or cyclic selection or balancing the load on computer servers are suggested for use.

    The implementation of remote execution in the NEST system is based on a network server process which resides in each computer connected by the network. The network server can be accessed from any computer. All server selection messages (adding/withdrawing a server to/from a pool, gathering information about servers' availability) are directed to the network servers, and it is their responsibility to update local databases.

When a computer advertises itself as a computer server, a remote execution dispatcher process is created at this computer. When a client selects a server, it must connect to the chosen server computer. This is performed in the following way. The client sends the connect message to the network server of the chosen computer. The server authenticates the client, and next, if authenticated, sends a response that causes a private communication channel to be established between the remote execution dispatcher at the server computer and the client computer. After that, the client initiates a remote execution by sending a remote execution request. The remote execution request can be sent in one message or in several messages. It contains the following information:

- the command to be executed,
- the environment of the process,
- the process group identification,
- the process identifier of the parent process,
- the disposition of signals,
- the priority,
- accounting data,
- other information which UNIX specifies as information to be preserved across an exec system call.

At the same time, at the client machine, receive descriptors are created for the current directory, root directory and any open files. These descriptors facilitate creation of send descriptors for the communication channels for these files at the server computer. To inform the server how to reach these receive descriptors, it is necessary to put adequate information together with the remote execution request. The last information, which is sent with the remote execution request, is used to create a channel to inform the process initiating a remote operation about its completion.

The process initiating a remote execution, after sending the request, changes its status to that of a kernel-level agent process and waits for a completion message to arrive. This means that the initiating process does not play any active role.

The remote execution dispatcher, after receiving a remote execution request, forks a remote execution server to service the request, and waits for more requests. The remote execution server uses information received in the request to create necessary channels for the current and

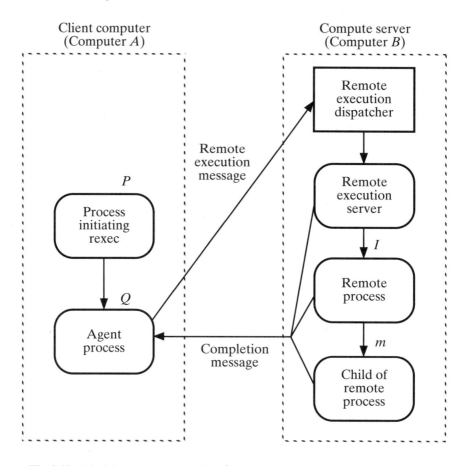

Fig. 8.12   Model of remote execution {adapted from Agrawal and Ezzat (1987)}.

root directories and open files, sets up appropriate ids, priorities and other information, and causes the remote process to be initiated.

The example process relationships for a case when process P forked a child Q at Computer A, and process Q in turns execs a remote operation '$l|m$' on Computer B is illustrated, following Agrawal and Ezzat (1987) in Fig. 8.12.

There are some important issues for NEST (they are not important for real distributed operating systems) connected with remote execution of processes: the fraction of the file system name space, signals and remote controlling terminal.

Files during remote execution could be accessed from:

- the computer on which the process originated, or
- from the local computer at which the process is executing.

The former solution is simple, but has performance problems. There is a high probability that the code for system commands (for example, nroff, cc) is replicated in every computer. Because of this, the latter solution is preferable. The authors have achieved their goal by defining two roots for every process, a default root and an alternate root. For a given process these roots differ when this process is executing remotely.

8.6 Migration of processes

Process migration in a distributed operating system is a facility to dynamically relocate a process from the processor on which it is executing (the source processor) to another processor (the destination processor). To execute such a process on a destination machine, a sufficient amount of a process's state has to be transferred. The need for process migration was identified by the end of the 1970s by Solomon and Finkel (1979), Finkel (1980), but only a few successful implementations have been reported by Lazowska *et al.* (1981), Rashid and Robertson (1981), Powell and Miller (1983), Walker *et al.* (1983), Theimer *et al.* (1985), Artsy *et al.* (1986), Douglis and Ousterhout (1987, 1989), Zayas (1987) and Walker and Mathews (1989). In general, process migration has proved to be a difficult facility to implement in distributed operating systems, but it received a lot of attention, and is surrounded by the controversy. These implementations show that pre-emptive process migration is possible. However, its complexity and overhead are higher than originally anticipated.

The basic idea of process migration is moving a process during its execution, so that it continues on another processor, with continuous access to all its resources. This operation may be initiated without the knowledge of the running process or any process interacting with it, this means migration is transparent. In other words, process migration should preserve all elements of computation and communication. However, there are two different solutions once a process is migrated out of a source processor. In the first, there are special links to the source processor to redirect messages to the migrated process; in the second, no trail or links are left. These problems will be discussed in detail later. When moving a process from one computer to another, an entire address space is moved. These process migration facilities can be called **address space migration facilities**. The systems mentioned in the previous paragraph use migration facilities of this type.

Should the candidate unit for moving be smaller than a process? The Emerald object-based language and system shows that this is possible (Jul *et al.* 1988). The principal goal of Emerald is to experiment with the use of mobility in distributed programming. Mobility is different from process migration in two respects:

(1) The unit of distribution and mobility is an object. Some of Emerald's objects contain processes, other objects contain only

data: arrays, records and single integers. This shows that the unit of mobility can be much smaller than in process migration systems. Thus, Emerald's object mobility subsumes both process migration and data transfer.

(2)   Emerald has language support for mobility.

Emerald processes are lightweight; we can say that Emerald supports **fine-grained** migration.

Two issues must be addressed in process migration. The first, a policy issue, is concerned with the selection of a process to migrate and determination of when and where it is migrated; it is addressed in the next chapter. The second issue is concerned with process migration mechanisms, in other words, how to migrate the selected processes to the destination computer.

Process migration mechanisms can be implemented at three different levels:

(1)   at the operating system kernel level;

(2)   outside the kernel; and

(3)   embedded in a compiler and runtime package.

The first and third levels are considered here. The second implementation, that is, (2), though interesting, is rather oriented towards network operating systems, and for this reason is not discussed here. One such implementation is described in Smith and Ioannidis (1989).

In the definition of process migration we emphasized the dynamic nature of relocation, in order to contrast this approach with methods required to achieve a balanced process distribution through initial placement. There are many algorithms developed to allocate processes statically. Static allocation is cheap. However, because distributed systems have a dynamic nature and the load fluctuates, static allocation does not improve their overall performance sufficiently.

8.6.1 Rationale for a process migration facility

Static process allocation limits the overall performance of a distributed system. The overall performance of a distributed system can be improved if processes may be dynamically allocated to processors.

There are several ways to improve the overall performance of a distributed system. One of them is to share the load among the set of available processors. As a result of load sharing and balancing a process can be completed earlier due to the utilization of otherwise idle or lightly-loaded processors. Thus, process migration may be used as a tool for dynamic load balancing among processors of a distributed system. The second way is to improve parallelism of applications. The result of this action is the minimization of the completion time of these applications. In these two cases, the process migration facility of the distributed operating system should be constructed in such a way that the distributed system achieves better overall throughput, in spite of the communication and computation involved in allocating a process to a remote processor.

Another way of improving system performance is to run processes which have some special resource requirements on those machines that can best fulfil such requirements. For example, special processors may perform Fast Fourier Transforms, Array Processing or Floating Point Processing. If a process requesting special resources is run on its source processor, access to non-local resources may result in a large communication overhead. Moving a process to the processor that provides the special resources may reduce system-wide communication traffic.

Process migration may also be advantageous in those cases where a process performs computations on data whose volume is larger than the process's size. This happens when performing operations on databases or in statistical analysis of large volumes of data. By moving a process rather than files, communication traffic is effectively reduced.

Process migration can be also used to improve the reliability of a distributed system, in particular, to aid fault recovery. This is particularly useful in the face of a certain class of faults about which advance notice can be achieved. In the case of a processor crash or a system shutdown, process recovery can be achieved by stopping the process, transporting its state to another computer, and restarting the process, transparently. In this case, the information necessary to transport the process should be saved in stable storage. Processes can also be moved to different computers to provide better failure coverage.

There are three additional reasons for providing mobility (fine-grained migration). The first is the possibility of moving data from one computer to another. This operation does not require having to explicitly package data and no separate message passing or file transfer mechanism is required. Second, mobility has the potential for improving the performance of remote invocation. This can be achieved by moving parameter objects to the remote computer for the duration of the invocation. Third, mobility can simplify distributed garbage collection by moving objects to computers where references exist.

8.6.2 Basic problems of process migration

There are many problems involved in the mechanism of process migration. The first group of problems relate to determination of the state of a process, and detaching a process from its current environment, transferring it with all its relevant context information, and connecting it with its new environment.

Determining the state of a process is not simple, because the process state is defined not only by the content in the process address space, that is, its internal state information which includes its text, stack, data segment, program counter and register contents, but also by local message queues, and the state of communication with remote processes (which includes the sending and receiving queues, and messages in transfer).

In general, it is easy to record internal state and local message queues because this information is local to a migrating process. However, it is very difficult to record the state of communication with remote processes. Fortunately, it is not necessary to record all message exchange simultaneously. It is only necessary to record all messages directed to the migrating process, and their order.

The next set of problems is connected with handling future communication directed to the allocated process. In one successfully implemented system (Powell and Miller 1983), there are special links to a source processor to redirect all messages transmitted to the migrated process, whereas in the second (Artsy *et al.* 1986), no trail or links are left. Approaches to handle correct message deliveries are discussed in Section 8.6.3.

The third group of problems is associated with making the new location of the process transparent to other processes and performing the transition without affecting the behaviour of the migrating process (operations in progress) or other processes. The problems in this context are of a different nature. In some systems, the state of the process is distributed among a number of tables, making it hard to extract entries and create corresponding entries on the destination computer. In many systems, some parts of the system interact with processes in a location-dependent manner. This implies that the operating system is not free to allocate a process at any time.

Some authors have emphasized that they were unable to experiment with process migration due to the lack of dynamic address translation (Solomon and Finkel 1979). Powell and Miller (1983) noted that in some systems, the presence of a machine identifier as part of the process identifier used in communication makes continuous transparent interaction with other processes impossible. Structured names imply location, which makes moving a process (object) harder because references to the moved object have to be updated. All these problems should be carefully analysed when designing a process migration facility.

Another set of problems is connected with the migration policy, which should define **when** to migrate **which** process to **where**, to achieve the best performance. Moreover, it is necessary in some circumstances to make a decision on **when** to pre-empt a migrated process from its current remote computer. These two '**when**' decisions are closely associated. The implementation of a migration policy requires collecting statistics, such as computer load, process usage of resources and communication links (connections) utilization.

A process migration facility may allow one or several processes (multiple migration) to migrate. There are some problems with the latter. One problem is connected with providing sufficient resources for all transferred processes. Another is generated by a wrong conception as to where the other end of the communication channel resides. A third problem is connected with the possible flooding of a lightly used computer, since the choice of a destination processor is made in a decentralized way.

Another problem associated with process migration is when a migrating process can begin its execution on a destination computer. This problem is generated by growing (in a linear fashion) costs of migrating, by direct copy, processes executing large programs. In such cases, the process virtual address space is large in proportion to the usable bandwidth of the communication medium. In the majority of systems providing a process migration facility, a process does not begin execution on the destination node until all of its state (direct copy) is transferred. An exception is the process migration facility built for the Spice environment at Carnegie–Mellon University, which allows the migrating process to begin execution on the destination almost immediately (Zayas 1987). This system uses copy-on-reference transfer to solve this transfer problem. These two possibilities are illustrated in Fig. 8.13.

All existing or designed process migration facilities are for homogeneous distributed systems. In distributed systems with computers of

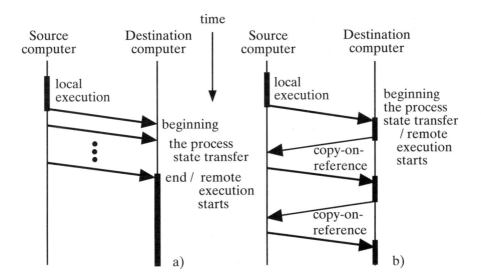

Fig. 8.13 Flow of execution: (a) the process does not begin execution on the destination computer until all of its state is transferred, (b) the process begins execution on the destination computer almost immediately.

the same type, process migration can be summarized as saving the process state on the source computer, and restoring it on the destination computer.

The most important thing is that both computers interpret the data in a consistent way. Some problems arise when an attempt is made to extend the notion of process migration to heterogeneous computers. In this case, the computers still save and restore the state, but they interpret the data in different ways. Thus, there is a translation problem when a process migrates between computers of different types. This problem is discussed in Maguire and Smith (1988).

Communication in a distributed computer system causes another problem for process migration. Process migration requires sending messages such as the process state and code, which increase communication traffic and may cause a deadlock which is similar to a communication deadlock. Thus, a process migration facility must ensure fair and deadlock-free process movement. Migration deadlocks in distributed systems are discussed in Chapter 10.

A designer of a process migration facility should find solutions to overcome all these problems.

8.6.3   Handling message delivery

It is difficult to record the state of communication of a migrating process and there is also the problem of handling future communication directed to a migrating process. So a solution needs to be found.

There are several approaches to handle problems associated with the communication state (present and future). Some rely on the reliability of the source computer, while others do not use such assumptions. Three approaches can be distinguished:

- message redirection,
- message loss prevention, and
- message loss recovery.

Message redirection
According to the message redirection approach, when a migrating process is suspended on the source computer for migration, all known (if any) names and locations of remote processes, with which a migrating process communicates, are saved in the process state. Also the destination computer address is saved on the source computer.

The process is moved to the destination computer. However, processes communicating with the migrating process are not informed about the migration intent. This implies that they will still send messages to the old location, which is to the source computer. When a process is suspended and migrating, all messages addressed to it are saved. After the process is resumed on the destination computer, these buffered messages are forwarded to its new location. The saved names and locations are used to send messages after resumption.

The migrated process running on the destination computer does not inform other processes about its new location. Thus, all processes send messages to the source computer. The source computer is responsible for forwarding these messages to the destination computer.

The message redirection approach can only be used if the source computer is reliable after process migration. If a process migrates several times, it must rely on several computers to forward messages correctly. This results in an increase of communication traffic, and generates communication dependency.

Message loss prevention
In this case, a migration facility on the source computer informs processes with which a migrating process communicates about the intent of moving a process. This takes place before process migration. When a process is migrating, messages addressed to it are buffered. After the process resumes, a migration facility on the destination computer resumes communication with migration facilities on other computers, the new address is passed. Hence messages to the migrated process are sent directly to the destination computer. This shows that migration facilities must cooperate at both process suspension time and resumption time.

Note that because migration facilities on different computers must cooperate, the message loss prevention approach is more complicated than the message redirection approach. However, communication traffic is much lower, and the migrated process does not depend on its source computer.

Message loss recovery
In this approach, a migration facility on the source computer does not save the destination computer address. Moreover, processes with which a migrating process communicates are not informed about the intent to move a process. All messages in transit during migration are ignored; they are lost.

However, the names and addresses of remote processes with which a migrating process communicates are saved. After resuming on the destination computer, the process establishes connections with remote processes cooperating with it before migration. Finally, message recovery is initiated.

Note that this approach does not need cooperation between migration facilities at the suspension time. The approach is simple and fast. This implies that this approach can be used in systems where it is critical to migrate processes quickly, when the source computer has detected a failure.

8.6.4 Design decisions

Different design decisions have been made when developing process migration facilities for different systems. We will present and analyse design decisions for process migration on the basis of such systems as DEMOS/MP (Powell and Miller 1983), V-system (Theimer *et al.* 1985), Charlotte (Artsy *et al.* 1986), Sprite (Douglis and Ousterhout 1987) and Emerald (Jul *et al.* 1988).

The design of a process migration facility can be based on the following issues:

- policy–mechanism separation,
- mechanism–mechanism independence,
- transparency,
- pre-emption,
- residual dependency avoidance,
- multiple migration,
- reliability of process migration, and
- efficiency.

Policy–mechanism separation
Separation of policy from mechanism is a very important issue in the design of operating systems. In process migration, policy deals with the definition of when to migrate which process to where. This means that the migration policy is connected with solving the problem of dynamic allocation of processes to processors. On the other hand, a migration mechanism provides facilities to embody this policy, that is, it gathers the statistics necessary to make policy decisions and performs the actual process migration.

The migration policy should be separated from mechanism and embedded at higher levels of a distributed operating system. Since a good migration mechanism does not have to be changed and must be effective to enable good overall performance in a distributed system, it should be performed by the kernel.

The separation of policy from mechanism is one of the most important process migration design principles of Charlotte, and is in use in DEMOS/MP.

Mechanism–mechanism independence
The process migration mechanism, in particular the statistics gathering and process migration, should be designed in such a way as not to interfere with other kernel mechanisms. This guarantees that several mechanisms are simple and easily modified. In particular, the process migration protocol should not interact with the interprocess communication

protocol. Moreover, migration of a process should result in minimal interference with its execution and the execution of the rest of the system.

Transparency

Processes should be location-transparent. This means that migrating processes should be provided with a network-transparent execution environment so that execution on a destination processor is the same as execution on a source processor (execution environment means the names, operations and data with which the process interacts during execution). Thus, migration is transparent to the migrating process. Moreover, migration should be transparent to the processes connected to the migrating process. This means that processes connected to the migrating process will not be affected. They can continue to communicate with this process or to destroy the communication. In general, the migrating process sees the same execution environment before and after migration.

To achieve migration transparency, a migration facility must satisfy the following conditions:

(1)   No extra code needs to be added inside any process to handle exceptions caused by process migration;

(2)   The resources referenced and accessed by a migrating process must be identified correctly;

(3)   The migration operations performed by a migration facility must be hidden from user processes.

When these conditions are met when a process is migrated, the process is said to be **transparently migratable**.

Such location transparency was achieved in Charlotte, V-system, and DEMOS/MP.

Pre-emption

The owner of a workstation has priority in its utilization. Thus, when the owner returns or runs processes which dramatically increase the computational load, all executing migrated processes must move to new destination computers to improve workstation performance. This means that a process migration facility should allow a sequence of process movements.

Residual dependency avoidance

It is necessary to distinguish between execution dependency and communication dependency. A migrating process should not depend on a source computer when it is executing on a destination computer. If this condition is not fulfilled the migrating process imposes a load on its source computer, and by the way decreases the benefits of migration.

It is necessary to avoid leaving any processor or data communication link skeleton in the source computer to handle communication redirection to the migrated process. This implies that all processes having links with a migrating process should be told the new address before the transfer is completed.

The avoidance of execution dependency was a design principle taken into consideration by the authors of V-system, while communication independency was implemented successfully in a migration facility in Charlotte. DEMOS/MP does not provide facilities to achieve communication independency.

Multiple migration

When discussing process migration problems, we said that a migration facility may allow the migration of one or several processes – multiple migration – to a single computer, since each computer in a distributed system is autonomous. Multiple migration increases the level of concurrency, but the migration policy becomes a more complicated task. This is because of the lack of accurate knowledge of the state of the distributed system (load, utilization of communication links). Charlotte provides facilities to perform multiple migration.

There are two general problems associated with multiple migration:

(1) When a number of processes are moved to a single computer, this computer has to have sufficient resources for all these migrating processes; and

(2) A lightly loaded or idle computer, chosen as a destination node, may become a heavily loaded one.

Overcoming these two problems can be achieved with an efficient and reliable negotiation protocol.

Reliability of process migration

The process migration facility should be designed and constructed in such a way as to survive any single computer crash. Migration should be aborted when either the source or destination computer crashes. A good discussion of reliability issues can be found in Artsy *et al.* (1986).

Efficiency

Efficiency is one of the major design issues of a process migration facility. Efficiency may be expressed in time, since it is the most critical resource when a process is executed. The following factors influence the performance of a process movement operation:

- the time for selecting a process to be migrated,
- the time for the determination of a destination computer,
- the time for setting up and later destroying a new execution environment,

- the time for moving a process, and
- the time spent in forwarding system calls and rearranging the communication between the migrating process and other processes.

These times and elements of the distributed systems which have an influence on them should be analysed very carefully when a process migration facility is designed or tuned.

8.7 Process migration mechanisms

Process migration can be divided into two main phases:

(1)   collecting necessary statistics, and

(2)   performing process transfer.

These phases can be implemented as two separate modules. The first is connected with migration policy, in that the policy determines the data to be collected and the frequency of this operation. Process transfer depends on the migration mechanism.

Collecting statistics
The design of an efficient method of collecting statistics and of the migration decision system is still an open research problem. However, there are some results which can be considered as milestones in this area.

In Charlotte, to decide when to migrate which process to where, the kernel of a distributed operating system can collect the following statistics:

(1)   **Computer load** – which consists of the number of processes and communication links, whether currently active or not, the average CPU load, and the average network load.

(2)   **Process resource usage** – which consists of the average and total CPU and network utilization of each process, and its total communication to local and remote processes (expressed in number of packets).

(3)   **Communication link statistics** – for the most active links per process. It gives total numbers of packets sent and received over each link.

A migration decision could additionally be based on information gathered for memory and CPU scheduling, and available information on communication load. Other suitable statistics which can be collected are presented in Chapter 9, which covers several distributed scheduling algorithms.

In general, information used to determine 'when to migrate which process to where' involves the state of the source computer and states of destination computers. Moreover, processor loading, memory demand for each computer, total communication load for each process and communication load are required. It is also possible for a process to request its own migration and define its destination computer.

Statistics can be collected in three different modes:

(1) **Event sampling** – Events such as message completion or process termination are instrumented to record their statistics.

(2) **Interval sampling** – A sample is taken of the current CPU load, expressed in the number of ready-to-run processes, and the network load, expressed in the number of messages awaiting transmission, at fixed time intervals.

(3) **Periodic statistics** – The average of several interval samples is calculated at a larger time interval.

Performing process transfer

Once the decision 'when to migrate which process to where' has been made, migration is performed by the kernel in several steps. Our presentation of process migration is based on the process migration mechanisms described in Powell and Miller (1983), Artsy *et al.* (1986), Finkel and Artsy (1989), Artsy and Finkel (1989), Theimer *et al.* (1985), and Zayas (1987). We will compare the most important features of these mechanisms.

8.7.1 Process migration mechanism in DEMOS/MP

DEMOS/MP is a distributed operating system developed at the University of California, Berkeley (Powell and Miller 1983, Miller *et al.* 1986). It is a message passing, process-based system. Messages are passed by means of links associated with a process. Links are managed by the kernel; the kernel participates in all link operations even though conceptual control remains with a process. Since a link always points to its creator process, links are context-independent.

The DEMOS/MP distributed operating system was one of the first to offer full transparency. The DEMOS/MP process migration facility was based on two characteristics of the DEMOS/MP system; the uniform and location-independent communication interface, and the fact that the kernel can participate in message send and receive operations in the same manner as a normal process. To deal with the communication state and future communication, DEMOS/MP's migration facility uses the message forwarding approach.

Migration in the DEMOS/MP distributed operating system is performed in two basic steps: negotiation and process moving.

Negotiation

The kernel of the source computer sends a migration offer to the destination computer. The message should contain information necessary for process migration.

If the destination computer has the necessary resources for the new process, its kernel replies with a 'migration accepted' message. Otherwise, the destination computer sends a refusal, and the decision 'when to migrate which process to where' has to be made again.

Moving a process

If the decision has been made to migrate, the moving operation can proceed. This operation is performed in the following steps.

(1)   **Remove the process from execution** – The process is marked as 'in migration'. If this process is in the ready state, it is removed from the run queue. However, no change is made to the recorded state of the process (whether it is suspended, running or waiting for message), since the process will at least initially be in the same state when it reaches its destination computer. Messages arriving for the migrating queue will be placed in its message queue. Process components of DEMOS/MP are illustrated in Fig. 8.14.

(2)   **Ask destination kernel to move process** – Since in DEMOS/MP, the process migration is performed by the kernel of the destination computer, the source computer sends a message asking that the remote kernel transfer the process to its computer. This mes-

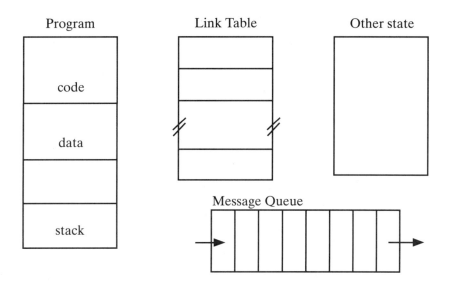

Fig. 8.14   Components of a DEMOS/MP process {adapted Powell and Miller (1983)}.

sage contains all necessary information to migrate a process: the size and location of the process's resident state, swappable state, and code.

After the completion of this operation, the next steps of process migration are controlled by the destination kernel (up to the forwarding of messages – Step 6).

(3) **Allocate a process state on the destination computer** – The destination kernel creates an empty process state. This state is similar to the state of that allocated during process creation except that it has the same process identifier as the migrating process. All necessary resources are allocated at the same time.

(4) **Transfer the process state** – The state of the migrating process is copied by the destination kernel into the empty process state. This operation is performed using the move data facility.

(5) **Transfer the program** – The destination kernel copies the memory (code, data and stack) of the migrating process into the destination process. Again, this operation is performed using the move data facility. After that, the destination kernel notifies that the process is established and returns control to the source kernel.

(6) **Forward pending messages** – Upon being notified that the process is established on the new computer, the source kernel re-sends all messages that were in the queue, or that have arrived when/since the process migration started. Before sending these messages, the source kernel has to change the location part of the process address to reflect the new location of the process. The structure of a process address is illustrated in Fig. 8.15.

(7) **Clean-up process's state** – The source kernel removes all state for the process which was transferred and space for memory and tables is reclaimed. Only a forwarding address is left on the source

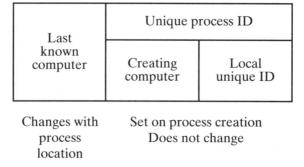

Fig. 8.15 Structure of a process address {adapted from Powell and Miller (1983)}.

computer to redirect messages to the new location of the process. The forwarding address is a degenerate process state which contains only the last known location of the process to which it was migrated. This is a very important feature of the process migration facility of DEMOS/MP. After completing this work, control is returned to the destination kernel.

(8) **Restart the process** – The process is restarted in whatever state it was in before being migrated. The process on the destination computer may now receive messages. The only part of the distributed operating system that knows the new location of the process is the kernel of the source computer. Restarting the process completes the work of the destination kernel. We can say now that process migration has been completed.

Fig. 8.16 illustrates the steps in transferring a process from the source computer to the destination in the DEMOS/MP environment (* denotes a process 'in migration').

Message forwarding

There is one very important problem of process migration in DEMOS/ MP, namely message forwarding. In process migration, it must be ensured that all pending, enroute and future messages arrive at the process's new location. Problems could arise through leaving a forwarding address on the source computer to forward messages to the process at its new location. There are three cases to consider:

(1) **Messages sent but not received before the process finished moving** – These messages were in the process's waiting message queue on the source computer when the process restarted on the destination computer. These messages are forwarded immediately as part of the migration operation.

(2) **Messages sent, after the process is moved, using old link** – These messages are forwarded as they arrive. This operation is performed using a forwarding address (Fig. 8.17).

(3) **Messages sent using a link created after the process moved** – These links, created after the process is moved, contain the same process identifier, and the last known computer identifier is that of the new computer. This case is very simple.

In all these cases, messages can be forwarded correctly and all messages sent to the process at its new location will be delivered. However, indirect transmission of messages to the migrated process degrades overall system performance, because a forwarding address process can be a bottleneck and transmission times are longer. This contradicts the use of process migration to improve overall distributed system performance. An alternative solution to message forwarding is needed.

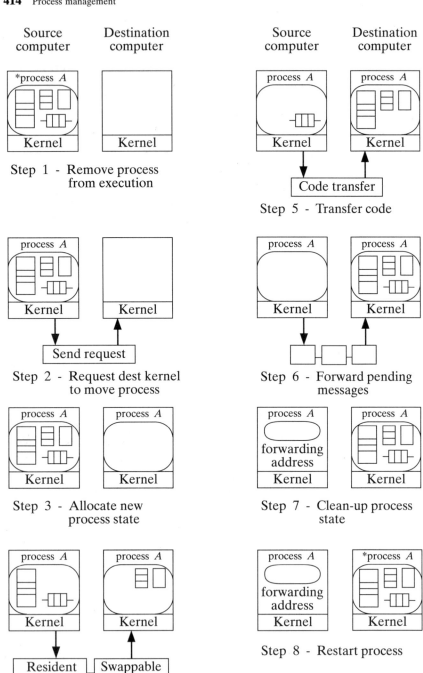

Fig. 8.16 Steps in a process transfer {adapted from Powell and Miller (1983)}.

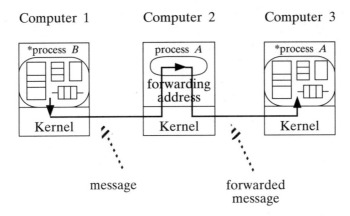

Fig. 8.17 Message sent through a forwarding address {adapted from Powell and Miller (1983)}.

There are two possible solutions. One is based on the concept that all messages addressed to the migrated process are returned to their senders as not delivered. In this system no forwarding process is required in the source computer. However, kernels of all senders have to perform some actions to find the new location of the migrated process.

The second solution is based on updating links. By updating a link we mean updating the process address of the link. As a result of this operation, the unique identifier is not changed, but the computer location is updated to specify the new computer. Updates of all links of a migrating process can be performed easily to all processes which during migration do not send messages. Since some messages could be in transit, some forwarding mechanism is required. It was suggested that links should be updated as they are used, rather than all at once (Fig. 8.18).

This update operation is performed by the kernel of the source computer when forwarding messages, by sending a special message containing the process identifier of the sender of the message, the process identifier of the intended receiver (the migrated process) and the new location of the receiver. Unfortunately, these solutions were not implemented in DEMOS/MP. In the next subsection we show how to improve the process migration facility to avoid forwarding messages.

8.7.2 Process migration mechanism in Charlotte

Charlotte is a distributed operating system which offers a uniform, location-transparent message-based communication facility. Processes communicate with each other through links (Finkel and Artsy [1989], Artsy and Finkel [1989]).

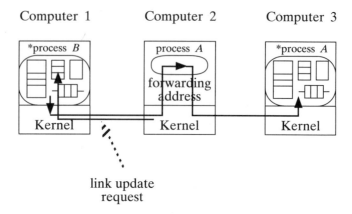

Fig. 8.18 Updating a link after a message forward {adapted from Powell and Miller (1983)}.

One of the most important differences between DEMOS/MP and Charlotte is that in the latter, once a process is migrated out of the source computer, no forwarding addresses or trail of stubs is left to perform future communication. The source kernel deletes all data structures relevant to the migrating process. The process migration facility of this system mainly requires readdressing the process's communication links. Moreover, in Charlotte, a process to be migrated must be 'frozen', that is, its activity is suspended and all external interactions with this process are deferred.

The Charlotte process migration facility may be characterized by three important features:

(1) It separates the decision-making mechanisms (located in user processes) from the migration mechanism, which is embedded in the kernel.

(2) Migration is transparent to the migrating process as well as to processes connected to it.

(3) The migrating process can be pre-empted at any time. An interrupted process can be moved to another computer.

An efficient and simple implementation of pre-emptive migration was achieved due to the features of the Charlotte interprocess communication. This interprocess communication is very flexible, and allows concurrent communication over multiple links, selectivity, message cancellation and link transfer.

The Charlotte migration facility is an addition to the underlying kernel. All kernel facilities are kept as independent as possible. Because of this any changes are relatively easy to do. Note however, that the Charlotte kernels are responsible for migration mechanism (detaching, transfer and reattach migrating process), and for providing a policy system (the Starter – see Chapter 14) with load statistics.

To implement the migration mechanism, three lightweight processes (threads) were created in the kernel:

(1)   the first process to handle the new service calls,

(2)   the second to accomplish phases of migration, and

(3)   the third to collect and report statistics.

Process-kernel interface

The process kernel interface was extended by adding four process migration services:

(1)   Start or stop gathering statistics.

(2)   Migrate a particular process to a selected computer (**MigrateOut**).

(3)   Accept a particular process moved from its source computer and allocate memory to it (**MigrateIn**). This call can be used to preapprove migration.

(4)   Cancel a migration in progress if possible.

Statistics

The Charlotte kernel collects statistics which include:

- data on computer load: number of processes, links, CPU and network loads;

- the age, state, CPU utilization, communication rate of individual processes; and

- the most active links, in particular, packets sent and received.

These statistics are collected periodically with an interval of 50 to 80 ms, and reporting period of 100 intervals. The overhead for collecting statistics is less than 1 per cent of total CPU time.

The mechanism

In Charlotte, after a process is selected, process migration is performed by the kernel in three phases: negotiation, transfer and clean-up (establishment). The message exchange carried out in the first phase is illustrated in Fig. 8.19. This figure shows links between a process to be migrated, P_1, and remote processes P_2, and P_3.

(1)   **Negotiation** – The kernel of the source computer sends a migration offer to the destination computer. If the offer is accepted (message 2), the decision is passed to the kernel in message 3 (it is

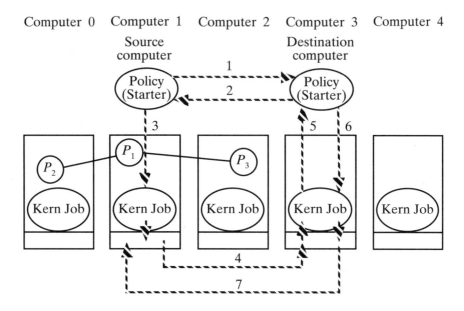

Computer 0   Computer 1   Computer 2   Computer 3   Computer 4

Fig. 8.19 Process migration in Charlotte {adapted from Artsy and Finkel (1989)}.

either a direct service call if the Starter runs on the source computer, or a message to the KernJob, which converts messages from remote processes into service calls).

Next, the thread responsible for accomplishing the three phases of migration sends to the destination computer message 4, which specifies the size of the process segments, its link table, its current active links, information about the process's CPU and network utilization.

If the destination computer has the necessary resources for the new process, then message 5, which includes the same information as message 4, is sent to the controlling Starter of the destination computer. The Starter issues a **MigrationIn** call (message 6), all necessary resources are reserved (to avoid deadlock and flow-control problems), and the kernel forks an internal task to accept the process's image across the network. Finally the kernel replies with a migration accepted message (message 7). This is the commit point of the process migration action. Otherwise, the destination computer sends a refusal, and the decision 'when to migrate which process to where' has to be made again. In this case, both kernels clean up their migration-related state.

Note that before the commit point, a Starter can successfully cancel the migration. This means that message 7 contains **Rejected**.

Computer failure has minimal effect on migration if it happens before the commit point. The migrating process is not transferred if the destination computer crashes. When the source computer crashes, the migrating process dies. If one of the two computers crashes, the other cleans up its state.

(2) **Transfer** – During this phase the migrating process is frozen. Relevant data structures are assembled and transferred together with the address space of the process. Transfer is performed in three steps:

(a) **Image transfer** – The kernel of the source computer transfers the image of the process to the destination computer. It is stored directly in the space reserved by the kernel during the negotiation phase.

(b) **Link update** – The kernel of each of the migrating process's link ends (in Fig. 8.19 the links between process P_1 and processes P_2, P_3) is told the new logical address of the link. Each kernel that receives a link update message must acknowledge the message. Once all acknowledgements have been received, it is safe to start transferring the process's data structures, since no more messages will be received across its link. This transfer is performed by the source kernel (recall that the transfer is performed by the destination kernel in DEMOS/MP).

It is very important that until this point, all messages received for a migrating process at the source computer are buffered by the kernel. The headers are transferred with the process at the next step. The data are not retransferred. The other kernel simulates a kernel-buffer cache miss when a migrating process is ready to receive them. At this stage we can see the next very important feature of Charlotte – from this point, the destination kernel might receive messages for the migrating process, even before the process's image and state are fully received. This implies the need for buffering all these messages by the destination kernel until the next phase.

At this stage there is an inconsistency in the link states. Some of the kernels know the new address, some do not. So messages can be sent to the source computer as well as to the destination one.

(c) **State transfer** – All kernel data structures relevant to the process (process descriptor, link descriptors, descriptors of pending and completed events and received messages) are transferred in packets. The source kernel marshals only the necessary data items (in particular dereferences pointers that use kernel virtual or physical addresses). These pointers will be reinstalled by the other kernel upon receipt.

(3) **Clean-up** – After sending all packets, the source kernel deletes all data structures relevant to the migrating process. On the other hand, the destination kernel, after receiving all packets, copying and/or marshalling back, adds the new process to the appropriate (ready or waiting) list. All buffered messages are reactivated, first those received by the source kernel. The migration has completed.

8.7.3 Process migration mechanism in the V-system

In the previous subsection, we showed how the performance and reliability of process migration can be improved by avoiding forwarding messages. However, the performance of process migration depends on the time during which a migrating process is frozen. Here, we present one solution to deal with this problem. This solution has been implemented in the V distributed operating system.

The V distributed operating system was developed at Stanford University (Cheriton 1984, 1988). It is a message-based system which provides uniform local and network communication. Our discussion of the facility for process migration in the V-system is based on Theimer *et al.* (1985).

Basic features of process migration facility

Theimer and his co-workers address the following three issues in their design:

(1) Processes should have a network-transparent **execution environment**. The names, operations and data with which the process interacts comprise this environment. In this context, some problems occur with directly-addressed hardware devices.

(2) The V migration is based on the atomic transfer of a copy of the process state to another host. Atomic transfer is necessary to ensure that the existence of multiple process copies cannot be detected by other system components.

(3) The migrating process should not depend on the previous location. This means that correct message delivery uses the message loss recovery approach.

As noted in Section 8.5, the V-system has a **remote execution facility** which is implemented by a **process group mechanism**. The V-system also provides a process migration facility, which is referred to as **preemptable remote execution facility**. These two facilities have a lot in common; for example, the destination computer is found using the same mechanisms employed for remote execution.

Process migration in the V-system is migration of the logical host containing the process. A logical host is defined by an address space in which multiple V processes may run. This means that when a process is migrating, its child processes are also migrating, unless a child process is already executed remotely from its parent process.

In the V-system, as in Charlotte, a process to be migrated must be 'frozen', that is, its activity is suspended and all external interactions with this process are deferred. However, this simple solution generates some problems: freezing the state may suspend the execution of a process in the logical host for too long; significant overhead may be incurred by retransmissions during an extended suspension period.

The authors propose a special mechanism, called **pre-copying**, to reduce the effect of these problems. Pre-copying means copying most of the logical host state before freezing it. As a result, the time it is frozen is reduced. However, multi-megabyte virtual address spaces imply that the amount of state generates a data transfer problem.

The mechanism

The first stage of process migration in the V-system, as in other systems, is the location of a destination workstation. This operation is performed via interprocess communication with members of a process manager group. After a new workstation that is willing and able to accommodate the logical host to be migrated is located, the following steps are performed.

(1) **Initialization on the destination computer** – Descriptors, sent by the source computer, allow the destination kernel to create a new copy of the logical host. This new copy has a different logical host-id. The different identifiers allow both copies to exist and be accessible at the same time. The new identifier is changed to the original logical host-id during the process of completing a copy (Step 3).

(2) **Pre-copying the state** – After completing Step 1, the state of the migrating logical host is pre-copied to the new logical host. This copying operation is executed at a higher priority than all other programs on the source computer to prevent interference with the pre-copy operation.

(3) **Completing the copy** – Once pre-copying the state is completed, the logical host is frozen and the copy of its state is completed. Freezing is a very sensitive operation because although execution can be suspended within a logical host, there are still messages sent from remote computers.

Request messages are queued for the recipient process. A 'reply-pending' packet is sent to the sender on each retransmission (as is done in the normal case). When the logical host is deleted from the source computer after the logical host migration, all queued messages are discarded – the sender has to retransmit its message to the destination host. Moreover, all other senders use the new binding of logical host to host destination address, which is broadcast when the logical host is migrated. Reply messages are handled by discarding them and relying on the retransmission capabilities of the IPC facilities.

The last part of copying the state consists of copying its state in the kernel server and program manager. That is done by replacing the kernel state of the newly created logical host with that of the migrating one. At this state the identifiers are changed also.

After completion of this operation there are two frozen identical copies of the logical host. Operations on both of them are suspended, hence the rest of the system cannot detect these two copies. The source kernel still sends responses with reply-pending packets and retransmits 'send' requests, thereby preventing timeouts.

(4) **Unfreezing the new copy and rebinding references** – At this stage the new copy of the logical host is unfrozen and the old copy on the source computer is deleted. A process identifier is bound to a logical host, which is in turn bound to a physical host via a cache of mappings in each kernel. The new binding can be broadcast at the time the new copy is unfrozen. Process migration is completed.

Results of the performance experiments performed on these three distributed operating systems with process migration facilities, DEMOS/MP, Charlotte, and V, show that the cost of this operation depends on interprocess communication facilities and the size of a computation's context.

8.7.4 Improving performance with 'copy-on-reference approach'

The preceding discussion shows that in process migration the performance depends not only on interprocess communication facilities but also on the amount of time during which a process is not able to execute because it is frozen. We saw that pre-copying may be used to reduce this freeze time. However, this technique suffers from one drawback: it may increase the total time for migration.

All of the process migration facilities described suffer from another major problem that as programs grow, the migrating cost grows in a linear fashion. Thus, moving the contents of a large address space stands out as the bottleneck in process migration. It dominates all other costs (Zayas 1987).

To deal with this problem, a solution which allows execution to begin on the destination computer almost immediately has been proposed in Zayas (1987). The approach is to perform a **logical transfer**, which requires only portions of the address space to be physically transmitted. Thus, instead of moving the entire contents at migration time, an individual on-demand page (IOU) for all or part of the data can be sent. This implies that when a migrating process executing on the destination computer attempts to reference 'owed' memory pages, it will result in the generation of requests transmitted to the source computer to copy in the desired blocks from their remote locations. Thus, this approach can be referenced as a demand-driven one. It has two important consequences: context transmission times during migration are greatly reduced with this demand-driven **copy-on-reference** approach; and these times are virtually independent of the size of the address space.

A process migration facility based on the demand-driven **copy-on-reference** approach has been developed for the Spice environment at Carnegie–Mellon University (Zayas 1987). It was possible to develop such a facility due to the integration of the interprocess communication and memory management facilities in the Accent distributed operating system. In particular, it was possible through the use of **copy-on-write** virtual memory mechanism by the interprocess communication facility. (This mechanism is described in Chapter 5.)

Copy-on-reference mechanism

To develop the copy-on-reference mechanism in Accent, a new segment class, called the **imaginary segment**, was introduced. The data of an imaginary segment is accessed through the interprocess communication system rather than by a direct reference to physical memory or a hard disk. Each imaginary segment is associated with a **backing IPC (interprocess communication) port**. This port provides memory management services for the imaginary segment. Every process in the Accent environment may create an imaginary segment based on one of its ports, map all or part of it into its address space, and pass this memory to another process via an interprocess communication message. Thus, this process transmits an 'IOU' for the region's data, promising to deliver it as needed. The role of the backing port in this operation is very important. It continues to field page request messages aimed at the imaginary objects until all references to it die out.

The introduction of imaginary segments requires the facility for determining the accessibility of any given virtual address range. Such a facility must be provided by the operating system. In Accent, this necessary addressing information is provided by **Accessibility Maps**, called AMaps. They describe the entire process address space.

The migration mechanism

Accent's migration facility is based on the copy-on-reference mechanism. Special migration primitive operations, which automatically separate out the context portions eligible for copy-on-reference moving, have been developed. These operations, which are used by the **Migration-Manager** process for context delivery to the destination computer, are presented in List 8.1.

ExciseProcess

which allows the complete context of an active process to be removed from its current computer. This process delivers a process context in two separate interprocess communication messages, ready for transfer to the destination computer.

InsertProcess

which uses two context messages to recreate the process. The embedded port rights are passed to the new incarnation. The process address space mappings are restored based on AMap and RIMAS (Real and Imaginary Memory Address Space). Finally, the reconstituted process is placed into the kernel queue representing the original execution status.

List 8.1   Context delivery operations.

Every computer of the Spice system which takes part in process migration runs two processes:

(1)   A **MigrationManager** server – with the task of accepting and executing commands to perform migrations.

(2)   A **NetMsgServer** process – with the task of providing transport services to support copy-on-reference access via imaginary segments. This service is provided by changing its message fragmentation and reassembly algorithms to account for imaginary subranges.

In process migration under Accent, one can distinguish three stages:

(1)   Packaging and unpackaging the named process context at the source and destination computers. At this stage, the **ExciseProcess** primitive is used to acquire the process context.

(2)   Transferring the context between the computers. This operation is performed by sending two context messages to the **MigrationManager** server at the destination computer.

(3)   Executing the process on its new computer. Executing the process is proceeded with by running **InsertProcess** primitive to reconstruct the target process.

It has been shown that copy-on-reference transfers reduce the time spent in the transfer phase. Remote execution times increased only moderately. The overall performance has been improved.

8.8   Object mobility

The migration facilities presented in the preceding section allow only one process to be moved from one computation environment to another. The unit of movement is a process. However, sometimes there is the need to move data from node to node without having to explicitly package data. The data to be moved can be of different types, such as arrays and integers. This is the main reason for studying migration of processes as well as data by the research team at the University of Washington (Jul *et al.* 1988). Mobility has the potential for improving the performance of remote invocation by moving parameter objects to the remote computer for the duration of the invocation; it can also simplify distributed garbage collection by moving objects to computers where references exist.

The natural construct which allows processes and data to be treated uniformly is the object. To distinguish process migration from moving objects in a distributed system, the authors refer to the latter as **object mobility** (or fine-grained migration). The study of object mobility is a major goal of the Emerald project. Emerald is a distributed object-based language and system (Black *et al.* 1987).

It is well known that object-based distributed operating systems have poor performance. Further, although object mobility increases the generality of a distributed system, its performance is reduced. The ensuing discussion of object mobility follows Jul *et al.* (1988).

8.8.1   Basic concepts of Emerald's object mobility

The unit of distribution and mobility in the Emerald system is the object. An object has four components:

(1)   a unique network-wide name;

(2)   a representation, the data local to the object, which consists of primitive data and the references to other objects;

(3)   a set of operations that can be invoked on the object;

(4)   an optional process – Emerald processes are light-weight processes.

Objects that contain a process are **active**. Otherwise, they are passive data structures.

The Emerald mobility concepts are integrated into the language. This results in the possibility of extensive cooperation between the compiler and the run-time system. This leads finally to large gains in efficiency over previously discussed systems.

In particular, object mobility in Emerald is provided by a small set of language primitives. These primitives are shown in List 8.2.

Locate an object (for example, 'locate X' returns the node where X resides);

Move an object to another node (for example, 'move X to Y' collocates X with Y);

Fix an object at a particular node (for example, 'fix X at Y');

Unfix an object and make it mobile again following a fix (for example, 'unfix X');

Refix an object by atomically performing an Unfix, Move, and Fix at a new node (for example, 'refix X at Z').

List 8.2   Emerald language primitives.

These primitives are closely associated with the concept of location, which is encapsulated in a **node** object. A node object is an abstraction of a physical machine. To specify a location either a node object or any other object must be named. When a non-node object is specified, the location is the node on which this object resides.

Another issue, closely associated with mobility of an object containing references, is deciding how much to move. An object is part of a graph of references. Thus, a programmer can specify the movement of a single object, several levels of objects, or the entire graph. Moreover, a programmer may wish to specify explicitly which objects move together. In Emerald this problem is solved by allowing a programmer to attach objects to other objects. This attachment operation is transitive.

A process in the Emerald system is a thread of control/lightweight process that is initiated when an object with a process is created. A process can invoke operations on its objects or on any object that it can reference. A process, which can be seen as a stack of activation records, is illustrated in Fig. 8.20.

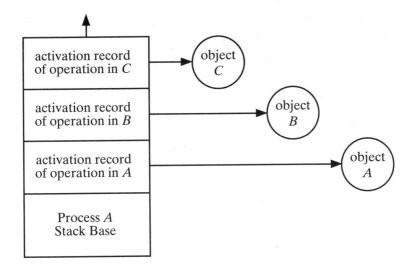

Fig. 8.20 Process stack and activation records {adapted from Jul *et al.* (1988)}.

When invoking an operation remotely, the problem is with parameter passing semantics. The Emerald system uses call-by-object reference parameter-passing semantics for all local as well as remote invocations. However, access by a remote operation to an argument may cause an additional remote invocation. The question is how to overcome this problem.

Emerald provides a solution, because its objects are mobile. It is thus possible to move argument objects to the computer of a remote invocation and to avoid many remote references. Such a move depends on

- the size of the argument object,
- other current or future invocations of the argument,
- the number of invocations that will be issued by the remote object to the argument, and
- the relative costs of mobility and local and remote invocation.

8.8.2 Moving objects

Recall that there are two basic problems of process migration:

(1)   since the entire state of a process may be distributed through a number of data structures, extracting the entire state is a difficult task;

(2)   a process may have variables that directly refer to open files, windows, etc.

These tasks may be a bit simpler in distributed object-based operating systems. This is because

- objects define the boundaries of all system entities;
- since resources are objects, addressing is standardized and location independent.

There are no restrictions imposed on object movement in Emerald. As a result, it is not always possible to know the location of a given object. This implies the need for either keeping track of the current locations of objects, or for locating them when required. Keeping track of object locations is expensive, and in practice unnecessary. Emerald uses a system based on the concept of forwarding addresses.

A forwarding address is a part of an object descriptor. Another part of an object descriptor is a unique network-wide object identifier. A forwarding address is a tuple (timestamp, node), where the node is the last known location of the object and the timestamp is the age of the forwarding address. The timestamp is used when there are conflicting forwarding addresses for the same object. The address associated with the most recent timestamp is valid. Thus, when an object is moved from node *A* to node *B*, both of them have to update their forwarding addresses for the object. Other nodes are not informed. This shows the difference between Emerald's forwarding addresses and DEMOS/MP's forwarding addresses.

Another problem of object mobility in the Emerald system is finding and translating references (all of the direct addresses). Emerald uses templates for an object's data areas describing the layout of the area. These templates are generated by the Emerald's compiler and stored with the code in the concrete type object that defines the object's operations.

Moving data objects

Objects that do not have any active invocations are the simplest objects to move. The operation is performed in the following way:

(1) The source kernel builds a message, with a head containing the data area of the object to be moved. This data may contain pointers to local as well as global objects. The second field of a message contains translation information. This information is used by a destination computer in mapping location-dependent addresses.

(2) The message is transmitted to the destination computer.

(3) The message is received. On receipt, the destination kernel allocates space for the moved object, copies the data areas into the newly allocated space, and builds a translation table that maps the source addresses into addresses in the newly allocated space.

Moving process activation records

In general, moving an active object is performed in a manner similar to moving data areas as described above. However, there is one problem. In Emerald, moving a process object is associated with moving a process activation record. Given an object to move, the problem is which activation records must be moved with it. Thus, finding the correct activation records requires a list of all active invocations for a named object.

The architects of the Emerald object mobility facility analyse two solutions:

(1)   The simplest solution requires each activation record to be linked to the object on each invocation and to be unlinked on invocation exit. Finding an invocation requires only a simple list traversal. Unfortunately, this solution increases the invocation overhead.

(2)   Creating the list only at move time which eliminates the invocation-time cost. The disadvantage of it is that all activation records on a node must be searched.

The authors adopted an intermediate solution. The interested reader is encouraged to find details on this and other aspects of object mobility in Jul *et al.* (1988).

8.9   Migration in heterogeneous systems

Until now we have discussed process migration and object mobility in systems composed of homogeneous computers. Interesting questions arise when one attempts to extend the concepts of process migration and object mobility to systems of heterogeneous computers. In such a heterogeneous environment, process migration means not only saving the state information on the source computer and restoring it on the destination one, but also data translation.

Data translation between two processors requires that each processor be able to convert the data from the remote processor type into its private format. Adding a new processor of a different type implies the need for translation between its own representation and those of other processors. Thus, if there are n different types of processors, the complexity of translation, and the number of pieces of translation software (Fig. 8.21), is $O(n^2)$. This implies that adding each new processor type to a distributed system is an extremely difficult task.

The complexity of translation can be reduced if a translation process is based on a standard representation for the transport of data. This implies that a new processor needs only to be able to convert data to and from the standard form (Fig. 8.22).

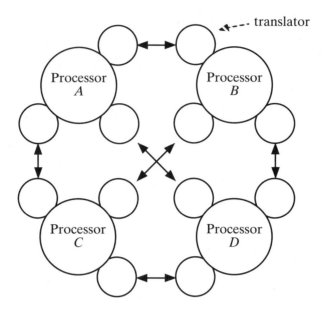

Fig. 8.21 Data translation performed on one-to-one basis.

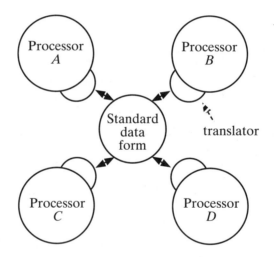

Fig. 8.22 Data translation using standard representation.

In summary we can say that process migration between heterogeneous processors requires an **external data representation**. Such an external data representation must address the problem of different representations for such data as characters, integers and floating point numbers.

Among many problems of data translation, one which we are interested in here is how to deal with different precisions and magnitudes of floating point representations in systems based on external data representation. These two parts of a floating point number should be treated differently because the side effects caused by an external data representation affect these two components differently (Maguire and Smith 1988).

Exponent

Suppose there are two different processors. Processor A uses an exponent of length $E_A = 8$ bit, and processor B uses an exponent of length $E_B = 16$ bits. The external data representation designed by users of processor A, provides an exponent of length $E_{edr} = 12$ bits. For simplicity of analysis we can assume that all three processors use the same number of bits for the mantissa.

A process migrating from processor A to processor B does not experience any problem in representing its floating point data. This is because $E_A < E_{edr} < E_B$.

On the other hand, when a process migrates from processor B to processor A, the external data representation cannot contain it ($E_{edr} < E_B$). If inadequate error handling exists, such a migrating process may not have meaningful data when it reaches processor A. This implies that a process migration facility should not allow process migration in such cases.

A very similar situation arises in the case where the length of the exponent on the source processor B, is shorter than on the destination processor A, even though the external representation is adequate, that is, $E_A < E_B < E_{edr}$. We see that the external data representation handles the number. However, the destination processor cannot.

This leads to the conclusion that a process can safely migrate only to destination processors on which exponents are at least as large as on the source processor. In this case, the external data representation should be treated as a virtual destination node.

Mantissa

Assume again that there are two processors of different architectures. Processor A uses a mantissa of length $M_A = 32$ bits, and processor B uses an mantissa of length $M_B = 64$ bits. The external data representation uses a mantissa of length $M_{edr} = 48$ bits. Let us assume that all three processors use the same number of bits for the exponent fields.

A process migrating from processor A to processor B is again in a good situation. It does not experience any problem in representing its floating point data – there is no loss of precision. This is because $M_A < M_{edr} < M_B$.

However, a process migrating from processor B to processor A is of concern. Moving in this direction implies throwing away half of the bits of data – 16 bits at the stage from processor B to the external data representation and another 16 when converting the external data representation to the destination processor. Thus, computation on processor A will be carried out in 'half-precision'.

Finally, we can say that the external data representation must have sufficient precision to handle the largest mantissa. Moreover, a user who wishes to migrate a process from a source processor which has larger mantissas than the destination processor should be aware that computation precision will decrease.

Note that here we only signalled the basic problems of data translation. The reader interested in identification of other problems should consult references on computer architecture and data representation in computer systems.

8.10 Summary

A process management system together with memory management and interprocess communication systems provides the execution environment for processes.

In centralized operating systems, process management deals with mechanisms and policies for sharing a processor among a number of competing processes. To achieve this, a number of operations on processes are provided. They allow processes to be created, run, named, suspended, synchronized, killed and scheduled. Only process scheduling addresses policy.

In distributed operating systems, process management mainly deals with mechanisms for sharing computation resources spread around a network among all processes. To achieve this goal it is also necessary to provide mechanisms, local and global, and some policy, to perform the same operations on processes as in centralized operating systems.

By nature distributed operating systems allow us to improve the overall performance of a system due to load sharing, load balancing and accessing remote peripheral resources. New and proper operations on processes should thus be possible. These operations are remote execution of a process and process migration (called also pre-emptable process execution).

There are two basic issues in the design of remote execution and/or process migration facilities: mechanisms and policy. Implementation of these issues should be separated. Policy deals with deciding 'which process, when, and where' to move. These aspects are discussed in the next chapter. Mechanisms deal with actual implementation of remote process execution and process migration.

Process migration mechanisms can be implemented at three levels: at the operating system kernel level, outside the kernel, or embedded in a compiler and run time package.

Different levels of granularity in process migration can be identified: address space migration, in which a unit of migration is one process, and fine-grained migration, in which a unit of movement is an object, for example, data of different types such as arrays or integers, and lightweight processes.

There are some basic problems of process migration. The most critical and difficult are determining the state of a process to be migrated, detaching a process from its current environment, transferring it to the destination computer, and connecting it with its new environment.

The state of a process consists of the process address space, local message queues and the state of communication of a process with remote processes. The last two of these generate the problems of how to handle current and future communication addressed to a migrating process: or in other words, how to handle message delivery.

There are three approaches used to handle message delivery to a migrating process: message redirection, message loss prevention and message loss recovery. The first approach can be used in environments where source computers are reliable, because they have to support residual communication dependency. This approach is simple but increases communication traffic. The second approach is more complicated than the first, but does not impose any special requirements on computer reliability. However, it requires close cooperation of process migration facilities on different computers. The third method does not need any cooperation between migration facilities. It requires a simple facility and provides fast migration. Therefore it can be used in systems subject to computer failures.

In process migration mechanisms it is possible to distinguish three phases: collecting necessary statistics (periodically, randomly, when some events happen), negotiation with potential destination computers and performing process transfer.

In some developed process migration mechanisms, a process to be migrated must be frozen, which means its activity is suspended and communication is deferred. Because freezing generates some problems (for example, a process can be suspended too long) pre-copying can be used. Performance can also be improved by using a copy-on-reference mechanism.

Process migration in heterogeneous environments is more complicated than in homogeneous ones, and sometimes even not feasible. This is because it requires not only performing migration operations required in a homogeneous environment, but also data translation.

Bibliography

Agrawal R. and Ezzat A.K. (1987). Location Independent Remote Execution in NEST. *IEEE Transactions on Software Engineering,* **SE–13**(8), 905–12

Almes G.T., Black A.P., Lazowska E.D. and Noe J.D. (1985). The Eden System: A Technical Report. *IEEE Transactions on Software Engineering,* **SE–11**(1), 43–59

Andrews G.R. (1981). Synchronizing Resources. *ACM TOPLAS,* **3**(4), 405–30

Andrews G.R. and Schneider F.B. (1983). Concepts and Notations for Concurrent Programming. *ACM Computing Surveys,* **15**(1), 3–43

Artsy Y. and Finkel R. (1989). Designing a Process Migration Facility. The Charlotte Experience. *Computer,* **9**, 47–56

Artsy Y., Chang H.Y. and Finkel R. (1986). *Process Migrate in Charlotte.* Computer Sciences Technical Report No. 655, University of Wisconsin–Madison

Bagrodia R. and Chandy K.M. (1985). A Micro-Kernel for Distributed Applications. In *Proceedings of the 5th International Conference on Distributed Computing Systems,* Denver, Colorado, pp. 140–149

Berglund (1986). An Introduction to the V-System. *IEEE Micro,* 35–52

Bershad B.N. and Levy H.M. (1988). A Remote Computation Facility for a Heterogeneous Environment. *Computer,* **21**(5), 50–60

Birrell A.D. (1989). *An Introduction to Programming with Threads.* Digital Systems Research Center, No. 35

Black A., Hutchinson N., Jul E., Levy H. and Carter L. (1987). Distribution and Abstract Types in Emerald. *IEEE Transactions on Software Engineering,* **SE–13**(1)

Brinch Hansen P. (1978). Distributed Processes: A Concurrent Programming Concept. *Communications of the AC,* **21**(11), 934–94

Burns A., Lister A.M. and Wellings A.J. (1987). A Review of Ada Tasking. *Lecture Notes in Computer Science, No. 262,* Springer-Verlag

Cheriton D.R. (1984). The V Kernel: A Software Base for Distributed Systems. *IEEE Software,* pp. 19–42

Cheriton D.R. (1988). The V Distributed System. *Communications of the ACM,* **31**(3), 314–33

Cheriton D.R. and Mann T.P. (1989). Decentralizing a Global Naming Service for Improved Performance and Fault Tolerance. *ACM Transactions on Computer Systems,* **7**(2), 147–83

Conway M. (1963). A Multiprocessor System Design. In *Proceedings of the AFIPS Fall Joint Computer Conference,* pp. 139–146

Dannenberg R.B. (1982). Resource Sharing in a Network of Personal Computers. *Ph.D. Thesis.* Department of Computer Science, Carnegie–Mellon University

Dennis J.B. and van Horn E.C. (1966). Programming Semantics for Multiprogrammed Computations. *Communications of the ACM,* **9**(3), 143–55

Dijkstra E.W. (1968). *Cooperating Sequential Processes in Programming Languages.* New York: Academic Press

Douglis F. and Ousterhout J. (1987). Process Migration in the Sprite Operating System. In *Proceedings of the 7th International Conference on Distributed Computing Systems,* Berlin, West Germany, pp. 18–25

Douglis F. and Ousterhout J. (1989). Process Migration in Sprite: A Status Report. *Operating Systems Technical Committee Newsletter,* **3**(1), 8–10

Finkel R. (1980). *The Arachne Kernel.* Technical Report TR–380, University of Wisconsin

Finkel R., Solomon M., DeWitt D. and Landweber L. (1983). *The Charlotte Distributed Operating System.* Computer Sciences Technical Report #502, Computer Sciences Department, University of Wisconsin–Madison

Finkel R. and Artsy, Y. (1989). The Process Migration Mechanism of Charlotte. *Operating Systems Technical Committee Newsletter,* 3(1), 11–14

Gehani N. (1983). *Ada: An Advanced Introduction.* Prentice-Hall

Hoare C.A.R. (1978). Communicating Sequential Processes. *Communications of the ACM,* 21(8), 666–77

Jul E., Levy H., Hutchinson N. and Black A. (1988). Fine-Grained Mobility in the Emerald System. *ACM Transactions on Computer Systems,* 6(1), 109–33

Lazowska E.D., Levy H.M., Almes G.T., Fisher M.J., Fowler R.J. and Vestal S.C. (1981). The Architecture of the Eden System. In *Proceedings of the 8th Symposium on Operating Systems Principles,* Pacific Grove, California, pp. 148–59

Liskov B.H. and Scheifler R. (1983). Guardians and Actions: Linguistic Support for Robust, Distributed Programs. *ACM Transactions on Programming Languages and System,* 5(3), 381–404

Maguire G.Q. and Smith J.M. (1988). Process Migration: Effects on Scientific Computing. *SIGPLAN Notices* 23(3), 102–6

Miller B.P., Presotto D.L. and Powell M.L. (1986). *DEMOS/MP: The Development of a Distributed Operating System.* Computer Sciences Technical Report #650, Computer Sciences Department, University of Wisconsin–Madison

Ousterhout J.K., Cherenson A.R., Nelson M.N. and Welch B.B. (1988). The Sprite Network Operating System. *Computer,* 21(2), 23–36

Peterson J.L. and Silberschatz A. (1985). *Operating Systems Concepts.* Addison-Wesley

Powell M.L. and Miller B.P. (1983). Process Migration in DEMOS/MP. In *Proceedings of the Ninth ACM Symposium on Operating Systems Principles,* Bretton Woods, New Hampshire, pp. 110–19

Rashid R.F. and Robertson G.G. (1981). Accent: A Communication Oriented Network Operating System Kernel. In *Proceedings of the Eighth Symposium on Operating Systems Principles,* Pacific Grove, California, pp. 64–75

Rashid R., Tevanian A., Young M., Golub D., Baron R., Black D., Bolosky W. and Chew J. (1987). *Machine-Independent Virtual Memory Management for Paged Uniprocessor and Multiprocessor Architecture,* Draft, Computer Science Department, Carnegie–Mellon University

Schroder W. (1987). A Distributed Process Execution and Communication Environment for High-Performance Application Systems. Experiences with Distributed Systems. *Lecture Notes in Computer Science,* (309), Springer-Verlag, pp. 162–188

Smith J.M. (1988). A Survey of Process Migration Mechanisms. *Operating Systems Review,* 22(3), 28–40

Smith J.M. and Ioannidis J. (1989). Implementing Remote **fork**() with Checkpoint/restart. *Operating Systems Technical Committee Newsletter,* 3(1), 15–19

Solomon M.H. and Finkel R.A. (1979). The Roscoe Distributed Operating System. In *Proceedings of the Seventh Symposium on Operating Systems Principles,* Pacific Grove, California, pp. 108–113

Theimer M.M., Lantz K.A. and Cheriton D.R. (1985). Preemptable Remote Execution Facilities for the V-system. In *Proceedings of the Tenth ACM Symposium on Operating Systems Principles,* Orcas Island, Washington, pp. 2–12

Walker B., Popek G., English R., Kline C. and Thiel G. (1983). The LOCUS Distributed Operating System. In *Proceedings of the Ninth ACM Symposium on Operating Systems Principles,* Bretton Woods, New Hampshire, pp. 49–70

Walker B. and Mathews R.M. (1989). Process Migration in AIX's Transparent Computing Facility (TCF). *Operating Systems Technical Committee Newsletter,* **3**(1), 5–7

Wegner P. and Smolka S.A. (1983). Processes, Tasks, and Monitors: A Comperative Study of Concurrent Programming Primitives. *IEEE Transactions on Software Engineering,* **SE–9**(4), 446–62

Zayas E.R. (1987). Attacking the Process Migration Bottleneck. In *Proceedings of the Eleventh ACM Symposium on Operating Systems Principles,* Austin, Texas, pp. 13–24

9 Resource allocation

User names	File service	Security	
	Collaboration of file servers Transaction service Directory service Flat file service Disk service	Access control	C o m m u n i c a t i o n
Name distri-bution	Resource allocation	Deadlock detection	R e s o u r c e p r o t e c t i o n
Name resolu-tion	Algorithms for load sharing and load balancing	Process synchro-nization	
		Capa-bilities	s e c u r i t y & Authen-tication
System names	Process management Operations on processes: local, remote Process migration	Access lists	Key manage-ment
Ports	Interprocess communication (and memory management) Interprocess communication primitives: Message Passing or Remote Procedure Call, or Transactions; Links or Ports	Info flow control Security kernel	Data encryp-tion
Address-es			
Routes	Transport protocols supporting interprocess communication primitives		Encryp-tion protocols

R esource allocation is one of three issues of resource management in operating systems; the other issues; deadlock detection and resolution; and resource protection and communication security are discussed in following chapters.

Resource allocation is a complex problem in centralized operating systems. In distributed operating systems there are extra complications, caused by physical distribution of the resources, communication delays, natural redundancy and the possibility of partial failures, and by the lack of global state information. For these reasons, relatively little work has been done on resource allocation, and several basic problems remain to be solved.

We begin by introducing general concepts of resources and resource management systems. We then look at how resources need to be described so that they can be managed efficiently, and present a taxonomy of resource management systems.

Different types of resource management systems are considered next. Centralized server based managers, distributed server based managers, and agent based resource managers are all able to provide a variety of services. Some other resource management systems only provide access to a single type of service.

The processor is an especially important type of resource. Distributed scheduling algorithms deal with the allocation of processes to available processors and the distribution of the workload. In Chapter 8 we presented mechanisms that support distributed scheduling, including remote execution of processes and process migration. In the last part of this chapter we discuss policy questions: how to find an idle workstation or/and lightly loaded computer, and when to migrate a process. This involves the study of load sharing and load balancing algorithms. Load sharing, which deals mainly with hunting for idle processors, improves performance locally; load balancing strives to improve performance globally.

Basic classifications of load sharing and load balancing algorithms are introduced, and several algorithms are presented.

9.1 Resources and resource management in distributed systems

In defining a distributed operating system in Chapter 1 we emphasized the management aspects of such a system and said that a distributed operating system should control network resource allocation to allow their use in the most effective way. To analyse these problems we should be familiar with the terms 'resources' and 'management of resources' in distributed computer systems.

9.1.1 Resources

Recallect that a **resource** is each reusable, relatively stable hardware or software component of a computer system that is useful to system users or their processes, and because of this it is requested, used and released by processes during their activity.

The resources provided by a computer system are usually grouped into two categories:

(1) **physical resources** – which are the permanent physical components of a computer system, such as processor, main memory, I/O devices, internal devices (clocks and timers) and external memory (disks and tapes);

(2) **logical resources** (also referred to as **software resources**) – which are collections of information stored within physical resources (main memory, external memory) such as processes, files, shared programs and data, and procedures.

In a distributed computer system all these resources are physically distributed. Moreover, in these systems there are also other resources such as identifier space, buffer space, and access to communication channels (bandwidth).

All the resources just listed can be referred to as low level resources, directly available on a distributed system. However, a user is usually interested in high level resources, such as a compiler service, a linking service, an edit service and an operating system instance. High level resources are built upon one or more subresources in a multilevel fashion. They are provided by a distributed operating system, in particular its resource management component; alternatively, clients may construct them based on a knowledge of mechanisms to construct them from the basic resources.

Resources must be described in such a way that clients may offer, request, and provide them in a consistent manner. The description of resources should express their functionality, structure, properties, allocation aspects and access possibility. This can be done by providing a set of one or more attributes. Attributes are used by the resource management system in matching client requirements to attributes of available resources.

Resources may be modelled as objects. An object type is defined by its

(1) **specification** – which is visible to the user and defines the syntax and semantics of a set of primitive operations applicable to the object type; and

(2) **implementation** – which is hidden from the user, and supports the operations defined in the specification.

An object can be active, which means it can change its own state and the states of other objects, or passive, which means it cannot change state on its own but only through an active object.

In our discussion we do not distinguish these two object states and they are used interchangeably. It should be remembered that in some circumstances the object approach may be more natural than the process approach as a basis for discussion.

9.1.2 Overview of resource management

Both physical and logical resources should be managed. Resource management is (Mullender 1984):

- planning and organizing the provisions of resources and identification of (i) where resources may be located, (ii) their availability, and (iii) their cost;

- the control of the use of, and access to, resources according to allocation, optimization and authentication rules;

- the task of ensuring that resources remain accessible and that they function correctly; and when this objective cannot be achieved, of ensuring that suitable signals are available which indicate failures.

The principles underlying the management of resources apply whether systems are centralized or distributed. Resource management should support their use in a convenient, effective and fair manner. The last two objectives imply the need for controlled sharing of resources. However, approaches, methods, and algorithms of resource management in distributed computer systems are different from those in centralized computer systems. The differences are due mainly to the physical distribution, which is manifested by a number of factors.

Physical separation implies the distribution of status information about all resources being managed. The collection of the status information of all resources in a system defines the global state of a distributed system. In centralized systems, global state information is located in one place. This implies that changes to this information can be made very quickly. Tables contain complete and up-to-date information about all resources.

In distributed systems, storage of information about all resources can be either centralized or distributed. Maintaining accurate global state information (in tables) in the former case is difficult because the distribution of sources of this information requires the transfer of data; this implies delays in table update. The table manager has to make resource management decisions without accurate global state information. Sometimes a decision made in such a situation can cause more problems than not making any decision.

When information about resources is distributed, usually decisions have to be made locally. These decisions are not globally optimal, and sometimes may generate problems. Some coordination is required to alleviate these problems. However, coordination requires transfer messages, and this introduces delays, additional computations, and in general, decreases performance of the total system. The problem of managing resources without complete and up-to-date global state information is very difficult.

Resource management in distributed systems is also difficult because of the problem of locating resources, since they are scattered around and may be mobile. We have noted that distribution improves the reliability of a total system. However, partial failures may affect the operations of other parts of the system. Moreover, they can generate inconsistency of data which may lead to contradictory management decisions. Management is also more complicated in heterogeneous distributed systems.

There are other issues of resource management. Before a client process can access a resource or service, it must determine its location. When it requests a low level resource, it can be accessed, if available, nearly immediately. However, when a user process is interested in a higher level resource, it must be constructed from low level ones. Some resources may not be accessible as a result of a crash. The resource management system should be able to detect such resources and perform or request a cleanup or recovery operation. Management processes should be based on a fair and efficient policy.

9.1.3   Performance criteria

Resources in a distributed computer system should be allocated mainly with performance or availability in mind. In the former case, the allocation should be carried out in such a way that low delay, high throughput and low migration costs are achieved.

Delay is usually defined as the time interval from when a process is ready to send a message (request, response) to when the first useful message reaches its destination. Delay does not depend only on the transmission properties of the interprocess communication primitives, their implementation, and supporting transport protocol, but also on the way resources are located, managed and accessed.

There are two other time-oriented performance measures: **waiting time** for a service (maximum and average), and **response time** (maximum and average) which is the amount of time elapsed from task submission to task completion. Note that all these time oriented measures are indications of processor load. The response time depends on:

- time dependent factors, such as resource demands, instruction mix, and the number of processes executing on a processor; and

- processor dependent factors, such as computer architecture, speed and operating system strategies.

Throughput is defined as the number of bits that reach the destination in a defined time interval. Both maximum and average throughput are relevant. Like delay, throughput is affected not only by the transmission properties of the communication system, but on the amount of overhead bits that must be transferred between different objects to locate, manage and access resources.

Resource allocation is associated with some costs. For example, to migrate a process it is necessary to gather and process statistics, exchange messages, and carry out some computations (load sharing and/or load balancing algorithms). This results in communication and computation overheads of resource allocation.

It is difficult to design a resource allocation facility in a distributed computer system that provides low delay, high throughput and low costs. However, resource allocation facilities can be designed to achieve a tradeoff between these three criteria. There are two issues of concern: the time to allocate a resource (for example, migrate a process off its source computer), and the ability of the migrated process to communicate with other processes.

In the following sections we present some mechanisms and algorithms that can be used when designing a resource management facility for a given computation environment.

9.2 Resource description

Resources of a wide variety must be viewed in a consistent manner. Thus they must be described in a consistent way. Resources must be described such as to allow a resource management system to match client resource requests to parameters of available resources. The following information can be used to describe resources: attributes, resource factors, data for resource access and properties for allocation.

9.2.1 Attributes

From a user's point of view the functionality of resources is their most important feature. Attributes can be used to describe the functionality of a resource. The most fundamental attribute is **type** (**class**). It specifies the basic type of a resource, for example, a file, process, processor, printer, compiler, file server or print server.

To determine a resource more precisely a number of **additional** attributes are provided. For example a file can be a source C, Pascal, or Fortran program, or executable code. A processor may be Motorola

68020 or MicroVax. A resource may be replicated. If there are a number of copies of a file, it is very convenient to have a copy number.

The type and additional attributes are specified by a user when requesting resources. A resource management system matches these attributes to parameters of resources that are available. It is preferable to place no interpretation on attributes; this approach allows the addition of new attributes, and thus resources, to the distributed system.

In a computer system, some resources are closely associated with each other. For example some compilers are available on chosen processors, and a processor is associated with a memory of a given capacity. This implies that a resource management system, when searching for a resource with given attributes, must also scan attributes of subresources.

In addition to a resource copy, there are attributes, also known as resource **factors**, which can be used to indicate the variance in instances of resources of a particular type. These factors can be used by a resource management system in determining the most appropriate way of satisfying a resource request. Craft (1985) lists the following resource factors:

(1)   **quality** – in general, it is difficult to quantify the quality of a provided service (it is possible to quantify the quality of printing) and because of this it is usual to order instances based on their performance or usefulness;

(2)   **allocation time** – the approximate time which will elapse between deciding how to obtain the resource and its being ready to allocate;

(3)   **cost** – can be used for accounting and determines the charge for the use of the resource; and

(4)   **communication delay** – indicates the 'remoteness' of a resource accessed through bridges and gateways.

Resources have names. Different naming conventions, in particular unique identifiers and attributed names, were presented in Chapter 7.

9.2.2   Data for resource access and properties for allocation

Resources belong to their 'owners'. These owners may allow other client processes to access these resources, but only to a limited extent. Data used to determine access rights can be closely associated with names (capabilities) or stored in special data structures (access lists). Naming aspects of capabilities are discussed in Chapter 7 and protection of resources is detailed in Chapter 11. Here we consider only one special case that relates to resource protection and construction.

There are three protection oriented problems which relate to one of the resource management issues presented earlier, namely higher level resource construction:

(1)   checking rights of a request to create a higher level resource; a process has to have the right to access a resource creator or server;

(2)   checking rights of a requesting process to access low level resources to be used to create a higher level resource; and

(3)   attaching access rights to a newly created higher level resource.

Because resources may be allocated to requesting processes, some data must be used to describe the properties for allocation. For example, one flag is to indicate whether and when a resource is allowed to be moved (allocated) after being created. When a resource is reusable, it is necessary to indicate that it recovered from the previous allocation to reallocate it. In the case of replicated objects, it should be indicated whether an object is replicated or not. In the former case the management system may ensure consistency of all object copies after every update of a copy (an attribute value 'absolute') or consistency may be achieved with an unpredictable delay (an attribute value 'eventual'). Based on such information, a resource management system can make decisions efficiently.

9.3   Taxonomy of resource management systems

Resource management in distributed computer systems is the central and the most complicated design issue because of the physical distribution, characteristics of resources, and possible diversity of resource management systems. In this section a taxonomy of resource management systems is presented.

9.3.1   Resource classes

Resources in distributed systems generate a number of interesting management problems because:

- they are varied, and often have a multi-level nature,
- they are available in different locations, being distributed among many nodes of a network from where they are requested, and
- the stock of available resources varies dynamically.

Services and data objects
Resources in distributed systems may be:

(1)   **Services** – A service presents a procedural interface to the user. A particular type of a service to an *a priori* unknown client (user) is provided by subsystems called servers.

Recall from Chapter 4 that the difference between a service and a server is that a service is a software entity running on one or more machines; and a server is the service software running on a single machine.

(2) **Data objects** – A data object is generally a handle to stored data which must be presented to the appropriate service for interpretation.

Both services and data objects can be structured. The primary structure associated with services is that of multiple layers, while structuring in data objects is similar to data structuring in programming languages.

An example of a structured service is a compiler service supported by an operating system shell supported in turn by a raw computer. An example of a structured data object is a user session environment, consisting of an individual's terminal capabilities, authentication token set, and personal filing system root index.

Sharable resource characteristics

The nature and the types of sharable objects may be characterized by object mobility and replication. Object mobility determines whether and when they are allowed to move after being created. The following levels of object mobility may be distinguished.

(1) **Absolute mobility** – Objects may migrate from computer to computer at any time, even while performing operations (active objects – processes) or being used (passive objects – data). Recall that processes in the V-system may migrate during execution.

(2) **Conditional mobility** – Objects must be quiescent in order to be moved. There must not be any ongoing operations being performed on them or by them. Eden is an example of a distributed operating system which allows objects to be moved, but only when they are not active.

(3) **Immobility** – Object cannot move. The Cambridge Resource Manager is an example of a system in which objects are immobile.

The class of replicated objects characterizes resource management systems according to whether or not logical sharable objects may have several locations in order to increase their availability and reliability. Thus, there are systems that support replication, such as LOCUS, and others that do not such as the V-system, Eden. Systems that support consistency can be divided into:

(1) **Absolute** – which ensure consistency of all object copies after every update of a copy. This means that the object update is accepted only after a commit point has been reached.

(2) **Eventual** – in which consistency is not enforced after an object update but is guaranteed to be achieved with an unpredictable delay.

Resource access and control

Resources may be classified according to the ways in which they can be located and controlled.

Recall that a resource is located using its name. Thus, each resource reference requires name resolution. This is a difficult task in the case of immobile resources. It is even more complicated in the case of mobile objects. Location dependency can make the location task easier. However, the communication overhead is so high that this solution should be avoided. Location methods can be divided into four groups, based on the information provided to locate an object (a complete description of location problems can be found in Chapter 7):

(1) **Self-location** – The system uses location information provided in the name of the object. This method is in use in the V-system.

(2) **Local cache** – Each host stores (caches) the location information locally. There is no guarantee that all copies are consistent. Data inconsistency can be caused by object migration and failures. The Newcastle Connection uses this method to locate objects.

(3) **Broadcast** – Information about the location of a given object is obtained from a computer on which a resource resides, in response to a broadcast query. The Eden distributed operating system is based on this location method.

(4) **Specialized server** – A specialized server is responsible for mapping the object name to its location. An example of a system based on such a method is Grapevine.

One of the most important tasks of resource management is resource control. A resource can be controlled solely by the computer on which it resides, or a control may be location independent. Thus, the alternatives are

(1) **Local** – A controlling system and a controlled object must reside on the same computer. In Eden, objects are controlled locally.

(2) **Remote** – Objects that reside on different computers are controlled remotely. The Cambridge Distributed System is an example of a system that allows remote control of resources.

9.3.2 Classes of resource management systems

Resource management systems in distributed operating systems take on different forms. The diversity of these forms is generated by:

(1) reasons for the development of computer networks, in particular local computer networks. Recall that these reasons are the decreasing costs of processing units, in particular, microprocessors,

and the high costs of peripheral units such as disks and plotters which imply a need for sharing of these resources.

(2)   distribution of resources among nodes of a distributed system. This can imply that the global system state may also be physically distributed.

(3)   the nature of resource management in distributed systems.

It is natural to distribute a management system physically. The problem is with the logical distribution of a resource management system.

Logically centralized or distributed management system?
A management system can be logically centralized or distributed: a resource management system is said to be distributed if there is a physical distribution of resource management as well as a logical one. A physical distribution does not require explanation. A logical distribution generates the question, when do we deal with logical distribution? The answer to this question can be elaborated on the basis of an analysis of the distributed kernel of a distributed operating system and is as follows: We deal with logical distribution when all management units (managers) share the same responsibilities. The problem is whether a logically distributed management system is good enough.

Let us consider now some aspects of distribution of resources, that must be taken into consideration when designing a resource management system.

(1)   Object availability depends on the local availability of information about this object. Both embedding the name or location of an object's manager in its name, and using local caches, make object migration very difficult. Forwarding pointers, which can alleviate this problem, generate communication overhead and are sources of failures.

(2)   Object replication generates a difficult problem of data consistency. This is aggravated by the large number of copies spread around a distributed system. This problem will get worse as the number of computers (and naturally copies) grows.

(3)   Replicating name databases in each computer of a distributed system not only generates the consistency problem, but also requires large amounts of memory, and thus complicates name resolution.

(4)   Better utilization of the system resources requires more sophisticated object selection and manipulation mechanisms. However, distribution of global state information makes it virtually infeasible to implement such complex procedures.

Given these shortcomings of a logically distributed scheme, why not use a logically centralized, global system to manage sharable resources in a distributed computer system? We answer this question in the following sections.

Models for resource sharing

Resource sharing is based on one of the following two basic models:

(1)   a distributed file system (DFS) model, or

(2)   a service-request model.

The DFS model has been used to build software products, and also as a paradigm for sharing in systems in high-performance workstations, for example in Andrew (Morris *et al*. 1986). This approach is used also in distributed operating systems, though it is extended to distributed processes and other objects. LOCUS (Popek and Walker 1985) is based on this approach.

The DFS model is useful because single-computer applications can be moved onto a network easily. DFS systems also provide network transparency. There are two basic configurations of DFS based systems. To the first belong those distributed systems in which any computer can offer files for use by other computers. In the second configuration there are distinguished node(s), on which all sharable files reside: these are **file servers**, specialized only in one function, or using specialized hardware or operating systems.

Note that many DFS based systems belong also to the class of network operating systems. Examples are NFS (Sandberg *et al*. 1986), RFS (Rifkin *et al*. 1986), Andrew (Morris *et al*. 1986), Cedar (Gifford *et al*. 1988) and Sprite (Nelson *et al*. 1988).

A service-request model is becoming more and more popular in larger, more dispersed systems. This model is embedded in distributed operating systems. It has advantages over the DFS model because:

(1)   Owners of data do not always trust direct sharing (Dannenberg and Hibbard 1985). They prefer providing services, to allow specialized and constrained uses of data.

(2)   Users prefer to use specialized servers to run processes requiring specialized resources. This allows the use of workstations or personal computers to run interactive tasks guaranteeing short response times.

(3)   Administrative control of a resource corresponds to physical access to the server.

(4)   Resources can be used remotely even in a heterogeneous environment.

9.3.3   Basic tasks of a resource management system

There are two main tasks of a resource management system in a distributed operating system:

(1)   A resource management system should accept requests from clients (users, processes) for desired resources and make an appropriate allocation from its pool of resources. If necessary, the system should construct the desired resource from available ones. The user should be able:

(a)   to inquire of the resources available from the resource management system so as to know how best to satisfy its requirements;

(b)   after allocation of the desired resource, to use functions provided by the resource management system to manipulate it, such as list information about it, return it or restart it.

(2)   A resource management system should assist those clients wishing to offer resources to the community:

(a)   resources offered should be accepted and included by the resource management system in its pool of available resources;

(b)   users which offer their resources for community use should be allowed to control their utilization by some way of monitoring and eventually reclaiming them.

At the level of resource management we deal with decentralized systems rather than distributed systems: there is an asymmetrical structure to the system in that different processors and different services are available at different locations. This has a very strong influence on the form of the resource management systems in distributed operating systems. It is, however, possible to develop a distributed management system in which all computers connected by a network share the same responsibilities.

9.4   Resource managers

One of the main tasks of a resource management system is resource allocation among requesting user processes. In practice the task is to give user processes access to a resource or service. The access can be to an idle processor, a lightly-loaded processor, a printer server or a mail server.

We distinguish two basic groups of management systems. To the first belong those systems that are able to provide a variety of services and resources. The second group give user processes access to a single service (single resource) only: this can be an idle workstation, in general an idle processor; a lightly-loaded processor; or a printer. The systems belonging to the second group use load balancing and/or load sharing as basic part of distributed scheduling algorithm.

It is obvious that systems that are able to provide a variety of services are more complicated and require more information to make a management decision. Moreover, the second group can be seen to be a subset of the first. These two groups are discussed separately because in a real distributed operating system it can be reasonable to use a system from the second group solely to decrease management overhead. This section deals with the first group of resource management systems; the second group is dealt with in Sections 9.5 and following.

Resource managers can also be classified on the basis of the type of service provided to clients, viz

- whether a server or agent approach is used for the manager,
- whether resources are allocated statically or dynamically,
- whether the management is centralized or distributed.

9.4.1 Server based centralized resource managers

The management of resources can be either centralized or distributed. In the former case, all resources are managed by a logically-centralized resource manager. Such a resource management system has been proposed by Zhou and Zicari (1988). This manager performs two basic tasks:

(1)   it maintains a database of sharable object information, and

(2)   it coordinates resource sharing.

Features of centralized managers

A logically centralized resource manager has a number of very important advantages. It is easy to keep reasonably up-to-date information and to make globally optimal allocation decisions. To achieve this, resources have to be registered with the resource manager to make them sharable. Because of centralization, information does not have to be distributed or polled. A distributed system based on a logically centralized resource manager can be easily extended – an additional entry has only to be put into resource information database. Processes requesting objects do not have to locate resource themselves; they inquire of the resource manager to receive information about the requested resources. Resources can be widely available and efficiently utilized, since the resource manager uses global knowledge.

On the other hand, a logically centralized resource manager suffers from some serious problems. First, the reliability of this system is low. Failure of the resource manager can seriously impair the normal operation of a distributed operating system. Second, a logically centralized resource manager is a potential performance bottleneck. Third, the autonomy of the individual objects and hosts is threatened because of the existence of a centralized manager. Fourth, it is impossible to maintain the exact state of the system, because it changes all the time and because of the physical separation of the manager database and the managed objects.

Fortunately, these problems can be alleviated. The very first design consideration is oriented towards object types to be managed by a logically centralized resource manager. Such a manager should not be involved in the management of single sharable resources, such as files, which can be managed by higher level objects such as servers. Objects suitable for management by this class of managers are services, that is, such types of objects as file servers, printer servers and computational servers. This approach considerably restricts the size of database of manageable object information.

Reliability and performance can be improved if a logically centralized resource manager is implemented as a replicated system. Maintaining consistency is not a difficult task since the size of the database is reasonably small. Performance can be improved significantly by using caching.

Since the objects in a distributed system can belong to separate client groups, their interests may conflict, and hence local autonomy of objects is desirable. Autonomy of groups in the system based on a logically centralized resource manager can be achieved if the manager acts as a coordinator. A coordinator balances the needs of these parts, and at the same time allows the full utilization of the available resources.

Because the objects managed by a logically centralized resource manager are restricted to high-level objects – servers – maintaining the system state is not too complicated a task. Moreover, objects change their states slowly or only very infrequently. Finally, servers (file server, printer server) do not migrate, and their hosts are stable for very long periods.

Organization of centralized resource managers

Two management levels can be distinguished in systems based on a logically centralized resource manager. The logically centralized manager is responsible for high-level objects, that is, servers. All low-level objects are managed by servers at a lower level of a management structure.

The logical structure of a logically centralized resource manager is illustrated in Fig. 9.1.

The manager is accessed through a common interface. The major task of this module is to route a request to the object type-specific management module. This routing operation is based on the type of the

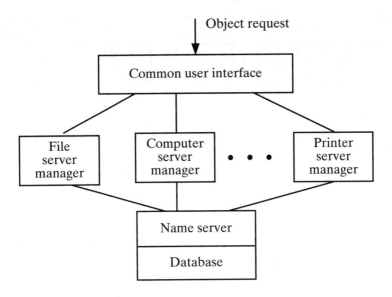

Fig. 9.1 Logical structure of a centralized resource manager.

request. The relevant manager module contains all the knowledge about a particular type of object and the corresponding algorithms. Thus, information can be easily changed. All manager modules access the object database through a name server, through a set of basic queries. With this structure it is easy to add new object types.

9.4.2 Server based distributed resource managers

In this case, all resources are divided into classes, also called pools, based on services offered to user processes. Each class is managed by a server (manager). This implies the existence, among others, of the following pools and their managers:

(1) Processor pool and processor manager. This pool contains all available processors, their memories, peripherals and compiler services;

(2) File server pool and file server pool manager;

(3) Printer server pool and printer server pool manager; and

(4) Plotter pool and plotter pool server manager.

The resource management system in the Cambridge Distributed Computer System is based on a set of resource pools and their managers (servers). The first Resource Manager for this distributed system was

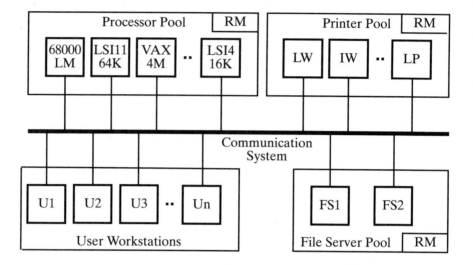

Fig. 9.2   Pools of resources and their managers: RM – Resource Manager, U – User, FS – File Server, LW – Laser Writer, IM – Image Writer, LP – Line Printer.

developed by A. Herbert (Needham and Herbert 1982) for simple management of the Processor Bank only. The extended version of the Resource Manager was developed by Craft (1983, 1985) to take a more general view of resources as multi-level structured objects. Our discussion of server-based distributed resource managers follows Craft.

An example of pools of resources and their managers is illustrated in Fig. 9.2.

To enable access to all resources in such a system, it is necessary that each manager has a specific name known to all client processes (users), or that each manager knows the locations of all other managers, or that there is a manager dispatcher which stores the locations of all pool managers.

Behaviour of the system

The behaviour of the management system is as follows. A request from a client (user, process) for desired resources can be directed to either:

(1)   the resource pool manager (server) which manages a requested resource, or

(2)   the closest pool manager which, after recognition, sends it to an appropriate resource pool manager, or

(3)   to the manager dispatcher which, after recognition, sends it to an appropriate resource pool manager.

This implies that each resource is described by a set of **attributes**, represented by unique identifiers. One attribute should describe the type of a resource, whereas the others are qualifying attributes.

Let us consider the behaviour of a resource manager in more detail. For each resource in the public pool, the resource manager maintains an entry in its **Resource Table**, containing information necessary to manage the resource. This table is searched by the resource manager when it tries to satisfy an incoming resource request. The resource manager can enter a new resource it has constructed into the Resource Table and can delete any resource if necessary. Any authorized client that offers a resource to a community may enter or delete a resource in the Resource Table.

The general model of negotiations between processes and a resource manager is illustrated in Fig. 9.3.

A user process sends a request containing attributes of a required resource to the known address of either the centralized resource dispatcher (message 1) or resource-type-oriented manager (message 2). In the former case, the dispatcher, after recognition of the resource type, sends a request to the relevant resource manager.

When the relevant resource manager receives a resource request, it searches the Resource Table. If a requested resource is not available, that is, resource manager does not have it in the Table, it will try to determine alternative ways of obtaining the resource. This means either finding a resource equivalent to the requested one or combining existing resources to construct a target resource. The latter is based on resource recipes to construct a functionally-equivalent resource.

When the requested resource is available or a target resource has been constructed, it is entered in the Resource Table and then allocated to the client process (Fig. 9.3b).

Design issues

One of the most fundamental problems of a management system based on distributed resource managers is reliability: If the resource manager of a given type of resources crashes, resources of this type are inaccessible. The second problem is associated with manager availability and total system performance. Although these are not as critical as in logically centralized systems, resource managers which are accessed very often (for example, file server manager) may become a performance bottleneck. These shortcomings of single-copy-based systems lead to the idea of multiple copies of the resource managers.

Replication of resource managers has several advantages:

- Distribution can increase the availability of a service because a faulty component need not cause disruption in services if the remaining components have sufficient information to reconfigure.

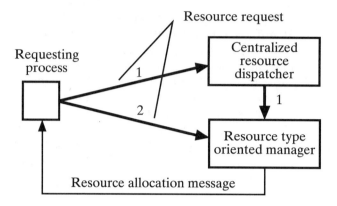

a) Resource management communication (1- this communication takes place only if the resource management system is abased on the centralized dispatcher which redirects a request to a resource-type oriented manager)

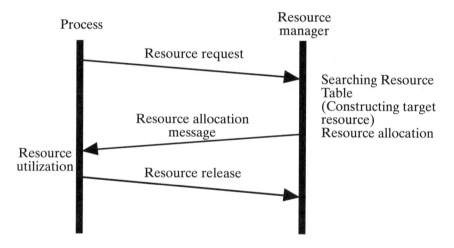

b) Resource management messages

Fig. 9.3   Resource negotiation.

* A distributed service can be more tolerant to failures, and more easily extended and contracted than a centralized one.

Because several resource managers are active at once, and all of them have complete and updated copies of resource tables, any request can be directed to any of these managers and will be served.

However, there are problems created by replication of resource managers. The most important is consistency of data stored and used by all managers. Since this problem is very similar to the problem addressed when discussing systems based on a logically centralized resource manager, it will not be discussed here.

9.4.3   Agent based resource managers

Another solution to the resource allocation problem is based on the **agent** approach (originally called the Butler approach). This is described in Dannenberg (1982), Dannenberg and Hibbard (1985) and Nichols (1987). The concept is strongly influenced by concerns about autonomy and protection. In this approach control is distributed among computers and the policy of any computer is dictated by its owner.

The architecture of an agent based resource manager
An agent is a process that enables users to control their system, and at the same time, to allow sharing of resources, that is, it controls the access to resources of a remote computer, and also provides protection. Thus, it helps user processes to borrow resources and supervises guests. The agent allows client processes to invoke operations on remote computers. More generally, it allows a process to invoke arbitrary services. This means that the agent supports the sharing of information as well as resources. The agent based resource manager approach has much in common with the remote procedure call concept.

The agent based resource manager approach creates a distributed resource management system since it allows the sharing of resources of any or all computers connected to a given network, by any of the processes allowed to access those resources. Following the principle of autonomy, a separate instance of the agent is executed by each computer. To create a nearly symmetrical management system it is necessary to have two agents located in two different computers: the local agent, and the host/remote agent, as illustrated in Fig. 9.4.

This figure shows that at least two computers, local and remote, are involved in sharing. A client process that runs on the local computer must use remote resources to complete. Thus, these resources have to be borrowed. A borrowing operation is performed by a local agent on behalf of the client. The local agent communicates with a remote agent which runs on a computer that is able to provide the necessary resources or services. The remote agent creates one or more processes, called guests, that work on behalf of the client process.

In summary, the two most important features of the agent based resource management approach are:

(1)   A requesting client process communicates only through an agent which provides the requested remote services; a remote (host)

Local computer   Remote computer

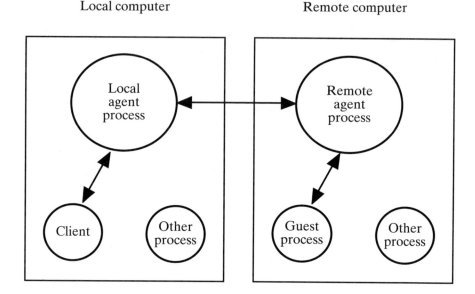

Fig. 9.4   Relationship between client, local agent, remote agent, guest and other processes.

agent represents a remote computer in lending requested resources (or providing requested services);

(2)   A guest process working on behalf of the requesting process is
created in the remote computer when a resource or service is provided for a remote client.

Thus, agents can be regarded as independent but cooperating processes,
rather than as a single distributed process. To show the cooperation of
these processes, it is necessary to analyse the jobs of both a local and a
remote agent.

The job of the local agent is to perform the following actions:

(1)   Get a request for some services from a client process. The request
specifies the configuration required by the client (for example, a
request for compilation would contain the name of the compiler,
the list of computer resources, information for exceptional condition handling, request to use the remote computer file system);

(2)   Locate a remote computer with the required resources;

(3)   Negotiate with that computer to borrow the resources;

(4)   Invoke the service requested by the client;

(5)   Handle the exception conditions (resource revocation, and location of a new host and deportation of the guest process) in a way that is transparent to the client and guest.

The job of the remote agent process is to lend resources and protect the interests of the computer owner. In particular it performs the following actions:

(1)   Receive a borrowing request from an agent;

(2)   Analyse the request to determine whether the resource can be granted;

(3)   Create an appropriate execution environment for the guest process (creating a new process and supplying the guest with capabilities to access other components of the system, according to the request specification, for example, network connections to the client so that the guest and the client can communicate directly);

(4)   Exception handling, for example, attempts to access resources which the guest was not allowed to utilize, revocation of rights.

Resources

The types of resources which the client process is interested in can be divided into the following groups:

(1)   resources related to services requested, for example, access to the local file system,

(2)   abstractions of the physical computer, for example, processes, disk pages, CPU time,

(3)   resources related to revocation, for example, a warning before revoking any rights can be considered as a resource.

Configuration specification

Before sending a request for remote services or operations (in other words, invoking a remote operation), a **configuration specification** is required. The specification should contain at least the name of the operation or service, and the resources required. In general, it is necessary to specify a configuration that names a number of system components and their interconnections. This information should be transferred in a request message to the remote agent.

The following four aspects of a configuration specification should be taken into consideration.

(1)   **Definition of the desired resource or service** – In the simplest case, a service can be provided by a server process. After issuing a user name of a server, a naming facility resolves this name, and

finally provides a port that represents the remote agent that works on behalf of the server.

(2) **Parameter passing to the server** – After the location of the server, parameters are placed into appropriate request message fields and sent off.

(3) **Specification of resource requirements** – Based on the received request parameters, the server specifies resources and services that it can offer to a client process. An important part of the resource representation is the specification of how revocation should be handled.

(4) **Specification of additional subsystems for the environment in which a guest process can run** – Additional subsystems that are necessary to perform the requested operation are defined. For example, if completion of a requested operation requires a file server, its port has to be specified.

Negotiation of resources

One of the most important functions of the local and remote (host) agents is to negotiate the terms under which the resource sharing will take place. Negotiation is the process of establishing the client's intentions and assuring that they will be met. During a negotiation process, an agent informs a potential host about the resources requested by a client, while a host establishes limits to the amounts of resources a guest can use. Moreover, a client has to be authorized to use resources on a remote computer.

The main goal of negotiation is to ensure that the guest has the resources which are necessary to complete the tasks of the client process. This requires that the host agrees not to revoke any resources or rights granted during negotiation, except under unusual circumstances. When resources must be revoked, or a guest exhausts the available resources, it is necessary to provide some form of recovery.

Another goal of negotiation is to increase the likelihood that a guest will be able to use resources effectively, and thus improve the performance of the total distributed system. The latter problem is associated with the problem how to find a remote (host) computer which can perform a remote operation or provide a service. The solution of this problem depends on the naming facility, in particular on the structure of the naming system (see Chapter 7) and load sharing and load balancing algorithms.

Thus, in the negotiation process it is possible to distinguish the following elements:

(1) informing a given (potential) host about the resources required by the client,

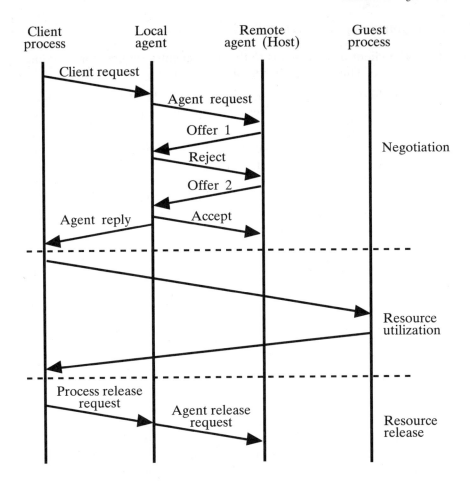

Fig. 9.5 Negotiation and resource utilization messages.

(2)   establishing limits to the amount of resources that a guest process can use,

(3)   authorizing a client to use resources on a remote computer.

The negotiation process can be performed on the basis of the protocol illustrated in Fig. 9.5. (This figure also contains messages sent while performing a remote operation.)

From this figure one can distinguish three phases in providing remote resources or services in an agent based resource management system:

(1)   negotiation,

(2)   resource utilization, and

(3)   resource release.

The negotiation process is as follows:

(1) The client process sends to the local agent a request for a remote service. This request can be of two forms:

   (a) Short request which contains only the maximum requirements for the services or resources to perform the remote operation;

   (b) Long request which contains the maximum requirements for the services or resources, as well as the minimum acceptable amount of resources if a client may be willing to accept fewer resources. Sending the long request simplifies searching for a suitable computer and the whole negotiation process could be performed in a shorter time;

(2) Assuming that a host computer has been found, the local agent sends the client's request to the remote agent residing in that computer;

(3) The host agent sends a reply containing a list of available resources and rights, and reserves those resources until receiving an acceptance response (subject to timeout);

(4) The local agent accepts the offer, if the list of available resources matches the client's request, or rejects the offer.

Revocation

It has been pointed out that the main goal of negotiation is to ensure that the guest process has the resources which are necessary to complete the tasks of the client process. This means that the host agrees not to revoke any resources or rights granted during negotiation, except under unusual circumstances. Such circumstances can arise, for example, a guest program running too long when the host needs to regain control over its own computer, or a guest exhausts the available resources, or the guest attempts to access resources without rights. This implies the need for resource revocation. Thus, an important part of negotiation is the determination of how resources will be revoked if necessary, and definition of methods for handling resource revocation.

Resource revocation can be related to resource types or guest actions. There are the following alternatives:

(1) Completion of the tasks of the client process is possible but in a longer time period (for example, running a program) and/or at a lower quality level (for example, printing); or

(2) Completion of the tasks of the client process is impossible, although in special cases a time deadline can be defined to allow a guest process to achieve a given state.

In general, the resource revocation methods should be such that recovery from revocation is possible. To ensure recovery, the process which will suffer from resource revocation should be informed (warned) early enough. This action is very important in real-time systems because of response time requirements.

In case (1) a process can accept a decreased performance – the guest process is continued, or it can start looking for another host which can offer resources satisfying process requirements. If the process finds such a host, it stops running all processes created by the guest process, and removes them as well as the environment created for the guest.

In case (2) two revocation mechanisms are possible. First, a guest process can be deported, but the guest state is encoded so resources cannot be reclaimed. Second, a guest process can be aborted, if the client process or its agent has been warned and did not take any action. All processes created by the guest and the environment created for the guest are removed. The guest state is not encoded so resources can be reclaimed.

Dannenberg (1982) discusses three distinct methods to be used to handle resource revocation: warning, deportation, and termination.

Warning gives a guest process a chance to perform application-specific recovery actions. This is performed by augmenting the guest's current resources by a set of warning resources and notifying the guest of the change. This gives the guest the greatest amount of flexibility in recovering. However, the warning resources are finite because the host cannot trust the guest process to observe the issued warning.

Deportation is the act of removing a guest from the source computer, and moving and reconstructing it at an alternate computer in a transparent way. Deportation is performed in the following three circumstances:

(1)   guest process attempts to overdraw an account,

(2)   **deport** flag was set in the guest rights returned from the invoke operation, and

(3)   **warning** was not requested or the guest's warning rights are exhausted.

Deportation is performed in the following steps:

(1)   the location of the state of the guest process,

(2)   the translation of the guest's state to a form suitable to be transferred to the destination computer, and

(3)   the reconstruction of the guest on the destination computer.

Deportation of a guest process is illustrated in Fig. 9.6. It can be seen that deportation is similar to process migration.

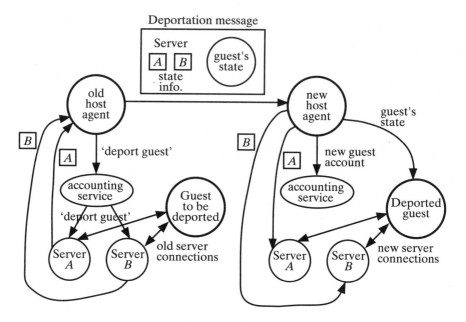

Fig. 9.6   Deportation of a guest process {adapted from Dannenberg and Hibbard (1985)}.

Termination is the third method of handling revocation. This method of revoking resources is used when warning or deportation were not requested, or if they failed. When the guest process is aborted, an explanation is sent to the agent.

In summary, warning is the most flexible method, but it requires the development of application-specific handlers. Deportation is an application-independent method. It is less efficient and less flexible than warning. Termination is the simplest method of handling revocation. However, it may make recovery in a distributed process more difficult.

The agent based approach for sharing resources has been implemented on the Spice personal computing environment at the Carnegie–Mellon University Computer Science Department (Dannenberg and Hibbard 1985). The Information Technology Center of the same university developed another system for sharing resources based on the butler approach, called the Butler (Nichols 1987). The most important feature of this system is that it can run on 'off-the-shelf' operating systems without modification of the kernel or the application programs. Because the solution of the Butler does not extend the agent based resource management system concept presented above, we will not discuss it further. Details on this system can be found in Nichols (1987).

9.5   Load sharing

So far general problems of resource management have been considered. No particular computer resource was discussed specifically. Now we orient our consideration towards some particular resources in a distributed system. One of the basic resources managed in any computer system, in particular in a distributed system, are processors. So the next step is to consider problems and methods for processor scheduling in distributed operating systems.

9.5.1   Load sharing and load balancing

As mentioned in the previous chapter on process management mechanisms, there are two components in a distributed scheduling policy:

(1)   a local scheduling discipline which determines the allocation of a processor among its local processes, and

(2)   a load distributing strategy that is responsible for the distribution of the system workload among the computers of a distributed system by means of process migration and remote execution.

Local scheduling is well understood and will not be discussed further. In this section we consider a load distributing strategy.

We recall that workstations equipped with powerful processors are private resources of the users who control access to them. On average, the processing demands of the users are much smaller than the capacity of the workstations they own. These workstations are idle during many hours of a day. Mutka and Livny (1987b) analysed the use of a group of workstations over five months, and found that only 30 per cent of their capacity was utilized. A large amount of capacity was available not only during the evenings and on weekends, but also during the busiest times of the day.

On the other hand, some users are in the situation where the computation capacities of their workstations are too small to meet their processing demands. They have to wait for long periods for completion of their background computations. Moreover, the response time of their interactive jobs does not satisfy them. Because of this, such users would like to use idle and/or lightly loaded workstations to improve the performance of their computations.

This leads to the policy problem, which can be stated as follows: **which** process should be moved to **where** and **when**, to improve performance. This performance could be measured, as we saw in Section 9.1.3, as average throughput, delay or response time of the overall system, or for a single process or user. Solutions to this problem belong to one of the following groups: **load sharing** or **load balancing**.

Allowing processes to get computation service on idle workstations is called **load sharing**. Algorithms for load sharing form the first class of a load distributing strategy. The most important feature of load sharing is that it provides a local solution, that is, it improves performance indices of only few users and their processes.

The second class contains algorithms for **load balancing**. Load balancing algorithms strive to equalize the system workload among all computers of a distributed system – performance indices are improved globally. The most important difference between these two classes of load distributing is that whereas load sharing is based on migration of processes only to idle computers, load balancing may require migration of processes even when no computers are idle.

This section addresses load sharing and its problems. Load balancing is discussed in Section 9.6.

There are two aspects associated with load sharing. The first is when to migrate processes to idle remote processors; the answer is simply when the processing demands of a user are greater than the computation capacity of his/her workstation. The second problem is how to find an idle remote processor. As we saw in Section 9.3.1, location methods can be divided into four groups based on information provided to locate an object.

(1)   **Self-location** – A system uses location information provided in the name of the object.

(2)   **Local (cache)** – Each host stores (caches) the location information locally. There is no guarantee that all copies are consistent. Data inconsistency can be caused by object migration and failures.

(3)   **Broadcast** – Information about the location of a given object is obtained from a computer on which a resource resides, in response to a broadcast query.

(4)   **Specialized server** – A specialized server is responsible for performing the task of mapping the object name to its location.

Load sharing systems can use different scheduling structures, ranging from centralized to distributed. In a centralized approach, the system should gather information about the location of idle computers, the processes waiting for remote execution and for how long, the parameters of processes being currently executed and where. Based on this information, the system can decide which process is granted which remote workstation. However, this approach suffers from two major drawbacks. First, there is the problem with maintaining an accurate state of the system, mainly because of distribution. Second, a centralized system is critically subject to failure.

In a system based on a distributed approach, idle processors are assigned by several workstations cooperating to conduct a scheduling policy. Each workstation searches for idle processors. Because of competition between requesting processes running on different computers, negotiations or some synchronization methods are required. Because of communication overhead and suboptimal assignment, this approach is less efficient than a centralized one. However, it does not suffer from the drawbacks of the former.

All these load sharing systems can also be described as systems hunting for idle processors. Hunting can be performed on the basis of many different organizations of the set of idle processors. The following are the most interesting and feasible.

(1)   Processors are organized in a logical hierarchy;

(2)   Processors are organized in a logical ring;

(3)   Processors are not organized in any special structure; and

(4)   Condor – a hunter for idle workstation.

These organizations which are all independent of the physical structure of the network are now discussed in turn.

9.5.2   Logical hierarchy of processors

A logical hierarchy of processors was proposed for the MICROS distributed operating system (Wittie and van Tilborg 1980). This scheme is not completely distributed, but it is feasible. MICROS was designed with the following goals in mind:

(1)   The development of principles of organization that can be extended to control network computers of thousands of nodes;

(2)   The development of a system which is able to support a multiuser environment with a dynamically varying mix of large and small jobs, and to tolerate hardware failures in local regions;

(3)   The development of a distributed operating system that does not depend on a fixed topology; and

(4)   The development of mechanisms that allow for migration or replication of processes or databases within the network to relieve overloaded communication lines.

These goals had a very strong influence on the organization of the MICROS operating system, particularly on the structure of the processor (resource) management system.

The global organization of MICROS

Since MICROS is a system to control thousands of computers, centralized resource tables cannot be utilized. Moreover, any centralized man-

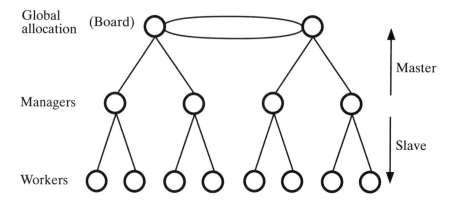

Fig. 9.7 A logical hierarchy of processor management nodes.

agement task will eventually run out of processing power and communication bandwidth as the number of directly controlled computers grows. A centralized system is also very sensitive to the failure of the computer storing the central resource database and running management tasks. This implies the need for a distributed system for resource (in particular, processor) allocation.

A proposed resource allocation structure is a hierarchy of network nodes organized as a truncated tree of nodes (Fig. 9.7). Such a management hierarchy can be found in corporate, military, academic and other realistic social organizations. This implies that some of the nodes are workers and some of them are managers. Worker-processors are globally accessible. In Fig. 9.7, circles represent nodes in the network and arcs represent management connections between them. These connections do not directly correspond to physical communication links.

The lowest nodes (worker-processors) in the tree are responsible for two major functions. They perform user tasks and handle input/output devices that are connected to the network. An upper node manages processors (resources) and provides local control for the nodes within its subtree of the network hierarchy (directly below it). The designers assessed the number of levels in the management structure in the following way. Assuming that one computer can manage about ten other lower level processors of similar speed, the number of levels in a truncated tree containing N nodes is about $\log_{10}(N)$.

Although processors are globally accessible, they are managed in nested pools. Such tasks as monitoring, scheduling and allocation of each processor associated with a lower-level node are performed by one or more of the mangement bodies (processors) in the chain between the worker-processor and the top of the hierarchy. Note that there is no topmost node controlling the entire set of computers (network).

The hierarchy can be greatly extended, with the number of levels growing logarithmically with the number of workers. This implies that communication and processing overload grow. To avoid communication and processing overloads, normally each node in the tree exchanges control messages one level upward (with its 'master') and one level downward (with its 'slaves'). However, physical connections with nodes of other levels is not excluded. Moreover, to avoid overloads, nodes in each higher level of the organization only keep summaries of the resource information known to the nodes in the next lower level (for example, low-level managers know which user task nodes are idle, but their master only knows how many nodes were idle at the time when each low-level manager made report).

Dealing with failures of managing nodes

There is one very important and characteristic problem of this processor organization: 'What can happen if a managing node fails completely?' This problem can be solved in the following ways, depending on the level of a managing node:

(1)   A single master node would make the network too vulnerable to a failure of that node. This implies the need for more nodes at the highest level of the organization. These nodes form a global control board. Each of the board nodes regularly passes summary information to other board members to protect against hardware failures.

(2)   If a lower-level manager node fails completely, the master above it can communicate with the slaves below it. This communication is necessary to elect one of the slave nodes as a new manager and to reconstruct lost resource management data.

In general, the system is self-repairing, and can survive failures of both workers and managers. An efficient network hierarchy can be selected regardless of the actual topology of physical communication links between nodes of the network.

Load sharing method

The allocation of processors, when a job requiring m processes appears, is as follows. For simplicity, we assume that all processors are monoprogrammed (as in MICROS) and that jobs can be created at any level of the organization tree.

(1)   A job requiring m processes implies that the system has to allocate m processors for it.

(2)   Each manager knows approximately the number of available workers in its subtree. The exact number of available workers is not known because summary information is only passed at certain intervals.

(3)   If the number of available workers w is sufficient, that is, $w \geq m$, the manager reserves a number of them for a given job and creates an environment for all m processes.

(4)   If the number of available workers w is not sufficient, the manager passes the request upward in the tree to its boss. If the boss cannot handle the task, the request continues upward until it reaches a level that has enough available processors at its disposal. Allocation of processors is then performed and the processors are marked as unavailable.

It is obvious that if more than one manager can allocate processors, deadlock can occur. This implies the need for a synchronization mechanism.

9.5.3 Logical ring

The second organization which can be used for load sharing (processor hunting) is based on a virtual ring concept (Goscinski 1987). In this case all processors are organized into a logical ring of network nodes (Fig. 9.8). In this figure, circles represent nodes in the network and their logical connections are represented by arcs.

The organization of the system

As in the MICROS distributed operating system, the structure is independent of the physical topology of the network. Moreover, there is no supervisor node. This implies that this scheme is completely distributed.

Each node of the network can be a worker as well as a manager. This means that each node can request the necessary number of other

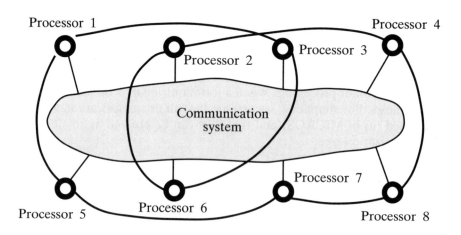

Fig. 9.8   Logical ring based organization of processors.

nodes to perform a given user task; also, when it is idle it can be at the disposal of any other node. A job can be created in any node of the network.

Hunting for an idle computer is based on the virtual ring connection. A token circulates among nodes. Only a node that possesses a token can hunt for an idle computer and perform resource management functions on the hunted computers (referred to as slaves). However, other connections among nodes are not excluded. Thus, manager computers can also communicate with their slaves directly or based on multicast or broadcast addresses.

Algorithm looking for idle processor

To implement processor hunting (allocation), the token is passed around the virtual ring. If a job requiring m processes appears in any node this node must wait for the token. When a node receives the token it may perform hunting and allocation functions, keeping the token. The node passes the token to its successor after completing its hunting functions.

The allocation (hunting) manager can work in the following way. For simplicity, assume that all processors are monoprogrammed. In this case a job requiring m processes needs m processors to be allocated for it. First the manager must find the necessary number of available processors.

(1) Because the nodes do not keep information about availability of all other nodes of the network, the manager must check all nodes by broadcasting an inquiry message. If a processor is available (idle), it sends a confirmation message and the manager reserves it.

   (a) The processor is released if during a given timeout it does not receive a message requesting creation of an environment for a process of a task.

   (b) If the number of available processors is less than the number of processors necessary to complete the task, the manager releases the available processors; (however, the manager can decide to use them and run a task less efficiently).

(2) The manager passes the token to its successor in the logical ring.

(3) If the number of available processors is m or acceptable, then the manager performs allocation of all necessary processors and creates computing environments in the slave processors.

(4) The slave processors are released after completing requested tasks.

There is another hunting method based on the virtual ring organization. In the case just described the token is a special message that does not contain any special information, and its possession allows a node to start hunting operations. In the second method, the token carries information about the availability of all processors registered in the virtual ring. Moreover, each computer stores a table which allows the mapping of logical ring names (position in the virtual ring) to communication identifiers (for example, port).

This allocation manager works in the following way. Let us assume again that a job requiring m processes needs m processors to be allocated for it. In this method the first step of the above algorithm is different (other steps are identical), and is as follows:

(1') After receiving the token, the manager counts the number of idle (available) computers, say k, in the distributed system. If $k \leq m$ then it registers their virtual ring addresses and sets in the token the relevant idleness (availability) bits to zero.

For the virtual ring organization, two types of failures must be considered: token loss and node failure. If the token is lost, it is necessary to elect a process to generate a new token. In the second case, a new logical ring must be established. There are a number of different algorithms for election and for reconstructing a logical ring; we do not discuss this topic further.

9.5.4 Free organization of processors – worm programs

A very special organization for hunting for idle computers and for replicating a process for each additional computation, called a **worm** program, was proposed by Shoch and Hupp (Shoch and Hupp 1982). Worm programs were also studied in Kindberg *et al.* (1987). The motivation for worms was generated by the observation that in local computer networks peripheral resources (disk drives and printers) are shared, but no attempt is made to share the processing load among the available processors.

The authors emphasize that 'the worm programs were an experiment in the development of distributed computations: programs that span machine boundaries and also replicate themselves in idle machines'. In general, a worm is a distributed system program that dynamically allocates resources and moves from computer to computer.

The worm approach has the following attributes:

(1) full and balanced utilization of distributed system resources, in particular processors, homogeneous and heterogeneous;

(2) parallel processing;

(3) tolerance of processor failure; and

(4) adaptability to short- and long-term network changes.

Worm programs were initially constructed for a homogeneous computing environment at the Xerox Palo Alto Research Center. The system of over 100 Alto computers connected by an Ethernet local area network was held together by the Pup architecture of internetwork protocols. Because many of the computers remain idle for lengthy periods, especially at night, they can be used effectively by constructing a system which hunts for idle computers.

The authors emphasize that almost any program can be modified to incorporate the worm mechanisms. However, running a worm depends on computer users, who must have confidence that their files will not be invaded and penetrated.

The organization of the system

A worm is a computation which lives on one or more computers. The processes on individual computers are described as **segments** of a worm. Worms may have only one segment or may be formed of a number of segments (Fig. 9.9). The segments of a worm communicate with each other. They can join and leave the computation. If one segment fails, other segments of the worm have to find another idle computer, create a computation environment, and add this new segment to the worm.

Two basic cases can be identified:

(1)   In the simplest case each segment of a worm carries a number indicating the number of processors (computers) which constitute the whole worm.

(2)   In the most advanced form of a worm the number of segments, that is, the number of necessary computers on which this worm lives, is not declared. The size of a worm can grow depending on the computation.

In both cases, the worm mechanism is responsible only for hunting an idle computer, and gathering and maintaining the segments of the worm. Application processes are built and run on top of this mechanism.

The worm segments broadcast resource requirements and then create new segments on consenting hosts. The worm mechanism should be seen as an allocation mechanism on which the user task is built. This mechanism gathers, releases and maintains the segments of the worm according to the requirements of the task. Because tasks can change in time, computers join and then leave the computation. The worm moves through the network.

The segments in a worm communicate with each other for two main purposes:

(1)   If one segment fails, the remaining pieces must find another available computer, initialize it, that is, create a computing environment, and add it to the worm.

(2)   When there is a need to extend or decrease the size of the worm to complete the task.

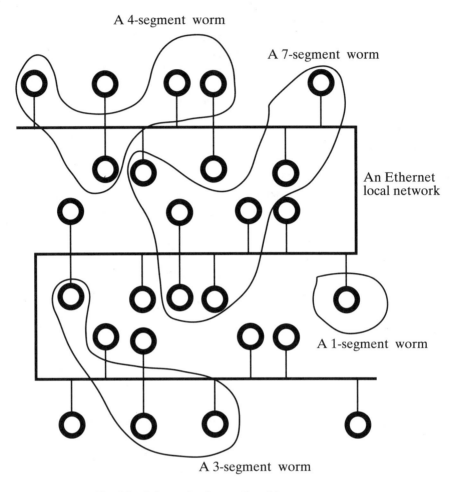

Fig. 9.9 Schematic of several multisegment worms.

The primary worm program is organized with three main components:

(1)   the initialization code to run when it starts on the first computer,

(2)   an initialization code to be run on any subsequent computer, and

(3)   the main program.

A worm life

There are three stages in the life of a worm program: locating an idle computer, releasing a computer and controlling the worm.

Locating an idle computer   First of all a worm must obtain its full component of segments to complete a user task in the most effective way. It must find some number of idle computers. If the number of available machines is less than the optimum for a given task, the worm expands, and runs the task, but not so effectively.

None of the computers connected to the network knows the global state of the system. This implies that the starting computer and each subsequent segment of the worm must locate an available computer, reserve it, create a computing environment and start another segment.

Location of an idle computer can be performed by sending probe 'inquire' messages to individual computers or by broadcasting an inquire message. In the first case the problem is how to determine which computer to probe next when looking for an additional segment. This problem can be solved in many different ways. One method, used by the authors of the first worm, is based on a very simple procedure: a segment begins with its own local host number and simply works its way up through the address space.

Each available computer sends an acknowledgement and reserves itself for a given period of time. If the requesting computer does not confirm its request by sending a message requesting creation of a computing environment during this period, the reservation is released.

Since multiple worms might be competing for the same idle computer, some synchronization mechanism should be used.

Releasing a computer   When a segment of a worm is finished with a computer, it returns that computer to an idle state. This operation should start a procedure, that allows other computers to treat this computer as available (for example, a diagnostic program).

Controlling the worm   The growth of a worm should be controlled while maintaining stable behaviour. A solution to this problem is still an open research question.

9.5.5   The Condor scheduling system

One of the most interesting and advanced systems that hunts for idle workstations is the Condor scheduling system (Litzkow *et al.* 1987). Condor allows idle workstation capacity to be used effectively. The system combines the results of two major projects:

(1)   The design of a scheduling algorithm that allows fair access to remote capacity for those users who use the system lightly in spite of large demands by heavy users (Mutka and Livny 1987*a*). As a result, the Up-Down algorithm has been developed; and

(2)   The development of remote execution facilities. As a result, the Remote UNIX facility has been developed (Litzkow 1987).

The Condor system was designed with the following issues in mind.

(1)   A user should not be aware that his/her jobs are executed remotely, nor where they are executed. The placement of background jobs should be transparent to the user.

(2)   A job should be restarted automatically and completed on another idle workstation, if a remote computer fails.

(3)   All users expect to have their background jobs completed in the shortest time. Thus, remote workstations should be accessed on a fair basis.

(4)   The mechanism implementing the system should consume very little computation and memory capacity.

(5)   The system should allow remote execution of long and very long jobs.

(6)   The system should not interfere with users and their local activity.

The system organization

The authors of the Condor system decided to structure the process (job) scheduler in such a way that it lies between a centralized, static approach and the fully distributed approach. The scheduling structure follows the principle that workstations are autonomous computing resources, managed by their owners. This structure is illustrated in Fig. 9.10.

The figure shows that on each workstation a local scheduler runs and there is a background process (job) queue. One workstation also holds a central coordinator. User processes are placed in the background process queue. A process state information is stored individually by each workstation. Moreover, each workstation schedules its own processes. The central coordinator is responsible for assigning computation capacity of idle processors to requesting workstations. These workstations use this capacity to schedule their processes.

The assignment of capacity is based on the knowledge of which processor is idle and which workstations have waiting background processes. The coordinator gathers this information periodically (every two minutes in the Condor system implementation). On the other hand, each local scheduler monitors its processor to check whether it is idle. If the local user has resumed using the workstation and a remote background job is running on this workstation, the local scheduler immediately preempts the background job. As a result, the user can have computation capacity under his/her control.

This short description of the Condor scheduling structure shows that process migration and remote execution play very important roles in converting idle workstations into computation servers. The workstations operate under the Berkeley BSD 4.3 UNIX operating system. To achieve compatibility between local and remote job execution, the Remote UNIX (RU) facility has been developed.

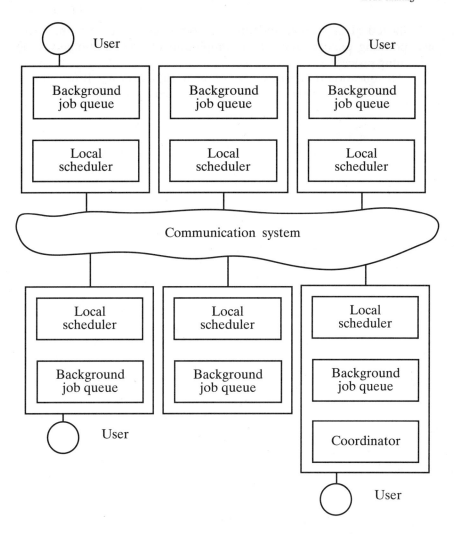

Fig. 9.10 The scheduling structure of the Condor system.

The Remote UNIX (RU) facility possess one important and unique feature that distinguishes it from other process migration facilities. This feature is **checkpointing**. Litzkow and his co-workers emphasize that the process migration facilities of such systems as V kernel, Sprite, and NEST were not specifically designed to execute long jobs remotely. In these systems intermediate results are not saved if there is no idle computer to move the process. Thus, pre-emption of a remote background job that is computationally intensive and runs for a long period can be critical for a user and very expensive. Checkpointing is an operation of saving the state of a process when it executes, so that it can be restarted at any time, and on any computer in the system. Thus, checkpointing enables successful completion of computationally time consuming processes.

The question that arises now is how to fulfil user needs for remote computation power. This problem can be solved by a proper scheduling algorithm.

Scheduling algorithm

Access to remote idle processors should be fair. This means that light users should be able to get access to remote workstations when they request it and heavy users should not be permitted to grab all available computation capacity for long periods. In the Condor system environment, fair access to idle processors is provided using the specially designed Up-Down algorithm.

The algorithm used by the coordinator trades off the computation capacities users have been assigned with the time they have waited to receive them. This is achieved using a schedule index maintained for each workstation in the following way. When remote capacity is allocated to a workstation, its index is increased. The index is decreased when a workstation requests remote computation power, but is denied access to it.

To assign a background job waiting on a given workstation to an idle remote processor, the coordinator uses the priority of each workstation. The priority is determined by the value of the workstation's index. The assignment operation is as follows:

(1)   Initially, assign the index for each workstation to zero. Update the indexes of the workstations periodically, using the approach given above.

(2)   The coordinator checks periodically whether any workstation has new jobs to be executed remotely.

(a)   If a workstation with higher priority has a job to execute, and there are no idle workstations, the coordinator pre-empts a remotely executing job from a processor with lower priority.

(b)   Checkpoint the pre-empted job.

(c)   Assign the newly available capacity to the job of the workstation with the higher priority.

Further details of the algorithm are given in Mutka and Livny (1987a). The performance of the Condor hunting system is presented in Litzkow et al. (1987). We do not discuss these results here. However, there are some issues associated with remote job execution that should be raised.

Remote execution of background processes requires their placement on the remote idle workstation's disk. This operation usually consumes a large amount of disk space. Users rarely manage their disk space carefully and their disks are often almost full so, if a workstation is idle, it does not necessarily mean that a job can be executed by its idle processor. The disk may not have enough free space for the background process(es). Thus, the coordinator must gather not only information about idle processors, but also must know how much disk space is available.

There is an additional disk space issue. The lack of local disk space may restrict the number of background jobs to be run remotely and concurrently, since checkpoint files of remotely executing jobs are stored locally. The local disk space situation can be improved if file servers can store these checkpoint files.

Another issue raised by Litzkow and his co-workers relates to the no interference design requirement. The question is whether a remote execution of a job should be checkpointed immediately when an owner resumes activity, and the remote job killed, or the processor is immediately returned but disk space occupied by a remote job is not released until the checkpoint files are moved. Such a checkpoint operation is performed if the processor does not become available within a defined period. The latter approach is supported by the observation that workstations that are identified by the coordinator as idle have a common feature that their unavailable intervals are usually short. On the other hand, this approach contradicts the requirement that remote jobs do not interfere with local activities. This led the authors to the new strategy of taking checkpoints of remote executions periodically. Moreover, when an owner resumes activity on a computer running a remote process, this process is killed immediately. This strategy minimizes any interference and the only computation lost is that between the process's last checkpoint and the time it was pre-empted.

Since there is no published comparison of the four processor allocation organizations presented here, it is impossible to suggest which organization should be used in what circumstances. This problem is currently under study.

9.6 Load balancing

Until now, we have discussed the problem of load sharing (also referred to as hunting for idle workstations). However, the solution of the load sharing problem is a local solution. It improves performance indices of only a few users and their processes. Thus, there is the need for sharing processors not only when they are idle, but also when some processors are lightly loaded and others are heavily loaded.

Load balancing is part of the broad problem of resource allocation. The problem of load balancing (referred to also as distributed

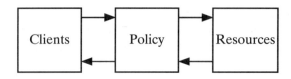

Fig. 9.11 The relationship between clients, policy and resources in resource management problem.

scheduling) is how to distribute processes among processors connected by a network to equalize the workload among them. While load sharing uses process migration only when there is an idle processor, balancing the workload may require migration even when no node is idle.

Before we deal with load balancing, we should clarify three basic terms in common use in the literature: load balancing, distributed scheduling and resource allocation. There is often an implicit distinction between these terms; is there any real distinction?

Let us have a closer look at the resource management problem (Casavant and Kuhl 1988a). We recall that resource management is a policy used to access and use resources effectively and efficiently by clients (processes, active objects). Thus, in this problem one can distinguish the following components: clients, resources and policy. Their relationship is illustrated in Fig. 9.11.

If we observe the behaviour of the system illustrated in Fig. 9.11 from the resources' point of view, we see the resource allocation problem. On the other hand, the behaviour of the system from the clients' point of view leads to the scheduling problem – in a distributed environment, the distributed scheduling problem. Thus, resource allocation and scheduling are merely two terms describing the same resource management problem but from two different points of view.

Load balancing is that part of a distributed scheduling policy which is responsible for the distribution of the system workload among the processors through process migration. Thus, load balancing strongly reflects client requirements. However, despite the fact that load balancing is a narrower term than distributed scheduling, because it reflects and covers different approaches, we use 'load balancing' and 'distributed scheduling' interchangeably in the following presentation.

Because a client wants to access a named resource quickly and efficiently, but does not wish to experience huge overheads, a system that performs policy functions must fulfil two client requirements:

(1) performance – how well resources are managed by the system, and

(2) efficiency – how difficult or costly it is to access and use a resource through the system.

9.6.1 Load balancing problems

The strategic goal of load balancing, that is, moving processes to equalize the system workload, generates some basic questions. These questions, oriented towards the transfer policy and location policy that are basic components of load balancing, are as follows:

- When to migrate processes to balance the system workload?

- How to compare workloads of different computers to decide which one should be offloaded first, while others must wait?

- Which process from a chosen computer should be moved?

- Which computer is the best destination for a process to be migrated?

- Which computer should be involved in searching for a lightly loaded (even idle) computer? Should it be the source computer for a given process, or should lightly loaded computers perhaps offer their services?

- When are the scheduling/load balancing decisions to be made?

- Which parameters should be taken into consideration in making the decisions required by the abovementioned questions?

- What can happen when data is not available or out of date?

- Should the data necessary to make these decisions be gathered and stored centrally, or in a distributed manner?

- Should computers cooperate in making decisions or not? If so, what mechanisms should be needed to update system state in relevant computers?

- What is the tradeoff between performance and overhead (costs) of making scheduling/load balancing decisions?

- How can one avoid overloading a lightly loaded computer?

There are a huge number of techniques, methods and algorithms for load balancing. Unfortunately, they are presented in the literature using inconsistent and even contradictory terminology, different problem statements and different methods. This makes it difficult to compare the resulting systems and give good answers to the above problems. Thus, first of all it is necessary to classify load balancing algorithms, based on an appropriate (small and concise) set of features.

9.6.2 Taxonomies of load balancing

The first taxonomy of load balancing (scheduling) in distributed computing systems was proposed by Casey (1981). It is a hierarchical classification of schedulers that reflects research results up to 1980. Since then a large number of additional distinguishing features have been identified. These features allow further differentiation between approaches to load balancing.

One such feature is associated with the type of node that takes the initiative in the search for a lightly-loaded computer. A taxonomy of load balancing algorithms that uses this feature and classifies them into source-initiative based strategies and server-initiative based strategies has been presented by Wang and Morris (1985). Those authors also characterized algorithms according to the degree of information dependency involved. An additional set of characteristic features of load balancing algorithms has been identified by Fogg (1987). Based on these features a flat classification of algorithms was presented.

Another taxonomy that reflects the latest results in the area of distributed scheduling was proposed by Casavant and Kuhl (1988*a*). Their taxonomy agrees with Casey's classification, but provides a more detailed and complete look at load balancing. Thus, their taxonomy is a hybrid of

(1)   hierarchical classification scheme – used as far as possible to reduce the total number of classes, and

(2)   flat classification scheme – used when the descriptors of the system may be chosen in any arbitrary order.

Despite Casavant and Kuhl's claim that their taxonomy is the most complete and general, we will use not only their classification structure but also that presented by Wang and Morris (Wang and Morris 1985). To define different classes of load balancing algorithms, we also use Chen (1987), Eager *et al.* (1986), Krueger and Livny (1987), Ni *et al.* (1985), Shen (1988) and Zhou (1988).

9.6.3   Hierarchical classification

A hierarchical classification of load balancing algorithms is illustrated in Fig. 9.12 (Casavant and Kuhl 1988*a*).

We discuss several classes of algorithms below, following this classification. Note that because local scheduling is described in numerous papers, we focus our discussion on global scheduling (load balancing).

Global distributed scheduling algorithms can be divided into two large groups: static and dynamic. This division is based on the time at which the scheduling/load balancing decisions are made. Static algorithms are discussed in Section 9.7, and dynamic algorithms in Section 9.8.

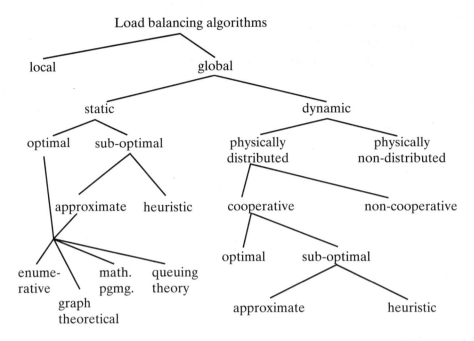

Fig. 9.12 Hierarchical classification of load balancing algorithms {adapted from Casavant and Kuhl (1988)}.

9.7 Static load balancing algorithms

Static load balancing, also referred to as task placement, uses algorithms which find the location for all processes before they start execution. A process does not move from a processor if it has begun execution – there is *a priori* assignment of processes to processors. Process transfer decisions are made deterministically or probabilistically, based on some probabilistic patterns. The current state of the total distributed system is not taken into consideration.

The principal advantage of static load balancing is its simplicity, because system state information need not be maintained. It is also effective when the workload can be sufficiently well described before making a decision. However, it fails to adjust to fluctuations in the system load. Moreover, it suffers from poor resource utilization.

There are two different classes of assumptions made by researchers of load balancing algorithms, and they generate two classes of algorithms:

(1) Unrealistic or impractical assumptions about processes that are to be executed and/or the execution environment, for example, pro-

cessing time of each process is known, communication traffic and cost between each pair of processes is known;

(2) The realistic assumption that nothing about the future behaviour of a process is known.

9.7.1 Optimal versus suboptimal

Static load balancing is simply a mathematical problem, matching the state of the system and resource requirements against some performance indices (criterion function). The following measures are in common use:

(1) minimizing total process completion time,

(2) maximizing utilization of resources, or

(3) maximizing system throughput.

Global, static, optimal load balancing algorithms are described for example in Chou and Abraham (1982), Ma *et al.* (1982), Ramamoorthy *et al.* (1972) and Shen and Tsai (1985). These algorithms have been developed based on queuing theory, mathematical programming (branch and bound) and graph theory.

Because of the size of a typical distributed system (large number of processes, processors, and other resources that impose some restrictions) static load balancing is a complex computation problem. Thus, obtaining optimal solutions can be very expensive and in many cases not feasible in a reasonable time period. This leads to the use of suboptimal solutions. There are two general categories of suboptimal solutions: approximate and heuristic.

9.7.2 Approximate versus heuristic

The approximate approach uses the same mathematical and computational model for the algorithm, but searching for a solution does not cover the whole solution space. This means that the goal is not finding an optimal solution but only a satisfactory one. Searching for only a 'good' solution decreases the taken time. It is the principal advantage of this class of algorithms. The problem is how to determine that a solution is good enough.

The following factors determine whether this approach is worthy of pursuit:

(1) availability of a function to evaluate a solution;

(2) the time required to evaluate a solution;

(3) the ability to judge according to some metric the value of an optimal solution; and

(4)   availability of mechanism for intelligently pruning the solution space.

Global, static, suboptimal, approximate load balancing algorithms have been described in Bannister and Trivedi (1983) and Lo (1984). The former algorithm is based on mathematical programming, the latter on graph theory.

The second category of suboptimal algorithms is based on heuristic search strategies. One of the most important features of these algorithms is that assumptions about *a priori* knowledge concerning processes and system loading are more realistic. Moreover, computation time and the amount of system resources required to find solutions based on these algorithms is reasonable.

Some global, static, suboptimal, heuristic load balancing strategies are described in Chu *et al.* (1980), Efe (1982), Gabrielian and Tyler (1984), Kruskal and Weiss (1984) and Ward and Romero (1984).

9.7.3   Optimal and suboptimal-approximate techniques

Both optimal and suboptimal-approximate solutions are based on the same formal computational models. These models can be developed based on the following mathematical areas: mathematical programming; graph theory; queuing theory; and solution space enumeration and search. (See Fig. 9.12 in Section 9.6.3.)

We will not analyse or present any of the algorithms belonging to the static branch of the hierarchical taxonomy as they do not result in good performance in distributed computer systems. This is simply because they do not take into consideration the current state of the system and the workload fluctuation.

9.8   Global dynamic load balancing algorithms

In static load balancing, decisions regarding the location of processes are made before they are executed. These decisions are based on assumptions about the processes that are to be executed (execution time) and the execution environment (current load, transfer times and communication costs). In practice, this information is usually not known – only a very little *a priori* knowledge is available.

Dynamic load balancing attempts to equalize the system load dynamically as processes are created and resumed. These algorithms allow processes to migrate to remote computers once they have begun execution. The goal of this migration is to find the 'best' locations for all processes existing in the distributed system. 'Best' here is used in the sense of a given performance index (indices) and existing restrictions. The decisions are made using the information on the current system state, that is, each computer should know the states of other computers.

Finding a dynamic solution is much more complicated than finding a static one. It requires gathering and maintaining system state information. However, dynamic load allocation can achieve good performance by making process migration decisions utilizing current system load indices. A problem closely associated with gathering and maintaining system state information is where the decision is to be made.

9.8.1 Distributed versus nondistributed

This issue involves whether the status information of all the processors and execution environments is to be collected at one location, and a scheduler used to dispatch processes to suitable locations for processing, or whether the decision making process is to be physically distributed among the processors that utilize information stored in many places.

The most important feature of making decisions centrally is simplicity. However, such systems suffer from a number of drawbacks. The first drawback is that gathering information and maintaining an up-to-date system state in one central location, can lead to a large time overhead, since there are transfer delays and messages may be lost. It is a very serious problem – it is well-known from the theory of optimization that decisions based on information that is not up-to-date can be worse than no decisions. The second drawback is the low reliability of such systems: failure of the node on which the load balancing is done results in the collapse of the entire management system.

Global dynamic centralized (physically nondistributed) load allocation is discussed for example in Chow and Kohler (1979) and Ousterhout *et al.* (1980).

A globally distributed load allocation system does not suffer from the above drawbacks. The bottleneck of collecting status information at a single site is avoided and schedulers can react quickly to dynamic changes in the system state. If one computer running a scheduler fails, others can continue their decision jobs, with the total load balancing system working at a reduced performance level. The distributed nature of a decision system generates some basic design issues. The first is the relationship between distributed decision components.

9.8.2 Cooperative versus non-cooperative

In a global physically distributed load allocation system, many components are involved and responsible for making decisions. If these distributed components cooperate in decision making, we deal with cooperative algorithms. All computers work toward one common system-wide goal though each of them is responsible for a portion of the scheduling task.

On the other hand, if computers make decisions independently of each other, the algorithms are called non-cooperative. Because the components act as autonomous entities they are oriented only towards individual goals. As a result, their decisions only affect local performance. Moreover, independently-made decisions can contradict each other and generate resource conflicts.

In the class of global physically-distributed cooperative algorithms it is possible to identify so-called 'bidding' algorithms. The basic concept lying behind this group is negotiation between components and submitting bids for contracts. To maintain consistency with the hierarchical taxonomy we do not discuss this group of algorithms here. They are discussed in detail in Section 9.9.

The great majority of global physically-distributed load allocation algorithms utilize cooperation among the scheduler's distributed components. We discuss this class of algorithm below. Some non-cooperative algorithms are described in Klappholtz and Park (1984) and Reif and Sprirakis (1984); we do not discuss them further.

9.8.3 Lower sub-branches of the dynamic branch

Global physically-distributed cooperative algorithms, just like static algorithms, can provide optimal or suboptimal solutions (load balancing decisions). Optimal decisions can be optimal locally or globally. When optimal solutions are computationally infeasible, it is necessary to use suboptimal solutions.

As for static algorithms, suboptimal dynamic solutions can be approximate or based on heuristics; and algorithms can be based on mathematical programming, queuing theory, graph theory, and solution space enumeration and search.

The lower levels of the hierarchical classification are the same for both static and dynamic algorithms.

9.9 Flat taxonomy of load balancing algorithms

Some descriptors of the load balancing algorithms cannot be chosen in a hierarchical way. This was the main reason for the development by Casavant and Kuhl of a flat classification. In this discussion we follow the structure used in Casavant and Kuhl (1988a) and results of work presented in Eager et al. (1986, 1988), Shen (1988), Smith (1980), Stankovic and Sidhu (1984), Wang and Morris (1985) and Zhou (1988).

9.9.1 Adaptive versus non-adaptive

This classification is associated with the kind of data used to make a decision. More precisely, whether only information on the current state is used, or the previous behaviour of the system together with the current state are used to make decisions.

An adaptive scheduler is one that modifies, that is, changes dynamically, its algorithms and parameters used to implement the scheduling policy according to the previous and current behaviour of the system. This is performed in response to previous decisions made by itself, which means it is based on the history of system activity. Note that this scheduling is also called probabilistic.

Stankovic and Sidhu (1984) developed a scheduling algorithm that considers many parameters when making decisions. The scheduler observes the response of the system to initial values of the parameters. As a result, it ignores some of these parameters if it thinks that they provide no information about change in system state; and changes the weight given to other parameters, if the changes they imply are not consistent with those implied by the rest of the parameters.

On the other hand, a non-adaptive scheduler (also called state-dependent policy) does not modify its basic control mechanism on the basis of the history of system activity.

One should note that the term 'adaptive load balancing' is also used to describe dynamic load balancing. This can be found in Eager *et al.* (1986, 1988).

The results of studies of both state-dependent and probabilistic strategies show that state-dependent strategies perform better, but have higher overhead. Moreover, probabilistic strategies are sometimes insensitive to dynamic changes in system load, resulting in suboptimal performance.

It is obvious that state information used in state-dependent strategies must be readily available and up-to-date, because decisions based on outdated or inaccurate state information can degrade performance.

9.9.2 Bidding

Bidding is an approach used for selecting a remote computer, which can be the destination computer for a migrating process. Bidding is performed when a computer does not have accurate information about states of other computers, or the information it has does not allow it to identify a good destination computer for a selected process. The concept behind the bidding approach is negotiation between components of a load balancing system (cooperative agents) and submitting bids for contracts.

A bidding negotiation has four features:

(1) it is a local process that does not involve centralized control,

(2) information is exchanged in both directions,

(3) each peer-to-peer negotiation component evaluates the information from its own perspective, and usually is based on a surplus in the resources needed by a process to be migrated, and

(4) final agreement is achieved by mutual selection.

Each computer in a distributed system is responsible for one of the two functions of the bidding process:

(1) **manager** (also called a local agent) – it works on the behalf of a process, trying to find a location for its execution,

(2) **contractor** (also called a remote agent) – it represents a remote computer which is able to work for a process from another computer.

Computers are not designated *a priori* as managers or contractors – the function can be changed dynamically during the course of making decisions. A computer may even perform both functions simultaneously for different contracts.

The bidding system works in the following way:

(1) The manager announces the existence of a process to be executed by broadcasting, or multi-tasking, or directing an **task announcement** (request for bid) message. At the same time its computer can receive announcement messages from other managers.

(2) Available contractors evaluate received announcements and submit bids on those for which they are suited.

(3) The manager evaluates received bids and awards contracts to the nodes it determines to be the most appropriate. The contracts are multicast to the bidders. It can also happen that there is no bid available for a given process. In this case contracts are not awarded.

According to the bidding mechanism, a contractor is allowed to partition a task and award contracts to other computers in order to improve performance. In this case the contractor becomes a manager.

There are a number of important features of load balancing algorithms based on bidding. The first is that the effectiveness and performance of these algorithms depends on the amount and type of information exchanged during negotiation. The second is that all computers have full autonomy; managers can decide to which computer to award a contract, and contractors have the freedom to respond to announcement messages by sending or not sending bids, and if sending to which manager.

Global physically-distributed cooperative algorithms utilizing the bidding approach are discussed in Casavant and Kuhl (1984), Ramamritham and Stankovic (1984), Stankovic and Sidhu (1984), Stankovic (1985) and Ramamritham *et al.* (1989).

9.9.3 Source-initiative versus server-initiative strategies

A basic problem of load balancing is when process migration should be performed, and which node could initiate this process to balance system load.

Wang and Morris (1985) propose a taxonomy of load balancing algorithms that is based on the type of a node that takes the initiative in the global search for a lightly-loaded or heavily-loaded computer. Indirectly, this taxonomy addresses the problem of when to start load balancing.

The taxonomy is based on a logical model in which nodes are divided into two groups: sources that generate tasks to be processed, and servers that process these tasks. A single computer (node) may be both a source and/or server. The logical model is illustrated in Fig. 9.13.

In a distributed system the problem is which computers can look for lightly loaded ones. The division of nodes given above leads to

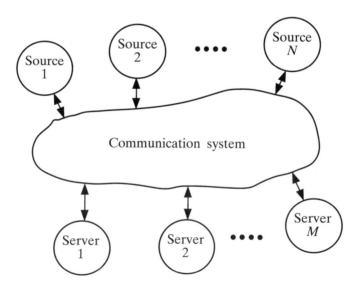

Fig. 9.13 Node type initiative based model of a distributed computer system.

source-initiative and server-initiative strategies. If the source overloaded node is responsible for finding a remote location for process execution, the strategy is called source-initiative. On the other hand, if a server looks for and requests processes from overloaded computers, the strategy is called server-initiative.

There are two major differences between these two classes of algorithms. The first is that in a source-initiative algorithm, queues tend to form at the server, whereas in a server-initiative algorithm, queues tend to form at the sources. The second is that in source-initiative algorithms, load balancing decisions are usually made at task arrival epochs (or a subset thereof), whereas in server-initiative algorithms, load balancing decisions are usually made at task departure epochs (or a subset thereof).

One of the most important conclusions presented in Eager *et al.* (1986), Wang and Morris (1985) is that with the same level of information available, server-initiative algorithms have the potential to outperform source-initiative algorithms. Moreover, source-initiative algorithms should be used in systems with light to moderate loads; server-initiative algorithms should be used in systems with light load, but only if the process migration costs are comparable under these two strategies or are not significant.

Eager and his co-workers (Eager *et al.* 1986) note that server-initiative algorithms are best supported by process migration. This is because processes may be transferred upon the server's request. Another study of server-initiative and source-initiative algorithms is reported in Zhou (1988).

9.9.4 Classification based on the level of information dependency

Another classification of dynamic load balancing algorithms is closely associated with node type taxonomy. This classification is based on the level of information dependency that is embodied in a strategy for selecting a remote node. The level of information dependency that is embodied in a strategy means the degree to which a source node knows the status of servers or a server knows the status of sources.

Seven levels of load balancing algorithms, classified by information dependency, have been identified in Wang and Morris (1985). This number of levels is arbitrary. The information levels have been arranged so that the information of a higher level subsumes that of the lower level.

The lowest level is represented by 'blind' algorithms which do not require any information. Examples of algorithms of the next levels are: partitioning algorithms, random splitting or service algorithms, cyclic splitting or service algorithms, join the shortest queue (JSQ) or serve the longest queue (SLQ). To the highest level belong these algorithms which require extensive information, for example, global first come first served (FCFS) or shortest task first algorithms.

These algorithms are based on the following information:

(1)　randomized parameter;

(2)　sequence state – the place where a previous task was sent in the case of source-initiative algorithms, or the place from where the previous task was picked up in the case of server-initiative algorithms;

(3)　server busy/idle (source-initiative algorithms) or source queue emptiness (server-initiative algorithms);

(4)　server queue lengths (source-initiative algorithms) or source queue lengths (server-initiative algorithms);

(5)　departure epochs of completed tasks at servers, or arrival epochs of tasks at sources; and

(6)　completed and remaining task at servers, or execution times of tasks at sources.

A list of these parameters shows also in a natural way the information used by algorithms of subsequent levels, since, as we said above, the information of a higher level subsumes that of the lower level.

One can expect that an increase in the level of information available allows the construction of better algorithms, which improve the performance of the total system. This is only true to some extent, because at some stage

- more information exchanged by scheduler components increases communication costs, overloads communication lines, and

- more sophisticated and complex software may become necessary; this generates higher computation overhead.

The problem can be stated differently, by asking what level of complexity is appropriate for dynamic load balancing algorithms. In this context, the following four location policies can be studied:

(1)　**Random** – it uses no information about the state of other computers; a process is sent to another randomly selected computer. Thus, no exchange of state information is required when a decision relating to the location of a migrated process is made. The disadvantage of this policy is that it is easy to send a process to an inappropriate computer (for example, overloaded).

(2)　**Threshold** – it collects and uses a small amount of information about a potential destination computer. According to this policy a computer is selected at random, and tested whether its load after transferring the process exceeds its threshold. If not, a process is migrated, otherwise, the policy is repeated.

(3) **Shortest** – it collects and uses more information than the previous algorithm and makes the 'best' choice. In this case a number of computers are selected at random and each is tested to identify its queue length. The process is migrated to the computer with the shortest queue, unless it is larger than the threshold. Otherwise, the originating computer must run the process.

(4) **Focused** – it collects and uses more information than the previous algorithm and makes the 'best' choice. In this case a number of computers are selected at random and each is tested to identify the estimated surplus in the resources. The node with the highest surplus needed by the migrated process, if big enough, is selected, and treated as the destination computer. This policy implies the need for periodical calculation of the resource surplus.

According to Eager *et al.* (1986) and Ramamrithan *et al.* (1989) experience with these algorithms shows that:

(1) Extremely simple scheduling policies, that is, policies that collect a very small amount of state information and use this information in very simple ways, provide dramatic performance improvement relative to no load balancing.

(2) The performance achieved with these simple policies is close to that which can be expected from complex policies. Complex policies are those that collect a large amount of information and attempt to make the 'best' choice given this information.

(3) Effective load balancing can be achieved without extensive state information. Moreover, extensive state information can be detrimental to system performance (increased costs of communication and computation).

(4) These results are valid over a wide range of system parameters.

9.9.5 Non-pre-emptive versus pre-emptive policies

Global dynamic load balancing systems are non-pre-emptive if they assign only newly-created processes to computers, that is, processes are not reassigned once they commence execution (Barak and Shiloh 1985, Chen 1987). This class of systems is also called non-migratory (Eager *et al.* 1988). The process is not migrated even though its run-time characteristics, or the run-time characteristics of any other process, change such that nodes become computationally unbalanced.

Pre-emptive load balancing systems, also called systems with migration, are those in which processes in execution may be interrupted, moved to another computer, and resumed in a new computation environment. These operations are performed whenever anomalies appear in the work loads of the computers. Thus, the system can adapt to workload fluctuations.

We recall that migrating processes during execution, though complicated, is feasible. But are there performance benefits offered by pre-emptive (migratory) load balancing beyond those offered by non-pre-emptive (non-migratory) load balancing. It has been emphasized that the adaptability mentioned above allows both an increase in throughput and a decrease in process response time Bryant and Finkel (1981) and Barak and Shiloh (1985). This problem was also studied by Eager, Lazowska, and Zahorjan (Eager *et al.* 1988). As a result of their study they present the following conclusions:

(1)   There are probably no conditions under which pre-emptive (migratory) load balancing could yield major performance improvements beyond those offered by non-pre-emptive (non-migratory) load balancing. This is particularly true with respect to the advantages of systems utilizing non-pre-emptive policies over systems which do not provide any load balancing.

(2)   Migratory load balancing can offer modest additional performance improvements only under some fairly extreme conditions. These conditions are characterized by high variability in both job service demands and the workload generation process.

(3)   The benefits of pre-emptive (migratory) policies are not limited by their costs, but rather by the inherent effectiveness of non-pre-emptive (non-migratory) load balancing.

These results show that although many interesting results have been received, they contradict, and there is the need to carry out more study in this area.

It is clear that choosing a suitable load balancing strategy is a very difficult task. In the following sections we present requirements that should be taken into consideration in carrying out a study or design algorithms for load balancing, and present some scheduling policies.

9.10   Characterization of load balancing algorithms

The taxonomies of load balancing presented in Section 9.6 provide a background for a more detailed study of some specific algorithms. Before we survey some of them, it is worth creating a background for their discussion and stating some important requirements for their study and design.

9.10.1 Performance

In Section 9.1.3 there was discussion of some general aspects of improving performance in distributed systems. Here, the issue is addressed once more with reference to some work done in the area of load balancing.

Load balancing algorithms should improve system performance. Computer performance is not easily defined, however, and there are also user performance expectations to be met. In general, the goal of load balancing policy is to distribute the computation load, transparently to a user, to achieve the best computer performance and to meet user performance expectations. This is difficult to assess, however, as there is no single performance objective for computer systems, and it is difficult to determine user performance expectations. It is also difficult to assess the efficiency of a load balancing facility, that is, the amount of overhead associated with the load balancing facility itself.

Usually, users are interested in the quality of service provided to their processes and they want to be treated fairly. Fairness may imply that a load balancing policy is non-discriminatory. This means that variations in the quality of service which is received by all processes in the system should be strictly random. The problem is how to measure the quality of service.

These problems are closely associated with the selection of performance indices for a computer system.

In order to solve load balancing problems it is necessary to solve an optimization problem. In general, there are three major performance indices for distributed scheduling:

(1) **System throughput** – this index is oriented mainly towards computer performance, but can also be used to assess stream processing systems.

(2) **Wait time** – defined as a total amount of time a process spends waiting for resources, and **wait ratio** – defined as the wait time per unit of service. These indices reflect user performance expectations in addition to being oriented towards computer performance. In this group of performance indices are mean wait time, mean and standard deviation of process wait time and wait ratio, and the correlations between wait ratio and service demand and between wait time and service demand. These measures are used in Krueger and Livny (1987).

(3) **Response time** of the distributed system – this index is oriented mainly towards user performance expectations. A performance index closely associated with response time is mean execution time (used by Barak and Shiloh [1985] and Chen [1987]).

Two factors largely determine the efficiency of the load balancing facility:

(1)   the cost of exchange of load estimation messages, coordination of processes involved in a potential process migration, negotiation messages, process transfer, and of transmitting the results from the remote computer, and

(2)   processor cost, for load estimation based on measurement of current load, and for packing data for transmission and unpacking it upon reception.

These costs should be minimized.

Which of these costs has more influence on the efficiency of a load balancing facility? It depends on the speeds of the processors and the communication system, and their interrelation. Eager and his co-workers report (Eager *et al.* 1986) that in their computation environment (Ethernet), in contrast to previous papers on load balancing, the cost of a process transfer is low, but it can be represented as a processor cost rather than as a network communication cost.

9.10.2   Characteristics of load balancing algorithms

A load balancing strategy should have certain desirable properties. The most important are:

(1)   Optimal overall system performance, defined as total processing capacity being maximized while retaining acceptable delays;

(2)   Fairness of service, defined as uniformly acceptable performance provided to jobs regardless of the source on which the job executes;

(3)   Failure tolerance, defined as robustness of performance in the presence of partial failures in the system;

(4)   Accommodation ability, defined as the degree to which a strategy accommodates reconfiguration and extension;

(5)   Good performance of the system under incidental conditions (overload).

Global dynamic load balancing algorithms should be developed with regard to the following six characteristics, which have a strong impact on performance (Fogg 1987):

(1)   **Load estimation** – The load on the computer involving processes being executed and those awaiting execution. Load estimation

should include processor, process and environment characteristics.

(2) **Information exchange between computers** – A computer transmits load information to inform remote computers of its current state. The amount of information exchanged involves a tradeoff between having a high level of detail (for example, information about every process) and minimizing the volume of network traffic.

(3) **Load information and transmission patterns** – A computer should send load information to every remote computer, as this provides the greatest number of potential destinations for migrating processes. Two addressing patterns can be used: one-to-one or one-to-many. The problem of how often load estimates should be sent to remote computers is still an open problem. An algorithm's transmission pattern should involve a tradeoff between the volume of network traffic and the desire to communicate with every node in the system.

(4) **Decision basis for moving tasks** – A decision mechanism should be used for determining whether a particular process is performing well or not on a given computer.

(5) **Receiver's knowledge of migrating tasks** – It is preferable for a destination computer to know about incoming processes before they arrive. Possessing this information helps to avoid some of the problems of out-of-date information.

(6) **Stability** – This relates to the amount of schedulable resource being consumed while the system state is changing, but not moving toward a better state (Casavant and Kuhl 1988b). Stability is a common issue of all dynamic systems. We say that a system is stable if it produces a bounded response to a bounded input. In the case of load balancing, an input is an externally-induced change in the overall system state.

   A distributed scheduling algorithm can be said to be stable:

   (a) if the response time to any 'reasonable' burst of arrivals of processes does not exceed some bound,

   (b) if the load on two computers do not differ by more than $\alpha\%$,

   (c) if it does not generate processor thrashing (exchange of a process without any productive work).

Casavant and Kuhl emphasize that in order to improve the response time in the case of at least one class of algorithms they studied, a certain amount of instability is desirable (Casavant and Kuhl 1988b). This statement is in accordance with results observed in the study of mechanical systems (for example, air planes).

9.10.3   Components of load balancing algorithms

Dynamic distributed load balancing algorithms consist of four basic components:

(1)   **The information gathering policy** – This component specifies system state information (the kind and amount of information) and maintains this information (for example, processor load, lengths of queues, process oriented information, history of system workload). The information gathering policy provides information to the two other components.

(2)   **The transfer policy** – This component determines whether a process is eligible for load balancing, that is, whether to run a process locally or remotely. This decision is based on task parameters, processor load and other information.

(3)   **The location policy** – This component determines to which computers eligible processes should be moved.

(4)   **The negotiation component** – The above three components of distributed load balancing algorithms are not isolated from analogical components of other computer systems. They interact in various ways, in general through the negotiation component; for example, it sends requests for bids, receives bids, and sends contracts.

The internal interaction of these components is illustrated in Fig. 9.14. This figure also shows that the results of a negotiation process are passed to the transfer policy and location policy components, and thus influence the final decisions made by computers.

9.10.4   Message priorities in systems with load balancing facilities

Load balancing requires the exchange of many messages between computers involved in this operation. In addition to regular messages exchanged between communicating processes, there are messages containing state information (statistics), negotiation messages (for example, bit for request messages), result return messages and process migration messages. These messages must be prioritized, to achieve the best performance.

Regular messages are assigned the highest priority, because they represent 'basic blood circulation' in a distributed system. The priorities of other messages are determined by considering their relative importance in the process of improving performance, and the overheads in terms of additional costs: communication costs measured for example using delay units, and computation costs measured in percentage of CPU utilization.

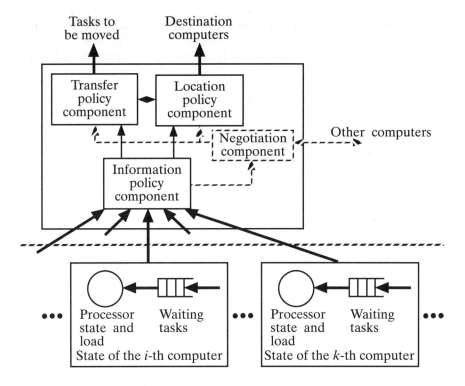

Fig. 9.14 The components of a load balancing algorithm and their interactions.

This results in the following ordering of message priorities (listed in decreasing order of importance):

(1) process migration,

(2) negotiation, and

(3) gathering data state information and statistics.

Note that communication traffic can be reduced if for example negotiation and data state information and statistics messages are piggybacked to regular messages.

9.11 A survey of selected load balancing algorithms

Having considered taxonomies, requirements and components of load balancing algorithms, it is time to look at some algorithms that have been constructed or studied. Space limitations prevent us from describing all of them in detail. Thus, instead of presenting each algorithm in a few lines, we have chosen to look in this section at five representative algorithms that fall into the hierarchical classification. Another two algorithms, from the flat classification, are discussed in Section 9.12.

The following load balancing algorithms have been chosen for discussion:

(1)   Bryant and Finkel's algorithm (also called the pairing algorithm). Pairs of processors exchange processes (Bryant and Finkel 1981).

(2)   Barak and Shiloh's algorithm (also called the vector algorithm). Processors maintain load vectors (Barak and Shiloh 1985).

(3)   Stankovic and Sidhu's algorithm (also called the bidding algorithm). (Stankovic and Sidhu 1984). Computers cooperate using a bidding approach.

(4)   SLA which is based on stochastic learning automaton (Stankovic 1985).

(5)   BDT which is based on Bayesian Decision Theory (Stankovic 1985).

9.11.1   Bryant and Finkel's algorithm

Bryant and Finkel's algorithm is a dynamic and physically distributed algorithm. To make a decision, computers cooperate by sending negotiation messages. The decisions are suboptimal, and a heuristic approach is used to find a solution. This distributed algorithm improves performance locally. It has been chosen because it is a good example of a cooperation based algorithm.

The strategy works in the following way.

(1)   A computer C_A sends a query to one of its nearest neighbours C_B to form a temporary pair, which enables a controlled, stable environment suitable for job migration. The query has two purposes:

(a)   it informs the computer C_B that C_A wishes to form a pair, and

(b)   it contains a list of processes and time consumed by each process for C_A. The time consumed by each process is used by a load estimation procedure to estimate the remaining time requirement of the process.

(2) C_B, after receiving the query, can perform one of three options:

(a)   rejecting C_A's query; this implies that C_A must send a query to another neighbour;

(b)   form a pair with C_A; this implies that C_A as well as C_B reject all incoming queries until the pair is broken;

(c)   postpone C_A when C_B is in a migrating state, that is, sending processes; this implies that C_A must wait until C_B forms a pair with it, or rejects it – C_A cannot query anyone else.

(3) After establishing a pair, the computer with the larger load (for example, C_A) proceeds to select a process ($i, i = 1, \ldots, p_A$, where p_A is a number of processes on C_A) to migrate to the other computer. This operation can be done on the basis of the expected improvement of response time for each process, denoted k_i, using the following formula:

$$k_i = T_{Ai}/(T_{Bi} + T_{ABi})$$

where T_{Ai} is the expected response time of process i when it is run on its source computer C_A,

           T_{Bi} is the expected response time of process i when it is run on destination computer C_B,

           T_{ABi} is a transfer time of process i from computer C_A to computer C_B.

The expected response time of process $T_{Ai}, i = 1, \ldots, p_A$, can be found using the estimation of the remaining time requirement $T_E(i)$; the time to complete a process equals the time used so far, T; and is calculated on the basis of the following algorithm:

$T := T_E(i);$
for all $j, j = 1, \ldots, p_A$ **do**
begin
    if $T_E(j) < T_E(i)$
       then $T := T + T_E(j)$
       else $T := T + T_E(i)$
end;
$T_{Ai} := T;$

(4) If no process can expect better performance on computer C_B, that is, when $k_i < 1$, for all $i, i = 1, \ldots, p_A$, then computer C_A informs C_B of this fact and the pair is broken. Otherwise, the process which can expect the best improvement is selected and migrated. This procedure is repeated for all remaining processes, until no processes can expect better performance on computer C_B.

This algorithm cannot be classified as either a source-initiative or server-initiative algorithm. Either computer in a pair can select a process to be migrated, and initiate its migration.

9.11.2   Barak and Shiloh's algorithm

Barak and Shiloh's algorithm is a global, dynamic load balancing algorithm. Moreover, it is distributed in the sense that each computer uses the same policy. This algorithm does not use an *a priori* knowledge of estimates on the resources that each process requires. Each computer maintains information about the load of a small (fixed) number of other computers. This information is frequently exchanged using a randomly selected path. Thus, this algorithm belongs to the class of cooperating algorithms. This algorithm has been chosen for presentation because of its simplicity – load balancing is provided by reducing the variance of loads between computers of a distributed system. Barak and Shiloh's algorithm is a server-initiative algorithm.

Barak and Shiloh assumed that:

(1) N is the number of computers in the system, and N is a large number;

(2)   there is a direct communication link between any pair of nodes.

The load balancing policy consists of three distinct components: the processor load algorithm, the information exchange algorithm and the process migration algorithm. Here we only discuss policy oriented algorithms, which are the first two.

The processor load algorithm is used by each computer to monitor and estimate its own local load on a continuous basis. The load is computed every atomic unit of time q, and it is averaged over a period of time t. Thus, $L(0)$ is a load estimate of the local computer and this value is updated periodically. This information forms the first component of a small, fixed sized (size l) load vector L. The remaining components hold load values of an arbitrary subset of processors.

The information exchange algorithm is responsible for the continuous exchange of the load information (load vectors) between computers; $L(j)$ denotes the j-th component of the load vector, $0 \leq j \leq l - 1 -$ it is the load estimate of the j-th computer. Portions of the load vector L are frequently exchanged using a randomly selected path, in a way similar to the worm program. Such exchanges provide sufficient and up-to-date load information to each computer.

The algorithm has been constructed in such a way that newly arrived load information is placed in positions which guarantee that only the latest load values are maintained. The information exchange algorithm works in the following way. Every unit of time on each computer

(1)   updates its own load value,

(2)   chooses at random another computer i, $1 \leq i \leq N$,

(3)   sends the first half of the local load vector, denoted L_r, to computer i.

After receiving a portion of a load vector, each computer:

(1)   uses the received vectors to estimate the load of each computer. To do this, the receiver first merges each vector received with its

own load vector, L, according to the following mapping:

$$L(2i) := L(i) \qquad 1 \leq i \leq l/2 - 1$$

and

$$L(2i + 1) := L_r(i) \qquad 0 \leq i \leq l/2 - 1$$

(2) estimates the load of a computer by finding the average number of processes requesting service in each quantum. This result can be used to estimate the response time of that processor.

(3) migrates a process to the computer that provides the lowest estimated response time. A special process in each computer periodically causes all other processes to consider migration.

The scope of performance improvement depends on the value of l. If l equals the number of nodes in the network, N, this algorithm is optimal globally.

This algorithm does not work efficiently when a large number of processes is suddenly created. In this case, the algorithm's limit on the number of migrating processes (one process per load-balancing cycle) implies excessively loaded computers in an otherwise unloaded system.

An improvement of the algorithm is reported in Barak *et al.* (1989). The following elements were considered and used to improve the original algorithm:

(1) Utilization of two load numbers per computer: a local load which reflects the true load of the computer, and an export load of which other computers are told. The difference between these two load values helps to establish stability in the system.

(2) Monitoring by each processor of its utilization, which is the fraction of time the processor is available for executing processes.

(3) Making the following adjustments:

  (a) when the local load reduces, the export load is decreased more slowly than the local load to lessen the effect of short-lived load fluctuations,

  (b) the export load is increased by an amount equal to a CPU-bound process for each arriving process as soon as the decision for migration is made.

(4) The decision to consider migration is made as soon as new load information arrives.

9.11.3 Stankovic and Sidhu's algorithm

Stankovic and Sidhu's algorithm also belongs to the class of global, dynamic, physically distributed algorithms. This algorithm requires cooperation between computers, utilizing a bidding approach to make a decision. Decisions made are suboptimal and heuristic. They are based on the history of system activity. This algorithm is included in this survey as an example of a bidding and adaptive algorithm. Note that Stankovic and Sidhu's algorithm is a source-initiative algorithm.

The heuristic utilizes prior information concerning the known characteristics of processes. These characteristics are resource requirements, special resource needs, process priority, precedence constraints and the need for clustering and distributed groups.

The algorithm utilizes the McCulloch–Pitts evaluation procedure (MPEP). This procedure is based on a decision cell which has a number of excitators and inhibitors as inputs, and a single value output. The output is the sum of the excitators, or zero if any of the inhibitors are set.

The algorithm works in the following way:

(1) All processes local to a given host are periodically evaluated using a MPEP to decide whether to transmit a bid request for a particular process. The input to the MPEP includes both process and network characteristics.

(2) If the output from the MPEP is above some threshold, then the process is performing well in the current environment. Otherwise, if the output is non-zero, the process should be moved because it performs poorly. If the MPEP returns zero, as a result of setting one of the inhibitors, the process may not move.

(3) When at least one process in a host needs to be moved, the host computer broadcasts the so-called 'request for bids' (RFB) to all other computers within a distance $i, i = 1, \ldots, n$, where n is the diameter of the network (treated as a parameter of the algorithm).

   (a) The RFB message is sent for each process which needs to be moved.

   (b) The RFB contains all of the characteristics of the potential migrant. Thus, all request receivers can run the MPEP to determine whether the process would run well (that is, the MPEP value should be above the threshold) if it were migrated.

(4) After some predefined time period t, all responses to the RFB message are adjusted by the cost of transferring the process. The best bid is then considered as a potential destination computer. One additional test is performed before any action is taken:

   (a) The MPEP value for the given process is tested. If the process is still performing poorly, then the process migrates to the winning bidder, otherwise it remains in the current computer.

(5)   If during the time period t no suitable bids are received, the distance i to send the RFB message is incremented, and the whole algorithm is repeated.

It is necessary to emphasize two facts. First, the adaptive part of this algorithm is that it dynamically modifies the number of hops that a bid request is allowed to go, depending on current conditions. Second, load balancing algorithm improves the performance with a scope depending on n. If n equals the number of nodes in the network, this algorithm is optimal globally.

9.11.4   Stankovic's algorithm based on Stochastic Learning Automata (SLA)

This algorithm belongs to the class of global, dynamic, and physically-distributed algorithms. Computers cooperate to make a decision. Decisions are based on a heuristic approach. The algorithm adapts to its parameters, based on the history of system behaviour. It utilizes a network of stochastic learning automata which make use of feedback information that identifies whether a previous load balancing decision was beneficial or not. This algorithm is included in this survey because it contains an explicit mechanism for dealing with some aspects of stability. Note that it belongs to the class of server-initiative algorithms.

Each computer of the distributed system:

(1)   Contains a load balancing algorithm; each algorithm is modeled as an SLA.

(2)   Has an optimal load defined (in wait queue plus one in execution). If the computer has less than this number of processes in execution or in its waiting queue, it is underloaded; if more, it is overloaded. This is an extension to the original concept of stochastic learning automata (Narendra and Thathacher 1974) and is called the measure of goodness.

In performing load balancing it must be possible for each computer to recognize underloaded computers, that is, it must be possible to identify network states.

(1)   If there are N computers, we would have 2^N possible states. This is the worst case.

(2)   To provide quicker balancing in the network and to address stability, the algorithm uses a heuristic that reduces the number of states, by recognizing a limited number of underloaded computers at a time. These states are called network-wide states.

(3)   A basic SLA has a probability vector with which it selects possible actions. This model has been extended by adding the concept of

network-wide states, so that there is one probability vector for each network-wide state. Thus, the vectors of actions and probabilities of a basic SLA now becomes a matrix, with one row for each network-wide state. This is also an extension to the original concept of stochastic learning automata and is called network-wide states of nature.

The operation of the scheduling algorithm is as follows:

(1) Each computer periodically, with period T1, checks its own status (underloaded or overloaded) and broadcasts this status to all other computers.

(2) This information is used by each computer to determine the network-wide state which the particular computer is observing at this time. This determines the probability vector to use and the action set associated with this vector to use in transmitting tasks in this time period.

(3) In parallel, the load balancing algorithm checks, with period T2, whether the computer is overloaded. If it is, it will transmit only one process to another computer, which is chosen probabilistically (on the basis of the probability vector currently in effect).

(4) When the destination computer receives the migrating process, it decides to reward or penalize the action based on the effect the arrival of this new process has on its own load.

(5) The decision (reward or penalty) is transmitted back to the source computer which updates the probability vector to take account the effect of the action (the probability is decreased if the action is penalized, or increased when the action was rewarded).

The performance improvement given by this algorithm depends on the heuristic in use.

9.11.5 Stankovic's algorithm based on Bayesian Decision Theory (BDT)

Stankovic's algorithm is a global, dynamic algorithm that requires cooperation between computers to make a decision. Solutions are suboptimal and are achieved utilizing a heuristic approach based on Bayesian Decision Theory. It is a physically-distributed load balancing algorithm, supported by a central monitor unit. The task of the monitor is to collate status information and inform individual computers about changes to the environment. Thus, it does not use a fully distributed approach. However, it is considered here because it has two interesting and unique features. The first is that loss of the control unit will not greatly affect the performance of the whole algorithm (according to Stankovic). The second is its architecture: the load allocation function is divided into two parts: a decentralized job scheduler (DJS) and a decentralized process scheduler (DPS).

The role of the DJS, which is composed of multiple entities and distributed, is as follows. Taking that fact into account that each computer maintains a wait queue of incoming jobs:

(1)   The DJS tries to keep the number of waiting jobs at each computer roughly equal, in order to improve response time, and to do this with low execution-time cost. This is achieved through job reassignment;

(2)   It maintains state information about the network in order to continually adapt to the state of the network. However, the DJS has no knowledge about the characteristics of incoming jobs.

To decrease the overhead of the DJS, it is run infrequently. This is possible because cheap monitor nodes (shown in Fig. 9.15), and an inexpensive heuristic are used.

In practice, only one monitor works constantly. The second monitor is used only when the first fails. The adaptation heuristic is based on Bayesian Decision Theory. Thus, these monitors are able to deal with the dynamics of the system.

The DPS decides which waiting jobs are activated. The DPS deals with multiple modules of a job, their resource requirements, clustering concerns, and assignment during execution of the job (process). Jobs (in

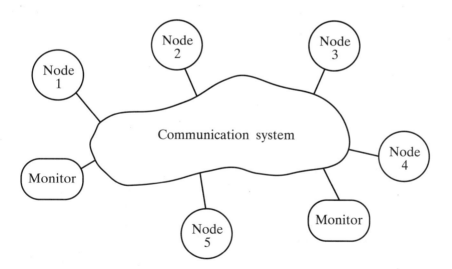

Fig. 9.15   Monitors supporting a load balancing algorithm in a distributed system.

the case of the DJS) and modules (in the case of the DPS) may migrate any number of times, up to some predefined limit. The Stankovic paper deals only with using Bayesian Decision Theory as a basis for the DJS. The DPS is not discussed.

This Bayesian Decision Theory algorithm is in many ways similar to SLA. The most important difference is that there is no immediate feedback from other computers attached to the network. Moreover, a distinction is made between the network-wide state and what a host computer observes to be the state, called its observation.

The operation of the load balancing algorithm is as follows:

(1)   Each computer sends (with period P) to the monitor:

    (a)   its observation of the network-wide state, and

    (b)   its status, that is, number of local processes.

(2)   On the basis of this information, the monitor calculates:

    (a)   the true network-wide state, and

    (b)   for each computer, the state given any observation.

This means that for any observation, the monitor calculates the most likely real network-wide state.

(3)   The monitor transmits (with period S) this vector to each computer.

(4)   Each computer broadcasts (with period T) estimates of the workload of all other computers, so that each computer can make an observation of the network-wide state.

(5)   When the computer has made an observation, an action is performed: the action may be, for example, do nothing, migrate one process to computer A. The type of action is determined by a static utility function in which the action with the highest utility is preferred.

Stankovic (1985) shows that the parameters P and T can be tuned to achieve optimum performance for a given cost.

9.11.6 Comparison of algorithms

The survey highlights a number of interesting issues. The first is that load estimation techniques require further study. There are two aspects of such investigations. The first is efficiency and feasibility. Only Barak and Shiloh's load estimation method is simple enough to be effectively used in real distributed operating systems; no other technique seems to be fully practical and accurate. The second aspect is associated with the quality of estimation. It is well-known that without a good load estimate it is impossible to achieve optimum or near optimum performance. It seems to us that the use of the MPEP procedure is promising, though there can be problems with quantification of some of the parameters.

The second issue is associated with information exchange between distributed components of a load balancing algorithm. There are three aspects of information exchange: the amount of information exchanged, the timeliness of this information and the pattern of information exchange. The surveyed algorithms (and others in the literature) can be divided into two classes. To the first class belong these algorithms that exchange detailed information about individual processes (Bryant and Finkel's algorithm and Stankovic and Sidhu's algorithm). These algorithms use a great amount of information to make a decision but do not specifically deal with the concomitant increase in network traffic. In the second class are algorithms that require the exchange of a relatively small amount of information, that is, only about the overall state of a processor (Barak and Shiloh's algorithm, Stankovic's algorithms utilizing SLA and BDT). These algorithms are simpler than those belonging to the first class, and the network traffic is less.

Solutions to load balancing problems can also suffer from the problem of out-of-date information. This problem is caused by transmission delays between decision-making components (distances between computers), and the amount of exchanged information. Only Bryant and Finkel's algorithm can guarantee that exchanged information is not out-of-date. This is because the algorithm allows computers to communicate only with their closest neighbours. However, solutions are only locally optimal.

The information exchange required for a given load balancing algorithm must be balanced between the volume of network traffic and the desire to communicate with every computer in a distributed system. One-to-one communication increases the volume drastically although it allows all components involved in making decisions to know the state of the total system. One-to-many (broadcast) communication is the solution, but not all networks are provided with this efficient form of distribution of information. Such algorithms as those developed by Stankovic and Sidhu, and Stankovic using SLA and BDT, are the closest to a one-to-many pattern.

There is a lack of serious study to find out which class of algorithms provides better performance. We believe that it would be more beneficial to adopt the approach used in the first class of algorithms, for two reasons. First, it allows more accuracy in load balancing decisions; second, the performance increase achieved using algorithms of the first class should outweigh the performance loss due to increased network traffic. However, a reader must bear in mind that costs of transfer oriented computation can be higher than costs of communication (Eager *et al.* 1986). Information exchange problems require further investigation.

The next design issue is associated with decision bases for migrating a process. In general, load balancing algorithms use load estimation values to decide on the destiny of processes. The algorithms can be again divided into two classes. The first class consists of those algorithms that make decisions based on the characteristics of individual processes. The algorithms developed by Bryant and Finkel (expected improvement, using the expected response time as a metric) and Stankovic and Sidhu (threshold value) are good examples. In general, this class of algorithms requires the evaluation of the characteristics of many processes. Thus, they are expensive but provide better performance. To the second class belong algorithms that are independent of individual processes. In Stankovic's algorithm based on SLA a process is migrated if its computer is overloaded. The algorithm can adapt to changes due to the immediate feedback. Because of the lack of feedback, the algorithm based on BDT is less dynamic. Moreover, there is no explicit decision mechanism. Generally, algorithms of this class require only simple table lookups to make a migration decision.

An issue which is closely associated with moving processes to balance system load is the amount of knowledge about a migrating process that a destination computer has. Algorithms in which the destination computer has no knowledge of an impending reception of a migrating process include Barak and Shiloh's algorithm, Stankovic and Sidhu's algorithm, and Stankovic's algorithms based on SLA and BDT. These algorithms can fall victim to out-of-date information, and as a result can perform unwanted process migrations.

In Bryant and Finkel's algorithm the destination computer knows it is about to receive a migrating process from the list of migrating processes sent to it before the pair is broken. Thus, any subsequent query by the destination computer includes the list of migrating processes. This implies that all calculations are based on up-to-date information about an environment. This knowledge increases the chance of making beneficial migration decisions.

The last issue is stability. Although Stankovic's algorithm addresses stability directly, Bryant and Finkel's algorithm is the most stable. However, it should be noted that this algorithm is optimal only locally. Stability theory indicates that the size of the environment in which decisions are in force is associated very strongly with stability. Thus, this issue should also be the subject of further study.

9.12   Examples of flat taxonomy-based algorithms

In the previous section, when surveying algorithms that fall into Casavant and Kuhl's hierarchical taxonomy, we considered two characteristics that are associated with the flat classification. Those were the form of cooperation between components involved in decision making, that is, bidding, and the history of system action, that is, adaptive solutions. However, we noted earlier that bidding can be classified as a subclass of cooperative algorithms.

In this section we characterize another aspect of the flat classification: the type of node that takes the initiative in the global search for a lightly-loaded processor. This categorization describes solutions as being source-initiated or server-initiated. Some algorithms investigated in Wang and Morris (1985) which belong to this class were presented briefly in Section 9.6.5. Here, we present another four, the first three being source-initiative algorithms, and the fourth a server-initiative algorithm. All of them were studied by Zhou (Zhou 1988). All these algorithms utilize the same transfer policy.

9.12.1 Transfer policy

The transfer policy of all the source-initiative and server-initiative algorithms is based on the computer load threshold T_l and the process execution time threshold T_{CPU}. When the local load of a given computer is at or below T_l all processes are executing locally. Otherwise, all the processes arriving at the computer and with execution time above T_{CPU} are eligible for migration to carry out load balancing.

Because it is difficult to predict execution time, processes can be classified into two categories: those that are worth considering for migration (big), and those that are not (small).

9.12.2 CENTRAL – a source-initiative algorithm

The CENTRAL algorithm requires that there be one computer designated as the **load information center** (LIC). The center receives load updates every P seconds from all the other computers, and works as a central load balancing decision maker.

The algorithm works in the following way.

(1)   A computer uses the transfer policy to find a process that is eligible for migration.

    (a)   if there is a process eligible for migration, the computer sends a request together with the current value of its load (queue length) to the LIC.

(2)   After receiving a request, the LIC:

    (a)   selects the computer with the shortest queue length (destination computer),

    (b)   informs the originating computer about the destination computer,

   (c)   increments its version of the load of the destination computer by one.

(3)   The originating computer moves the selected process to the destination computer.

This algorithm is based on the assumption that the loads of all the computers are known to the placement decision maker, though with some delay. Of course, this assumption generates big overhead costs.

   The following algorithms do not gather as much information as CENTRAL algorithm and use less system state information. This implies that overhead costs are smaller.

9.12.3   THRHLD and LOWEST – source-initiative algorithms

THRHLD and LOWEST are very similar algorithms. The THRHLD algorithm works as follows.

(1)   A computer finds a process eligible for migration.

(2)   If there is a process eligible for migration, a number of randomly selected computers, up to a testing limit L_p, are interrogated.

(3)   Received responses containing current load T_i, $i = 1, \ldots, L_p$, are checked against the load threshold T_l.

(4)   If there are computers such that $T_i < T_l$, the process is migrated to the first of them that is found. Otherwise, the process is executed locally.

The LOWEST algorithm works nearly identically. The difference is in the last two steps of the location policy. Instead of using a threshold for finding a destination computer, the process which is loaded most lightly is selected.

9.12.4   RESERVE – a server-initiative algorithm

This algorithm is based on process reservation. It works in the following way.

(1)   After completing a process, a server (any computer which may act as a server) checks its local load T_i.

(2)   If the load is below T_l, that is, $T_i < T_l$, the computer probes other computers to register up to R reservations at R computers with loads above T_l.

(3)   An inquiring computer stores the outstanding reservations in a stack. Thus, when a process is found to be eligible for load balancing, the top reservation on the stack is used as the address of the destination computer.

(4)   If the load of a given computer is above T_l, this computer sends a process to the destination computer, which in practice is the most recent reservation. If the load of a given computer falls below T_l, all its reservations are cancelled.

The simulation results obtained by Zhou (1988) indicate that the best performance (average response time) is achieved using the CENTRAL algorithm, followed by LOWEST, THRHLD and RESERVE. The bad performance of the server-initiative algorithm is due partially to the restrictions on initial process placement.

9.13 Summary

Resource management is one of the basic and most important problems of operating systems. It is a complex problem in centralized operating systems, and even more complicated in distributed operating systems. There are three resource management issues: resource allocation; deadlock detection, prevention and avoidance; and resource protection. This chapter has considered resource allocation.

Resource allocation in distributed operating systems is a complex problem because of physical distribution of the resources, communication delays, natural redundancy and the possibility of partial failures, and the lack of global state information.

We know how to solve problems associated with allocation of processors and peripheral devices in centralized computer systems. In the area of distributed systems, relatively little work has been done on resource allocation. The situation is better in the area of allocation of processors (workstations). However, finding an idle or lightly-loaded workstation or computation server, and other necessary resources, and making them available to a process requesting a given service in real systems, are still basic problems.

For performance reasons, resources should be allocated in such a way as to minimize response time, waiting time, or delay, achieve high throughput, and minimize computation and communication overhead of resource allocation, for example, process migration.

Management systems allocating resources to processes can be divided into two groups. To the first group belong those which are able to provide a variety of resources. The second group contains those systems which provide access to a single type of resource. The latter group is mainly oriented toward processor/workstation allocation.

Resources belonging to the former group can be provided by two different types of resource managers. The first are centralized and distributed server based managers; the second are agent based resource managers. This means that some structural aspects of resource allocation systems have to be considered when designing a resource allocation facility. These aspects are associated with means of implementation of resource allocation algorithms.

The second group of resource allocating systems deals with single resources, and general computation resources (processors, workstations). The problem of allocating a single computation service can be seen as a distributed scheduling problem. In this area one can be involved in load sharing, which mainly deals with finding idle processors and is sometimes called hunting for idle processors, and in load balancing algorithms. The most important difference between these two approaches to distributed scheduling is that whereas the former improves performance locally, that is, for a few users and their processes, the latter approach strives to improve performance globally.

The load sharing and load allocation problem can be stated as the problem of searching for a process to be migrated, selecting a remote computer for the migrating process, and determining when process migration should be performed.

Load sharing systems can be organized differently using different logical connections of processors. The most interesting are a logical hierarchy of processors, logical ring of processors, worm based organization, and Condor, a hunter for idle workstations.

Load balancing algorithms can be classified using several features. There are two basic classifications: hierarchical and flat. According to the former classification, to improve performance in a distributed system with load fluctuation, global, dynamic, and physically distributed load balancing algorithms should be used. Computers should cooperate, and solutions, to be feasible, are suboptimal (they use approximate or heuristic approaches).

If cooperating computers do not have accurate data they could use bidding to select a remote computer. Server-initiative and source-initiative strategies can be used to determine which computer could initiate load balancing.

Load balancing algorithms consist of four basic components: the information gathering policy, the transfer policy, the location policy and the negotiation policy. There are a number of algorithms which show the most important features of load balancing, and components of load balancing algorithms. From them one can identify necessary data to be gathered, problems of their implementation, and possible performance improvement. Note that these algorithms or their modifications can also be used with systems providing a variety of services.

Bibliography

Bannister J.A. and Trivedi K.S. (1983). Task Allocation in Fault-Tolerant Distributed Systems. *Acta Informatica,* **20**, 261–81

Barak A. and Shiloh A. (1985). A Distributed Load-Balancing Policy for a Multicomputer. *Software—Practice and Experience,* **15**(9), 901–13

Barak A., Shiloh A. and Wheeler R. (1989). Flood Prevention in the MOSIX Load-Balancing Scheme. *Operating Systems Technical Committee Newsletter,* **3**(1), 24–7

Bryant R.M. and Finkel R.A. (1981). A Stable Distributed Scheduling Algorithm. In *Proceedings of the 2nd International Conference on Distributed Computing Systems,* 314–23

Casavant T.L. and Kuhl J.G. (1984). Design of a Loosely-Coupled Distributed Multiprocessing Network. In *Proceedings of the 1984 International Conference on Parallel Processing,* pp. 42–45

Casavant T.L. and Kuhl J.G. (1988). A Taxonomy of Scheduling in General-Purpose Distributed Computing Systems. *IEEE Transactions on Software Engineering,* **SE–14**(2), 141–54

Casavant T.L. and Kuhl J.G. (1988). Effects of Response and Stability on Scheduling in Distributed Computing Systems. *IEEE Transactions on Software Engineering,* **SE–14**(11), 1578–88

Casey L.M. (1981). Decentralized Scheduling. *The Australian Computer Journal,* **13**(2), 58–63

Chen R. (1987). *A Dynamic Job Scheduling System for a UNIX Based Distributed System.* Report No. UIUCDCS–R–87–1382, Department of Computer Science, University of Illinois at Urbana-Champaign, Urbana, Illinois

Chou T.C.K. and Abraham J.A. (1983). Load Redistribution Under Failure in Distributed Systems. *IEEE Transactions on Computers,* **C–32**(9), 799–808

Chow Y.C. and Kohler W. (1979). Models for Dynamic Load Balancing in a Heterogeneous Multiple Processor System. *IEEE Transactions on Computers,* **C–28**(5), 334–61

Chu W.W., Holloway L.J., Lan M.T. and Efe K. (1980). Task Allocation in Distributed Data Processing. *Computer,* **13**(11), 57–69

Craft D.H. (1983). Resource Management in a Decentralized System. In *Proceedings of the Ninth ACM Symposium on Operating Systems Principles,* Bretton Woods, New Hampshire, pp. 11–19

Craft D.H. (1985). Resource Management in a Distributed Computing System. *Ph.D. Thesis,* Technical Report Computer Laboratory, University of Cambridge

Dannenberg R.B. (1982). Resource Sharing in a Network of Personal Computers. *Ph.D. Thesis,* Department of Computer Science, Carnegie–Mellon University

Dannenberg R.B. and Hibbard P.G. (1985). A Butler Process for Resource Sharing on Spice Machines. *ACM Transactions on Office Information Systems,* **3**(3), 234–52

Eager D.L., Lazowska E.D. and Zahorjan J. (1986). A Comparison of Receiver-Initiated and Sender-Initiated Adaptive Load Sharing. *Performance Evaluation,* **6**(1), 53–68

Eager D.L., Lazowska E.D. and Zahorjan J. (1988). The Limited Performance Benefits of Migrating Active Processes for Load Sharing. In *Proceedings of the 1988 ACM SIGMETRICS Conference on Measurement and Modelling of Computer Systems,* pp. 63–72, Santa Fe, New Mexico

Efe K. (1982). Heuristic Models of Task Assignment Scheduling in Distributed Systems. *Computer,* **15**, 50–6

Fogg I.S. (1987). *Distributed Scheduling Algorithms: A Survey.* Department of Computer Science, University of Queensland

Gabrielian A. and Tyler D.B. (1984). Optimal Object Allocation in Distributed Computer Systems. In *Proceedings of the 4th International Conference on Distributed Computing Systems,* pp. 84–95

Gifford D.K., Needham R.M. and Schroeder M.D. (1988). The Cedar File System. *Communications of the ACM,* **31**(3), 288–98

Goscinski A. (1987). *Distributed Operating Systems.* Department of Computer Science, The University of New South Wales

Kindberg T., Sahiner T. and Paker Y. (1987). Worm Programs, NATO ASI Series F28. *Distributed Operating Systems. Theory and Practice,* (Paker *et al.* eds.) pp. 355–379, Springer-Verlag

Klappholtz D. and Park H.C. (1984). Parallelized Process Scheduling for Tightly-Coupled MIMD Machines. *1984 International Conference on Parallel Processing,* pp. 315–321

Krueger P. and Livny M. (1987). *Load Balancing, Load Sharing and Performance in Distributed Systems.* Computer Science Technical Report #700, Computer Science Department, University of Wisconsin–Madison

Kruskal C.P. and Weiss A. (1984). Allocating Independent Tasks on Parallel Processors. Extended Abstract. In *Proceedings of the 1984 International Conference on Parallel Processing,* pp. 236–240

Litzkow M.J., Livny M. and Mutka M.W. (1987). *Condor: A Hunter of Idle Workstations.* Computer Science Technical Report #730, Computer Science Department, University of Wisconsin–Madison

Lo V.M. (1984). Heuristic Algorithms for Task Assignment in Distributed Systems. In *Proceedings of the 4th International Conference on Distributed Computing Systems,* pp. 30–39

Ma P.Y.R., Lee E.Y.S. and Tsuchiya J. (1982). A Task Allocation Model for Distributed Computing Systems. *IEEE Transactions on Computers,* **C–31**(1), 41–7

Morris J.H., Satyanarayanan M., Conner M.H., Howard J.H., Rosenthal D.S.H. and Smith F.D. (1986). Andrew: A Distributed Personal Computing Environment. *Communications of the ACM,* **29**(3), 184–201

Mullender S.J. (1984). *Distributed Systems Management in Wide Area Networks.* Report CS–R8419, Department of Computer Science, Centre for Mathematics and Computer Science

Mutka M.W. and Livny M. (1987). Scheduling Remote Processing Capacity in a Workstations-Processor Bank Computing System. In *Proceedings of the 7th International Conference on Distributed Computing Systems,* Berlin, West Germany, pp. 2–9

Mutka M.W. and Livny M. (1987). Profiling Workstations' Available Capacity for Remote Execution, Performance'87. In *Proceedings of the 12th IFIP WG 7.3 Symposium on Computer Performance,* Brussels, Belgium

Narendra K.S. and Thathacher M.A.L. (1974). Learning Automata—A Survey. *IEEE Transactions on Systems, Man, and Cybernetics,* SMC–4, July

Needham R.M. and Herbert A.J. (1982). *The Cambridge Distributed Computing System.* Addison-Wesley Pub. Co.

Nelson M.N., Welch B.B. and Ousterhout J.K. (1988). Caching in the Sprite Network File System. *Communications of the ACM,* **31**(3), 134–54

Ni L.M., Xu C.-W. and Gendreau T.B. (1985). A Distributed Drafting Algorithm for Load Balancing. *IEEE Transactions on Software Engineering,* **SE–11**(10), 1153–61

Nichols D.A. (1987). Using Idle Workstations in a Shared Computing Environment. In *Proceedings of the Eleventh ACM Symposium on Operating Systems Principles,* Austin, Texas. *Operating Systems Review,* pp. 5–12

Ousterhout J., Scelza D. and Sindhu P. (1980). Medusa: An Experiment in Distributed Operating System Structure. *Communications of the ACM,* **23**(2), 92–105

Popek G.J. and Walker B.J. [eds.] (1985). *The LOCUS Distributed System Architecture.* Cambridge, MA: M.I.T. Press

Ramamritham K. and Stankovic J.A. (1984). Dynamic Task Scheduling in Hard Real-Time Distributed Systems. *IEEE Software,* pp. 65–75

Ramamritham K., Stankovic J.A. and Zhao W. (1989). Distributed Scheduling of Tasks with Deadlines and Resource Requirements. *IEEE Transactions on Computers,* **C–38**(8), 1110–23

Reif J. and Sprirakis P. (1984). Real-Time Resource Allocation in a Distributed System. *ACM SIGACT/SIGOPS Symposium on Principles of Distributed Computing,* pp. 84–94

Rifkin A.P., Forbes M.P., Hamilton R.L., Sabrio M., Shah S. and Yueh K. (1986). RFS Architectural Overview. In *Proceedings of the USENIX Conference,* Atlanta, GA, pp. 248–259

Sandberg R., Goldberg D., Kleinman S., Walsh D. and Lyon B. (1986). Design and Implementation of the Sun Network File System. *Sun Microsystems Report,* Mountain View, CA 9404

Shen S. (1988). Cooperative Distributed Dynamic Load Balancing. *Acta Informatica,* **25**, pp. 663–676

Shen C.C. and Tsai W.H. (1985). A Graph Matching Approach to Optimal Task Assignment in Distributed Computing Systems Using a Minimax Criterion. *IEEE Transactions on Computers,* **C–34**(3), 197–203

Shoch J.F. and Hupp J.A. (1982). The 'Worm' Programs—Early Experience with a Distributed Computation. *Communications of the ACM,* **25**(3), 172–80

Smith R.G. (1980). The Contract Net Protocol: High-Level Communication and Control in Distributed Problem Solvers. *IEEE Transactions on Computers,* **C–29**(12), 1104–13

Stankovic J.A. (1985). An Application of Bayesian Decision Theory to Decentralized Control of Job Scheduling. *IEEE Transactions on Computers,* **C–34**(2), 117–30

Stankovic J.A. and Sidhu I.S. (1984). An Adaptive Bidding Algorithm for Processes. Clusters and Distributed Groups. In *Proceedings of the 4th International Conference on Distributed Computing Systems,* pp. 49–59

Wang Y.T. and Morris R.J.T. (1985). Load Sharing in Distributed Systems. *IEEE Transactions on Computers,* **C–34**(3), 204–17

Ward M.O. and Romero D.J. (1984). Assigning Parallel-Executable, Intercommunicating Subtasks to Processors. In *Proceedings of the 1984 International Conference on Parallel Processing,* pp. 392–394

Wittie L.D. and van Tilborg A.M. (1980). MICROS, A Distributed Operating

System for MICRONET, A Reconfigurable Network Computer. *IEEE Transactions on Computers,* **C–29**(12), 1133–44

Zhou S. (1988). A Trace-Driven Simulation Study of Dynamic Load Balancing. *IEEE Transactions on Software Engineering,* **SE–14**(9), 1327–41

Zhou S. and Zicari R. (1988). Object Management in Local Distributed Systems. *The Journal of Systems and Software,* **8**, pp. 283–295

10 Deadlock detection

		Security	
User names	File service		C s
	Collaboration of file servers	Access control	o e
	Transaction service		m c
	Directory service		m u
	Flat file service		u r
Name distribution	Disk service	R p e s o u r c e	n i c t a y t i o n
	Resource allocation	Deadlock detection	
Name resolution	Algorithms for load sharing and load balancing	Process synchronization	&
		Capabilities	Authentication
System names	Process management Operations on processes: local, remote Process migration	Access lists	Key management
Ports	Interprocess communication (and memory management)	Info flow control	Data encryption
	Interprocess communication primitives: Message Passing or Remote Procedure Call, or Transactions;	Security kernel	
	Links or Ports		
Addresses	↕		
Routes	Transport protocols supporting interprocess communication		Encryption protocols

D eadlock handling, in particular deadlock detection and resolution, is the second major issue of resource management in distributed operating systems. This is simply because resource allocation may result in deadlock. It is also very closely associated with concurrency. A deadlock can occur in any multiprogramming, multiprocessing, or distributed system. Because deadlock is a real problem that can cause expensive, time-dependent hang-ups or failures in these systems, its handling is one of the most important research and development problems.

In a distributed system, as in a centralized one, there are a number of processes that compete for the same limited resources. If a process requests a resource, and this resource is not available at that time, then the process enters a waiting state. A situation may arise where the process may never change its state. This waiting situation can happen if the requested resources are held by other waiting processes. This situation is called deadlock, and processes are said to be deadlocked.

Deadlock is the time-dependent state of permanent blocking of a set of processes which either interact directly, by communicating with each other, or indirectly, by competing for resources.

To remind the reader of this basic concept, Fig. 10.1 shows an example of simple deadlock involving two processes and two resources (physical or logical). Process P1 requests and holds resource R1, and then requests resource R2. On the other hand, process P2 is programmed to work in the opposite order: first it requests and holds resource R2, and then it requests R1. If both processes obtain their first resource before either requests its second, deadlock can happen. Neither process can proceed, and neither will release a resource unless forced by the operating system.

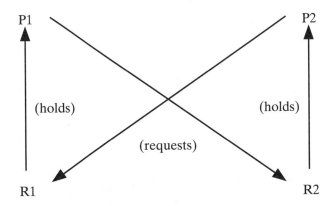

Fig. 10.1 A simple deadlock cycle.

The figure shows one of the key properties of deadlock, namely circular wait among processes that hold some processes while requesting others (here it is a chain of the form P1, R2, P2, R1, P1). This chain does not necessarily imply a deadlock. There could be more than one instance of one resource type, and a resource instance could be released by a process outside the chain. However, if there is only one instance of a requested resource type, a chain loop is equivalent to a deadlock.

The deadlock problem can be considered not only from the perspective of an operating system (physical and logical resources), but also from a database transaction–processing perspective (database entities, for example, a record). Deadlock in a database can be defined as a situation in which each transaction in a set of transactions is blocked waiting for another transaction in the set, and therefore none will become unblocked unless there is external intervention. Thus, in this chapter we will deal with deadlocks in distributed operating systems as well as in distributed databases, but in a uniform way.

Deadlocks in a computer system can be handled using three different approaches: prevention, avoidance, and detection and resolution. Here, we only consider deadlock detection and resolution in distributed systems, for reasons given in Section 10.1.

The key problem is how to detect deadlock. In general, the logic of deadlock detection is to search for cycles in the process/transaction-resource graph. This is a complex process, particularly in distributed systems. To help us identify problems associated with deadlock detection and determine methods and algorithms, some classifications are needed.

Thus, in this chapter we present various classifications of deadlocks and deadlock detection algorithms in distributed systems (operating systems and databases) and create a uniform framework for the discussion of these algorithms. In Section 10.2, we introduce two basic deadlocks: resource and communication deadlocks. We also discuss migration deadlock, which is similar to the deadlock which occurs when processes cooperate by exchanging messages. In Section 10.3, we present models of deadlock using a wait-for-graph (WFG) which is a mathematical model of resource requests.

Deadlocks can be detected using centralized, hierarchical and distributed schemes. These are briefly characterized in Section 10.4. Deadlock detection algorithms can be based on such concepts as path-pushing, edge-chasing, diffusion computations and global state detection. These concepts are discussed in Section 10.5. Four classes of distributed deadlock detection algorithms, developed from these concepts, are also characterized. Some aspects of deadlock resolution are discussed in Section 10.6. Finally, the most representative detection and resolution algorithms are discussed.

10.1 Methods of deadlock handling

There are three methods for handling deadlocks: deadlock prevention, deadlock avoidance, and deadlock detection and recovery. Which of these approaches can be used to deal with resource deadlocks in distributed computer systems?

10.1.1 Deadlock prevention

Deadlock prevention takes a variety of forms, most of which impose constraints on the ways in which processes request resources in order to prevent deadlock. There are three basic schemes:

(1) All resources which a process will need must be acquired at once before processing begins. This requirement cannot always be satisfied, not only in distributed systems but also in centralized environments, since the resource needs of a process may be data dependent and not precisely known at the start of processing. Acquiring all possible resources by a process decreases system concurrency, so it is very impractical.

(2) A process must release all its resources before requesting new ones. This implies that resources needed concurrently must be requested and allocated as a group.

(3) Resources are ordered linearly. This implies that a process must request them in that order. It is evident that this scheme would prevent the deadlock shown in Fig. 10.1.

There are two disadvantages of deadlock prevention. First, preallocation of resources reduces concurrency. Second, additional overhead is created by evaluating the safety of the request. The advantage of deadlock prevention is that it does not require a process restart or transaction rollback due to deadlocks.

In summary, deadlock prevention is considered impractical except for systems which have a predefined structure.

10.1.2 Deadlock avoidance

Deadlock avoidance involves the maintenance of information about processes and related resources in a process–resource graph. This graph reflects the current allocation of resources to processes, and incorporates potential requests as well. Deadlock avoidance algorithms determine from the graph where there is a valid sequence of actions that enables all processes to run to completion; if this can be determined, a resource allocation strategy that avoids deadlock can be derived. In other words, deadlock avoidance does not require determining resources *a priori*. Processes can run unless a requested resource is unavailable. As a result of this, when conflict arises processes can wait.

Deadlock avoidance thus requires some advance knowledge of the resource usage by processes. In a distributed operating system this information is distributed around a network, and its collection is inefficient. Incorporating potential requests in the process–resource graph is also a complex operation.

In summary, deadlock avoidance is not practical in distributed operating systems; any attempt to avoid deadlocks is inefficient.

10.1.3 Deadlock detection and resolution

In systems using deadlock detection and resolution, processes are allowed to wait for requested resources without restriction. This, as we know, can result in deadlock. Therefore deadlock must be detected and resolved correctly and efficiently.

This requires maintainance of information on processes and related resources, usually in the form of a process–resource graph. The nodes of the graph represent processes or resources. The edges indicate whether a resource has been allocated to a process, or a process is waiting for a resource. If a process waits for some time, deadlock can be suspected. The process–resource graph is analysed by a deadlock detection algorithm.

Deadlock detection algorithms can be centralized, hierarchical or distributed. We discuss these schemes in Section 10.4.

There are two main disadvantages of deadlock detection algorithms. The first is the overhead generated by detection of cycles in a process–resource graph. The second is the cost of deadlock resolution, mainly the cost of interrupting and restarting a process after deadlock.

Many deadlock detection algorithms for distributed systems have been proved incorrect. One of the main reasons is the lack of specification tools. The design and implementation of new algorithms is important; more research is needed in the area of algorithm specification and verification.

The correctness of a deadlock detection algorithm depends on two factors:

(1)   all deadlocks must be detected in a finite time; and

(2)   if a deadlock is detected, it must indeed exist.

Another problem associated with deadlock detection algorithms is practicality. This leads to the next research area – performance evaluation of deadlock detection algorithms. Very few papers address this problem.

Deadlock detection and resolution can be performed by searching for cycles in a process–resource graph. This approach is feasible in centralized systems. However, it is not efficient in distributed systems because the maintenance of a global process–resource graph for the entire system is not efficient. Resource deadlock detection and resolution can be practical if algorithms can be used which do not require a global graph to be built and maintained. Algorithms for resource deadlock detection in distributed systems need not differ from these used in centralized computer systems. However, the lack of shared memory makes the construction and the maintenance of various graphs used for deadlock detection the source of significant bookkeeping and, possibly, of performance problems.

The first two methods ensure that deadlocks never occur, while the third method allows the system to enter a deadlock state. In this case, an operating system must examine the system state to determine whether a deadlock has occurred, and if so to recover from the deadlock.

Many algorithms have been developed and published for deadlock avoidance, prevention, or detection in centralized systems. One can say that the deadlock problem in those systems has been essentially solved. The problem of deadlock reappeared with the advent of distributed systems. Unfortunately, the most important features of distributed systems, such as lack of global memory and non-negligible message transmission delays, make centralized techniques for solving deadlock problems expensive. Thus, it is necessary to re-evaluate the area of solving deadlock problems for distributed operating systems.

Some theoretical work has been done in the area of the detection of deadlocks in distributed systems but few papers on deadlock prevention and avoidance in distributed systems have been published. Moreover, they are not general enough, since they are oriented toward special classes of resources; Hac et al. (1989) deals with files; Peacock (1989) deals with message buffer pools.

In summary, deadlock avoidance is a complicated and expensive operation. In the area of (distributed) operating systems it is mainly of theoretical interest. Prevention can be used in some batch processing operating systems, however, it is not considered feasible in interactive operating systems and databases. Detection and resolution is generally recommended to handle deadlocks in distributed systems.

Many published algorithms for detecting and resolving deadlock in distributed systems have subsequently been shown to be incorrect. This indicates the compexity of the problem in distributed systems and queries the applicability of results thus far obtained.

10.2 Deadlock in distributed systems

We have defined deadlock as the time-dependent state of permanent blocking of a set of processes which communicate with each other, or compete for resources. This implies that there are two kinds of deadlocks in distributed systems (Chandy *et al.* 1983):

(1) resource deadlocks, and

(2) communication deadlocks.

Resource deadlock has been the subject of research by many authors, but communication deadlock has not been studied as extensively. Few algorithms to detect deadlocks among communicating processes have been published.

Another form of deadlock that can arise in distributed operating systems is migration deadlock. Migration deadlock is discussed later in this section.

Before we discuss different types of deadlock in distributed systems, we look at resource and communication deadlocks in centralized systems (both operating systems and databases).

10.2.1 Resource and communication deadlocks in centralized systems

Communication deadlock can occur in a set of processes communicating by messages, where a process waits to communicate with any other process from this set. A nearly identical situation can happen in a database which utilizes majority locking. In this case, a transaction that is blocked can proceed when any other transaction releases its lock on a parent of the granule in question.

In the case of a resource deadlock, a process becomes unblocked only after receiving all the resources for which it is waiting. Thus, if a process invokes concurrent slave (children) processes, the originating process is blocked until all children terminate.

For the case of a process/database model in which a process/transaction is either active or waiting for exactly one resource, there is no distinction between resource and communication deadlock. They reduce to the same concept.

There is one very important difference between resource and communication deadlock detection in centralized systems and distributed systems – simplicity. Centralized deadlock is simpler to detect, because the operating system has a total view of the whole system. In a distributed system, each site has only a local view of the whole system. To create a global view, which is required to detect deadlocks involving more than one site, cooperation among sites is required.

10.2.2 Resource deadlocks in distributed systems

The resource deadlock problem has usually been studied in the context of distributed databases. In such systems, a transaction can access non-local data by invoking slave transactions at sites where these data are stored. These transactions may run concurrently with each other. The originating transaction is blocked until **all** slave transactions terminate. Terminating all transactions is the basic feature of the resource model.

Menasce and Muntz (1979) developed a commonly used model for studying deadlock detection algorithms for distributed databases. According to this model, a database is distributed among N computers, $S_1, S_2, \ldots, S_N$, connected by a network. This network is reliable and fully connected. Users interact with the database via transactions. There are M transactions, $T_1, T_2, \ldots, T_M$. A transaction which involves resources at a local computer is called local, as opposed to a distributed transaction which involves resources at several remote computers. It is assumed that a transaction is implemented by a collection of processes with at most one process per computer. A local operating system or controller C_j at each computer S_j schedules processes, manages resources, and carries out communication. A process is denoted P_{ij}, which means that it works on behalf of transaction T_i on computer S_j.

Let us assume that one transaction T_i is running. In this case, when a process P_{ij} needs a remote resource managed by a controller C_m, its controller C_j must send a request to a process P_{im} via controller C_m. If the resource is available, P_{im} acquires it from C_m, and sends a message to P_{ij} (via C_m and C_j) stating that the resource has been acquired. P_{ij} may proceed with its computation only after it has received positive replies to all of its requests for resources.

When process P_{ij} in transaction T_i no longer needs a resource managed by controller C_m, it communicates via C_j and C_m with process P_{im}, which is responsible for releasing the resource to C_m.

A process is said to be:

(1) **blocked** when it is waiting to acquire a resource; more precisely, from the time it issues a resource request until it receives a grant message for the requested resource, and

(2) **executing** otherwise.

A process is permanently blocked if it never receives a grant message for which it is waiting, this means it never receives access to a requested resource. While a process is blocked it may not send any request or grant messages. However, it may send and receive other messages or perform other tasks, that are, for example, related to deadlock detection.

It is assumed that messages sent by any controller C_i to C_j arrive sequentially and in finite time. It is also assumed that if a single transaction runs by itself in the distributed database, it will terminate in finite time and release all resources. When two or more transactions run in parallel, however, deadlock may arise.

In the following presentation, for notational simplicity we assign a single identifying subscript to a process. Thus, P_i denotes the i-th process. The problem is not altered at all by this notation change, since all the processes in the system are merely renumbered with $1, 2, 3, \ldots$.

Now we define deadlock, based on the concept of dependency. A process P_j is said to be **dependent** on another process P_k if there exists a sequence (**seq**) of processes $P_j, \ldots, P_k$, where each process in **seq** is blocked and each process (except the first) in **seq** holds a resource for which the previous process in **seq** is waiting. A process P_j is said to be **locally dependent** on P_k if all the processes in **seq** belong to the same controller. If P_j is dependent on P_k then P_j must remain blocked at least as long as P_k remains blocked.

Thus, process P_j is deadlocked if it is dependent on itself or on a process that is dependent on P_j. In either case, deadlock exists only if there is a cycle of blocked processes each dependent on the next process in the cycle. Thus, resource deadlock is a circular wait condition that can occur in a distributed computer, if resources are requested when needed while already allocated resources are still being held.

It can be seen from the above definition and example that resource deadlock is a traditional deadlock which arises because processes may wait permanently for resources held by each other. The problem has been studied mainly in the context of distributed database systems by Gligor and Shattuck (1980), Gray (1978), Menasce and Muntz (1979), Obermarck (1982) and Badal (1986).

Resource deadlock detection algorithms function by detecting cycles in the dependency graphs of blocked processes. A number of distributed algorithms for resource deadlock detection have been developed. In general, these algorithms pass information about process demands in an attempt to maintain relevant parts of the global wait-for graph on each node. Papers by Menasce and Muntz (1979), Gligor and Shattuck (1980), Obermarck (1982) and Badal (1986) discuss this in more detail. We introduce the wait-for graph (WFG) model when we discuss deadlock detection algorithms in Section 10.3.

10.2.3 Communication deadlocks in distributed systems

Communication deadlock can be easily defined, based on the communication model. The communication model is an abstract description of a network of processes which communicate via messages. This model does not have any explicit controllers or resources, since controllers are implemented by processes, while requests for resource allocation, cancellation and release are implemented by messages.

Associated with every blocked process is a set of processes called its **dependent set**. A process is said to be **blocked** when it is waiting for a message. A blocked process may start execution upon receiving a message from **any** process in its dependent set. A process is **permanently blocked** if it never receives a message from any process in its dependent set. If a process does not receive a message, it changes neither its state nor its dependent set. A process is said to be **terminated** if it is blocked and its associated dependent set is empty.

Based on these definitions, it is possible to define communication deadlock. A non-empty set S of processes is said to be **deadlocked** if all processes in S are permanently blocked. In general, deadlock occurs among a set of processes which communicate directly when they are blocked waiting for messages from other processes in order to start execution, but there are no messages in transit between them.

It is not possible to detect permanent blocking in the following situation. Process P is waiting for a message from process Q, and Q is currently executing and will send a message to P only upon completion of a loop. In this situation process P appears to be permanently idle if process Q's loop computation is non-terminating. Moreover, because detection of permanent blocking of this type amounts to solving the halting problem and hence is undecidable, it is necessary to assume that P is not permanently blocked since Q may send it a message some time in the future. This leads to the following operational definition of deadlock.

A non-empty set S of processes is **deadlocked** if and only if

(1)   All processes in S are blocked;

(2)   The dependent set of every process in S is a subset of S; and

(3)   There are no messages in transit between processes in S.

A process is **deadlocked** if it belongs to some deadlocked set.

When there are no messages in transit between any pair of processes in S, none of the processes will ever receive a message. This implies that all processes are permanently idle, or deadlocked. A process which suspects that it may be deadlocked must query other processes to determine whether it is indeed deadlocked.

In general in the communication model, upon receiving any one resource, a process sends cancellation messages if necessary and starts waiting for a new set of resources. The communication deadlock model is both more abstract and more general; it is applicable to any message communication system. This model has been studied by the researchers Chandy and Misra (1982), Bracha and Toueg (1984), Misra and Chandy (1982a, 1982b) and Cidon et al. (1987).

Algorithms for communication deadlock detection were, in general, inspired by work on parallel graph algorithms by Dijkstra and Scholten (1980) and Chang (1982). In this class of algorithms simple messages are passed from one process to another. The global wait-for graph is not explicitly built up, but a cycle in the graph will utimately cause messages to return to their initiators, thus alerting them to the existence of a deadlock.

10.2.4   Comparison of resource and communication deadlocks

There are some major differences between the resource model and the communication model. The first difference is that in the communication model, a process can know the identity of those processes from which it must receive a message before it can proceed with further computations. This implies that the process has enough information to perform deadlock detection. In the resource model, the dependence of one transaction on actions of other transactions is not directly known. It is only known whether a transaction is waiting for a given resource or whether a transaction holds a given resource. Only the controllers can deduce that one transaction is waiting for another. This difference implies that the agent of deadlock detection in the two environments cannot be the same.

The second difference between the resource model and the communication model is manifested in conditions for activation. In the former, a process can proceed with execution after receiving **all** its requested resources. In the latter case a process can proceed when it can communicate with *at least one* of the processes for which it is waiting. This difference implies different algorithms.

We noted earlier that resource deadlock arises when there is a **cycle** of blocked dependent processes. A communication deadlock occurs when there is a **knot** of blocked dependent processes. A vertex *i* of a directed graph is said to be a knot if all vertices that can be reached from *i* can also reach *i*. Intuitively, no paths originating from a knot have 'dead ends'.

Finally, communication deadlock is more general than the resource deadlock. This is because the resource model can be simulated by a communication model.

10.2.5   Migration deadlock

In Chapters 8 and 9 we discussed the requirements and mechanisms of process migration in distributed systems. It is obvious that because this process requires resources, they have to be managed in a proper way. Thus, process migration mechanisms must ensure fair and deadlock-free process movement.

Migration deadlock can arise because each computer is only able to support a limited process load. Filali and his co-workers derived two process migration properties for a distributed system where processes communicate by means of rendezvous (Filali *et al.* 1987). The first is that migration is allowed only if the destination computer is available. Another, called the fairness property, implies a preliminary safety property, namely no migration deadlock. This implies the need for detection or prevention of such deadlocks.

Two types of migration deadlock can occur in a distributed system where the process load on a given machine is restricted to some maximum value:

(1)   local, which can occur on a single computer, and

(2)   global, which involves several computers.

The latter is very similar to communication deadlock.

Local migration deadlock

Local migration deadlock occurs when a process required to satisfy a pending rendezvous on a computer cannot migrate because the destination computer is full.

To illustrate this situation let us assume that a computer has a load capacity for two processes. These two slots are occupied by a migrating task M1 and a resident process P1. Suppose M1 has called P1 and P1 has called a non-resident migrating task M2. This dependency sequence is shown in Fig. 10.2.

However, M2 cannot migrate, because the computer is full. This implies that P1 is blocked calling M2 and M1 is blocked calling P1.

To define deadlock formally, it is necessary to analyse a dependency graph. This graph is constructed only when the computer is computationally full and every process on it is blocked. The dependency graph distinguishes between migration deadlock and deadlock caused by the internal behavior of user processes.

There is a local migration deadlock if the constructed dependency graph is a knot including all the migrating processes on the computer and at least one absent process.

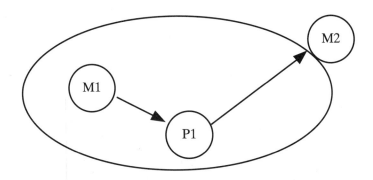

Fig. 10.2   The dependency sequence {adapted from Filali *et al.* (1987)}.

The dependency graph is constructed in the following way:

(1)   The computer is considered as a serially reusable resource – it is represented graphically as a square node and called a computer node. To this node is associated a non-negative integer representing the available slots on the computer.

(2)   A process on a computer is represented as a circular node, called a process node, and a directed edge from the computer node to the process node.

(3)   The representation of a pending rendezvous depends on its kind:

(a)   a rendezvous call (for example, process P1 has called a process M2) is represented as a directed edge from the caller node to the called node; in the case when the called process is not present on the computer, a corresponding node is added;

(b)   an accepted rendezvous (for example, a process T1 accepts a rendezvous) is represented as a directed edge from every potential rendezvous caller node to the accepting node, since every process can call this rendezvous.

(4)   For each absent process P, the fact that P has to acquire a slot before migration is represented by a directed edge from P to the computer node.

The dependency graph for the example of Fig. 10.2 is illustrated in Fig. 10.3. The graph clearly shows a knot and thus indicates a migration deadlock.

Global migration deadlock
Global migration deadlock occurs on a distributed computer system if

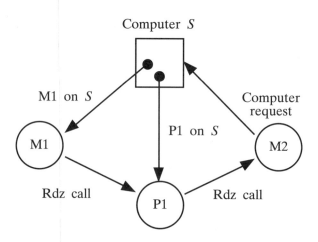

Fig. 10.3   Dependency graph for Fig. 10.2 {adapted from Filali et al. (1987)}.

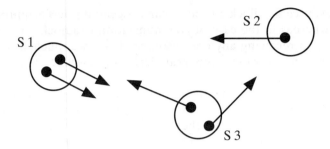

Fig. 10.4   Global migration deadlock {adapted from Filali et al (1987)}.

(1)   every computer is computationally full, and

(2)   at least one process on every computer in the system wants to migrate toward another computer.

Note that global migration deadlock is very similar to communication deadlock. We recall that there is a communication deadlock in a system of processes communicating by messages, modelled by a directed graph, if there exists a knot in this graph.

Let us use a directed graph again to model migrating processes in a distributed system and to define migration deadlock formally. The vertices of the graph represent the system's computers. There is a directed edge from vertex S_i to vertex S_j if a process wants to migrate from computer S_i to S_j.

The following example illustrates this situation. The computers S_1, S_2, and S_3 are overloaded (computationally full). Processes in this distributed system want to migrate to either S_1, S_2, and S_3, as illustrated in Fig. 10.4. However, they cannot, because there is migration deadlock.

There is a global deadlock in a distributed computer system if a directed graph which models this system in the way presented above is a knot. This is not proven here; a proof sketch can be found in Filali *et al.* (1987). The definitions of communication and migration deadlock are so similar that we can always treat the migration deadlock as a special case of communication deadlock. This shows once again the generality of communication deadlock.

10.3   Models of deadlock

The division into two basic deadlock models in message communication systems, resource and communication deadlocks, is not good enough if one wants to detect deadlock efficiently, using proper algorithms. Thus, there is the need to utilize some special features of applications. One of them is a type of resource request. We recall that in the case of resource deadlock a process can proceed if it has acquired all resources, whereas in the case of communication deadlock a process can proceed upon receiving any one resource. Thus, we touched on the resource problem. However, this granularity of resource requests is too general.

The discussion in this section of a hierarchy of resource models that can be used to classify deadlock detection algorithms according to the complexity of the models they permit is based on models of deadlock presented by Knapp (Knapp 1987) and literature that introduced these models. We start from very restricted forms and go to models with no restrictions. We characterize these models formally using a wait-for-graph (WFG) which is a mathematical model of resource requests.

Note also that detection algorithms based on the use of WFGs differ in how and where the graphs are maintained and what messages are sent from computer to computer.

10.3.1   The wait-for-graph model

A wait-for-graph (WFG) belongs to a class of directed graphs. The vertices of this graph are used to model processes. Directed edges in the graph represent blocking relations between processes. A vertex with outgoing edges corresponds to a blocked process. Formally, there is an edge in the WFG from process P_{ij} to P_{kj} if controller C_j has a request from P_{ij} for resources held by P_{kj}. This edge is called an **intracontroller** edge. There is also an edge from P_{ij} to P_{im} if P_{ij} is waiting for a grant message from P_{im} (that it has acquired a resource managed by C_m). This type of edge is called an **intercontroller** edge.

A deadlock is indicated by a cycle in the WFG. There are two aspects which have to be signalled at this stage. The first is that the precise definition of the term cyclic structure depends on the deadlock model. Another, the indication of deadlock by a cycle depends on the deadlock model adopted. The relationship between deadlocks and WFGs is presented in the following sections.

10.3.2   One-resource model

The one-resource model is the simplest request model. In this model a process can have at most one outstanding resource request at a time. This implies that the maximum outdegree of the relevent WFG is 1.

To find deadlocks in a system which is modelled by the one-resource model it is necessary to find a cycle in the WFG.

The one-resource model has been used in theoretical studies of database systems (Bernstein *et al.* 1987). A simple algorithm for deadlock detection in a system described by the one-resource model has been developed by Mitchell and Merritt (1984). This algorithm is described in Section 10.7.4.

10.3.3   AND model

The AND model is more general than the one-resource model. According to the AND model a process is permitted to request a set of resources. The process remains blocked until it is granted all the resources it has requested. Therefore, requests of this type are called AND requests. Notice the similarity between the AND model and the resource model discussed in Section 10.2.2.

The nodes of the WFG constructed for a system modelled by the AND model are called AND nodes. These nodes may have outdegree greater than 1. As in the one-resource model, to find deadlocks in the AND model it is necessary to find a cycle in the WFG.

A formal definition of deadlock in the AND model was given by Chandy and Misra (1982). It is identical to that given in Section 10.2.2 for resource deadlock; process P_i is deadlocked if it is dependent on itself or on some process that is dependent on P_i.

More precisely, process P_i is **dependent** on another process P_j if there is a sequence **seq** $= P_i, P_{i1}, P_{i2}, \ldots, P_{in}, P_j$ of processes such that each process in **seq** is blocked and each process (except the first) in *seq* holds a resource for which the previous process in **seq** is waiting. A process P_i is **locally dependent** on P_j if all the processes in **seq** belong to the same controller. If P_i is dependent on P_j than P_i remains blocked at least as long as P_{ij} remains blocked. We say again that P_i is deadlocked if it is dependent on itself or a process that is dependent on itself. In summary, deadlock exists only if there is a cycle of blocked processes.

Deadlock detection algorithms for the AND recognize deadlock by finding cycles of blocked processes, each dependent on the next one in the cycle. There is no guarantee that all deadlocked processes will be detected, since a process might be outside the cycle but dependent on a process in the cycle. Fig. 10.5 shows a process (P_{53}) that is deadlocked, but is outside the cycle, and so is will not be detected as deadlocked.

Note that deadlock in the one-resource model is defined in the same way. There is only one restriction, as emphasized in the previous section, that a process can have only one outstanding request at a time. In the WFG it is manifested by one outgoing edge.

A number of deadlock detection algorithms have been proposed for the AND model. They can be found in Chandy and Misra (1982), Chandy *et al.* (1983), Menasce and Muntz (1979) and Obermarck (1982). Some of them are described in Section 10.7.

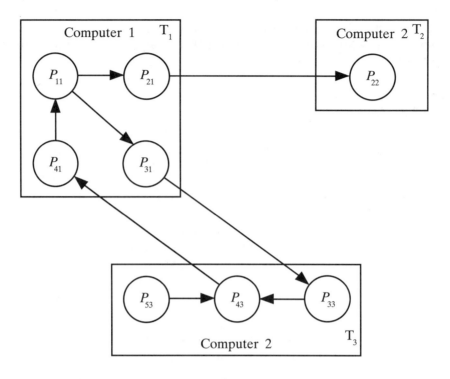

Fig. 10.5 Example of WFG {adapted from Knapp (1987)}.

10.3.4 OR model

The OR model is an alternative to the AND model of resource request. It is also referred to as the communication model. In this model it is insufficient to discover a cycle in the WFG to detect deadlock; instead, deadlock detection involves finding knots in the WFG.

To illustrate this, let us use the example of the WFG utilized by Knapp and shown in Fig. 10.5. Suppose all requests are OR requests; the nodes are called OR nodes. In this case transaction T_1 is not deadlocked becasue P_{22} has no outgoing edges. Thus, after T_2 releases the resource it holds, T_1 can continue. Thus, a knot indicates a deadlock (Chandy et al. [1983] and Knapp [1987]).

Algorithms for deadlock detection in the OR model can be found in papers by Misra and Chandy (1982a, 1982b), Chandy et al. (1983) and Natarajan (1986). Some of them are also described in Sections 10.7.5 and 10.7.6.

10.3.5 AND–OR model

The AND and OR models have been generalized in the AND–OR model (Knapp 1987). The basic concept of this model is that AND–OR requests may specify any combination of *and* and *or* in the resource request. For example, let us assume that *a*, *b*, *c*, and *d* are resources that exist on different computers. A request for (*a and* (*b or c*)) *and d* is possible.

Note that there is no familiar construct of graph theory to describe a deadlock in the AND–OR model in terms of the WFG. Deadlock in the AND–OR model can be detected by repeated application of the test for OR model deadlock, assuming that deadlock is a stable property. This stable property means that deadlock does not go away by itself. However, this is not an efficient strategy. Hermann and Chandy (1983) have developed a more efficient algorithm.

10.3.6 $\binom{n}{k}$ model

A generalization of the AND–OR model is the $\binom{n}{k}$ model. This allows the specification of requests to obtain any k resources from a pool of n available resources. It is possible to show that every request in the $\binom{n}{k}$ model can be expressed in the AND–OR model.

The formal definition of deadlock and an algorithm for deadlock detection in the $\binom{n}{k}$ model was published in Bracha and Toueg (1983).

10.3.7 Unrestricted model

The most general request model is the unrestricted model, in which no underlaying structure of resource requests is assumed. Only the stability of deadlock is required. The advantage of looking at the deadlock problem using the unrestricted model is that it aids in analysing the design problem. This means that properties of the underlying database computations (for example, degree of concurrency) are separated from concerns about properties of the problem (stability of deadlock). As a result, all the general algorithms can be used to detect other stable properties as well. However, the algorithms dealing with the general model are computationally very heavy because there are no assumptions about the underlying structure of the database computation.

The reader interested in this model is referred to Chandy and Lamport (1985), Chandy and Misra (1986) and Helary *et al.* (1987).

10.4 Centralized, distributed or hierarchical deadlock detection

Deadlock can be detected utilizing centralized, distributed or hierarchical schemes. Detection and resolution requires maintaining information on all processes and related resources. This information must be monitored, and cycles in the process–resource graph must be checked. In a distributed environment these operations are expensive.

10.4.1 Centralized scheme

In the centralized scheme, one single controller is responsible for deadlock detection. This means that all information represented by the process–resource graph is maintained by the single controller. This controller is responsible for running the deadlock detection and resolution algorithm.

A major advantage of a centralized scheme is that data is gathered and maintained in one central location. On the other hand, centralized deadlock detection algorithms are subject to failures of the central detector. Heavy traffic to and from the central detector can result in a performance bottleneck, which limits the overall performance of a distributed system. Moreover, data can be out-of-date because of communication delays and lost messages.

These typical drawbacks of centralized systems are not the only reasons for pursuing alternatives. Bernstein *et al.* (1987) discuss one feature which is purely oriented towards deadlock detection in distributed systems: for typical applications most WFG cycles are very short. For most applications, over 90 per cent of WFG cycles are of length 2. This means that most deadlocks involve only two computers. Bernstein and his co-workers give the theoretical reasons for this; Gray *et al.* (1981) present similar figures based on an empirical study.

A centralized detector has to spend a significant time to gather and assemble all the local WFGs. This implies that a distributed deadlock might remain undetected for a long time.

Centralized deadlock detection algorithms have been developed by Chu and Ohlmacher (1974), Gray (1978) and Ho and Ramamoorthy (1982). In the last of these, periodically a node is chosen as a central controller responsible for deadlock detection.

10.4.2 Distributed scheme

One way to overcome the problems presented above is to distribute the information relating to processes and resources; no single computer has all the information. One boundary solution is for each computer to only maintain information relevant to its own operations. Gathering information is then much faster than in a centralized scheme, but global deadlock can be overlooked. To detect deadlocks, information must be passed between computers. The problem is how to pass relevant information – this is discussed in Section 10.5.

Another solution is for each computer to have all information on resource allocation and requests. This can lead to two problems. The first is maintaining consistency. Using outdated information can lead to detecting false deadlocks. Interrupting processes to resolve false deadlocks is expensive, measured in computation time and wasting of system resources. The second problem is that the same deadlock can be detected by two systems. How should this be dealt with.

A distributed detection algorithm should involve sharing enough information to avoid these two boundary solutions. This results in algorithms that involve minimal costs. These costs are measured in terms of messages exchanged between remote facilities involved in deadlock detection (controllers), and computation overhead. Note that if detection is distributed, and most deadlocks involve only two processors, then remote facilities should be able to communicate quickly and detect a deadlock almost immediately.

Another reason for developing and utilizing distributed deadlock algorithms is that they are not necessarily more complex and harder to implement then centralized ones. This has been demonstrated by Mitchell and Merritt (1984).

10.4.3 Hierarchical scheme

It is possible to impose a hierarchical organization on deadlock detection facilities (controllers) running on different computers. This leads to a hierarchical deadlock detection scheme. More precisely, this scheme is based on providing several layers of hierarchy, namely local, regional and global. Each node tries to detect and resolve its deadlocks locally. A higher layer controller is only involved in detection if a local controller identifies that its processes are waiting for resources provided by another local computer. In this case relevant information is sent to the higher layer controller coordinating these local controllers. Deadlock detection should be provided by a facility running on a computer as close as possible to the computers involved in the deadlock.

Examples of hierarchical deadlock detection algorithms are those developed by Menasce and Muntz (1979) and Ho and Ramamoorthy (1982).

10.5 Basic concepts for distributed deadlock detection algorithms

The previous sections identified three classifications of distributed deadlock detection algorithms. The first was based on models for deadlock. It leads to algorithms for detecting resource and communication deadlocks. The second classification is based on request models. This classification has a number of features in common with the first. The third classification divides algorithms into three groups: centralized, distributed and hierarchical.

A fourth classification is based on the particular concepts on which distributed deadlock detection algorithms have been (and can be) developed. These concepts are:

(1) path-pushing,

(2) edge-chasing,

(3) diffusing computations, and

(4) global state detection.

This classification leads to four classes of algorithms.

10.5.1 Path-pushing algorithms

Path-pushing algorithms are based on an explicit global WFG. Each computer of a distributed system builds its own simplified form of the global WFG. This operation is performed by sending its local updated WFG to a number of neighbouring computers every time a deadlock computation is carried out. This procedure is repeated until some computer constructs a simplified but sufficient form of the global WFG to detect deadlock or to establish that no deadlocks are present. The sending around of paths of the global WFG is the main feature of this scheme, and is the basis of the term **path-pushing algorithms**.

Many algorithms have been developed using the path-pushing approach. Unfortunately some of them are defective, despite being 'proved' correct. The most influential algorithm, developed by Menasce and Muntz (Menasce and Muntz 1979) was proved defective by Gligor and Shattuck (Gligor and Shattuck 1980). Another algorithm was published in Ho and Ramamoorthy (1982); Jagannathan and Vasudevan (Jagannathan and Vasudevan 1982) proved that this algorithm is also incorrect. The algorithm developed by Obermarck (1982) is also incorrect, as stated in Elmagarmid (1986).

Other path-pushing algorithms were presented in Bracha and Toueg (1984), Chandy and Misra (1982), Choudhary *et al.* (1989) and Roesler and Burkhard (1989).

The failure of many of these algorithms is not astonishing. Chandy and Lamport (1985) state that this may be because relationships among local process states, global system states and points in a distributed computation are not well understood. Another consequence of this lack of understanding is that most of these algorithms depend on 'freezing' the underlying computation for the time the deadlock detection goes on. As a result, in most cases the picture of the assembled global WFG is inconsistent.

10.5.2 Edge-chasing algorithms

Let us assume that we have a distributed graph structure. The problem is how to verify the presence of a cycle in such a structure. The verification can be provided by propagating special messages called **probes** along the edges of the graph. These probe messages are distinct from request messages and grant messages. Thus, when the initiator of a probe message receives a matching probe, it knows that it is on a cycle in the graph.

The most useful feature of this approach in connection with deadlock detection is that the executing processes can discard any probe messages they receive, while blocked processes propagate the probe along their outgoing edges. Mitchell and Merritt (1984) modified this method by sending probes upon requests and in the opposite direction of the edge.

The edge-chasing approach is also used in Chandy and Misra's algorithm (Chandy and Misra 1982).

10.5.3 Diffusing computations

The development of algorithms using the concept of diffusing computations is based on the pioneering work by Dijkstra and Scholten (Dijkstra and Scholten 1980) and Chang (Chang 1982) carried out nearly at the same time. Our presentation follows Dijkstra and Scholten (1980) and Knapp (1987).

The basic idea of this approach is that a diffusing computation is activated, for example, by a transaction manager (initiator) that suspects a deadlock. This diffusing computation is superimposed on the underlying database computation. The initiator declares deadlock if the diffusing computation terminates.

The diffusing computation has one characteristic feature in the case of distributed deadlock detection: the global WFG is implicitly reflected in the structure of this computation. However, the actual WFG is never built explicitly.

A diffusing computation grows as a process sends **query** messages, and shrinks as a process receives **replies**. These messages are used only for deadlock detection purposes, and so are distinct from resource requests and grant messages. The root (initiating process) sends queries (called engaging queries) to its successor to start a diffusing computation. A process, on receipt of the engaging query, sends queries to its successors. Each process is able also to receive replies from its successors and to send replies to its predecessors. Note that queries always travel in the directions of the graph edges, whereas replies always travel the oposite way. It is required that the number of queries received along an edge always be at least the number of replies sent in the opposite direction. The difference between these numbers is called the **deficit** of an edge.

A process is in its natural state if the deficits of all incoming and outgoing edges are zero. The diffusing computation terminates if the root returns to its natural state. In other words, when a diffusing computation shrinks back to its root, it terminates.

The problem of how to detect termination is discussed in Apt (1986), Dijkstra *et al.* (1983), Francez and Rodeh (1982) and Huang (1988).

Now we can define the relationship between deadlock detection and a diffusing computation. A blocked process can determine whether it is deadlocked by initiating a diffusing computation. If the initator receives replies to all the queries sent, then it is deadlocked. A number of processes may initiate a diffusing computation at the same time.

Algorithms based on the diffusing computation approach can be found in Chandy and Misra (1982), Chandy *et al.* (1983), Chang (1982), Dijkstra *et al.* (1983), Misra and Chandy (1982*a,b*) and Chandy and Misra (1986).

10.5.4 Global state detection

Deadlock detection algorithms can also be based on the global state detection approach. This approach was proposed by Chandy and Lamport (1985). In this paper they present algorithms by which a process in a distributed system can determine a global state of the system during a computation.

Recall that when discussing the path-pushing approach we noted that many algorithms are incorrect. The reason for this is that the relationships among local process states, global system states and points in a distributed computation are not well understood. The major contribution of Chandy and Lamport's work is the definition of these relationships.

The basic notion of Chandy and Lamport's approach is a consistent global state that can be determined without temporarily suspending the underlying computation (which is also referred to as the system). The underlying computation is a collection of processes (these processes can be thought of in database terms as transaction managers and transaction agents). Processes communicate by sending messages, for example, resource requests and grants. This communication is managed according to an underlying protocol. Some events, namely the sending and receipt of messages, must be distinguished. The set of events $\{e\}$ in the system is denoted by E.

The **local state** of a process P consists of the history of all events that occurred on P. These events are partially ordered according to Lamport's happened-before relation, denoted by $\rightarrow$ (see Chapter 6).

Chandy and Lamport use the following formalization. A cut c of E is a partition of E into two sets P_c and F_c, standing for past and future, respectively. A cut of a distributed system is illustrated in Fig. 10.6.

A cut is said to be **consistent** if F_c is closed under $\to$. A consistent cut defines a consistent state. This implies that consistent cut and consistent state can be used interchangeably. Intuitively, consistent cuts are those that do not contain a send event in F_c with the corresponding receive event in P_c.

Fig. 10.6 shows that $P_c = \{e_1, e_3, e_4, e_7, e_8, e_9, e_{10}\}$ and $F_c = \{e_2, e_5, e_6\}$. Moreover, since F_c is closed under $\to$, c is a consistent cut.

Using the above definitions, we define a special type of consistent state which is the global state of the distributed system. The global state S_t is the collection of all the local states of the processes at time t. This state cannot be observed because this would require an outside observer to record the local states of the processes instantaneously. Thus, the global state is a theoretical construct. However, consistent states can be obtained from within the system.

The extension of the happened-before relation ($\to$) to consistent states is defined as follows. Let S_1 and S_2 be consistent states. We say $S_1 \to S_2$ if P_{S_1} and P_{S_2}. Now, we define the reachability relation between states. Let S be a consistent state of a distributed system and e is an event such that $P_S \cup \{e\}$ defines a consistent state S'. Then S' is reachable from S, and is denoted $S \mid\!-^e S'$.

A sequence of events **sched** $= (e_1, e_2, \ldots, e_n)$ is said to be a schedule, if $S \mid\!-e_1 S_1 \mid\!-e_2 S_2, \ldots, \mid\!-e_{n-1} S_{n-1} \mid\!-e_n S'$. We denote this as $S \mid\!-^{\text{sched}} S'$. It is possible to prove (Chandy and Lamport 1985) that:

Lemma 10.1. If $S \to S'$, then there is a schedule **sched** such that $S \mid\!-^{\text{sched}} S'$.

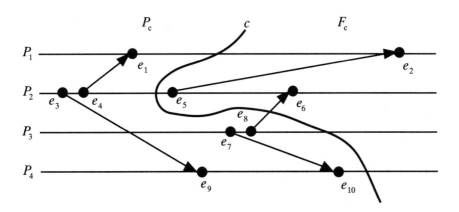

Fig. 10.6 A cut of a distributed system {adapted from Knapp (1987)}.

In the context of deadlock detection, the state of the system is a WFG, and schedules are schedules of WFG transformations. A process (transaction) is said to be **deadlocked at time** t if it is deadlocked in WFG_t, that is, the WFG at time t. The following lemma (Bracha and Toueg 1983) allows us to apply a distributed deadlock detection algorithm to consistent WFGs instead of WFG_ts.

> *Lemma 10.2.* If WFG $\rightarrow$ WFG' and process v is deadlocked in WFG, then v is deadlocked in WFG'.

This is the fundamental lemma on which deadlock detection algorithms can be developed. One algorithm based on this approach has been developed by Bracha and Toueg (Bracha and Toueg 1983).

10.6 Some aspects of deadlock resolution

As we noted earlier, many attempts have been made to provide methods and algorithms for handling deadlocks in distributed systems. We say that detection and recovery is the recommended approach to handle deadlocks.

Many algorithms based on this approach have been developed. However, these attempts have not been entirely successful. Many of these algorithms fail to work correctly, and their feasibility is questionable – they exhibit poor performance. Another very important limitation of some of these algorithms is that they do not provide a full solution to the problem. It is not enough to detect deadlocks – deadlocks must be resolved. For example, the algorithms published in Bracha and Toueg (1987), Chandy and Misra (1982), Chandy *et al.* (1983) and Gray (1978) do not indicate how to eliminate deadlock after it is detected.

Attempts to provide algorithms which detect and resolve deadlock given in Gligor and Shattuck (1980), Menasce and Muntz (1979), Obermarck (1982), and Sinha and Natarajan (1986) have also not been successful. The main reason for this lies in the inability of these algorithms to restore the WFG to a consistent state after resolving the deadlock (Elamagarmid 1986). This can result in either detecting false deadlocks or failing to detect real ones.

One algorithm which not only detects deadlocks but also resolves them is presented in Roesler and Burkhard (1989). This algorithm has been proved correct.

10.7 A survey of deadlock detection algorithms

One of the most important features of deadlock detection algorithms is correctness. Correctness depends on two conditions:

(1) **Progress property** – every deadlock must be eventually detected.

(2)   **Safety property** – if a deadlock is detected, it must indeed exist.

Message delays and out-of-date WFGs can cause incorrect deadlock detection. Such deadlocks are called **phantom deadlocks**.

Selected deadlock detection algorithms will now be discussed. Some of them have been proved to be incorrect. This was emphasized when we discussed deadlock types and classifications of deadlock detection approaches and algorithms. They are still worth presenting, both for historical reasons, and second, because of their influence on the development of other algorithms.

10.7.1   Gray's algorithm – centralized deadlock detection

In centralized deadlock detection, there is one distinguished node referred to as the central detector, which is designated as being responsible for the detection of global deadlocks. The deadlock detection algorithm developed by Gray (Gray 1979) belongs to a class of centralized algorithms. It deals with resource deadlocks. This algorithm looks for cycles in the global WFG, and belongs to the class of AND models. Our presentation follows Gray (1979).

Basic concept
According to Gray's algorithm, each node has its local deadlock detector which maintains a graph called the transaction_wait_for (TWF) graph.

(1)   The nodes of the TWF graph are transactions and resources (locks).

(2)   The edges of this graph are directed and are constructed in the following way:

   (a)   if resource (lock) R is granted to transaction T then draw an edge from R to T;

   (b)   if transaction T is waiting for resource (lock) R then draw an edge from T to R.

(3)   There is a deadlock if and only if the transaction_wait_for graph has a cycle. This implies that deadlock detection becomes an issue of building the transaction_wait_for graph and searching it for cycles.

(4)   The local deadlock detectors running in each node detect deadlocks among transactions which run exclusively in each of those nodes. Moreover, the local deadlock detectors of each node have to agree on a common protocol in order to handle deadlocks involving distributed transactions (global deadlocks).

Fig. 10.7 may help in understanding Gray's concept. Transaction T1 has two processes P1 and P2 in two nodes Node1 and Node2, respectively. P1 is session-waiting for its co-process P2 to do some work. P2 needs

Node 1

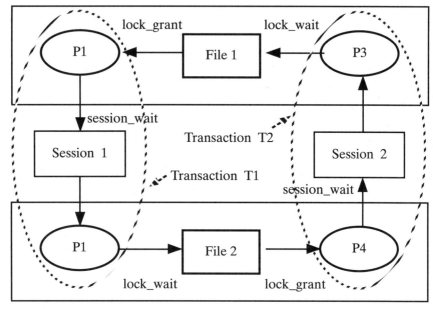

Node 2

Fig. 10.7 Global resource deadlock {adapted from Gray (1979)}.

access to file File2 in Node2 to do this work. But File2 is locked exclusively by another process P4 of Node2, so P2 is in lock–wait state. This implies that transaction T1 is waiting for File2. Transaction T2 is in a similar state – it waits for File1. Thus, transaction T1 is waiting for File2 which is granted to transaction T2 which is waiting for File1 which is granted to transaction T1 – global deadlock has occured.

The global deadlock detector is in session with all local deadlock detectors and coordinates their activities. The global deadlock detector can run in any node, but the best location for it is that which minimizes its communication distance to the resource (lock) managers.

To handle global deadlocks, the notion of a transaction_wait_for graph must be generalized. In this case the nodes of the graph represent processes and resources. They are connected by edges of the graph that are constructed in the following way.

(1) Draw a directed edge from a process to a resource if

    (a) the process is in lock–wait for the resource,

    (b) the process is in session–wait for the resource (session).

(2) Draw a directed edge from a resource to a process if

    (a) the resource is lock granted to the process.

Thus, for the model under discussion, we can see that

(1)   a local deadlock is a cycle of the following form

lock_wait → .... → lock_wait

(2)   a global deadlock is a cycle of the form

lock_wait → .... → session_wait → lock_wait → .... → session_wait.

An algorithm for deadlock detection can be activated, whenever anyone waits, either continuously or periodically.

(1)   The cost of deadlock detection every time anyone waits is a sum of the cost of continual maintenance of the transaction_wait_for graph and almost certain failure since deadlock is rare.

(2)   The cost of periodic deadlock detection is the cost of detecting deadlocks late. This type of detection is even more important for a distributed system than for a centralized one. The cost of detection is much higher in a distributed system.

Deadlock detection algorithm
To detect global deadlocks, the global deadlock detector is started in some specific node. The global detector is in session with all local deadlock detectors. Its basic task is the coordination of activities of these local deadlock detectors.

Global deadlock detection is carried out in the following way:

(1)   Each local deadlock detector tries to find all **potential global deadlock paths** in its node. This searching is performed by enumerating periodically all

session_wait → lock_wait → .... → session_wait

paths in its node by working backwards from processes which are in session_wait. Starting at such a process it sees if some local process is locked waiting for this process. If there is such a process, the deadlock detector searches backwards looking for some process which has a session in progress.

(2)   When such a path is found, the local deadlock detector sends a message to the global deadlock detector, containing the following information:

(a)   sessions and transactions at endpoints of the path and their local pre-emption costs,

(b)   the minimum cost transaction in the path and the node's local pre-emption cost.

(3)   Periodically, the global deadlock detector

(a)   collects these messages,

(b) glues all these paths together by matching up sessions,

(c) enumerates cycles and selects victims just as in the local deadlock detector case.

It should be noted that the cost of a distributed transaction is the sum of the costs of its partition elements. The global detector approximates this cost by summing the costs of the transaction partitions known to it.

(4) When a victim is selected, the resource (lock) manager in the victim's node is informed of the deadlock. The local resource (lock) manager in turn informs the victim with a deadlock return.

There is a problem when a node crashes. We should distinguish two cases.

(1) If a node with a local deadlock detector crashes, then its partition of the system is unavailable. In this situation, its co-processes in other nodes can wait for its recovery or they can abort.

(2) If a node with a global deadlock detector crashes, then no deadlocks will be detected until the node recovers. The resource (lock) manager can nominate a new global deadlock detector whenever the node of the current one crashes.

The following features of centralized deadlock detection can be identified:

(1) Centralized deadlock detection is conceptually simple, but the design of an efficient algorithm does not appear to be a simple task.

(2) The cost of constructing and maintaining the transaction_wait_for graph is high.

(3) This approach is very vulnerable to failures of nodes hosting the global deadlock detector.

(4) Some practical problems, such as the removal of false deadlocks, can be easily solved.

(5) Centralized deadlock detection may be practical and efficient for local area networks, but is likely to be too expensive for wide area networks.

10.7.2 Menasce and Muntz's algorithm

Menasce and Muntz (1979) developed two algorithms, which deal with resource deadlock, and are based on the AND model. The first algorithm is based on a hierarchical approach to detect deadlock. They also presented a distributed deadlock detection algorithm which has been proven by Gligor and Shattuck (1980) to be incorrect and impractical.

Hierarchical deadlock detection is carried out by a logical hierarchy of deadlock detectors, and is an extension of centralized deadlock detection.

The most important features of the hierarchical deadlock detection algorithm proposed by Menasce and Muntz are that

(1) it does not require that a global graph be built and maintained, and

(2) it lends itself to an optimization whereby deadlocks can be detected by a node which is located as 'close' as possible to the nodes involved in the cycle.

The last point implies that deadlock detection is based on searching for the existence of cycles in the graph.

Note that the Menasce and Muntz algorithm is the first which used a condensed transaction-wait-for graph. In this graph, the vertices represent transactions, and edges reflect relationships between transactions.

To present the hierarchical deadlock detection algorithm a formal model of transaction processing must be introduced.

Formal model of transaction processing

The model is nearly identical to the model described in Section 10.1.2. Modifications have been made to reflect the style of the Menasce and Muntz algorithm.

A transaction which involves data at a single node is said to be a local transaction. A distributed transaction involves resources at several nodes. Distributed transactions are implemented as a collection of processes (called transaction incarnations) which act on behalf of the transaction.

Recall that a transaction can be in two different states: active and blocked. A transaction is blocked if its execution cannot proceed because a required resource is being held by another transaction. Otherwise, the transaction is active.

The state of execution of all transactions in the system is depicted by a graph model called transaction_wait_for (TWF) graph. The nodes of the transaction_wait_for graph are transaction incarnations. They are labeled by the pair (transaction_name, node_name) (T, N). This provides unique global names.

(1) There is a directed arc from node (T_i, N) to node (T_j, N) if the incarnation of transaction T_i in node N is blocked and waiting for the incarnation of T_j to release a resource needed by T_i. (T_i, N) is in 'resource_wait' for (T_j, N).

(2) There is a directed arc from node (T, N_i) to node (T, N_j) if the incarnation of transaction T in node N_i is blocked and waiting for

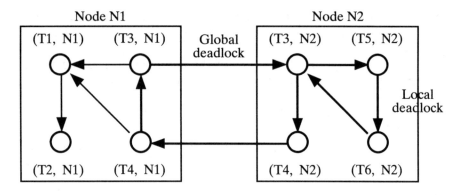

Fig. 10.8 A transaction wait_for_graph for a two–node network.

a message from the incarnation T in node S_j. (T, N_i) is in 'message_wait' for (T, N_j).

A resource deadlock occurs in the system if and only if a cycle in the transaction_wait_for graph exists. An example of the transaction_wait_for graph with two deadlock (local and global) is shown in Fig. 10.8.

Basic concepts of the algorithm

The basic concepts are presented in two stages. The first is very general, showing the basic cooperation of hierarchically arranged nodes, and the second is more formal allowing us to present the algorithm formally.

In the Menasce and Muntz hierarchical approch, nodes are formed into a hierarchical (or tree-like) structure. The lowest level nodes (N_{11}, N_{12}, N_{13}, N_{14}, in Fig. 10.9) maintain local TWF graphs.

Low level TWF information is merged and maintained by upper level nodes, that is, N_{21}, N_{22}, which work as controllers for nodes N_{11}, N_{12}, and N_{13}, N_{14}, respectively. N_3 acts as a controller for nodes N_{21} and N_{22}.

The problem is how these nodes cooperate when they are detecting deadlock. Let us assume that node N_{13} must wait for a transaction carried out on node N_{14}. In this case, an output port is added to the TWF graph at N_{13}, and a corresponding input port to the TWF graph at N_{14}. When N_{13} checks for cycles and finds a path between the output port at N_{13} and input port at N_{14}, it sends this path, which is a potential global deadlock, to controller N_{22}. N_{14} works in the same way, and as a result also transmits the path to N_{22}. Having information from the nodes involved, N_{22} can detect deadlocks caused by transactions between N_{13} and N_{14}. Additionally, if the information from N_{13} waits for a transaction on N_{21}, the TWF graph created at N_{22} must be sent to the higher level controller, that is, N_3, which assembles all the information from lower levels to detect deadlock.

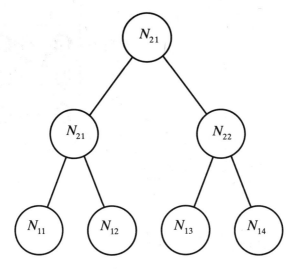

Fig. 10.9   Hierarchy of nodes for deadlock detection.

This general presentation shows that hierarchical resource dead-lock detection uses a hierarchy of controllers (deadlock detectors). Moreover, the Menasce and Muntz model is based on the assumption that we can partition the global database, DB, into disjoint local data-bases (DB_i) (subdatabase), where each local database is associated with one and only one node.

(1)   A local controller LK_i is assigned to each local database DB_i.

(2)   Each local controller LK_i maintains a transaction_wait_for graph, TWF (LK_i).

    (a)   This graph contains all the nodes of the global TWF graph associated with transaction incarnations local to LK_i.

    (b)   Moreover, each TWF graph of a local controller contains two special types of nodes (output_port nodes, and input_port nodes) which are associated with the arcs of the global TWF which join incarnations in two distinct controllers.

These nodes are defined in the following way:

    (i)   A node in the TWF graph of LK_i is called an output_port, $O(LK_i, T)$ in TWF(LK_i), if the global TWF contains an out-going arc from an incarnation of transaction T local to LK_i into a nonlocal incarnation of T.

    (ii)   A node in the TWF graph of LK_i is called an input_port, $I(LK_i, T)$ in TWF(LK_i), if in the global TWF there is an incoming

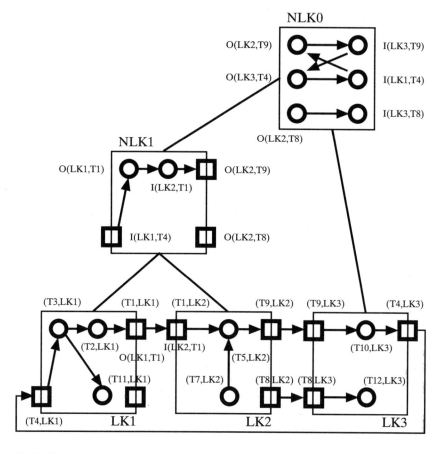

Fig. 10.10 A hierarchy of controllers {adapted from Menasce and Muntz (1979)}.

arc into an incarnation of transaction T local to LK_i from a nonlocal incarnation of T.

(3) Nonlocal controllers maintain an input_output_ports (IOP) graph. Nodes of this graph are associated with input and output ports of local controllers, refered to as i_nodes and o_nodes respectively.

(a) The input_output_port graph (IOP) for controller NLK$_i$, denoted IOP(NLK$_i$), is defined in the following way:

(i) Arcs go only from i_nodes to o_nodes and vice versa.

(ii) Let **Oa** be an output port from a local controller in the subtree rooted at NLK$_i$ and **Ib** be the corresponding input port to another local controller in the same subtree. In this case there is an arc from o_node **Oa** to i_node **Ib**.

(iii)   There is an arc from the i_node **Ia** to o_node **Ob** in IOP(NLK$_i$) if there is a path from an input port **Ia** to an output port **Ob** of a son of NLK$_i$.

(iv)   An input (output) port of IOP(NLK$_i$) is also an input (output) port of a local controller in the subtree rooted by NLK$_i$.

(b)   A hierarchy of controllers is illustrated in Fig. 10.10. In this figure, the ouput port O(LK1, T1) and the input port I(LK2, T1) correspond to an arc in the global TWF from (T1, LK1) to (T1, LK2). The dashed lines indicate arcs in the global TWF which are represented at the upper levels of the hierarchy. There is an arc from O(LK1, T1) to I(LK2, T1) in the IOP of NLK1 since O(LK1, T1) is an output port of LK1 and I(LK2, T1) is its corresponding input port in LK2. LK1 and LK2 are in the subtree rooted by NLK1. There is an arc from I(LK1, T4) to O(LK2, T9) in NLK0 since in NLK1 there is a path between I(LK1,T4) and O(LK2, T9). The input port of IOP(NLK1) is also an input port of LK1.

(c)   In addition, Menasce and Muntz's algorithm requires the definition of the **lowest common ancestor** between controllers K1, K2, . . . , Kn, denoted LCA(K1, K2, . . . , Kn), which is the common ancestor between them at the lowest level in the hierarchy (the root is at the highest level).

The algorithm
The hierarchical deadlock detection algorithm developed by Menasce and Muntz is given in Fig. 10.11.
   The algorithm of hierarchical deadlock detection presented above requires that nonlocal controllers be kept up-to-date either continuously, periodically, or after connections between input and output ports have persisted longer than some threshold.
   The algorithm of hierarchical deadlock detection has two properties:

(1)   Deadlocks which involve resources of a single subdata base DB$_i$ are detected by the formation of a cycle in the TWF of the local controller associated to DB$_i$. This property follows directly from Rule 1 of the algorithm.

(2)   Deadlocks which involve resources controlled by the local controllers LK1, LK2, . . . , LK$_i$ are detected by the formation of a cycle in the IOP graph of the nonlocal controller which is the lowest common ancestor between the LK$_i$'s. The proof of this property can be found in Menasce and Muntz (1979).

Rule 1 – Transaction incarnation T requests a local resource

The requested resource R is in the same subdata base as the transaction incarnation T. Let Lk_i be the controller for resource R.

> *Rule 1.1:*   Assume the resource cannot be granted. Let {T1, T2, . . . , Tk} be the set of transactions which currently hold resource R. Add an arc from (T, LK_i) to (T_j, LK_i) for $j = 1$ to k. Check the TWF graph at LK_i for the existence of cycles.
>
> *Rule 1.1a:*   If cycles are formed, then one or more local deadlocks have been detected and an appropriate action is required for deadlock resolution.
>
> *Rule 1.1b:*   The addition of the arcs mentioned in Rule 1.1 may have created one or more paths between input and output ports of LK_i. For each such path, send the (input_port, output_port) pair which delimits the path to the parent of LK_i.

Rule 2 – Transaction T requests a nonlocal resource

The requested resource R is in a different subdata base from the previously requested resource R. Therefore, it has to be acquired by an incarnation of T local to R. Let LK_i be the controller for the previously requested resource and let LK_i be the controller for resource R. The incarnation of T at LK_i becomes blocked and waiting for a message from the incarnation of T at LK_j. The node (T, LK_i) is now an output port of the TWF graph at LK_i, and the node (T, LK_j) is an output port of the TWF graph at LK_j.

> *Rule 2.1:*   An arc from $O(LK_i, T)$ to $I(LK_j, T)$ is created in the IOP graph of the lowest common ancestor between LK_i and LK_j.
>
> *Rule 2.2:*   An o_node labeled $O(LK_i, T)$ is added to the IOP graph of each controller in the path between LK_i and $LCA(LK_i, LK_j)$. Each such o_node is also an output port of the corresponding IOP graph.
>
> *Rule 2.3:*   An i_node labeled $I(LK_j, T)$ is added to the IOP graph of each controller in the path between LK_i and $LCA(LK_i, LK_j)$. Each such i_node is also an input port of the corresponding IOP graph.

The algorithm followed by a nonlocal controller NLK_i is described by Rule 3 below.

Rule 3 – An arc is added to $IOP(NLK_i)$.

Fig. 10.11 Menasce and Muntz's algorithm {adapted from Menasce and Muntz (1979)}

Rule 3.1:   If a cycle is generated by the addition of the new arc, then a global deadlock has been detected and an appropriate action is required to resolve it.

Rule 3.2:   If no cycle was generated, check whether any input-output port connection has been generated in IOP(NLK$_i$) and report the endpoints of any such connection to the parent of NLK$_i$.

Fig. 10.11 (Cont.)

The advantage of the hierarchical Menasce and Muntz algorithm is that it detects many deadlocks at a relatively low level. This means that message passing overhead is reduced to a minimum.

This algorithm can suffer from two drawbacks: overload or crash of controllers. The first problem can be overcome by introducing dedicated nodes. The second is more serious, because it requires reconfiguration of the hierarchy.

10.7.3 Badal's algorithm

We emphasized earlier that there are a number of distributed deadlock detection algorithms developed based on the path-pushing approach. Many of them have been shown to be defective, despite being 'proved' correct.

One distributed deadlock detection algorithm based on the path-pushing approach was developed by Obermarck (Obermarck 1982). This algorithm was proposed for the AND model; thus it allows the detection of resource deadlocks. Obermarck provided a correction proof, but his algorithm and proof subsequently were shown to be incorrect (in the sense that false deadlocks can be detected) by Elmagarmid (Elmagarmid 1986). Despite this deficiency, many researchers describe Obermarck's algorithm for historical reasons.

Another algorithm belonging to the same class, which can be seen as an extension of the Obermarck's algorithm, was proposed by Badal (Badal 1986). It seems that this algorithm is not defective. We present Badal's algorithm because it has several interesting features:

(1)   it requires fewer messages than other published algorithms;

(2)   it differs from other algorithms in that it uses the concept of a lock history carried with each transaction;

(3)   it is based on the notion of intention locks.

Deadlock detection is a three-staged process.

Basic concepts of Badal's algorithm

Badal's algorithm is based on the following assumptions:

(1) Transaction execution is based on a distributed model.

(2) Each transaction has a node (site) of origin (Sorig); Sorig is the node at which the transaction entered the system.

(3) If a transaction requires a remote resource, it migrates to the node where this resource is located. To perform a migration, it is necessary to create an agent at the remote node. The transaction agent then executes and may either create additional agents, start commit or abort actions, or return execution to the original node.

(4) An agent can be in one of the following three states:

(a) **inactive** – An inactive agent is one that has done work in a node and has created an agent in another node, or one that has returned execution to its creating node and is awaiting further instructions (commit, abort or become active again).

(b) **blocked** (waiting) – A blocked agent is one that has requested a resource that is locked by another agent.

(c) **active** – An active agent is one that is not blocked or inactive.

Each transaction or agent has a globally unique identifier that indicates its node of origin.

(5) Transactions are well-formed and two-phase, that is, any active agent can release a lock only after the transaction has locked all resources it needs for its execution, and only after it has terminated its execution; the active agent is notified to release the lock during two-phase commit.

(6) The information contained in a lock table for a resource includes:

(a) the transaction or agent ID and transaction node of origin,

(b) the type of the lock, and

(c) if possible, the resource (and type of lock) that the transaction holding a lock intends to lock next.

(7) There are the following types of locks:

(a) exclusive write (W),

(b) shared read (R),

(c) an intention lock (I) which indicates that a transaction wishes to aquire a lock on a resource, either to modify it (IW) or to read it (IR).

(8)   The intention locks are placed:

    (a)   in the resource lock table, when an agent is created in a node of a locked resource that it requires, or when a resource in the same node is requested but is already locked by another transaction;

    (b)   in the lock table of the last locked resource(s), if the transaction can determine which resource(s) it intends to lock in a remote node in its next execution step.

(9)   The rules for locks are:

    (a)   any number of transactions or agents may simultaneously hold shared read locks on a particular resource, but only a single transaction or agent may hold an exclusive write lock on a resource (conventional locking).

    (b)   any number of intention locks may be placed on a resource (any number can wait for a resource).

(10)   There is a lock history (LH) for a transaction. LH is a record of all types of locks on any resources that have been requested or are being held by that transaction. Lock histories are in use for three reasons: in some cases to avoid global deadlocks; to support the selection of victim transactions for rollback; and to avoid detection of false deadlocks.

(11)   Two types of resources are considered:

    (a)   Type I resources whose intention lock can be determined from a remote node, that is, the transaction can determine the remote resource lock granularity and its mode before migrating to the node of the remote resource (usually those whose level of granularity is the whole resource).

    (b)   Type II resources whose intention lock granularity and mode can be determined after the transaction has migrated to the remote node (for example, pages of a file in a distributed database system).

There are two types of global deadlocks:

(1)   **Direct global deadlocks** – The global deadlock of two transactions T1 and T2 is **direct** when T1 and T2 deadlock in two nodes that are also the last nodes in which T1 and T2 executed, that is, they were not blocked. This implies that if T1 and T2 executed only in two nodes, they can generate only direct global deadlocks.

(2)   **Indirect global deadlocks** – An indirect global deadlock is one that is not direct.

A deadlock can be detected by Badal's algorithm either by:

(1)   constructing the transaction_wait_for (TWF) graph using the lock histories of transactions that are possibly involved in a deadlock cycle; or

(2)   directly from the wait_for_strings (WFSs).

The WFS is both a list of transaction_waits_for_transaction strings (each transaction waits for the next transaction in the string), and a lock history for each transaction in the string. The deadlock can be detected directly from the WFS without constructing the TWF graph by simply detecting whether any transaction occurs more than once in the WFS list. This condition is equivalent to having a cycle in the TWF graph. (In the algorithm the phrase **check for deadlock** means the detection of a cycle or cycles in the TWF or in the WFS.)

Each node has a distributed deadlock detector (copy of the same algorithm) that detects deadlocks for transactions or agents in that node. These detectors can work simultaneously. The algorithm uses a staged approach to deadlock detection. This approach relies on the observation, previously noted, that cycles of length 2 occur more frequently than cycles of length 3, and so on.

There are two types of deadlock cycles:

(1)   Those that can be detected using only the information available in one node. This type is divided into two levels of detection activity:

    (a)   Level 1 which checks for possible deadlock cycles every time a remote resource is requested and another transaction is waiting for a resource held by the transaction making the remote resource request. This is fast and inexpensive. This level was designed to detect most cycles of length 2. Some more complex deadlocks can also be detected, but it depends on the deadlock cycle topology. Level 1 can efficiently detect direct global deadlocks of cycle length 2.

    (b)   Level 2 which attempts to detect a deadlock by using the lock tables of all resources in the node. This is more complex and time consuming than level 1 and is run if a requested resource is not available after a defined number of units of time;

(2)   Those that require internode messages to detect. This type forms

    (a)   Level 3 which detects all deadlocks that require internode communication.

Badal's algorithm uses one very important feature (optimization) whereby the WFS is sent to the node to which the awaited transaction has migrated only if the first transaction in WFS has a higher lexical ordering than the transaction that has migrated.

(1)   When a node deadlock detector receives a WFS, the latest lock history is substituted for any transaction for which the detector has a later version.

(2)   Next, the detector constructs a new TWF graph or WFS and checks for cycles. If a cycle is found, it must be resolved. If any transactions are waiting for other transactions that have migrated to other nodes, the current node must repeat the process of constructing and sending TWF's or WFS's to the nodes to which the transactions being waited for have migrated, subject to the constraints of optimization. If these transactions are in this node and active, deadlock detection activity can cease.

(3)   The deadlock detection activity will continue until a deadlock is found or it is discovered that there is no deadlock.

The algorithm
Badal's algorithm uses the following definitions:

IL	intention lock;
$W(x)$	exclusive write lock on resource x;
$R(x)$	shared read lock on resource x;
$IW(x)$	intention lock(write) on resource x;
$IR(x)$	intention lock(read) on resource x;
Sorig(T)	node of origin of transaction T;
LT(R)	lock table for resource R;
LH(T)	lock history for transaction T;
next	field in lock table reflecting the resource a transaction intends to acquire next;
current	field in lock table reflecting the lock currently held by a transaction.

The distributed deadlock detection algorithm is given in Fig. 10.12.

1)   {*This step is executed any time a transaction or agent requests a remote resource, or when it determines that it will require a remote resource. The lock table of the resource that the transaction is currently using is checked to see whether any transactions are waiting for that resource. If so, the lock histories of all transactions requesting and holding the resource are combined into a TWF graph or a WFS and a check for cycles is made. If no cycle is found, T collects the new WFS and causes an agent to be created in the node of the requested resource.*}

Fig. 10.12   Badal's algorithm {adapted from (Badal 1986)}

(a) If a type I remote resource is required, place an appropriate IL entry in the lock table of the current resource (the last resource locked by T, if any) and in LH(T).

(b) {*Start level one detection activity in current node.*}

Construct a TWF graph or WFS from the lock histories of all transactions holding and requesting R, and if a type I remote resource is requested, check for deadlock.

(c) If no deadlock is detected:

(i) Have an agent created in the node of the requested resource and ship the WFS (generated at step 1(b) or step 4(a)) there.

(ii) Stop.

(2) {*This step is executed each time a local resource is requested, either by an agent (transaction) already in that node or by a newly created agent. If the resource is available, appropriate locks are placed and the resource is granted. Otherwise, intention locks are placed in the lock table of the requested resource and in the lock history of the requesting transaction. If the resource is not available after a delay, the probability that there is a deadlock is higher, so the algorithm shifts to another level of detection. It now uses lock histories from each blocked or inactive transaction in the node, as well as from any WFSs from other nodes that have been brought by migrating transactions. If there are no cycles in the new TWF graph or WFS, and the resource is still unavailable after a pre-defined delay, the probability of deadlock is very much higher, but the current node has insufficient information to detect it. The algorithm the progresses to the third level of detection (step 3).*}

(a) If resource R is available: {*lock it*}

(i) Place an appropriate lock in lock table of resource R and in LH(T).

(ii) Stop.

(b) If the resource is not available: {*Start level two detection activity.*}

(i) Place an appropriate IL in the lock table of resource R and in LH(T), and delay for X time units.

(ii) If the resource is now available:

• Remove IL from lock table and LH(T).

• Go to step 2(a).

Fig. 10.12(Cont.)

(iii) If the resource is not available: {*Continue level two activity.*}

- Construct a TWF graph or new WFS using the lock histories of the transactions in the WFSs that have been sent from other nodes, and the lock histories of all blocked or inactive transactions in this node; then check for deadlock.

- If any deadlock is found, resolve the deadlock.

- If no deadlock is found, delay for Y units.

- If the requested resource is now available, go to step 2(a).

- If the transaction being awaited is in this node and active, stop.

- If the resource is still not available, go to step 3 {*Start level 3 detection activity*}.

(3) {*The wait_for message generated by this step consists of a collection of substrings. Each substring is a list of transactions, each waiting for the next transaction in the substring. The substring also lists the resources locked or intention locked by each transaction in the substring. This step includes the optimization presented above.*}

(a) {*Start level 3 detection activity.*} Construct a new WFS either by condensing the latest TWF graph or by combining all WFSs.

(b) Send the WFS to the node to which the transaction being awaited has gone if the awaited transaction in each substring has a smaller identifier than the first transaction in that substring. Then stop.

(4) {*This step is executed only after a wait_for message has been received. The lock histories of the transactions in the WFSs previously received from other nodes, and the lock histories of any blocked or inactive transactions in this node are used to generate a new WFS or TWF graph. If deadlock is detected, it is resolved; otherwise there is still insufficient information to detect a cycle, and another iteration must be performed. The algorithm repeats by transferring control to step 3. If the transaction being waited for is still active, the algorithm stops.*}

If wait_for message received:

(a) {*Start level 3 detection activity.*} Construct a TWF graph or a new WFS from the lock histories of the transactions in the

Fig. 10.12 (Cont.)

WFSs from other nodes and from the lock histories of all blocked or inactive transactions in this node. (Use the latest WFS from each node.) Check for deadlock. If deadlock is found, resolve it.

(b) If an awaited transaction has migrated to another node that is different from the one that sent the WFS message, go to step 3. {*Repeat WFS generation.*}

(c) If the awaited transaction is active, stop.

Fig. 10.12 (Cont.)

Badal's algorithm has the following features:

(1) It is able to detect deadlock with a smaller number of internode messages than other existing algorithms for distributed computer systems. For the scenarios analyzed by Badal, this algorithm requires from 0 to $N - 1$ (where $N = \Sigma_{k-1}^{n} (n - k)$) messages for resources of type I and from 0 to N messages for resources of type II, where n is the number of transactions and nodes involved in the deadlock cycle.

(2) It can detect the most frequent deadlocks with a minimum of internode messages.

(3) This algorithm has a constant overhead due to the amount of information in the lock tables and to the required frequent checking for cycle-length-2 deadlocks.

10.7.4 Mitchell and Merritt's algorithm

Mitchell and Merritt (Mitchell and Merritt 1984) developed an algorithm for deadlock detection in the one-resource model. This algorithm is simple, elegant and easily implemented. It is based on the edge-chasing algorithm, in which each process uses a public and private label to detect deadlock. However, probes are sent upon request and in the opposite direction of the edges in the WFG. Another distinctive feature of this algorithm is that only one process in a cycle will detect deadlock, generally simplifying deadlock resolution. Here, we describe only the first version of Mitchell and Merritt's algorithm. The reader can find the modified algorithm for a system with priorities in Mitchell and Merritt (1984).

The system model

The system is described by the WFG. Since each process waits for one resource at a time, the outdegree of the WFG is one. Each node of the WFG has two labels (local variables). The first is a **private** label. This

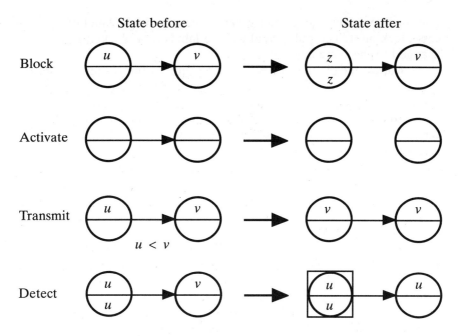

Fig. 10.13 The possible state transitions {adapted from Mitchell and Merrilt (1984)}.

means that it is unique to the node, though not constant. However, it is non-decreasing over time. This can be achieved by keeping the low-order bits of the label constant and unique while increasing the higher-order bits when desired. In Fig. 10.13, the private label is indicated by an index in the lower half of the circle denoting the node. The second label is a **public** one. This label represents a number that can be read by other processes, and the same value can be in several nodes. In Fig. 10.13, it is indicated by an index in the upper half of the circle denoting a node.

Deadlock detection

The state of the system is given by the global WFG. This graph is maintained by four non-deterministic state transitions, which are illustrated in Fig. 10.13. These state transitions define the deadlock detection algorithm. In the figure, $z = inc(u, v)$, where $inc(u, v)$ gives a unique label greater than both u and v, and labels not mentioned explicitly remain unchanged. Initially, private and public labels are the same for each process.

Block creates an edge in the WFG. It occurs when a process begins to wait on some resource held by another process. Two messages are needed: the resource request and a message informing the blocked process of the public label of the process it is waiting for. Both the public and private labels of a blocked process are increased to a value greater than their previous values and greater than the public label of the process blocking it. The public and private labels of a blocked process are changed to the same new value.

Activate means that a process has acquired the resource from the process on which it was blocked, or a process has timed out and ceased waiting, or a process failed. As a result, an edge disappears.

Transmit occurs when the blocked process reads the public label of the process on which it is blocked. This means that the blocking process propagates its public label in the opposite direction of the edges by sending a probe message. If the blocked process receives a probe with a label smaller than its own public label it simply ignores it. Otherwise, the process replaces its label with the one it just received. Thus, the largest label in the wait-for-graph chain migrates in the opposite direction along the edges of the WFG.

Detect occurs when a probe with the public label of the initiating process comes back to the initiating process. This means that this probe made a whole circle, and indicates a deadlock. Thus, a cycle of N processes will be detected after N − 1 **Transmit** operations. Moreover, only one process in a cycle will detect deadlock. In the case of deadlock, a process can simply abort or release its resources to break it, or it can initiate some other deadlock resolution scheme.

Note that this algorithm can detect all existing deadlocks. Moreover it does not detect false deadlocks in the absence of process failures. We do not present a proof of the correctness of the algorithm; one can be found in Mitchell and Merritt (1984) or Knapp (1987).

10.7.5 The CMH algorithm

An algorithm for the OR (communication) model has been proposed by Chandy, Misra and Haas (Chandy *et al.* 1983). It is based on a diffusion computation approach. A blocked process can determine whether it is deadlocked by initiating a diffusion computation. Several processes may initiate diffusion computations at the same time. This algorithm also applies the concept of edge-chasing. Our presentation of the CMH algorithm follows Chandy *et al.* (1983), Adams (1986) and Knapp (1987).

Basic concepts

Before presenting the basic concepts of the CMH algorithm, it is worth recalling a couple of assumptions and basic definitions associated with the communication model.

(1) The communication model does not assume the existence of explicit controllers (or resources). It does require that controllers must be implemented by processes, and that requests for resources, allocation, cancellation and release must be implemented by messages.

(2)   Every idle process is associated with a set of processes called its **dependent set**. An idle process can start executing upon receiving a message from any other process in its dependent set. An idle process can change neither its state nor its dependent set if it has not received a message.

(3)   A process is **terminated** if it is idle and its associated dependent set is empty. The basic CMH algorithm assumes that processes do not terminate, fail, or abort.

On this basis, Chandy, Misra and Haas have given an intuitive definition of a deadlocked set of processes. A non-empty set S of processes is deadlocked if all processes in S are permanently blocked. A process is permanently blocked if it never receives a message from any process in its dependent set.

The problem is that detection of permanent blocking in some situations amounts to solving the halting problem, and hence is undecidable. For this reason, the authors adopted an operational definition of deadlock.

This definition states that a nonempty set S of processes is deadlocked if and only if

(1)   all processes in S are blocked;

(2)   the dependent set of every process in S is a subset of S; and

(3)   there are no messages in transit between processes in S.

A process is deadlocked if it belongs to some deadlocked set.

The goal of the deadlock detection algorithm is to allow a blocked process to determine if it is deadlocked. This determination is performed using a deadlock (diffusing) computation which is initiated by the process when it enters its blocked state. The deadlock computation is distinct from the underlying computation for which deadlock is being detected. This means that processes may exchange messages for the deadlock computation even when they are blocked, because the state is blocked in reference to the underlying computation. The process which initiates a deadlock computation is called an **initiator**.

The example of a system of processes illustrated in Fig. 10.14 as a graph, can be used to identify the basic concepts of deadlock detection using the CMH approach. In this graph, processes are represented by nodes. The executing process is shown as a double circle.

The figure shows that the set of processes $\{B, C, D\}$ is deadlocked. What should be done to detect deadlock? Let us assume that process B, which is blocked for some time while waiting for a resource, begins to suspect that it may be caught in a deadlock circle. It initiates a deadlock computation by sending a query to every process in its dependent set,

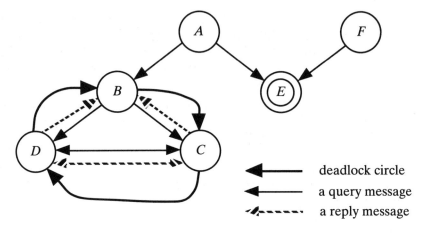

Fig. 10.14 System of processes modelled by a graph.

that is, to processes C and D, and after that it blocks when waiting for the two corresponding replies.

If a process which receives a query is not blocked, it simply ignores the inquiry. If it is blocked, it sends a query to a process with which it is blocked. Thus, in our case, process D, upon receiving the query from B, sends a query to process C. On the other hand, process C, upon receiving the query from process B, sends a query to D. After receiving the query from D, process C sends a reply to process D. Similarly, process D sends a reply to process C, after receiving the query from C. Next, both of them send a reply to process B. Once process B receives these two replies, it declares itself deadlocked.

Let us assume now that process A initiates a deadlock computation. It will not receive a reply matching the query sent to process E. Therefore, process A will not declare itself deadlocked. Suppose that process E later sends a message to process F and then blocks waiting for process C. Process A will then be deadlocked (along with processes B, C, D and E). Unfortunately, process A might never learn it is deadlocked without initiating another deadlock computation. Thus, it may be more efficient to have processes C or D break the deadlock, and for process E to know that it cannot possibly break the deadlock by acting alone.

The example shows clearly that this is edge-chasing, with messages being sent along the edges of an implicit global WFG. If a query returns to the originating process, a deadlock (a cycle) exists. If, after a reasonable time, no query message is received, the originator concludes that there is no deadlock; it continues to wait for the requested resource.

The basics of the algorithm

The example given in Fig. 10.14 shows that a deadlock computation is based on two messages: query and reply. These messages are of the form:

(1)   query(i, m, j, k) – at most one message of this form, and

(2)   reply(i, m, j, k) – at most one reply message of this form to the query message,

where:

> i   is the index of the process which initiated the deadlock computation, P_i,
>
> m is the sequence number (counter) which is incremented by one each time process P_i initiates a new deadlock computation; it is used to ensure old queries do not interfere with any newer ones initiated by the same process,
>
> j   is the index of the process which sends the particular query; thus, P_j is a sender,
>
> k   is the index of the process which will receive the query; thus, P_k is a receiver.

The deadlock computation can be briefly described as follows. An initiating process after sending a query message to all processes in its dependent sets is blocked waiting for replies. All queried processes send queries to each other. Upon receiving expected replies, each queried process in the dependent set sends a reply message to the initiator. An executing process discards any queries received.

The deadlock computation has the following properties.

(1)   If process P_i is deadlocked when it initiates its m-th deadlock computation, then it will receive reply(i, m, j, i) corresponding to every query(i, m, j, i) that is sent.

(2)   If the initiator P_i has received reply(i, m, j, i) corresponding to every query(i, m, j, i) that is sent, then it is deadlocked.

Thus, if the initiator receives one reply for each query sent out, then the initiator is deadlocked. Otherwise, if the initiator has not received all replies within a timeout period T, it assumes that it is not deadlocked. However, this algorithm does not work correctly when conditions such as network failures, a large backlog of messages, or a process being aborted, prevent any reply from being received within the timeout period T.

Each process maintains four arrays of local variables. Each array is one-dimensional of length N, where N is the number of processes in the system. These arrays are as follows:

> latest(i)   The variable latest(i) is the largest sequence number m in any query(i, m, j, k) sent or received by P_k. Initially, latest(i) = 0, for all i.

engager(i)   The variable engager(i), where $i \neq k$, is the identity, say j, of the process which caused latest(i) to be set to its current value m by sending message query(i, m, j, k) to process P_k. The initial value of engager(i) is arbitrary.

num(i)   The variable num(i) is the total number of messages of the form query(i, m, j, k) sent by P_k, minus the total number of messages of the form reply(i, m, j, k) received by P_k, where $m =$ latest(i) and j is arbitrary. Note that num(i) means that P_k has received replies to all queries of the form (i, m, k, r) that P_k sent, where $m =$ latest(i).

wait(i)   The variable wait(i) is true if and only if P_k has been idle continuously since latest(i) was last updated. Initially wait(i) is false, for all i.

The algorithm

The CMH algorithm is presented in Fig. 10.15.

There are some important features of this algorithm.

(1)   If a process is deadlocked when it initiates a query computation, it will eventually declare itself deadlocked. Also, if every process initiates a new query computation whenever it becomes idle (or idle for time T_1), at least one process – the last process in the set to become idle – in every deadlocked set will report 'deadlock'.

(2)   This algorithm does not guarantee that every process in the deadlocked set discovers or is informed that it is deadlocked. Once a process declares itself deadlocked, it only knows that the processes in its dependent set are also deadlocked. The processes in the deadlocked set must be discovered/notified by other means.

(3)   If e is the number of communicating pairs in the system, no more than e queries and replies will be required for a single process to declare itself deadlocked. If N is the number of processes in its dependent set, then $e \leq k*N$. In a system where k is O(N), the CMH algorithm requires O(N^2) queries and replies for each complete query computation.

(4)   This algorithm is easy to implement, since each message (query, reply) is of fixed length and requires few computational steps.

(5)   This algorithm is attractive for reasons of performance as well as correctness, since the overhead for deadlock detection computations and the message traffic associated with deadlock detection is generated primarily when processes are idle.

(6)   The CMH algorithm does not require any particular structure among the processes.

(1)   For an idle process P_i, to initiate a query computation:
{*An idle process initiates a query computation by sending queries to processes in its dependent set. The basic idea is that an idle process on receiving a query should propagate the query to its dependent set if it has not done so already. It counts the number of queries sent out.*}

```
begin
    latest(i) := lastest(i) + 1; wait(i) := true;
    send query(i, latest(i), i, j) to all processes P_j in P_i's dependent set S;
    num(i) := number of elements in S
end
```

(2)   For an executing process P_k: On becoming executing, set wait(i) := false, for all i. An executing process receives a query – An executing process discards all queries received. An executing process receives a reply – An executing process discards all replies received.

(3)   For an idle process P_k, upon receiving query(i, m, j, k):
{*A process P_k receives a query with initiator i, sequence number m, and sender* j. *Local variables* latest(i), engager(i), num(i), *and* wait(i) *refer to the variables of process P_k*}

```
if m > lastest(i)
then    begin
            lastest(i) := m;
            engager(i) := j;
            wait(i) := true;
            for all processes P_r in P_k's dependent set S send query(i, m, k, r);
            num(i) := number of processes in S;
        end
else    if wait(i) and m = latest(i)
        then send reply(i, m, k, j) to P_j
```

(4)   Upon receiving reply(i, m, r, k):

```
if m = latest(i) and wait(i)
then    begin
            num(i) := num(i) − 1;
            if num(i) = 0
            then if i = k
                then declare P_k deadlocked
                else send reply(i, m, k, j) to P_j where j = engager(i)
        end
```

Fig. 10.15 The CMH algorithm {adapted from (Chandy *et al.* 1983)}

Some deficiencies of the CMH algorithm can be addressed. Adams (1986) established the following goals to guide the development of improved variants of the CMH algorithm:

(1)   All true deadlocks should be detected, with no false detections.

(2)   Once a process in a deadlocked set declares itself deadlocked, it should know the identity of the other processes in the deadlocked set.

(3)   A process which has initiated a query should receive some type of response confirming the presence or absence of deadlock.

(4)   The number of queries and replies should be minimized.

(5)   The amount of information passed during query computations should be increased.

(6)   A query computation should identify all minimal deadlocked sets in the reachable set of the initiator. Any process declaring deadlock should also learn if it must take some action to break the deadlock.

(7)   During the course of the query computation, at least one process in each minimal deadlocked set should also learn the identity of all other processes in its minimal deadlocked set, since at least one process from the minimal deadlocked set will be involved in a scheme to break the deadlock. By identifying all processes in a minimal deadlocked set, an optimizing deadlock breaking scheme can be more easily implemented.

Five new algorithms which achieve these goals are presented in Adams (1986).

10.7.6   Natarajan's algorithm

Natarajan proposed (Natarajan 1986) an algorithm for detecting communication deadlocks which, like the CMH algorithm, does not require any particular structure of processes. Natarajan's algorithm is also based on diffusion computations. The major differences between these two algorithms are as follows:

(1)   In the Natarajan algorithm, the additional storage required within each process for deadlock detection is much less than in the CMH algorithm.

(2)   The Natarajan algorithm is based on periodic retransmissions of signals for deadlock detection.

(3)   The Natarajan scheme does not require any storage whose size is a function of the network size.

As a result, the Natarajan algorithm is suitable not only for an environment with statically created processes but also for an environment where processes are created dynamically. Our presentation follows Natarajan (1986).

The basic concepts of the algorithm

Natarajan developed his algorithm using a communication model which is slightly different from that presented earlier. To simplify the study of the algorithm, we present some basic features of the model:

(1)   A distributed program is a network of computing agents (processes in terms of the CMH communication model) which communicate via message passing.

(2)   Associated with each agent is a collection of input ports (to receive messages) and output ports (to send messages).

(3)   An output port of an agent can be connected only to an input port of another agent.

(4)   A communicant of a port P of an agent is another agent that has a port Q connected to P. Q is called the correspondent of P.

(5)   Inter-agent communication is synchronous; that is, an agent can send (receive) a message through an output (input) port P only if the communicant of the port is ready to receive (send) the message through the correspondent of P.

(6)   To communicate with any one of its several communicants, an agent initiates a communication transaction using one or more of its ports, called the candidates of the agent. The communicants of the ports are called the candidate communicants of the agent.

(7)   The transaction completes when the agent synchronizes and communicates with one of the candidate communicants. The transaction fails if the agent and its candidate communicants are members of a group of agents that is communication deadlocked.

Natarajan characterized communication deadlock with the following set of definitions:

(D1)
The communication transactions initiated by two agents **do not match** with each other if no candidate of either agent is the correspondent of a candidate of the other.

(D2)
A group of agents, each of which has initiated a communication transaction, is a **closed group** if

(a) each agent in the group is a candidate communicant of some agent in the group, and

(b) all candidate communicants of an agent are members of the group.

(D3)
A closed group of agents is deadlocked if the transaction initiated by each member agent does not match with those initiated by its candidate communicants.

A graph theoretic interpretation of a communication deadlock is as follows.

(1) A directed graph is used. Each node denotes an agent, and a directed edge is drawn from one node to another if the former is waiting to communicate with the latter.

(2) An agent is communication deadlocked if the corresponding node N in the graph is in a knot; that is, all nodes that are reachable from N can also reach N.

(3) The problem of deadlock detection is thus to detect if an agent is in a knot.

The main assumption in Natarajan's concept is that agents can detect deadlocks during the course of their communication transactions. It is desirable, as in the CMH algorithm, that only one agent among the deadlocked group detects the deadlock, to make deadlock resolution simple.

For the purpose of designing a distributed deadlock detection algorithm, communication deadlock is characterized by states of ports. A port P of an agent can be in one of three (not necessarily exclusive) states. Assuming that C is the communicant of P,

(1) P is Active if C has not initiated a communication transaction, or C has initiated a transaction and is attempting communication with P.

(2) P is Inactive if C has initiated a communication transaction, but is not attempting communication with P.

(3) P is Quiet if C has initiated a communication transaction, but is not attempting communication with P, and further, each candidate of C is in Quiet state.

An agent is involved in a communication deadlock if it observes that each of its candidates is in Quiet state. The informal justification is as follows: an agent can complete its current communication transaction only if at least one of its candidate communicants attempts a matching transaction. Since

(1)   no candidate communicant of the agent is attempting a maching transaction because they are in Quiet state, and

(2)   each candidate communicant is unable to complete its current transaction since all its candidate are in Quiet state,

no communication is possible. This means that a deadlock has occurred.

The state of a candidate port is determined by an agent on the basis of certain **control messages** exchanged with the communicant of the port. (Control messages are distinct from the messages (of **basic communication**) exchanged between agents as part of their computation.)

The agent determines the state of P depending on the response received.

(1)   A port P is Active (Inactive) if the communicant sends a response Active (Inactive), that is, it has (has not) initiated a transaction for which the correspondent of P is a candidate.

(2)   A more elaborate protocol is needed to enable an agent to determine that a port is in a Quiet state, by propagating queries and responses successively through a chain of agents. It is not necessary that every query generated by an agent be propagated as above. Determining which queries to propagate and when to propagate them are the essential aspects of the deadlock detection algorithm.

Phases of the deadlock detection scheme

The deadlock detection scheme developed by Natarajan consists of two (possibly overlapping) phases.

Phase 1   The agents come to agreement on which agent should be the detector. The following technique is used to elect the detector in a distributed manner:

(1)   Each communication transaction is assigned a unique identification, called CommId .

(2)   Every agent that is attempting commuication sends queries periodically to its candidate communicants.

(3)   The response Inactive received from a communicant contains the value of a variable, DeadlockId, of the communicant. Initially, DeadlockId of an agent is set to the CommId of the current transaction of the agent; when a response Inactive(X) is received, DeadlockId is updated to max(DeadlockId, X).

(4)   When a group of agents is deadlocked, they retransmit queries forever, and eventually DeadlockId for each agent converges to the

maximum CommId's. Then, the agent whose transaction has the largest CommId becomes the detector.

Phase 2 The detector initiates a deadlock computation, which is then propagated by other agents, and responses are sent back to the detector. The communication network is assumed to be reliable, and no message sent is lost.

(1) An agent uses two kinds of control messages, called **signals** and **responses** which are port directed.

(2) For every signal sent, an agent receives a response from the communicant of the port. However, there are also responses not prompted by signals.

    (a) An agent can send a signal to a port only if a response has been received for a previous signal sent on the port. However, an agent can send signals on several ports in parallel, and at any time may have responses outstanding on several ports.

    (b) An agent uses the following signals and responses:

        (i)   Query and Detect signals, to determine the states of the candidates.

        (ii) Active, Inactive, and Quiet responses, as replies to Query and Detect signals.

        (iii) Idle response (not prompted), to indicate that a candidate is in the Quiet state.

In addition to these signals, an agent sends many other kinds of signals and responses in order to synchronize with a communicant during a transaction. These control messages will be not considered here.

The algorithm
The deadlock detection algorithm developed by Natarajan is given in Fig. 10.16.

The following comparisons may be made between the Natarajan algorithm and the CMH algorithm.

(1) Both algorithms are based on the same principle:

    (a) An idle process initiates a deadlock computation by sending queries to its dependents, that is, the processes with which it is attempting communication.

    (b) If a process receives a query when it is idle, it propagates the deadlock computation to its dependents.

        If a process receives a query for a computation that it has initiated or propagated, it sends a reply.

    (c)   When a process receives replies from all dependents for a query, it sends a reply to the process that sent the query to it, unless it has initiated the query, in which case it detects a communication deadlock.

There are some major differences.

(1)   In the CMH algorithm:

    (a)   An idle process, if it receives a query, always propagates the query to its dependents without checking if the initiator of the deadlock computation and the process are already waiting for each other (directly or indirectly).

    (b)   This implies that each process has to store information regarding all queries received by it (four arrays are required within each process, and the size of each of them is equal to the total number of processes in the system).

    (c)   A knowledge of the number of processes is required.

    (d)   The CMH algorithm is oriented towards a network of processes that is configured statically.

(2)   In Natarajan's algorithm:

    (a)   There are no such arrays. Their effect is achieved by periodic transmission of Query and Detect signals.

    (b)   At any time, an agent is involved in only one deadlock computation.

    (c)   An agent propagates a Detect signal corresponding to a deadlock computation only if the initiator of the computation and the agent are already waiting for each other.

    (d)   This algorithm is suitable for an environment where agents are created dynamically.

    (e)   In terms of the number of messages exchanged for detecting a communication deadlock, both algorithms are comparable.

10.7.7 Bracha and Toueg's algorithm

Bracha and Toueg developed an algorithm based on the global state detection approach for the $\binom{n}{k}$ model (Bracha and Toueg 1983). The need for a model of this type is seen from the following:

(1)   In operating systems (centralized and distributed), processes can request k special resources (disks, printers, tape drives, etc.) out of a pool of size n. A process can proceed only if it gets k of these resources.

(1)   When an agent initiates a communication transaction, the transaction is assigned a unique identification, CommId, generated using a logical clock (or counter). A unique CommId is generated by incrementing the clock, and obtaining a pair (ClockValue, NodeId), where NodeId is is the unique identification number of a node.

(2)   Each agent uses the following variables:

- CurrentId – identifies the current communication transaction initiated by an agent.

- DeadlockId – identifies the deadlock computation with which the agent is currently involved.

- Detecting – a Boolean variable which, if true, indicates that the agent has either initiated or propagated a deadlock computation.

- Initiator – identifies the port of the communicant which got the agent involved in the current deadlock computation.

Signals and responses sent by an agent include a parameter DRef to indicate to the communicant the value of DeadlockId of an agent.

(3)   When an agent initiates a transaction, it does the following:

- Detecting:= false;
  DeadlockId:= CurrentId ;

- It sends Query(DeadlockId) signals periodically on its candidate port until it synchronizes, or Detecting is true. When Detecting becomes true, the agent sends Query(DRef) signals periodically instead of Query.

(4)   When an agent receives a Query(DRef) signal on a port P, it does the following:

>   **if** not communicating **or** P is a candidate
>   **then** reply Active (undef) {undef is an undefined value}
>   **else** reply Inactive (DeadlockId)

(5)   When an agent receives an Active (undef) or Inactive (DRef) response on a port P for a Query signal (i.e., when Detecting is false), it does the following:

```
if Active received
then Set state of P to Active
else begin
        Set state of P to Inactive;
        DeadlockId:= max(DeadlockId, DRef);
        if all candidates are in Inactive state
            and (CurrentId = DeadlockId)
        then begin {Initiate a deadlock computation}
                Detecting:= true;
                Initiator:= self
            end
    end;
```

Fig. 10.16   Natarajan's algorithm {Natarajan (1986)}

Note that when Detecting is true, the agent sends Detect signals periodically.

(6) When an agent receives a Detect (DRef) signal on a port P, it does the following:

```
if P is a candidate
then reply Active (undef)
else  if not Detecting
      then  begin
                 if all candidates are in Inactive state and (DRef = DeadlockId)
                 then begin {Propagate the deadlock computation}
                          Detecting:= true;
                          Initiator:= the correspondent of P
                      end;
                 reply Inactive (DeadlockId)
            end
      else  if (Dref = DeadlockId) and the correspondent of P is not Initiator
            then {already propagated the computation}
                 reply Quiet (DeadlockId)
            else reply Inactive (DeadlockId);
```

(7) When an agent receives a response on a port P, after it has initiated or propagated a deadlock computation (i.e., when Detecting is true), it acts as follows:

```
if (Quiet or Idle response received) and (DRef = DeadlockId)
then begin
         Set state of P to Quiet;
         if all candidates are in Quiet state
         then if Initiator = self
              then deadlock detected
              else Send Idle (DeadlockId) to Initiator
     end
else if  Active response received
     then begin {Abort the deadlock computation}
              Detecting:= false;
              Reset the state of all candidates to Inactive
              Set state of P to Active
          end
     else {Inactive response}
        if DRef > DeadlockId
        then begin {Abort the deadlock computation}
                 Detecting:= false;
                 DeadlockId:= DRef ;
                 Reset the state of all candidates to Inactive
             end;
```

After an agent aborts its deadlock computation, it sends Query signals periodically instead of Detect signals.

(8) Due to parallel queries, it is possible that an agent may receive Quiet or Idle responses after it has aborted a deadlock computation (i.e., when Detecting is false). The agent discards such responses.

Fig. 10.16 (Cont.)

(2) In distributed databases, to maintain their consistency with replicated files, we showed in Chapter 4 that to read (write) a replicated file, a process must read (write) k_r (k_w) copies out of the n
copies of the file such that $k_r + k_w > n$. Recall that to read or write
a file copy, a process must request and obtain a lock on this copy.
This implies that reading (writing) a file generates k_r-out-of-n (k_w-
out-of-n) locking requests.

(3) In the most general case, a process can make requests described
by the formulae with AND, OR, and k-out-of-n connectives.

Bracha and Toueg give three versions of the algorithm. The first assumes synchronous communication between processes and that the
WFG is static. In the second algorithm, the authors have relaxed the
constraint on synchrony. However, since the state of an edge incident on
a process must still be known to that process in order for the algorithm
to be correct, the second version is also synchronous. The third algorithm is essentially constructed in two parts. The first determines a
global snapshot of the WFG. This operation is performed using Chandy
and Lamport's technique (Chandy and Lamport 1985). The second part
uses the snapshot and one of the first two algorithms to detect deadlock.
Here, we restrict our presentation to the first version of the deadlock
detection algorithm.

Basic concepts

According to the $\binom{n}{k}$ approach, a process can request an arbitrary AND-
OR combination of $\binom{n}{k}$ requests. (Note that both AND and OR requests
are special cases of the k-out-of-n request, $\binom{n}{k}$; an AND request corresponds to $k = n$, an OR request corresponds to $k = 1$.) This allows us to
restrict our consideration to systems where processes issue only a single
k-out-of-n request.

A process can be either active or blocked. An active process,
which requires k resources to proceed, may issue $\binom{n}{k}$ requests by
transmitting n request messages. These messages may be sent to n processes that can act on behalf of the requesting process, or simply to managers of n resources. All these n resources form a dependent set of
resources, denoted **dependent**. Upon issuing these requests, the process
becomes blocked. It waits until it acquires at least k resources from the
dependent set (or until the action requested is carried out by at least k
processes). A blocked process cannot send any further request messages.

It is obvious that only active processes can carry out a requested
action. Thus, if a process from **dependent** is active, it sends a reply
message to the requesting process to notify it that its request is granted.
The requesting process becomes active again after receiving k reply
messages. It then sends **relinquish** messages to the remaining $n - k$ processes to relinquish the requests made to them.

The global state of the system of processes is modeled by a WFG. Thus, the **relinquish** messages are necessary because each process must know both its outgoing edge set and its incoming edge set. Deadlock in the $\binom{n}{k}$ model is defined in terms of the WFG, as was shown in Section 10.4.4.

A process P is deadlocked in a WFG, which is denoted G, if there is no schedule **sched** such that $G \mid -^{\text{sched}} G'$ and P is executing in $'$.

Before presenting the algorithm we present a number of relevant comments.

First of all, this static algorithm consists of two phases:

(1)   a notification phase, in which processes are notified that a deadlock detection algorithm has started, and

(2)   a granting phase, in which active processes simulate granting of requests.

These nodes which are not made active by the second phase are deadlocked nodes.

Second, the first algorithm developed by Bracha and Toueg is a nested invocation of diffusing computations, with a slight twist. This twist is that a process leaving its natural state remembers that it did so. Only the first query it ever receives will be engaging, whereas all subsequent queries are answered immediately with a reply. The latter is performed even if the process has returned to its natural state. This behaviour implies a reduction in the number of messages which are exchanged during an invocation of the algorithm. Another implication, a negative one, is that many of the nice properties of diffusing computations are lost and the proof of correctness becomes messy and almost incomprehensible.

Bracha and Toueg's algorithm has one very distinctive and novel feature in comparison with the other algorithms. In this algorithm a diffusing computation always terminates, and when that happens, every process knows whether or not it is deadlocked.

The algorithm
The deadlock detection algorithm developed by Bracha and Toueg can be described as a nesting of two instances of an algorithm similar to a diffusing computation. This algorithm is called **Closure** by the authors.

The **Closure** algorithm starts when some process, which is called the initiator, suspects that it is deadlocked (this can happen after a long wait for a request to be satisfied). The algorithm consists of two phases, equivalent to performing the following two procedures:

(1)   **Notify** – processes are notified that a deadlock detection algorithm has started; and

(2)   **Grant** – processes simulate the granting of requests. The **Grant** phase is nested within the **Notify** phase.

The algorithm is started when an initiator calls the **Notify** procedure. It terminates when this procedure call terminates. At termination, the initiator test a local variable free$_{\text{initiator}}$ to identify whether it is or not deadlocked. If free$_{\text{initiator}}$ = true then it is not deadlocked in the static WFG. Every process P has its own local variable free$_P$. The value of free is established by simulating the propagation of grant messages through the WFG.

More formally, the algorithms can be described in the following way. Initiator i starts to propagate queries to find the set S of all reachable executing processes; this action is the result of the **Closure** procedure call. All the other processes in S should also call the **Closure** procedure, either spontaneously or following the reception of a **notify** message.

(1)   Each process P from the set S ($P \in S$) simulates granting all the resources it holds that the other processes are waiting for.

(2)   The grants are propagated and the number g of simulated grants received at each reachable process Q is compared with the number r of resources needed by Q to start executing again. If $g < r$, then Q will never get enough grants; this means that it is deadlocked.

Bracha and Toueg proved that the algorithm always terminates and that at termination each process knows whether it is or not deadlocked. However, the proof is based on operational arguments, and no invariants are given.

One feature of Bracha and Toueg's algorithm is that the level of concurrency is very low. Because snapshooting is used, the WFG proceeds off-line, and there is no true concurrency between deadlock detection and the underlying computation. Moreover, the algorithm proceeds in phases. This implies that the deadlock computation is performed sequentially.

The second of Bracha and Toueg's algorithm cannot be correct; this was demonstrated in Knapp (1987). The reader interested in a detailed description of all three algorithms and their correctness proofs should refer to Bracha and Toueg (1983, 1984) and Knapp (1987).

10.7.8   Comparison of deadlock detection algorithms

A deadlock detection algorithm is a vital part of a distributed operating system. This implies that it should be performed on-line. This requirement imposes some restrictions on the message complexity of a distributed deadlock detection algorithm. The best level at which to compare the complexity of the algorithms presented is the request model level.

The algorithms based on the following three request models: one-resource, AND-, and OR- model have worst-case complexity of $O(N^2)$, where N is the number of nodes in the WFG. In the case of the AND-OR algorithm, at most $O(N^3)$ messages are needed. However, such an algorithm is vulnerable to an exponential blowup if $\binom{n}{k}$ requests are cast into AND-OR form. The algorithm for the $\binom{n}{k}$ model itself has a worst-case complexity of $O(N^2)$, as in the case of more basic models. However, this can only be achieved if the deadlock detection is performed off-line from the application computations. One can say that in general the complexity of the presented algorithms is comparable.

10.8 Summary

Deadlock handling is one of the most important and critical parts of resource management in distributed systems. Why is it so important?

In a computer system several processes (transactions) may compete for a finite number of resources. If a requested resource is not available, a process waits for it. However, a situation may arise where waiting processes will wait indefinitely, because requested processes are held by other waiting processes. This situation is called deadlock, and these waiting processes are said to be deadlocked.

There are three methods for handling deadlocks: prevention, avoidance, and detection and resolution. Handling deadlocks in centralized systems is a complex task, but it is even more complicated in distributed systems. This is due mainly to generic features of distributed systems: the lack of up-to-date data on the state of all processes and related resources, and communication delays.

Detection and resolution is the recommended approach to handling deadlock in distributed systems (distributed operating systems and distributed databases). This method requires maintaining information on all processes and the resources that they hold, in the form of a process–resource graph. This information is monitored by a deadlock detection algorithm, which checks for cycles in the graph. Because of distribution, this operation can be expensive.

In distributed systems, since deadlock is the time-dependent state of permanent blocking of a set of processes which compete for resources, or communicate with each other, two kinds of deadlocks can be identified: resource and communication deadlocks. The latter kind of deadlocks has not been studied so extensively as the former one. The third kind of deadlock, migration deadlock, can be seen as a subclass of communication deadlock.

To detect and resolve deadlock efficiently it is not enough to know whether it is resource or communication deadlock. It is necessary to utilize some special features of applications. One of these features is the kind of resource request. Models based on this issue lead to the classification of deadlock detection algorithms. We described the following models: one-resource model, AND model, OR model, AND-OR model, $\binom{n}{k}$ model, and unrestricted model.

Deadlock can be detected and resolved utilizing centralized, distributed, or hierarchical algorithms.

Deadlock detection and resolution algorithms can be developed based on the following concepts: path-pushing, edge-chasing, diffusion computation and global state detection.

A number of algorithms for deadlock detection and resolution have been developed. However, many attempts have not been successful – some of these algorithms do not work correctly, and some do not provide a full solution to the problem, since they do not resolve deadlock after its detection. There is a lack of unified means by which researchers may specify their algorithms. This implies that more research in the area of specification and verification of deadlock detection and resolution algorithms is needed.

Another problem associated with deadlock detection and resolution algorithms is their performance. Almost all algorithms contain a time-critical parameter that affects their overhead and efficiency (for example, in the CMH algorithm, it is the length that a process waits for a resource before it decides to send an inquiry message). Almost no work has been done in the area of evaluating the performance of existing algorithms.

Bibliography

Adams R.A. (1986). Distributed Deadlock Detection for Communicating Processes, *Ph.D. Thesis,* Department of Computer Science, University of Illinois at Urbana-Champaign, Report No. UIUCDCS–R–86–1282

Apt K.R. (1986). Correctness Proofs of Distributed Termination Algorithms. *ACM Transactions on Programming Languages and Systems*, **8**(3), 388–405

Badal D.Z. (1986). The Distributed Deadlock Detection Algorithm. *ACM Transactions on Computer Systems*, **4**(4), 320–37

Bernstein P.A., Hadzilacos V. and Goodman N. (1987). *Concurrency Control and Recovery in Database Systems,* Reading, Mass. Addison-Wesley

Bracha G. and Toueg S. (1983). *A Distributed Algorithm for Generalized Deadlock Detection.* Technical Report TR 83–558, Cornell University, Ithaca, N.Y.

Bracha G. and Toueg S. (1984). A Distributed Algorithm for Generalized Deadlock Detection. In *Proceedings of the Third Annual ACM Symposium on Principles of Distributed Computing,* Vancouver, B.C. 285–301

Bracha G. and Toueg S. (1987). Distributed Deadlock Detection. *Distributed Computing*, **2**, 127–38

Chandy K.M. and Misra J. (1982). A Distributed Algorithm for Detecting Resource Deadlocks in Distributed Systems. In *Proceedings of the ACM Symposium on Principles of Distributed Computing*, Ottawa, 157–64

Chandy K.M., Misra J. and Haas L.M. (1983). Distributed Deadlock Detection. *ACM Transactions on Computer Systems*, **1**(2), 144–56

Chandy K.M. and Misra J. (1986). An Example of Stepwise Refinement of Distributed Programs: Quiescence Detection. *ACM Transactions on Programming Languages and Systems*, **8**(3), 326–43

Chandy K.M. and Lamport L. (1985). Distributed Snapshots: Determining Global States of Distributed Systems. *ACM Transactions on Computer Systems*, **3**(1), 63–75

Chang E.J.H. (1982). Echo Algorithms: Depth Parallel Operations on General Graphs. *IEEE Transactions on Software Engineering*, **SE–8**(4), 391–401

Choudhary A.N., Kohler W.H., Stankovic J.A. and Towsley D. (1989). A Modified Priority Based Probe Algorithm for Distributed Deadlock Detection and Resolution. *IEEE Transactions on Software Engineering*, **SE–15**(1), 10–17

Cidon I., Jaffe J.M. and Sidi M. (1987). Local Distributed Deadlock Detection by Cycle Detection and Clustering. *IEEE Transactions on Software Engineering*, **SE–13**(1), 3–14

Chu W.W. and Ohlmacher G. (1974). Avoiding Deadlock in Distributed Data Bases. In *Proceedings of the ACM National Conference*, 156–60

Dijkstra E.W. and Scholten C.S. (1980). Termination Detection for Diffusing Computations. *Information Processing Letters*, **11**(1), 1–4

Dijkstra E.W., Feijen W., and van Gasteren A.J.M. (1983). Derivation of a Termination Detection Algorithm for Distributed Computations. *Information Processing Letters*, **16**(5), 217–19

Elmagarmid A.K. (1986). A Survey of Distributed Deadlock Detection Algorithms, *ACM SIGMOD*, **15**(3), 37–45

Filali M., Padiou G. and Planque A. (1987). *Safety of Task Migration in a Distributed Operating System Nucleus, Local Communication Systems: LAN and PBX*. Elsevier

Francez N. and Rodeh M. (1982). Achieving Distributed Termination Without Freezing. *IEEE Transactions on Software Engineering*, **SE–8**(3), 287–92

Gligor V.D. and Shattuck S.H. (1980). On Deadlock Detection in Distributed Systems. *IEEE Transactions on Software Engineering*, **SE–6**(5), 435–40

Gray J.N. (1978). *Notes on Data Base Operating Systems, Operating Systems: An Advanced Course*, Springer-Verlag

Gray J.N., Homan P., Korth H.F. and Obermarck R.L. (1981). *A Straw Man Analysis of the Probability of Waiting and Deadlock in Database Systems*. Technical Report RJ 3066, San Jose, California, IBM Research Laboratory

Hac A., Jin X. and Soo J.H. (1989). A Performance Study of Deadlock Prevention Algorithms in a Distributed File System. *Software—Practice and Experience*, **19**(5), 461–89

Helary J., Jard C., Plouzeau N. and Raynal M. (1987). Detection of Stable Properties in Distributed Applications. In *Proceedings of the ACM Symposium on Principles of Distributed Computing*, Vancouver, 125–36

Hermann T. and Chandy K.M. (1983). *A Distributed Procedure to Detect AND/ OR Deadlock*. Technical Report TR LCS–8301, Department of Computer Science, University of Texas, Austin

Ho G.S. and Ramamoorthy C.V. (1982). Protocols for Deadlock Detection in Distributed Database Systems. *IEEE Transactions on Software Engineering*, **SE–8**(6), 554–7

Huang, S.T. (1988). A Fully Distributed Termination Detection Scheme. *Information Processing Letters*, **29**, 13–8

Jagannathan J.R. and Vasudevan R. (1982). A Distributed Deadlock Detection and Resolution Scheme; Performance Study. In *Proceedings of the Third International Conference on Distributed Computing Systems*, Miami, Florida, 496–501

Knapp E. (1987). Deadlock Detection in Distributed Databases. *ACM Computing Surveys*. **19**(4), 303–28

Menasce D.A. and Muntz R.R. (1979). Locking and Deadlock Detection in Distributed Data Bases. *IEEE Transactions on Software Engineering*, **SE–5**(3), 195–202

Misra J. and Chandy K.M. (1982). Termination Detection of Diffusing Computations in Communicating Sequential Processes. *ACM Transactions on Programming Languages and Systems*, **4**(1), 37–43

Misra J. and Chandy K.M. (1982). A Distributed Graph Algorithm: Knot Detection. *ACM Transactions on Programming Languages and Systems*, **4**(4), 678–86

Mitchell D.P. and Merritt M.J. (1984). A Distributed Algorithm for Deadlock Detection and Resolution. In *Proceedings of the Third Annual ACM Symposium on Principles of Distributed Computing*, Vancouver, 282–4

Natarajan N. (1986). A Distributed Scheme for Detecting Communication Deadlocks. *IEEE Transactions on Software Engineering*, **SE–12**(4), 531–7

Obermarck R. (1982). Distributed Deadlock Detection Algorithm. *ACM Transactions on Database Systems*, **7**, 187–208

Peacock J.K. (1989). Deadlock Avoidance in Loosely-Coupled Multiprocessors with Finite Buffer Pools. *Operating Systems Review*, **23**(2), 20–4

Roesler M. and Burkhard W.A. (1989). Resolution of Deadlocks in Object-Oriented Distributed Systems. *IEEE Transactions on Computers*, **38**(8), 1212–24

Sinha M.K. and Natarajan N. (1985). A Priority Based Distributed Deadlock Detection Algorithm. *IEEE Transactions on Software Engineering*, **SE–11**(1), 67–80

11 Resource protection

			Security	
User names	File service			
	Collaboration of file servers Transaction service Directory service Flat file service Disk service	Access control	C o m m u n i c a t i o n	s e c u r i t y
Name distri-bution	Resource allocation	Deadlock detection	R e s o u r c e	p r o t e c t i o n
Name resolu-tion	Algorithms for load sharing and load balancing	Process synchro-nization		
		Capa-bilities	& Authen-tication	
System names	Process management Operations on processes: local, remote Process migration	Access lists	Key manage-ment	
Ports	Interprocess communication (and memory management) Interprocess communication primitives: Message Passing or Remote Procedure Call, or Transactions; Links or Ports	Info flow control	Data encryp-tion	
Address-es		Security kernel		
Routes	Transport protocols supporting interprocess communication primitives		Encryp-tion protocols	

D istributed operating systems allow users to achieve their computing goals efficiently, largely through the sharing of resources. Not all users have rights to access all resources, however. Moreover, there could be users who want to read data in transfer or alter data to disrupt the cooperation of other users. There could also be users who would like to masquerade as other users, and exchange messages with eligible users.

This implies the need for protecting resources, securing communication and authenticating users. These three issues together are seen as the third important aspect of resource management in distributing operating systems. In the following sections, when considering broadly this aspect of resource management, we will use the term security. We will specify its component issues when dealing with specific aspects of security.

Distributed system security is a broad and complex topic which involves not only such advanced aspects as access control, communication security and authentication measures, but also more conventional measures: physical, electromagnetic emanation, procedural and personal security. The importance of security in distributed systems grows as more sensitive information is stored and processed by computer systems, and transferred over networks. As one can expect, because of sensitivity of information, security entails moral issues imposed on society, and legal issues, where control is legislated. However, in this chapter we do not consider any moral or legal issues associated with information security; rather we deal only with technical issues.

A computer system must not only be secure, but this feature must be demonstrable to users who will rely on it. Implementing data security measures in a centralized computer system is a complex task. Developing a convincing user demonstration is also difficult. In distributed systems these two tasks are complicated still further, as extra security problems are created. For example other processes can influence a user's process when they run remotely, and the physical distribution of data opens up the possibility of **passive** and **active** line tapping on the communication medium. Fig. 11.1 shows a processor reading signals coming on the line and, from them, constructing new signals which go onwards to the destination.

There are three major aspects to security in distributed systems:

(1) **resource protection** – protecting objects in the distributed system from unauthorized access;

(2) **communication security** – safeguarding information transmitted between computers connected by communication media; and

(3) **user authentication** – assuring the receiver that the message came from the reputed source and that it has travelled to him without being modified.

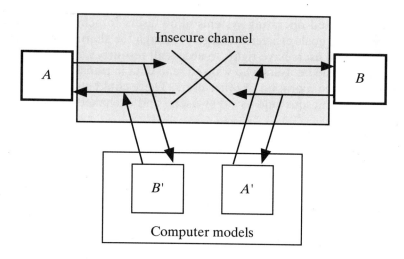

Fig. 11.1 Active line tapping.

This chapter introduces general issues of security, and then focuses on mechanisms that prevent unauthorized access to computer and communication resources. These mechanisms are referred to as protection mechanisms. To improve readability we decided to move other security issues, that is, security aspects in communication system and authentication, to the next chapter.

Section 11.1 characterizes the goals of security and the types of violations that must be guarded against, and presents three taxonomies of security. Section 11.2 introduces four access control approaches: the access matrix model, lattice model, information flow models and a security kernel. Their basic concepts, advantages and drawbacks are discussed in detail in Sections 11.3 to 11.5. This discussion is followed by presentation and discussion of implementation aspects of these four approaches. Sections 11.6 to 11.10 discuss the implementation of the access matrix model using access control lists and capabilities; passing and revoking access rights are considered in detail. Section 11.11 presents a simple method for implementing information flow control, using a 'clearance capability'. Finally, an implementation of a distributed security kernel is described in Section 11.12.

11.1 Basic aspects of security and common violations

In this section we examine places of common violations in distributed systems, and taxonomies of security.

11.1.1 Issues of security

Security in computer systems deals with five main goals:

(1) **Secrecy** – to ensure that information is only disclosed to authorized users. Each user of a computer system must be able to keep data secret. Mechanisms should be provided so that no other user is able to access it.

(2) **Privacy** – to ensure that information is used according to its original goals. Users must be guaranteed that if they give information to somebody else, it is used for the purpose for which it was given.

(3) **Authenticity** – to prove the identity of the entity; data provided to users must be authentic. This means that if data appears to come from a given source S, the user must be able to verify that S was indeed the sender of that data.

(4) **Integrity** – to ensure that information is not changed. Neither the system, which stores and transmits data, nor unauthorized users should be able to corrupt that data.

(5) **Availability** – to ensure that authorized users can make effective use of a computer system.

However, some users (unauthorized and even authorized) try to obtain access to system objects (processes, resources, data). Fig. 11.2 shows common places of attack in distributed systems. This figure shows that access to data must be controlled in the case where processes run locally as well as when they run remotely. For example, process P1 is not allowed to access Data2, but has rights to access Data1. Process P3 may remotely access Data1 located on Computer2 (as well as local Data1) but is not allowed to access remote data, Data2 stored on Computer2. Moreover, data must be securely transmitted through communication lines. As we can see in Fig. 11.2, an intruder may attack this part of a distributed system passively or actively. Finally, access to the computer facility must be controlled, since there are persons who do not have rights to use it.

Intruders can use the following methods to obtain unauthorized access to data:

(1) **Leaking** – An intruder has an accomplice (a legitimate user) who leaks information to him/her. The prevention of leaking is very difficult. The problem of making sure that information cannot be leaked to the outside world is called the **confinement problem** (see Section 11.3.5).

(2) **Browsing** – An intruder attempts to read all information stored in a system, passively attacking communication media to read all the packets in transfer. This intruder does not modify data.

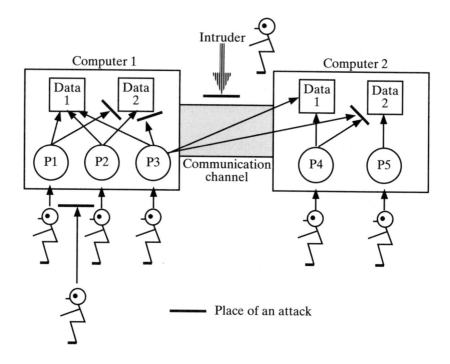

Fig. 11.2 Places of common violations in a distributed system.

(3) **Inferencing** – An intruder tries to steal information by reading stored data, listening to data in transfer, and getting protected information from a legitimate user, that is, the above two methods are used together. For example, the intruder attempts to read encrypted information by applying a derived encryption key.

(4) **Masquerading** – An intruder or a program may masquerade as an authorized user or program in order to gain access to system objects (data, resource). A masquerading program is called a Trojan Horse (see Section 11.3.5).

11.1.2 Taxonomies of security

Both applications and users of computer systems need to characterize the level of security which is offered by that system. There are three basic taxonomies of security which can be used for this purpose.

The first taxonomy we describe here was introduced by the Department of Defence U.S. (DoD 1983). It provides a yardstick that can be used to distinguish computer systems that are 'more secure' from those that are 'less secure'. The Trusted Computer Evaluation Criteria (the so called Orange Book) introduced the Trusted Computing Base

(TCB) which is the totality of protection mechanisms in a computer system responsible for enforcing security policy. It includes software, firmware and hardware, and nothing outside the TCB should be able to cause security violation.

The main goal of the Orange Book was to encourage manufacturers to provide more trustworthy operating systems. It classifies secure systems into four divisions labelled A (most secure) to D (insecure).

(1) **Division D: Insecure** – This division groups products that have not been evaluated. The systems provide only minimal protection. Some systems would not even achieve this category because they do not try to implement a security policy (for example, DOS).

(2) **Division C: Discretionary Protection** – Systems of this category provide for discretionary (need-to-know) protection. There are two subcategories:

    (a) **Class C1: Discretionary security protection** – This provides for separation of users and data, with mechanisms to protect one user's files from unauthorized accesses by other users.

    (b) **Class C2: Controlled access protection** – At this level login is required, as is auditing of security events, and isolation of the security mechanisms.

(3) **Division B: Mandatory (Nondiscretionary) Protection** – In this division security is enforced by the TCB. It must check all access to all objects and enforce security policy. The reference monitor concept (see Section 11.5.1) must also be implemented. There are three subcategories:

    (a) **Class B1: Labelled security protection** – Classification labels must be attached to all objects, and the system must enforce the security policy by allowing access by subjects to only those objects less classified than the clearance level of the user.

    (b) **Class B2: Structured protection** – These systems must be written from scratch with a formal security policy model. This model must be documented. Each communication channel used by communicating processes and which may be exploited in a manner that violates the system's security policy and its bandwidth must be identified. At this level security gets serious.

    (c) **Class B3: Security domains** – The TCB must satisfy the reference monitor requirements. Security domains are introduced. A security domain is (i) a list of users or groups with access privileges to an object, and (ii) a list of users and groups for which no access should be granted.

(4) **Division A: Verified Protection** – This requires complete formal design of the system. It is oriented toward classified information.

    (a) **Class A1: Verified design** – This does not provide any extra features over B3. However, the complete formal design method it requires provides a very high level of assurance that the system is completely secure.

The second taxonomy we consider here was introduced by Voydock and Kent (1983). They classified security violations into three classes:

(1) **Unauthorized release** (called also **disclosure**) of information – intruders may derive the meaning of data;

(2) **Unauthorized modification** of information – intruders alter data. Note that it is not necessary to read data to alter it. It is very difficult to protect against modification; only detection is possible;

(3) **Denial** of resource usage – where users cannot access a requested resource even though they are eligible to do so. For example, an intruder floods the network with packets, resulting in denial of network bandwidth to legitimate users.

The third taxonomy we consider here was introduced in Wulf *et al.* (1981). They considered the security of the Hydra operating system in terms of:

(1) **Mutual suspicion** – which addresses selective access to objects. A programmer needs some guarantee that, except through execution of his/her program, other users cannnot access his information stored in a system;

(2) **Modification** – which addresses the problem of reconciling reliability with privilege. A system must be constructed in such a way that users trust that its subsystem fulfils its specifications, just as they trust that the subsystem maintainers do not distribute amplification templets indiscriminately;

(3) **Conservation** – which addresses the problem of limiting the propagation of capabilities;

(4) **Confinement** – which addresses the problem of limiting the propagation of information;

(5) **Initialization** – which combines aspects of all the previous problems.

Note that the first classification and partly the third one are oriented towards resource protection mechanisms. We do not use them directly when discussing these aspects. Such terms are introduced to allow the reader to see the applicability of the Orange Book taxonomy in distributed operating systems. Our discussion on communication security and authentication carried out in Chapter 12 is based on the classification put forth by Voydock and Kent.

11.2 Access control approaches

Protection within a computer system is required if the system resources are to be shared by a number of mutually supicious users. Such sharing may involve arbitrarily long timescales. This is because protection is required for both users of the system, and information stored by users in the system.

Protection, which is one of the major problems of resource management, can be described as follows. Protection is the control of access to the resources, that is, controlling **who** can perform **which operations** and on **what objects**.

A computer system may be viewed as a collection of processes and resources. In this context, the role of protection in the computer system is to provide a mechanism for the enforcement of the policies governing resource use; those policies can be: fixed in the design of the system, formulated by the management of the system, or defined by the individual users. If we have a good protection model and methods of implementing it for a single, physically isolated system, we would like to apply this to a distributed system by setting up distributed access control mechanisms. However, the desire to provide flexible and controlled sharing of resources in a distributed system implies the need for additional access models and techniques.

There are a number of approaches for controlling access to resources, based on different access control models (also called schemes). A distributed system must be not only secure, but must be also demonstrably secure. Formal models are needed by researchers and designers as a tool to convince others of the security of their systems. Access control approaches for computer protection are based on abstractions of operating systems structures, or on military security concepts. The access matrix model, which is well known to readers familiar with operating systems for stand alone computers, is representative of the former approach.

Access control models can be implemented as:

(1) **Discretionary access control systems** – In systems which belong to this class, access to an object (resource) can be granted or denied to any user at the discretion of the 'owner' of the object. Thus, a discretionary policy contains security rules that can be specified at the option of each user.

(2) **Nondiscretionary access control systems** – In systems which belong to this class, access to an object (resource) can be granted or denied based on the classification of information and the clearance of a user. Thus, a nondiscretionary policy contains mandatory security rules that are imposed on all users.

The approaches we will describe treat the protection problem from different perspectives, and provide different levels of detail in their specifications. Before presenting them, we discuss some basic concepts and trends. This discussion follows Denning and Denning (1979), Kent (1981), Landwehr (1981), Rushby and Randell (1983) and Maekawa *et al.* (1987).

The access matrix model

The access matrix model was proposed by Lampson (Lampson 1971) as a generalized description of operating system protection mechanisms. It provides a general representation of access control policies in which the access rights of each user to each object (resource) are defined as entries in a matrix. In a distributed system, the objects could be physical objects such as computers, hosts, terminals, and printers to which access is controlled, as well as logical objects within computers and hosts to which access is traditionally controlled in centralized systems, for example, files, and processes. The latter can be included in the matrix as a service to hosts. The access matrix model can be implemented as a discretionary access control system.

The most important features of the access matrix approach are that access is controlled through classification of users and information, and that users' access to information is controlled without regard to the semantics of the information in question. Only the rights of users to access objects are checked. The basic disadvantage of the access control approach in computer systems is its vulnerability to attack by Trojan Horse programs.

In many real systems (military, banking, medical, trading), classified information is involved. This implies that the semantics of the information must be considered. Therefore, the access matrix approach is not adequate. It must be extended or new models must be developed.

The lattice security model

The lattice security model is an extension to the access matrix model to include classifications, clearances and rules concerning the classifications. In this security model, objects are assigned classifications and subjects are assigned clearance. This model was derived from the military classification system, which reflects the structure of military security levels. However, the lattice model can be used in commercial systems. The lattice model can be implemented as a nondiscretionary access control system.

A lattice is a finite set, together with a partial ordering on its elements such that for every pair of elements there is a least upper bound and a greatest lower bound (Birkhoff and Bartee [1970] and Landwehr [1981]). In the context of security, there is a set of partially ordered access classes from which user clearance and object classifications are selected.

A good example of a lattice model is the Bell and LaPadula (Bell and LaPadula 1973) model which has been summarized in two axioms:

(1) No user may read information classified above his clearance level ('No read up');

(2) No user may lower the classification of information ('No write down').

A problem of the Bell and LaPadula model is lack of elegance.

Information flow model

The information flow model, introduced by Denning in 1976 (Denning 1976), is also based on the lattice security concept. However, instead of requiring a list of axioms governing users' accesses, this model requires that all information transfer is subject to the flow relation among the security classes. Thus, the focus is on flow of information from one object to another rather than on individual accesses to objects.

The advantages of this approach are added flexibility in analysing flow over storage channels and the ability to analyze flow at a fine-grained level. The information flow model has an elegance lacking in the Bell and LaPadula model.

A security kernel mechanism

Schell (Landwehr 1981) proposed an approach to computer security based on defining a small subset of a system that would be responsible for its security. It is assumed that:

(1) this subset would monitor all accesses,

(2) it would be correct, and

(3) it would be isolated, so that its behavior could not be tampered with.

This approach is called a security kernel mechanism. Note that Bell and LaPadula's model grew out of work on the security kernel mechanism.

The general concept of this approach fits well with notions of operating system kernels and layered abstract machines. Thus, the security kernel would be the innermost layer of the system responsible for all the security-oriented operations. If such a security kernel is small (as it should be) it is possible to examine it for flaws and demonstrate its correctness. However, in real general-purpose operating systems, it is difficult to identify and isolate all of the security-oriented functions without creating a fairly large and slow 'kernel'.

Kernel-based secure systems have been studied intensively in the context of distributed systems by Rushby and Randell (Rushby and Randell 1983). They propose that secure systems be conceived as distributed systems in which security is achieved:

(1) partly through the physical **separation** of its individual components, and

(2) partly through the **mediation** of trusted functions performed within some of these components.

11.3 Access matrix model

The access matrix model, which provides a basic framework for protection based on abstraction of operating system structures, was developed by Lampson (Lampson 1971), and improved by Graham and Denning (Graham and Denning 1972), and Harrison, Ruzzo and Ullman (Harrison *et al.* 1976). The presentation here follows Graham and Denning (1972).

The access matrix model is simple and general, and it allows a variety of implementation techniques. It is widely used in centralized computer systems, and continues to be a subject of further research. The take-grant models of Bishop and Snyder (1979) and Bishop (1981) and the model of data security used in Popek and Farber (1978) are access matrix models. It has been extended for use in distributed systems.

11.3.1 Basic concepts of the access matrix model

A protection system controls access to resources, based on the identity of the accessing entities. More specifically, the access matrix model is concerned with three basic components:

(1) A set of passive **objects** – the resources to be protected. Associated with each object is a **type** (for example, process, file, line printer, a host, terminal on a network) which determines the set of **operations** that may be performed on it (for example, start, kill, read, delete, print).

(2) A set of active **subjects** – the individuals wishing to access and perform operations on objects. Depending on the system, subjects may be users, processes or procedures. Normally we are interested in subjects that are **processes**. Subjects are also objects since

they too must be protected. A subject can be defined as a pair (process, domain) where a domain is the protection environment in which a process is executing. Of course, a process can change domains when executing.

(3)   The set of access rules governing the manipulation of objects by subjects – these can be regarded as relations between subjects and objects. Thus, associated with each (subject, object) pair is an **access right** which defines the set of operations that this particular subject may perform on this particular object. A **domain** can be seen in this context as the set of objects that a process can access at any given time.

The system maintains, in a **protection state**, all information that specifies the rights, that is, types of access, that subjects have to objects. To describe a particular system, the following must be defined:

(1)   the representation of the domain of a process in the protection system, and the actual enforcement of the protection rules; and

(2)   the circumstances under which a process can move from one domain to another and the ways in which such moves can occur, that is, can it gain and lose access rights as a result of executing certain types of operation?

The simplest and most natural representation of protection can be in the form of of an **access matrix**, denoted AM, that holds the rights for each (subject, object) pair. Such a matrix is usually sparse. In an access matrix

(1)   the rows represent domains,

(2)   the columns represent objects,

(3)   each entry in the matrix consists of a set of access rights, and

(4)   the entry **access**(i, j) defines the set of operations that a process, executing in domain D_i, can invoke on object O_j.

Thus, the access matrix can be seen as recording the protection state of the system. An example of an access matrix is illustrated in Fig. 11.3.

The entry **access**(i, j) can define a form of access such as the right to kill a process, to read data, to write data, to obey programs, to load a queue, to append data to a file, to send data out on a particular communication line, and other access forms.

Each type of object has associated with it an object monitor. Based on the access matrix, each access to an object is validated in the following way:

(1)   A subject S wants to perform an operation Op on object O.

Subjects	Objects			
	S_1	S_2	O_3	O_4
S_1	terminate	wait, signal, send	read	
S_2	wait, signal, terminate			read, execute write
S_3		wait, signal, receive		
S_4	control		execute	write

Fig. 11.3   Access matrix.

(2)   The triple (S, Op, O) is formed by the system and passed to the object monitor of O.

(3)   The object monitor looks for the attributed Op in AM$[S, O]$. If present, access is permitted and the operation Op is allowed to proceed; otherwise, a protection violation occurs.

The correctness of the object monitors is crucial because they determine the correctness of the system, assuming that the identification of a subject is unforgeable.

The access matrix is not particularly useful for the systems, because of the way in which the protection facility is used. As we said above, it is very sparse. Many objects are accessible only to their owners, so many columns of the table contain only one entry. A real system must devise ways of storing the information contained in the access matrix more compactly, and in such a way that it can be retrieved easily when needed.

There are four important issues associated with the access matrix model: dynamic protection structures, levels of sharing, the trust issue and the confinement problem. All of them are briefly considered below. Dynamic protection structures are discussed in more detail because they are closely related to **revocation**, which is a very important matter in distributed systems.

11.3.2   Dynamic protection structures

The association between a subject and a domain may be **static**, if the set of resources available to the subject is fixed throughout its lifetime, or **dynamic**. Static protection structures are a simpler problem to solve.

If the association between a subject and a domain is dynamic:

(1)   a mechanism must be available to allow a subject to switch from one domain to another,

(2)   the content of a domain can be changed.

If the second case is impossible, we can create a new domain and use the first.

Domain switching can be controlled by including domains among the objects of the access matrix. This means that the access matrix is itself a protected object controlled by a distinguished monitor called the **access matrix monitor**. When changing the content of the access matrix, an operation on an object, that is, the access matrix, is performed. The access matrix monitor may transfer, grant, read, or delete access rights upon authorized requests from subjects. Since each entry in the access matrix may be individually modified, we must consider each entry in the access matrix as an object to be protected.

Consider the operations that are possible on the new objects (domains and the access matrix) and how we want processes to be able to execute these operations:

(1)   Processes should be able to switch from one domain to another.

(2)   Domain switching from D_i to D_j is allowed, if and only if the access right

switch $\in$ **access**(i, j).

Allowing controlled change to the content of the access matrix entries requires three additional operations: **copy, owner, control**.

(1)   The ability to copy an access right from one domain (row) to another is denoted by appending an asterisk (*) to the access right. The **copy** right only allows the copying of the access right within the column, that is, for the object for which the right is defined. There are two variants of this scheme:

    (a)   When a right is copied from **access**(i, j) to **access**(k, j), it is removed from **access**(i, j). This is the transfer of a right rather than a copy;

    (b)   Propagation of a **copy** right may be limited. This means that when the right $R*$ is copied from **access**(i, j) to **access**(k, j), only the right R (not $R*$) is created. For example, this implies that a process executing in domain D_k cannot further copy the right R.

The system may select only one of these **copy** rights, or may provide all three by identifying them as separate rights: **copy, transfer,** and **limited-copy.**

(2) The **owner** right controls adding new rights and removing some rights.

If **access**(i, j) includes the **owner** right, then a process executing in domain D_i can add and remove any right in any entry in column j.

(3) A mechanism is needed to change entries in a row – the **control** right is only applicable to domain objects.

If **access**(i, j) includes the **control** right, a process executing in domain D_i can remove any access right from row j.

Changes to the protection state are modeled by a set of commands. These commands specify by a sequence of actions that change the access matrix. Graham and Denning (1972) proposed the commands which are given in List 11.1.

---

transfer
a subject that has Op* access to an object may transfer a copy of the attribute to another subject.

grant
allows the owner of an object to grant any attributes (with exception of the owner attribute) to another object.

delete
allows subject S_0 to delete access attributes to object O by another subject S provided that either subject S is under control of S_0 or object O is owned by S_0.

read
allows a subject to read a cell of the access matrix.

create object
allows any subject to create a nonsubject object.

delete object
allows the deletion of an object by its owner.

create subject
allows any subject to create a subordinate subject. The creating subject becomes the owner (by virtue of create object) and the new subject is in control of itself.

delete subject
allows the deletion of a subject by its owner.

List 11.1 Commands for specifying sequence of actions that change the access matrix.

We can define a protection system as a system which consists of the following two parts:

(1)   an access matrix which for a given sets of subjects and objects defines a finite state of generic rights R, and

(2)   a finite set of commands.

A protection system is said to be safe if access to objects (for example, files) is impossible without the concurrence of the owner. However, the owner can give away certain rights to his/her objects; a protection system allowing this is not strictly safe. Thus, weaker conditions must be considered. This leads to systems which enable users to keep their own objects 'under control'.

Moreover, the user should be able to determine whether a user action, such as, giving away a right, can lead to the further leakage of that right to truly unauthorized subjects. Unfortunately, for a given fully general access matrix this protection problem, known as the confinement problem, is undecidable. Before we discuss the confinement problem, we consider levels of sharing and the trust problem.

11.3.3   Levels of sharing

The following levels of sharing are permitted by the access matrix model defined in this section:

(1)   No sharing at all (complete isolation) – it is easily seen that this can be provided by the access matrix model.

(2)   Sharing copies of data objects – this level of sharing can be accomodated in the access matrix model because different subjects can be permitted to access different copies of the same object.

(3)   Sharing originals of data objects – to show this possibility, let us assume that subject S_1 agrees to share an object O_S with subject S_2. This can be carried out in the following way. Subject S_1 executes the command **transfer** right R *to* S_2, or **grant** R *to* S_2. It is obvious that S_2 cannot obtain access rights to any other subject accessible by S_1.

(4)   Sharing untrusted programs among trustworthy subjects – let us assume now that subjects S_1 and S_2 are trustworthy. S_1 decides to share a program O_S with subject S_2, but wants to be able to revoke S_2's privilege to share O_S. The O_S program can access an object X, and S_2 requires the same access to X. However, S_2 does not trust O_S and therefore needs to guarantee that O_S will not access any of S_2's objects.

Graham and Denning proposed a solution to this problem based on the concept of an indirect access attribute.

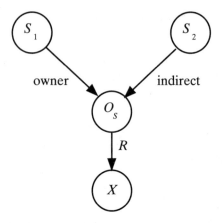

Fig. 11.4   Use of indirect attributes {adapted from Graham and Denning (1972)}.

Indirect access as illustrated in Fig. 11.4 has the following characteristics:

(a)   An indirect attribute applies only to subjects. It may be granted by the owner of a subject.

(b)   If S_2 has indirect access to O_S, then it is able to access objects accessible to O_S in the same way as they would be accessed by O_S. However, S_2 may not acquire for itself direct access to the objects, but may read (not acquire) access attributes possessed by O_S.

(c)   The owner of O_S, that is, S_1 may revoke S_2's indirect access to O_S at any time.

Another solution to this problem is based on switching (Maekawa *et al.* 1987).

(5)   Sharing among untrustworthy subsystems – this problem can be solved using the same approach used to share untrusted objects among trustworthy subjects. This is illustrated in Fig. 11.5.

11.3.4   The trust problem

It is clear from Section 11.3.3 that the access control system is correct if trustworthy subjects are involved, or some control can be placed on trustworthy subjects (programs). However, the presence of untrustworthy subjects generates some problems that cannot be solved by the access matrix model. The problems are:

(1)   An attribute passed from one subject to another can be further passed. Can the second subject be trusted?

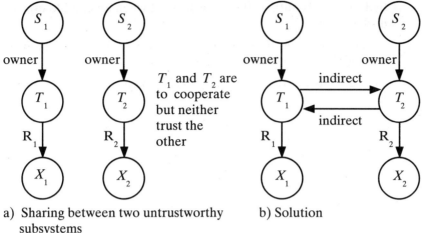

a) Sharing between two untrustworthy subsystems b) Solution

Fig. 11.5 Sharing between untrustworthy subsystems {adapted from Graham and Denning (1972)}.

(2)   The **read** attribute is all-powerful in the sense that it does not prevent a reader from making a copy of the resource and granting others **read** access to this private copy.

(3)   If two untrustworthy subjects conspire, the first may execute its rights on behalf of the second.

(4)   If subjects are shared, the owner of a subject can gain illegal access to the subject's indirect attributes, which may have been granted by yet a third subject.

These problems show that the element of trust is necessary in the access matrix model.

11.3.5   The confinement problem

In the previous sections we demonstrated that protection problems are considerably more complex in the case when programs are shared than in the case of sharing data objects. The problem and difficulty can be exemplified by the possible presence of a **Trojan Horse**.

The Trojan Horse

A Trojan Horse is a piece of code that is intentionally placed in a program to perform extra functions in addition to the normal goals of this program. The extra function might be to copy confidential information.

A Trojan Horse program can be either:

(1)   a secrecy threat if, for example, it invisibly sends copies of classi-

fied files to its author; this is performed when an eligible user see his/her files;

(2)   an integrity threat if, for example, it alters or destroys data when an eligible user accesses it; and/or

(3)   an availability threat if, for example, it makes some part of a system inaccessible.

More precisely, Trojan Horse programs contain two parts:

(1)   instructions which are the attacker's aim, and

(2)   instructions which cause the Trojan Horse programs to spread around a distributed system, and attack either previously unaffected computers, or previously innocuous programs.

These spreading attacks are called 'worms' and 'computer viruses'. The mechanism of a worm was discussed in Chapter 9. A worm program can damage a distributed system by sending multiple copies of itself over all communication links, overloading the system and degrading performance, or by undertaking more sophisticated attacks after arrival at a network node.

A computer virus is a type of integrity threat. A program infected by a virus contains Trojan Horse instructions. When an infected program is executed, the Tojan Horse locates one or more uninfected programs, and inserts inself into those programs so that they are now infected. The virus spreads further when these newly infected programs are executed.

In summary, many systems have mechanisms allowing programs written by some users to be used by other users. If these programs are executed in a domain which provides the access rights of the executing user, they may misuse these rights by running a Trojan Horse. There is a leak of information which should be prevented.

We do not discuss worms and computer viruses in detail here. The reader can refer to Cohen (1987) and Chess (1989).

The confinement problem

Confinement is defined as allowing a borrowed program to have access to data, while ensuring that the program cannot release information.

A program that cannot retain or leak information is said to be memoryless or confined. The prevention of information leakage is called the **confinement problem**. In other words, the problem is to eliminate every means by which an authorized subject can release any information contained in the object it has an access to, to some subjects which are not authorized to access that information. If, for a given protection system, it can be demonstrated that no such mechanism exists, that system is not susceptible to Trojan Horse attacks.

The confinement problem was studied by Lampson (Lampson 1973), who proposed two rules which are sufficient to ensure confinement: total isolation and transitivity. They can be expressed in the following way. Confinement can be ensured by restricting the access right of a borrowed program, provided this program does not retain information or output any information other than by its formal parameters. If a program retains or outputs information through other channels, protection cannot be ensured by access control alone.

Three channels that can be used to leak information can be identified:

(1) **Storage channel** – for those objects that are shared among processes, for example, file system;

(2) **Legitimate channel** – for those objects that a process normally uses to convey information, for example, messages, parameters, printed output; and

(3) **Covert channel** – for those objects normally not intended for information transfer, for example, a program might vary its paging rate or control its execution time in some way to send an observing process confidential information.

11.4 Information flow models

The major disadvantages of protection systems based on access matrices are that they may be vulnerable to Trojan Horse attacks, and that, in general, it is impossible to determine whether unauthorized information flows exist, that is, the confinement problem is undecidable. Another disadvantage of access matrix-based systems is that the semantics of information to be accessed is not considered. Thus, it is necessary to find suitable and viable restrictions according to which the security of a system will not only be decidable, but the system will be secure.

11.4.1 Denning's model – the lattice security model

Fortunately, it is possible to extend protection systems based on the access matrix in such a way that the protection state is determined by a definition of the secure flow of information. This approach was derived from a general security policy similar to that in use in military organizations, and is commonly referred to as the **lattice security model**. This extension is premised on the ability to impose a classification scheme on both objects and subjects. Moreover, the confinement problem is decidable in the context of the lattice security model. The following discussion of the lattice security model is derived from Denning (1976), Kent (1981), Landwehr (1981) and Maekawa *et al.* (1987).

Denning's lattice model of secure information flow is based primarily on the definition of an information flow model. This model is defined by

$$FM = \langle N, P, SC, \oplus, \rightarrow \rangle$$

where:

N   is the set of logical storage **objects** (for example, files, segments, program variables);

P   is a set of **processes**, which are subjects (active agents) responsible for all information flow;

SC   is a set of **security classes** which correspond to disjoint classes of information; each object is bound to a security class, users may be bound to security classes referred to as 'security clearances', and each process may also be bound to a security class;

$\oplus$ a **class-combining operator** is an associative and commutative binary operator that specifies, for any pair of operand classes, the class in which the result of any binary function on values from the operand classes belongs;

$\rightarrow$ a **flow relation** is a relation defined on a pair of security classes as follows: for classes A and B, we write $A \rightarrow B$ if and only if information in class A is permitted to flow into class B. Information is said to flow from A to B whenever information associated with class A affects the value of information associated with class B. Denning considered flows which result from operations that cause information to be transferred from one object to another (for example, copying, assignment, message sending, parameter passing). This includes flows along legitimate and storage channels.

The security requirements of this model are as follows. A flow model FM is secure if and only if execution of a sequence of operations cannot give rise to a flow that violates the relation $\rightarrow$.

The flow model components SC, $\rightarrow$, and $\oplus$ form a universally bounded lattice under certain assumptions. They follow from the semantics of information flow, that is, either that no generality is lost by them or that they are required for consistency. The latter means that all flows implied by a permissible flow should also be permitted by the flow relation.

An example of a linear ordered lattice is illustrated in Fig. 11.6. Another, more complicated structure which satisfies the lattice property is also given in Denning (1976).

The lattice illustrated in Fig. 11.6 is a lattice with lower bound L and upper bound H since the following assumptions are fulfilled. SC is finite, $\langle SC, \rightarrow \rangle$ is a partially ordered set, SC has a lower bound L such that $L \rightarrow A$ for all $A \in SC$, and $\oplus$ is a least upper bound operator on SC, and these assumptions imply the existence of a greatest lower bound operator, denoted $\otimes$. The latter in turn implies the existence of a unique upper bound H.

Let us now illustrate the application of the Denning's model and demonstrate the extension to the access matrix model. This requires that:

(1) each object is assigned a **classification** (unclassified, confidential, secret, top secret); this classification denotes the security level of the information content (this can be illustrated by a lattice given in Fig. 11.6);

(2) each subject is assigned a **clearance** to access certain classes of information. The term **security level** used denotes the clearance of a subject or classification of an object;

(3) each object and each subject may be affiliated with a **compartment** that categorizes the information content for the object and represents a need-to-know classification for the subject, and

$$SC = \{A_1, \ldots A_n\}$$
$$A_i \longrightarrow A_j \text{ iff } i \leq j$$
$$A_i \oplus A_j \equiv A_{\max(i,j)}$$
$$A_i \otimes A_j \equiv A_{\min(i,j)}$$
$$L = A_1$$
$$H = A_n$$

Description   Representation

Fig. 11.6 Linear ordered lattice {adapted from Denning (1976)}.

(4)   the **security class** SC of an object or subject is specified by a pair
       (A, B), where A is the clearance or security level and B is a com-
       partment designation.

A secure flow of information is defined by a partial order imposed on
the set of security classes. This implies that access controls are governed
by the ordering of security classes; a subject S is allowed access to an
object O if and only if two conditions are satisfied:

(1)   S has the appropriate clearance relative to the class of the object
       O.

(2)   The compartment designation for S is contained in the compart-
       ment designation for O. (This condition is an application of the
       principle of **least privilege** or **need-to-know**.)

There is a certification mechanism for verifying the secure flow of information through a program. It also exploits the properties of a lattice
structure among security classes. Because this topic does not relate directly to problems discussed in this chapter, we will not discuss it here.

11.4.2   Bell and LaPadula's model – flow-secure access controls

In 1970s the US Air Force sponsored the construction of some prototype security kernels and some formal models for computer security.
Bell and LaPadula's model (Bell and LaPadula 1973) is a result of that
research. The following description is similar to that given in Landwehr
(1981) and Maekawa *et al.* (1987).

Bell and LaPadula represented the security kernel as a finite state
machine, and the security rules defined allowable transitions from one
'secure' state to the next. Their model is the best known use of flow
control to implement access control.

In addition to the objects and subjects of the access matrix model,
Bell and LaPadula's model includes the security classes of the military
security system. Thus, each object has a classification, and each subject
has a clearance and a current security level. The current security level
may not exceed the subject's clearance. These classes are used to control
the manner in which the access control matrix may be modified.

Four modes by which a subject may access an object are defined
by the access matrix. The subject is allowed to perform one of the operations on an object. These operations are given in List 11.2.

Moreover, there is also a **control** attribute (which is like an ownership flag) which allows a subject to pass to other subjects some or all of
the access modes it possesses. The control attribute itself cannot be
passed to another object.

read-only
>   the subject can read the object but not modify it;

append
>   subject can write the object but cannot read it;

execute
>   subject can execute the object but cannot read or write it directly; and

read-write
>   subject can both read and write the object.

List 11.2 Operations performed on an object.

The protection state is considered secure if the following two fundamental axioms hold:

(1) **The simple security property** – Reading information from an object O by a subject S requires $SC(S) \geq SC(O)$, that is, the clearance of the subject must be greater than the classification of any object to be read.

(2) **The *-property** ('**star-property**') – Appending information to an object O by subject S requires $SC(S) \leq SC(O)$, and both reading and writing of an object O requires $SC(S) = SC(O)$, whereas reading requires that $SC(S) \geq SC(O)$.

Moreover, if SC denotes the security class of an object or the current security class of a subject, then a subject S can read an object O_1 and write an object O_2 only if $SC(O_1) \leq SC(S) \leq SC(O_2)$.

Bell and LaPadula also gave the rules to change or access the access control matrix. These rules are presented in List 11.3.

Each rule has an associated set of restrictions to ensure that the **simple security policy** and ***-property** are satisfied.

There have been extensions made to the Bell and LaPadula model. They are as follows:

(1) **Hierarchies**, introducing hierarchies of objects such as files, directories.

(2) **Integrity policy**, allowing control of unauthorized 'upgrading' of information.

(3) **Database management systems**, in particular:

(a) extension of the concept of classification of elements of a relational database,

---

get (read, append, execute, read-write) access
  used by a subject to initiate access to an object in the
  prescribed mode.

release (read, append, execute, read-write) access
  used to release previously initiated access.

give (read, append, execute, read-write) access
  used by a subject to grant access to a specified object to another subject.

rescind (read, append, execute, read-write) access
  used by a subject to reduce the allowed access that some
  other subject has to a specified object.

create object
  used by a subject to activate an inactive object (if the object
  does not exist, then it must first be created).

delete object
  used by a subject to deactivate an object.

change security level
  used by a subject to alter the current security level of the
  specified object.

List 11.3   Rules to change or access the access control matrix.

(b)   the development of the concept of integrity as a formal dual
      to security, and

(c)   the development of a directory structure that partitions ob-
      jects according to level of classification.

(4)   The development of **automated program verifiers**.

Despite these extensions, the Bell and LaPadula model still has several
restrictions. Details on this topic can be found in Maekawa *et al.* (1987).

11.5   A security kernel mechanism

In Section 11.2 we introduced the concept of a security kernel mechanism. It is a small subset of a system that is responsible for the system
security. It is assumed that:

(1)   this subset would monitor all accesses,

(2)   it would be correct, and

(3)   it would be isolated so that its behavior could not be tampered with.

It is necessary to emphasize very strongly that the concept of a security kernel mechanism although it is treated as a general model, is very closely associated with computer implementation. That is because it is based on the concept of the **reference monitor** which allows for the incorporation of a specific set of security policies.

11.5.1   The concept of the reference monitor

The abstract notion of the reference monitor was adopted from the models of Lampson (Lampson 1971). In the reference monitor, subjects make reference to objects using a set of access authorizations (reference monitor database). Note that every reference to information or change to authorization must go through the reference monitor. The reference monitor is illustrated in Fig. 11.7.

The reference monitor concept defines subjects, objects, a reference monitor database (also called an authorization database) and security audit. As Fig. 11.7 shows, subjects are users, processes, or job streams who wish to gain access to objects. Objects are files, programs, terminals or tapes that contain information.

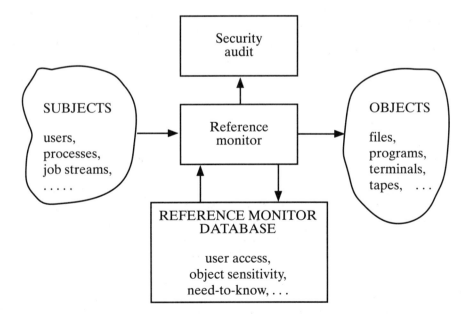

Fig. 11.7   Reference monitor.

The reference monitor database consists of many types of security data, such as user access, object sensitivity, need-to-know. This database provides information to the reference monitor on which subjects are authorized to access which objects.

The security audit mechanism allows users and security managers to monitor and gather information on a variety of events that represent access attempts, successful or not, in order to identify efforts to penetrate security barriers.

The reference monitor concept is used in most implementations of protection models. The most direct application is in a security kernel, which is described in the next subsection. The place of this concept in implementations of other protection models is not so straightforward. This is because different programs can function as part of the reference monitor mechanism, there are different ways of association of subjects with users or processes working on their behalf, and different objects contain sensitive information. Thus, some computer systems can be trusted but others cannot.

11.5.2 The security kernel

The concept of the reference monitor fits well with the notions of operating system kernels and layered abstract machines. Thus, the security kernel is one realization of the reference monitor abstraction. It forms the innermost layer (implemented in hardware and software) of the system, and it is responsible for all security-oriented operations. If the security kernel is small, as it should be for performance reasons, it should be possible to examine it for flaws and demonstrate its correctness. However, in real general-purpose operating systems it is difficult to identify and isolate all of the security-oriented functions without creating a fairly large and slow 'kernel'.

One of the basic features of the kernel security approach is that a system using it can only support a specific set of protection policies. This implies the need for the precise definition of protection policies: all the permissible modes of access between subjects and objects should be identified.

The protection policy enforced by a security kernel is expressed as a set of mathematical rules that constitute a formal security model. These rules must address both discretionary and non-discretionary policies. The problem is whether the model of the policy is complete. To determine this, it is necessary to consider two key issues:

(1) A model of a policy must define the information protection behavior of the total system. Modelling distinct operations with respect to individual assertions about a protection mecha-

nism does not address overall system security, and can be misleading.

(2) A model of a policy must include a 'security theorem' to ensure that the behavior defined by the model always complies with the security requirements of the applicable policy.

The model of policy enforced by most security kernels has been derived from the Bell and LaPadula model. Recall that each subject and object is given an access (security) class. These classes, organized in a lattice, are used to determine whether a subject is allowed to access an object. Moreover, two non-discretionary rules are used:

(1) the **simple security property**, which prohibits users from directly viewing data that they are not entitled to see, and

(2) the ***-property**, which helps to prevent illicit indirect viewing of objects; this property explicitly addresses the problem of Trojan Horse.

These rules are used primarily to prevent the unauthorized disclosure of information. To protect information from improper alterations, the model also includes integrity properties. Integrity rules prevent subjects with a given integrity class from modifying objects of higher integrity or being affected by objects of lower integrity.

Another problem is how to distinguish different users within the same access class. The non-discretionary rules do not provide such a protection policy. Therefore, discretionary rules are included in the model to provide the required type of protection policy. These rules allow authorized users to arbitrarily grant and revoke access rights to information based on user names or other information.

One restriction of this model is that it does not address a threat known as **denial of service** (for example, crashing a system or making it unresponsive). For this reason, rules dealing with denial of service in the security kernel approach are difficult to formalize.

11.6 Implementation of the access matrix

In an access matrix, subjects are usually represented by rows and objects by columns. The access rights that appear in the entries of the matrix correspond to the operations that can be performed on the objects. One could naively say that implementation of an access matrix is very simple. Indeed, it could be. However, it would be very inefficient, and expensive since the access matrix is usually sparse. Moreover, in distributed systems there is another very important factor that complicates implementation: subjects and objects are located on different sites.

Before we consider how to implement an access matrix efficiently, we need to look at some design principles.

11.6.1   Design principles

Saltzer and Schroeder proposed some design principles for protection of centralized systems (Saltzer and Schroeder 1975). They remain appropriate in the context of distributed systems (Kent 1981).

(1)   **Economy of mechanisms** – dictates the use of the simplest possible design that achieves the desired effect. Protection mechanisms must be built in the system and should be part of the system design process. Moreover, protection mechanisms should be small in the sense that their correct implementation can be verified.

(2)   **Fail-safe defaults** – requires that access decisions should be based on permission rather than exclusion. Thus, arguments must be made as to why objects should be accessible, rather than why they should not.

(3)   **Complete mediation** – requires that every access to every object must be checked using an access control data base for authority. This principle enforces a system-wide view of access control.

(4)   **Open design** – requires that the design of the protection mechanisms should not be secret. Moreover, these mechanisms should not depend on the ignorance of the potential attacker, but rather on the possession of protected information. This principle is not accepted in the context of military security.

(5)   **Least privilege** – requires that every subject should be given only those access rights (should operate using the least set of privileges) which are necessary to complete its task. If the access requirements change, the subject should switch domains. Access rights should be acquired only by explicit permission. This principle serves to limit the damage caused by accidents, errors or subversion of a component of a system.

(6)   **Acceptability** – requires that the protection mechanisms must be easy to use so that users can apply them automatically. Otherwise, they are likely to be unused or incorrectly used. This principle is important in discussing the suitability of various access control approaches as well as authentication procedures.

11.6.2   Implementation methods of an access matrix

Direct implementation of the access matrix is impractical due to the sparseness of the matrix. Taking into consideration this feature, the design principles listed above, and features of distributed systems, three general access control schemes (implementations of the access matrix) to protect resources in distributed computer systems have been proposed: access control lists, capabilities and a lock/key mechanism.

(1) **Access control list** – A scheme which is the result of decomposing the matrix by columns. An object monitor, which is responsible for the control of direct access to an object is associated with each object. Thus, the access control list associated with the object enumerates the subjects that have access rights to this object and determines those rights. A typical example of the use of access control lists is file directories.

The advantages of this scheme are:

(a) for a given object it is possible to easily and efficiently determine which subjects have access rights; and

(b) revocation of privileges is inexpensive.

The disadvantage is that it is difficult to determine the access rights of a given subject.

(2) **Capabilities** – A scheme which is the result of decomposing the matrix by rows. In this scheme, associated with each subject is a list that defines the objects to which the subject has access rights and determines those rights. As we saw in Chapter 7, capabilities in distributed systems are associated directly with names, and capability is supplied with a request in a message to an object monitor (server).

The advantage of this scheme is that for a given subject it is easy to determine the set of objects that can be accessed and the access rights.

The disadvantages are:

(a) for a given object it is difficult to determine which subjects can access it and what access rights they have; and

(b) revocation of privileges is a complicated task, and the operation can leave a number of copies of obsolete capabilites in the system.

(3) **Lock/key mechanism** – A scheme which combines the advantages of both access control lists and capabilities (Gifford [1982], and Maekawa *et al.* [1987]). To achieve this, each subject S is stored with a capability list. However, in this case the capability is a pair (O, K), where O denotes an object that can be accessed by subject S, using the key K. On the other hand, each object is associated with an access control list, which consists of pairs (L, A), where L denotes a lock and A denotes an access attribute. This list is also called a lock list.

When a subject S makes an attempt B to access object O, the protection system performs the following perations:

(a) the pair (O, K) from the subject S's capability list is passed to the monitor of O;

(b) the access to object O is permitted by its monitor if and only if there is a pair (L, A) on the lock list such that $K = L$ and B is a subset of A.

Note that these schemes strive for general purpose protection, yet do not have any definitive criteria for what is security relevant. Thus, the mechanisms in these systems essentially provide a computer with special security features.

Another aspect should also be pointed out. Although techniques for implementing the access matrix, in particular with access control lists and capabilities, in a centralized (single) computer system have long been established, little has been done to extend them to distributed systems. Only a small number of distributed operating systems provide protection mechanisms: Hydra uses capabilities (Almes and Robertson 1978), Accent uses capabilities (Rashid and Robertson 1981), Butler uses access control lists and the location of access (Dannenberg and Hibbard 1985), Amoeba uses capabilities (Mullender and Tanenbaum 1986), Apollo uses access control lists (Levine 1986), Mach uses capabilities (Sansom *et al.* 1986) and Andrew uses access control lists (Satyanaryanan 1989).

Note that only access control lists and capabilities have been used in distributed operating systems. For this reason, only these mechanisms are discussed in the following sections.

11.7 Access control lists

This section discusses implementations of access lists in distributed operating systems, and looks at methods of passing rights.

11.7.1 Implementation aspects

The access list scheme is based on the following concept for the implementation of an access matrix. This concept is identical for centralized operating systems and distributed operating systems.

(1) Each column in the access matrix is implemented as an access list for one object (empty entries can be discarded);

(2) The resulting list for each object consists of ordered pairs

< domain, right >

which define all domains with a non-empty set of access rights for that object. These access rights are usually denoted by positive numbers.

In other words, each object O is associated with a list of pairs $(S, A[S, O])$, one for each subject S that is allowed to access the object.

In practice, this approach is not used often. In real systems, it is sufficient to specify domains and assign sets of rights to each class of domains. Usually, there are few classes. For example, in UNIX and UNIX-like distributed operating systems, there are three classes of domain associated with each object· **owner**, **group** and **others**. Only the owner can change rights.

An access list-based system can use either process names or unique identifiers, as subject identities in the pairs. This information is passed to an object monitor (server), which stores an access control list, together with the operation request. However, the subjects still need to maintain references to the objects which they can access. This implies that two lists have to be maintained.

Whenever an operation M is to be executed on an object O_j within domain S_i, that is, by named subject S_i, an object monitor (resource server) searches the access list for object O_j, looking for an entry $<S_i, R_k>$, where $M \in R_k$. In other words when a subject (process) attempts access to a resource, its name or unique-identifier is used to search a list of all agents allowed to access the resource. If the entry is found, if the subject is on the list and it has access rights, the operation is allowed to continue; otherwise, an exception error is raised. These actions are illustrated in Fig. 11.8.

Note that it is possible to compose an access control list of two sublists:

(1)   a list of **Positive Rights** – as in conventional access control lists, an entry in this list indicates possession of set of rights, and

(2)   a list of **Negative Rights** – an entry indicates denial of those rights; if conflict occurs, denial overrides possession.

Such access control lists are used in Andrew (Satyanaryanan 1989).

There are some very important features of a protection system based on the access list scheme. The first is that the access list is checked on every access. From the security point of view, this is a very desirable feature. However, when the access list is long, this checking results in a considerable overhead. This drawback can be overcome by associative searches or the use of a cache store to maintain access list entries only for the active subjects.

Access rights can be granted to a subject by inserting a new reference in the subject's list and inserting the subject's identity plus permitted operations in the object's access list.

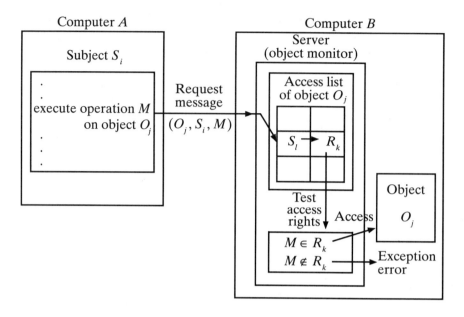

Fig. 11.8 The utilization of an access list in a distributed operating system.

Rights can be revoked simply by removing the corresponding entry from the access list of a given object. If an access control list contains lists with both **Positive Rights** and **Negative Rights**, revocation can still be done by removing a user from an access list. However, that user can be a member of more groups that bestow rights on the object. Thus, the protection domain must be modified to exclude the user from those groups. Discovering all groups that the user should be removed from, performing this operation at the master site, and propagating this information to all other sites, is a time-consuming process. Thus, negative rights can reduce the window of vulnerability, because changes to access lists are effective immediately. The member can be deleted from the groups later.

Determination of who may access a particular object and how, is straightforward. It may be noticed that, since each object is associated with its access list, objects can be grouped for the purpose of naming, or searching. This grouping is independent of any desired grouping for protection. It is also seen that maintaining such attributes as ownership and control is easy.

This short presentation of access lists in a distributed system shows that the operating system does not require any special modification and no message field has to be added. The implementation is straightforward.

11.7.2 Passing rights

We now consider passing access rights in a protection system with access lists.

 Let us assume that subject A wishes to pass to subject B access rights to a resource. In this case A sends a message to the resource server requesting the addition of B to the resource access list with certain access rights. That is illustrated in Fig. 11.9a. Before adding B to the list, the server checks to ensure that A possesses a superset of the access rights being passed. This is done by comparing A's identifier (that is, ei-

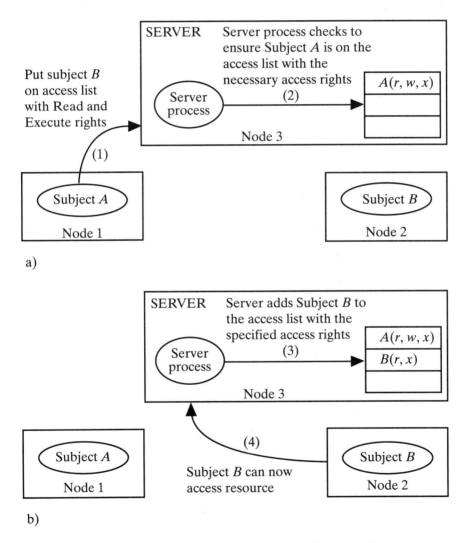

a)

b)

Fig. 11.9 Passing access rights in a system using access lists.

ther A's name or identifier supplied in the request) with those on the access list. If the identifier is found on the list associated with a superset of the access rights being passed, the identifier of B, associated with the access rights being passed, is added to the list (Fig. 11.9b).

Access lists can store either process names or identifiers. If process names are stored on access lists, the passing of access rights between processes requires the action of the resource server. This can decrease performance, in particular when a distributed application requires frequent process creation with the concomitant passing of access rights. On the other hand, if a resource server uses unique identifiers to pass access rights, the efficiency of distributed computations is greatly improved. That is because access list update is necessary only when access rights are passed between processes. To ensure that identifiers cannot be forged or stolen and then used, they must be protected using cryptographic techniques.

It should be emphasized that the use of process identifiers does not completely support the principle of least privilege because a process has access to all resources available to a principal, not just to those necessary to perform its function.

11.8   Capabilities

Capabilities are another form of implementation of the access matrix. Rather than associate the columns of the access matrix with the objects as in access lists, we can associate each row with its domain.

Recall that capabilities are associated directly with names, in particular, with system names (computer-oriented identifiers). This aspect was highlighted in Chapter 7. We defined a capability as an unforgeable ticket which specifies one or more permission modes, and allows its holder to access a named object. A capability combines a reference to an object with the access permission.

Possession of a capability means that access is allowed with the mode of access associated with the capability. To execute operation M on object O_j, the process executes the operation M, specifying the capability (pointer) for object O_j as a parameter.

Comparing capability based access control to access lists shows that capabilities support closer adherence to the principle of least privilege, and allow the passing of access rights between processes and principals without mediation by the resource server. Access lists tend to give slower caching as a search is required to find the appropriate right, but allow easier alteration of rights.

In Chapter 7 we discussed three types of capabilities: tagged, partitioned and sparse. We noted that tagged and partitioned capabilities are oriented towards centralized computers, in particular to hardware implementation. Only sparse capabilities can be used in distributed systems to name objects and protect them. There are two reasons for using the sparseness approach in distributed operating systems:

(1) It does not require capabilities to be distinguished from data – capabilities are bit strings of a defined length;

(2) Because kernels of user computers cannot be trusted, capabilities cannot be stored in the kernels, as they can in centralized systems. A protection mechanism which provides a trusted solution in distributed systems can be constructed based on the sparseness of some object identifier space.

11.8.1 Basic implementation aspects of capabilities

Capabilities in a distributed environment cannot be protected by kernels because a user does not trust the security of a distributed operating system. It is impossible to make assumptions about the ability of these systems to prevent attempts to forge or insert copies of stolen capabilities. Thus, capabilities might as well be stored in user process memory. The problem then arises of how these capabilities can be protected.

The simplest means of capability protection with simple passwords or encryption can protect against forgery to some extent. It is not possible to protect against capabilities, appearing in dumps or on terminals, being seen by unauthorized persons, and then being reinserted into another computer. Additional protection mechanisms are needed.

Watson and Fletcher (Watson and Fletcher 1980) discuss such a mechanism in the context of two types of capabilities: **uncontrolled** and **controlled**.

(1) **Uncontrolled capabilities** – If a subject possesses such a capability, it means that it has right of access. The access rights are represented by that capability. Capabilities of this type are protected against forgery with passwords or encryption.

(2) **Controlled capabilities** – Capabilities of this type can only be accepted if from a legitimate holder. They can be protected in three different ways:

    (a) with access lists,

    (b) with encryption using the legitimate holders address or other attribute as part of the key, or

    (c) with 'capability lists' named by the origin address; in this case the controlled capability is logically a name appearing in a directory-like object maintained by the server.

The capability system should allow the sharing of an object by simply passing the appropriate capability, uncontrolled as well as controlled, in a message. Uncontrolled capabilities can be sent without additional mechanism. Sharing controlled capabilities by subjects, or using them by a chain of servers involved in satisfying a subject's original request, must be supported by validation, encryption, or authentication protocols (see Chapter 12).

In Section 7.8 we described the most representative sparseness-based capability system, from the naming point of view. Now, we discuss its protection aspects.

11.8.2   Encrypted signature capabilities

Encrypted signature capabilities were invented by Gligor and Lindsay (Gligor and Lindsay 1979) in order to develop a mechanism to allow the migration of typed objects, including capabilities.

A capability is composed of two basic parts: an object identifier and some rights information. This capability may be extended by including a signature string, that is, by adding some redundant bits. This extension adds sparseness to the capability. To migrate such a signed capability, it must be protected against forgery. This is achieved by encryption. Because an intruder can deduce the signature function from the three basic strings, all of them are encrypted using a key. This encrypted, signed capability may be stored in unprotected memory. The revalidation of the capability requires the kernel to decrypt the bits from memory using a secret key. This operation must be performed before checking the signature. The authors of this proposal emphasize that the DES encryption system is quite resistant to attempts to deduce the key. Thus, it is very difficult to forge without knowing the encryption key. This leads to two basic problems. The first is the protection of the encryption key, and the second is the key distribution problem. Key distribution is discussed in Chapter 12.

Gligor and Lindsay proposed two schemes for incorporating redundancy and ciphertext into the migrated representation. The first, called the **first migration scheme**, is illustrated in Fig. 7.12. The most important feature of this scheme is that the representation to be passed is constructed by encrypting both the capability and the signature. To reinstantiate a passed capability, the subject first obtains the capability and the signature by deciphering the migrated object. Next, the new signature is computed from the newly obtained capability. If the computed signature matches the deciphered signature, the capability is accepted.

When a capability is to be stored as cleartext, the first migration scheme is not useful. The **second capabilities migration scheme** must be used. This scheme is illustrated in Fig. 11.10.

In the case of the second migration scheme, the migrated capability representation consists of the cleartext capability concatenated with a signature which is constructed by encrypting the capability and dis-

Capability

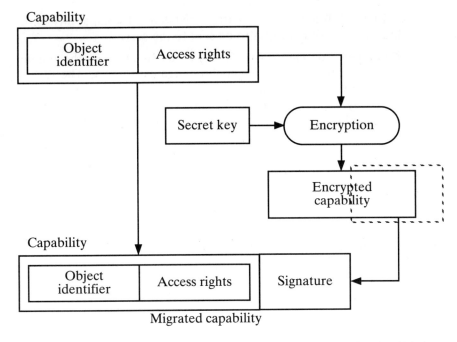

Fig. 11.10   Second capability migration scheme {adapted from Gligor and Lindsay (1979)}.

carding the first part of the encrypted capability. Thus, the signature cannot be computed without knowing the encryption key.

After receiving the protected capability, the capability is enciphered and the result is compared with the encrypted signature extracted from the received protected capability. The migrated capability can be accepted if the computed signature matches the migrated signature.

11.8.3   LLNL's capabilities

The Lawrence Livermore National Laboratory capability is used to protect unique local-identifier and server address (Watson and Fletcher 1980). This capability is illustrated in Fig. 7.8.

In addition to the server address and the unique local-identifier, the capability contains two fields which are protection oriented:

(1)   **Properties** – These are a set of standard bits and fields that indicate to a subject (client processes) the nature of the capability. Thus it is possible to indicate whether a capability is controlled or uncontrolled, resource type, access mode, resource lifetime or se-

curity level. It is state information included in the capability to reduce number of messages to be sent to the server.

(2) **Redundancy** or **password** – This guards (if present) the unique
local-identifier part of the capability against forgery. The idea is
that if any process tries to forge a capability, it will not be accepted by the server unless the password is correct. Encryption
and redundancy can also be used to provide protection.

In the LLNL system, the unique local-identifier has been made sparse.
This implies that without knowledge of this name a process cannot access the resource named. There is no information relating to passing
capabilities.

11.8.4 Amoeba's capabilities

An encrypted sparse capability is used in the Amoeba distributed operating system to protect the message ports (Mullender and Tanenbaum
[1986] and Tanenbaum *et al.* [1986]). The capability illustrated in Fig.
7.14 consists of four fields, two of which are used for protection.

(1) **Access rights** – a field which contains 1 bit for each permitted
operation on the named object.

(2) **Random** – a random number for protecting each object. This field
makes the capability sparse.

In Amoeba, the server port name has been made sparse; port names are
chosen randomly. This implies that if a process does not know a port
name, it cannot access the service behind the port. The ports are stored
in directory servers. Clients can encrypt ports for added protection before passing them to the directory service. Thus, a client requesting a
service has to give the name of the service, and this name is used to look
up the ports for that service.

Two necessary conditions for storing capabilities have been stated.
First, capabilities can be kept in a user's private directory. Second, if a
user does not divulge the capability for his private directory, he/she can
keep everything in it secret.

Mullender and Tanenbaum present a simple example of how capabilities are used. A client wishes to create a file using the file service,
write some data into the file, and then give another client permission to
read (but not modify) this file. Thus, this example illustrates capability
passing, which is a very important aspect of protection.

(1) First, the client sends a request message to the file server port
which specifies that a file is to be created. The request may contain a file name or account number. The information sent depends
on the nature of the file server.

(2)   The server then picks a random number, stores this number in its object table, and inserts it into the newly-formed object capability. It then sends a reply message. The reply would contain this capability for the newly-created (empty) file.

(3)   The client writes the file by sending a message containing the capability and some data.

(4)   The write request arrives at the file server. In this situation, the server uses the object number which is contained in the capability as an index into its tables to locate the object.

Several interesting object protection systems have been developed using this framework.

(1)   The simplest system is based on a random number stored in the file table when the object was created. The server compares this number to the number contained in the capability received together with data. If these numbers agree, all operations on the file are allowed.

This system is simple to implement. However, it has a major drawback in that it does not distinguish between operations that may be performed on an object (read, write, delete). To provide that distinction some modifications have to be made.

(2)   The modified system uses encryption and decryption for protection purposes. It works in the following way.

(a)   When a file (object) is created, the random number chosen and stored in the file table is used as an encryption/decryption key.

(b)   Next, the capability is formed. This operation is performed in stages. First, two numbers are taken: the rights field, which is initially all 1's indicating that all operations are legal, and the random number field, which contains a known constant (for example, 0). They are concatenated and treated as a single number. Second, the newly created single number is encrypted using the key just stored in the file table. Third, the encrypted value is put into the newly minted capability in the combined rights-random field.

When the capability is returned to be used, the server uses the unencrypted object number to find the file table and hence the encryption/decryption key. If the result of decrypting the capability leads to the known constant in the random number field, the capability is almost assuredly valid, and the rights field can be trusted.

One of the most distinctive advantages of the modified system is the ease of passing rights. The owner of the object can give an exact copy of the capability to another process simply by sending it the bit pattern with a permitted set of rights. To accomplish this task, the process must send the capability back to the server along with a bit mask and request the fabrication of a new capability whose rights field is the Boolean- and of the rights field in the capability and the bit mask.

Moreover, this system allows the selective passing of rights, since the owner of a capability can mask any operation that the receiver is not permitted to carry out. Finally, it decouples verification of rights from the security operations. Only the sender of the object operators need interpret the rights field.

This system has a minor drawback in that it requires going back to the server every time a sub-capability with fewer rights is needed.

(3) A third protection system has been proposed to avoid the drawback of the modified system. This system requires the use of a set of N commutative one-way functions, F_0, F_1, ..., F_{N-1}, which correspond to the N rights present in the rights field. Since the functions are commutative, it does not matter in what order the rights field bits were turned off. The rights field is not encrypted. This protection system works in the following way.

(a) When an object is created, the server picks a random number and puts it in both the file table and the random number field. Thus, this is performed in the same way as in the first protection system. All bits of the rights field are set to 1.

(b) The client process can delete permission K from a capability by replacing the number, R, with $F_k(R)$ and turning off the corresponding bit in the rights field.

(c) When the capability comes into a server to be used a new number is computed. The necessary operations are as follows: the server fetches the original random number from the field table, looks at the rights field, and applies the functions corresponding to the deleted rights to it.

(d) A comparison is made. If the computed number agrees with the number present in the capability, then the capability is accepted; otherwise it is rejected. The operations performed by all parties involved are illustrated in Fig. 11.11.

Note that although the rights field is not encrypted, an intruder cannot temper with this field; the server would detect it immediately.

Notice that there is no central record of who has which capability. However, it is easy to retract existing capabilities. To do this, the owner of

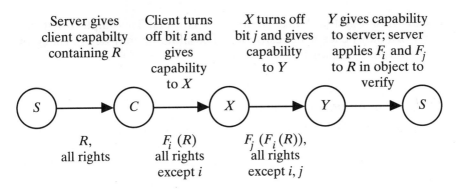

Fig. 11.11 Passing rights using capabilitities {adapted from Mullender and Tanenbaum (1986)}.

the object has to ask the server to change the random number stored in the file table. When this operation is to be performed it must be protected as any other operation. However, all existing capabilities are invalidated if the operation succeeds.

11.8.5 Password capabilities

Password capabilities are built in two parts – a unique object-identifier and a password (Anderson and Wallace 1988). A password capability is not encrypted and is defined as any string (128 bit value) that identifies some extant object and can be used to gain some access to it.

A password capability's integrity depends on the password. Its length (64 bit) makes it very difficult to guess. Because pseudo-random generators are of finite complexity and the output can be predicted, a hardware device is used as a source of unpredictable numbers.

The most important features of password capabilities are:

(1) There is no need to keep a secret key because there is no encryption;

(2) When a password capability is validated, the process is one of lookup and matching. In systems with encrypted capabilities the following operations have to be performed: lookup, decryption and matching;

(3) If someone does manage to procure a password capability, there is no way to manipulate the access rights. This implies that capabilities cannot be used to determine the value of any other capability to the object.

However, password capabilities have also a distinctive disadvantage: sharing capabilities is very difficult. There is no one key as in encrypted capabilities; a system has as many keys as users. This implies that one password may be a strong restriction. The situation may be alleviated by using multiple passwords.

11.8.6 Conditional capabilities

A conditional capability, which is a generalization of a conventional capability, is informally defined as an ordinary capability associated with a set of conditions (Ekanadham and Berstein 1979).

A conditional capability is a protected item which, in addition to a global identifier leading to the address of an object, contains two elements oriented towards protection (Fig. 11.12a):

(1)   **Access rights** – the set of access bits that determine which operations are allowed on this object via capability.

(2)   **Locks** – a set of unique numbers generated by the system to represent conditions. The lock is used to guarantee that the capability is exercised only when the condition is true.

To provide protection based on conditional capabilities, the system uses another protected item which contains a unique number generated by the system, referred to as a condition key. A condition key is shown in Fig. 11.12b).

When a conditional capability is referenced during an access, the protection system must check whether all conditions associated with it are satisfied. We say that a condition on a capability is satisfied if a corresponding key can be presented along with the capability. This means that in order to exercise a capability with a lock L_x, a matching key K_x must be presented. Thus the action of checking conditions is an operation of matching between locks and keys (a lock and key have to have the same unique number).

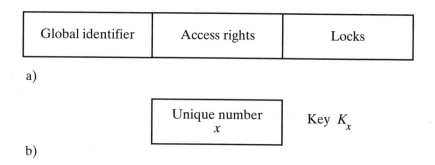

a)

b)

Fig. 11.12   Conditional capability: a) capability, b) a condition key.

The protection system provides three services oriented towards conditional primitives:

(1) Creation of capabilities – a capability is created along with an object; it has no locks at this time.

(2) Creation of a new condition key – the **Getkey** primitive creates a new condition key by incrementing a unique number generator and returning the new number x as a protected key K_x.

(3) Creation of a copy D of the parameter capability C — the **Addkey**(C, K$_x$) primitive returns a copy D of the parameter capability C with the additional lock L_x included in it. The capability C remains unchanged.

The protection system is responsible for validating each access to an object ($A:C$ denotes an instruction attempting an operation A on an object pointed at by capability C).

To show how a conditional capability is passed, we extend to distributed systems the example of amplification control presented by Ekanadham and Berstein. Consider a capability C stored in node P (Fig. 11.13).

Let us assume that C must be moved to another node Q but with the restriction that the object referenced be only accessible through node P.

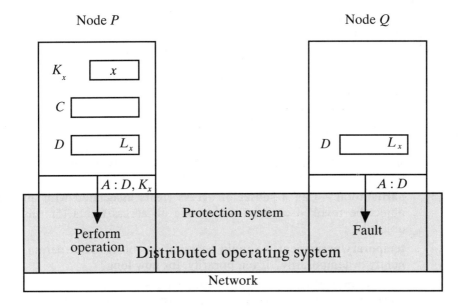

Fig. 11.13 Amplification using a conditional capability.

To solve this problem P obtains a key K_x using **Getkey** primitive. Next, it adds a lock L_x to C using the primitive **Addkey**(C, K_x). Let D denote the capability returned by this operation. The exercise of C is unconditional. Because of this D can be exercised only in conjunction with K_x. While D is transferred to Q, K_x is retained in P. This implies that the object can be accessed only through P. Thus, in order to perform an access, Q will have to call P, transferring D as a parameter.

11.9 Revocation of access rights

In a dynamic system, that is, one which allows transfer of access rights during the execution of a process and not just at its initiation, sometimes it may be necessary to cancel the access authority, that is to revoke access rights to objects that are shared by a number of different users.

11.9.1 Basic aspects of revocation

Protection mechanisms generate some overheads in checking the privileges of subjects when they attempt to access objects. In dynamic systems, these overheads involved in privilege transfer and revocation are considerably higher. Thus, protection systems which provide such services should be designed so that these overheads are minimal. One way of decreasing overheads is to make occasions for revocation exceptional and infrequent. This is in opposition to the frequent need to transfer access rights between cooperating processes. This implies that it would be efficient to pass access rights to those subjects, from which, with high probability, the privileges would not be revoked.

The following questions arise about revocation:

(1) **immediate/delayed** – When should rights be revoked? If revocation is delayed, for how long?

(2) **selective/general** – When an access right to an object is revoked, does it affect all users who have access to that object, or can we specify a select group of users whose access rights should be revoked?

(3) **partial/total** – Can a subset of access rights associated with an object be revoked or must we revoke all access rights for this object?

(4) **temporary/permanent** – Should access rights be revoked permanently or temporarily? If temporarily, for how long?

(5) **revocation methods** – In what way may access rights be revoked if a protection system is based on access lists and how may this operation be performed when capabilities are used?

It is obvious that revocation is appropriate when a subject detects or suspects a breach of trust, when a period of time has elapsed beyond which it is not desired to share objects, and where recovery from an error requires the revocation of access rights. It would be very difficult to give answers to the first four questions, simply because it depend on such matters as the conditions under which the access rights have been passed to other subjects to let them share some objects and the behavior of these subjects after receiving rights — they are matters of policy.

The last question is concerned with mechanisms, about which we can say something. As we have seen, revocation is easy if an access list scheme is in use. In this case access rights are simply deleted from the list. Capabilities present a much more difficult problem. Capabilities are distributed throughout the system, so they have to be found before they can be revoked.

11.9.2 Capability revocation

Very little has been done in the area of capability revocation in distributed operating systems. The work reported is oriented towards centralized systems, assuming the existence of tagged or partitioned environments. Variations of the following three methods have been used to implement revocation: keeping track of the locations of capabilities, forcing capabilities to evaluate through some map, and restricting the propagation of capabilities.

Redell and Fabry (Redell and Fabry 1974) proposed a revocation scheme referred to as a reduced tree, for use in tagged and partitioned environments. According to their scheme, a capability points to a map entry. There could be a chain of such maps organized so that the location of the object is determined.

The most interesting property of reduced tree based revocation is that it saves time and space, because it does not require the recording of the locations of capabilities. The number of map entries will be small if more literal copies are made rather than revocable copies when a new capability is constructed. A literal copy entails copying a capability from one protected location to another one, whereas a revocable copy requires making a new map entry. Another property of a reduced tree is that when revocation takes place, only map entries are changed. Moreover, it is not necessary to examine and modify possibly scattered locations in memory.

Gligor (Gligor 1979) proposed a propagation graph to support revocation. The locations of all capabilities and their copies are recorded in consecutive nodes to form a propagation graph for a given object. A propagation graph scheme can be used in both tagged and partitioned environments.

The most interesting property of a propagation graph based revocation is that, since the contents of the capability are used as a pointer into the object map, it is not necessary to follow paths in evaluating a capability's validity. As a result, there is no need for an associative cache to store evaluated addresses.

Some systems limit the propagation of capabilities. An example is Hydra (Wulf *et al.* 1981). Limiting the propagation of capabilities is carried out by checking the equivalent of a 'copy' bit in the access rights. Thus, any attempt to copy a capability without the copy right will fail. Revocation policies can be based on capabilities without the copy right. However, it is very difficult to derive capabilities with lesser access rights to an object if a capability without the copy right is used. On the other hand, protection systems with revocation mechanisms based on either reduced trees or propagation graphs can easily derive revocable capabilities with less rights from others. This is a distinct advantage of these two schemes over one using capabilities without the copy right.

It is impossible to prevent the propagation of sparse capabilities. First of all, schemes involving capabilities without a copy right are not useful. This is simply because sparse capabilities are values, that can be copied at will. Second, since the locations of all sparse capabilities cannot be recorded or controlled, it is impossible to implement a propagation graph in a sparse capability environment using Gligor's concept for revocation. Third, reduced tree mechanisms are also not useful, since it is impossible to distinguish between map entries for an object given in a single, sparse identifier.

Amoeba (Mullender and Tanenbaum 1986) has the most advanced protection system based on capabilities. In this system it is possible to invalidate all capabilities to an object by changing the random number field associated with the object identifier. This operation can be performed by a server. However, there is no support for selective or transitive revocation similar to the schemes discussed above. Since validating the capability depends on using a single record for all capabilities to an object, it is impossible to revoke a particular capability without revoking all other capabilities for a given object.

As well as those presented above, there are a number of different schemes for revoking capabilities:

(1)   **reacquisition** – Periodically, capabilities are deleted from each domain. A process may try to reacquire the capability if it finds that the capability was deleted;

(2)   **back-pointers** – A list of pointers is maintained with each object, pointing to all capabilities associated with that object. When revocation is required, these pointers can be followed, changing these capabilities as necessary;

(3)   **indirection** – The capabilities do not point to the objects directly, but indirectly. This means that each capability points to a unique entry in a global table, which points to the object. Revocation is implemented by searching the global table for the desired entry and deleting it;

(4)   **keys** – A key is a unique bit pattern which can be associated with each capability. It is defined when a capability is created and it cannot be modified or inspected by a process owning that capability. A **master-key** associated with each object can be defined or replaced with the **set-key** operation. When a capability is created, the current value of the master-key is associated with the capability. When the capability is exercised, its key is compared to the master-key, and if the keys match, the operation is allowed to continue; otherwise, an exception condition is raised. Revocation replaces the master-key with a new value by the **set-key** operation, invalidating all previous capabilities for this object.

In summary, methods for revoking capabilities are at an early stage of development and need further study.

11.10   Distributed matrix access control

There are two important aspects associated with distributed matrix access control: implementation and identifier protection.

11.10.1   Ways of implementing distributed access control

Distributed matrix access control can be implemented either by:

(1)   cooperating node operating system kernels, or

(2)   mechanisms supported in user processes.

When distributed access control is implemented by cooperating node operating system kernels, object identifiers or capabilities are stored in operating system kernel space. An authorized process can either act on behalf of a object or use a capability which has process-specific information, which is associated with it by the kernel. In identifier-based schemes, the kernel stores the object identifier in process state information not directly accessible to the process. In capability based schemes, the kernel maintains a capability list associated with each process.

When a process wishes to pass a object identifier or capability to another process, it makes a system call to the kernel requesting the specified operation. If the process receiving the access control information is a remote process, the kernel formats a message containing either the identifier or capability and sends it to the kernel of that remote process. That kernel either associates the identifier with the process or adds the capability to the process's capability list. The process passing the access control information must also inform the process receiving this information of the access control transaction. This requires the transmission of another message, one that moves between the two processes rather than between their kernels.

Object identifiers and capabilities should be protected by node kernels against surreptitious actions of other node kernels. That is done by cryptographic checksums. If all nodes exchanging access rights information trust each other, nodes are never compromised and all channels are protected against active and passive threats (to be discussed later); object identifiers and capabilities managed by operating system kernels do not then have to be protected by cryptographic checksums. Since these conditions are very rarely obtained, checksums are required when kernels manage distributed access control information.

When distributed access control is implemented by mechanisms supported in user processes, access control operates in the same manner as kernel-based access control, except that object identifiers or capabilities are stored in process space, while the cryptographic keying material used to protect them is managed by the node kernel. As a result, the identifiers and capabilities can be passed between processes without incurring message traffic between kernels. Process based distributed access control eliminates certain resource control and synchronization problems faced by kernel-based schemes, supports more efficient communications, and simplifies the node operating system kernels, while offering the same degree of security as kernel based mechanisms.

Note that in both cases capabilities or object identifiers are transferred in interprocess communication messages.

In summary, we can say that in commonly occuring operational environments, kernel-based distributed access control offers no security advantage over process-based distributed access control. Moreover, managing access control information in node kernels requires the transmission of two messages when a object identifier or capability is passed. One message goes from the source to the destination kernel, and the second from the source to the destination process. Because process-based distributed access control requires the transmission of only one message to pass a object identifier or capability, this scheme is cheaper and simpler.

11.10.2 Identifier protection

Both access control lists and capabilities need to trust that an identifier, the trusted identifier in the former, and the capability in the latter, cannot be forged or stolen. Encryption, other uses of redundancy, and as-

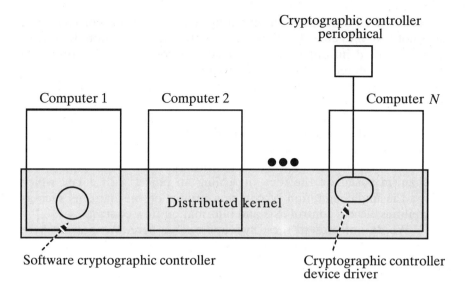

Fig. 11.14   Cryptographic controllers.

sumptions about what components (that is, local operating system, physical security and communications) can be trusted, form the basis for deciding which approach to use and how to create a workable system.

There must be a mechanism to prevent forgery and theft of data. One such mechanism is based on secret-key encryption. Secret-key encryption requires encryption/decryption keys that must be kept secret. The most important thing is that these keys must be secretly distributed and protected by each node of a distributed computer system.

One possibility is for each node to have a cryptographic controller, as illustrated in Fig. 11.14. The cryptographic controller protects the encryption keys and intermediate cryptographic results.

In summary, how well access control information is protected depends on the types of threats each protection scheme is intended to counter (for example, forgery protection, protection against theft of access control information); on the strength of the cryptographic algorithms, cryptographic information handling procedures, and the key management protocols supporting the schemes; and on the extent to which the protection schemes are enforced in the different parts of the distributed system.

11.11   Implementation of information flow control

We saw earlier that because discretionary access controls have some limitations, certain protection questions are undecidable (for example, the confinement problem). Moreover, the access matrix model, since it is a generalized description of operating system protection mechanisms, does not take into consideration the semantics of information. However, when classified information is involved, the semantics of information must be considered. For these reasons a lattice security model has been proposed and models based on the access control matrix have been extended.

The best known such model is Bell and LaPadula's model, which requires that the classification of information (object), the clearance of the user (subject), and rules concerning classifications must be known before an access can be granted. Gifford (Gifford 1982) proposed a mechanism based on the idea of sealing an object with a key which allows the implementation of common protection mechanisms such as capabilities, access control lists and information flow control.

We do not present these two approaches here. We present here an implementation which is an extension to capabilities, and modified access control lists, proposed by the author.

This protection system uses a **clearance capability**, which is a trusted identifier with additional redundancy for protection, and security level to provide clearance of a subject to access certain classes of information (to access certain objects). It has the form shown in Fig. 11.15.

The fields of a clearance capability are:

(1)   The **server address** which is the address of the server that manages the object (information).

(2)   The **object** identifier used by the server to identify and locate the specific object (information).

(3)   The **clearance** of a subject to access certain objects (certain classes of information). In other words, it is the security level of the subject.

(4)   **rights** which is a field containing one bit for each permitted operation on the object.

(5)   **random** which is a field containing a random number for protecting the capability.

Note that the last three fields are encrypted.

In a clearance capability-based protection system, a server does not have to maintain for each object a list of subjects which are allowed to access this object. However, the system must maintain one list whose

Server address	Object identifier	Clearancce	Rights	Random

Fig. 11.15   A clearance capability.

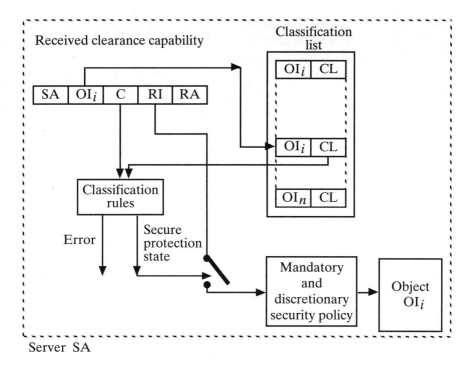

Fig. 11.16   A clearance capability-based protection system.

individual entries contain an **object identifier** and a **classification** assigned to this object. A clearance capability-based protection system is shown in Fig. 11.16.

This system works in the following way. When a capability is received, the content of the clearance field is compared against the classification of the requested object. At this stage rules concerning classifications, for example, the **simple security property** and the ***-property** (see Section 11.4.2), are used. If both properties hold, the protection state is considered secure; otherwise, the requesting subject is refused access. Next, if the protection state is secure the access rights field is compared against the requested operation to determine whether the requested access confirms to mandatory and discretionary security policy. If so, the request can be granted.

11.12   Implementation of a distributed security kernel

A security kernel mechanism was introduced in Section 11.2. and described in Section 11.5. Recall that this mechanism is based on the concept of a reference monitor and fits in well with notions of operating system kernels. The protection policy enforced by a security kernel is formed from a set of mathemetical rules which must address both discretionary and non-discretionary policies.

The first step in developing a kernel-based system is to identify the specific set of protection policies to be supported by the kernel. Because a given system is secure only with respect to some specific policy, the policy has to be precisely defined. This requirement distinguishes a kernel-based system from protection systems that are based on the access matrix model, for example, capability- and access list-based systems. The latter are oriented towards general-purpose protection. They do not have any definitive criteria for what is security-relevant; they essentially provide a computer with general protection mechanisms. On the other hand, the security-kernel approach explicitly addresses both policy and mechanism.

Security-kernel systems have the following problems:

(1)   The security kernel imposes some performance degradation because it provides an additional level of interpretation beneath the main operating system.

(2)   The division of an operating system into trusted and untrusted components is a complex and expensive task. It is hard to determine which functions of such operating system components as process management, resource management, I/O management, and file system management, are security relevant and must be in the kernel.

(3)   Security kernels for general-purpose operating systems tend to be complex. The reason for the significant performance degradation observed with security kernel-based systems is the lack of adequate hardware. With appropriate hardware and specific software, however, there is no reason that a security kernel-based system should perform worse than a non-security-kernel based system with similar capabilities.

In this section, we describe a distributed secure system designed by Rushby and Randell (Rushby and Randell 1983). Before doing so, we look briefly at a security kernels for centralized system.

11.12.1 Security kernel design in a centralized system

The structure of a security kernel-based general-purpose operating system with online, interactive users is illustrated in Fig. 11.17. There are three topics that should be addressed when designing a security kernel-based operating system: kernel/nonkernel trade-offs, trusted subjects and hardware/software features.

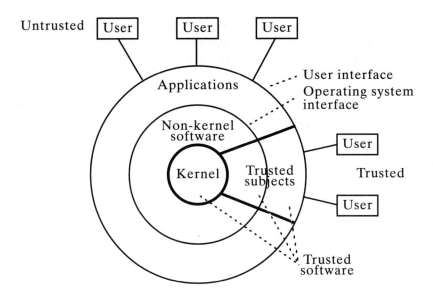

Fig. 11.17   The structure of a security kernel-based operating system {adapted from Ames *et al.* (1983)}.

It is difficult to determine which functions of such kernel-based operating system components as process management, resource management, I/O management, and file system management, are security relevant and must be in the kernel. In general, the kernel must handle those parts of an operating system that are involved in the management of resources which are shared by multiple subjects (processes, users). Examples of such resources are memory and disk space. If these resources are protected by the kernel, their locations are not visible to untrusted software. Non-kernel software implements those functions that provide useful common utilities but do not manage anything shared among users and those that address denial of service are outside the scope of the security policy. When deciding what to put into the kernel, it is necessary to make tradeoffs between performance, functionality, and complexity.

In many cases there is a desire for a security policy that is more oriented towards the needs of systems than that defined by the security model. This orientation policy may be only applied under special circumstances or to a special class of users. Such an extended policy implemented in a kernel is usually provided by a set of interfaces that can be invoked by certain **trusted subjects**. Trusted subjects are often implemented as asynchronous processes or as extensions of the kernel itself. Thus, if a running process is identified as a trusted subject, it may be able to perfom actions not permitted by the access checks built into normal kernel functions. Usually, trusted subjects are involved in the following two actions: performing system maintenance, and controlling the access policy that the kernel enforces for untrusted subjects.

Appropriate hardware and some specific software mechanisms can significantly improve the performance of a security-kernel-based system. In the following areas, special mechanisms have proved useful or necessary to support a security kernel-based operating system:

(1)   explicit processes give efficient support for multiprocessing and interprocess communication;

(2)   memory protection provides large segmented virtual memory, access control to memory, and explicitly identified objects;

(3)   execution domains provides minimum of three domains (user, supervisor and kernel) and efficient transfer of control between domains; and

(4)   I/O mediation gives control of access to I/O devices, to external media, and to memory by I/O processors.

Details can be found in Ames *et al.* (1983).

11.12.2   A secure kernel-based distributed system

The goal of a project described in Rushby and Randell (1983) was the study and development of a distributed system that provides a limited but useful form of multilevel secure operation. Rushby and Randell's approach involves interconnecting small, specialized, provably trustworthy systems, and a number of larger untrustworthy host computers. Each host computer provides services to a single security partition. The basic functions of the trusted components are:

(1)   the mediation of access and communication between the untrusted computers,

(2)   the provision of specialized services (for example, a multilevel secure file store), and

(3)   the ability to change the security partition to which a given host computer belongs.

There are two benefits of this approach to secure computing:

(1)   it does not require any modifications to untrusted host computers and it allows them to provide their full functionality and performance,

(2)   it enables the mechanisms of security enforcement to be isolated, single purpose and simple.

Principles and mechanisms

The reference monitor is a basic concept used in the development of secure systems. The reference monitor is a small, isolated, trustworthy mechanism which controls the behavior of untrusted system components, by mediating their references to external entities such as data and other untrusted components. Each requested access is checked against a record of the accesses that are authorized by the security policy for that given component.

Note that in the previously developed security-oriented systems, the above mentioned design issues: **separation** of secure from insecure objects and **mediation** have been confused and incorporated into a single mechanism – a security kernel. This could be considered as a weakness. Thus, it was necessary to make a strict logical and implementation distinction between separation and mediation.

Four different separation mechanisms are used by Rushby and Randell:

(1) **Physical** separation which is achieved by allocating physically different resources to each security partition and function. Distributed systems are well suited to the provision of physical separation. Security is achieved in these systems by providing trustworthy reference monitors to control communications between the distributed components and to perform other security-critical operations. However, provision of physical separation for each security partition and reference monitor could be very expensive. Thus, this separation is only used for untrusted host computers and for the security processors that maintain their trusted components.

(2) **Temporal** separation which allows the untrusted host computers to be used for different activities in different security partitions. This is possible due to the separation of all these activities in time.

(3) **Logical** separation which is provided by a **separation kernel**. There are a number of different separation and reference monitor functions, and some untrusted support functions. All of these functions are supported by the security processors by using a separation kernel. Thus, logical separation is used to separate the above mentioned functions. The separation kernels are can be relatively small, uncomplicated and fast, and allow simpler and more complete security verification than general-purpose security kernels.

(4) **Cryptographic** separation which uses encryption and related techniques (for example, checksum) to separate different users of shared communications and storage media.

Rushby and Randell's securely partitioned distributed system

A securely partitioned distributed system described in Rushby and Randell (1983) is shown in Fig. 11.18.

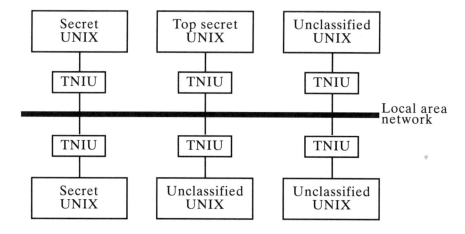

Fig. 11.18   A securely partitioned distributed system {adapted from Rushby and Randell (1983)}.

The securely partitioned distributed system is composed of standard untrustworthy UNIX systems interconnected by a local area network. Communication among UNIX systems is provided by the Newcastle Connection.

The assumption that each UNIX system is untrusted implies that the unit of protection must be these systems themselves. As a consequence, each individual system can be dedicated to a fixed security partition. Therefore, one might allocate one system to the Top Secret level, two systems to Secret level, and others to Unclassified utilization. The system also permits limited need-to-know controls. This can be provided by dedicating individual machines to different compartments within a single security level. For example, one of the secret systems could be dedicated to Finance and another to Personnel. Users assigned to computer hosts know that no security is guaranteed within those individual systems, and they cannot rely on authentication because there is no security within host computers – they are not trusted. This implies that each system must be controlled by physical or other external mechanisms.

Although individual UNIX-based host computers are not trusted, the key concept to Rushby and Randell's approach is to enforce security on the exchange of messages between systems. This is provided by placing a trustworthy mediation device between each system and its network connection. This device, called TNIU (Trustworthy Network Interface Unit) uses the Data Encryption Standard (DES) to protect information sent over the local area network.

The basic task of the TNIU is to permit communication only between computers which belong to the same security partition. This implies the need for division of the single UNIX system (UNIX United) into a number of disjoint subsystems. The second task of the TNIU is to provide a separation function to isolate and protect the legitimate host-to-host communication channels. In practice, controlling which host computers can communicate with one another is the task of a reference monitor. However, because the communication medium can be tapped or subverted, the TNIU must be involved in the separation.

Separation is provided cryptographically. The TNIU encrypts all communications sent over the local area network. Note that since communicating host computers are untrustworthy and may attempt to thwart the TNIU-provided cryptographic protection, the encryption must be managed very carefully to prevent clandestine communication between communicating units.

Readers interested in other aspects of the distributed secure system such as the multilevel secure file store or the accessing and allocation of the security partitions are encouraged to consult the original work by Rushby and Randell.

11.13 Summary

A distributed operating system provides services for remote communication, resource allocation, load sharing and balancing, and, if necessary, deadlock detection and resolution. However, not all users have the same rights to access computer system objects. Moreover, some users (intruders) want to tap passively a communication medium to read or actively change, or destroy exchanged messages. Some intruders try also to masquerade and exchange messages with eligible users.

This implies the need for security and security measures in a computer system. Security deals with such issues as: secrecy, privacy, authenticity, integrity and availability.

Applications as well as users of computer systems need to characterise the level of security offered by that system. There are three basic taxonomies of security. The first, introduced by the Department of Defence U.S., creates means to distinguish more secure computer systems from less secure ones, and to encourage manufacturers to provide more trustworthy operating systems. Voydock and Kent's taxonomy is based on security violations; three violations are identified: release and modification of information, and denial of resource usage. The Wulf *et al.*'s taxonomy is based on such terms as mutual suspicion, modification, conservation, confinement, and initialization.

Security in distributed systems covers three basic areas: protection mechanisms that prevent unauthorized accessing system objects based on access control approached, communication security, and user authentication. This chapter deals with protection mechanisms.

There are four fundamental access control approaches. The first is the access matrix model which is a generalized description of operating system protection mechanisms. It provides a general representation of access control policies in which the access rights of each subject (user, process) to each object (resource, process) are defined as entries in a matrix. This approach is simple and effective, but suffers from two drawbacks: it is vulnerable to Trojan Horse attacks, and it does not take into consideration the semantics of information.

The lattice security model includes classifications, clearances and rules concerning the classifications. It is an extension to the access matrix model. It was derived from the military classification systems, and is based on the lattice security concept. The best known example of this model is the Bell and LaPadula model.

The third approach, information flow models, is also based on the lattice model. The Denning model, instead of requiring a list of axioms governing users' accesses, requires that all information transfer is subject to the flow relation among the security classes.

A security kernel mechanism represents the fourth access control approach. The general concept of this approach fits well with notions of operating system kernels and layered abstract machines.

Although the access matrix is simple, its direct implementation would be very inefficient and expensive since it is usually sparse. Moreover, in distributed systems, subjects and objects are located on different computers. For these reasons two fundamental implementation methods of an access matrix are proposed: access control lists, and capabilities.

Access control lists are associated with objects. For a given object it is possible to easily and efficiently determine which subjects have access rights, and revocation of privileges is inexpensive. The disadvantage of access control lists is that it is difficult to determine the access rights of a given subject.

Capabilities are associated directly with names. They are supplied with a request in a message to an object monitor/server. There are a number of different types of capabilities. However, an encrypted sparse capability best suits the requirements of distributed systems. Capabilities have the advantage that for a given subject it is easy to determine the set of objects that can be accessed and the access rights. However, for a given object it is difficult to determine which subjects can access it and what access right they have. Revocation of privileges is also a complicated task.

A mechanism based on the idea of sealing an object with a key was proposed for implementing common protection mechanisms such as capabilities, access control lists, and information flow control. Another, simpler, implementation mechanism is proposed here based on the so-called clearance capability. This is a standard sparse capability extended by a field which contains the clearance of a subject.

Implementation of a distributed security kernel is a complex task. The basis for a distributed secure system proposed by Rushby and Randall is provided by four different separation mechanisms: physical, temperal, logical and cyrptographic separations.

It is necessary to emphasis that few distributed operating systems so far provide protection mechanisms that prevent unauthorised accessing of system objects. Only access control lists or capabilities have been used.

In summary, protection mechanisms for distributed operating systems require further extensive research.

Bibliography

Almes G. and Robertson G.G. (1978). An Extensible File System for Hydra. In *Proceedings of the 3rd International Conference on Software Engineering IEEE*

Ames S.R., Gasser M. and Schell R.R. (1983). Security Kernel Design and Implementation: An Introduction. *Computer,* **16**(7), 14–22

Anderson M. and Wallace C.S. (1988). Some Comments on the Implementation of Capabilities. *The Australian Computer Journal,* **20**(3), 122–33

Bell D.E. and LaPadula L.J. (1973). *Secure Computer Systems: Mathematical Foundations.* ESD–TR–278, 1, ESD/AFSC, Hanscom AFB, Bedford, MA

Birkhoff G. and Bartee T.C. (1970). *Modern Applied Algebra.* New York: McGraw-Hill

Bishop M. (1981). Hierarchical Take-Grant Protection System. In *Proceedings of the Eighth Symposium on Operating Systems Principles*, Pacific Grove, California

Bishop M. and Snyder L. (1979). The Transfer of Information and Authority in a Protection System. In *Proceedings of the Seventh Symposium on Operating Systems Principles,* Pacific Grove, California

Chess D.M. (1989). Computer Viruses and Related Threats to Computer and Network Integrity. *Computer Networks and ISDN,* **17**, 141–8

Cohen F. (1987). Computer Viruses: Theory and Experiments. *Computers & Security,* **6**, 22–35

Dannenberg R.B. and Hibbard P.G. (1985). A Butler Process for Resources Sharing on Spice Machines. *ACM Transactions on Office Information Systems,* **3**(3), 234–52

Denning D.E. (1976). A Lattice Model of Secure Information Flow. *Communications of the ACM,* **19**(5), 236–43

Denning D.E. and Denning P.J. (1979). Data Security. *Computing Surveys,* **11**(3), 227–49

DoD (1983). *Trusted Computer System Evaluation Criteria.* CSC–STD–001–83, Department of Defense, Computer Security Center

Ekanadham K. and Berstein A.J. (1979). Conditional Capability. *IEEE Transactions on Software Engineeing,* **SE–5**(5), 458–64

Gifford D.K. (1982). Cryptographic Sealing for Information Secrecy and Authentication. *Communications of the ACM,* **25**(4), 274–86

Gligor V.D. (1979). Review and Revocation of Access Priviliges Distributed Through Capabilities. *IEEE Transactions on Software Engineering,* **SE-5**(6), 575–86

Gligor V.D. and Lindsay B.G. (1979). Object Migration and Authentication. *IEEE Transactions on Software Engineering,* **SE-5**(6), 607–11

Goldstein, A. (1985). Operating Systems Offer Security Features to Control Computer Access. *Computer Technology Review,* 191–9

Goscinski A. and Pieprzyk J. (1989). Security in Distributed Operating Systems. In *Proceedings of IEEE and IE Australia Workshop on Computer Security and Reliability,* Sydney

Graham G.S. and Denning P.J. (1972). Protection: Principles and Practices. *Proceedings of the AFIPS Spring Joint Computer Conference,* **40**, 417–29

Harrison M.A., Ruzzo W.L. and Ullman J.D. (1976). Protection in Operating Systems. *Communications of the ACM,* **19**, 8, 461–71

Kent S.T. (1981). Security in Computer Networks. *Protocols and Techniques for Data Communication Networks.* Prentice-Hall, 369–432

Lampson B.W. (1971). Protection. *Fifth Princeton Conference on Information and Systems Sciences,* pp. 437–43

Lampson B.W. (1973). A Note on the Confinement Problem. *Communications of the ACM,* **16**(10), 613–15

Landwehr C.E. (1981). Formal Models for Computer Security. *ACM Computing Surveys,* **13**(3), 247–75

Levine P. (1986). The Apollo Domain Distributed File System. *Distributed Operating Systems: Theory and Practice,* NATO Advanced Study Institute, Turkey: Springer-Verlag

Maekawa M., Oldehoeft A.E. and Oldehoeft R.R. (1987). *Operating Systems. Advanced Concepts.* The Benjamin/Cummings Publishing Company, Inc.

Mullender S.J. and Tanenbaum A.S. (1986). The Design of a Capability-Based Distributed Operating System. *The Computer Journal,* **29**(4), 289–99

Nessett D.M. (1987). Factors Affecting Distributed System Security. *IEEE Transactions on Software Engineering,* **SE-13**(2), 233–48

Popek G.J. and Farber D.A. (1978). A Model for Verification of Data Security in Operating Systems. *Communications of the ACM,* **21**(9), 737–49

Rashid R.F. and Robertson G.G. (1981). Accent: A Communication Oriented Network Operating System Kernel. *Proceedings of the Eighth ACM Symposium on Operating Systems Principles,* Pacific Grove, California

Redell D.R. and Fabry R.S. (1974). Selective Revocation of Capabilities. *Proceedings of the International Workshop on Protection in Operating Systems,* IRIA, pp. 197–209

Rushby J. and Randell B. (1983). A Distributed Secure System. *Computer,* **16**(7), 55–67

Saltzer J.H. and Schroder M.N. (1975). The Protection of Information in Computer Systems. *Proceedings of the IEEE,* **63**, 1278–1308

Sansom R.D., Julin D.P. and Rashid R.F. (1986). *Extending a Capability Based System into a Network Environment.* Technical Report CMU–CS–86–115 Computer Science Department, Carnegie–Mellon University

Satyanarayanan M. (1989). Integrating Security in a Large Distributed System. *ACM Transactions on Computer Systems,* **7**(3), 247–80

Tanenbaum A.S., Mullender S.J. and van Renesse R. (1986). *Using Sparse Capabilities in a Distributed Operating System*. The 6th International Conference in Distributed Computing Systems, June 19–23, Cambridge, MA, 558–63

Voydock V.L. and Kent S.T. (1983). Security Mechanisms in High-Level Network Protocols. *Computing Surveys,* **15**(2), 135–71

Watson R.W. and Fletcher J.G., (1980). An Architecture for Support of Network Operating System Services. *Computer Networks,* **4**, 33–49

Wulf W., Levin R. and Harbison S.P. (1981). *HYDRA/C.mmp: An Experimental Computer System*. McGraw-Hill

12 Communication security and user authentication

			Security	
User names	File service			C s
	Collaboration of file servers Transaction service Directory service Flat file service Disk service		Access control	o e m c m u
Name distri-bution			R p e r	m r u i
	Resource allocation	Deadlock detection	s o o t	n t i y c a

Name resolu-tion	Algorithms for load sharing and load balancing	Process synchro-nization	u e
			r c
			c t
			e i
			   o
			   n
				t i
				i
				o
				n
				&
				  &

			Capa-bilities	Authen-tication
System names	Process management Operations on processes: local, remote Process migration		Access lists	Key manage-ment
Ports	Interprocess communication (and memory management)		Info flow control	Data encryp-tion
	Interprocess communication primitives: Message Passing or Remote Procedure Call, or Transactions;		Security kernel	
	Links or Ports			
Address-es	↕ ══════════════ ↕			
Routes	Transport protocols supporting interprocess communication primitives			Encryp-tion protocols

There is a growing awareness that information is a saleable commodity. Since more and more information is stored in computers, particularly in computers located in different places and connected by networks, one must ensure that unauthorized persons do not have access to information either at its storage location, or during transfers over networks. The goal of information security is to protect against the unauthorized disclosure, modification, or destruction of data stored in or transmitted by a computer system.

Implementing data security measures in a centralized computer system is a complicated task. Expansion into distributed systems has complicated the security issue still further. Moreover, the costs of developing and maintaining security measures in a distributed system is much higher.

An analysis of the basic aspects of security and common violations carried out in Chapter 11 shows that it is possible to identify not only the mechanisms to prevent accessing objects in a distributed computer system by unauthorized users, but also to provide **communications security** and **user authentication**.

We noted in Chapter 11 that distributed systems give rise to the additional need to protect the communication system because it can be regarded as open to **passive** line tapping and thus to the reading of data. **Active** line tapping in which data may be inserted onto the line or deleted from the line is also possible. These two strategies of attack on a communication system require that a secure distributed computer system not only provide protection mechanisms within a system, as in a centralized system, and secure communication, but also that these two systems be integrated to provide a coherent security system for the distributed system.

Note that the security of communication relies upon the communicating commonly suspicious users (processes) having knowledge of each others identities. This implies that authentication providing some level of assurance that the identities are as claimed, plays an important role in the provision of virtually all communication security services.

This chapter focuses on communication security and user authentication. We discuss these two security topics using the Voydock and Kent taxonomy. Section 12.1 deals with the factors complicating the application of security measures to distributed systems, and introduces the association model which can be used for a study of communication security. Next, we present threats to interprocess communication in distributed systems, in particular passive (release of traffic contents and traffic analysis) and active attacks (message stream modification, denial and delay of message delivery, and masquerade). Basic communication security goals are stated, that is, prevention of passive attacks and detection of active attacks.

Encryption has been used as a countermeasure against passive attacks, and in conjuction with protocols has been used to detect active attacks. Data encryption is therefore discussed in the following part of this chapter. In particular basic issues of symmetric and public-key cryptosystems are discussed, and major encryption techniques such as block ciphers and stream ciphers are introduced. Two representative cryptosystems, DES and RSA, are characterized.

Secure communication in a distributed system can be achieved through encrypting messages. This means that the sender and receiver have to be provided with matching keys. These keys must be produced and distributed securely. For this reason, key management problems and systems in symmetric and asymmetric cryptosystems are discussed. Finally, three communication security measures – link-oriented, end-to-end oriented, and association-oriented – are discussed.

Users communicating in a distributed system are suspicious of each other. There may also be intruders interested in masquerading as legitimate users to read information or submit false data. Countermeasures against these attacks can be provided by authenticating users. We discuss some elementary methods for message authentication. Authentication servers that allow the identification of communicating entities are briefly presented.

Finally, a summary of security services and mechanisms in distributed systems is given. This is followed by the presentation of secure communication protocols. In particular, the placement of security services in the ISO/OSI Reference Model and primitive security functions are discussed.

12.1 Basic problems of communication security

This section presents reasons for attacking distributed systems and lists security violations. Based on this, we discuss factors that make the application of security measures in a distributed environment so difficult. Next, we introduce a model (the association model) of an end-to-end data path through a distributed system. This model provides a context for the discussion of security threats to interprocess communication in distributed systems.

12.1.1 The factors complicating the application of security measures to distributed systems

There are a number of reasons for attacking distributed systems and breaching network security:

(1)   ease of sharing objects and the possibility of remote access to computer facilities;

(2)   the growing quantity and value of information transferred among connected computers, workstations, and servers; and

(3)   the development of new network technologies, which facilitates certain kinds of attacks on distributed systems.

An attacker (also called an intruder) may be either outside the user community, or a legitimate user of the distributed system. Such a person can perform the following security violations:

(1)   unauthorized release of information,

(2)   unauthorized modification of information,

(3)   unauthorized denial of resource use.

The distributed nature of a computer system and the classes of potential security violations create serious difficulties in applying security measures in distributed systems. A number of factors that complicate the application of security measures to a distributed environment have been identified. These factors are as follows (Andreasson *et al.* 1988):

(1)   Networks and computers connected to them are exposed to a large community of potential attackers. Users work at workstations or computers which can be located far from the location of their data. Processes which work on behalf of the users can run on remote computers. Thus, data has to be transferred among computers, workstations and servers. The problem is with authenticating all subjects, and controlling access to objects.

(2)   Networks, in general distributed computer systems, are dynamic. They are still evolving because of considerations of technological evolution, efficiency, throughput, error rates and economics. Distributed system security must fit into this framework.

(3)   Networks very often span administrative domains and tend to be administered hap-hazardly, if at all. This implies that objects on a network tend to be protected at the level of the least secure system in the distributed system.

(4)   Networks use different communications media. Some of them are susceptible to eavesdropping. The communications links are then regarded as open to passive line tapping and thus to the reading of data. Active line tapping is also possible and easy if some media are used. Encryption is used to protect information in transfer. However, this solution generates its own problem in the area of key administration.

(5)   Computer networks use a variety of communication protocols, which form different architectures. Security mechanisms must be embedded into the appropriate protocols and inserted into a

proper place in the architecture. The performance of the communications functions should not be adversely affected. However, differences among the architectures make it difficult to apply strong, network-wide security features.

(6)   The scope of a network grows erratically with new network connections: from as little as one user of a distributed system, to as much as a new network to further extend the existing distributed system. Such extensions together with weak administration can result in uncontrolled exposure.

There is also one philosophic problem. Whereas distributed systems foster general, flexible access giving a user great power, security seeks to impose limited access rules under rigidly-controlled conditions.

The types of measures provided for distributed computer system security vary widely, depending on the network environment. To select a proper security measure it is necessary first to evaluate the threat to communications in a distributed system, and then to select techniques appropriate for use in the given environment. These tasks should be performed using a proper model.

12.1.2   The association model

We consider here a connection between two processes, that is, a potentially bidirectional end-to-end data path through a distributed system. This connection is called an **association** (Kent [1981] and Voydock and Kent [1983]). The association model is illustrated in Fig. 12.1.

The model assumes that both ends of the association terminate in secure areas. However, the remainder of the association may be subject to physical attack. It is assumed that in this distributed system there is an intruder. This intruder is represented by a computer under hostile control, located in the communication path between the ends of the association. This implies that all messages must pass through the intruder.

It is important to notice that the association model is general enough in the context of network security to allow the discussion of se-

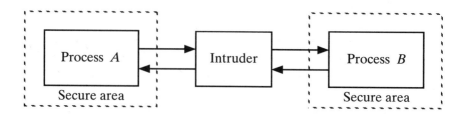

Fig. 12.1   The association model.

curity threats and countermeasures without regard to differences between connection and connectionless services.

12.2 Threats to interprocess communication in distributed computer systems

Before we discuss the threats to interprocess communication in distributed systems it is useful to analyse the possible locations of intruder attacks. We indicate the places at which an intruder can attack the security of a distributed systems in two figures.

Fig. 12.2 shows the physical path that messages travel between a user at a terminal, which is one end of the association, and the application program in a service host, which is the second end of the association.

As indicated by the arrows, an intruder attack can take place at any of the links on the message path. Moreover, any of the computers in the path can be the target of subversion carried out by the intruder. This can be achieved by modifying hardware or software, or by monitoring their electromagnetic emanations.

An intruder can attack communication media either passively or actively. Some media, because of their nature, are easy subjects for both types of attack (for example, telephone links). Other media can

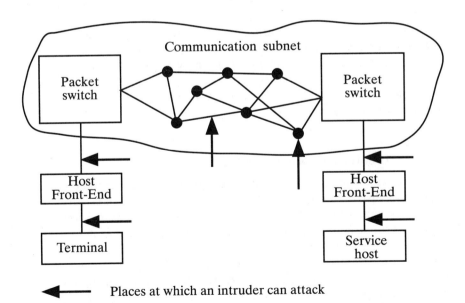

Places at which an intruder can attack

Fig. 12.2   Typical physical path of information transfer.

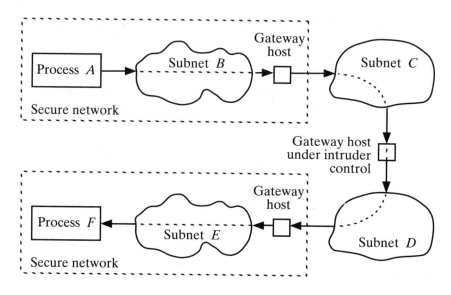

Fig. 12.3 Intruder in the internetwork environment.

only be attacked passively, because active attacks require expensive equipment and a high degree of technical sophistication. For example, satellite links can be intercepted very easily and with little risk to the intruder because satellite groundstation receivers are becoming very inexpensive, but actively interfering with data sent on satellite links is very difficult.

An intruder can also attack the security of a distributed system built from a set of secure and insecure networks connected by a gateway (an internetworking environment). This gateway provides the only communication path between processes executing in different secure environments. Since the gateway is in an insecure intermediate environment, the intruder can attempt to subvert it (Fig. 12.3).

12.2.1 Threats to network security

Interprocess communication threats are effected through unauthorized access to a distributed system. The locations at which such unauthorized access can take place have been identified in the previous section. To develop proper countermeasures against these threats it is necessary to identify and describe these threats.

There are several threats which take place when a distributed system is subject to the observation, modification, deletion, insertion, delay, recording, redirection, duplication or replay of messages travelling in the distributed system.

Passive attacks

In passive attacks an intruder observes messages containing application layer data which pass on a network, without interfering with their flow. There are two basic categories of passive attack: release of message contents, and traffic analysis.

(1) **Release of message contents** – A threat that occurs when the information contained in a message is leaked or stolen by some unauthorized agent or entity (for example, passive tapping of a communication channel). As a result, message contents can be released.

(2) **Traffic analysis** (called also *violations of transmission security*) – The unauthorized transfer of information by an entity (intruder) which observes when and where interprocess messages flow in a distributed system. The intruder can identify the location and identities of the communicating entities (processes). Moreover, he/ she can examine the length of messages and their frequency of transmission. For example, suppose an intruder observes messages transferred between two organizations and finds that some negotiations take place; if the intruder knows the topic these organizations are talking about, then traffic analysis may be of considerable value.

Active attacks

In the case of active attacks, the intruder performs a variety of processing on messages passing through the association. There are four basic categories of active attack: message stream modification, denial of message delivery, delay of message delivery, and masquerade.

(3) **Message stream modification** – This violation involves changing the message content when a message is transferred between two processes, and encompasses the replay, re-ordering, deletion and insertion of messages into an original message stream. Bogus messages can also be synthesized and inserted into the connection.

   In general, protocol control information (addresses) can be changed by the intruder, so that they can be sent to the wrong destination. The intruder can also change the data portion of a message, and can modify sequencing information. This means that message stream modification includes attacks on the authenticity, integrity and ordering of transferred messages.

(4) **Denial of message delivery** – This threat occurs when an intruder blocks message passing in an association between two communicating processes.

(5)   **Delay of message delivery** – This threat occurs when an intruder delays the delivery of message passing in an association between two communicating processes.

(6)   **Masquerade** – This comprises attacks in which an intruder establishes a connection between two processes under a false identity in such a way that one or both processes accept messages as if they were coming from a third process, or the intruder 'plays back' a recording of a previous legitimate association initiation sequence. Note that replay and insertion are the essence of masquerade.

A fundamental principle of security in an interprocess communication environment is the guaranteed identification of the sending process to the receiving process. The lack of such a guarantee leads to the threat of masquerade. Thus, if an intruder can perform operations in the distributed system in such a way that a receiving process can identify a message sent by the intruder as coming from another legitimate process, the intruder has successfully masqueraded as that legitimate process.

Countermeasures for the former attacks require secure identification of communicating entities. This issue interacts with authentication and security controls outside the association model. However, the identification problem must be dealt with from within the model. To fight the latter attack, it is necessary to include into the association initiation a mechanism that verifies the time integrity of the association.

12.2.2 Communication security goals

There are two main goals for the design of mechanisms to provide communication security:

(1)   prevention of passive attacks, such as release of message contents, and traffic analysis; and

(2)   detection of active attacks (spurious connection initiation or message stream modification, denial of message delivery, delay of message delivery and masquerade). Moreover, the communication security measures should not only detect active attacks, but also automatically recover from them if they are of a transient nature.

Encryption has been used as a countermeasure against passive attacks, thus addressing the release of message contents, and traffic analysis. Encryption, in conjunction with protocols, can also be used to achieve the second goal. In summary, the only way to provide security in distributed systems is by the application of cryptographic techniques.

12.3 Data encryption

Cryptography is the only known practical technique for guarding against security violations in network-based distributed systems. In addition, cryptography can be used for authentication, that is, for verifying the identity of the communicating principals to one another.

The primitive operation employed by cryptography is **encryption**. According to Seberry and Pieprzyk (1989) encryption is a special computation performed on messages, that converts them into a representation which has no meaning for any entities (processes) other than the designated receiver. Thus, some form of encryption is necessary for sending and storing data over communication media which are not secure. This implies that suitable encryption algorithms are a prerequisite to the development of secure network-based distributed systems.

Although the design and development of encryption algorithms are beyond the scope of this chapter, their critical importance to the development of all countermeasures to passive and active attacks in distributed systems means that an understanding of some basic characteristics of these algorithms is necessary.

12.3.1 Basic concepts of encryption

Encryption is a common safeguard for transmitting or storing data over media whose security cannot be guaranteed. It is associated with the transformation of an intelligible **message** (M) into an unintelligible form (C) with the help of a secret key (K_e), before putting it in the insecure medium. Thus, encryption is a mathematical function (encryption algorithm) with the following form

$$C = E(M, K_e) = E_{K_e}(M)$$

where E should be an easy-to-compute function. The keys should uniquely define the encrypted message, that is, $E_{K_1}(M) \neq E_{K_2}(M)$ if $K_1 \neq K_2$.

An encryption algorithm must have the property that the original data can be recovered from the encrypted data if the value of the key used is known. This means that there must exist a function D (decryption algorithm) such that

$$M = D(C, K_d) = D_{K_d}(C)$$

where K_d is a decryption key. Moreover, encryption and decryption algorithms must have the following property: $E_{K_e} - 1 = D_{K_d}$. This means that D is the inverse of E, that is, $D_{K_e}(C) = D_{K_d}[E_{K_e}(M)] = M$.

The input to the encryption algorithm, referred to as a **cipher**, is called the **message, cleartext** or **plaintext**, while the output from the algorithm is referred to as the **ciphertext** or **cryptogram**.

The keys must be kept secret and the ciphertext is 'compromised' if an intruder can deduce the key by analysing the information available ('public' information). The strength of a cryptosystem is measured by the level of difficulty (usually measured either by the time or number of elementary operations) of determining K_d, referred to also as resistance to attack. Attacks can be classified on the basis of the amount of public information available to an intruder:

(1) **Ciphertext-only attack** – The intruder has intercepted ciphertext material, or cipher (its structure), and has a general knowledge secondary information about the transmitted message (for example, statistical properties of the message source). A system whose security is not resistant to a ciphertext-only attack is considered inadequate or totally insecure.

(2) **Known-plaintext attack** – In addition to the information required for a **ciphertext-only** attack, the intruder has substantial amounts of plaintext and its corresponding ciphertext. A system which can resist a known-plaintext attack is considered to be secure.

(3) **Chosen-plaintext attack** – The intruder can see, in addition, ciphertext for any plaintext. Note that this attack is based on such favorable assumptions that compromisation under this attack does not indicate a realistic resistance of a security system. It is required by commercial and government agencies that the cryptosystem should be able to withstand a chosen plaintext attack.

Two very different notions of security against attack were considered. They imply the following systems:

(1) **Unconditionally secure** (or **theoretically secure**) – when K_d cannot be determined regardless of the available computer power; one of the results of Shannon's research was a very pessimistic conclusion that the amount of secret key needed to build a theoretically secure cipher is impractically large for most applications; and

(2) **Computationally secure** (or **practically secure**) – when determination of K_d is economically infeasible, in other words, compromisation of the system is beyond the economic means of any intruder.

It is important to notice that most practical ciphers must depend for their security not on the theoretical impossibility of their being broken, but on the practical difficulty of such breaking. (Note that federal agencies still seem to believe that hiding the algorithm is a good means of achieving security.) Following this we assume that the security of the system depends only on the secrecy of the keys and not on the secrecy of the encryption algorithm. Moreover, we assume that the cryptosystem used is computationally secure against a chosen plaintext attack, efficient and easy to use.

We have to emphasize here that cryptography provides security only in a probabilistic sense. The first reason for this statement is that all of the measures discussed in the previous section are based on the assumed inability of the intruder to subvert the encryption algorithm used in the attacked system. Second, even if the algorithm is not subverted, the measures used against active attacks are assumed to be infalliable, that is, active attacks will be detected with high probability.

12.3.2 Block and stream ciphers

There are two major classes of encryption techniques in use in distributed systems and computer applications: block ciphers and stream ciphers.

Block ciphers encrypt fixed-size blocks of bits under the control of a key that is often approximately the same size as the blocks being encrypted. The mapping must be one to one to make sure that each ciphertext block is unambiguously decipherable. Block ciphers are equivalent to classical simple substitution ciphers. This technique has one important disadvantage. The length of a message does not generally correspond to the block size of the cipher. Some means must be employed to resolve this mismatch. For example, the message may be fragmented into as many block-sized pieces as required, padding it to occupy an integral number of blocks. This padding implies wasting bandwidth and may also compromise security.

Stream ciphers perform bit-by-bit transformations on cleartext under the control of a stream of key bits, usually using some easily reversible operation (for example, addition modulo 2). Stream ciphers can operate on the stream of cleartext in real time. Each quantum of cleartext is enciphered as it is generated by combining it with a quantum from the key stream. The cipher used has an influence on the size of quanta precedent (commonly from 1 to 8 bits). Note that if the quantum size is chosen appropriately, stream ciphers provide a key stream that is exactly matched to the length of the message. As a result, the problem connected with padding cleartext to match block sizes is avoided.

Generally, it is easier to construct strong stream ciphers than strong block ciphers. However, strong stream ciphers are often constructed from strong block ciphers, because it is easier to implement and test block ciphers. The general approach to construction of a stream cipher using a block cipher is shown in Fig. 12.4. This approach is used in DES, presented in Section 12.3.3.

Stream ciphers have one very important feature – an error in a given block makes subsequent blocks undeciphereable. Block ciphers are thus usually preferred over stream ciphers.

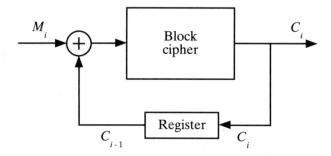

Fig. 12.4   Stream cipher based on a block cipher and ciphertext feedback.

12.3.3 Symmetric cryptosystems

A symmetric cryptosystem is a cryptosystem in which $K_e = K_d = K$, that is, either the same key is used at both ends of the channel or one key is easily derived from the other.

As a result, symmetric encryption requires a secure channel (low speed) by which the sender can inform the receiver of the key K used to encipher the message M. The encrypted message is transmitted through an insecure medium (high speed). This message is secure as long as the key is secret. This implies that the key is known only to authorized users. The symmetric cryptosystem is illustrated in Fig. 12.5.

The function f in symmetric encryption is designed to mask statistical properties of the cleartext. It should have two desirable characteris-

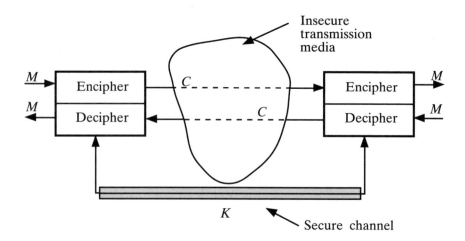

Fig. 12.5   Coventional cryptosystem.

tics from a protection point of view:

(1)   The probability of each symbol of the encrypted character set appearing in an encoded message E ideally is to be equal; and

(2)   The probability distribution of any pair of such characters is to be flat.

The difficulty of distributing keys has been one of the major limitations on the use of symmetric cryptographic systems. This implies that the communicating entities must be prepared to wait while the keys are being sent, or have made prior preparation for cryptographic communication.

The best known and most widely used symmetric cryptosystem is the Data Encryption Standard (DES), which was officially announced by the National Bureau of Standards in 1977 to be used by federal departments and agencies for protection of unclassified computer data. The algorithm was developed by IBM. It can be implemented as an LSI chip, which allows it to operate at a high data rate. The basic DES enciphering chain is illustrated in Fig. 12.6.

The DES is the example of a cipher designed in accordance with Shannon's diffusion and confusion principles (Shannon 1949). Diffusion means the spreading out of the influence of a single plaintext digit over many ciphertext digits so as to hide the statistical structure of the plaintext. Following this idea, the influence of a single key digit is spread over many digits of ciphertext. As a result, the difficulty of attacking the cipher is greatly complicated. Confusion means the use of enciphering transformations that complicate the determination of how the statistics of the ciphertext depend on the statistics of the plaintext.

The DES has several modes of operation, allowing its use as either a block or a stream cipher. In the most fundamental mode it is a block cipher operating on 64-bit blocks of plaintext, using a 56-bit key. Each block is independently enciphered, using transformation comprising 16 levels of substitutions and permutations. The input block – plaintext – is initially permuted by initial permutation IP: next it is subject to key-dependent computations, and finally is permuted again by the inverse of the initial permutation $IP = IP^{-1}$.

The same process is used when deciphering, except that the complex component is run backwards. Keys are used in reverse order. Details of the DES algorithm can be found in Diffie and Hellman (1979), Massey (1988) and Seberry and Pieprzyk (1989).

The DES is not universally regarded as a highly secure cryptosystem. In particular, there is a common concern that DES has too modest a key space (there are only 2^{56} keys) and therefore a brute-force attack on the system is possible. It has been suggested that a 128-bit key would

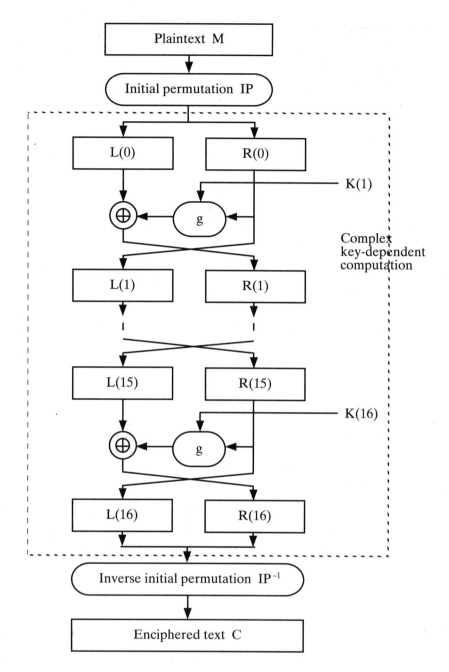

Fig. 12.6 DES enciphering chain.

make the DES virtually unbreakable (Denning and Denning [1979] and Brown [1987]).

12.3.4 Public-key encryption

A public-key cryptosystem was proposed by Diffie and Hellman (Diffie and Hellman 1976) as a variation of the conventional encryption that may, in some cases, have some advantages. In a public-key cryptosystem, the ability to encrypt messages under a given key is separated from the ability to decrypt those messages. This is a result of the most important feature of all public-key systems, which is that the key K_d used to decrypt a message is not equal to, and is impractical to derive from, the key K_e used to encrypt that message; in other words $K_e \neq K_d$.

In the public-key cryptosystem each user has a public key P which is published to everyone through a directory, and a secret key S which is not revealed to anyone. These keys define a pair of transformations, each of which is inverse of the other. The encryption algorithm need not be secret. Thus, both the public key and the encryption algorithm may be sent via insecure communication channels. This cryptosystem is called asymmetric, because different keys are used at the ends of the communication channel.

Communication between computers on the basis of the public-key cryptosystem is illustrated in Fig. 12.7.

In general, public-key encryption is more secure than symmetric encryption because no user need rely on the security of the computer network to safeguard his secret key, and public keys may be freely distributed without concern for secrecy.

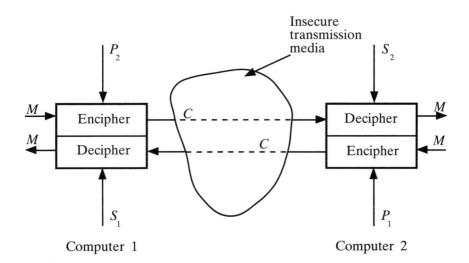

Fig. 12.7 Public-key cryptosystem.

However, although public-key encryption does not need a secure communication channel for key distribution, there is still a key authentication (management) problem. For example, an intruder, instead of trying to compute a secret key, can generate a new (P_i, S_i) and claim at the same time that the pair is genuine, and it has been created by the receiver. Now, if the sender uses the 'public' key P_i, the intruder can intercept and decrypt messages using the generated secret key S_i.

12.3.5   Rivest-Shamir-Adleman cryptosystem

The Rivest-Shamir-Adleman cryptosystem, referred also to as the RSA system, is the first published public-key cipher. It is based on the discrete logarithm problem and the factorization problem. This system is also a block cipher. It is a distinctive feature of the RSA system that messages, ciphertexts and keys (public and secret) belong to the set of integers. Suggested block sizes for the RSA system range from about 256 bits to 650 bits (80 to 200 decimal digits). Note that the block size should be approximately 320 to 380 bits to provide security comparable to the 56-bit DES key, assuming that DES keys can be recovered only via exhaustive search and RSA keys can be recovered via factoring.

The RSA system enciphers a message in the following way. The receiver generates a pair of keys (P, S) along with a pair of primes (p, q). It sends both the public key P and modulus of computation $N = p*q$ to the sender. The key S and the factorization of N remain secret and are known only to the receiver.

The sender enciphers a message M with P using the exponential function to produce a ciphertext

$$C = M^P (\bmod\ N)$$

and sends it to the receiver which is an owner of the public key.

The receiver deciphers the received ciphertext using the generated secret key S by applying exponentiation to retrive the original message,

$$M = C^S = (M^P)^S \bmod N$$

The last congruence is satisfied if $P * S = 1[\bmod\ \Phi(N)]$, where $\Phi(N)$ is the Euler function such that

$$\Phi(N) = \mathrm{lcm}(p - 1, q - 1),$$

where lcm stands for the least common multiplier.

It should be noticed that unlike the DES, there is no way of transforming the RSA system into a stream cipher while preserving the public-key characteristics of the system.

12.3.6 Limitations of encryption

Encryption can be used in many ways to protect information stored in or transmitted between entities in a distributed computer system. There are some practical limitations to the class of applications for which it is viable, however. These limitations are as follows.

(1) **Processing in cleartext** – Most operations performed on data require that the data be supplied in cleartext. This requires that cleartext data be protected.

(2) **Revocation** – Keys are similar to simple forms of capabilities and act as tickets. Holders may pass keys, just as capabilities may be passed. Selective revocation of access is a very complex problem, comparable with the complexity of revocation in protection systems. The only known method of revocation, that is, invalidation of all old keys, is to decrypt the data and re-encrypt with a different key. The problem is that this method is not selective.

(3) **Protection against modification** – It is very important to note that encryption does not provide any protection against inadvertent or intentional modification of data. Modification can be detected by including as part of the encrypted data a number of check bits. When decryption is performed, if those bits do not match the expected values, then the data are known to be invalid. In some cases when detection of modification is not enough protection (for example in large databases) error correcting codes could be applied to the data after encryption in order to provide redundancy. In some very special cases, when redundant data has been destroyed, it may be necessary to restore the data from archival records.

(4) **Key storage and management** – Key storage and management to protect a large number of long-lived data items separately is a formidable problem. Safe storage and archiving systems are essential.

   All participants in a secure network conversation must obtain matching keys to encrypt and decrypt the transmitted messages. A matching pair of keys forms an independent logical channel. It does not depend on other channels of the same type, and they are separated from channels created by network transmission protocols. Possession of the key admits one to the channel; it is unavailable if a user does not have a key. The problem is how to supply the keys necessary to create the corresponding necessary private channel.

Some of these problems are discussed in the following sections, to give the reader an idea of the power and weaknesses of encryption as a basic tool for developing countermeasures against passive and active attacks in distributed systems.

12.4 Key management in distributed systems

Secure communications in distributed systems can be achieved through encrypting messages. This requires that the sender and receiver of encrypted messages have to be provided with matching keys. These keys must be produced and distributed not just once, but continually. Only distributed systems in which information has a short lifetime (for example, computer control systems for military environments) are not in such a critical situation. In many systems, keys must be changed with the passage of time, or with the amount of traffic; in general, whenever communicating entities are feared compromised. Moreover, new users have to be provided with keys. On the other hand, when users withdraw, old keys must be retired. All these problems are the subject of key management.

The basic problem of key management is key distribution between communicating entities. This process should be carried out securely. There are two different approaches to key distribution. The first is used in systems based on symmetric cryptographic algorithms. It is called a conventional-key distribution. The second approach is associated with asymmetric cryptosystems.

12.4.1 Key distribution in symmetric cryptosystems

In a real distributed computer system key distribution has to be carried out using the same physical channels by which all exchanged data is transmitted. There is no special transmission medium for the key transfer. Thus, keys are sent in the form of cryptograms. Moreover, a user usually does not know in advance who will later want to communicate secretly with whom.

The usual solution to this key distribution problem is based on the **key distribution center** (KDC) which runs on a designated computer, or a set of computers. It is assumed that each user shares with the KDC a prearranged pair of unique keys. How keys are distributed, what can happen if a KDC crashes, and the like depend on the number of KDCs employed in a distributed system. Three forms of key distribution systems are possible: centralized key distribution, fully distributed key distribution and hierarchical key distribution.

Centralized key distribution
Centralized key distribution, the simplest form of key distribution, is based on a single KDC for the entire distributed system (network). This

means that the KDC for a system with n distinguished entities has to store n prearranged key pairs to provide secure communication. The price paid for this simplicity is reduced reliability. When the computer on which the KDC runs crashes or the network itself halts, it is impossible to establish any further secure communication. This drawback can be easily remedied by providing a redundant KDC. Such a center can be located on any computer which supports a secure operating system and provides appropriate key generation. Another drawback of the centralized key distribution is that the KDC can become a performance bottleneck.

A KDC operates in the following way. Suppose that a user A wants to securely communicate with user B. A and B each have a secret key, K_a and K_b, respectively, known only to themselves and the KDC. The messages involved in key distribution for this example are illustrated in Fig. 12.8.

The operations are as follows. To establish a secret channel, user A sends a request to the KDC in cleartext. The request contains the code for a request R_a and the identification name ID_a (message M1). In a response message (M2) encrypted with key K_a, the KDC sends to A

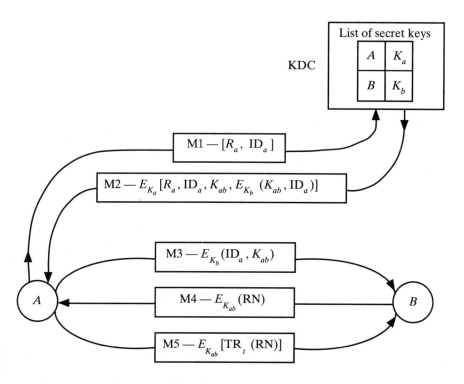

Fig. 12.8 A scheme for centralized key distribution.

the following information:

(1)   a copy of A's request, R_a;

(2)   the identification name of A, ID_a;

(3)   a key K_{ab} to be used to protect communications between users A and B;

(4)   a cryptogram of the pair (K_{ab}, ID_a) obtained for a key K_b shared between user B and the KDC, $E_{K_b}(K_{ab}, ID_a)$.

Thus, user A is the only one who can receive this information, and A knows that it is genuine. After receiving the message, A deciphers it and checks whether the name and the request copy match the originals. If so, user A sends the cryptogram $E_K(K_{ab}, ID_a)$ to user B (message M3). B deciphers the received cryptogram and retrieves both K_{ab} and the name ID_a. After this operation, both A and B have the same key K_{ab} which allows them to create a secure communication channel. First, to be sure that a received cryptogram was not a false one, user B initiates an authentication procedure. For this purpose, it sends A (message M4) a randomly chosen number RN encrypted under key K_{ab}, $EK_{ab}(RN)$. A decrypts the cryptogram and transforms RN by a previously-defined function $TR_t(RN)$, which depends on the time. This value is encrypted under K_{ab} and the obtained cryptogram is sent to user B (message M5). Now B knows that a secure channel can be created.

The performance of this exchange can be improved by avoiding two of the messages, and by storing frequently-used keys in cache memory.

Fully distributed key distribution

A fully distributed key distribution is based on the assumption that each host computer in a distributed system serves as a KDC for certain connections. These KDCs do not work independently; they cooperate during the process of deciding whether to allow the creation of a secure channel. However, if the users $A_1, A_2, ..., A_m$ of computers $C_1, C_2, ..., C_m$, respectively, intend to communicate securely, then only the KDCs that run on these computers have to be involved in the security decision making. This implies that each KDC must be able to communicate with all other KDCs in a secure manner. Thus, if a system has n computers, each of them keeps $n - 1$ keys which are used to communicate between KDC's. Thus $n*(n - 1)/2$ key pairs must be stored in a distributed system.

The decision making process is carried out in the following way. A user, who wants to communicate securely with another user, sends a request to the local KDC. The KDC chooses the key as in the case of the centralized key distribution, and distributes its decision to the other KDCs. Each KDC can decide whether the requested channel can be established and sends its decision to the originating KDC. The key is then distributed to the interested user if all the other KDCs accept the establishment of the channel.

The major advanatge of this approach is that the only nodes which must be properly functioning are those which support the intended user. Moreover, it permits each computer to use its own security policy if user software is forced by the local system architecture to use the network only through encrypted channels. If there is no possibility of using separate channels for host computer key distribution, a hierarchical key distribution system may be applied.

Hierarchical key distribution

As in the previous solution, KDCs run on their own computers. However, they are divided into the following three classes: local KDCs, regional KDCs and global KDCs. Hierarchical key control is distributed among these three classes of KDCs.

A local KDC is responsible for key distribution in its local environment, that is, those computers for which the pairs of keys have been prearranged. This implies that this local KDC can communicate securely with 'its' computers. KDCs situated within a region are subject to a corresponding regional KDC. Users who want to communicate securely within their local environment are served by their local KDC in the same way as by a centralized KDC. If they want to communicate with a user from another locale, their local KDC must send a secure request message to a regional KDC, using a prearranged channel. The regional KDC forwards the message to the appropriate local KDC which can communicate with the desired user. The same approach is used when a user wants to transfer a protected message to a user located in different region. At this stage a global KDC has to be involved in key distribution.

There are two advantages of hierarchical key distribution. The first is the limit it places on the combinatorics of key distribution. Each local KDC only has to prearrange channels for the potential users in its locale, whereas regional KDCs have to be able to communicate securely with local KDCs. The second is that local failures have only local consequences.

12.4.2   Key distribution in asymmetric cryptosystems

From the description of an asymmetric cryptosystem one might think that there is no need for key distribution. However, this is not correct. Indeed, any user can generate his/her own pair of keys and send a public key to another user via an insecure communication channel. Security of the secret key does not have to be compromised. Thus, there is no problem of key transmission via an insecure channel. However, a user who receives a public key wants to be sure that the cryptogram received is genuine. Thus, users must identify themselves using an authentication procedure.

An asymmetric cryptosystem needs a key distribution scheme for two other reasons. First, since the safety of the system depends critically on the correct public key being selected by a user, there must be an authority located in a separate place which maintains all public keys. Second, sometimes public keys must be changed, either because of the desire to replace a key which was used to send a large amount of data, or because a key has been compromised. Thus, the authority must be responsible for key change and distribution.

In the following presentation of a key distribution scheme in an asymmetric cryptosystem, we use Fig. 12.9, which shows the messages involved in such a scheme.

Assume that user A wants to talk securely to user B. Both users generated their key pairs (K_a, k_a) and (K_b, k_b), respectively. The secret keys k_a, and k_b are known exclusively to themselves. On the other hand, the public keys are known to the authority and stored in a key directory, KD. The KD has also a pair of keys (K_{kd}, k_{kd}). Public key K_{kd} is known to all users of a distributed system, whereas secret key k_{kd} is known only to the authority.

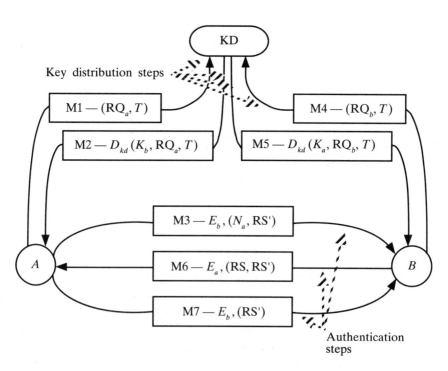

Fig. 12.9 A scheme for key distribution in an asymmetric cryptosystem.

User A begins by sending to the KD authority a timestamped message requesting secure communication with user B. (Using timestamps has also been proposed by Denning and Sacco (1981). Thus, a message contains a request RQ_a, and timestamp T (message M1). In response (message M2), the KD sends A a cryptogram (enciphered under the secret key of KD, k_{kd}) which contains the public key K_b of user B, a copy of the original request, and the timestamp. The KD encrypts this message only for authentication – everybody can read this message but nobody can change its contents. A decrypts the cryptogram using public key K_{kd}, and retrieves the contents. The timestamp is used for checking that it is not an old message, and that it contains B's current key. The copy of the original request allows users to verify that their original cleartext message were not altered.

User A now uses B's public key to send B a cryptogram $E_b(N_a,$ RS), where N_a is A's name and RS is a random sequence chosen by A (message M3). After deciphering the received cryptogram, user B knows that A wants to communicate securely. In order to get the authentic public key for user A, B sends to the KD timestamped message ($RQ_b,$ T') (message M4). The KD sends in response a cryptogram $D_{kd}(K_a, RQ_b,$ T'), which contains K_a, that is, the public key of user A (message M5). After deciphering the received cryptogram, B has the authentic public key of user A.

User B generates a new random sequence RS', creates a pair (RS, RS'), encrypts it under public key K_a of user A, and sends this cryptogram to user A (message M6). User A decrypts it using the personally owned secret key k_a and compares the original sequence RS with that received in the cryptogram. If these sequences are the same, A is sure that user B is authentic. Finally, A retransmits the random sequence RS' encrypted under K_b and sends it to user B (message M7). B decrypts $E_b(RS')$ and compares the received value of RS with the original one. If they are the same, B confirms the authenticity of A.

This scheme is based on seven messages, but four of them, those which retrieve the public keys, are not necessary when users use local cache memory to store their public keys. Thus, three messages are really needed. For other solutions to the authentication procedure the reader should consult also Meyer and Matyas (1982) and Davis and Price (1984).

12.4.3 Comparison between symmetric- and public-key distribution schemes

Both schemes presented require key distribution centers in order to establish a secure channel. Moreover, both schemes require the same amount of overhead to establish a connection (three messages). In general this amount is small in comparison to the number of messages for which such a connection will be used. These schemes can be modified to handle multiple users. However, the number of messages can be reduced to three by using caching.

It must be emphasized that the safety of these schemes depends only on the protection of secret keys in the symmetric cryptosystems and private keys in the public key cryptosystems. It is obvious that the KDCs in symmetric cryptosystems are very sensitive to illegal activities because all keys are stored there, and these keys are basic items of a security scheme. On the other hand, although public keys in asymmetric cryptosystems do not have to be protected, they are stored in an encrypted form, and can be obtained if a user knows the master key (K_{kd} in the above example). Thus, both schemes depend on upon the security of the secret key of the center.

In summary, both schemes used to support private communication are very similar.

12.5   Approaches to communication security

When dealing with communication security in a distributed system it is necessary to know to what extent we can provide security. This means that we have to identify communication security measures.

There are three basic approaches to communication security. They differ not only in their internal implementation characteristics, but also in the nature of the security they provide. These approaches are as follows:

(1)   **link-oriented** security measures, which provide security by protecting message traffic independently on each communication link;

(2)   **end-to-end** security measures, which provide uniform protection for each message all the way from its source to its destination;

(3)   **association-oriented** security measures, which are a refinement of **end-to-end** security measures.

These three measures are illustrated in Fig. 12.10.

12.5.1   Link-oriented security measures

Link-oriented security measures provide protection for all messages passing over an individual communication link between two nodes, regardless of the ultimate source and destination of the messages. Each of these links corresponds to a Data Link Layer of the ISO/OSI Reference Model. Usually, these links are not protected and thus are subject to

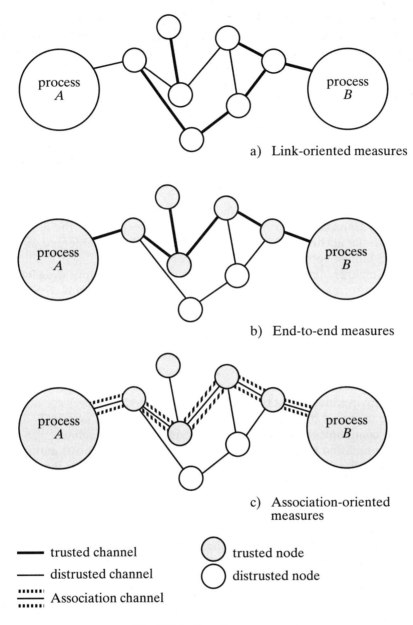

a) Link-oriented measures

b) End-to-end measures

c) Association-oriented measures

——— trusted channel ◯ trusted node

——— distrusted channel ◯ distrusted node

⋮⋮⋮ Association channel

Fig. 12.10 Security measures.

attack. We identified several possible links which can be the subject of attack in Fig. 12.2.

In computer networks which employ link-oriented measures, encryption can be performed independently on each communication link.

The protocol control information and the data can be encrypted. This implies that origin-destination patterns are masked. Message travel frequencies and length patterns can also be masked when a continuous stream of ciphertext bits is maintained between nodes. In this case all forms of traffic analysis are completely prevented. Moreover, using this technique does not degrade the effective bandwidth of the network because it does not usually require transmission of any additional information.

Note that a different encryption key can be used for each link, so that subversion of one link need not necessarily result in release of information transmitted on other links. Stream ciphers are generally used to encrypt the information.

Link-oriented protection measures have the advantage that they provide a transparent form of communication security for the hosts attached to the network. Thus, these measures can be implemented so that they are almost completely invisible to network users.

However, link-oriented measures suffer from some drawbacks. Because information is enciphered only on the links and not within the nodes they connect, the nodes themselves must be secure. Moreover, link-oriented encryption requires that all intermediate nodes must be physically secure. Subverting of one of the intermediate nodes exposes all of the message traffic passing through that node, despite any physical security precautions still in effect at the source and destination nodes. This means that link-oriented measures require that the entire open-system environment must be secure. Link-oriented measures are not applicable in packet broadcast networks, because there are no readily identifiable communication links within the communication subnet.

In addition to the initial costs of providing secure hosts and intermediate nodes, and the link-oriented measures, there is also the cost of maintaining the security of the nodes. This is another problem of link-oriented protection measures. Moreover, it is difficult to apportion the costs of link-oriented protection fairly. Note that some users of a distributed system may not want to rely for security services on the authorities controlling the communication subnet. This is especially true in an open-system environment, which is built of different networks usually controlled by diverse bodies.

For all of these reasons, link-oriented security measures do not appear to be appropriate as the basis for communication security in an open-system environment.

12.5.2 End-to-end measures

The goal of end-to-end measures is to protect messages in transit between source and destination nodes in such a way that subversion of any of their communication links does not violate security. The secure association is now a path between communicating processes. As we said before, link-oriented protection measures can be implemented so that they are almost completely invisible to network users. End-to-end measures usually extend beyond the communication subnet. Because of this they sometimes require a greater degree of standardization in the interfaces and protocols employed by those users.

The major advantage of end-to-end security measures is that an individual user or host can use them without affecting other users and hosts. This implies that the cost of using such security measures can be more accurately apportioned. Another advantage of these measures is that they can be used in packet-switched networks as well as in broadcast networks where link-oriented security measures are often not applicable. Finally, end-to-end measures are more naturally suited to users' perceptions of their security requirements because these measures rely on the security of equipment only at the source and destination of the association. In summary, end-to-end security measures are superior to link-oriented measures for an open-system environment.

12.5.3 Association-oriented measures

A communication network often provides its users with a medium for establishing virtual circuits (or connections) from source to destination. These were modelled in Section 12.1.2 as associations between communicating processes. This leads to the idea of providing security services oriented towards associations, and that each association is protected individually.

Association-oriented security measures constitute a refinement of end-to-end measures. Association-oriented security measures, as end-to-end measures, allow great flexibility in chosing the ends of associations for security purposes. They also significantly reduce the probability of undetected **cross-talk**. Such cross-talk can be induced either by hardware or software.

12.6 User authentication

In a distributed system, one user can send information to another user through a communication channel, which, unfortunately, may be under intruder control. Recalls that the intruder's activity can take different forms. In particular, the intruder can:

(1) record information and repeat it later during a spurious transmission session;

(2)   block an information flow;

(3)   change the information content (addresses, data); and

(4)   masquerade as the sender and insert a message synthesized by the intruder.

The communicating entities are interested in secure communications. The security of communication relies upon the communication entities having knowledge of each others' identities. Thus, the goal of message authentication is to detect attacks, by making it possible for the receiver to reliably determine the association to which a message belongs and the direction in which it is moving. In particular, the receiver wants to be able to determine that:

(1)   the message was sent by the genuine sender, and

(2)   the contents of the message were not changed when it was in transfer.

Moreover, the sender wants to know whether:

(1)   the message sent was received by the intended receiver, and

(2)   the contents of the message were changed.

This implies a need for the receiver to send acknowledgement messages. Again, the sender wants to know that the acknowledgement was sent by the intended receiver. Thus, the problem is with authenticity of messages, and indirectly with authenticity of communicating entities. In general, an authentication protocol must be used.

Authentication means verifying the identity of the communicating entities to one another in a secure manner. Simple extensions of methods for user identification by a centralized operating system are unacceptable. Each participant must send personal secret parameters (for example, password) and this operation give exposure to the receiver, which is a second participant and which can be an intruder.

In distributed systems all authentication schemes reduce to enabling each user to obtain or possess some information which makes it possible to identify the other. This information is secret; usually, encryption keys can be used for this purpose.

An authentication scheme must guarantee that if communicating entities really are who they say they are, then:

(1)   they will end up in possession of one or more secrets, or

(2)   they will become able to recognize the use of other entities' secret information.

If secret information is not yet known, one or both entities must obtain it from a place where it is held and easily accessible, for example, from an authentication server. This server also uses the authentication framework to meet its own needs for authentication, access control and other security services.

Authentication was mentioned in the section on key distribution schemes, as part of the process of establishing a secure channel. In this section we consider the authentication of each message received, and indirectly user authentication, because of fear of active attacks on transmitted messages.

There are different levels and types of authentication. In some environments it is enough to authenticate only the message, whereas in others there is the need for not only authentication but also for secrecy.

Different approaches may be used to protect against different threats, and may provide different levels of assurance. Note that the level of assurance needed depends on the 'cost' of undetected impersonation. These leads to two authentication methods:

(1) **simple** – based on simple password arrangements, and

(2) **strong** – based on cryptographic techniques.

In the second group one can identify the following authentication schemes:

(1) elementary authentication methods using both symmetric and public-key ciphers,

(2) authentication methods based on authentication servers,

(3) authentication methods based on subliminal channels, and

(4) authentication methods based on minimum (or zero) knowledge protocols.

Authentication methods can also be used for the generation of digital signatures. We discuss these five topics in the following subsections.

12.6.1 Simple authentication

A simple authentication method uses an authentication server, and relies on a user name and password. These two data items are transferred as cleartext. This method is illustrated in Fig. 12.11, and is performed in the following four steps.

(1) User A, who wants to communicate with user B, sends B a message M1 containing A's own user name and a password;

(2) User B sends the received name and password to the authentication server in message M2. The authentication server checks this password against that stored as an attribute within its entry for user A;

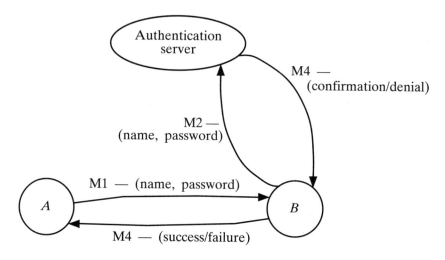

Fig. 12.11   A simple authentication.

(3)   The authentication server sends message M3 to user B confirming (or denying) the authenticity of user A;

(4)   User B sends message M4 to user A informing A of the success (or failure) of authentication.

Note that this authentication process is subject to passive as well as active attacks. All exchanged messages are sent in cleartext. Thus, an intruder can gather the information needed to subsequently masquerade as user A.

12.6.2   Elementary methods for user authentication

Assume that a message is sent on a communication channel and that its receiver wants to verify the authenticity of this message. The message authenticity in this case relies upon fixing the set of so called valid messages at both ends of the channel. This means that any message is said to be valid if it has a predetermined structure.

Elementary methods for message authentication can be based on either symmetric or public-key cryptosystems. Our description of these methods follows Seberry and Pieprzyk (1989).

Authentication based on symmetric cryptosystems

The concept of the elementary authentication scheme based on a symmetric cryptosystem is shown in Fig. 12.12.

Suppose that **M** is a set of all messages. The subset of M $\subseteq$ **M**, which is a set of valid messages, must be known to both communicating users. Security of valid messages, that is, those from set **M**, is not crucial.

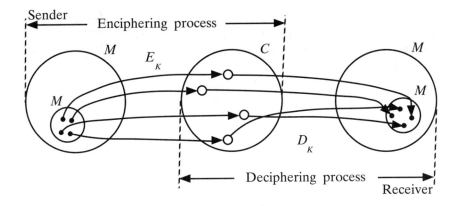

Fig. 12.12 The elementary authentication scheme based on a symmetric crypto-system.

Authentication is carried out in the following way. The sender, before sending message $M \in$ M, encrypts it under the key K, which is shared by both communicating entities. The receiver deciphers the received cryptogram $E_K(M)$ and checks the structure of the message obtained. If the message belongs to the set M, it is considered as genuine; otherwise is rejected. The correctness of the elementary scheme of message authentication relies on the secrecy of the key, and imposing a special message structure.

The latter requirement can be achieved for example in the following way. Suppose that M is a message whose authenticity is required. A pair (M, M_s) is created, where M_s is a subsidiary message. This pair now forms one message. The cryptogram $C = E_K(M, M_s)$ is sent to the second user. After decryption, the extracted part M_s is compared to the original M. If they are the same, M is said to be authentic.

This simple example shows the need for redundancy in the message source. Finally, the lack of secrecy means that authentication is impossible while using symmetric cryptosystems.

Authentication based on public-key cryptosystems
Public cryptosystems can also be used for message authentication if the sender generates the pair (K, k). The key k is kept secret, while the public key is sent via an insecure channel to the receiver (Fig. 12.13).

The receiver, after getting a cryptogram C, applies the public key K and retrieves message M. This message is said to be original. However, the following conditions must be fulfilled to assume that the authentication scheme works properly:

(1)   Generation of the pair of keys (K, k) must depend on calculation being in polynomial time.

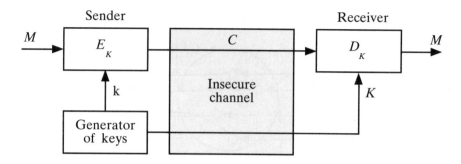

Fig. 12.13 The elementary authentication scheme based on a public-key crypto-system.

(2)   Calculations of both the cryptogram $C = E_K(M)$ and the message $M = D_E(C)$ must be easy, that is, they must run in polynomial time.

(3)   For a given pair <(a message and a suitable cryptogram), the public key K>, the computation of both the secret key k and the cryptogram for any different message must be intractable.

(4)   The public key K must be authentic, which means there must be a way to establish whether it has been generated by the sender.

The RSA system can be used for message authentication by shifting the key generator to the sender's computer. The RSA is the only public-key cryptosystem which can be used for both secrecy and authentication. Note that when the RSA system is used for authentication, the cryptogram C and the public key K are publicly known. Everybody can recreate a cleartext message. Thus, a public-key cryptosystem can provide secrecy or authentication. This implies that if one wants to have both, one has to use a public-key cryptosystem twice – once for secrecy and once for authentication.

The reader who wants to know more about public-key authentication schemes used for elementary authentication (such as those developed by Shamir, El Gamal and Rivest, Shamir and Adleman) should refer to Seberry and Pieprzyk (1989).

12.6.3   Authentication servers

The correctness of the elementary scheme of message authentication relies on the access and secrecy of the key: a secret key in the case of symmetric cryptosystems and a public key in the case of public-key cryptosystems. To achieve high performance in distributing and/or changing keys, key distribution centers (KDCs) are used. These centers are also called authentication centers (Birrell *et al.* 1986) or servers.

An authentication server is a server that can deliver identifying information computed from the requesting user's secret key. The main database for an authentication server is indexed by name. This implies that the management of authentication servers is related to the management of names. There could be either one central name registration authority, if a network is small, or multiple naming authorities in the case of an extended network. Each naming authority has to have an associated with it one or more name lookup servers and one or more authentication servers. The contents of these authentication servers are secret. It is generally agreed that a global authentication service, implemented as an authentication server, cannot be provided unless it is based on a global naming service.

Needham and Schroeder's authentication server utilizing symmetric keys

Needham and Schroeder (Needham and Schroeder 1978) proposed authentication protocols based on both symmetric keys and public keys. Their authentication servers perform strikingly similar functions to key distribution systems, symmetric and public-key, described in Sections 12.4.1 and 12.4.2, respectively.

If an authentication server uses a symmetric cryptosystem, then each communicating entity has a secret key, which is known to itself and the authentication server.

Setting up secure communication between two users, A and B, where A is an initiator, requires the generation of a message with two properties:

(1)   it must be comprehensible only to B, which means only B can use its contents for personal identification to A, and

(2)   it must be evident to B that it originated with A.

The authentication process using symmetric keys is illustrated in Fig. 12.14, and is performed in the following steps.

(1)   User A sends to the authentication server message M1 in clear-text, which contains the user's claimed identity, identity of user B, and a 'used only once' (called here a nonce) transaction identifier TI_a, that is, this message is of the form $\{A, B, TI_a\}$;

(2)   After receiving message M1, the authentication server looks up the secret identifying keys of both users, K_a and K_b, and computes a new key K_{ab} which will be used for conversation between A and B. Next it sends message M2 to user A. Message M2 is encrypted with A's secret key, K_a, and has the form $\{TI_a, B, K_{ab}, \{K_{ab}, A\}_{K_b}\}_{K_a}$;

(3)   After receiving this cryptogram, A decrypts it with its secret key, K_a, and finds key K_{ab}. If the decrypted message contains the in-

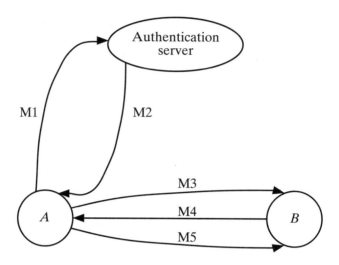

Fig. 12.14   Authentication using the Needham and Schroeder protocol with symmetric keys.

tended recipient's name, B, and the correct identifier, TI_a, user A sends to B message M3 which contains part of M2, encrypted with K_b, that is, message M3 has the form $\{K_{ab}, A\}_{K_b}$.

(4)   Only the genuine B, after receiving message M3, is able to decrypt it, and extract the conversation key K_{ab}. Both users now have the same conversation key; they also know that any communication received which is encrypted with K_{ab} must be originated by the second entity, and that any message sent with K_{ab} encryption will be understood only by the second entity. Moreover, B knows the identity of user A; it was authenticated by the authentication server.

(5) A and B are now in different positions regarding the utilization of the K_{ab} key before the current conversation. A is aware that this key was not used before; it is sure that any message encrypted with K_{ab} is legitimate. B is not in such a fortunate situation. Unless B remembers all keys previously used by A, B could suppose that this key is replayed. To guard against this possibility, B generates a nonce identifier for the transaction, TI_b, and sends it to A, as an encrypted message M4 under K_{ab}, that is, $\{TI_b\}K_{ab}$. B expects a reply, for example one less than TI_b to be sent.

(6) A, after receiving M4, calculates a new value, and sends to B message M5 of the form $\{TI_b - 1\}_{K_{ab}}$. This is sufficient to achieve mutual confidence and allows regular communication to start.

Note that this protocol requires five messages. This number can be reduced to three by keeping by each entity for regular partners, a cache with the following items: $K_{ab}, \{K_{ab}, A\}_{K_b}$.

Needham and Schroeder's authentication server utilizing asymmetric keys

Nedham and Schroeder also proposed an authentication protocol based on public keys. This protocol allows two entities to exchange two independent, secret keys. The authentication process is illustrated in Fig. 12.15.

Authentication using asymmetric keys is performed in the following steps.

(1) User A sends to the authentication server message M1 in cleartext, which contains the user's claimed identity, and identity of user B, to find user B's public key, that is, $\{A, B\}$.

(2) The authentication server sends in response to A message M2 of the form $\{PK_a, B\}_{SK_s}$, where PK_a and SK_s are the public key of user A and secret key of the authentication server, respectively. User A must obtain and store the public key PK_s of the authentication server. Thus, the received message M2 can be decrypted. If an intruder can provide an arbitrary value that is treated by A as PK_s, then the intruder can masquerade as the authentication server. It is important to notice that message M2 is encrypted to ensure its integrity, not to ensure secrecy.

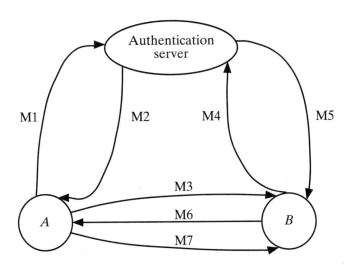

Fig. 12.15 Authentication using the Needham and Schroeder protocol with asymmetric keys.

(3)   *A* initiates communication with user *B* by sending message M3 of the form $\{I_a, A\}_{PK_b}$. It says that someone calling itself *A* wishes to establish communication, and sends secretly the nonce identifier I_a.

(4)   User *B* finds PK_a by sending to the authentication server message M4 in cleartext of the form $\{B, A\}$.

(5)   The authentication server sends in response to *B* message M5 of the form $\{PK_a, A\}SK_s$. This message, like message M2, is encrypted for integrity.

(6)   To start regular communication, a double handshake is needed to authenticate *A* and *B* to one another and to establish the time integrity for that regular communication. For this purpose *B* sends to *A* message M6 of the form $\{I_a, I_b\}_{PK_a}$, and *A* responds by sending message M7 of the form $\{J_b\}_{PK_b}$.

Note that this protocol requires seven messages (the protocol with symmetric keys requires only five messages). This number can be reduced to three messages if users store commonly used public keys. In this case messages M1, M2, M3, and M5 are not sent.

Birrell's authentication service

An authentication service developed by Birrell and his co-workers (Birrell *et al.* 1986) was part of a design for a global name service. In their authentication server there is no global trust. Moreover, only symmetric cryptosystems are considered.

The name service is based on a hierarchical name space, which is formed of directories. Directories are connected into a tree structure with a single, global root (as in the UNIX operating system). Each directory provides multiple mutable mappings from a 'simple-name', denoted usually by a character string, to a set of values.

The name service possesses the following features. Each directory may be replicated, and each replica is maintained by a name server. Each name server maintains some set of directory replicas. Moreover, each directory in the name service is permanently and uniquely identified by a UID (Unique Identifier). Thus, a name presented to the name service consists of the identifier of some directory (referred to as the root of the name), and a path from that directory. Such a path consists of a sequence of simple names for the directories that form the path.

Note that this name service can be used for authentication straightforwardly when the name service is uniformly trusted. Authentication protocols for such a case have been published in Bauer *et al.* (1983), Denning and Sacco (1981), Needham and Schroeder (1978) and Voydock and Kent (1983). The authentication service described here does not fulfil this requirement – there is no global trust.

The basic element of an authentication service is a set of **secure channels** which are provided by the name service. A secure channel is established when a pair of users share a key. Thus, users who want to communicate secretely via a secure channel have first to get a key. On the other hand, each user registered in the name service has a secure channel to each personal directory. This channel is based on the user's personal secret key, which is stored by itself and also stored in the user's directory entry. Thus, there is one-to-one correspondence between users and directory entries.

Directories are also associated. Each directory has a secure channel to the directory's parent, which is formed in the same way as a channel between a user and its directory. Thus, a directory, in this respect, behaves just as any other user.

Let us assume that at some stage two users, A and B, possess the key K_{ab}, which forms secure channel between them. The problem is to what extent can user A trust a channel (in practice the key K_{ab}) received from another source, AC. User A should trust the channel only as much as it trusts AC. The following statement (originally in the form of lemma) plays an important role in the authentication service.

If A receives a message M along a secure channel, then A should believe the message, subject to trusting the user at the other end of the channel, that is, B, and the source who gave A the channel, that is AC.

The authentication scheme is based on this statement and the algorithm, referred to as the forwarding algorithm, which allows us to compose secure channels to form a new secure channel. For example, if we have two secure channels, the first from A to B, and the second from B to C, than we can construct the third channel from A to C, subject to trusting B.

In summary, the most distinctive feature of the authenticating scheme developed by Birrell and his co-workers is that it ensures that each entity to the authentication knows who is being trusted, and that it is possible to achieve two-way authentication without trusting the entire global authentication service.

12.6.4 Authentication based on minimum (or zero) knowledge protocols

All the authentication approaches we have discussed are based on the identification of originality of transmitted messages. Proving that a message is original also shows that the sender knows the correct secret keys, confirming to the receiver that the sender is genuine. The distinctive feature of these approaches is that parties identifying themselves have to reveal their knowledge.

However, in some circumstances we are interested in verifying a sender's knowledge rather than in direct user authentication. In other words, we want communicating parties to prove their identity by demonstrating their knowledge, but without revealing that knowledge. Zero-knowledge protocols are an effective and elegant technique which allow proof of identity based on a limited amount of information transferred from a prover A to a verifier B. There are two basic classes of these protocols. To the first class belong schemes that require a minimum amount of knowledge to be revealed (Goldwasser *et al.* 1985). To the second class belong those schemes which allow the identification of process to be carried out without revealing any knowledge (Feige *et al.* 1988). The basic idea of these schemes is to replace 'knowledge' by 'knowledge about knowledge'. Thus, the goal of a user is not to prove that it possesses the knowledge of the secret information by sending a message, but to demostrate that it has the necessary knowledge to solve a given problem in a short time.

Authentication based on minimum knowledge concepts has been proposed and developed in the Kerberos system (Steiner *et al.* 1988). This system is used by the Athena's file system to authenticate users. Users prove their identity not by sending keys (secret information) over a network, but by answering encrypted challenges (questions) from a server. Of course, the server knows the shared secret. In particular, the server, after receiving a request (message M1), encrypts a challenge (question) C with the shared secret key K and transmits it to the client which requested a service (message M2). The client receives the challenge, decrypts it, answers the challenge, say $f(C)$, and sends an encrypted response to the server (message M3). The client is served if the challenge response is correct. Note that the challenge is never repeated. This authentication process is illustrated in Fig. 12.16.

The reader interested in authentication based on minimum (or zero) knowledge protocols should refer to such works as Goldwasser *et al.* (1985), Chaum (1987) and Feige *et al.* (1988).

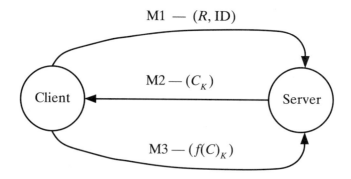

Fig. 12.16   Authentication based on minimum knowledge protocol.

12.6.5 Digital signatures

In some circumstances (military orders, bank transactions, contract negotiations), the author of a digitally represented message wants to sign it in such a way that the signature has properties similar to an analog signature written on a hard copy. Popek and Kline (Popek and Kline 1979) list the following properties of a digital signature:

(1) **Unique** – Only the author should be able to create the signature.

(2) **Unforgeability** – Generation of authentic signatures by persons, who want to forge signatures, should be impossible; if an intruder tries to forge signatures, that intruder must face intractable computational problems.

(3) **Authenticity** – There must be a way to demonstrate conclusively the validity of a signature in case of dispute, even long after authorship.

(4) **No repudiation** – It must not be possible for the author of signed correspondence to subsequently disclaim authorship.

(5) **Low cost and high convenience** – Low cost and simple methods are prefered.

The generation of signatures should be such as to allow any dispute as to the authenticity of signed messages (documents) to be unambiguously resolved. Taking this into consideration, authentication methods can be divided into the following two classes:

(1) methods of direct signature authentication – applied only by receivers, and

(2) methods of indirect signature authentication – in addition to the senders and receivers, there are third parties who can solve possible disputes.

Different methods of signature generation which belong to the above classes have been developed, based on both symmetric and public-key cryptosystems. For further information see Popek and Kline (1979) and Seberry and Pieprzyk (1989).

Note that digital signatures can also function as message authentication codes – successful decryption shows both the authenticity of the sender and that the message was not interferred with in transit. Thus, digital signatures are applicable to both communication security and user authentication.

12.7 Security services and mechanisms in distributed systems

In previous sections we have discussed basic aspects of security in distributed systems. We have considered threats, classification of attacks and approaches to communication security. We also discussed some basic concepts of data encryption that can be used to construct countermeasures against communication threats. In particular, we discussed classes of cryptosystems, major encryption techniques, some encryption algorithms for both symmetric and public-key cryptosystems, selected aspects of key management, (or key distribution,) and authentication schemes.

We have seen that there are three basic types of security measures in distributed computer systems: link-oriented, end-to-end, and association-oriented. Each of these depends on security protocols. Since communication protocols are the subject of standardization, these security protocols should be seen in the context of a standard network architecture. The ISO/OSI Reference Model was described in Chapter 2 as a basic standard network protocol architecture.

In this section, to summarize all these aspects and to create a background for the discussion of encryption protocols, we present how, where, and what security services and security mechanisms should be considered in distributed systems.

12.7.1 Security services

In the Trusted Computer System Evaluation Criteria (TCSEC) published by the National Computer Security Center (NCSC) and the OSI Secure Protocol Reference Model drafted by the ISO, the following security services are recommended (Abrams and Jeng, 1987).

Identification
Peer entities must be identified. Each access to a Protocol Data Unit (PDU), that is, a message at a given layer of the protocol architecture, must be mediated, based on the entity's identity and on the classes of information that the entity is authorized to deal with.

Peer entity identification
It is the task of the network to ensure that a data exchange is established with the addressed peer entity and not with an intruder who attempts to masquerade or replay a previous exchange. Moreover, the network must ensure that the sender of data is the one claimed (data origin authentication).

Peer entity authentication is an appropriate measure against attempts to create a session under a false identity. This authentication can also be used to protect against playing back a previous legitimate session initiation sequence. Playback attacks can be discovered by verifying that a session initiation is being attempted in real time.

Peer entity authentication generally follows identification, that is, establishing the validity of the claimed identity. Identification, authentication, and authorization information (for example, passwords) must be protected by the network.

Access control

This security service provides against unauthorized use of resources accessible via the ISO/OSI. As such it is closely associated with resource protection, discussed in the previous chapter. Access control requires a set of rules that are used by the system to determine whether a given entity has rights to access specific distributed system resources (for example, communication resources, information, processing resources). The rules may specify both discretionary and non-discretionary access control. Thus, it is possible to effectively protect sensitive or classified information.

Discretionary access control According to the TCSEC, discretionary access control is a means of restricting access to resources based on the identity of entities and/or groups to which they belong. The ISO/OSI security addendum (discussed further in Section 12.8) uses the term identity-based security policy to refer to discretionary access control.

Non-discretionary access control According to the TCSEC, non-discretionary access control is a means of restricting access to resources based on the sensitivity (as represented by a label) of the information contained in the resources and the formal authorization (clearance) of entities to access information of such sensitivity.

Marking Access control labels must be associated with protocol-data-units (messages) and network entities. Thus, it must be possible to mark every PDU with a label that reliably identifies its sensitivity level.

Since resource protection was discussed in detail in Chapter 11 we do not discuss access control any further in this chapter.

Data confidentiality

This service provides for the protection of data from unauthorized disclosure, in particular, the release of message contents and analysis of traffic. The release of message contents can be prevented by applying encryption mechanisms. The problem is at what layer this service should be provided. We are interested in communicating entities and in end-to-end measures; the Transport Layer is the lowest layer with end-to-end significance. Key distribution must also be considered. The granularity of key distribution is a tradeoff between convenience and protection. The finest granularity employs a unique key for each session; the coarsest granularity employs the same key for all sessions during a time period.

Traffic flow security is concerned with masking the frequency, length and sender-destination patterns of communications between entities, that is, protection of the information that might be derived from observation of traffic flows. Encryption can be used to restrict disclosure above the Transport Layer. However, host computers are not concealed.

Confidentiality has the following features:

(1) confidentiality of all user-data on a specific protocol layer connection,

(2) confidentiality of all user-data in a single connectionless datagram,

(3) confidentiality of selected fields within the user-data of a PDU (message), and

(4) traffic flow security.

Communication integrity

This service provides protection of data against active attacks such as modification, insertion, deletion or replay of data. Communication protocols offer some protection against these attacks as part of their reliability features. However, they are not designed to counter hostile attacks.

To act against these attacks, it is necessary first to develop systems that allow the detection of message stream modification. This detection is hierarchically organized into integrity, ordering and authenticity. Integrity mechanisms use cryptography. Countermeasures for authenticity are based on uniquely identifying a session and its PDUs. The following approaches are also employed: selection of a unique key for each session, proper selection of an initialization vector in encrypting each end-to-end data path, and addition of protocol fields. Message-ordering countermeasures are developed using a unique sequence number and session identification protocol field. The Transport Layer and its protocols are the best place for countermeasures against message stream modification.

A communications integrity service must detect integrity violations. It may work at any of the following levels:

(1) integrity of a single connectionless PDU; this allows one to determine whether a received message has been modified;

(2) integrity of selected fields within a single connectionless PDU;

(3) integrity of selected fields transferred over a connection; this allows the determination of whether the selected fields have been modified, inserted, deleted or replayed;

(4) integrity of all user-data on a protocol layer connection; this allows the determination of whether any PDU of an entire PDU

sequence has been modified, inserted, deleted or replayed, but with no recovery attempted; and

(5) integrity of all user-data on a protocol layer connection, but with recovery.

Service availability

This service must provide protection against denial of communications service, in the form of blocking or drastically delaying messages. A countermeasure is based on active verification that a communication path is not under attack. Availability services may include:

(1) detection of conditions that would degrade service below a specified minimum, and reporting of this fact;

(2) service continuity in the event of equipment failure and actions by persons and processes not authorized to alter the data; and

(3) detection of conditions that would degrade service below a specified minimum, reporting this fact, and automatic adaptation.

Non-repudiation

This service is closely associated with service availability. Non-repudiation prevents the sender from disavowing a legitimate message or the receiver from denying reception of a message. Thus, the system must provide either or both of the following:

(1) the receiver is provided with proof of origin of data; thus, will prevent any attempt by the sender to falsely deny sending the message or its contents; and

(2) the sender is provided with proof of delivery of data; thus, will prevent any attempt by the receiver to falsely deny receiving the message or its contents.

Accountability

Detection of attacks and provision of countermeasures are one side of a coin. Another is intruder hunting. Thus, audit information must be selectively kept and protected, so that actions affecting security can be traced to the responsible intruder.

12.7.2 Security mechanisms

The first stage in designing a security system for a distributed computer system is to select the security services that will be provided. The second stage is to select mechanisms to implement these services. The ISO/OSI security addendum gives the security mechanisms, which are presented in List 12.1.

1. **Encryption** – based on encryption algorithms;
   - Link encryption
   - End-to-end encryption
   - Symmetric cryptosystems
   - Public-key cryptosystems
   - Key management

2. **Digital signature** – requires two procedures: signing the data unit, and verifying a signed data unit;

3. **Access control** – based on the identity of an entity to determine its access rights;
   - Access control lists
   - Passwords
   - Capability lists
   - Credentials
   - Labels

4. **Data integrity** – requires the sender to append to a data unit additional information which is a function of the data itself;
   - Checksums, for example, a block check code, or a cryptographic checkvalue, which may be encrypted
   - Sequencing and/or timestamping

5. **Authentication** – proves the identity of the entity;
   - Cryptographic means
   - Passwords

6. **Traffic padding** – to provide various levels of protection against traffic analysis;

7. **Routing control** – by which routes are chosen dynamically or statically so as to use only physically secure networks, links, etc.;

8. **Notarization** – gives assurance of some properties of the data communicated such as its origin, integrity, time, and destination; this mechanism is provided by a third party notary which is trusted by communicating entities.

List 12.1   List of service mechanisms.

Table 12.1 Relationship between security services and mechanisms {adapted from (Buffenoir 1988)}.

Service	Security mechanism							
	1	2	3	4	5	6	7	8
Peer entity authentication	C	B	n	n	Y	n	n	n
Data origin authentication	C	B	n	n	n	n	n	n
Access control service	C	n	Y	n	n	n	n	n
Confidentiality	Y	n	n	n	n	n	Y	n
Traffic flow confidentiality	A	n	n	n	n	A	Y	n
Data integrity	C	B	n	Y	n	n	n	n
Non-repudiation	C	Y	n	A	n	n	n	A

Y — mechanism is adequate
n — mechanism is not appropriate
A — to be used simultaneously for providing a service
B — mechanism which provides more than what is necessary
C — mechanism which can be used in conjunction with another to provide a service

The relationship between security services and mechanisms is shown in Table 12.1. In this table mechanism numbers represent the numbers used in List 12.1.

With this general presentation of security services and mechanisms behind us, we can now discuss security protocols and their placement in the ISO/OSI architecture.

12.8 Secure communication protocols

As we emphasized in Chapter 2, network communication protocols have a large influence on the flexibility and bandwidth provided by a network. In this chapter we have seen that encryption facilities provide a potentially large set of secure (logical) channels, which are managed by encryption protocols. Thus, the secure communications protocols (also called encryption protocols) also have significant impact on distributed system architecture and performance.

Any encryption protocol must answer the following questions:

(1) How is the channel established from the sender (encrypter of a cleartext message) through the insecure communication channel, to the receiver (decrypter of the cryptogram) and back?

(2) How are message addresses passed by the sender around the encryption facilities to the network without providing a path by which message data can be inadvertently or intentionally leaked by the same means?

(3) What facilities are provided for error recovery and resynchronization of the protocol?

(4) How is a security channel closed?

(5) What is the interaction between the encryption protocol and the network protocol?

(6) How is the encryption protocol to be implemented; in particular, how much software is needed to implement it? What is the influence of this software on the network security?

Communication channels and security channels can be managed independently. This implies that many of the communication oriented questions can be ignored by the encryption facilities. The next step is to consider the relationship between these two classes of protocols, and present some distinct features of the encryption protocols. The discussion is based on the ISO/OSI Architecture.

12.8.1 Placement of security services in the ISO/OSI Model

A proposed security addendum to the OSI architecture has been prepared by the Ad Hoc groups of the American National Standards Institute (ANSI) and the International Standards Organization. The security services that may be located in the ISO/OSI Model are listed in Table 12.2.

The ISO 7498–2 standard security services listed in the table can be described in the following way (Barker and Nelson 1988):

- **Data origin (connectionless oriented) authentication** confirms source (sender) of data;

- **Peer entity (connection oriented) authentication** confirms identity of entities (sender, receiver) at the time of usage; it protects against masquerades and replay of previous messages;

- **Access control** prevents unauthorized use of resources (for example, communications resources, reading, writing or deletion of information, and execution of processing resources) accessible via the OSI architecture;

Table 12.2 The placement of the security services in the ISO/OSI Model {adapted from (Buffenoir 1988)}.

OSI Layer							Service
1	2	3	4	5	6	7	
		X X	X X			X X	1. IDENTIFICATION/AUTHENTICATION - Data origin (Connectionless) - Peer entity (Connection)
		X X	X X			X X	2. ACCESS CONTROL - User agent authorization - Peer entity authorization
		X X X	X X X			X X X X	3. INTEGRITY - Connection integrity with recovery - Connection integrity without recovery - Selective field connections integrity - Connectionless integrity
X X	X X	X X X	X X			X X X X	4. CONFIDENTIALITY - Connection - Connectionless - Selective field - Traffic flow
						X X	5. NON-REPUDIATION - Originator - Recipient

- **Connection integrity (with and without error recovery)** detects modification, insertion, deletion or replay of data within a sequence, that is, the service protects data against active threats in connection-oriented systems;

- **Selective field connectionless integrity** provides integrity within selective fields within a single message; that is, the service protects some fields of the data message against active threats in connectionless systems;

- **Connectionless integrity** provides integrity within a single message; that is, the service protects data against active threats in connectionless systems;

- **Connection confidentiality** protects all user data on a connection from disclosure;

- **Connectionless confidentiality** protects user data within a message from disclosure;

- **Selective field confidentiality** protects selected fields of user data within a message or within a connection from disclosure;

- **Non-repudiation with proof of origin** the receiver is provided with proof of the origin of data; it protects against any attempt by the sender to falsely deny sending the data or its contents;

- **Non-repudiation with proof of delivery** the sender is provided with proof of delivery of data; it protects against any subsequent attempt by the receiver to falsely deny receiving the data or its contents.

This set of services provides countermeasures against passive and active attacks such as masquerade, replay, modification and denial of service in distributed systems.

Although this table defines a number of security services and their placement in the OSI architecture, the addendum is not adequate for an implementation, for three reasons. First, it would be too expensive to provide all security services at all layers as specified in Table 12.1. Second, if one implementing body chose to implement a service at one layer and another body chose to implement the same service at at a different layer, then there is no compatibility between peer layers of the OSI Model. Third, standards for implementing the security services are not yet fully specified.

The following steps should be taken when selecting the layer(s) for implementing selected security services:

(1)   choose a basic set of security services to be implemented;

(2)   choose a minimum number of layers in which these services will be implemented;

(3)   select the ISO/OSI layers in which the chosen security services will be implemented.

When carrying out this process the following factors must be taken into consideration:

(1)   The number of layers affected by security should be minimized;

(2)   The communication services provided by the chosen communication layer extended by adding the security service, should be compatible with communication services provided before the extension;

(3)   The overall cost of providing the chosen security services is minimized.

12.8.2 Primitive security functions

Branstad (Branstad 1987) proposes to use some primitive functions to implement ISO/OSI security services. These functions are defined in List 12.2 (the set of calling parameters are in square brackets, and the results returnd after listed are enclosed in curly brackets.

authenticate [id; authenticator] {result; status}
verifies that the authenticator does correspond with the claimed id by searching the local Secure Management Information Base and responding with the correct result and status.

authorize [id; type; resource] {result; status}
verifies the authorization of id with the indicated type for access to the requested resource and sets the correct result and status.

encipher [pt; length; keyname] {ct; length; status}
encrypts a message beginning at pt for the indicated length into cryptogram beginning at ct for the indicated length, using the key associated with keyname, and sets the resulting status.

decipher [ct; length; keyname] {pt; length; status}
decrypts a cryptogram beginning at ct for the indicated length into message beginning at pt for the indicated length, using the key associated with keyname, and sets the resulting status.

computemac [data; length; keyname] {mac; status}
computes a Message Authentication Code (mac) on the data of indicated length, using the key associated with keyname, and sets the resulting status.

verifymac [data; length; userid; keyname; mac] {result}
computes a Test Message Authentication Code (tmac) on the data of indicated length, using the key associated with keyname, and sets the correct result to indicate if tmac is identical with the input mac.

sign [data; length; userid; keyname] {signature; status}
computes a signature on the data of indicated length for the user indicated by userid, using the key associated with keyname, and sets the resulting status.

verifysignature [data; length; userid; keyname; signature] {result; status}
computes a Test Signature (signature) on the data of indicated length for the user indicated by userid, using the key associated with keyname, compares it with signature, and sets the correct result and status.

List 12.2 Primitive functions to implement ISO/OSI security services {adapted from (Branstad 1986)}.

12.8.3 The status of standardization

Successful implementation of computer communications depends on standardization. This is also true of secure protocols. The status of standardization of secure protocols is as follows:

(1) Some propretiary or nationally standardized systems have been implemented, mainly for transaction and point-of-sale systems [AS–2805.1/4];

(2) CCITT and ISO have published recommendations regarding Message Handling Systems [CCITT 1986], [ISO–8502–2]. These recommendations specify procedures for authentication, confidentiality, and key distribution and management.

(3) Research is in progress on secure protocols for the future Integrated Services Digital Network [Presttun 1987].

The state of standardization in the area of the ISO/OSI Architecture is as follows:

(1) **The Physical Layer** – A Draft International Standard [DIS–9160] has been published.

(2) **The Network Layer** – A working document [WG3/N152] has been prepared and will be forwarded as a DIS in 1990.

(3) **The Transport Layer** – A working document [WG3/N153] has been prepared and will be forwarded as a DIS in 1990.

(4) **The Presentation Layer** – A working document [WG3/N154] has been prepared and will be forwarded as a DIS in 1990.

Moreover, several schemes for authentication and digital signatures are under development.

12.9 Summary

Distributed system security includes not only mechanisms that prevent access to system objects by unauthorized users, but also communication security and authentication. The former safeguards information transmitted between remote processes (users), and the latter assures the receiver of a message that the message came from the reputed source.

The development of countermeasures against security threats in communication systems requires a model which can be used to discuss these security threats and countermeasures. Such a model is the association model.

An intruder can attack any element of a communication path (association) between communicating entities (for example, communication links, intrermediate nodes and gataways). These attacks can be passive, lead to release of message contents, and traffic analysis. Attacks can also be active; the following active threats are identified: message stream modification, denial of message delivery, delay of message delivery, and masquerade.

Encryption can be used as a countermeasure against passive attacks. Encryption in conjunction with protocols can be used to detect active attacks. There are two major encryption techniques: block ciphers and stream ciphers. Block ciphers encrypt fixed-sized blocks of bits under the control of a key that is often approximately the same size as the block it encrypts. The mapping is one-to-one. Stream ciphers transform cleartext bit-by-bit under the control of a stream of key bits, usually using some easily reversible operation. Generally, it is easier to construct strong stream ciphers than strong block ciphers.

There are two classes of cryptosystems: symmetric and asymmetric, also called public-key encryption. A symmetric cryptosystem is one in which either the same key is used at both ends of a communication channel, or one key is easily derived from the other if two keys are used. In a public-key cryptosystem each user has both a public key, and a secret key which is not revealed to anyone. These keys define a pair of transformations, each of which is the inverse of the other. The best known and most widely used symmetric cryptosystem is the DES (Data Encryption Standard). RSA (Rivest-Shamir-Adleman) is the best known public-key cryptosystem.

For secure communication in a distributed system, messages must be encrypted. This requires that both the sender and receiver are provided with matching keys. The keys must be securely produced and distributed between communicating entities. Key distribution can be based on symmetric or asymmetric cryptographic algorithms, using the same physical channels by which all regularly exchanged data are transmitted. This requires sending keys in cryptograms. In symmetric cryptosystems, keys can be maintained using centralized, distributed and hierarchical approaches. Key distribution in an asymmetric cryptosystem can be carried out using a centralized key centre.

There are three basic security measures: link-oriented, end-to-end, and association-oriented. The first provides security by protecting messages independently on each communication link. The second provides uniform protection for each message on the way between the sender and receiver, and the third measure is a refinement of the end-to-end measure, and is oriented toward connection-oriented communication.

Users of a distributed system are mutually suspicious. This implies that before they start a regular exchange of messages, they want to verify each other's identity in a secure manner. Thus, authentication services must be provided. Different authentication approaches may protect against different threats, and may provide different levels of assurance.

There are two basic authentication methods: simple, which is based on a simple password arrangement, and strong, which is based on cryptographic techniques. The second group of methods includes the following authentication schemes: elementary – built using both symmetric or public-key cryptosystems; authentication servers; methods using minimum (or zero) knowledge protocols; and digital signatures. In some environments (for example, military, banking) authentication as such is not enough – digital signatures must also be used.

To standardize security countermeasures the following services must be taken into consideration: identification of peer entities, access control, data confidentiality, communication integrity, service availability, non-repudiation, and accountability. The following mechanisms are standardized: encryption, digital signatures, access control, data integrity through checksums, sequencing and/or timestamping, authentication, traffic padding, routing control, and notarization.

All services but non-repudiation can be placed in the Application, Transport, and Network Layers of the ISO/OSI Reference Model. Confidentiality can also be placed in the Data Link and Physical Layers. Some primitive security functions, which are important from a distributed operating system point of view, are also proposed for standardization.

Bibliography

Abrams M.D. and Jeng A.B. (1987). Network Security: Protocol Reference Model and the Trusted Computer System Evaluation Criteria. *IEEE Network Magazine*, **1**(2), 24–33

Andreassen A.L., Leighton W.J. and Schreiber D.F. (1988). Information Security: An Overview. *AT&T Journal*, 2–8.

AS-2805.1/4 Australian Standards — Electronic Funds Transfer

Barker L.K. and Nelson L.D. (1988). Security Standards — Government and Commercial. *AT&T Technical Journal*, May/June, 9–18

Bauer R.K., Berson T.A. and Feirtag R.J. (1983). A Key Distribution Protocol Using Event Markers. *ACM Transactions on Computer Systems*, **1**(3), 249–55

Birrell A.D., Lampson B.W., Needham R.M. and Schroeder M.D. (1986). A Global Authentication Service Without Global Trust. In *Proceedings of the 1986 IEEE Symposium on Security and Privacy*, Oakland, California, 223–30

Branstad D.K. (1986). Considerations for Security in the OSI Architecture. In *Networking in Open Systems*. Lecture Notes in Computer Science, No. 248, Springer-Verlag

Brown L. (1987). *A Proposed Design for an Extended DES*. Technical Report CS87/ Canberra: Dept. of Computer Science, The University of New South Wales

Buffenoir T. (1988). Security in the OSI Model. *Computer Networks and ISDN Systems*, **15**, 145–50

Burrows M., Abadi M. and Needham R. (1989). *A Logic of Authentication,* Systems Research Center Digital

CCITT. SG VII, (1986). *Draft Recommendation X.ds7, The Directory — Authentication Framework* Geneva

Chaum D. (1987). Demonstrating that a Public Predicate Can Be Satisfied Without Revealing Any Information about How. In *Proceedings of CRYPTO 86*. Lecture Notes in Computer Science, 263, Springer-Verlag

Davis D.W. and Price W.L. (1984). *Security for Computer Networks: An Introduction to Data Security in Teleprocessing and Electonic Funds Transfer*, New York: Wiley and Sons

Denning D.E. and Denning P.J. (1979). Data Security. *Computing Surveys*, **11**(3), 227–49

Denning D.E. and Sacco G.M. (1981). Timestamps in Key Distribution Protocols. *Communications of the ACM*, **24**(8), 533–6

Diffie W. and Hellman M. (1976). New Directions in Cryptography. *IEEE Transactions on Information Theory*, **IT–22**(11), 644–54

DIS-9160. ISO Draft International Standard–Information Processing–Data Encipherment–Physical Layer Interoperability Requirements.

Feige U., Fiat A. and Shamir A. (1988). Zero-Knowledge Proofs of Identity. *Journal of Cryptology*, **1**(2), 77–94

Goldwasser S., Micali S. and Rackoff C. (1985). Knowledge Complexity of Interactive Proof Systems. *Proceedings of STOC*, 291–304

ISO–8502-2, (1987). CCITT Draft Recommendation X.402, ISO Working Document for DIS 8502-2–MHS/MOTIS–Overall Architecture

Kent S.T. (1981). Security in Computer Networks. *Protocols and Techniques for Data Communication Networks* Prentice-Hall, 369–432

Massey J.L. (1988). An Introduction to Contemporary Cryptology. *Proceedings of the IEEE*, **76**(5), 533–49

Meyer C.H. and Matyas S.M. (1982). *Cryptography: A New Dimension in Computer Data Security* New York: Wiley and Sons

Muftic S. (1988). Security Mechanisms for Computer Networks. *Computer Networks and ISDN Systems*, **15**, 67–71

Needham R.M. and Schroeder M.D. (1978). Using Encryption for Authentication in Large Networks of Computers. *Communications of the ACM*, **21**(12), 993–9

Nessett D.M. (1983). A Systematic Methodology for Analysing Security Threats to Interprocess Communication in a Distributed System. *IEEE Transactions on Communications*, **COM–31**, 1055–63

Popek G.J. and Kline C.S. (1978). Design Issues for Secure Computer Networks. *Operating Systems. An Advanced Course*, (Bayer, R. Graham, R. M. and Seegmuller, G. eds.) Springer-Verlag

Popek G.J. and Kline C.S. (1979). Encryption and Secure Computer Networks. *Computing Surveys*, **11**(4), 331–56

Presttun (1988). *Presttun: Integrating Cryptography in ISDN*, Lecture Notes in Computer Science, CRYPTO–87, Springer-Verlag

Seberry J. and Pieprzyk J. (1989). *Cryptography: An Introduction to Computer Security*. Prentice–Hall

Shannon C.E. (1949). Communication Theory of Secrecy Systems. *Bell Systems Technical Journal*, **28**, 656–715

Steiner J.G., Neuman C. and Schiller J.I. (1988). Kerberos: An Authentication Service for Open Network Systems. *Usenix Conference Proceedings*, Dallas

Voydock V.L. and Kent S.T. (1983). Security Mechanisms in High-Level Network Protocols. *Computing Surveys*, **15**(2), 135–71

WG3/N152 (1987). *ISO/IEC/JTC1/SC20/WG3 Working Document—Data Cryptographic Techniques—Conditions for Practical Operations in the Network Layer*, ISO

WG3/N153 (1987). *ISO/IEC/JTC1/SC20/WG3 Working Document—Data Cryptographic Techniques—Conditions for Practical Operations in the Transport Layer*, ISO

WG3/N154 (1987). *ISO/IEC/JTC1/SC20/WG3 Working Document—Data Cryptographic Techniques—Conditions for Practical Operations in the Presentation Layer*, ISO

13 File service

	File service		Security	
User names	File service		Security	
	Collaboration of file servers Transaction service Directory service Flat file service Disk service		Access control	C o m m u n i c a t i o n
			R e s o u r c e	p r o t e c t i o n
Name distri-bution	Resource allocation	Deadlock detection		
Name resolu-tion	Algorithms for load sharing and load balancing	Process synchro-nization		&
			Capa-bilities	Authen-tication
System names	Process management Operations on processes: local, remote Process migration		Access lists	Key manage-ment
Ports	Interprocess communication (and memory management) Interprocess communication primitives: Message Passing or Remote Procedure Call, or Transactions; Links or Ports		Info flow control Security kernel	Data encryp-tion
Address-es	↕ ↕			
Routes	Transport protocols supporting interprocess communication primitives			Encryp-tion protocols

s e c u r i t y

In distributed systems created from a set of single-user computers connected by a local area network and/or high bandwidth wide area networks, there are economic reasons for sharing resources in addition to the requirements for sharing by applications. The management of shared resources is an important service that should be provided by a trusted authority. Such a trusted authority is a distributed operating system, and in particular a server implemented in one of the computers connected to the network.

As emphasized in Chapter 4, a distributed system can be developed based on one of two models: the integrated model of distributed computing and the server-based model. According to the former model, all users and application processes have the same view of the system. This means that they see it as a single integrated whole, not a collection of individual computers and devices. However, autonomy is not sacrificed to achieve integration – the system provides mechanisms that permit a high degree of cooperation and sharing. In an integrated model-based distributed system, each computer runs a complete (but highly configurable) set of standard software which (potentially) provides it with all needed facilities. LOCUS (Walker *et al.* [1983], Popek and Walker [1985], and DOMAIN Leach *et al.* [1985], Levine [1987]) were built following the integration model.

On the other hand, in a server-based distributed system, services are provided by designated computers (servers). These computers run special purpose software tailored to providing some single service built from a number of small services.

Recall that a server is a subsystem that provides a particular type of service to *a priori* unknown client processes. There is a difference between a service and a server. A service is a software entity running on one or more machines, and a server is the service software running on a single machine. A client can be defined as a software layer between the basic network communication subsystem and the application software, a layer relatively application-independent, but file-service dependent. The clients of a server normally run on separate computers. In some special cases a client can share the same computer with the server. Discussions in this chapter relate to server-based distributed systems.

One of the primary functions of an operating system is providing a file storage capability. Users assess the quality of a distributed system compared with a centralized system mainly on services provided by the file system. A file system is used both to provide information sharing, and for economic reasons.

This chapter is concerned with file service and its closely-associated directory service. Note that file and directory services are not discussed in detail, since this is adequately covered elsewhere (Braban and Schlenk [1989], Coulouris and Dollimore [1988], Fridrich and Older

[1985], Gifford *et al.* [1988], Leach *et al.* [1985], Levine [1987], Mullender and Tanenbaum [1985], and Sturgis *et al.* [1980]). Interested readers should consult these excellent references.

The following issues are introduced in this chapter: general classifications of file servers, some implementation aspects, basic file and directory services, that is, those which provide primitive facilities to construct a wide range of file systems, some aspects of shared files based on research and design issues introduced in Chapters 4 and 6, such as transactions, atomic actions, recovery, replication, and synchronization, and finally, selected aspects of collaborating servers.

13.1   Basic aspects of file services and servers

This section presents both classifications of file services and servers and some implementation aspects.

13.1.1   Classifications of file servers

A file server is one of the most important servers in a distributed system. It supports processing performed on the several computers, facilitating the sharing of files and databases as well as providing a basis for building other types of servers needed by users such as print server or name server.

The influence of the use of servers on the general shape of a distributed computer system is substantial, going far beyond the financial benefits mentioned above. As soon as facilities that are necessary for most computations are provided in this way, individual computers become less autonomous and the network much more important. Moreover, there are advantages in having a certain uniformity of services (for example, uniform way of archiving and backup for files).

In addition to supporting the sharing of data and databases, a file server provides other services by supporting the following:

(1)   **Automatic backup and recovery** – Backup is performed as a preventative measure against storage media failure and user errors. Because the corresponding recovery procedures require some training and daily attention, the user should be released from such duties.

(2)   **User mobility** – A file service makes it possible to use different computers at different times. It is necessary when:

(a)   a computer fails,

(b)   some users may need computers at more than one location, and/or

(c)   computers are managed as a common pool.

In summary, a file server makes it feasible to provide a working environment independent of the computer used, or its location, without the necessity of physically relocating secondary storage devices.

(3)   **Diskless workstations** – Diskless workstations are desired for two reasons:

(a)   for low-cost personal computers and/or workstations (connected to a network), the cost of a disk drive can be more expensive than the processing units,

(b)   mechanical storage devices are often noisy and generate heat, which should be avoided in a working environment.

There are four main approaches to classifying file servers. According to the first approach, there are two major classes of file servers:

(1)   **True file server** – is a complete filing system that recognizes textual file names and manages file directories for its user.

(2)   **Storage server** – stores data in unstructured objects that are accessible only by primitive identifiers.

In both cases the term file server is widely established.
     The second classification divides file servers into three categories – simple file server, universal file server, and server providing database management support – in terms of three design parameters: unit of data access, unit of locking, and scope of atomic update. These parameters have the most significant impact on the complexity of file server design. These three categories are presented in Table 13.1.
     A third classification of file services distinguishes two kinds of file services: traditional and robust.

(1)   **Traditional file service** – offered by nearly all centralized operating systems, that is, files can be opened, read, and rewritten in place. Updates are usually implemented by the file server by simply overwriting the relevant disk block.
      Concurrency control, if there is any, usually involves locking entire files before updating them.

(2)   **Robust file service** – is aimed at those applications that require extremely high reliability and whose users are prepared to pay a significant penalty in performance to achieve it. They generally offer atomic updates and similar features lacking in the traditional file services. A robust file service normally includes traditional file service as a subset.

Table 13.1   Categories of file servers.

	Simple file server	Universal file server	Database management support
Unit of' data access	File	Sequential subset of bytes	Record
Unit of locking	File	File	Record or variable
Scope of atomic update	File	Multiple files	Multiple files
		(Multiple servers)	

The fourth classification of file servers, which is closely associated with the first one, takes remote file access into consideration. There are two forms of remote file access.

(1)   **Explicit file transfer** – which provides the most basic service; a client must invoke a file transfer utility to transfer a remote file before or after its use. Some of these systems perform limited data conversion to mitigate the effects of heterogeneous hardware and file formats. Some of them also use access control mechanisms and authentication to provide protection. Connection-based file transfer protocols such as FTP and FTAM are used.

These servers suffer from the following drawbacks: a client cannot execute a remotely-stored program, the access granularity is a file, and clients must remember the location of a desired file. In summary, explicit file transfer is an inconvenient and time-consuming way of file accessing.

(2)   **Distributed file systems** – in which file location is transparent to clients, who refer to files by name. The system locates the server storing a referred file, performs security oriented operations (for example, authentication), synchronizes access to the file, and finally transfers the data. For performance reasons some data and directory information are cached, and for reliability reasons some files can be replicated.

13.1.2   Implementation aspects of file servers

The overall performance of a distributed system depends on file server efficiency, whose implementation plays a very important role in this aspect.

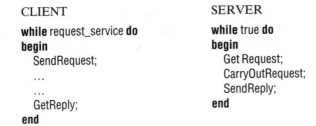

CLIENT

while request_service **do**
begin
   SendRequest;
   ...
   ...
   GetReply;
end

SERVER

while true **do**
begin
   Get Request;
   CarryOutRequest;
   SendReply;
end

Fig. 13.1 The structure of the simplest server based system.

The structure of the simplest server, organized as a single process, is illustrated in Fig. 13.1.

This model exhibits two important features: it is very simple conceptually and easy to implement, and all requests received have to be carried out sequentially. The latter means that the server is blocked when carrying out one request, and requests from other users must wait for the completion of a service requested by the first user. The utilization of a server based on this approach is very low. An improvement of throughput in such a server can be achieved by using one of two forms of concurrency.

(1)   The communication and the request handling by a server processor can be performed concurrently. This is possible if a table of received requests is maintained. Such a solution can be effective, but the software is complicated and poorly structured.

(2)   The entire service and communication functions can be implemented as a set of processes where each of them is capable of accepting new requests for work. This scheme requires some method of locking shared data to prevent races.

The most efficient approach to constructing a file server is to divide it into several parts, each implemented as a separate mediumweight process. As the reader may recall, these medium-weight processes share global data (for example, file system tables and buffers) but have their own program counters and stacks. The problem is in determining what is the best division of the whole file system. This and other aspects associated with the file system parts are discussed in the following sections.

13.2 Basic services provided by a file system

In Chapter 4 we noted that files represent a convenient way of viewing programs and data from both the logical user and the physical storage view point. Thus, files need a method for control and management at the system level. In particular, the following major functions have to be performed: block (disk) service, file service and directory service. Note that this is a very simplified picture of a file system.

The key issue in the design of a file system for centralized as well as for distributed systems is the problem of system decomposition. This includes the definition of specific functional units and the placement of such units, and their interaction. These operations must be considered in the context of file system design goals.

13.2.1   Design goals of a distributed file system

The basic distributed file system design goals are as follows:

(1)   **Diversity of application** – A file system should be able to support the whole range of applications.

(2)   **File system semantics** – The semantics of a distributed file system should be easy to understand. This implies that the interface to the file system must be simple, the number of commands be as small as possible, that the user sees the concept of a file and knows how to use the mechanisms provided.

(3)   **Matching user requirements** – A file system should provide only those services to a user that match his/her requirements. Thus, the user should not have to pay for those features and relevant mechanisms they do not need.

(4)   **Consistent naming** – Every object (user, process) in a distributed system uses the same text name for a file regardless of where the referencing object is located. This results in the possiblility of accessing a particular file anywhere in the distributed system.

(5)   **Location transparency** – A file should be moveable in a distributed system without having to change all name and process references to that file. This implies that a user name should not bind the specified file to a particular computer.

(6)   **Transparent access** – A file system should allow processes to access remote files in the same way as local files. Moreover, processes should not need or be able to recognize whether a file is remote or local.

(7)   **Data consistency** – A file system must guarantee the integrity of data. Users competing for access to a file must be protected by some form of concurrency control. Changes to files must never be lost.

(8)   **Consistent authentication** – The identity of a user must be recognized by other co-operating users, as well as server processes requested to provide a service for a requested process. A user

should be treated in the same way regardless of current physical location.

(9) **Information protection** – Information stored in a file system should be protected against non-authorized access, reading, changing, or deletion. Passing rights to access the file should be performed safely, that is, the receiver of rights should not be able to pass them further if he/she is not allowed to do that. In general, to encourage sharing of files between users, the protection mechanisms should allow a wide range of policies to be specified.

(10) **User mobility** – A user should be able to access any file from any workstation in a distributed system, and the performance characteristics should not discourage the users from accessing their files from workstations other than the 'home' one.

(11) **Performance** – Performance of a distributed file system should be such that users would not see differences between a distributed system and a timesharing system using similar resources. This means that the level of file system performance must be at least as good as that of an equivelent lightly-loaded time sharing system.

(12) **Availability** – The failure of a computer or some single element of a network should not affect the entire community of distributed system users. It is acceptable that only small groups of users can suffer from a temporary lack of service.

(13) **Crash recovery/High reliability** – User processes and servers must be able to recover easily from computer crashes and network problems in order to mount remote files from many different servers. Mechanisms should be provided to access files and carry out operations on them in a reliable way.

(14) **Scalability** – The system's growth should not cause serious disruption of service or loss of performance to users.

(15) **Accommodating different storage media** – A file system must be able to accommodate several different storage media.

13.2.2 Architecture of a centralized file system

In a centralized operating system, the following basic services are provided: block (disk) service, file service and directory service. These functions are not usually separated although they are arranged in a hierarchical way, as illustrated in Fig. 13.2.

The (disk) service, file service, and directory service are performed by the following modules:

(1) **Device module** – which performs disk I/O and buffering;

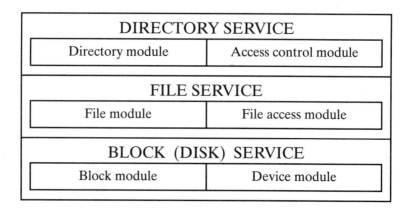

Fig. 13.2   Architecture centralized file system.

(2)   **Block module** – which accesses and allocates disk blocks;

(3)   **File module** – which relates file identifiers (IDs) to particular files;

(4)   **File access module** – which reads and writes the file data or attributes;

(5)   **Access control module** – which checks rights for the operations requested; and

(6)   **Directory module** – which provides the required mapping between file text names and references to files, that is, file IDs.

The problem is whether this hierarchical model can be used in a distributed system and whether the basic services and their functional modules fulfil the requirement of users of both the distributed systems, and the distributed systems themselves.

13.2.3   Architecture of a distributed file system

A distributed file system should provide, in general, the same services as a centralized file system, that is, block service, file service and disk service. However, for reasons of performance, reliability, and distribution the following additional issues and services should be considered: replication and multiple copy update, transactions and atomic action control, naming of distributed objects, and the placement and location of files in a distributed file system.

Now, the problem is how these issues should be seen in the context of the distributed file system as a whole, and how they should be placed in the overall architecture.

An analysis of the distributed file systems described in Braban and Schlenk (1989), Brown *et al.* (1985), Leach *et al.* (1985), Levine

(1987), Mullender and Tanenbaum (1985), Fridrich and Older (1985), Sandberg (1986), Gifford *et al.* (1988) and Satyanarayan *et al.* (1985) show that their development is based on different architectural models. However there are some common elements that allow us to propose a general architecture, useful for research purposes. This architecture is illustrated in Fig. 13.3.

Note that while in a centralized file system the basic services are usually not separated, in a distributed system there is a division of responsibilities and file system functions are handled by separate services.

The services of a distributed file system are performed by the following modules:

(1) **Device module** – which performs disk I/O and buffering;

(2) **Block module** – which accesses and allocates disk blocks;

(3) **Caching module** – which caches recently obtained results of disk operations and remote operations;

(4) **File module** – which relates file identifiers (ID's) to particular files;

(5) **File access module** – which reads and writes the file data;

(6) **Attribute access module** – which reads and writes file attributes;

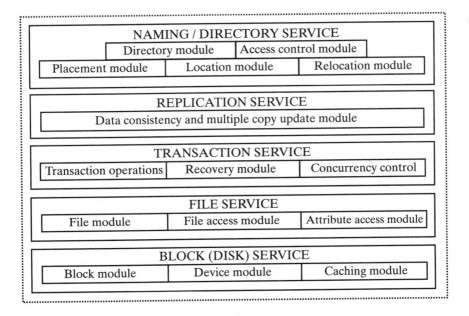

Fig. 13.3 Architecture of a distributed file system.

(7)   **Transaction operations module** – which provides a transaction mechanism to allow grouping of elementary operations so as to execute them atomically;

(8)   **Recovery module** – which provides recovery mechanism after failure;

(9)   **Concurrency control module** – which provides concurrency control mechanisms to ensure that object consistency is preserved and that each atomic action is completed in finite time;

(10)   **Data consistency and multiple copy update module** – which improves the performance of a file system when files are shared, by maintaining data consistency and providing a multiple copy update mechanism;

(11)   **Directory module** – which resolves user names by providing the required mapping between file user (text) names and references to files, that is, system names, file ID's;

(12)   **Access control module** – which checks rights for the requested operations;

(13)   **Placement module** – which selects the server to hold a newly created file;

(14)   **Location module** – which finds the location of the server managing a referenced file;

(15)   **Relocation module** – which improves the performance of the file system by relocating files.

All services of a distributed file system and their modules are discussed briefly in the following sections.

13.3   Disk service

A block (disk) service provides a logical view of a disk storage system. This service also enables a single storage system to be shared between different file services. The disk service is concerned with reading and writing raw disk blocks without regard to how they are organized. Moreover, facilities must be provided to delete and truncate files. A block service is also responsible for maintaining the frequently used blocks in a memory buffer. Typical commands are to allocate and write a disk block, or to return a capability or address so that a block can be read later.

In many distributed file systems the disk service is separated from the file service. In general, this separation makes it easy to combine different methods of storage, and different storage media. Moreover, a disk service can combine high speed with high reliability by using caching and dual storage.

13.3.1 File storage

Different conceptual models of a file are used by different file systems. According to the simplest model, a file is an unstructured sequence of data; there is no substructure known to the file server. A more structured model assumes that a file is an ordered sequence of records, which can be of different size. These records can have keys and can be separately addressed. The most advanced model of a file models it as a tree. Each tree node may have both, or either, a key and a data record.

In this chapter, a file is modeled by a file server as a sequence of modifiable data items of a given size. When a file is created, space must be allocated for it. This space is recovered when a file is deleted or truncated. The size of a file can change when operations on it are performed. Thus, dynamic allocation of storage is required to allow files to grow and shrink.

In addition to data items, files also have **attributes** that describe them. Each attribute has a name, a type and a value. Some attributes are created when the file is created and do not change. Others can be changed by users. A third group of attributes are maintained and changed by the file server. Examples of file attributes are: file name, allowed operations, access control data, date and time of creation, date and time of last file modification, owner, and encryption key.

Files are stored in addressible blocks of storage whose size is fixed by the storage device, typically between two and eight kbytes. This explains the existence in the disk service of the block module, which is responsible for the allocation, reading and writing of blocks. Block operations in distributed systems can be implemented either in a software module as a part of the file server software, or as a separate service.

The use of a block service offers some advantages in the implementation of a shared file service:

(1)   Differently-specified file services can coexist and share the same disk storage device in a single distributed system.

(2)   A variety of disks and other media can be used.

(3)   The implementation of the file service can be separated from disk-specific optimizations and other hardware concerns.

In a system based on the block approach, a file is stored in a non-contiguous set of blocks of storage. This implies the need for recording a sequence of pointers to the blocks of which each file is composed. This sequence of pointers is stored in a separate data structure called the **file**

File index

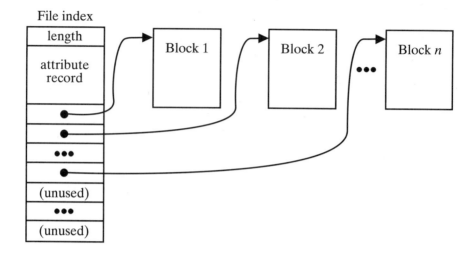

Fig. 13.4 The storage structure of a single file.

index. The file index must be organized in such a way that both sequential and random access to the items of a file are supported. The storage structure of a file is illustrated in Fig. 13.4.

This figure shows that the file attributes, although stored with the file, are not included in the file contents. This is because they are subject to different access controls. The attribute record is maintained and used by the directory service. There is also another item stored in the file index, namely the **file length**. It should be noticed that these data are stored with the file rather than with the file name in the directory. This is because many directory systems allow files to be referenced by more than one name.

The block service is usually implemented with commands that allow a user to allocate, deallocate, read and write blocks of data. Each of this blocks is protected; thus, if a block is allocated to one user, another user cannot access it without permission. To implement atomic actions on files, the block writing operation should be an atomic operation, with a confirmation after storing the block on disk. Moreover, to allow the file service to realize concurrency control polices, a simple locking facility on individual blocks should be implemented in the block service.

13.3.2 A caching system

The performance of any system supported by external memory suffers from disk access operations and remote operations, which are very time consuming; it is necessary to avoid them whenever possible. This motivates the development of a software system, called a caching system, that reduces the cost of file access by storing recently-used blocks in local memory, and reuses them when it can be ascertained that they are still valid. Note that not only data but also file attributes are cached and reused if they are still valid.

A cache is a set of local copies of blocks or remote data. One possible placement of a cache in a disk service and the relationship between them and a disk driver is illustrated in Fig. 13.5.

An external memory cache is an area of main memory which is organized as an array of blocks. The size of each block is the same as the size of a block on the disk. Each cache block has an associated cache pointer. These pointers are checked on every read operation. If the cache pointer is present, the cache block is read. Otherwise, the cache is loaded with the contents of the block from the disk and the associated cache pointer is updated. Thus, subsequent read operations that require that same block use the cache.

A buffer cache can be maintained either by a file server in its memory or in the memory of a client computer. Note that when the cache is large enough, the ratio can exceed 90 per cent; this eliminates a large portion of the disk accesses. The most serious problems are how to avoid overloading a cache and how to maintain reliability in the case of file server crashes. These are not discussed here; the interested reader should reference for example Coulouris and Dollimore (1988).

The client-memory-based caching can improve performance even better, as was presented in Howard *et al.* (1988), Kazar (1988), Nelson *et al.* (1988), Ousterhout *et al.* (1988), Satyanarayanan *et al.* (1985) and Schroeder *et al.* (1985). The caches on client computers can be either on their local disks or in memory. Moreover, not only blocks, but also entire files, can be cached.

Several problems arise in introducing a cache system. The most serious is how to maintain consistency between blocks cached in more than one location. Cache is said to be **consistent** if it contains an exact

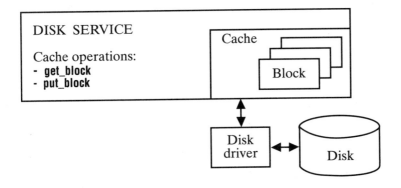

Fig. 13.5 The relationship between cache, disk service and disk driver.

copy of data. The problem of keeping local cache copies up to date when changes are made in remote locations is called the cache consistency problem.

There are three basic solutions to the cache consistency problem:

(1) **Passive** – This solution assumes that the system does nothing; only users are informed to be careful.

(2) **Server maintains cached objects** – The server keeps track of which client has which blocks and files in its cache. When a client modifies a block or a file, it informs the file server. The file server informs the other clients that the particular block or file is invalid and must be removed from their cache.

(3) **Server monitors object access** – Clients can only cache files in their caches. A client informs the file server when opening a specific file, indicating whether this is to be opened for reading or for writing. The server takes no action if the file is open by all clients for reading. If only one client opens a file for writing and there are no readers, the server also does not react. However, when a second client opens a file, the server asks the first process to upload the file back to the server and to cease caching it. This implies that the second open operation is blocked until the upload is completed. Because heavily shared files are rarely updated, this solution is reasonably efficient. This strategy is used in the ITC Distributed File System (Satyanarayanan *et al.* 1985). The discussion of different approaches to the cache consistency problem in real systems is also presented in Gifford *et al.* (1988).

In summary, a caching facility in a distributed file system should address the following design decisions as discussed by Nelson *et al.* (1988), Levy and Silberschatz (1989):

(1) granularity of cached data,

(2) the place of maintaining the client's cache – main memory or local disk,

(3) the manner of propagating of modifications on cachewd copies,

(4) the ways of determining of consistency of cached data.

13.3.3 Unique file identifiers

Every file maintained by a file system has at least one user name and a unique system name. File servers use only system names. As noted in Chapter 7, a system name can take several different forms, for example, a capability or a unique object (file) identifier. In the following discussion we use only unique file identifiers. Note that **unique file**

identifiers (UFIDs) are used to refer to files when performing file service operations.

UFIDs are usually long integers of a fixed length. This allows the file server to map them to the data in the files. These identifiers are unique among all of the files in a distributed system and should be generated in a way that makes them difficult to forge. It is important to notice that the UFID does not have to act as a file address. This means that it need not contain any information concerning the address of the server managing it, nor its location in disk storage.

In Chapter 7 we showed how to generate a UFID. Different methods are presented in Needham and Herbert (1982), and Leach *et al.* (1983). All these methods are based on a relatively large, sparsely populated space. A UFID constructed using these methods is illustrated in Fig. 13.6.

This UFID is constructed by concatenating the following fields:

(1)   the address of the server which created the file,

(2)   a timestamp from the server's clock, or

(3)   an integer which represents the consecutive number of a file created by this server, and

(4)   a random number to provide sparseness.

Such UFIDs have the following advantages in a distributed file system (Levine 1987):

(1)   they are completely location independent;

(2)   each UFID unambiguously identifies a single file system object;

(3)   UFIDs may be passed between processes and from computer to computer without having to be examined and transformed at each step;

(4)   the address of the server is necessary only to guarantee uniqueness and not for locating the object in the network.

Recall that the UFID constitutes a capability or a key. This fact is used when developing a method to access a file. However, more advanced protection can be provided by embedding an access right field in the UFID. Protection aspects are discussed in Chapter 11.

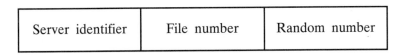

Fig. 13.6   An example of the UFID.

13.3.4 File location

Clients of a disk service do not need to know the home location of the files. Performing an operation on a file requires specifying its UFID and a page, or an offset within this file. This information is sent in a request message to the file server, which translates it to obtain the location of the file index and the file blocks.

Thus, it is the responsibility of a disk service to locate a specific file and to make files stored at different computers of a distributed system equally available. This operation is illustrated in Fig. 13.7.

Fig. 13.7 shows that if the specified file is local, the disk service module performs the I/O operation; otherwise, a request is sent to the file home server. This method of file location is used in DOMAIN (Levine 1987).

This file block reference method should be fast because is performed once for every request. Moreover, this method ensures that the file service requests are stateless (stateless servers are discussed in Section 13.4.4).

The retrieval of the location of a file, that is, the translation process, can be expressed as follows:

UFID → location of file

There are two basic translation methods: two-step translation and one-step translation.

Two-step translation   The first step of a two-step translation process gets the pointer to the relevant file index:

UFID → block pointer of file index

In the second step, the file index is accessed to get the block pointer for the required block b in the file:

b → block pointer for block b

A two-step-translation-based system can be developed from two basic organizations. In the first, each UFID contains a pointer to the

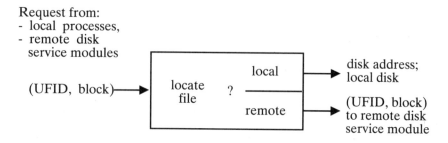

Request from:
- local processes,
- remote disk
  service modules

(UFID, block) →

locate file ?

local → disk address; local disk

remote → (UFID, block) to remote disk service module

Fig. 13.7   File location in a distributed system.

first block of the relevant file index; no file location map is required. The second organization is based on a file location map which stores UFIDs and the corresponding file index block pointers.

One-step translation One-step translation requires the file location map and the file index to be combined as a single table. This implies that the location retrieval process is performed according to the following formula:

UFID $\times b \longrightarrow$ block pointer for block b

One-step translation is used in the Xerox Distributed File System (XDFS) system (Mitchell and Dion [1982], Sturgis *et al.* [1980]), and two-step translation is used in the Cambridge File Server (CFS) as discussed in Dion (1980) and Needham and Herbert (1982).

DOMAIN uses a searching algorithm and relies on a special database to find files, given only their UFID (Levine 1987). The technique depends on receiving a list of likely locations from the so-called **hint manager**. This manager catagorizes UFIDs by the address of the creation server. Each category is associated with a list of servers at which UFIDs of that category have been found before – this information is stored in the hint manager database. This database is permanently updated. Thus, to perform the search for a particular UFID the disk service module retrieves the appropriate server list from the hint manager and iterates through it until it finds the file. According to Levine, the algorithm works because in practice files move infrequently from the server at which they were created.

13.3.5 Service functions provided by a disk service

A disk service manages and accesses the contents of a large collection of disk blocks. It enables clients to:

(1) obtain new blocks,

(2) release blocks that are no longer required, and

(3) transfer data into and out of blocks; checksums are used to detect errors.

These services can be provided by the disk service operations. Disk services of different distributed file systems provide different set of operations. As an example, we propose primitive operations based on the File System for the PM (Parallel Modules) system (Braban and Schlenk 1989) and DOMAIN (Leach *et al.* 1985). These operations are presented in List 13.1.

---

allocate_block()
allocates a new block and delivers its pointer.

free_block(Block)
releases Block.

get_block(Block)
the Block is read at a given address on disk, stored in a free buffer of the cache, and a copy is sent to the user process. No access to the Block is made if the Block is already in the cache.

put_block(Block, Data)
Data stored in the cache is copied on to disk at the given address Block.

flush_block(Block)
removes Block from the cache.

List 13.1 Block service operations.

When designing the service functions to be provided by a disk service, several aspects should be considered. First, the size chosen for the block pointer. This value is important because it determines the maximum number of blocks that can be stored by the block server. Second the size of blocks. In general, a tradeoff problem has to be solved since the use of small blocks improves the utilization of disk storage when there are many small files in a file system. On the other hand, the use of large blocks reduces the effect of latency and the complexity of the file index for large files. Thus, access time is reduced. Third, because file system performance depends on the size of a block and the sizes of files, the best solution can be achieved by providing a number of different block sizes. Fourth, a disk service should be designed so as to ensure that the files they hold are accessible after all kinds of system failures except the most catastrophic. This implies at least that the file location map and the file indexes must be recoverable if the system fails while updating them, or a disk error occurs resulting in an invalid block. This leads to the fifth design aspect: **stable storage**. Stable storage is an approach designed to ensure that any essential permanent data will be recoverable after any single system failure. This may be failure during a disk write operation, or damage to any single disk block. Thus, stable storage is achieved by writing each disk block of data to two separate disk blocks. This guarantees that at least one block is correct when a computer or disk fails. The stable storage approach is used in the XDFS.

13.4 File service

A file service provides its clients with an abstraction consisting of files, each of which is a linear sequence of data items (records). The data items may be system-defined or user-defined. Possible operations are reading and writing records, starting from some particular place in the file. The client is not concerned with how and/or where the data in the file are stored or with any relationships between files.

A distributed file service enables users to access files without copying them to a local workstation disk. Moreover, if diskless workstations are used, the file service provides permanent data storage.

The main goal of a distributed file service is to offer filing facilities of at least the same generality as those found in centralized file systems (see Birrell and Needham [1980], Coulouris and Dollimore [1988], Spector and Kazar [1989] and Mullender and Tanenbaum [1985]). This goal can be achieved by providing a general-purpose, efficient set of operations.

13.4.1 Mutable and immutable files

Two types of files can be stored by file servers: mutable and immutable files. A file is said to be mutable if there is for it just one stored sequence that is altered by each update operation. The files provided in centralized operating systems are mutable files. File servers such as XDFS and CFS also provide mutable files.

An immutable file is one that cannot be modified once it has been created except to be deleted. The second important property of an immutable file is that its name may not be reused. This implies that the name of an immutable file signifies the fixed contents of the file, not the file as a container for variable information. In Gifford *et al.* (1988) it has been emphasized that sharing only immutable files makes it easy to support consistent sharing. Moreover, it makes it easy to implement a distributed file system. Sharing immutable files means that the local cache facility can ignore the possibility of remote files changing.

Note that each file is represented by a history of immutable versions. The immutable file is not updated. A new version is created each time a change is made to the file contents, and the old version is kept unchanged. Sometimes only a record of the difference between versions is stored, to minimize the storage required. Old versions are removed when there is a shortage of disk space.

Immutable files are sources of two potential problems: increased use of disk space and increased disk allocation. The reader interested in the utilization of immutable files is encouraged to study the Cedar File System (CFS) in Gifford *et al.* (1988).

13.4.2 File service operations on data

A file contains data, and has attributes. This implies that there are two separate sets of operations, one to deal with data and the other to deal with attributes. A set of operations that deal with data are available to a user to manipulate files.

---

create() → File
> creates a new file of length 0 with the specified name File, establishes its attributes, and delivers a UFID for it.

open(File)
> opens the existing File that can be used to perform **read**, **write**, and other operations on this file.

copy(fromFile, toFile)
> copies file fromFile to file toFile.

get_size(File)
> returns the File's size after setting a lock on the file properties.

read(File, offset, count, buffer)
> reads up to count bytes of data from File starting offset bytes and puts them contiguously into buffer; or

read(File, pageRun, buffer)
> reads data from the File pages described by pageRun and puts it contiguously into buffer.

write(File, offset, count, buffer)
> writes count bytes of data from buffer to File beginning offset bytes from the beginning of the file; or

write(File, pageRun, buffer)
> writes data from buffer to the File pages described by pageRun.

close(File)
> terminates access for actions to be taken on the File.

delete(File)
> removes the File from the file store. An error occurs if the File is currently open.

List 13.2 File service operations.

An analysis of distributed file systems presented in Brachan and Schlenk (1989), Brown *et al.* (1985), Folts (1989), Gifford *et al.* (1988), Levine (1987), Leach *et al.* (1985), Mukherjee *et al.* (1988) and Sandberg (1986) shows that there is a set of commonly used operations on files and their data. These operations are given in List 13.2.

13.4.3   File service operations on attributes

The file service maintains a set of attributes for each file, such as date of creation, type, date of last access, date of last modification, file ownership and access list. These attributes are regarded by the file service as an uninterpreted sequence of bytes, which may be stored and retrieved.

An analysis of the references used in Section 13.4.2 shows that the following operations on file attributes are in use List 13.3.

---

read_attribute(File)
   returns the values of the attributes of the File.

write_attribute(File, Attribute)
   writes (modifies) the existing value of the attribute (mode, UFID, size, access time, modification time, etc.)

List 13.3   File attribute operations.

The file service, directory service, and the user are responsible for setting the contents of the attributes part of a file. In particular, the directory service determines the internal structure and the values stored in the attributes section. They are identical for all files managed by a particular directory service.

13.4.4   Operational properties of file systems

Two properties of operations on the data of currently open files are important in the construction of a distributed system: idempotency, and stateless.

Idempotency
An operation is said to be **idempotent** if its effect when executed more than once is the same as for a single execution. Certain errors caused by computer failures and communication delays may lead to repeated executions of some operations (for example, remote procedure call). If re-

petition may have an uncertain effect, the server must prevent it by implementing duplicate suppression. If the operations are idempotent, then overheads due to duplicate suppression may be avoided. However, repetition of operations can degrade system performance.

Stateless file servers

The above discussion concerning idempotent file operations leads to the problem of which site, that is, the file server or the client, should maintain both the state of files when performing operations on them, and the information on all past requests.

A server which does not maintain its internal state is known as a **stateless server**. In this case, the parameters necessary to carry out an operation on a file is stored by the client, and is passed to the server in a request message. The server does not keep track of any past request. After opening a file the index to this entry is returned to the client for use in subsequent request.

An example of state information is the read-write pointer. In a centralized operating system, the kernel can hold this pointer for each open file in a process table. If a file server stores this information for each client, then two unfortunate situations may arise. If the server crashes, this information may be lost; when the server re-starts the client program might continue its task unaware of this crash and produce inconsistent results. On the other hand, a client program may also crash; the server is then left holding information that is wrong but cannot be easily withdrawn. Thus, when the program re-starts, it might produce inconsistent results. Clearly, operations that do not rely on the stored state in the file server can simplify its design.

In summary, the stateless server based approach also satisfies crash recovery; when a server crashes, the client retransmits only its request message until a response message is received. When a client crashes, no recovery is necessary for either the client or the server.

On the other hand, if a state is maintained by the server, called a **stateful** server, recovery is much harder. This is because both the client and the server need to reliably detect crashes: the client must detect server crashes in order to rebuild the server state; the server must detect client crashes in order to discard any state it is holding for the client.

A stateless server has also some disadvantages. If the client holds the state then problems arise if the server moves the file. Moreover, if information in a file can be updated concurrently by several clients, simple stateless servers are inadequate. There are some consistency constraints. Thus, a file server should support atomic transactions on files. This may require the retention of some state information, such as locks. However, this information is used only by the file server and will be removed when the transaction has been completed or after the server or client crashes.

In general, it is difficult to implement normal file system semantics in a stateless way. This can be observed in such cases where for example a user removes an open file, or changes its protection mode. In both cases the client can do nothing with this file.

13.5   Transaction service

If the basic file service is used concurrently by a number of processes to read from and write data to the same file, unpredictable effects on the file can result. Moreover, if a client or file server fails, undetected errors can be produced. To avoid these problems, the file service should support **transactions** and an **atomic transaction service** must be pro-.vided. This implies that the file service should be extended to provide a mechanism that allows operations on files to be grouped (for example, **create**, **open**, **write**, **close**) into a transaction, using such primitives as **begin_transaction** and **end_transaction**, to execute them atomically. An example of an transaction is illustrated in Fig. 13.8.

When a client process wants to be provided with a service, it sends a **begin_transaction** request to the file server. Usually, the **begin_transaction** primitive allows both the checking of whether this client has permission to start a transaction, and the starting of a transaction. If a transaction can be opened, the server returns a result message with a unique transaction identifier, transID; all further messages within the transaction must carry that identification (in Fig. 13.8, file oriented primitives do not show this parameter, for simplicity).

After opening a transaction, file oriented operations (for example, **create**, **open**, **read**, **write**, **close**, **destroy**) can be performed. After completing these operations, the client will send the **end_transaction** request to close the transaction. The system completes the transaction and sends a response to the client.

As noted in Chapter 4, two requirements must be satisfied by a system supporting atomic transactions. The first is that each transaction must be **recoverable**: when a client or server stops for whatever reason,

begin_transaction

> **create**(File);
> **open**(File);
> **read**(File, pageRun, buffer);
> **write**(File, pageRun, buffer);
> **close**(File);

end_transactions(transID)

Fig. 13.8   Example of a transaction.

begin_transaction

   create(File);
   open(File);
   read(File, pageRun, buffer);
   write(File, pageRun, buffer);
   close(File);

end_transaction(transID)

(a)

begin_transaction

   create(File);
   open(File);
   read(File, pageRun, buffer);
   write(File, pageRun, buffer);

abort_transaction(transID)

(b)

SERVER
ABORTS →
   create(File);
   open(File);
   read(File, pageRun, buffer);
   write(File, pageRun, buffer);

(c)

Fig. 13.9 Transaction life histories: (a) successful, (b) aborted by client, (c) aborted by server.

then changes to files within the transaction must either be completed or files must be returned to their state before the transaction was started. Thus, all the **create, open, write,** and **delete** operations within a single transaction must be done completely or not at all. Second, the result of concurrent execution of a number of atomic transactions must be the same as if these transactions had been done serially in some arbitrary order, that is, the results must be **serially equivalent**.

In summary, a **transaction service** needs to be provided. A transaction service can be regarded as an extension to, or a variation of, a file service that provides atomic actions on some or all of its files. An atomic transaction is achieved by cooperation between the client process and the transaction service. Thus, the client process specifies the sequence of operations which are to be performed in one transaction and the transaction service must preserve the atomicity of the entire sequence.

Recall that a transaction may be successful or it may be aborted by either the client or the server. If the transaction has progressed normally the client is informed by the server that the transaction is **committed**. Otherwise, the transaction is aborted. Three posssible scenarios for transactions are illustrated in Fig. 13.9.

The fact that a transaction can be aborted implies that all of the file update operations must be performed in a **tentative** manner. This means that these update operations are performed in such a way that they may either be permanently recorded or undone.

13.5.1 Transaction service operations

We have defined a transaction service as that class of file service which supports transactions on its files. To complete our discussion of transaction services, we provide a list of transaction service operations, which were proposed in Brahan and Schlenk (1989), Brown *et al.* (1985), Eppinger and Spector (1988), Fridrich and Older (1985), Mukherjee *et al.* (1988), Paxton (1979) and Sturgis *et al.* (1980).

The commonly used transaction service operations are given in List 13.4.

---

begin_transaction
> creates a new transaction and delivers a unique TransID. This identifier is used in the other operations in the transaction.

end_transaction(TransID)
> commits a transaction; the returned result indicates whether the transaction has committed, failed, or whether the transaction is inactive because it was aborted.

abort_transaction(TransID)
> aborts the transaction; all files open for this transaction are unlocked and the state of the transaction is changed to inactive.

List 13.4 Transaction service operations.

13.5.2 Recovery after failures

The atomicity of transactions is threatened by two factors:

(1) Failures of processes and computers. Three types of failures are identified:

   (a) transaction failures which may result from entering erroneous data values or erroneous processing;

   (b) system failures, which may be caused by a bug in the database management system code, an operating system fault, or a hardware failure;

   (c) media failures, in which some portion of the secondary storage medium is damaged.

(2) Concurrency.

This section briefly presents some aspects of recovery after failures.

There are two commonly-used approaches to recovery: the intentions list approach and the file version approach. Before discussing these approaches, it is necessary to consider some aspects of the transaction operations. In both recovery approaches, a transaction consists of two phases (Fig. 13.10) with three associated states: **tentative, committed,** and **aborted.**

The first phase This phase starts when the server receives an **begin_transaction** request from the client and ends when **end_transaction** is received. During this phase the transaction is in the tentative state. Thus, the server makes tentative copies of changed items in the files. Only during the first phase can a transaction be aborted. Since client's files are not permanently affected by operations of the aborted transaction, the only thing to be done by the server is to make tentative copies of changed items in the files.

The second phase This phase starts after the server receives an **end_transaction** request. If previously discussed conditions are fulfilled, the committed state is entered, and the tentative values of the changed items are made permanent by inserting them into appropriate places of the files. Of course, this phase must be atomic. Otherwise, the aborted state is entered and the server informs the client that the transaction has failed.

The intentions list approach
In the intentions list approach (see Brown *et al.* [1985], Gray [1978], Lampson [1981], Mukherjee *et al.* [1988] and Sturgis *et al.* [1980]) the server makes a list of all actions (called an intentions list) for each transaction. This list of actions will be performed by the server only after a transaction is committed.

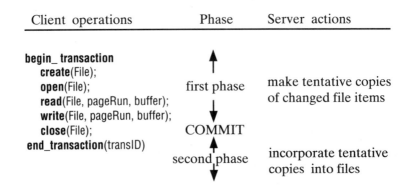

Client operations	Phase	Server actions

begin_ transaction
    create(File);
    open(File);
    read(File, pageRun, buffer);
    write(File, pageRun, buffer);
    close(File);
end_transaction(transID)
	first phase
	
	COMMIT
	second phase
		make tentative copies
		of changed file items
		
		incorporate tentative
		copies into files

Fig. 13.10 The two phases of a transaction.

The intentions list (called the recovery log by Gray) can be regarded as a log of the operations of a transaction. The list contains a record for each operation (for example, **write**) that will make changes to files. Thus, when for example a **write** operation is performed, its intention is stored in the intentions list rather than making updates to the file involved. The construction of an intentions list is illustrated in Fig. 13.11.

The figure shows that a transaction state flag is associated with the intentions list. Thus, during the first state the **commit flag** is set to **tentative**. This state is changed to **committed** or **aborted** when the request **end_transaction** is received. This state change operation must be performed as an atomic action.

In general, to have transactions on files in a system based on paged memory, it is necessary to keep different versions of pages around. In a system based on the log approach, these pages are stored in log records and are incorporated into files only by copying. Moreover, in such a system a file that allows update under a transaction is incorporated as a log plus a file in an underlying file system that does not implement transactions.

The intentions list and the commit flag are stored in stable storage separately from the files involved in the transaction. Intentions list can be written and erased atomically. This recording has to be done in such a way that it will remain intact after a server has crashed or halted. Thus, if a crash occurs, all existing intentions lists are discarded during recovery from the crash. Next, each list is carried out and erased. This guarantees that a transaction completes correctly.

The reader interested in details of the intentions list approach should refer to Brown *et al.* (1985) and Hagmann (1987).

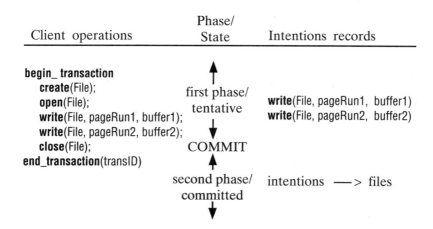

Fig. 13.11 Construction of an intentions list.

The file version approach

In the file version approach (see Gifford *et al.* [1988], Mullender and Tanenbaum [1985] and Reed [1983]) the server makes new versions of the files containing the changes. If the transaction commits, the new version of the file is used; otherwise it is discarded.

A file may have a sequence of versions which are the results of file modifications. Each of these versions is written only once and is tentative. This sequence forms a chronological history of the file. A transaction can modify more than one file. In this situation, there is a tentative version for each file. When the server commits the transaction, the most recently committed version of the file becomes the current version. The previous current version is added to the sequence of old versions.

When two or more concurrent transactions have accessed the same file, two kinds of conflicts may arise:

(1) **A version conflict** – which occurs when concurrent transactions access the same file, but none of the data items modified in any of the transactions have been accessed or modified by the other transaction. This kind of conflict can be resolved by a merging action.

(2) **A serializability conflict** – which occurs when two or more concurrent transactions are allowed to access the same data items in a file, and one or more of these accesses is a **write** operation. Locking can be used to prevent this kind of conflicts. They are resolved when they occur by timestamping.

When implementing file versions in a computer system based on paging memory, the shadow pages technique can be used to make new versions of files.

To characterize the shadow page approach, let us recall that a page is a fixed length byte sequence in a file. A page (a block) is identified within a file using a page number. A page is usually stored in a disk sector. To store mappings of the pair <UFID, page number> to disk sector, a file map is used. The file map is used by the file system to find the correct sector to perform operations on the relevant page. Allocation is performed based on an allocation map that contains the free or allocated status of every sector.

In a system based on the shadow page approach a file is updated by updating the file map. This is performed in the following way. The file system allocates a new sector, writes the new page value there, and modifies the file map. This implies that each next operation on this page is based on the new sector rather than the old one.

Thus, in a file system which provides a transaction service, if the client commits the transaction, the change to the file map is made permanent, and the old sector is freed. If the transaction is aborted, the file map is restored to its previous state and the new sector is freed. Before either of these two happens, the page exists in two versions: the new but uncommited page and the old, tentative, page called the shadow page.

In summary, in a system based on the shadow page approach different versions are stored as pages that are incorporated into files by modifying the file map. Note that there are many variations of the shadow page approach. They can be distinguished by the management of the file map and the allocation map.

The question is which approach – the log, or the shadow page – is preferable. The shadow page implementation requires less I/O operations – each page is written only once – whereas the log implementation writes data first to the log, later reads data from the log and writes to the underlying file. On the other hand, the shadow page implementation must also update the nonvolatile file map: this operation is not performed in a log approach based system. We do not discuss other advantages and disadvantages of these two approaches here. The reader is encouraged to consult Brown *et al.* (1985).

13.5.3 Concurrency control

In Chapter 6 we noticed that if the system is not to fail, all concurrency control mechanisms must ensure that consistency of objects is preserved, and each atomic action is completed in finite time.

This can be achieved if transactions are run so that their effect on shared data is serially equivalent. Serial equivalence of transactions can be achieved by a file server by serializing access to data items. However, the shared portion to which access must be serialized should be the smallest possible part of a file. This is very important because if larger parts of a file or even an entire file are serially accessed by processes, then concurrency is reduced.

Concurrency control problems can be solved by the following three commonly-used approaches:

(1) **Locking** – Using this approach, a server sets a lock on each data item of a file before it is accessed on behalf of the first transaction which wants to access it. Each lock is labelled with the transaction identifier. Thus, only the transaction which locked the data item can access it. Other transactions must wait until the data item is unlocked. The data item is unlocked, that is, the lock is removed when the transaction is completed (committed or aborted).

(2) **Optimistic concurrency control** – According to this approach, which is based on the hope that no access conflicts will occur, the server allows a transaction to proceed to the end of the first phase. However, before it is committed the server checks to see if the

transaction has used the same data items as an earlier transaction. If a conflict occurs, the transaction must be aborted and restarted.

(3)   **Timestamps** – A server based on this approach records the most recent time of reading and writing for each data item. Each transaction compares its own timestamp with that of the data item. This comparison is used to determine whether the current operation can be performed or not. Transactions are aborted and restarted when they are too late to do an operation on a particular data item in a file.

It is important to notice that each transaction has its own record of changes (tentative values/copies). Moreover, each transaction is unable to observe another transactions' tentative values.

13.5.4   Implementation of a transaction service

Some elements of the implementation of a transaction service are now presented. Together with the issues just introduced, this should provide a complete picture of the implementation of a transaction service.

First of all, we introduce some operations for working on an intentions list. Next, we present the implementation of locks for concurrency control in combination with an intentions lists. Finally, we briefly discuss the actions required when a transaction commits in the presence of locks and an intentions lists. In these implementations, the shadow pages technique is used. It is important to notice that the shadow pages are accessible to the transaction that has created them.

Implementing intentions lists

The operations that can change the contents of a file are **create**, **write** and **delete**. Thus, an entry must be made in the intentions list for each of these operations. The entry consists of a record of the information necessary to do the **create**, **write** and **delete** operations.

Each transaction has an intentions list, which is maintained by the transaction service in the form of a list of **intentions records** in stable storage. The intentions record records the following:

(1)   the type of the operation, that is, **create**, **write** and **delete**;

(2)   the transaction identifier,

(3)   the file and block (page) to which the intention refers,

(4)   pointer to the block that holds the shadow page, and

(5)   shadow length of a file.

Some operations for storing and accessing intentions records that may be used only within the server are presented in List 13.5:

> **get_intention**(Operation, TransID, File, Page)
> if the intentions list for the transaction with TID TransID contains an intention to perform the Operation on Page of File, returns a pointer the intention record.
>
> **set_intention**(Operation, TransID, File, Page)
> records an entry in the intentions list for TransID.
>
> **List 13.5** Operations on intentions records.

Locks

Locks can be used to provide concurrency control in transaction service operations. We assume for simplicity that locks are applied at the level of pages. Thus, the server maintains a set of locks for each page of a file. There are the following types of locks: read and write. The set may contain several read locks, one write lock, or no locks associated with each page.

The operations required on locks in the DOMAIN system (Leach *et al.* 1985) are shown in List 13.6:

> **lock**(TransID, File, Page, LockType)
> waits on the lock condition variable, LockFree, if there is a lock set on the Page of the File that conflicts with LockType.The boolean 'locked' is returned true if the page is locked.
>
> **relock**(TransID, File, Page, LockType)
> sets a new lock of type LockType on Page of File.
>
> **unlock**(TransID, File, Page, LockType)
> removes the lock and signals if there is a lock of type LockType on Page of File on behalf of the transaction TransID. This allows any transactions waiting in a **lock** for Page to proceed.
>
> **List 13.6** Lock access functions.

These lock operations are used in the implementation of transaction service operations, such as **write, read**. When more than one transaction tries to modify a lock concurrently, conflicts between them can occur. To avoid such conflicts the operations should be protected by a monitor. As a result, only one transaction at a time can execute **write, read** or

unlock, and the scope for concurrency within the server is restricted quite severely. However, it should be noticed that since locks are associated with particular pages, two transactions conflict when they are accessing locks on the same page. Therefore, a number of monitors can be instantiated. In this case each monitor may be executing a **write** or a **read** concurrently on a different file or a different page of the same file.

The commit phase of a transaction

The following operations are performed by the transaction server in the second phase of a transaction:

(1)   transfer the data in the shadow pages into appropriate files,

(2)   release the locks, and

(3)   recover the storage used to represent the transaction record and intentions list.

Recall that all these operations must be performed completely, even if the server or the client crashes.

   To perform these operations the server must know the state of transactions. Thus, a transaction record which contains two items, the transaction identifier and the commit flag, is associated with each active transaction. (The commit flag records the current phase of the transaction: **tentative, committed** or **aborted**.) All these records are maintained by the server.

13.5.5   Selected aspects of a distributed transaction service

In a distributed system based on one local area network or on a number of linked local area networks there could be more than one file server. However, a client should not need to be aware that there are a number of servers, that they are geographically distributed, and that files are located in any of them in particular. All these servers should collaborate to provide an integrated file service transparent with respect to location, distribution, and replication of files.

   In such a system, a distributed transaction service can be seen as an extension to the transaction service which supports transactions that involve files managed by several servers. This extension should be done in such a way that the distribution of the files involved in a transaction is transparent to the client. The servers that perform file operations forming a joint transaction may communicate to coordinate their actions. In particular, the actions of the servers must be coordinated when the transaction commits in order to achieve reliability and concurrency control over the entire set of these operations. Despite this, clients requests to access and update a file involved in a transaction are sent to the server that stores and manages the file. Such an approach avoids the additional communication overhead which would otherwise arise if all requests were directed to one single server.

Distributed transactions with a coordinating server are implemented in the XDFS file service (see Mitchell and Dion [1982], Sturgis *et al.* [1980]), based on the concepts introduced in Israel *et al.* (1978). When a client needs to access files on more than one file server in a single transaction, it opens this transaction by sending an **begin_transaction** request to any server. The server performs **begin_transaction** and returns the transaction identifier. The selected server becomes the **coordinator** for the transaction.

The coordinator reports to the primary server for the transaction so that they can coordinate later. The identity of the primary server is a part of the transaction identifier, which appears in the response to the original **begin_transaction**. The coordinator is also responsible for aborting or commiting the transaction, and adding other servers called **workers**. However, gathering workers is a client task, which sends a call to a server to join the transaction as seen in List 13.7.

---

add_server(TransID, coordinator _serverID)
informs a server that it is involved in the transaction TransID.

List 13.7   Transaction service operation.

This operation is an extension to a set of the transaction service operations listed in Section 13.5.1. After receiving an **add_server** request from a client, a server calls the coordinator to inform it of its intention to join the transaction. Next, the worker records the coordinator's identifier, makes a new transaction record containing the transID, and initializes a new intentions list to record the updates to local files from the transaction. The coordinator stores a list of all the other servers involved in the transaction.

When a distributed transaction ends and is due to enter the second phase, it must be committed or aborted. At this point the servers involved in this transaction must communicate to decide whether the transaction should be committed or aborted. Thus, first the coordinator sends an inquiry **can_commit?** to each worker in the list. If all of the servers can commit the transaction, the coordinator tells each worker to commit its transaction by sending a **do_commit** request. After this, each server must complete the transaction according to the joint decision. A worker confirms that it has committed the transaction by sending **have_committed**. The two-phase commit algorithm (presented in Chapter 6) can be used to commit multi-server transactions. Such an algorithm is used in the XDFS system.

The basic problem of a service based on communicating servers is how to guarantee its security, that is, how to protect the integrity of a distributed transaction. Because we do not want any other process than the coordinator to call **do_commit**, some information must be passed between a worker and the coordinator. For example, a worker could use a **capability** in the **new_server** call for this purpose. A worker will commit its transaction if it receives a **do_commit** call containing the **capability** it issued. Of course, other methods providing security between communicating entities can be used (see Chapter 12).

In this monograph we do not discuss in detail multi-server commit or the implementation of distributed transactions in which the treatment of recovery and synchronization is combined using timestamps. Readers can refer to Israel *et al.* (1978), Reed (1983), Svobodova (1984) and Coulouris and Dollimore (1988).

13.6 Selected issues of replicated file services

There are two classes of collaborating file servers which can provide integrated, distributed file service:

(1)   file servers managing partitions of the total set of files in the distributed system, and

(2)   file servers supporting replicated files.

Performance and reliability reasons may force the designer of an integrated file service to use replicated files. A replicated file is a file which has a number of copies which are located in separate servers. The provision of replicated files can improve performance by reducing communication traffic and improving response time by providing clients with local copies, and enabling several clients to access the same file serviced by different servers, thereby improving system throughput.

File replication also improves reliability by increasing system availability, by making it possible to access the same file on more than one server; this reduces the effect of server and communication failures.

The provision of replicated files reduces the importance of the three problems mentioned before, but generates another problem known as the **multi-copy update problem**. Maintaining consistency among copies when a replicated file is updated is the major design problem of a replicated file system. This implies the need to associate either a timestamp or a version number with each replicated copy of a file. Moreover, the access and update algorithms must ensure that up-to-date versions are used. (Problems associated with timestamps, and some solutions to them, are discussed in Chapter 6.)

It is also obvious that replicated file systems should be transparent. This means that a replicated file service must function exactly like a non-replicated file service, but exhibit improved performance and reliability.

As mentioned earlier, file replication can be used to improve the performance of a file service when files are shared. The improvement can be achieved by allowing several copies of the same file to be placed and managed by different servers. The main problems of a replicated file service are data consistency and multiple copy update.

There are two basic approaches to file replication: the master/slave strategy and distributed update control. These two strategies can be distinguished from each other in that the former requires a distinguished master copy, whereas the latter does not.

13.6.1 The master/slave strategy

In a system based on the master/slave strategy there is one distinguished (master) server and several secondary (slave) servers for each replicated file. The master server stores a master copy of the file. It also services all the update requests. Each slave representative of the file is updated by taking copies from the master copy or by receiving information about changes from the master server. This strategy can be used in applications in which files are changed infrequently, and changes can be accepted at a central point. The Sun Yellow Pages (YP) service (Sun 1987) is an example of the master/slave strategy.

13.6.2 Distributed update control

In some applications, files are updated frequently by clients at different locations. In this case an approach based on a distinguished master copy is not a useful solution. This is because:

(1) updates must continue even when some of the servers containing copies of a file are unavailable, and

(2) it may not be desirable to update all copies immediately for performance reasons.

This leads to the need for a distributed update control mechanism. A mechanism of this type should allow any server which maintains a copy of a file to accept changes to that file and to issue those changes to the other copies in such a way that clients have a consistent view of the data. Moreover, the distributed update control mechanism should resolve conflicting updates and ensure consistency of the replicated files. Replication of files should be transparent to the user. This implies a replicated file should always be seen as a single file by the user.

To provide a replicated file service, each server which holds a copy of a replicated file should maintain a list of copies which contains at least the UFIDs and the server identifiers of the replicated files. The set of copies that compose a replicated file is called a **file suite**.

Since it may not be desirable to update all copies of a file immediately, servers must be able to determine, based on version numbers or timestamps, whether copies are up to date before a read operation is performed. If version numbers are used, a server which receives a request to perform a read or write operation on a replicated file can request version numbers from other servers listed in the file suite. The latest version number among version numbers received belongs to the current version of a file.

The problem is how many copies of a file should be updated immediately. This problem has no single solution. Existing solutions are based on voting, using two basic voting methods: majority voting (known also as majority consensus) and weighted voting (also called majority consensus with weighted voting). These voting methods were described in Chapter 4.

13.7 Naming/directory service

A naming facility manages user names and their mappings into the system names that are meaningful at the machine level. This allows files to be referenced by text string names. It is very important to logically separate the storage policy and mapping rules from the underlying facility that manages files (and transactions) that the names represent.

Recall that system names should be unique throughout a distributed system. User names should also be uniform so that the name of a file does not change from one computer to another. However, every user should be allowed to name personal files without any knowledge of names used by other users. This can lead to different user names for the same file or the same user names for different files. A naming service should be developed in such a way as to enable these contradictory requirements to be fulfilled. The response is a hierarchical tree name space.

Files usually belong to their owners who created them. The file system should provide a protection service to stop unauthorized access to files. However, many files are shared. This implies that a protection system should allow for sharing and this should be provided at different levels of user granularity (for example, owner, group, others).

In a distributed system there could be more than one file server. However, a client should not need to be aware of this fact, nor that these servers are geographically distributed, nor that files are located in any of them in particular. This results in file servers collaborating to provide an integrated file service transparent to location, distribution, and replication of files.

13.7.1 Naming schemes

In distributed file systems, there are three main approaches to naming schemes (Levy and Silberschatz 1989):

(1) **Simple naming** – According to this approach, files are named by some combination of their local name and server name. As we emphasized in Section 13.3.3, this guarantees uniqueness of a wide naming space. This naming scheme is used in Ibis (Tichy and Ruan 1984).

(2) **Mounting remote directories to local directories** – This approach gives the appearance of a coherent directory tree. Note that only the attached, remote directory can be accessed transparently. This naming scheme is used in Sun's NFS (Sandberg 1986).

(3) **Single global name space** – According to this approach, which provides the total integration between the component file systems, a single global name structure spans all the files in the system. Different variations of this approach are used in LOCUS (Walker *et al.* [1983] and Popek and Walker [1985]), and Sprite (Ousterhout *et al.* 1988).

13.7.2 Directory service

The directory service is concerned with naming and protecting files. This service typically provides objects called directories, that map ASCII file names onto the file identifiers (UFIDs) used by the file service. A directory is mostly a file and a set of functions which distinguishes it from an ordinary data file, allowing this file to be seen as a fixed sized record file, each record coresponding to an entry in the directory. Since the directory service is a client of the file service, its mappings are stored by the file service. Thus, each directory has a UFID. The directory service protects files, utilizing an access list for each file to ensure that UFIDs are not given to the wrong clients. Since the directory service is separate from the file service a variety of directory services can be developed and used for a single file service.

The division of responsibilities between file service and directory service is based upon the use of UFID for access to the contents of files. Thus, when a file is created for the requesting client, the file service allocates a new UFID for it. Then, this client can request the directory service to record the UFID and its text (user) name. As a result, the client can request access to the file by providing its user name to the directory service.

A hierarchical tree name space is commonly used in many centralized systems (e.g., UNIX). It guarantees uniqueness of names, and efficient name resolution. A hierarchical tree name space was also developed for LOCUS (Popek and Walker 1985), DOMAIN (Leach *et al.* 1985) and the File System for PM (Braban and Schlenk 1989).

In the DOMAIN name space, directories are at the nodes and files at the leaves. A single component name is resolved in the context of

---

create_dir(Dir, ParentDir)
  creates a new directory Dir in the directory ParentDir.

open_dir(Dir)
  opens the Dir directory

read_dir(Dir, Name, AccessMode)
  Locates the text name in the directory and returns the relevant UFID; reports an error if it cannot be found or if the client making the request is not authorized to access the file in the manner specified by AccessMode.

insert(Dir, Name, File)
  adds the (Name, File) pair to the Dir directory.

un_name(Dir, Name)
  removes the entry containing Name from the directory. If Name is not in the directory: reports an error.

change(OldDir, OldName, NewDir, NewName)
  changes the entry containing OldName to a NewName.

get_names(Dir, Pattern) —> NameSeq
  returns the set of all of the the names in the Dir directory that match regular expression given by Pattern.

close_dir(Dir)
  closes the Dir directory

delite_dir(Dir, ParentDir)
  removes the empty directory Dir from the directory ParentDir.

ch_dirAttr(Dir, Attributes)
  changes attributes of the Dir directory; allows the modification of the access control list associated with this directory.

List 13.8 Directory service operations.

---

the particular directory by finding its associated UFID. The absolute name of a file is an ordered list of component names, which, when resolved starting from 'root' directory leads to the UFID of the file. Note that 'root' is network-wide distinguished directory. This implies that an absolute path name is valid and unique throughout the entire distributed system. In a hierarchical tree name space, other forms of name can also be used. These are the so called relative names. These names are used for convenience since absolute names can be very long.

The directory service can be better described by introducing its operations. This presentation of operations of a directory service follows Braban and Schlank (1989), Sandberg (1986) and Spector and Kazar (1988).

A set of directory service operations is listed in List 13.8.

13.7.3 Access control

Access control requires the directory service to access and update the file attributes. On the other hand, the directory service should provide an operation which enables clients to inspect the file attributes. Since each file has an owner and the owner's userID is recorded in the attributes, the directory service should also provide operations which allow the owners of files to grant and revoke access rights to other users.

The problem is who can access directories and can perform such operations as **read_dir**, **insert**, **change** and **un_name**. Since the directory service is the owner of all the files which contain its directories, it is allowed to perform all file service operations on them. Thus, the directory service can create, write, read and delete the mappings between file names and their UFIDs.

On the other hand, it is obvious that when users have separate private directories, the UFID of the directory may be regarded as a capability. Thus, no further access control is required. Only when directories are shared is some access control needed. A simple access permission scheme used for files can be applied in this situation.

Since other aspects of access control such as access control lists have been discussed in Chapter 11, they will not be discussed further in this section.

13.7.4 Placement and location of files in a distributed file service

In a distributed system there could be more than one file server. However, a client should not need to be aware that there are a number of servers, that they are geographically distributed, and that files are located in any of them in particular. All these servers should collaborate to provide an integrated file service transparent to location, distribution and replication of files.

When file servers hold partitions of the total set of files, usually each partition is associated with a particular application and the servers are placed at separate locations. A given file server manages its partition independently from other servers. The file service presented in Section 13.5 can be used for this purpose. The client is not aware of the location of the server holding the files. There are three basic problems. The **placement problem** arises when a file is created and a server must be chosen to hold it. The **location problem** arises when a client wishes to refer to a given file – a server which holds this file must be found. The **relocation problem** arises when files need to be relocated for performance reasons.

To solve these three problems it is necessary to provide additional services within a naming service responsible for the placement of newly created files, the location of referenced files, and the relocation of files. A schematic system providing these services is illustrated in Fig. 13.12.

This figure shows that the basic task of a file service in the distributed systems with a number of servers managing partitions of the total set of files is to locate a file. Moreover, each server suffers from the same drawbacks with respect to a given file partition as a centralized file server: poor performance and low reliability.

In a basic distributed file service, when a client creates a file, one server has to be selected to hold and maintain this file. The selection can be performed automatically or can take into consideration the client's preferences. In the case of an automatic placement algorithm, the loca-

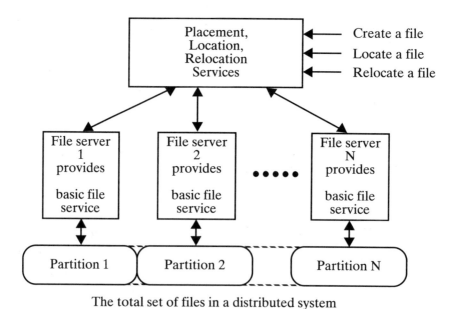

The total set of files in a distributed system

Fig. 13.12   Placement, location and relocation services.

tion is chosen to minimize comunication delay between the client and server, or to optimize the storage utilization across all of the servers. The selected server generates a new UFID which contains its own server-ID, and manages the file.

To reference a file, a client has to know the location of the file server that manages the required file. There is no problem if files do not move. However, if a file can move between servers, a location algorithm must be used to determine its current location. This information is retained by the client for future reference until the file is again moved. Successful access by a client must never depend on the holding of a current location token. Rather, the access algorithm must transparently update the location token whenever access is requested.

To support placement and location the primitive operations given in List 13.9 can be used.

---

place(File)
> finds the 'best' file server for File.

locate(File)
> finds the node address of the home server of File.

List 13.9   Primitives for collaborating files servers.

Different systems use different location algorithms. For example, in the Apollo DOMAIN operating system, as we said earlier, a separate file locating service determines the locations of files based on their UFIDs (Leach *et al.* 1983). The locating algorithm uses the following hints about file location: the birthplace, a hint file stored in each client computer, and a directory service. The last is based on the assumption that files are stored in the same server as the directory they are in. Another approach is used in LOCUS (Popek and Walker 1985). In this system each file is assigned to a **synchronization site**, which is a server that records a mapping from the UFID to the server that is currently storing the file. This implies that one of the fields of the file's UFID contains the address of its synchronization site, and that this reference remains constant. Thus, the file can be moved from one server to another, but information about its current location must be updated at the synchronization site each time it moves.

13.8   Analysis of file server designs

Many file servers have been designed and implemented. These systems are based on different solutions to the problems of data access, concurrency control, serializing transactions, deadlock control and recoverability. An overview of these servers can be found in Svobodova (1984), Hac (1985), Levy and Silberschatz (1989) and Satyanarayanan (1989). There are pros and cons to every solution, and not all of these solutions are independent of each other. Moreover, a file server can be designed in several different ways depending on the application.

13.8.1 File servers reviewed

The following systems will be reviewed:

(1) XDFS (Xerox Distributed File System) from Xerox PARC (see Sturgis *et al.* [1980], Mitchell and Dion [1982]). This was a result of an extensive research project in designing a very robust, multiple server system. XDFS is a file service running on several servers accessed by clients in the Xerox Internet. Each file has a unique identifier (a large integer) generated when a new file is created. XDFS does not include directory facilities, but a directory service is provided as a client of it.

(2) CFS (Cambridge File Server) (see Dion [1980], Mitchell and Dion [1982], Needham and Herbert [1982]). This system was developed at the University of Cambridge as an attempt to implement a 'universal' file server for clients that are general-purpose operating systems (CAP [Wilkes and Needham 1979] and TRIPOS [Richards *et al.* 1979]). It supports other servers in the Cambridge Distributed Computing System, above all the name server, the boot server and the authentication server. CFS provides both files and indexes, which are structures designed to hold identifiers of files.

(3) FELIX (Fridrich and Older 1981, 1985). This is a general-purpose file server developed at Bell–Northern Research. The first version of this system was implemented in extended Pascal, and its first client was an existing UCSD Pascal file system. The second version is an object-oriented file system which consists of the original FELIX and a client layer that implements various abstract objects. It provides full-scale dynamic concurrency control.

(4) SWALLOW (Reed and Svobodova 1981, Svobodova 1981). SWALLOW is a distributed data storage system designed in early 1980 at the Laboratory for Computer Science at the Massachusetts Institute of Technology. SWALLOW was intended to provide atomic transactions on multiple files and multiple servers. It is based on a model of stored objects. This model supports the coexistence of multiple versions of an object and an automatic selection of versions of objects used by a transaction. SWALLOW consists of two components: repositories – the actual shared ser-

vers; and brokers – modules running in each client computer. SWALLOW design first explored the benefits of immutable files.

(5) CMCFS (Carnegie–Mellon Central File System) (Svobodova 1984) was designed in early 1980. This system puts strong emphasis on filing and access control. It planned to provide two different kinds of update: an update of an entire file – create a new version of the file; and a transaction update – allow several transactions to use and update the same version of a file.

(6) The file system of LOCUS (Mueller *et al.* 1983, Popek *et al.* 1981, Walker *et al.* 1983) was developed at UCLA in 1981. LOCUS is a UNIX-like distributed operating system, including a so-called 'integrated' distributed filing system in which each computer can act as a client and a server. Each computer contains a part of the total filing system, which can be accessed by client programs running in any other LOCUS node. Principle features of LOCUS are a high degree of location transparency, a high level of reliability and availability, and good performance. Operations on files can involve the following sites: the using site – the client computer which issues requests and receives responses; the storage site – the place where files are stored, and the current synchronization site – which records the locations of files and is responsible for the synchronization of concurrent accesses to them.

(7) The Apollo DOMAIN system was developed by Apollo Computer Inc. in 1979 (Leach *et al.* [1983, 1985] and Levine [1987]). DOMAIN is a distributed architecture of workstations and servers connected by a token ring network. Both local and remote files (in general, objects) are addressed by a unique identifier (UIDs), and referenced and accessed by clients in the same way. The DOMAIN system implements a single level storage for accessing all objects. Open files are mapped into the virtual address space of client processes. However, all access to the single-level store is through the kernel. The DOMAIN system is based on an integrated model in which each computer runs a complete set of system software providing a file service, directory service and other data management services which support transparent access to data. This is one of the most distinctive features of DOMAIN. Access to objects is transparent.

(8) F-UNIX (Luderer *et al.* 1981) is a remote shared server for a distributed UNIX file system, developed at the Bell Laboratories. A client, called S-UNIX, can access several F-UNIX servers and its own local files in a transparent way. Each client communicates with the F-UNIX servers via a virtual circuit switch. This system has been used mainly to study virtual circuit switching as the basis for a distributed system design.

(9)   The Sun Network File System (NFS) (Sandberg [1986], Osadzinski [1988]) provides transparent, distributed file service based on networked UNIX systems. However, it is designed to be easily portable to other operating systems (MS-DOS, VMS) and machine architectures (IBM PC). Moreover, the NFS allows sharing of files in a network of non-homogeneous computers. It uses an External Data Representation (XDR) specification to describe protocols in a computer and system independent way. The NFS design consists of three major pieces: the communication protocol; the server side – because the NFS server is stateless, when servicing a request it must commit any modified data to stable storage before returning results; and the client side – which provides an interface to NFS that is transparent to applications. In NFS, names are not location independent. NFS does not provide replication.

(10)   The file system of DEMOS (Powell [1977], Powell and Miller [1983]). This system was a part of the DEMOS operating system developed at Los Alamos Scientific Laboratory.

13.8.2   Review of file servers

We will review the systems presented above from the point of view of their approaches to the problems of data access, concurrency control, serializing transactions, file replication, deadlock control, recoverability and communication protocols.

Data access

There are a variety of data access units, that is, the fraction of a file that can be transferred to/from clients as a result of a single **Read/Write** operation, in several file servers. The unit of data access can be a file (SWALLOW), a sequential subset of a file (CFS, CMCFS, DEMOS), a page (FELIX, LOCUS, DOMAIN), a logical block (NFS), or a subset of a page (XDFS).

A mechanism for access control is necessary to protect files from unauthorized access. In a capability-based system, usually the file identifier is used as the capability. In an identity-based system (access list control), the identity of the user is also required. CFS, FELIX, LOCUS, and SWALLOW have a capability-based scheme, whereas CMCFS, XDFS, DOMAIN, and directory access in FELIX are identity-based.

File system structure

File systems usually consist of a multilevel tree of fixed-sized blocks (CFS, FELIX, LOCUS, CMCFS, DOMAIN, DEMOS). They may also consist of a multilevel tree of variable-size blocks (SWALLOW), or of a set of fixed-sized blocks (XDFS).

File management

Clients use two basic facilities that enable them to refer, access and manage files: file storage and directory storage. They can cooperate in two basic ways depending on the structure of the file servers. In XDFS and CMCFS a directory server is a client of the file server. In CFS, LOCUS, DOMAIN, FELIX, the file server includes special features for implementing directories.

Concurrency control

Any policy for concurrency control must allow transaction-type access to shared files. Concurrency control can be handled by the file system (CFS, FELIX, LOCUS, SWALLOW, XDFS, DOMAIN, DEMOS) or by the user (CMCFS).

CFS provides a simple form of atomic transaction, which allows only a single file in each transaction. Transactions may also include multiple files, as in XDFS and SWALLOW. Also, multiple files in multiple servers may be included in transactions (XDFS, SWALLOW). The XDFS file service supports atomic transactions including any number of files on several cooperating servers. In this system, every file operation must be part of a transaction, which implies some difficulties when programming certain applications (Mitchell and Dion 1982).

CFS and FELIX can support only single-client transactions. On the other hand, XDFS and SWALLOW support multi-client transactions.

In DOMAIN, a two-layer approach to concurrency management is used. There is no waiting for locks, for they are either accepted or rejected immediately.

The unit of concurrency control (that is, the entity to be locked) is usually a file (CFS, FELIX, SWALLOW, DOMAIN, CMCFS); it can also be a page (that is, the unit of storage allocation) (CMCFS). XDFS provides concurrency control also using locking, but the locking scheme was designed to maximize concurrency by reducing granularity of locking – portions of data within files are locked.

LOCUS provides nested transactions in which all changes to a file are atomic. It also uses the shadow page technique for making tentative copies of files during transactions. The shadow page technique is also used in XDFS.

NFS does not support remote file locking. Instead, there is a separate RPC-based file locking facility, the so-called status monitor. The status monitor is important to stateless services because it provides a common view of the state of the network. In the case of concurrent access to remote files by multiple clients, since the NFS server maintains no locks beween requests and a write may span several RPC requests, two clients writing to the same remote file can receive intermixed data on long writes.

The usual concurrency control policies are:

(1)   single writer or single reader policy;

(2)   single writer or multiple readers policy; this approach is used in CFS, CMCFS, and DOMAIN; and

(3)   single writer and multiple readers policy; this approach is used in XDFS, FELIX, and SWALLOW.

The lock operation in DOMAIN supports two locking modes for objects: the above-mentioned single writer or multiple reader, and a co-writers lock mode which makes no restrictions on the number of readers and writers, but demands that they be located at a single network node.

Serializing transactions

The most popular protocols for serializing transactions are:

(1)   Two-phase locking (commit) protocols (XDFS, FELIX, CMCFS). In the first phase, a transaction acquires locks; in the second phase, it releases all locks. In XDFS the two-phase commit protocol is carried out by means of messages passed between the coordinator and the participating servers. It is based on novel time-limited breakable locks.

(2)   Timestamp-based protocols (SWALLOW). This protocol requires that all transactions have associated values of their arrival times and can access the file according to the monotonically increasing values of these times.

File replication

The file system associated with LOCUS provides facilities for file replication, maintaining consistency among copies, continued operation in the face of partitioning of the file system, and location transparency. File replication is achieved through containers, which are assigned to logical file groups. A container is a reserved space on a disk and is associated with a single physical file system.

In LOCUS, consistency among copies of a file is maintained through the use of file locks and a 'single writer, multiple readers' protocol. A file is made available for reading and writing even if some copies are not currently available. To allow this, a copy reconciliation mechanism is provided. It is based on version vectors.

DOMAIN provides a very special form of file replication – fast access to distributed data is achieved by caching it in the main memory. This service is provided by the object storage system. A timestamp-based version number scheme is used to support the cache validation mechanisms and provide version consistency. This form is different from replicating data by keeping copies on the disks in a number of servers, but the issue of synchronizing updates of multiple copies is similar.

In SWALLOW, there are no specific facilities provided for file replication. However, a simple replication scheme could fairly easily be added to this system.

Deadlock handling

The policies for deadlock control are:

(1) Deadlock prevention (FELIX). A transaction declares all files before starting.

(2) Deadlock detection and resolution (FELIX). A transaction (or a process) responsible for a deadlock is selected and pre-empted, and its locks are released; after a while, the transaction is re-started. The operating system includes a lock manager which detects and resolves deadlocks.

(3) Time-limited locks (XDFS). The transaction waits to acquire its locks only for a certain amount of time, and then is timed out; after a while, it retries to acquire its locks. This system is acceptable when the system is not heavily loaded. When the system becomes more congested, then more transactions timeout due to their waiting for system resources and locks, rather than because of a system deadlock.

(4) Ordering by timestamps (SWALLOW) determines whether a transaction may wait for locks without creating a deadlock. A decision about whether to wait for locks or to abort a transaction is made immediately when a transaction requests access to a file. This decision is made on the basis of the order of timestamps.

(5) None (CFS, CMCFS). In the case of conflict, the user chooses whether a request has to be rejected or to be queued. The latter decision may cause a deadlock.

Recoverability

The shadow-page technique is the most common solution to ensure recoverability (LOCUS and FELIX). The idea of this mechanism is that only the file pages which have been updated are written into free blocks on the storage device. The file page map then has to be updated to indicate the new mapping of file pages to storage blocks. Shadow pages and intentions logs are also used. This recoverability technique is used in XDFS and CFS. Tentative versions are used in SWALLOW.

After a crash, a server must complete all committed transactions and undo all aborted ones. However, work which is performed in the second case must be completed before the server resumes normal operation. It is necessary to ensure that clients do not see any data inconsistencies. Immediate recovery after a crash is performed in CFS, XDFS, and FELIX, whereas recovery is completed as needed in SWALLOW.

Communication protocols

The following protocols are used to communicate between users and a file server:

(1) A datagram (unreliable) protocol (XDFS, CFS, SWALLOW, DOMAIN, FELIX) which transmits a message in a single network packet. However, reliability can be built in at a higher level where necessary, using, for instance, idempotent operations or stateless servers (DOMAIN); and

(2) A virtual circuit protocol (F-UNIX) transfers a stream of basic network packets.

A user communicates with a remote server in several ways:

(1) in two steps based on the model send_request/receive_response model (CFS, FELIX, LOCUS, DEMOS),

(2) in three steps based on the RRA protocol, that is, send request/ receive_response/send_ acknowedgement (XDFS),

(3) in a single step using no-wait_send (SWALLOW), or

(4) using the Remote Procedure Call model (NFS).

The mechanism used to reclaim server resources from non-responding users may be:

(1) Single timeout per transaction (SWALLOW);

(2) Interrequest timeout (CFS, XDFS), where the timeout is associated with individual user requests;

(3) Communication subsystems (CMCFS), which detects non-responding users and aborts the affected transactions.

NFS uses a stateless protocol. The parameters to each procedure call contain all of the information necessary to complete a call. Thus, the server does not keep track of any past request. As a result, crash recovery is easy.

13.9 OSI file service

The three highest layers (Session, Presentation and Application) of the ISO Reference Model for Open System Interconnection (OSI) provide services to ensure that the incoming communication is understandable and processible. In particular, the Application Layer provides Application Service Elements (ASEs), that is, services that are required for a semantic exchange between user (application) processes. A number of ASEs have been developed just recently. Among them are File Transfer, Access, and Management (FTAM), Message Handling System (MHS), Virtual Terminal (VT), Distributed Transaction Processing (DTP), Job Transfer and Manipulation (JTM).

The File Transfer, Access and Management (FTAM) provides not only a file transfer mechanism but also such functions as remote access and manipulation of data, and a powerful file management capability. Following the ISO/OSI concept, the FTAM is based on the concept of a virtual filestore that defines the common structure to describe and execute file-related actions among different systems in the OSI environment. The FTAM Protocol was published in October 1988; protocol standard, ISO 8571.

A file in the FTAM context is a collection of meaningful information with a variety of properties. All files have attributes that describe them. A filestore is an organized collection of files, including their attributes and names, which reside at a particular open system. Table 13.2 shows the OSI virtual filestore attributes. This table indicates that some attributes are created when the file is created, others can be explicitly changed by user operations, and others are automatically maintained by the file server.

Attribute	when created	changed by user	maintained by server
File name	x	x	
Allowed operations (can be specified by the creator of a file	x		
Access control (specifies who may access the file, and how)		x	
Account number	x	x	
Date and time of file creation	x		
Date and time of last file modification	x	x	x
Date and time of last file read	x		x
Date and time of last attribute modification	x		x
Owner	x		
Identity of last modifier	x		x
Identity of last reader	x		x
Identity of last attribute modifier	x		x
File availability (used to indicate that there may be a delay when opening the file)	x	x	
Contents type	x		
Encryption key	x		
Size	x	x	x
Maximum future size	x	x	
Legal qualifications (might contain security classification code)	x	x	
Private use	x		

Fig. 13.2 The OSI filestore attributes.

The openess requires the filestore in the FTAM to be virtual. The virtual filestore is defined as an abstract model for describing files and filestores as a common basis for supporting communications among real systems. This has to be provided regardless of the design, technology and manufacture of the real system.

The capabilities of FTAM are defined by the operations that the virtual filestore is capable of performing. The operations listed in List 13.10 can be performed on whole files.

Create file
create a new file and establish its attributes.

Delete file
remove an existing file.

Select file
establish a relationship between the creator and and a particular file; pick a file for attribute management.

Deselect file
remove a file from access without deletion.

Open file
open a file for subsequent operations (reading or modification).

Close file
close an open file.

Read attribute
read a file attribute.

Change attribute
modify a file attribute.

List 13.10 The virtual filestore operations performed on whole files.

The operations given in List 13.11 can be performed on an open file. These operations are invoked by FTAM service primitives issued by a filestore client. Access control is based on attributes such as, client identity (access lists), or location of a client. The basic FTAM file structure is a multilevel hierarchy. Two special hierarchical subsets are accommodated: one-level (unstructured) and two-level (flat) files.

Locate
> locate a specified unit of data.

Read
> read data from a file.

Insert
> insert a new unit of data into the appropriate position in the file.

Replace
> substitute (overwrite) the contents of a unit of data.

Extend
> append data to some unit of data (record).

Erase
> delete the entire unit of data.

List 13.11   The virtual filestore operations performed on opened files.

13.10 Summary

There are a number of services provided by a distributed system, but one of the most important is the file service. In practice, users contact a computer system through the file service. This service is the main service used by users in accessing the total distributed system. Note that a file service is also necessary to support automatic backup and recovery, user visibility, and diskless instructions.

There are three main classifications of file servers. The first distinguishes true file servers, which are complete filing systems, from storage servers. Another classification distinguishes a traditional file service, which is offered by nearly all centralized operating systems, and a robust service, which is aimed at those applications that require extremely high reliability. The latter service generally offers atomic updates and similar features lacking in traditional file services.

The third classification is based on remote file access. There are two forms of remote file access: explicit file transfer in which a client must invoke a file transfer utility to transfer a remote file before or after its use; and distributed file systems in which file location is transparent to clients, files are referred to by names, source data and directory information are cached, and some files can be replicated.

Files represent a convenient way of viewing programs and data from both the logical user view and the physical storage view. This implies that files need a method for control and arrangement at the system level.

The following major functions must be performed in centralized systems as well as in distributed systems: disk service, file service, and directory service. These three functions are usually performed by the following modules: device, block, file access, access control, file module and directory. Whereas in centralized systems these three functions are usually not separated, in distributed systems there is a division of responsibilities of these three functions – three services handle these functions.

When dealing with disk service, the following issues must be considered: file storage, the caching system, unique file identifiers, file location and block service operations. The design of a flat file service deals with such issues as mutable and immutable files and file service operations on data and attributes. Directory service is mainly oriented towards performing operations of the directory service, and access control mechanisms.

Because many client processes should be allowed to read and write data in the same file concurrently, the file service should support transactions, and atomic actions should be provided. This requires special transaction service operations. Moreover, because of the possibility of failures, some recovery procedures must be implemented. There are two commonly-used approaches to recovery: the intentions list approach and the file version approach.

The connection of a number of various local area networks into one distributed system, and performance and reliability reasons, dictate the existence of collaborating file servers. There are two classes of collaborating file servers: those managing partitions of the total set of files in a distributed system, and those supporting replicated files.

Clients of the first class are not aware of the location of files. This generates three basic problems: placement, location and relocation. Data consistency and the multiple copy update problems are the basic issues to be dealt with when providing replicated file services. There are two basic approaches to file replication: the master/slave strategy and distributed update control. The main difference lies in the fact that the former requires a distinguished master copy, whereas the latter does not.

When assessing file servers the following aspects must be considered: data access units and mechanisms, file system structure, file management, concurrency control, serializability of transactions, file replication, deadlock control, recoverability and communication protocols.

ISO has put a lot of effort into ensuring that incoming communication is understandable and processible. In particular, the Application Layer provides Application Service Elements; services that are required for a semantic exchange between user processes. Among them is File Transfer Access and Management (FTAM). FTAM provides not only a file transfer mechanism, but also remote access and manipulation of data, and a file management capability.

Bibliography

Bernstein P.A. and Goodman N. (1981). Concurrency Control in Distributed Database Systems. *Computing Surveys,* **13**(2), 185–221

Birrell A.D. and Needham R.M. (1980). A Universal File Server. *IEEE Transactions on Software Engineering,* **SE–6**(5), 450–3

Braban B. and Schlenk P. (1989). A Well Structured Parallel File System for PM. *Operating Systems Review,* **23**(2), 25–38

Brown M.R., Kolling K.N. and Taft E.A. (1985). The Alpine File System. *ACM Transactions on Computer Systems,* **3**(4), 261–93

Coulouris G.F. and Dollimore J. (1988). *Distributed Systems. Concepts and Design* Addison-Wesley

Dion J. (1980). The Cambridge File Server. *Operating Systems Review,* **14**(4), 26–35

Eppinger J.L. and Spector A.Z. (1988). A Camelot Perspective. *UNIX Review,* **7**(1), 58–67

Folts H. (1989). OSI File Service. *IEEE Network,* **3**(2), 52

Fridrich M. and Older W. (1981). The FELIX File Server. In *Proceedings of the 8th ACM Symposium on Operating Systems Principles,* Pacific Grove, California, 37–44

Fridrich M. and Older W. (1985). Helix: The Architecture of the XMS Distributed File System. *IEEE Software,* **2**(3), 21–9

Gifford D.K., Needham R.M. and Schreader M.D. (1988). The Ceder File System. *Communications of the ACM,* **31**(3), 288–98

Gray J. (1978). Notes on Database Operating Systems, in Operating Systems. An Advanced Course. *Lecture Notes in Computer Science, No. 60,* Springer-Verlag, 394–481

Hac A. (1985). Distributed File Systems — A Survey. *Operating Systems Review,* **19**(1), 15–8

Hagmann R. (1987). Reimplementing the Cedar File System Using Logging and Group Commit. *Proceedings of the Eleventh ACM Symposium on Operating Systems Principles,* Austin, 155–62

Howard J.K., Kazar M.L., Menees S.G., Nichols D.A., Satyanarayanan M. and Sidebotham R.N. (1988). Scale and Performance in a Distributed File System. *ACM Transactions on Computer Systems,* **6**(10), 55–81

Israel J.E., Mitchell J.G. and Sturgis H.E. (1978). Separating Data from Function in a Distributed File System, *Operating Systems: Theory and Practice,* (Lanciaux D. eds.), North-Holland, 17–22

Kohler W.H. (1981). A Survey of Techniques for Synchronization and Recovery in Decentralized Computer Systems. *Computing Surveys.* **13**(2), 149–83

Kung H.T. and Robinson J.T. (1981). Optimistic Methods for Concurrency Control. *ACM Transactions on Database Systems,* **6**(2), 213–26

Lampson B.W. (1981). Atomic Transactions, in Distributed Systems — Architecture and Implementation. An Advanced Course (Lampson B.W., Paul, M. and Siegart H.J.), *Lecture Notes in Computer Science,* (105), pp. 246–64

Leach P.J., Levine P.H., Douros B.P., Hamilton J.A., Nelson D.L. and Stumpf B.L. (1983). The Architecture of an Integrated Local Network. *IEEE Journal on Selected Areas in Communications,* **SAC–1**(5), 842–56

Leach P.J., Levine P.H., Hamilton J.A. and Stumpf B.L. (1985). The File System of an Integrated Local Network. *ACM Computer Science Conference, New Orleans*

Levine P.H. (1987). The Apollo DOMAIN Distributed File System. *Distributed Operating Systems Theory and Practice*. (Paker *et al.* eds.) 241–60, Springer-Verlag

Levy E. and Silberschatz A. (1989). *Distributed File Systems: Concepts and Examples*. TR–89–04 Department of Computer Sciences, The University of Texas at Austin

Linington P.F. (1989). File Transfer Protocols. *IEEE Journal on Selected Areas in Communications,* SAC–7(7), 1052–9

Luderer G.W.R., Che H., Haggerty J.P., Kirslis P.A. and Marshall W.T. (1981). A Distributed UNIX System Based on a Virtual Circuit Switch. *Proceedings of the 8th ACM Symposium on Operating Systems Principles,* Pacific Grove, California,

Meister B., Janson P. and Svobodova L. (1985). File Transfer in Local Area Networks: A Performance Study. *The 5th International Conference on Distributed Computing Systems*, Denver, Colorado, 338–49

Melamed A.S. (1987), Performance Analysis of UNIX-based Network File Systems. *IEEE Micro, 7*(1), 25–38

Mitchell J.G. and Dion J. (1982). A Comparison of Two Network-Based File Servers. *Communications of the ACM. 25*(4), 233–45

Mueller E.T., Moore J.D. and Popek G.T. (1983). A Nested Transaction Mechanism for LOCUS. In *Proceedings of the 9th ACM Symposium on Operating Systems Principles,* Bretton Woods, N.H. 71–89

Mukherjee A., Kramer J. and Magee J. (1988). A Distributed File Server for Embedded Applications. *Software Engineering Journal*, (8), 142–8

Mullender S.J. and Tanenbaum A.S. (1985). A Distributed File Service Based on Optimistic Concurrency Control. *Proceedings of the Tenth ACM Symposium on Operating Systems Principles,* Orcas Island, Washington, 51–62

Needham R.M. and Herbert A.J. (1982). *The Cambridge Distributed Computing System*. Addison-Wesley

Nelson M., Welch B. and Ousterhout J.K., (1988). Caching in the Sprite Network File System. *ACM Transactions on Computer Systems, 6*(1)

Osadzinski A. (1988). The Network File System (NFS). *Computer Standards & Interfaces,* 8, 45–8

Ousterhout J.K., Cherensen A.R., Douglis F., Nelson M.N. and Welch B.B. (1988). The Sprite Network Operating System. *IEEE Computer, 21*(2), 23–36

Paxton W.H. (1979). A Client – Based Transaction System to Maintain Data Integrity. *Proceedings of the Seventh Symposium on Operating Systems Principles,* Pacific Grove, California, 18–23

Popek G., Walker B., Chow J., Edwards D., Kline C., Rudisin G. and Thiel G. (1981). LOCUS: A Network Transparent, High Reliability Distributed System. *Proceedings of the Eighth ACM Symposium on Operating Systems Principles,* Pacific Grove, California, 169–77

Popek G. and Walker B., ed. (1985). *The LOCUS Distributed System Architecture*. Cambridge, Mass: MIT Press

Powell M.L. (1977). The DEMOS File System. *Proceedings of the Sixth ACM Symposium on Operating Systems Principles,* 33–42

Powell M.L. and Miller B.P. (1983). Process Migration in DEMOS/MP. *Proceedings of the 9th ACM Symposium on Operating Systems Principles,* Bretton Woods, 33–42

Rake F., Tasker R. and Kummer P. (1984). Performance Measurements of an Ethernet Local Area Network. *Interfaces in Computing,* **2**, 221–6

Ramakrishnan K.K. and Emer J.S. (1986). A Model of File Server Performance for a Heterogeneous Distributed System. *SIGCOMM'86 Symposium on Communications Architectures and Protocols,* Stowe, Vermont, 338–47

Reed D.P. (1983). Implementing Atomic Actions on Decentralized Data. *ACM Transactions on Computer Systems,* **1**(1), 3–23

Reed D.P. and Svobodova L. (1981). SWALLOW: A Distributed Data Storage System for a Local Network. *Local Networks for Computer Communications* (West A. and Janson P. eds.), 355–73, North-Holland

Richards M., Aylward A.R., Bond P., Evens R.D. and Knight B.J. (1979). TRIPOS: A Portable Operating System For Mini-computers: *Software — Practice and Experience,* **9**(7), 513–26

Sandberg R. (1986). *The Sun Network File System: Design, Implementation and Experience.* Sun Microsystems, Inc.

Satyanarayanan M. (1989). *A Survey of Distributed File Systems.* CMU–CS–89–116, Department of Computer Science, Carnegie–Mellon University

Satyanarayanan M., Howard J.H., Nichols D.A., Sidebotham R.N., Spector A.Z. and West M.J. (1985). ITC Distributed File System: Principles and Design. *Proceedings of the 10th Symposium on Operating Systems Principles,* Orcas Island, 35–50

Schroeder M.D., Gifford D.K. and Needham R.M. (1985). A Caching File System for a Programmer's Workstation. *Proceedings of the 10th Symposium on Operating Systems Principles,* Orcas Island, 25–32

Spector A.Z. (1987). Distributed Transaction Processing and the Camelot System. *Distributed Operating Systems. Theory and Practice* (Paker Y. ed.) Berlin: Springer-Verlag, 331–53

Spector A.Z. and Kazar M.L. (1989). Uniting File Systems. *UNIX Review,* **7**(3) 61–70

Sturgis H., Mitchell J.G. and Israel J. (1980). Issues in the Design and Use of a Distributed File System. *Operating Systems Review,* **14**(3), 15–8

Sun (1987). *Sun Network File System (NFS) Reference Manual,* Mountain View, California: Sun Microsystems

Svobodova L. (1981). A Reliable Object-Oriented Data Repository for a Distributed Computer System. *Proceedings of the 8th ACM Symposium on Operating Systems Principles,* Pacific Grove, California, 47–58

Svobodova L. (1984). File Servers for Network-Based Distributed Systems. *Computing Surveys,* **16**,(4), 353–98

Tichy W.F. and Ruan Z. (1984). Towards a Distributed File System. *Proceedings of Usenix 1984 Summar Conference,* Salt Lake City, Utah, 87–97

Walker B., Popek G., English R., Kline C. and Thiel G. (1983). The LOCUS Distributed Operating System. *Proceedings of the 9th ACM Symposium on Operating Systems Principles,* Bretton Woods, N.H., 49–70

Wilkes M.V. and Needham R.M. (1979). *The Cambridge CAP Computer and Its Operating System,* New York: North-Holland

14 Survey of experimental distributed operating systems

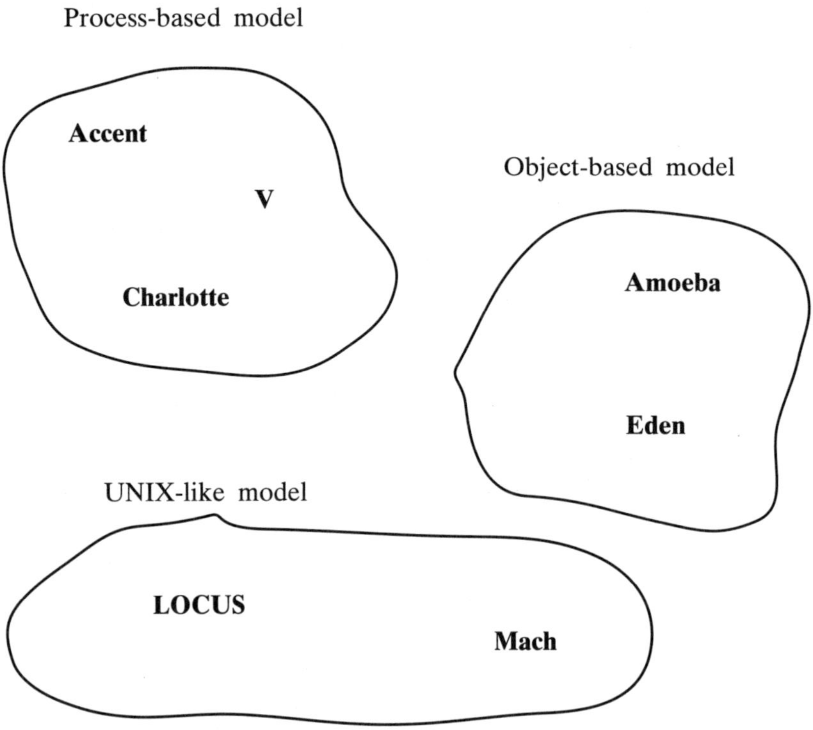

Process-based model

Accent

V

Charlotte

Object-based model

Amoeba

Eden

UNIX-like model

LOCUS

Mach

In previous chapters we have discussed individual aspects of distributed operating systems. We have not emphasized the design and implementation aspects which are relevant to the system as a whole. One of the goals of this chapter is to consider the overall design and implementation of a distributed operating system.

For several years, leading researchers in operating systems have advocated an anthropomorphic programming style using lightweight processes. On the other hand, in programming-language research, information hiding has been the guiding principle in the development of abstract data type systems. The latter has been used also during the 1980s in the development of operating systems, and in particular, distributed operating systems. There is also a third approach used to build operating systems – the UNIX-based approach. It is a process-based approach, but because it has some distinct features, it can be separated from the main stream.

Note that most distributed operating systems developed to date are in one of these two major categories: process-oriented systems – based on the concept of a process, or object-oriented systems – based on the concept of an object. At the level of policy the two models are equivalent. There is no logical difference between these models. Thus, logically each model has equivalent components. Processes in the former model can be mapped into objects in the latter. Moreover, these two systems use similar structuring and synchronization mechanisms, and similar operations. However, these systems differ at the level of mechanisms. Thus, these categories of systems are defined based on the mechanisms by which they implement the notions of functional entity and synchronization.

This chapter aims to survey the goals and most important features of several existing experimental distributed operating systems. This survey is based on the underlying interaction models they use. We will look at Accent, V, and Charlotte as examples of process-based systems; Amoeba and Eden as examples of object-based systems; and LOCUS and Mach as examples of UNIX-based systems. The description of each system concludes with comments on what has been learned from the relevant project.

The survey should be treated as an illustration of the concepts and solutions to the problems discussed in the previous chapters. In particular, it will help the reader to identify basic design assumptions and solutions of these experimental distributed operating systems, implementation of their concepts, and also their strong points and weaknesses. Moreover, it will be possible to identify how far the architects of these systems went, in comparison to the design and research issues discussed in the previous chapters.

14.1 Distributed operating systems to be surveyed

In the following sections we survey a number of distributed operating systems to identify their basic research and design issues and features. In deciding which systems to survey, the following selection criteria have been taken into consideration:

(1) The system should be well documented;

(2) Only implemented systems will be considered;

(3) The system should possess features which can influence and/or have influenced the development of other systems;

(4) Each category of distributed operating system (process-based, object-based, and UNIX-like) should be represented.

The most interesting and most representative distributed operating systems from the research and application point of view are:

(1) process-based: Accent, V-system, and Charlotte;

(2) object-based: Amoeba, and Eden;

(3) UNIX-like: LOCUS, and Mach.

Note that several distributed operating systems have been coupled to the UNIX system in an attempt:

- to extend it (LOCUS);

- to prove that the UNIX kernel can be completely rebuilt without loss of functionality and portability (Mach);

- to be a vehicle for UNIX in a distributed environment (Amoeba); or

- simply sit on top of UNIX (Eden).

14.2 Accent

Accent was developed as part of the Carnegie–Mellon Spice Project as a 'redo' activity on a RIG-like system taking into consideration limitations of the latter. Accent was built to support a large network of scientific personal computers. The presentation of Accent's project goals, research and design issues, and features follows its descriptions in Rashid (1981), Rashid and Robertson (1981), Rashid (1986), Fitzgerald and Rashid (1986) and Rashid (1987).

14.2.1 Design goals

Accent is a communication-oriented operating system designed to support:

(1) a large network of uniprocessor scientific personal computers, and

(2) the development of a fault-tolerant distributed sensor network.

Accent was built to conform to the following design constraints (viewed as essential to (1)):

(1) **Large problem decomposition** – modular decomposition of a problem into smaller modular units which can be run concurrently on a single processor or optionally distributed between several processors on a network should this be possible;

(2) **Multiple language support** – the system should support many language environments;

(3) **Protection** – because a system can run a number of processes, their interactions should be predictable to avoid chaos;

(4) **Rapid error detection and tools for transparent fault recovery, debugging, and monitoring** – tools for process monitoring and debugging should be provided to aid building a reliable distributed system;

(5) **Transparent access to resources** – all resources should be accessed transparently;

(6) **Uniform access to resources** – It should be possible for any feature provided by the kernel to be provided instead by a process;

(7) **Explicit representation of knowledge** – where possible, information about the functioning of processes is made explicit rather than procedurally embedded.

14.2.2 The Accent architecture

In 1986, Accent was used at CMU in a network of over 150 PERQ workstations supported by Ethernet (Rashid 1986). The operating system can be viewed as having a number of layers. Each workstation possesses an operating system kernel, which is the bottom layer. Each kernel supports a collection of processes, which form higher layers and provide successively more complex services. The Accent architecture is illustrated in Fig. 14.1.

The kernel provides an execution environment for processes running on its workstation. This includes:

(1) interprocess communication,

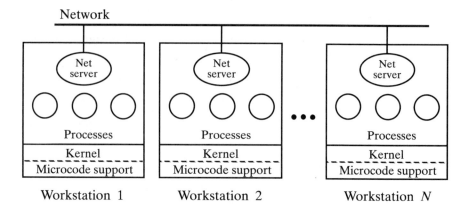

Fig. 14.1 The Accent architecture {adapted from Rashid and Robertson (1981)}.

(2)   virtual memory management, and

(3)   process management.

Moreover, the kernel provides:

(1)   the low-level functions of process creation and destruction,

(2)   access to devices through interprocess communication,

(3)   support for language and application specific microcode, and

(4)   rudimentary support for process monitoring and debugging.

Accent is organized around a protected interprocess communication system which allows processes to be bound together and provides a uniform interface at the system level. All services and resources in the system, including process management and memory management, are accessible through an interprocess communication facility. All resources throughout the network are accessed uniformly. Moreover, access to kernel-provided services is indistinguishable from access to process-provided resources.

14.2.3   Interprocess communication

The interprocess communication facility of the Accent kernel is defined in terms of communication between processes on the same machine. It can be extended transparently over a network by processes called network servers. The interprocess communication facility is defined in terms of two abstractions: ports and messages.

Ports

The interprocess communication facility is based on message passing, and is integrated with copy-on-write virtual memory management. Processes communicate indirectly through ports. A port is a protected kernel object: it is a basic transport abstraction provided by Accent. However, ports are not only communication objects but also are defined as capabilities. Logically, a port is a finite length queue of messages sent by a process. Many processes may send messages to a port, but only one process may remove messages from a port at a time. Access to a port (to either send or receive) is granted by receiving a message containing a port capability. Ports are used to represent all services or data structures.

Since ports are protected kernel objects, they cannot be directly manipulated or named by a process. Instead, the kernel provides processes with a secure capability to send a message to a port and/or to receive a message from it. A capability is a local name for a system object. A given process may have only one local name for a given port at a time. Port capabilities may be passed in messages, handed down to process children, or destroyed. When a port name is passed in a message, the system kernel maps that name from the local name space of the sending process into the name space of the receiver.

There are two primitives which allow performing operations on ports. These primitives are listed in List 14.1.

AllocatePort
   this call allows a process to create a port. The call creates a new port, allocates space for its queue of messages, and returns a local port name which refers to the created port. Logically, this name is an index into a correspondence table maintained by the kernel for each process. Initially, the port is owned by the creator. The creator also has receive access, which is distinct from ownership, to the port. Both rights can be passed to other processes if desired.

DeallocatePort
   this call allows a process to destroy a port, if it both owns and has receive access to it.

List 14.1   Ports primitives.

A process is automatically destroyed when its owner and the process with receive access to it die. In either case, processes with send access to that port are informed via emergency messages. Receive access is distinguished from ownership to allow a process to take over services or functions provided by other processes in the event that those processes die or malfunction.

Messages

Logically, an Accent message is a collection of typed data objects copied from the address space of the sender at the time of a message send call into the address space of the receiver when a receive call is performed. A message consists of a fixed length header and a variable size sequence of typed data objects to be transmitted. Fields of the header include:

(1)   the length of the entire message,

(2)   the specification of the type of a message,

(3)   both port capabilities (names): a capability for the destination (remote) port and, if a response is expected, a capability (a port name) which can be used for the response (for a local port),

(4)   an ID used for discriminating between different messages sent between the same processes; it allows the receiver to select an appropriate message structure for receiving it, and

(5)   a pointer to the stuctured data part of the message.

The variable part of the message is a list of typed data items. Each entry in the list has a type, size, and value. A single message may transfer up to 2^{32} bytes of by-value data.

The type of a message field specifies the kind of service it requires from the interprocess communication facility. The following service classes are provided: flow control, priority, sequentiality, reliability, maximum age and security.

Accent uses two different types of messages which play a dominant role in communication:

(1)   **Normal messages** – these are flow controlled, sequential, reliable, not secure, of lowest priority, and without maximum age. Normal messages are assumed to satisfy most communication requirements. This type of message is the default.

(2)   **Emergency messages** – these are specially flow controlled, sequential, reliable, not secure, of highest priority, and without maximum age. They are used in error handling (notification), special event processing, and debugging.

Messages of the same priority are queued using the FIFO strategy. However, high priority messages are queued before low priority messages.

Communication primitives

Accent's interprocess communication is based on only two primitive operations: **send** and **receive**. However, these operations themselves are quite flexible, particularly **receive**. Messages can be sent to a process at almost any time, even when the port is full. Thus, there is the need for mechanisms to check the state of its ports, to wait for activity on one or more of its ports, and to receive messages selectively. Moreover, it should be possible for a process to specify a maximum amount of time to wait for a message before reawaking.

Four primitives are provided to deal with these problems. These primitives are given in List 14.2.

Receive(SetOfPorts, Message, Timeout)
> waits for at most Timeout milliseconds and if during this period a message is available from any of the ports designated by SetOfPorts then the message is read into Message and a true value is returned;

MessageWait(SetOfPorts, Timeout)
> similar to Receive, but does not receive the pending message. It returns the list of capabilities of the ports from which the next messages could be received.

Preview(SetOfPorts, Message, Timeout)
> performs a similar function to Receive, but it reads only the header of the next waiting message and does not actually dequeue that message from the port queue.

PortsWithMessagesWaiting(SetOfPorts)
> checks the status of all ports and returns the set of ports with messages waiting.

List 14.2   Accent's waiting for messages primitives.

Network interprocess communication

Before we discuss a network server which provides a transparent network extension of interprocess communication, it is worth introducing the concept of an intermediary process. Let us assume that there is a need for communication between two distinct process groups, A and B. Since Accent's messages are sent to ports rather than processes and ports are only referenced indirectly by processes, it is possible to use one single process, N, to act as an intermediary. Communication via an intermediary process is illustrated in Fig. 14.2.

An intermediary process allocates ports which 'mirror' only those ports used by each of the two process groups.

Working as an intermediary process between A and B requires N to provide some means by which A and B can establish an initial connection. This could be done either through string name lookup or through some special function provided by N and known to A and B.

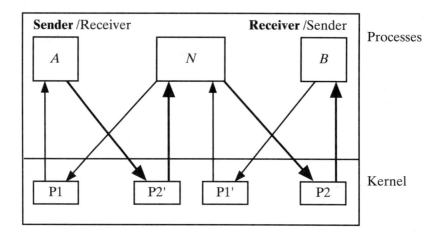

Fig. 14.2 Communication via an intermediary process; P1', P2' – 'alias' ports of P1 and P2, respectively {adapted from Rashid and Robertson (1981)}.

A network server can function much like the intermediary process. In a distributed system, process groups A and B are located on two different computers. This implies that there are two network servers, N_1 and N_2, which can communicate with each other across the network; they provide the correspondence between 'alias' ports. This concept does not require that the kernels know about the network. Network communication in Accent is illustrated in Fig. 14.3.

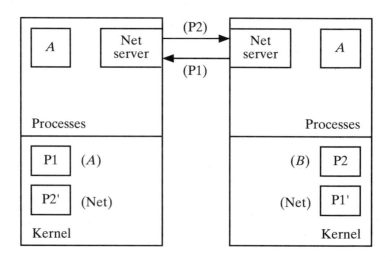

Fig. 14.3 Network communication {adapted from Rashid and Robertson (1981)}.

A network server provides some form of reliable, flow controlled communication between computers. The semantics of local interprocess communication is accommodated. Remote communication is distinguished from local communication based on a port which belongs to the network server. Thus, any process wishing to send a message to a process running on a remote computer sends it to the network server's port. The sender has to know the name of a port (possess its capability) of the destination process. In practice, this capability is a capability for a port owned by the network server on the remote computer, that is, P1'. In summary, communication between remote processes uses the fact that a network server fabricates a local port to correspond to a remote port.

Note that this interprocess communication is independent of the exact nature of connection, the protocol used, the topology of the network, and even the existence of multiple competing networks linking communicating computers: everything is hidden from the client process. Moreover, since the kernel can act like a process, the network server can be implemented in the Accent kernel. This results in improved efficiency of communication.

Ports can be passed between processes through a network server. The only requirement is that there be a way for network servers to know when a message contains a port capability (name). This scheme implies that an implicit network connection is sent along with each capability.

Message structuring in Accent is important in two major cases: first, as described above, for handling the transmission of port capabilities across networks and second, for data conversion in heterogeneous networks in which machines have widely varying data representations. To obtain greater location and implementation independence and to hide information on a machine involved in communications, this translation should be performed by the network server rather than the end processes.

14.2.4 Virtual memory management

Accent has one very distinct feature: virtual memory, file storage, and interprocess communication are integrated in such a way as to preserve the logical structure of interprocess communication. This results in performance advantages over previous communication based operating systems.

The result of the close association of virtual memory with interprocess communication is the possibility of allowing one Accent process to manage the virtual address space of another. The management can be performed either by allocating virtual memory from the kernel and sending it to another process, or explicitly managing page faults.

This possibility results in a clean, kernel-transparent mechanism for cross-network paging.

Accent provides a 2^{32}-byte paged address space for each process as well as for the operating system kernel. Disk pages and physical memory can be addressed by the kernel as a portion of its 2^{32}-byte address space. A virtual memory table is maintained for each user process and the operating system kernel. The kernel's address space is paged. All user process maps are kept in paged kernel memory. Note that only the kernel virtual memory table, a small kernel stack, the PERQ screen, I/O memory, and those Pascal modules required for handling the simplest form of page fault are locked in physical memory. The kernel code and symbol table information require 64K bytes.

To transmit a large amount of data, Accent uses memory mapping techniques rather than data copying to transfer information from one process to another within the same machine. In the case of transfer across a network, Accent provides the ability to allow memory to be sent copy-on-reference.

14.2.5 Process management

Process management, together with the virtual memory management and interprocess communication, provides the execution environment for processes running on a host computer.

The following issues were addressed in building the process management component of Accent:

(1) **Simple user interface** – The process system is simple. The **Fork** and **Terminate** primitives allow process creation and destruction. Processes can be monitored using the primitive **Status**, and controlled with **SetPriority, SetLimit** (sets a runtime limit), **Suspend**, and **Resume**.

(2) **Multiple language support** – Mechanisms are provided for supporting languages with different notions of process state. Different languages have different underlying microcode support. This implies that most of the process mechanisms are moved to the microcode level and supported by a **MicroKernel**. It consists of language-independent microcode support, including process queue management, process state switch and context swap, low level scheduling, I/O and interrupt support, and virtual address translation.

(3) **High performance** – The context swap mechanism (language independent) is quite fast; for instance, a context switch from one Pascal virtual machine to another requires only 50 microseconds.

(4) **Scheduling control** – The process scheduling facility provides time slice scheduling with sixteen priority levels. Pre-emption is provided to enable time critical processes to meet their demands. Aging is provided to support some degree of fairness in scheduling.

(5)   **Simple interrupt structure** – Accent does not use the traditional interrupt structure. Hardware interrupts are serviced in the Micro-Kernel, and processes waiting on service are simply awakened. If the awakened process is time-critical, pre-emptive scheduling is used. At the process level there is only the notion of a software interrupt. It is associated closely with interprocess communication: any receipt of a normal or emergency message will flag a software interrupt for the receiving process.

14.2.6 Naming

Accent uses local port naming (in contrast to the global [flat] naming space used for example in the V-system). It provides only local naming in the kernel. Remote messages must be interpreted by a server process outside the kernel.

In Accent, each process can receive messages at a number of ports. The identity of the receiving port is thus an implicit argument of every request, and ports subsume the uses of multiple capabilities. Note, however, that Accent ports are more general than multiple capabilities. This is because the right to read from a port can be passed from one process to another. On the other hand, the object corresponding to a given capability remains fixed.

All global entities are named uniformly by capabilities. This includes not only objects, but also nodes (machines), and checksites (disks). The designers of Accent believe that naming machines with capabilities reduces the number of location dependent primitives required and provides a convenient conceptual unity.

14.2.7 Lessons learned

The system seems to have been successful in meeting its design goals. The design constraints are also satisfied by:

(1)   providing the ability to create and control a large number of independent processes and to support a sophisticated form of interprocess communication;

(2)   supporting the notion of multiple, independent virtual address spaces and a virtual machine specification which can accommodate diverse interpretations of process state;

(3)   supplying address space protection to ensure that no process can affect another except through the use of interprocess communication.

(4)   supplying access protection in the communication facility itself to prevent unauthorized communication between processes;

(5)   defining interprocess communication such that it allows transparent debugging, monitoring, and fault recovery;

(6)   defining interprocess communication such that it allows transparent network extension independent of network hardware and protocol;

(7)   allowing all services except the basic communication primitives to be seen by processes as being provided through a communication interface;

(8)   structuring message communication to allow intermediary processes (for example, debuggers, protocol converters) to better interpret the contents and purpose of messages.

Accent can be seen as a relatively pure example of a communication-oriented operating system. The most interesting lesson learned from this project is that memory management can be effectively integrated with the interprocess communication system, so that access to all services and resources can be provided through the communication facility. Moreover, the use of virtual memory makes it possible to overcome limitations in the handling of large objects. In Accent, ports are defined to be capabilities as well as communication objects. The architects of Accent carried out performance studies of the interprocess communication system when cooperating with virtual memory support and file access facilities. No other performance studies have been reported.

14.3   The V distributed system

The V-system was developed by Cheriton and his co-workers at Stanford University as part of a research project to explore issues in distributed systems. This project was motivated by a classical phenomenon, namely, the increasing availability of powerful workstations, which can be seen as an alternative to traditional time-shared minicomputers.

This system is based on the client–server model. V is a compromise between process-based systems and object-based systems. It uses a block-oriented data model instead of the more traditional byte-oriented UNIX model. The V kernel is an outgrowth of experience gathered with the earlier systems, Thoth (Cheriton *et al.* [1979], Cheriton [1982]) and Verex.

The designers of the system wanted to prove:

(1)   that a powerful system can be built upon primitives that provide inexpensive process management and simple, fast, interprocess communication;

(2)   that for fast communication between two processes, synchronous

message passing provides the simple interface demanded, and that it can be implemented with the desired efficiency;

(3) that common system problems can be solved elegantly and efficiently with primitives that provide communication to and from groups of processes;

(4) that a uniform interface and protocol, reasonably independent of particular physical devices or intervening networks, can be defined to simplify the process of adding new services to the system;

(5) that principles for distributed operating systems are applicable to operating systems for multiprocessors.

The designers also believed that by building the V-system, they:

(1) provide an environment for developing and studying distributed applications (including extremely robust systems),

(2) determine the hardware and software facilities needed to built good tools,

(3) make utilization of these facilities easy for a novice and powerful for experienced users, and they will be portable, and finally

(4) allow better (faster, cheaper and more reliable) systems to be constructed using these facilities.

The major feature of V is an abstract division of responsibilities in the kernel. The kernel is responsible primarily for communication. Such facilities as file system, resource management and protection are provided by servers outside the kernel. It is also important that services are, in principle, ordinary user processes (the free market model of services).

The V distributed system consists of a collection of powerful Sun (Sun-1, Sun-2, Sun-3) and VAXstation-II workstations connected by either a 3M-bit or a 10M-bit Ethernet. A 'guest-level' implementation is possible for 4.2. BSD UNIX systems. The V environment also allows time-sharing or special-purpose computers and wide area networks to be accessed.

Our presentation of the project goals and the features of this system follows descriptions in Cheriton and Zwaenepoel (1983), Cheriton (1984), Tanenbaum and van Renesse (1985), Cheriton and Zwaenepoel (1985), Cheriton and Deering (1985), Theimer *et al.* (1985), Berglund (1986), Mason (1987), Finlayson and Cheriton (1987), Cheriton and Williamson (1987) and Cheriton (1988).

14.3.1 The architecture of the V-system

Software of V

The V distributed system is structured as a relatively small kernel, a set of service modules, various run-time libraries, and a set of commands. The architecture of the V-system is illustrated in Fig. 14.4.

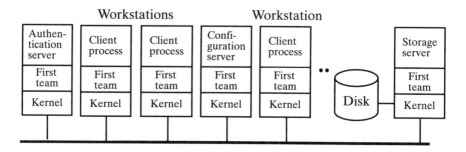

Fig. 14.4 The architecture of the V-system.

The kernel is distributed; this means that a copy of the kernel code runs on each machine of the system. This distributed kernel implements a program environment of many lightweight processes communicating by messages. The existence of a collection of computers and their network interconnection is transparent at the process level. The service modules implement services using the basic access to hardware resources provided by the kernel. For example, the V file server implements a UNIX-like file system using the raw disk access supported by the kernel. The run-time libraries implement conventional language or application-to-operating system interfaces (for example, Pascal I/O, C stdio).

Most of the servers run on each host, and these servers run on the so-called **first team**, which is started by the kernel after initialization. The first team includes the following servers: the exception server, the team server and the exec server. We will discuss them later.

The kernel

The V kernel is the heart of the V-system. It provides the following basic facilities: a network-transparent abstraction of address spaces, lightweight processes, and interprocess communication. It is a very important feature of the V kernel that these facilities are analogous to those provided by Multibus or S-100 bus back planes. The address space corresponds to a backplane slot. Thus, a program can be plugged into an address space independent of what is running in other address spaces. This can be done in the same way as a circuit board can be plugged in. Moreover, the lightweight process corresponds to the electrical power supplied by the backplane, and interprocess communication corresponds to the data and control lines of the backplane bus.

The V kernel performs three basic operations: interprocess communication, process and memory management, and device management. Each of these functions is implemented by a separate kernel module. Each module is replicated in each host, and handles the local processes, address spaces and devices. Each module is registered with the interprocess communication facility and is invoked from the process level using the standard interprocess communication facilities.

There are three major components of the V kernel:

(1) **the interprocess communication** allows the different system components to be connected. It is implemented with conventional system call traps;

(2) **the kernel server** provides the kernel process and memory management operations as a server accessed by the interprocess communication; and

(3) **the device server** provides access to devices through messages. This server uses the V I/O protocol for input and output with these devices.

Note that one of the major focuses of the V team research was exploring ways to achieve good interprocess communication performance.

14.3.2 Interprocess communication

Processes and communication between processes are major facilities provided by the V kernel. The V interprocess communication system uses remote procedure call-like semantics: messages are blocked, buffered, and are reliably delivered.

There are three types of V interprocess communication: message exchange, a data transfer that moves large amounts of data between processes, and multicast.

With message exchange, communication between processes is provided in the form of short fixed-length messages, as a result of the execution of the following primitives: **Send, Receive**, and **Reply**. The **Send** request message passes the equivalent of procedure arguments, and the **Reply** message returns the results. This sequence is referred to as a **message exchange**. These messages are 32 bytes in length. Because the receiver has the possibility to choose when it wants to reply to each message, it can receive and queue as many messages as it chooses. This allows sophisticated scheduling of message handling and replies.

There is also the possibility of performing a data transfer operation for moving large amounts of data between processes. This is the second type of interprocess communication. It also follows the procedure call paradigm. Moreover, the segment access operations are used primarily to access what are logically 'call-by-reference' parameters. To achieve this, the server process (the receiver) may execute one or more **MoveTo** or **MoveFrom** data transfer operations between the time the message is received and the time the reply message is sent back.

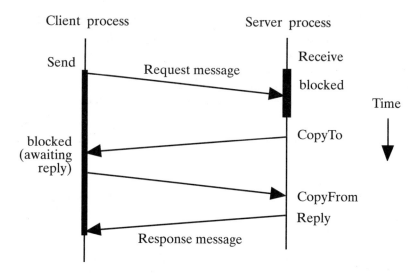

Fig. 14.5   Message exchange and data transfer in V.

Message exchange and data transfer operations between a client process and a server process based on this semantics for the first two types is illustrated in Fig. 14.5.

Note, that there are no per-packet acknowledgements for large data transfers. Instead there is only a single acknowledgement when the transfer is complete.

The V communication primitives which support the first two types of communication are presented in List 14.3.

Send(message, pid)
>   sends the 32-byte message specified by message to the process specified by pid. The reply message overwrites the original message area. A client can also pass read or write access in the message (it is a kind of pseudopointer) to a segment of its address space. This pseudopointer can be used to permit the server to read from or write to the client's memory. Such reads and writes are handled by the kernel using the **MoveFrom** and **MoveTo** primitives.

pid = **Receive**(message)
>   blocks the invoking process, if necessary, to receive a 32-byte message in its message vector. Messages are queued using the FIFO strategy until received.

(pid, count) = **ReceiveWithSegment**(message, segptr, segsize)
>   blocks the invoking process to receive a message as with

Receive. However, if a segment is specified in the message with read access, up to the first segsize bytes of the segment may be transferred to the array string at segptr, with count specifying the actual number of bytes received. Messages are queued until received.

Reply(message, pid)
sends a 32-byte reply contained in the message buffer to the specified process providing it is awaiting a reply from the server (replier). The replying process does not block.

ReplyWithSegment(message, pid, destptr, segptr, segsize)
sends the 32-bytes reply message as **Reply** does. However, it also transmits the short segment specified by segptr and segsize to destptr in the destination process's address space. A bit flag indicates whether the recovery procedure is at-least-once or exactly once.

MoveFrom(srcpid, dest, src, count)
copies count bytes from the segment starting at src in the address space of srcpid to the segment starting at dest in the active process's space. The process identified as srcpid must be awaiting a reply from the active process and must have provided read access to the segment of memory in its address space using conventions described in **Send**.

MoveTo(destpid, dest, src, count)
copies count bytes from the segment starting at src in the active process's space to the segment starting at dest in the address space of the destpid process. The destpid process must be awaiting a reply from the active process and must have provided write access to the segment of memory in its address space using the message conventions described under **Send**.

SetPid(logicalid, pid, scope)
associates pid with the specific logicalid in the specified scope, which is one of local, remote or both. Example logicalid's are fileserver, nameserver, etc.

pid = **GetPid**(logicalid, scop)
returns the process identifier associated with logicalid in the specified scope if any, else 0.

List 14.3 V interprocess communication primitives.

The third type of interprocess communication supports a one-to-many (one-to-a-group) model of communication, also called multicast. The multicast facility in V is used to transmit clock synchronization information in time servers, to request and distribute load information as part of the distributed scheduling mechanisms, as part of the V transaction atomic protocol, and in the replicated file update protocol.

A process group is a set of one or more processes identified by a group id. All these processes are equal. Moreover, group members may be on different computers. Any process can freely join or leave a group, and can be a member of multiple groups. Messages are delivered to all members, but only on a 'best effort' basis. The sender (client) is unblocked after receiving the first reply to its group message. The concept of a process group is supported by the V kernel with the operations given in List 14.4.

---

groupid = **AllocateGroupid**()
> allocates and returns a group identifier with the invoking process becoming a member of the new group. Group identifiers are identical in syntax and similar in semantics to process identifiers.

JoinGroup(groupid, pid)
> makes the process specified by pid a member of the group specified by groupid.

LeaveGroup(groupid, pid)
> removes the process specified by pid from the group specified by groupid.

pid = **GetReply**(replyMessage)
> returns the next reply message from a group **Send** in replyMessage and the identity of the replying process in pid. **GetReply** returns with pid set to 0. Additional reply messages for this transaction may be received, and, if any, will be returned on a later invocation of **GetReply**. All replies are discarded if when the process sends again.

List 14.4   Process group operations.

It is left to the sender to decide how many replies it wishes to receive and how long it is willing to wait for these replies. Group interprocess communication is illustrated in Fig. 14.6.

The V communication system is easy to use, because calls to servers are embedded in stubs. This implies that the caller just sees an ordinary procedure call. However, stub generation is not automated.

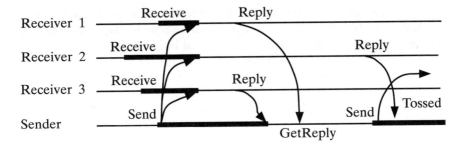

Fig. 14.6 Group interprocess communication.

Cheriton and Zwaenepoel (Cheriton and Zwaenepoel 1983) emphasize the following features of the V interprocess communication:

(1) Programming is easy due to the synchronous request-response pattern, which is similar to procedure calls.

(2) The distinction between small messages and the data transfer facility suits the observed usage pattern well: the first style of communication is very frequent whereas the latter is occasional.

(3) Synchronous communication and small, fixed-size messages reduce queuing and buffering problems in the kernel.

(4) The V message primitives are ill-suited in several ways for a network environment. The main reason for this is that the short, fixed-size messages make inefficient use of large packet sizes, which are typically used in local area networks.

It is necessary to emphasize very strongly that fast interprocess communication in the V-system is achieved not only by using relatively simple and basic interprocess communication primitives, but also due to using a transport protocol that was carefully designed to support these primitives. This transport protocol is called the VMTP protocol and was characterized in Chapter 3. The protocol is optimized for request-response behaviour. It supports multicast, datagrams, forwarding, streaming, security and priority. It was demonstrated by the V-system designers that network interprocess communication performance benefits from the use of the VMTP transport protocol.

14.3.3 Naming

The V naming facility is based on a three-level model, structured as character-string names, object identifiers, and entity identifiers.

Character-string names
The highest level of the naming facility assigns character-string names to objects. Permanent objects such as files are named using character-string

names. The designers of the V-system claim that the most efficient naming design from a communication point of view is to have each object manager implement names for its own set of objects (for example, each file server implements its own directory system). This means that character-string names are interpreted in some context. Each server manages its own context. This implies that operations on objects specified by name can be handled directly by the object manager without communication with a name server, provided only that the client can determine which object manager to contact, given an arbitrary name. This is the result of the fact that a name is generally only mapped as part of an operation on the object.

The advantages of this design are:

(1) efficiency;

(2) consistency between objects and the directory entries for the objects is simplified because both are implemented by the same server. This approach also eliminates the need for a client-visible unique object identifier returned by a separate name server and passed to the object manager.

(3) the object directory is replicated to the same degree as the object being named, because the directory is replicated when the manager is replicated.

(4) it facilitates incorporating 'foreign' or independently developed services, which typically already have their own directory system and (sometimes) their own syntax.

Given this background, the goal was the design of an efficient, reliable and secure mechanism, called the naming protocol. This protocol can be characterized as follows. Each server for a class of objects provides the name service for those objects; thus several object-specific name servers might reside on a workstation. Each object manager mounts its object directory into the global name space, by picking a unique global name prefix for the object directory, and adding itself to the **name handling (process) group**. Based on this, a client can locate the appropriate object manager for a given character string name by multicasting the **QueryName** operation to the name handling group. The number of multicast queries is reduced by each program maintaining a cache of name prefix to object manager bindings. In summary, the naming protocol ties these individual object manager directories into a system-wide name space and directory system.

The earlier V-systems distributed the responsibility for object naming among the systems object managers and used a name-mapping protocol, but did not provide a uniform global name space. Instead, each workstation was provided with a small, independent name server to store local aliases and the top level of the naming hierarchy. A set of conventions outside the naming system properly ensures that most workstations had similar views of the name space. The current system replaces these with the multicast name mapping mechanism and per-client name caches (Cheriton and Mann 1986).

File names, host names, and other high-level character-string names are implemented logically as a global directory providing uniform global interpretation of these names. This global directory is implemented using a decentralized approach, where each server implements the portion of the global directory naming the objects it implements, as shown in Fig. 14.7.

Thus, naming is regarded as a part of every service that provides objects with high-level names, as opposed to being provided by a distinguished name server.

In summary, the V naming protocol uses multicast:

(1)   to locate the servers that implement the correct portion of the name space so that the direct calls can be used.

(2)   to communicate with multiple servers simultaneously in the case that the specified portion of the name space is handled by more than one server.

Object identifiers

In the V-system, each object is referenced by an efficient object identifier. Using object identifiers enables one to avoid the overhead of character-string handling and look-up for each access. Object identifiers are

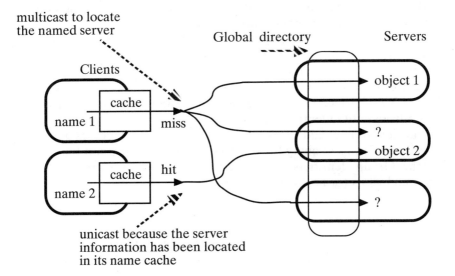

Fig. 14.7 The V naming directory {adapted from Cheriton (1986)}.

used to identify open files, address spaces and contexts or directories. Note that object identifiers are only used to identify objects whose lifetime does not exceed the lifetime of the service entity identifiers. This is because the entity identifier is invalidated when the process crashes.

An object identifier is structured as shown in Fig. 14.8. The **manager-id** is an interprocess communication identifier that specifies the object manager or one of its parts that implements the object; the **local-object-id** specifies the object relative to this object manager.

Entity, process and group identifiers

Entity identifiers are used at the bottom level of the V naming facility. These identifiers are fixed-length binary values. They are used to identify transport-level communication end points, and processes and groups of processes, because a process effectively has a single logical port on which to send and receive messages.

Process identifiers are unique within the context of a local network. On the SUN workstation, it is natural for the V kernel to use 32-bit process identifiers; the high-order 16 bits of the process identifier serve as a logical host identifier subfield, while the low-order 16 bits are used as a locally unique identifier. Thus, the V-system uses a global (flat) naming space for specifying processes (in contrast to the local port in the Accent naming system).

The use of an explicit host field in the process identifier allows distributed generation of unique process identifiers between machines, and allows an efficient mapping from process pid to network addresses. In particular, it is very efficient to determine whether a process is local or remote. This 'locality' test on process identifiers serves as the primary invocation mechanism from the local kernel software into the network interprocess communication portion.

Thus, the key property of entity identifiers that distinguishes them from the endpoint identifiers in other transport layer facilities is that they are host-address independent. That is, a process can migrate from one host to another without changing entity identifiers.

This design requires large entity identifiers and a mapping mechanism from entity identifiers to host addresses. The V kernel maps entity identifiers to host addresses using a cache of such mappings and multicast mechanisms to query the other kernel for mappings not found in the cache. Group identifiers are mapped many-to-one onto a range of multicast addresses (or host group addresses).

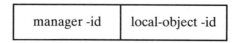

Fig. 14.8 The structure of the object identifier.

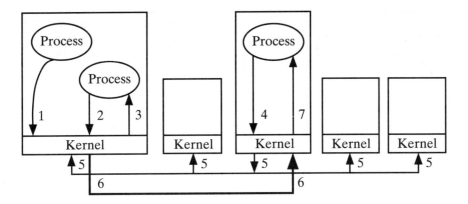

Fig. 14.9   Kernel naming primitives {adapted from Berglund (1986)}.

It is important to notice that a process can register its process identifier as corresponding to a particular **logical process identifier**. This is done by using the **SetPid** primitive (Step 1 in Fig. 14.9).

A logical process identifier is a well-known integer reserved for a specific kind of server. To learn the real process identifier, other processes can query the kernel with the well-known integer using **GetPid**. This allows a process to find out the pid of the kernel server. Note that this query can be performed by a local process (Steps 2 and 3) or can be done remotely (Step 4). In the latter case, a process broadcasts a request to all of the kernel servers (Step 5), but the response comes from the kernel server on the appropriate computer (Steps 6 and 7).

Note that the main naming operations and operations using names can be described as a (remote) procedure call to the server implementing the portion of the name space containing the name.

14.3.4   Process and memory management

This section deals with two basic problems: the management of processes and memory, which are basic resources of the V-system, and remote execution and migration.

The management of processes and memory

Operations to be performed on V processes and memory are implemented by the V kernel process server. It is a server implemented directly by the kernel. It is not a real process, but a collection of kernel service routines. Kernel server operations can be invoked by sending a message to a particular process identifier. Note that the kernel server must reside inside the kernel because the kernel is the kernel manager for processes.

A V process is a logical activity that sequentially executes instructions. A process, which is identified by a globally unique **process identi-**

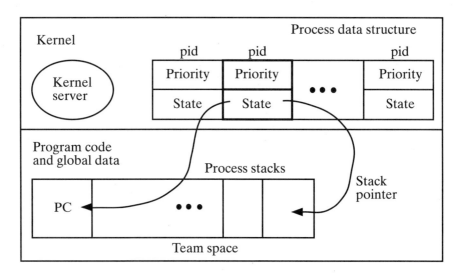

Fig. 14.10 A V-system process {adapted from Berglund (1986)}.

fier, or **pid**, is illustrated in Fig. 14.10. This figure shows that associated with each process is a priority, a state, a team space, and a stack. Processes are scheduled using a priority discipline. A process in a **ready** state with the highest priority is allocated the processor. The state is the machine state of the processor for that process. Processes are organized into groups called **teams**.

The team space is the area of memory to which the process has direct access. More than one process can be in a team space. Thus, all processes with the same team space are on the same team. All processes on a team must run on the same processor. Teams provide fine-grain sharing of code and inexpensive sharing of data between cooperating processes. The stack is an area in the team space that is used by the process.

newpid = **CreateProcess**(priority, initialpc, initialsp)
> creates a new process with the specified priority priority, initial program counter initialpc, and initial stack pointer initialsp, and returns its unique process identifier.

newpid = **CreateTeam**(priority, initialpc, initialsp)
> creates a new team with an initial or root process having the specified priority, initial program counter initialpc, and initial stack pointer initialsp, and returns its unique process identifier. This primitive is similar to **CreateProcess**() except the new process is created on a new team. The team address space and root process state are initialized using **SetTeamSize**(), **CopyTo**(), and **WriteProcessState**().

DestroyProcess(pid)
> destroys the specified process determined by pid and all processes that it created.

GetTeamSize(pid)
> returns the first unused location in the team space associated with pid, as set by **SetTeamSize**().

QueryProcessState(pid, state)
> copies the state of the process pid into the structure pointed to by state.

SetTeamPriority(pid, priority)
> sets the team priority of the team associated with pid to the specified priority and returns the previous team priority.

returnaddr = **SetTimeSize**(pid, addr)
> sets the first unused address for the team containing pid and addr.

WriteProcessState(pid, state)
> copies the specified process state record into the kernel state of the process specified by pid and returns pid.

MapTeamSpace(pid, addr, bytes, uio, blockno, mode)
> maps the team space associated with process pid starting at virtual location addr for the specified number of bytes with the specified uio starting at blockno block number. The following modes are possible read_only, copy_on_write, and read_write.

Delay(seconds, clicks)
> suspends execution of the invoking process for the specified number of seconds and clicks.

seconds = **GetTime**(clicksptr)
> returns the current time in seconds.

SetTime(seconds, clicks)
> set the kernel maintained time to that specified by seconds and clicks.

WakeUp(pid)
> unblocks the specified process if it is delaying using **Delay** and returns pid.

List 14.5   Process and memory management operations.

Processes in the V-system can be dynamically created and destroyed, by sending a message to the kernel server. Destroying a process results in all the processes created by it also being destroyed.

V kernel process and memory management operations are given in List 14.5.

Remote execution and migration in V

Because a facility providing remote execution and migration of processes in the V-system was discussed in Chapter 8, we only present some additional comments here reflecting distinct feature of V.

The V-system allows the execution of programs on workstations that are not being used. It does it by using the group communication facilities of the kernel, the team loading capability of the team servers, and the command parsing feature of the exec. Execution of a given program can be performed on a specified machine or on any idle machine on the network by appending to an **exec** command <machine_name> or @any, respectively. We will consider the latter here.

The exec, after receiving a command, does not ask the team server on its workstation to load a program given in the command, as in the local case. Instead it multicasts a request to a process group made up of all the team members running in the system (Step 1 in Fig. 14.11).

In the request message, the exec asks each team server to indicate whether it is available for remote execution. The response (Step 1') includes pid, amount of available memory, the percentage of processor time used recently, and whether anyone using the workstation has forbidden remote access.

The exec collects responses until it has found a suitable workstation. Then it sends a request (Step 2) to the remote team server. This

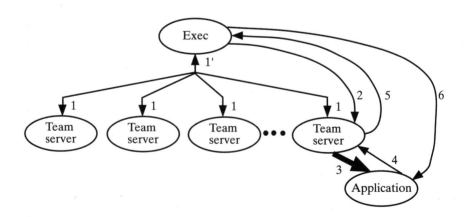

Fig. 14.11   Starting running a process remotely {adapted from Berglund (1986)}.

allows the execution to commence (Steps 3, 4, and 5). The distributed kernel allows the exec and a new program to interact with each other normally. Note that the team root message sent to the new team (Step 6) differs only in providing access to virtual terminals on the user's workstation instead of to ones on which the process runs.

14.3.5 Resource management

Each processor in the V-system has a dedicated function (for example, a workstation, a file-server, a printserver). This implies that V does not provide any form of dynamic processor allocation. Except for such key resources as processes and memory, V only manages I/O devices. These devices include the keyboard, mouse, disk, network (Ethernet) interface, serial line, and tape.

Device management is the responsibility of the kernel. However, it does not do this directly. The device server pseudoprocess inside the kernel provides access to and management of kernel-supported devices, as shown in Fig. 14.12.

If a process wants to perform an I/O operation, it has to learn the pid of the device server. This can be done by using the **GetPid** primitive. After this, the server is accessed via the interprocess communication operations, like the kernel server. The I/O access to all 'file-like' services is provided, similarly to UNIX, by using the V-system I/O protocol.

The V I/O protocol provides uniform transfer of data between a client process and the device server managing the data as a **file**. The file is a concept that refers to many different types of objects, which are viewed as readable or writeable. A uniform I/O object is characterized by an identifier, an owner process, an associated sequence of data blocks or records (which are numbered **nextblock** through **lastblock**, each of the size **blocksize** in bytes), and a set of generic attributes.

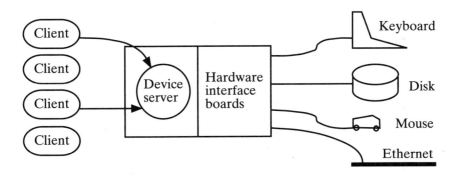

Fig. 14.12 The V device driver.

The protocol allows processes to read and write specific blocks on the device. The operations provided are given in List 14.6.

---

uio = **Create_UIO**(name)
      corresponds to a conventional **open**.

Query_UIO(name)
      corresponds to a conventional **reopen**.

Release_UIO(uio, mode)
      corresponds to a conventional **close**.

Read_UIO(uio, block_number, buffer, bytes)
      corresponds to a conventional **read**.

Write_UIO(uio, block_number, buffer, bytes)
      corresponds to a conventional **write**.

Set_UIO_Owner(uio, block_number, buffer, bytes)
      corresponds to **"pass file connection"**.

List 14.6 The operations of the V I/O protocol.

Note that UIO is an abstract object which provides a uniform interface to the underlying file or device, and a block abstraction of I/O (byte streams can be implemented by clients). Reading and writing specifies the required block rather than a current file position. This allows these two operations to be idempotent. This idempotency is important for efficient network file access because the V kernel can easily implement idempotent message transactions.

14.3.6 Services

A basic framework for implementing a variety of services in the V-system is provided by the kernel facilities, the naming protocol and the UIO interface. All service modules share some attributes in common:

(1) They are structured as multiprocess programs, exploiting the lightweight processes provided by the V kernel.

(2) Most of the service modules implement the V naming protocol and UIO interface.

(3) Client access to their services is provided entirely through the V interprocess communication primitives.

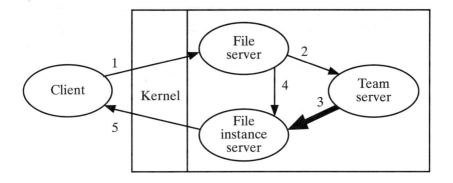

Fig. 14.13 The file server {adapted from Berglund (1986)}.

The file server

The file server implements the V system I/O protocol. It is not part of the operating system, but an ordinary user program running on top of the V kernel. The file server runs on a dedicated server computer (one that runs only servers) with mass disk storage. Because most of the workstations running the V-system do not have disks, the file server must provide file access for clients on the network.

The file server is a member of a group of servers. All of them share a well-known group id. The members of a file server group share a common buffer cache, which is used to store often-used blocks in main memory. A client which wants to access the file server must first identify a particular server's id. This can be done using the group id and the V naming protocol. Then the client can create or open a file by sending the file server a **Create_Instance** request (Step 1 in Fig. 14.13).

In Steps 2, 3, and 4 a process, called a **file instance server**, is created. This server will handle all subsequent requests dealing with the file. The response (Step 5) to the initial request contains the pid of the file instance server. This short description emphasizes one important feature, namely, the scheduling mechanisms built into the kernel are in fact scheduling file access by scheduling the processes associated with each file. After creation of an instance of a file, it can be read, written, and released by means of library routines that implement the rest of the V I/O protocol.

The V file server was derived from the Thoth file system (Cheriton 1982). Each file has a file descriptor. It is similar to an *i*-node in the UNIX system, except that the file descriptors are gathered into an ordinary file, which can grow as needed.

The authentication server

Security in the V distributed system does not fulfil the requirements imposed on computer systems working in a commercial environment.

The system works in a friendly research environment. Thus, the designers of the V-system assumed that the sanctity of the distributed kernel cannot be violated. Messages sent by the kernel on one computer cannot be tampered with by a user before they reach another kernel. To implement security in V, each user is issued an account name with a password and a user number. This number is associated with messages sent by processes running on behalf of the user.

Two resources are protected in the V environment: files and hosts. Files are protected by the file servers, and hosts by the team servers. To access protected resources, a user process must send a request for authentication to the authentication server (Step 1 in Fig. 14.14). The request message contains the user's account name and password. They are checked against an encrypted file on the file server (Step 2). If the passwords match, the authentication server returns an indication of success to the requesting process (Step 3). Next, the kernel of that user's workstation associates the user number with the process (Step 4). After the completion of these operations, every consecutive message sent by the newly authenticated process (and its children) will include the user number.

Any process can ask its kernel for the user number of any process that sends it a message. This can be used by the file server to determine whether a request to carry out operations on a file has come from an authorized process. Also the team server can use the number of its potential clients to determine whether it must start new processes on its workstation. Note that although any process can know the number of any other process, this does not give it any new priviliges, because only the kernel can set the user number field in a message.

The UNIX server
It is very useful to be able to use the complete capabilities of another system from a workstation running a given system (for example, the V system). The UNIX server is a program that allows this to be done by

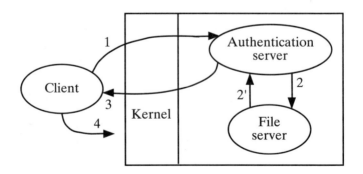

Fig. 14.14 The authentication steps {adapted from Berglund (1986)}.

running on a UNIX-based system. It simulates a V-system kernel and file server. UNIX system services are provided via the V-system kernel's interprocess communication primitives. The UNIX server is constructed in such a way that, to workstations running the V kernel, it appears to be a standard V file server, but one that provides UNIX file access via the V I/O protocol. The UNIX server is illustrated in Fig. 14.15.

To be served by the UNIX server in order to access a UNIX file, a client process must receive its user number from the authentication server (Step 1). A request with this user number is sent to the UNIX server (Step 2). The UNIX server maps the user number to a UNIX account accessible to that client. Next, it forks a copy of itself (Step 3) and passes the privileges of the user (Step 4) and effectively gives a pid to the forked UNIX server. As a result, upcoming requests can be directed to it. The new pid is returned to the client process (Step 5). This pid is used as long as it wishes to access a UNIX file.

Other servers

The Internet server implements the TCP/IP suite of protocols. It uses the basic network access provided by the kernel device server. This server uses services provided by the V kernel for lightweight processes, real-time scheduling, accurate timing and fast interprocess communication. The Internet server is loaded on demand in V rather than permanently configured in the standard system.

The printer server has a number of interesting features. It supports spooling of print jobs even if it runs on a diskless node. This is achieved by exploiting V network interprocess communication to write files to network file servers. Moreover, it supports multiple client proto-

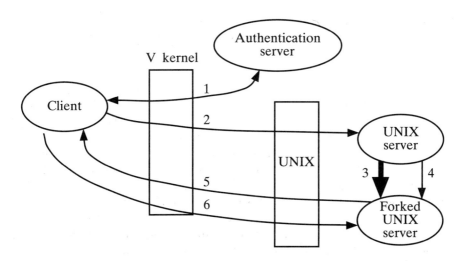

Fig. 14.15 The UNIX server {adapted from Berglund (1986)}.

cols. This allows submitting print files using either V interprocess communication and the UIO interface or using TCP connections.

Other servers of the V-system are the pipe server, the display server and a log server.

14.3.7 Lessons learned

The V-kernel has been in use at Stanford University for over five years as a basis for a variety of projects, including the research project on distributed operating systems. The V-system has reached a reasonable level of utility and maturity. It is distributed under licence by Stanford University and is in use at several universities, research laboratories and companies. The kernel handles communication, but no disk access, no display access, and no memory management. These functions are relegated to servers. Local and remote interprocess communication are handled identically. This implies that when two local processes communicate, it is grossly inefficient. In general, the V kernel is a good example of an efficient message passing kernel. Its performance is considered nearly optimal (Welch 1986). The use of messages is similar to the way the RPC protocol uses messages. V-system provides pre-emptable remote execution and process allocation facilities.

The V-system was used extensively to study the relationship between network protocols and the interprocess communication system, and group addressing based on broadcast and multicast services provided by the network. In particular, the V kernel performance was studied extensively. These studies prove that a kernel/server-based system is a good way to build a high-performance distributed system. A lot of work has been done to make the system fast, and the goals of the V project as presented above have been achieved. It seems to us that V-system is one of the most interesting project carried out in the distributed operating system area.

14.4 Charlotte

Charlotte is a distributed operating system developed by Finkel and his co-workers at the University of Wisconsin-Madison. It is a direct descendent of the Arachne (originally called Roscoe) distributed operating system (Solomon and Finkel 1979). Charlotte was designed for the Crystal loosely-coupled multicomputer network, which contains 20 VAX-11/750 and 780 computers running Berkeley UNIX 4.2. These hosts are connected by an 80 Mbps token ring, called Pronet. Each node runs a basic software nugget, which provides low-level internode communication facilities.

Charlotte was intended as a test bed for developing techniques and tools for exploiting large-grain parallelism to solve computationally-intensive problems. All software is written in a local extension to Modula, except for startup code, which is written in assembler, and some of the interprocess communication code, written in C. Charlotte includes unique interprocess communication mechanisms and process management services.

The following constraints were applied when designing Charlotte:

(1)   Charlotte will run on a multicomputer.

(2)   Charlotte must support a wide variety of application programs.

(3)   Policies and mechanisms will be clearly separated. (The designers placed mechanisms in the kernel, replicated in each machine. Policies are governed by utility processes.)

The overall goals of the project were simplicity and function:

(1)   **Charlotte will provide adequate functionality** – The commmunication facilities should be appropriate to application programs which cover various communication paradigms.

(2)   **Charlotte will be simple** – This property refers to both the kernel and the utility processes. According to the designers, Charlotte is intended to be minimal and efficient, easily implemented and easily used.

Our presentation of the project goals and the features of the Charlotte distributed operating system follows its descriptions in Finkel *et al.* (1983), Finkel *et al.* (1986), Artsy *et al.* (1984, 1986, 1989), Finkel and Artsy (1989) and Finkel *et al.* (1989).

14.4.1   Software architecture

The software architecture of Charlotte contains three levels, as illustrated in Fig. 14.16. The lowest level is the **kernel**. An identical copy of the kernel resides on each computer. The kernel provides interprocess communication, process control (multiprocessing), and mechanisms for scheduling, storage allocation and migration. A single kernel supports all the processes on its computer. Services are requested by processes by issuing **kernel calls**. They appear much like subroutine calls to processes written in Modula. The **KernJob** process also exists on each computer. This process provides process-control functions to other processes through the message-based interprocess communication interface.

Utility processes, which concentrate all policies of Charlotte, form the second level of the software architecture. They cooperate to allocate

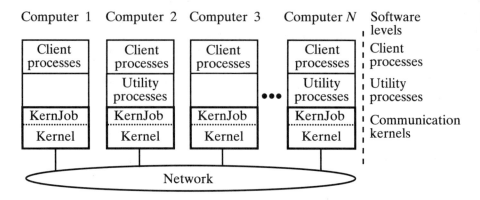

Fig. 14.16 Software architecture of Charlotte.

resources, provide higher-level services such as file and connection services, and enforce control policies such as medium to long term-scheduling, process placement and migration. These processes are designed in such a way that each process controls a policy on its own set of machines, and they need not reside on each node. The processes that control the same resources on different machine sets communicate with each other to achieve global policy decisions. It was reported in 1984 (Artsy *et al.* 1984) that the following utility processes had been developed: a program starter (manages memory), a file server, initial-linkup server (Connector), a directory server (SwitchBoard), and a command interpreter. Charlotte needs at least one copy of each utility to function fully.

The third level of the architecture contains client processes. They are supported by the interprocess communication mechanism provided by the kernel and utility functions from utility processes. Processes communicate with the kernel by kernel calls, some which are restricted to special utilities.

14.4.2 Interprocess communication

Interprocess communication in Charlotte is unique, since it combines the addressing features of capabilities and the transmission facilities of message-based communication.

Links

Charlotte's interprocess communication is based on the concept of a **link**. A link, as we recall from Chapter 5, is a connection between two processes, each of which has a capability to one end of the link. Full-duplex links are used in the Charlotte system. This means that both processes can perform all link operations concurrently. A process never refers to another process directly – it presents a link identifier, which is a small integer local to the process. This identifier is used by the kernel to index an entry in the link discriptor (peer-process capability table). Every kernel maintains such a link discriptor for all the processes on that computer.

Each entry in the table contains:

(1) static information about the link: type, state, local-end address (source) and remote-end address (destination). An address is a triple of node (computer) identifier, process identifier, and system link identifier;

(2) information concerning a current **Send** operation: send state (S_State), send buffer;

(3) information concerning a current **Receive** operation (as for **Send**).

Link-oriented primitives (kernel calls) provided in the Charlotte system are given in List 14.7.

MakeLink(var end1, end2 : link)
  constructs a new link with the creator holding both ends. The creator can transfer one end to a client or a server or transfer both ends to two processes.

DestroyLink(myend : link)
  destroys the link at one end. The process at the other end is notified of this event. That process can still obtain the result of previously sent communication requests, however, it cannot send new ones. The other end is disposed of only when that process explicitly calls **DestroyLink**.

List 14.7 Link-oriented primitives.

The designers of Charlotte decided to use duplex links for two reasons. First, such models of communications as a client-server, master-slave, and remote procedure call require information to flow in two directions. Second, the kernel at the receiving end sometimes needs to know the location of the sending end (for example, to send a message to warn that the receiving end terminated or moved).

The link abstraction is supported by the kernel. This implies that sending messages between two remote processes requires cooperation between the kernels of the two ends of the link. Charlotte communication layers are illustrated in Fig. 14.17.

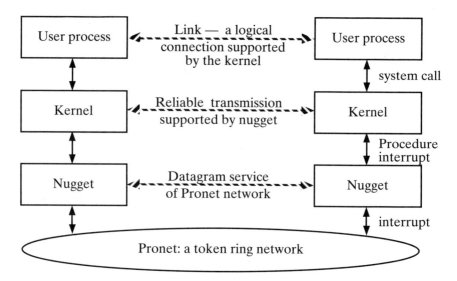

Fig. 14.17 Communication layers in the Charlotte system {adapted from Artsy *et al.* (1984)}.

Communication primitives

Processes communicate using messages, that is, packages of information of any length. The internal structure of a message is ignored by the kernel. Buffers are used in communications. A buffer is an area in the addressing space of a process that contains, or is expected to receive, a message. Process communication in Charlotte is:

(1) **non-blocking** – a process can continue executing while the kernel is transmitting a message on its behalf;

(2) **unbuffered** – a message can only be transmitted when the receiver provides a place to put it; and

(3) **synchronous** – processes are not interrupted by the arrival of messages or the completion of sent messages.

Interprocess communication primitives provided in the Charlotte distributed operating system are presented in List 14.8.

Note that a process can transfer possession of any link ends it holds to another process, even a remote one. This is achieved by enclosing that end in a message sent across a different link. The sender loses its ownership, and the receiver of the message gains possession of that end. Such a transfer of a link end is seen by a process as an atomic action. The transfer of a link end allows communication structures to be changed dynamically.

The Charlotte kernel does not provide buffering. Buffer allocation is handled within the domain of each process instead of within the

---

Send(L : link; buffer : address; length : integer; enclosure : link)
    posts a send operation on a given link end, optionally
    enclosing another link end.

Receive(L : link; buffer : address; length : integer)
    posts a receive operation on a given link end. L can be a
    specific link or AnyLink.

Cancel(L : link; d : direction)
    attempts to cancel a previously-started **Send** or **Receive**
    operation. L can be AnyLink.

Wait(L : link; d : direction; var e : description)
    waits for an operation to complete. L can be a specific
    link or AnyLink. The direction can be Sent, Received, or
    either. The description returns the success or failure of
    the awaited operation, its link, direction, number of
    bytes transferred, and the enclosed link (if any). (**SendWait**
    and **ReceiveWait** primitives, which combine **Send** and **Receive**
    with **Wait** are also supported.)

GetResult(L : link; d : direction; var e : description)
    asks for the same information returned by **Wait**, however
    does not block if the operation has not completed.
    GetResult is a polling mechanism.

List 14.8 Interprocess communication primitives.

---

kernel. The highest degree of concurrency between senders and receivers would be offered by providing an unlimited number of intermediate buffers. However, in practice, a system provides only a finite number of buffers to store messages. The buffer pool requires deadlock prevention or detection techniques.

14.4.3 Synchronization

Basic communication activities in Charlotte never block. The **Send** and **Receive** calls initiate communication, but do not wait for completion. This implies that a process can issue **Send** or **Receive** requests on many links without waiting for any to finish. Processes can perform work while communication is in progress.

Issuing the **Send** and **Receive** calls is synchronous: a process knows at what time the request was issued. On the other hand, completion is asynchronous: the data transfer may occur at any time in the future. There are three facilities to deal with this asynchrony:

(1)   versions of **Send** and **Receive** are available that block until they complete;

(2)   a process may explicitly wait for a **Send** or **Receive** to finish; and

(3)   a process may poll the completion status of a **Send** or **Receive**.

14.4.4   Naming

Each process in Charlotte has its local identifier. As a result, a process in the Charlotte system can be located using a logical address, which is the triple: machine number (1 to n, where n is the number of machines in the system), process identifier and link number.

Processes in Charlotte do not refer to each other directly, but only through the links that connect them. A process does not see a process identifier and machine location of the other end of a link. The kernel maintains full, up-to-date information about the links held by processes it controls. This implies that absolute information is in use, but it is not necessitated by the communication semantics which have been chosen.

Charlotte's links are capability-based names. Capability-based naming facilitates experimentation in migration for load balancing. These names have advantages and disadvantages. The advantages of using this kind of naming are both protection and flexibility. Links, as we said earlier, are bound dynamically to processes. This implies that it is easy to change communication patterns in order to reconfigure the system or to reallocate resources. There are two basic disadvantages: the lengthy initial setup episode, and the cost of validating and associating the capacity with the destination process in every communication.

Naming services are provided by a name server called the Switch-Board. Any server process can register itself with a SwitchBoard (with a set of patterns). On the other hand, any client process can ask a Switch-Board to locate a server described by a pattern. Since Charlotte uses links, the SwitchBoard returns a link to that server.

14.4.5   Process management

There are two distinct issues in Charlotte's process management: operations on processes and memory management, and process migration.

Operations on processes

Processes in Charlotte are created by KernJob (this and other utility processes will be discussed later) through the restricted **MakeProcess** call. It returns a process identifier, which is later used to control the process. However, the creation of new child processes is managed by the Starter.

This utility process manages memory and is also responsible for a set of nodes. A parent process wishing to create a new child sends a message to a Starter naming a file which contains the executable code for that child. The Starter sends a request to KernJob on the appropriate computer to execute **MakeProcess** on its behalf. **MakeProcess** arguments indicate the memory requirements of the new process: where it starts in physical memory and how long it is.

The **Terminate** kernel call causes termination of a process. All links owned by the terminated process are destroyed. If a process executes on a remote computer, the KernJob on this computer is notified and may take some action (in particular, destroy any control link for the process).

The following other operations can be performed on Charlotte's processes: **Suspend**, **Resume**, **Inspire**, and **Expire**, with a process identifier parameter.

Active processes are scheduled using the round-robin strategy, with a fixed quantum (1/20 second). This is the short-term scheduling algorithm. A process can be deactivated by the holder of a control link as part of a long-term scheduling policy.

Charlotte's processes do not share memory. The **GetMemoryMap** kernel call is used by the KernJob to identify the initial arrangement of memory. This information is passed to the Starter to assume its responsibility of managing memory. Processes are described by Object Modules in the form used by Berkeley UNIX Version 4.1. When the Starter loads a process, it allocates sufficient room for combined text, data, and bss areas. A process cannot request more space. Moreover, Charlotte does not support paging.

Process migration

Process migration in Charlotte was designed:

(1)   to provide a testbed for the study of load sharing policies and migration algorithms in distributed operating systems, in other words to evaluate algorithms used to determine '**when** to migrate **which** process to **where**',

(2)   to enhance Charlotte's function as a testbed for research in distributed algorithms; and

(3)   to demonstrate the feasibility of an efficient implementation in the context of powerful but complex interprocess mechanisms.

The process migration facility was embedded into Charlotte in such a way that no changes to its major features and structure were made, and the behavior of processes and users was not affected. Because we presented Charlotte's process migration facility in Chapter 8, we will not discuss it further here. However, we will emphasize those aspects which illustrate the decisions made by the designers.

The process migration facility has a number of important features:

(1)   The decision-making (policy) facility is separated from the migration mechanism. The former is implemented at the utility process level, whereas the latter is embedded in the kernel.

(2)   Migration is transparent to a migrating process as well as to the processes connected to it. The migrating process sees the same computational environment before and after moving. Processes can either communicate with the migrating process (although with a small delay), destroy or move their connection with it.

(3)   Migration can be aborted in the middle. Moreover, the migrating process can be rescued under certain circumstances when either the source or the destination computer crashes.

Process migration is performed by two cooperating utility processes: the KernJob and the Starter. The KernJob (remember, this resides on each

---

HandShake(what : action_type, buffer : address)
> called by the KernJob to request the kernel to start or stop collecting statistics.

MigrateOut(who : process, where_to : machine)
> called by a Starter process, either directly if it resides in the source machine, or indirectly through the KernJob of that machine.

MigrateIn(which : (process, machine), Accept : boolean, memory_blocks : list of (address, size))
> called by a Starter process either directly or via the KernJob, as before. The purpose of this call is to let the Starter that controls the destination machine approve or disapprove a migration request that has been announced to the Starter by the kernel of the destination machine, or to preapprove a migration attempt after negotiating it directly with the Starter that controls the source machine. (process, machine) refers to the source machine. If the Starter agrees to accept a process, the Starter furnishes a list of memory blocks (the process's image will be copied into these blocks).

CancelMigrate(which : (process, machine))
> tries to retroactively terminate a MigrateOut or a MigrateIn request. This primitive has not been implemented.

List 14.9   Process migration primitives.

computer) provides a path between the kernel and processes that need control over that kernel's process. Process migration is one of the tasks performed by the Starter.

As well as policy–mechanism separation and transparency, the following principles have been used to design the process migration facility: mechanism–mechanism independence, reliability, concurrent multiple migration possibilities, and no stub left behind.

The kernel collects the following statistics: machine load (number of processes and links, the average CPU load, the average network load), process resource usage (the average and total CPU usage and network utilization of each process, its state, and its total communication to local and remote processes), and link statistics (the number of packets sent and received over each link). These statistics are gathered in three different modes: event sampling, interval sampling and periodic statistics.

The new kernel calls added to support process migration are presented in List 14.9.

Since the process migration protocol is presented in Chapter 8 we do not dicuss it here further.

14.4.6　I/O management

It is an important feature of the Charlotte system that most high-level input and output are provided by utility processes. Only some low-level facilities are provided by the Charlotte kernel.

Two routines are provided for low-level control of the console terminal on each machine. They are:

- **PutChar**: this call adds the character to a list of characters ready to be printed out; and

- **GetChar**: this call gives the caller the next character. The caller is blocked if necessary.

The kernel echoes all characters on the terminal.

14.4.7　Utilities

To keep the Charlotte kernel efficient, concise and easily implementable, the designers decided that only interprocess communication and process control should be included in it. All other services are implemented through utility processes. To support the kernel these processes wait for requests coming from client links. We describe here the following utility processes: the KernJob, the Starter, the SwitchBoard, the FileServer and the Connector.

The KernJob

The KernJob is logically part of the kernel. This process resides on every computer and acts as a representative of the kernel on this node for other processes. Calls are made by ordinary messages, which come from processes on any node, whereas kernel calls are directed to the kernel on the same node as the process. For instance, the Starter (the main client of the KernJob), which may reside on a different node from the processes it controls, uses the KernJob as an intermediary for manipulating these processes. This Starter also uses the KernJob to create a process. The processes submit their requests to the KernJob through **control links**.

The following process control services are provided by the KernJob:

(1) Getting the memory allocation map of the node machine: **GetMemoryMap**. This information is used by the Starter during both initialization and failure recovery;

(2) Getting the existent process description: **GetProcessDesc**. This information is also used by the Starter during both initialization and failure recovery;

(3) Making a new process: **MakeProcess**; and

(4) Exercising control over the created process: **Peek, Poke, Inspire, Expire, Status, Suspend** and **Resume**.

All these services are accomplished through the privileged calls allowed only for the KernJob. Moreover, the KernJob maintains a table that associates control links with processes.

The Starter

The Starter is responsible for creating new child processes for clients. However, only registered Starters on the SwitchBoard can provide services to the clients. Not every node needs a Starter, because each Starter may control a number of nodes. The Starter maintains information about all the nodes it serves. This includes current memory allocation and current process states on each node. Moreover, a Starter periodically exchanges information about computation load with other Starters through Starter links.

A client who wants to start a child process must send a request to a Starter. Therefore, it must have a link to a Starter. Such a link can be obtained from the SwitchBoard, in response to the **Locate** request.

Thus, the client sends a child creation request message on the link to the Starter. This message must contain a file name that corresponds to an object file (in UNIX a.out format), and may also contain a request for a control link for the created child process. The Starter communicates with the FileServer to obtain the text and data, stored in the indicated file, for the child process.

However, the Starter does not create a child immediately. The clients' Starter link is passed around the squad of Starters in order to find a good place to make a new process. Because the Starter maintains information about all its nodes, it can decide on which node and where in memory of this node to place a new process. Thus, if a good place is found, the link remains connected to the Starter responsible for that node. This Starter finally performs the process creation. At this stage, the Starter communicates with the KernJob on the appropriate machine to cause the child to start and to have the proper contents. Note that the link can also remain with the Starter that decides that the requested process cannot be created.

If Starter completes the child creation, a control link is returned to the client. This link allows the parent process to exercise some degree of control over its child.

The SwitchBoard

The SwitchBoard allows processes to exchange links, because it works as a name server. Thus, any process can register a link under a given character string name with a SwitchBoard. The SwitchBoard also allows any process to locate a link (and thus a server) registered under a given name. A number of SwitchBoards may be active at a time. This implies the need for their cooperation to satisfy client requests.

Request messages sent to the SwitchBoard and response messages received from the SwitchBoard have several fields, as indicated in List 14.10.

Request
> used by: (i) a client process to name the particular service it requires – the **Register** and **Locate** requests; (ii) the SwitchBoard to indicate either success, the constant SB_SUCCESS, or failure, the constant SB_FAILURE.

Arg
> used by: (i) a client process to carry auxiliary arguments; (ii) the SwitchBoard in the case of failure, to contain an error code.

Name
> used by: (i) a client process to hold the character string name that is to be registered or located, (ii) the Switch-Board in the case of failure, to contain an error message.

SearchLen
> used to specify the maximum searching length.

SearchHist
> used to return the list of the searched SwitchBoards.

List 14.10 Fields of messages used in communications with SwitchBoards.

The FileServer

The FileServer squad has two implementations. The first converts the file access requests to calls to a UNIX process residing on the host. The second converts requests to calls to the WiSS (Wisconsin Storage System) file server computer in the Crystal network.

To service clients, the FileServer must be registerd with the Switch-Board. The client wishing to read or write a file must acquire a link to the FileServer from the SwitchBoard. Having a link, a process can communicate with the FileServer directly.

Open files are represented by links which connect the clients and the FileServer. In the case of the read operation, the FileServer reads from the file and sends data across the link. When a file is opened for writing, the FileServer accepts messages across the link and transfers them to the physical device. In both cases, control information may flow in the other direction on the link.

File service is provided by the squad of processes. Any of these processes can potentially access any file. However, each process in the squad can only access a subset of the files directly. Therefore, any request outside its jurisdiction is transparently forwarded to the file server process that can handle it. This means that the link to the client process is passed along with the request – the client and the responsible file server can communicate directly.

The FileServer provides services to manipulate a file. Because UNIX files are used in the implementation, the operations are identical to such UNIX operations as **open**, **read**, **write**, **create**, and **seek**.

The Connector

The Connector is a utility process which enables an initial linkage to be established within a group of processes. It is implemented as a free-standing utility registered with the SwitchBoard. When a parent process wishes to create a process group, it sends the file name of a **connection description file** to a Connector. This file contains the names of the object files to execute and their inter-relationships. The Connector sends a request to the Starter to load these files. The Starter starts the processes. Each process should start with a call to the library routine **Linkup**. This is used to communicate with the Connector in order to receive the initial link set.

14.4.8 Lessons learned

The following lessons have been learned from this project. First, that very complex interprocess communication semantics should be avoided (a distinctive feature of Charlotte, oriented as it is towards large-grain parallelism to solve computationally-intensive problems). Second, that simple primitives interact in complex ways. Third, that it is not easy to make use of asynchronous primitives. Fourth, that while an interprocess communication facility makes it possible to write highly-concurrent programs, such programs are prone to subtle programming errors. Fifth, that absolute distributed information is hard to maintain. And last, that it is possible to construct an efficient process migration facility to provide load balancing and to improve response time. Only the performance of the process migration facility was studied in this project. On the other hand, complex application problems were studied extensively and intensively. The results of this study could be interesting to the designers of parallel processing systems.

14.5 Amoeba

Amoeba is a research project on distributed operating systems. This project is being carried out at the Vrije University in Amsterdam under the direction of Andrew Tanenbaum. Its major goal is to investigate capability-based, object-oriented systems. It is important to notice that the Amoeba distributed operating system was designed to be used. Some research issues addressed by the project were:

(1) how to to put as much of the operating system as possible into user processes;

(2) how to use a processor pool; how to integrate workstations and a processor pool; and

(3) how to connect multiple Amoeba sites into a single coherent system using wide-area networks.

The design constraints of the Amoeba project are that:

(1) All the Amoeba computers run the same kernel. This kernel provides message passing services and little else.

(2) The kernel should be kept small for two reasons: to enhance its reliability, and to allow as much as possible of the operating system to run as user processes, providing for flexibility and experimentation.

(3) There is a free market model of services.

Amoeba uses the object-oriented model for distributed computing, together with remote procedure calls and lightweight processes.

The Amoeba system runs on a collection of Motorola 68020 computers connected by a 10 Mbps Ethernet. The second network supported by Amoeba is the Pronet token ring. Ethernet and Pronet can be connected by a bridge. Amoeba has been also ported to such different CPUs as NS32016, 8088, VAX, and PDP-11. To allow UNIX programs to run on Amoeba, a library has been written. A number of utilities, including compilers, editors and shells are operational.

Our presentation of Amoeba's project goals and features of this system follows descriptions in Tanenbaum and Mullender (1984), Mullender and Tanenbaum (1985, 1986), Mullender and van Renesse (1985), Tanenbaum and van Renesse (1985, 1986, 1987), Tanenbaum et al. (1984, 1986), Mullender (1985, 1987), Shizgal (1987), van Renesse (1988) and van Renesse et al. (1989).

14.5.1   Architecture of the Amoeba system

The architecture of the Amoeba distributed system consists of four basic components, as illustrated in Fig. 14.18. The first component is the workstation, one per user. Each workstation runs window management software, which allows a user to carry out tasks requiring fast interactive response. The second component is the processor pool. Each processor can be dynamically allocated when needed. After use, it is returned to the pool. The third component is the specialized servers. The main servers are directory, file and block servers, database servers, bank servers and boot servers. The fourth component is a gateway.

All of the Amoeba machines run the same copy of the kernel. The Amoeba kernel provides only the bare minimum of services. Its main tasks are communication services (message-transasction facilities), process management and access path to peripherals. Most services run in

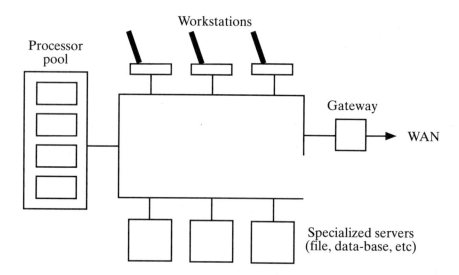

Fig. 14.18   The Amoeba architecture {adapted from Tanenbaum and van Renesse (1985)}.

user space. For example, a file service is a user-space service with no special privileges.

The Amoeba system has been developed from several basic concepts. As we noted earlier, Amoeba is an **object-oriented** distributed operating system, that is, files, directories, disk blocks, processes, bank accounts, and devices are objects. Each object is owned by some service and managed by the corresponding server processes.

To carry out an operation on an object, a client process sends a request message to the server process that manages that object, and then blocks. The server performs the requested operation on the object. When the operation is complete the server sends a response message to the client. This unblocks the client process. This request/response exchange is called a **transaction** by the designers (it is not a database transaction). The Amoeba system provides **at-most-once** execution of transactions.

Another basic concept of Amoeba is the **remote procedure call**. Remote procedure calls are implemented by assembling an operation code and its arguments in a request message, which is sent to the appropriate server. The client process blocks while the server is working, whereas the server blocks while it is waiting for a request. A transaction is performed by the server. The results of running the procedure are returned to the client in a response message.

In the Amoeba system simultaneous multiple transactions are possible. To handle them, a process can be subdivided into lightweight processes known as **threads**. There is a thread for each request. This results in a server process that can handle multiple requests simultaneously. Also, a client process can perform several transactions at the same time – it has to have one thread per transaction. Threads are only rescheduled when the currently-running thread blocks. This means that threads are non-pre-emptive. This avoids race conditions and simplifies programming.

The next basic Amoeba concept is a **capability**. All objects in this system are named and protected by cryptographically-secure capabilities. Capabilities and transactions provide a uniform interface to all objects in Amoeba. It is important to notice that users view the Amoeba environment as a collection of objects, named by capabilities, on which they can perform operations.

14.5.2 Interprocess communication

Communication between clients and servers is supported by three layers. The highest, the Transaction Layer, is responsible for reliable delivery of requests and replies. To guarantee the arrival of these messages, it uses the Port Layer and timers. The Port Layer deals with the location of services, the transport of 32K byte datagrams (packets whose delivery is not guaranteed) from source to destination, and enforces the protection mechanism. The lowest layer, the Physical Layer, deals mainly with electrical and mechanical aspects of data transfer. These three layers are implemented by the kernel and hardware. Only the Transaction Layer interface is visible to users (clients and servers).

The message passing mechanism is implemented by the Port Layer. It may be implemented as a set of system calls, or as a set of subroutines in user space. The interface between user programs and the port layer is simple. The calls for sending and receiving messages, and for the creation of ports are given in List 14.11.

---

put(putport, srcport, signature, buffer)
   sends a message stored in buffer to a port named putport; a response is expected on port srcport. This call is the same for clients and servers.

get(getport, srcport, signature, buffer)
   receives a message from a port named srcport on a port named getport, and puts received data into a buffer. This call is the same for clients and servers.

makeport(getport, putport)
   creates ports. This call is issued by servers.

List 14.11   The Amoeba message passing calls.

The Amoeba transaction-oriented communication between clients and servers is based on a minimal remote procedure call model. The communication primitives are presented in List 14.12.

---

get_request(req-header, req-buffer, req-size)
   by calling this primitive a server awaits a new request message specifying a header, req-header, and a buffer, req-buffer, of a given req-size in which to receive the message.

put_reply(rep-header, rep-buffer, rep-size)
   sends back a reply of rep-size, which is stored in rep-buffer.

do_transaction(req-header, req-buffer, req-size, rep-header, rep-buffer, rep-size)
   a client invokes this primitive to send a request message by specifying the capability of the object to be operated on and the operation code in the request header.

List 14.12   The Amoeba communication primitives.

These primitives are not embedded in a language environment with automatic stub generation. They are implemented as small library routines that are used to invoke the kernel directly from C programs.

The basic message primitives are blocking. Request and replies are delivered reliably. A reliable delivery service is provided transparently by the kernel. Messages are not buffered. An unexpected message is discarded. After timeout, the sending kernel tries again. Retransmissions are performed a defined number of times. Thus, Amoeba guarantees that messages are delivered at most once. The return status of the **do_transaction** primitive can be one of three values:

(1)   the request was delivered and has been executed;

(2)   the request was not delivered and hence not executed; or

(3)   the status is unknown: the request was sent, but any contact to the server was broken afterwards.

Although the basic communication primitives are blocking, special provision is made for handling emergency messages. If a user does not want to wait for completion of a request, it should be possible to abort all the processes working on behalf of the initial request. In order to do this, an Amoeba terminal is able to generate and send a special **exception** message, which causes an interrupt at the receiving process. This message forces the receiving process to stop working on the request and to send an immediate reply with the status code of REQUEST ABORTED. If more servers are involved in performing the request, the **exception** message is recursively propagated, forcing each server to finish immediately.

Amoeba's requests and reply messages consist of two parts: a header of 32 bytes and a buffer of up to 30 000 bytes. They will be changed to 64 bytes and 1 gigabyte respectively. A request header contains a capability of the object to be operated on, the operation code, and parameters to the operation (8 bytes). A reply header contains an error code, a limited area for the result of the operation (8 bytes), and a capability field that can be used to return a capability (for example, as the result of the creation of an object).

To contact a service, a client sends a message to a port. Every service has one or more ports. A port is a large number (typically 48 bytes). Ports are known only to the server processes that comprise the service and to the service's clients. There are ports generally known to all users (for a public service), and those which are kept secret (used by ordinary users). Knowledge of a port is taken by the system as evidence that the sender has a right to communicate with the service. This is not enough, however, so protection and naming are discussed in the following section.

14.5.3 Naming and protection

All Amoeba objects are named and protected by capabilities. A capability has 128 bits, and is composed of four fields, as shown in Fig. 14.19.

48	24	8	48	Number of bits
Server port	Object number	Rights	Check field	Fields

Fig. 14.19 An Amoeba capability {adapted from Tanenbaum and van Renesse (1985)}.

(1) **The server port** – 48 bit sparse address which identifies the server process that manages the object. A server can choose its own address.

(2) **The object number** – an internal 24 bit identifier used by the server to distinguish among its objects. The server port and the object number together uniquely identify an object.

(3) **The rights** – 8 bits which determine which operations on the object are permitted by the holder of this capability.

(4) **The check field** – a 48 bit number that is used to protect the capability against forging and tampering.

Thus, each object has a globally unique name, contained in its capabilities, which is used to access and address it. Note again that one field of the capability, called the server port, specifies the service that manages objects of its type. Since these ports do not carry information about the whereabouts of the associated server process, a locate mechanism is necessary to find a server for a service. The mechanism for locating ports in local area networks is based on broadcast queries, 'where are you?'. For locating ports in wide area networks, it uses a different mechanism because these networks do not provide a broadcast facility. They are based on sending messages to locate a port. One research result indicates that using totally unstructured names does not scale well, and the authors of the Amoeba system are working on details of a hierarchical port name space, in which a service indicates in what domain its servers must expect their clients. Thus, ASCII string-to-capability mapping and storage are handled by directory servers for convenience.

When an object is created by a server, the requesting process is given a capability for it. A process can only carry out operations on the object using this capability (for example, starting or stopping a process). A bit map in the capability shows which operations the holder of the capability is permitted to use.

Capabilities are managed entirely by user processes. They are protected cryptographically. There are no kernel-maintained tables or mechanisms for protection. When creating a requested object, a server picks an available slot in its internal tables and puts the information about the object there, together with a newly-generated 48 bit random number. The object number field of the capability is loaded with the index into the table. The contents of the rights field together with the random number, are encrypted and the result is stored in the check field. When a request message with a capability arrives, a server checks this capability by encrypting its rights field together with the random number in the server's tables. The result is compared with the check field in the capability.

Capabilities are stored in directories. A directory is a set of <ASCII string, capability> pairs. Each directory is also an object, and as such is managed by the directory service. Note that directory entries may contain capabilities for other directories, resulting in the ability to construct an arbitrary naming graph. The following operations can be performed on capability directories: entering and deleting directory entries, listing a directory, and making inquiries (asking for the capability corresponding to a presented ASCII string).

The Amoeba naming scheme has the following features:

(1)   It is flexible. A directory may contain capabilities for an arbitrary mixture of object types and locations.

(2)   It is uniform, that is, every object is controlled by a capability.

(3)   It allows for the building of a hierarchical directory tree, or more general naming graphs. This can be achieved because a directory entry can be for another directory. Moreover, a directory may also contain a capability for a directory managed by a different directory service. Note that it is possible to distribute objects over directory services in an arbitrary way, if the directory services have the same interface with the user.

Owners of Amoeba objects can pass rights to these objects by simply giving a copy of the capability to another process. Passing restricted rights (for example, read-only access) is also possible but more difficult. In general, as the reader recalls, there are some problems with revocation of rights in capability based systems. This problem is effectively solved in Amoeba. The capabilities and objects are organized in such a way that no central record is kept of who has which capabilities. However, in this situation, the owner of an object can ask the server to change the random number stored in the file table. (Of course, this operation must be protected with a bit in a rights field.) The effect of changing the random number is that all existing capabilities are instantly invalidated.

14.5.4 Process management

Process management mechanisms in Amoeba allow downloading, process migration, checkpointing, remote debugging, and emulation of alien operating system interfaces. Process management facilities are realized by two main services:

(1)   Kernel Service, which implements local segments and is a kernel-based service; and

(2)   Process Service, which uses segments to implement a system-wide segment abstraction. It is a user-space service.

These services can be augmented by other user-space services, such as Debug Service, Load-Balancing Service, UNIX-emulation Service and Checkpoint Service.

The Kernel Server

To realize the process abstraction in Amoeba, the kernel manipulates three kinds of basic objects: a **process**, which is a virtual address space, a **segment** which is part of a process, and a **thread**.

The state of a process consists of its memory content which is in the form of a collection of segments, and a **Process Descriptor** which contains the additional state, program counters, stack pointers and system call state.

A **segment**, which is an object managed by the Kernel Service, is a named linear section of memory. When the Kernel Server is requested to create a segment of a given length, it allocates the necessary amount of memory, and returns to the requester a capability for it. The requester becomes the owner of this newly-created segment and can manipulate it. Afterwards, the segment can be mapped into a process's address space, using a **map** request. The **map** request includes a data structure, called a segment descriptor, as shown in Fig. 14.20.

Segments may be unmapped and can also be deleted. Segments cannot migrate; they are created and deleted on the same processor.

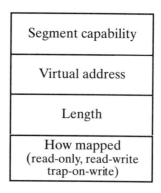

Fig. 14.20   Segment descriptor {adapted from Mullender (1987)}.

Segments are necessary to create processes. To create a process, the parent process sends a **CreateSegment** request with the parameters shown above. The capability returned by the Kernel Server is required by the parent to perform **write** operations to load data into the segment. The segment and load operation is repeated until all the child process's initial segments have been constructed. Thus, this cycle can be repeated three times, that is, for the child process's text, data, and stack segments.

To create the child process (thread), the parent process then performs a **MakeProcess (MakeThread)** operation. As parameters, the parent has to provide capabilities for the child's segments. The server returns a process capability for the child. This capability is used when the process is to be started, stopped, and generally manipulated.

The same primitives can also be used to build a set of processes that share text and/or data segments. This is useful for constructing servers that consists internally of multiple miniprocesses, called thread. Threads share text and data. Each of these processes (threads) has its own stack and program counter. This implies that when one of these tasks blocks on a remote procedure call, the others are not affected and are free to handle new requests. Such threads can be consolidated into a process.

The Kernel Server creates and manages processes. A process is created after receiving a **CreateProcess** request with a **process descriptor** as the parameter. The process descriptor describes the initial state of the process by describing the state of its threads, the address space in which these threads will run, and the processor on which the process must run. The process descriptor is illustrated in Fig. 14.21.

The process descriptor's fields are:

(1) **The host descriptor** – which describes the kind of processor the process runs on.

(2) **The scheduling field** – which is used to provide scheduling information from the previous host to the next one when a process migrates.

(3) **The exception handler** – which gives the port of the service which handles exceptions if they occur.

(4) **The segment descriptors** – there is one descriptor for each segment in the process's address space.

(5) **The thread descriptors** – one descriptor for each thread in the process; it gives the state of each thread in the process.

The interface with the Kernel Server for process management contains a number of requests and system calls. They are given in List 14.13.

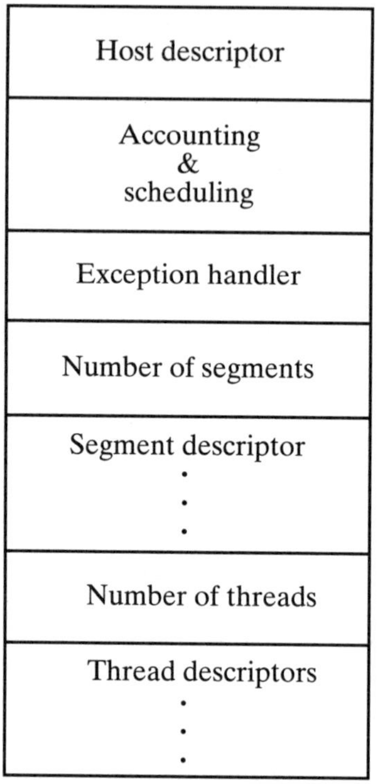

Host descriptor
Accounting & scheduling
Exception handler
Number of segments
Segment descriptor • • •
Number of threads
Thread descriptors • • •

Fig. 14.21   Process descriptor {adapted from Mullender (1987)}.

Transactions with Kernel Service

Segment management

   CreateSegment(ProcessCap, SegmentDesc) → SegmentCap
      creates a segment and returns SegmentCap.

   WriteSegment(SegmentCap, ptr) → ack
      loads data from a buffer referenced by ptr into a segment
      named SegmentCap and returns ack.

   ReadSegment(SegmentCap, ptr)
      reads data from a segment named SegmentCap and puts it
      into a buffer pointed to by ptr and returns ack.

   MapSegment(ProcessCap, SegmentDesc)
      maps a segment described by SegmentDesc into a process
      named ProcessCap and returns ack.

UnMapSegment(ProcessCap, VirtualAddr) → ack
  unmaps a segment from a process's address space and
  returns ack.

DeleteSegment(SegmentCap) → ack
  deletes a segment named SegmentCap and returns ack.

Process creation, running and deletion (process may delete itself)
  CreateProcess(KernelCap, ProcessDesc) → ProcessCap
  creates a process described by ProcessDesc on behalf of a
  client and returns ProcessCap. However, the process
  descriptor's segments capabilities must refer to existing
  segments.

RunProcess(ProcessCap, ProcessDesc) → result
  runs a process described by ProcessDesc.

DeleteProcess(ProcessCap) → ProcessDesc
  deletes a process named ProcessCap and returns ProcessDesc.

Interrupting process
  Signal(ProcessCap, SignalType, Parameter) → ack
  interrupts a process named ProcessCap by a signal of type
  SignalType with a Parameter and returns ack.

Kernel system calls

Thread management
  MakeThread(ProgramCounter, StackPointer) → ack
  creates a thread and returns ack. The new thread will start
  execution at the address indicated by the ProgramCounter.

ExitThread()
  deletes itself by issuing this call. It does not return.

Synchronization
  P(Semaphore)

  V(Semaphore)

  Sleep(Condition)
  puts a thread to sleep.

  WakeUp(Condition)
  wakes up every thread sleeping on the condition.

List 14.13 Kernel requests and system calls for process management.

The Process Server

The Kernel Server is responsible for creating a process. This is performed by creating and writing a segment, followed by a request to make a process containing a list of created segments. However, since the Kernel Server implements only local segments, there is no kernel mechanism to write into a remote segment.

The Process Server uses segments to implement a system-wide segment abstraction. These segments are referred to as **global segments**. Two global segments have the same name if they have the same contents.

The most important task of the Process Server is to cause processes to be executed on a host that it serves. This operation is performed by the Server after it receives a **RunProcess** request. It is important to notice the difference, namely, that the Process Descriptor contains global segment capabilities, whereas the Kernel Server's Process Descriptor must contain local segment capabilities.

Another task of Process Servers is to initialize segments by mapping them in their own address space, writing into them, and unmapping them again. Segment contents can be fetched from a remote server by doing a transaction. These tasks and associated attributes play an important role in process migration.

The process migration mechanism is implemented by Process Servers. (Note that a process migration policy is made at a higher level of service.) The basic assumption is that when a process moves from one machine to another, the Process Server at the old machine (denoted **OldProServer**) makes the memory contents and process description available to the Process Server on the new host (denoted **NewProServer**). The **NewProServer** loads the process into memory and starts it executing.

There is one element which plays a very important role in process migration. Every Process Server has an internal Segment Server thread which serves requests from remote clients to obtain the contents of segments. When the contents of a given segment are needed, the Segment Server maps them into its virtual memory and replies to those requests using the reply buffer in the mapped segment.

Let us assume now that the **OldProServer** received a request to move the process to the **NewProServer**. The general concept of the migration algorithm is as follows:

(1)   **OldProServer** sends a signal to the process. This causes the Kernel Server to freeze this process in its tracks, and to send a process descriptor to **OldProServer**.

(2)   **OldProServer** creates global segment capabilities for the process's segments. Segments whose contents (may) have changed must be given new, unique capabilities. Those segments whose contents have not changed may retain their previous global capability.

(3)   The Segment Server provides its service.

(4)   **OldProServer** sends the process descriptor to **NewProServer** in a **RunProcess** request. The local segment capabilities are replaced by global segment capabilities.

(5)   **NewProServer**, after receiving the **RunProcess** request, examines the global segment capabilities to see whether it already has any of them. If so it uses them, otherwise it creates and maps them into its address space.

(6)   It sends **ReadSegment** requests with the reply buffer in the mapped segment to the Segment Server at **OldProServer**.

(7)   It copies a process's memory contents over the Ethernet.

(8)   **NewProServer**, after completion of the copy operation, replaces the global segment capabilities in the process descriptor by the appropriate local ones and starts the process with a **CreateProcess** request.

(9)   The process executes on its new host.

(10)   **NewProServer** returns a reply to **OldProServer**. **OldProServer** deletes the process with a **DeleteProcess** request issued to the Kernel Server.

(11)   Migration is completed.

Note that while migration is in progress, the process on **OldPro-Server** is frozen. This implies that the kernel replies to all messages directed to it with a 'try again later, this process is frozen' message. When messages come after the process has been deleted, the kernel replies with 'this port is unknown at this address'. As a result of this reply, the sender will start a **locate** operation to find the process.

Other process management services
In Amoeba, when a process traps because of an exception, a debugger is invoked. The Debug Server is a user-space process. This server does not have any special privileges. It can reside on the same kernel as the faulty process, or it can be run remotely. In the latter case, the Debug Server needs some help from the Process Server.

The task of the Program Server is the provision of new process. It stores the binary codes of the programs running in Amoeba into files. It also makes them available to Process Servers such that the Program Server appears to them as a Process Server. If a program is downloaded over the network, it uses the same mechanisms as migration.

14.5.5   Resource management

The most distinctive Amoeba resources to be managed are processes and the processor pool. Resource management in Amoeba is performed in a distributed way. Capabilities are used for these purposes. Each machine (workstation, pool processor) runs a resource manager process. This process controls that machine. To keep the system kernel as small as possible, the management system of the processor pool has been placed outside the kernel. Since this service is associated with process scheduling, it is provided by the Process Server.

To control the processor pool, the Process Server keeps track of which processors are free and which are not. Based on this information the Process Server allocates processes to processors, and controls migration. If an installation wants to multiprogram the processor pool machines, the Process Server manages each process table slot on a pool processor as a virtual processor. The concept of a 'process image' containing all the information necessary to run a process (memory, registers, capabilities), is introduced so that process migration and swapping among processes can be handled in a unified way.

Another very important element of the resource management mechanisms is the bank service. This service implements objects called 'bank acounts' with operations to transfer virtual money, possibly in multiple currencies, between accounts and to inspect the status of accounts. There are two bank accounts: individual and business. Usually, users have their individual accounts, each user having one account. The virtual money on these accounts is used to pay for CPU time, disk blocks and all other resources. Business accounts are used by services to keep track of who has paid them and how much.

14.5.6 Security

Two solutions are proposed by the designers to provide security in networks connecting machines running the Amoeba distributed operating system. The first, and simplest, requires a special hardware device or a protected kernel. The second solution is general – it uses a public key cryptosystem.

Security based on one-way functions
Security based on one-way ciphers requires inserting a (small) hardware device between the user machines and the communication medium, as is illustrated in Fig. 14.22.

The interface providing network security uses one-way ciphers. A **one-way cipher** is a function f which is publicly known but computationally infeasible to invert. This means that given $f(x)$ it is very difficult to deduce x.

To achieve the necessary security, the getport and putport are associated with each other using the formula:

putport = f(getport)

When a process creates a new service, it calls **makeport** which picks a randomly chosen number from a large (that is, sparse) address space,

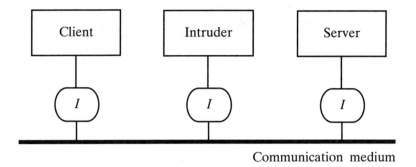

Communication medium

Fig. 14.22 Network security provided by the hardware interface (I – interface).

and uses it as the getport. Next, using the one-way function, it computes the putport. This putport is given to selected clients to use when communicating with the server.

To receive messages, the server does a **get** on the getport. It passes the getport to the interface, where the corresponding putport is computed. Afterwards, the putport is stored in a table in the interface. When a destination port in a transmitted message matches the stored putport value, the message is copied to the interface and passed to the host. Note that the port to be used by the server to reply to the client can be safely included in the client to server message.

Because an intruder cannot derive the server's getport from the publicly known putport, and is not able to pick getports at random due to the sparseness of the port space, messages can be securely transmitted between clients and servers.

The one-way function mechanisms can also be used to send **signed** messages. To do this, a process selects a **private signature** by calling **makeport**. Note that a signature is just another port, although it is not necessarily used as such. The private signature is encrypted and is treated as a **public signature**. The public signature can now be given to another process which uses it to identify the sender of message.

Secure message transmission using one-way functions is illustrated in Fig. 14.23.

The security method presented above can be also used in networks in which the routing is done using physical machine numbers rather than the port matching with associative memory system, as well as in star-shaped networks. Note that since all the machines in a network have protected operating system kernels, the interface can be located in the kernel.

Security based on a public key cryptosystem
To send messages securely in an insecure environment, ports and messages should be encrypted. The method proposed by the Amoeba designers uses a public key cryptosystem in such a way that every service

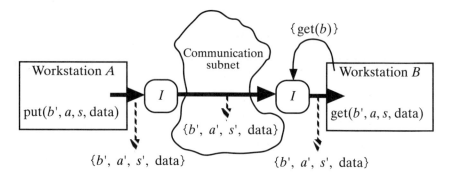

Fig. 14.23 Passing a message containing a destination port b', a source port a, and a signature port s, from workstation A to workstation B. I indicates an interface, getports are indicated by a, b and s, and putports by a', b', and s {adapted from Mullender and Tanenbaum (1984)}.

uses the public key for the encryption of messages and the private key for decryption.

Each port (created by the **makeport** primitive) consists of:

(1)   a port-identifier (port-id), which is used for identification of the port (it is kept secret), and

(2)   an encryption key (putport) or a decryption key (getport).

These keys are used to encrypt and decrypt messages. Messages are headed by the port-id in plaintext, to allow a receiving process to find out which key should be used. The port-id should be long enough to preclude the possibility of two agents accidently choosing the same port name.

14.5.7   A distributed file service

Amoeba has several kinds of block, file and directory services. A file service is one of the most important services provided by a computer system. Taking this into consideration, the Amoeba architects attempted to build a file service which would be suitable for many different aplications: ordinary 'plain' files, hierarchically structured files, replicated files, databases, source code control systems.

The following issues were taken into consideration when designing file services:

(1)   The Bauer principle, which says 'you should not pay for those features you do not need'.

(2)   The file server should be easy to understand. The interface to it must not only be simple (with few commands), but also clients

must have a simple conception of the structure of the file, and how to use it.

(3) The distributed file server should be suitable for an Amoeba environment. It should use the protection provided by Amoeba's ports and capabilities.

(4) Storage services should be developed and provided to a user according to the open operating system approach. Many storage services should be available, they should be structured hierarchically, and a choice of which file server to use is up to the user. An example of a storage service hierarchy in an open system, and the placement in such a hierarchy of the Amoeba file server is shown in Fig. 14.24.

An Amoeba file system is a collection of processes with no special privileges. This system is highly modular and depends heavily on capabilities.

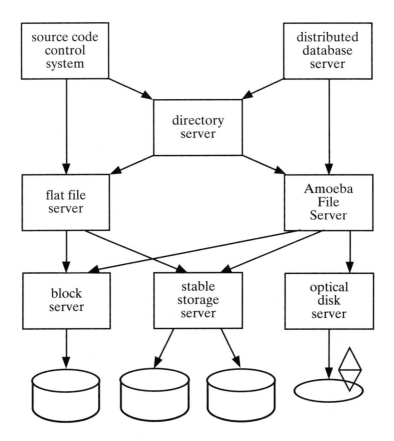

Fig. 14.24 An example of a storage service hierarchy in an open system {adapted from Mullender and Tanenbaum (1985)}.

Block service

The Amoeba block service is responsible for managing raw disk storage. Because it also provides an interface to the outside world, file servers are relieved of the responsibility of coping with the details of a disk's functions. At this level, there is no concept of a file. The block server primitives provide a convenient object-oriented interface for file servers to use. The principal primitives (operations) are given in List 14.14.

---

allocate
> allocates a block, writes data into it, and returns a capability to this block.

free
> frees the block named by a given capability.

read
> reads the block named by a given capability and returns the data contained in it.

write
> writes the data into the block named by a given capability.

lock
> locks or unlocks the block named by a given capability using a given key.

List 14.14   Block service primitives in Amoeba.

The **lock** primitive, which allows clients to lock individual blocks, forms a sufficient basis for file systems to develop more elaborate locking schemes. There is also another primitive, **recovery**. This operation allows a file server that has lost all of its internal tables in a crash to rebuild its entire file list from scratch. It uses for this purpose the account numbers of all blocks (the same as are used by clients in **allocate** operations) which are stored in a place not accessible to clients, and it requires searching of the entire disk using all the returned capabilities.

It is interesting that each block is stored by two servers on two different disk drives. This implies that on request to allocate and write a block, the block server which received a request (say A), allocates a block on its disk, then sends a request with data and the chosen block number to the second block server (B). This second server writes the block to disk at the address indicated by A, and replies with an acknowledgement message. After receiving the acknowledgement, server *A* writes the data in its own block, and returns a block identifier to the client. Note that allocate collisions may occur when two clients allocate a block simultaneously, one on server *A* and one on server *B*, and *A* and *B* accidently choose the same number. Moreover, write collisions may occur when two clients write the same block via different block servers. Fortunately, these collisions are detected before any damage is done, because writes are performed on the companion disk first.

File service

The Amoeba File Service was developed for the Amoeba distributed operating system. It implements the file system as a tree of pages, whose subtrees are files, and uses a combination of an optimistic concurrency control mechanism and a locking mechanism to prevent conflict in simultaneous updates.

The Amoeba File Service implements optimistic concurrency control by a version mechanism. The basic model is that a file is a time-ordered sequence of versions, where each version is a snapshot of the file made at a moment determined by a client. The current state of a file is contained in the **current version**. At any instant, exactly one version of the file is the current version. **Committed versions** represent past states of a file, whereas **uncommitted versions** represent possible future states of the file. A file and a version are accessed by their **file capability** and **version capability**, respectively. Atomic updates on files are bracketed by creating a version and committing a version. Committing a version makes that version the current one.

If a client wants to use a file, it sends a request message to a file server. This message contains a file capability and a request to create a private version of the current version of the file. The server returns a capability for the new version. This version looks to a client like a block to block copy. In practice, the file is not really copied block to block. Instead, when a new version is created, a table of capabilities (pointers) to all the file blocks is created. This means that the capability for the new file version is a capability to this version table. When a block is modified in the new version, a new block is allocated using the block server, it replaces the original block, and its capability is inserted into the version table. It is necessary also to set a bit to indicate that the block is new. This mechanism is called 'copy on write'.

Versions created and modified by a client are called **uncommitted versions**. At any time there is a possibility that the current version could have many uncommitted versions created by different clients. A client, after completing work on a personal version, asks the file server to **commit** this version, thus making it the current version. The commit succeeds if the version from which the version to be committed was derived is still current at the time of the commit. If it is not, and other clients want to make their versions current, the Amoeba authors propose to use the concept of **serializability**. This concept does not require locking. It works because most updates, even on the same file, do not affect the same parts of the file, and hence do not conflict. As a result performance of the system is improved.

The Amoeba file system is represented as a large tree of pages. The structure of this file system is illustrated in Fig. 14.25.

Note that Amoeba files, unlike files in most file systems, form a nested structure. This means that a subtree whose root page is inside another subtree may be treated as a file within another file. For example, A and B are subfiles of file C.

Caching is an important form of optimization, and the Amoeba File Service is especially suited for caching. This is because each version behaves like a private copy of a file that cannot change without the owners consent. Thus, both Amoeba file servers and their clients can maintain a cache, which for the most recently used versions of a set of files, contains collections of blocks. This implies that when a new version is created, a client or a server examines its cache to determine whether there are any blocks from a previous version of the file that can still be used.

In summary, the Amoeba File Service combines a number of concepts from the operating systems' world, the distributed systems' world,

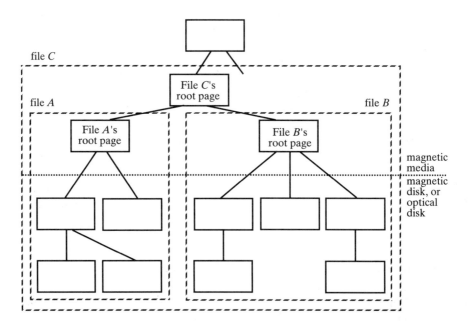

Fig. 14.25   The tree structure of the Amoeba file system {adapted from Mullender and Tanenbaum (1985)}

and the database world. This service possesses some very distinctive features and advantages.

(1)   Distributed file servers have been constructed using optimistic concurrency control. It is a very novel solution which allows the system to be always in a consistent state, with a maximum of concurrency in accessing files. Moreover, there is no necessity for recovery after a crash: no rollback is required, no locks have to be cleared, no intention lists have to be carried out.

(2)   When a large update must be carried out on a heavily shared file, starvation may occur. However, the situation can be improved by using the locking mechanism. This means that a file is locked when it is known that the update is large.

Moreover, the Amoeba architects suggest organizing the file system in such a way to avoid frequent updates on super-files. Each small file should be self contained as much as possible to have most updates performed on small files. This results in a large degree of concurrency.

(3)   End-user processes and Amoeba File Server processes should maintain block caches.

(4)   The Amoeba File Service provides mechanisms that allow both sophisticated and simple applications to use its services efficiently.

(5)   The Amoeba File Service is suitable also for a file system on write-once media, such as optical disks.

Directory service

A directory service is needed to provide symbolic naming. The main task of the directory service is to manage directories. Each directory contains a collection of (ASCII name, capability) pairs. The following basic operations can be performed on directory objects: asking for a capability associated with a given ASCII name, entering and removing (ASCII name, capability) entries from directories. These operations can be performed if a client presents to the directory server the capability for a directory. Using these primitives, and a few others, it is possible to build up arbitrary directory trees and graphs.

14.5.8   Lessons learned

The design goals have been achieved. The authors wanted to develop a functional distributed operating system to prove that it is possible to construct such a system, and to show that such a system can be powerful enough to be used in different applications to provide services requested by a user. Architects of the Amoeba system presented several guidelines on how to design a distributed operating system. Their published works on this topic are oriented towards qualitative as well as quantitative aspects. This distributed operating system is one of the most interesting of the experimental systems.

14.6 Eden

The Eden system was developed at the University of Washington in Seattle. The goal of the Eden system was to investigate logically-integrated but physically-distributed operating systems. The underlying philosophy of Eden involved constructing a system based on the principle of one user and one workstation (no processor pool), but with a high degree of multi-user, system-wide integration. The second fundamental goal of the Eden project was to provide support through the system for the community of computer scientists involved in building advanced distributed applications.

The authors of Eden emphasized in 1981 that they were not concerned with supporting a network of heterogeneous nodes, and with the concomitant problems of communicating abstract values among such nodes. Moreover, they were not concerned with extreme resistance to malice. This does not mean that they ignored protection issues – they used the object model, which uses capabilities. They meant that their system was to be designed for computer scientists, not for bank applications. They were also not concerned with extreme reliability.

Eden is based on the object model. All objects are accessed by capabilities, which are protected by the Eden kernel. However, Eden objects contain not only passive data, as for example Amoeba objects do, but use the active object paradigm. This means that each object consists of a process and an address space. There are two parts to invoking an object: sending a message to the server process in the object, which executes the requested routine, and returning the results in reply. Objects are mobile, but at any instant an object and all the processes it contains reside on a single workstation.

Our presentation of project goals and features of this system follows its descriptions in Lazowska *et al.* (1981), Black (1985), Almes *et al.* (1985), Tanenbaum and van Renesse (1985 or 1987) and Almes and Holman (1987).

14.6.1 The hardware architecture and software structure of the Eden system

Eden was implemented in a number of stages. Initially, the Eden hardware architecture involved a number of powerful workstations based upon the Intel iAPX 432 processor connected by an Ethernet local area network. The underlying architecture considered at that stage was iMAX, and the designers wanted to use Extended Ada. Special-purpose servers such as conventional time-sharing computers, high-resolution hard-copy output devices, gateways, and file servers were interfaced to the system through node computers. This architecture is illustrated in Fig. 14.26.

In the second stage, a centralized VAX/VMS version (called Newark because it was far from Eden) was written in Pascal. This system supported multiple processes per object but did not have automatic stub generation. After evaluation, a new implementation was written on top of UNIX instead of VMS. That version was called Eden 1.0. A new programming language, called EPL, was developed to support Eden's programmers. This stage of the system development was followed by a port of the system to 68000-based Sun workstations, also on top on UNIX rather than on the bare hardware. UNIX is used to provide processes and virtual address spaces, to load code into those address spaces, and to provide access to the disk and the network. Putting Eden on top of UNIX made system development easier and assisted users in migrating from UNIX to Eden. However, this solution leads to poor performance. Note that V and Amoeba run on bare 68000's and that in Amoeba, UNIX is put on top of a distributed kernel.

Eden's integrated environment is created by a collection of software systems which operate on a distributed set of node computers. The Eden system was designed to have as much system software as possible outside the kernel. The Eden kernel is implemented as a UNIX user process.

The kernel supports the object programming base of the system. For example, it provides primitives for object and type manager creation, object addressing and invocation, and intra-object communication and synchronization. There is no hierarchical structure of the system outside the kernel. However, it is possible to envision several logical

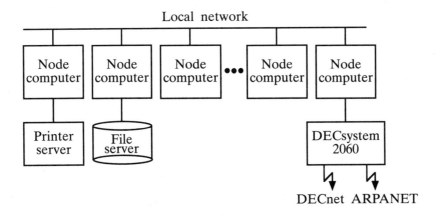

Fig. 14.26 The hardware architecture of the Eden system.

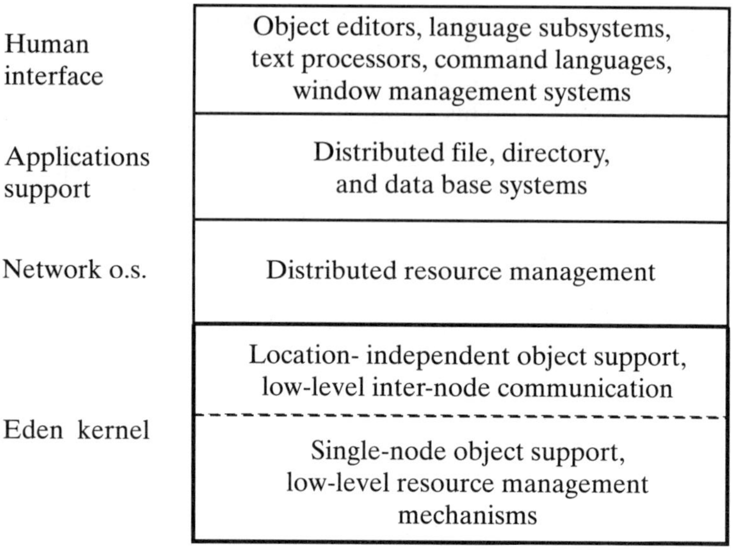

Human interface	Object editors, language subsystems, text processors, command languages, window management systems
Applications support	Distributed file, directory, and data base systems
Network o.s.	Distributed resource management
Eden kernel	Location- independent object support, low-level inter-node communication
	Single-node object support, low-level resource management mechanisms

Fig. 14.27   Eden software structure.

levels of support for the programming environment. This is shown in Fig. 14.27.

The Eden kernel is meant by its designers to be a software interface supplying location-independent object support. As the designers state, the kernel is below the level of the typical operating system interface.

The kernel consists of several layers. Some of them are constructed as Eden objects. All user programs, as well as traditional system software (filing, directory, record management and database systems) are built using only the kernel-supplied object primitives.

14.6.2 Basic concepts of Eden

Eden was based on the object model. It is a descendant of Hydra (Wulf *et al.* 1981). All 'traditional' programs and physical and logical resources are represented as objects. There are no pure data objects – Eden objects are supported by active processes. An Eden object may be seen as an instance of an abstract data type. Because there are some differences between Eden's objects and those of other systems and languages, the designers refer to them as Ejects (for **Eden Ob**jects). An Eject is composed of four parts, as illustrated in Fig. 14.28, and has several characteristics.

(1)   **name** – a system-wide, unique-for-all-time, unforgeable binary

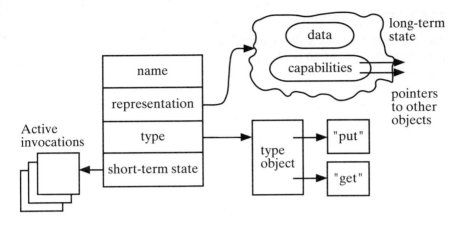

Fig. 14.28 An Eden object {adapted from Lazowska *et al.* (1981)}.

identifier for the Eject; the name is location independent, although it may indicate where the object was created. If an Eject wants to communicate with another Eject it has to know its name.

(2) **representation** – consists of data and capability segments that form the Eject's long-term state; these segments contain the data structures that implement any data abstraction.

(3) **type** (Edentype) – describes a set of routines that define the set of invocations to which the Eject will respond, and maintain the abstraction of which this Eject is a single instance. The type field contains a capability for another object in the system, a type manager – its representation consists of instruction segments that define the operations allowable on object instances.

(4) **short-time-state** – unique to each object instance, includes any temporal data, synchronization information, and processor state necessary to maintain one or more executing invocations.

(5) **invocations** (threads of control).

Eden objects are fundamental units of distribution, and are the smallest units that can be moved by the kernel from one node to another. Each Eject has its own thread of control and may be thought of as active at all times. Eden objects refer to one another by means of capabilities.

Recall that the underlying system of Eden is Berkeley UNIX running on VAXes. Each active Eject executes within a separate UNIX process with its own address space. This process is managed by the Eden kernel using UNIX facilities.

14.6.3 Communication in Eden

The following additions have been made to the UNIX kernel: an inter-process communication package, an Ethernet driver, and a simple module to compute timestamps. The interprocess communication package is the one used in Accent (Rashid and Robertson 1981). The interprocess communication mechanism is used by the kernel to communicate with an Eject. This communication and process management model, provided by the kernel, result in isolation of Ejects from each other during execution and prevent spreading bugs among Ejects. Moreover, this design allows the kernel to add new Edentypes and Ejects while the system is running.

Ejects communicate with one another by means of **invocations**, that is, messages sent from one Eject to another requesting a particular action and a reply. Thus, Eden's communication is a remote procedure call-like one: parameters are passed and the caller's thread of control is suspended pending completion of the invocation.

Eden uses facilities provided by the Eden Programming Language (EPL). This language was derived from Concurrent Euclid, a dialect of Toronto Euclid that provides multiple processes and Hoare monitors.

There are three layers of support for invocation: the EPL translator's role in invocation, the synchronous invocation level, and the asynchronous invocation level. The arrangement of functions among these levels must satisfy the following criteria:

(1)   Each of the EPL processes within an Eject must be able to synchronously invoke other processes, without blocking.

(2)   On the other hand, each Eject must be able to wait for invocation requests, and after their arrival to allocate them to a process for service.

(3)   The allocation of requests to processes must be done such as to avoid deadlock.

(4)   It must be easy for the EPL programmer to set up the sending and receiving operations.

(5)   Invocations must be as efficient as possible.

The EPL translator's role in invocation
The main tasks of the highest level of support of invocation are declaring and using invocation procedures. To ease these tasks, Eden uses facilities provided by EPL. Three essential functions are involved in this level:

(1)   **Parameter packaging** – This function is performed by the ESCII (Eden Standard Code for Information Exchange) facility. The facility allows operation names and parameter lists to be packaged into self-describing data structures.

(2) **Stub generation for the invoked Eject** – When a given EdenType is compiled, the translator builds a version of **CallInvocationProcedure** (usually, it is called directly by the Edentype programmer) tailored to the invocation procedures it defines. One of the tasks of this newly built procedure is to unpackage incoming ESCII's.

(3) **Stub generation for the invoking Eject** – At the same time, the translator generates a stub for each invocation procedure exported by the object of the compiled Edentype. These stubs are included in each Edentype that invoked that object. The stubs include calls to the ESCII packing routines and also to **SynchInvoke**. **SynchInvoke** is a lower-level invocation support routine. It helps in handling outgoing invocation messages.

SynchInvoke
> is used within the stubs generated by EPL. It invokes an Eject denoted by a 'target' capability, and waits for the reply to arrive. Note that only the calling EPL process blocks during the call.

ReceiveOperation
> is used directly by the programmer. It is called by an EPL process in order to wait for an incoming invocation request. This process blocks during the call. **Receive-Operation** takes a set of operations as an argument; however, it returns only when a request for one of these operations is present.

ReceiveAny, ReceiveSpecific
> are used when universal or singleton sets are desired, respectively.

CallInvocationProcedure
> is used directly by the programmer. It is called by an EPL process that has received an incoming request and wishes to call the appropriate invocation procedure. **CallInvocationProcedure** unpacks the parameters from the invocation request message, checks them for compatibility with the invocation procedure, makes the call, and executes a ReplyMsg (supported by the asynchronous invocation level).

List 14.15 Major procedures of the synchronous invocation level.

The synchronous invocation level

The synchronous invocation level is provided by a procedure library within each Eject. This level uses both services of the lower synchronous invocation level, and EPL processes and monitors, to provide invocation facilities that can block a single process at the EPL level.

Three major procedures, given in List 14.15, are used.

The asynchronous invocation level

The asynchronous invocation level is provided by the kernel. There are two sending primitives and one receiving procedure. These procedures are described in List 14.16.

AsynchInvoke

sends the invocation request message to the target Eject. It does not wait for a reply, but returns an **InvocationHandle** to the caller. This is used by the caller to recognize the reply when it arrives as a result of the **ReceiveMsg** call.

ReplyMsg

sends an invocation reply message back to the invoking Eject.

ReceiveMsg

receives the next invocation request or reply message. If no message is present, the call returns immediately. UNIX software interrupts are used to notify the user of the message arrival. An EPL process can block until the arrival of such an interrupt.

List 14.16 Procedures of the asynchronous invocation level.

14.6.4 Concurrency

Synchronization in Eden is associated with communication and is considered in terms of concurrency control. Eden's designers do not directly consider synchronization of processes wishing to access sharable resources. Eden provides concurrency at two levels. Different objects running on different processors may execute in parallel, and multiple lightweight processes and structures for concurrency control are available within each object.

Processes provided by the Eden Programming Language communicate through monitors. The Eden designers do not claim that this mechanism is better or worse than other language mechanisms (for example, Ada tasks or rendezvous). The selection of primitives was completed in a natural way during the development of EPL. However, they emphasize that the processes and monitors of EPL have been a major success.

One object can manage many remote activities simultaneously. This shows the importance of concurrent processes within one object. Many remote activities must be managed simultaneously when one is using multiple objects in a computationally intensive task and when one is making calls on remote services.

14.6.5 Naming and protection

Capabilities are used in Eden for naming and protection. All global system entities, that is, objects, Edentypes, machines (nodes), and disks (checklists), are named uniformly by capabilities. The only available form of interaction with an object is by the invocation of one of the operations defined by the object. Only a user who has a valid capability with appropriate rights can request a service from an object.

There is a uniform naming and protection scheme throughout the Eden system. Capabilities are not typed – they are checked at run time. An Eden capability consists of two fields: an identifier (system-wide, unique-for-all-time, location independent) and rights, as illustrated in Fig. 14.29.

Capabilities are invoked directly and may be stored in any object. Capabilities can be grouped together by a mechanism provided by directories. Each directory entry contains the ASCII string by which a capability is accessed, and the capability itself. These directories can be accessed by users by invoking the directory object with one of the valid operations (add entry, delete entry, lookup string and rename capability).

Eden capabilities are protected by the kernel. Users keep copies of capabilities in their own address space for their own use. They are pure data and they can be modified and stored anywhere. However, when a user requests a service from an object, the capability is checked against its copy kept in a protected table maintained by the kernel, and if it does not match this copy, access to the object is denied.

An Eden capability is not interpreted by the system itself. This task is performed by the object, which is free to interpret each bit as it sees fit. There are sixteen different access rights for each object. On the

Fig. 14.29 An Eden capability.

surface this seems to be generous, but the designers emphasize that the rights space is inadequate. This is because rights interact with the abstract type system, resulting in only sixteen access rights for the whole system.

The Eden system provides a location-independent address space. This implies that an invocation can be issued without knowledge of the destination Eject location. However, since there is a need to refer to machines and disks, and they are named with capabilities, a concept supported by the location dependent primitives was introduced, known as **co-location** – a pair of capabilities must be co-located by the system. Ejects can get location information from the kernel. The kernel maintains a cache of the locations of remote Ejects and of the status of other Eden machines. This helps in the mapping of capabilities into physical locations. Ejects are capable of making location changes.

14.6.6 Eject management

Primitives for creating new Ejects and types are provided by the kernel. The kernel creates and manages the UNIX processes used to implement Eject active forms. A new Eject can be created by another Eject.

Ideally, an Eject should be active. However, it is not always active, either because it or its computer has crashed, or because it has explicitly deactivated itself in order to economize on the use of system resources. Thus, an Eject has two manifestations: an **active representation** (with its system-level process) and a **passive representation**. The passive representation consists primarily of a disk file. All invocations are implemented by an active representation. However, only the passive representation can survive a crash.

An Eject can perform a **Checkpoint** operation. This operation creates a passive representation, that is, a data structure designed to endure system crashes. This means that the data in a passive representation should be sufficient to enable the Eject to reconstruct its long term state. Acquiring and releasing active and passive representations are illustrated in Fig. 14.30.

The figure shows that when an Eject is created, only an active representation exists. Thus, it can execute and engage in invocations. However, it does not have its state saved in permanent store. This implies that if this Eject were to **Deactivate**, or if the system were to crash, it would vanish and it could not be invoked again. If another Eject with a capability for the vanished Eject attempts to invoke it, the invocation fails. The kernel does not make any attempt to remove such 'dangling' capabilities. An Eject having a passive representation will be deallocated only by an Eden garbage collector.

Performing a **Checkpoint** operation results in the following actions: opening a passive representation of an Eject, writing its state in a series

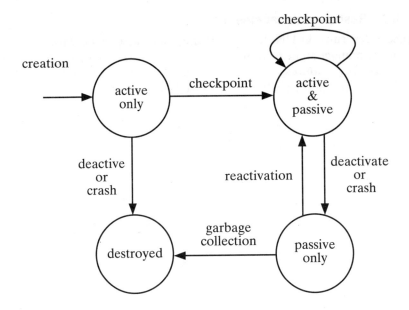

Fig. 14.30 Transitions between active and passive representations {adapted from Almes *et al.* (1985)}.

of **PutData** calls, and completing the passive representation with a call. The Eject then has its state and identity on permanent store. If this Eject **Deactivates** or crashes, its active representation vanishes, but the passive representation remains. If the Eject having a passive representation is invoked by another Eject, then the kernel reactivates it, that is, it constructs a new active representation which will receive the invocation.

Only passive Ejects can move (Black 1985). This implies that in order to move, an Eject must first request that its next reactivation occur on another machine, and then deactivate itself.

The provision within an Edentype of multiple processes and synchronous invocation rather than a single process and asynchronous invocation is Eden's additional feature. It allows parallelism to be achieved in a straightforward manner. Multiple processes play an important role in Edmas – The Eden Distributed Mail System. For example, the simplest Eject within Edmas, such as a MailMessage, has three processes: one that handles incoming invocations, one that **Deactivates** the Eject after it has been idle for a certain amount of time, and the **Dispatcher** process. In some cases of Ejects with multiple processes (for example, DistributionList Ejects) deadlock can occur, since they may refer directly or indirectly to themselves. Some care is necessary to ensure termination and avoid deadlock.

14.6.7 Resource management

Since Eden runs on UNIX, most of the issues associated with low-level resource management have not yet been dealt with. However, some issues have been addressed. One of them is location. The notion of location is captured in the abstraction referred to as a **node**. A node is an Eject that supplies:

(1)   virtual memory to store the segments of active Ejects, and

(2)   virtual processors to execute invocations.

An abstract node corresponds roughly to a real node computer. However, one real computer may support several node Ejects, or a multiprocessor may support one Eject node. At any instant, each active Eject is supported by exactly one node, which supplies hardware resources and receives and processes invocations for the Eject.

An active Eject can request the right to pass responsibility for its resources to another node. This can be performed by the kernel-supplied **move** operation. Moreover, some Ejects may have the ability to make location decisions for other Ejects in the system. On the other hand, some Ejects can be frozen to improve performance and make the location process efficient. A frozen Eject has its representation immutable, but it can still receive invocations.

Another resource management issue arises when an Eject is created, namely, where to put this Eject. Usually, it is put on the same computer as the Eject that created it, unless an explicit request has been issued to put it somwhere else.

Storage management has also been the subject of some work. The problem of storage management appears in the Eden system in two different contexts:

(1)   For each Eject, the EPL run-time system manages a heap used by the EPL data structures; these structures are allocated and deallocated by explicit primitives issued by the EPL compiler. The storage is reclaimed from the heap by means of explicit deallocation.

(2)   Storage management is provided for Ejects themselves. When an Eject is created by the kernel, it allocates storage for the Eject from its own heap and gives the Eject its own address space. Moreover, it manages the user capabilities for the Eject such that it is possible to find all capabilities by scanning the kernel's data structures. The storage is reclaimed from the heap via garbage collection.

14.6.8 Services

Unlike the V-system and Amoeba, the Eden system does not have special computers dedicated as servers. However, each computer can support file Ejects, for local users as well as for remote users. Eden provides a number of services. They are implemented as application systems. The most mature systems are The Eden File System (EFS), The Eden Distributed Mail System (Edmas), and The Eden Appointment Calendar System.

The Eden File System

Conventional sequential files are not part of the Eden kernel. Such a file is simply an Eject that allows its contents to be read and written using Eden Transput System, that is, a system that is not a part of the kernel but allows input and output operations to be performed independently of physical devices. The contents of a file Eject are maintained on stable storage by the **Checkpoint** facility.

A file service in the Eden system is quite different from most other systems. Because in Eden each file Eject contains within it the processes needed to handle operations on it, the file contains the server rather than the server containing the file. This implies that for each file in existence there is a running process. Because this solution is very expensive, optimization is used in implementation. When a file is not open, its processes are dormant and do not consume resources. Thus, such a file Eject can execute a checkpoint sequence and acquire a passive representation. However, it is necessary to have the means to keep capabilities for all checkpointed Ejects. The Edentype Directory provides the required service. When a file is opened, the kernel will reactivate this Eject.

This atypical solution of the file service has its advantages and disadvantages compared with the traditional one-server-many-files solution. The advantages are: that the complicated, multithreaded file server is eliminated, and that files can be moved freely about all the nodes in the system. Thus a file might be created in one node and then migrated to a remote node where it will be used. The main disadvantage is poor performance, since all the processes for the open files consume resources. Moreover, fetching the code for the first file to be opened on a computer is slow.

The Eden File System provides two facilities to a user of a sequential file: nested transactions and atomic update. A user wishing to keep several versions of a document (rather than to enter several files in a directory) enters a single VersionManager Eject. When a client Eject opens an output stream to the VersionManager, a new sequential file is created. This file reads from the client Eject. As a result, when the file is completed it becomes the latest version known to the VersionManager. When the VersionManager is opened for reading it provides a stream from the latest version of the file.

Replicated files in Eden are supported by the transaction facility. If a client wishes to update several files atomically, it first creates a TransactionManager Eject. The TransactionManager opens all the VersionManagers that are to participate in the transaction. After that, the sequence of operations is as follows: the new updated files are created and closed, and their capabilities are passed to the TransactionManager. If at this stage the client asks the TransactionManager to abort the transaction, it simply **Deactivate**s itself; nothing in the file system has yet been changed. If the transaction is to be committed, the Transaction-Manager performs a two-phase commit with the VersionManagers, makes sure that all the new versions are safely stored on disk, and then checkpoints itself. In effect, the TransactionManager acts as the commit record for the transaction.

The reader interested in details of the Eden File System can refer to Jessop *et al.* (1982) and Pu *et al.* (1986).

Edmas – The Eden Distributed Mail System

The Eden Distributed Mail System (Edmas) was one of the first applications built on top of Eden. It was developed with two goals in mind (Almes and Holman 1987):

(1) to determine whether Eden could be used to build distributed applications which are cleanly structured, extensible, and location independent, and

(2) to learn about the structuring of mail systems generally.

Mail systems consist of two parts: a user interface that allows mail to be sent and read, and a transport and storage system. The Edmas designers concentrated their efforts mainly on the latter. They constructed this system from two principal Edentypes: the MailBox and the MailMessage. The user interface is implemented using another two Edentypes and some UNIX facilities. Such Edentypes as the Directory and the DistributionList were also used.

An Eject of type MailBox implements the mail message abstraction. A mail message (a sequence of characters) is implemented as a Mail-Message Eject. Its long-term state comprises such fields as a **From**: field, a **To**: field, a **Subject**: field, and a **Text**: string containing a message text string. MailBox uses a model which requires delivering mail to a mailbox, and storing mail until the owner picks it up.

Both MailMessages and MailBoxes are Ejects and are referred to by capabilities. This implies that MailBox Ejects need to store the capability for a MailMessage, rather than a copy of the message itself. Also the **To**: and **From**: fields are stored as capabilities for MailBoxes rather than as string names. The **From**: field is the capability of the message creator; the **To**: field is a list of capabilities for the addressees' Mail-Boxes. Because users use string names, the user interface provides another way of referring to them, by using the type Directory which maps strings to capabilities.

The operations which can be performed on MailMessage objects are given in List 14.17.

Set and **Append**
> call objects to compose the message by initializing the various conceptual fields;

Get
> retrieves these fields;

Deliver
> indicates the end of the composition process. It has two effects. First, the MailMessage freezes itself, by setting a boolean variable called IsFrozen. IsFrozen means that any further requests to alter the fields will be refused. Second, the MailMessage tries to deliver itself to all the MailBoxes.

List 14.17 The operations performed on MailMessage objects.

Each MailBox object represents the personal mailbox for some Eden users. The long-term state of a MailBox contains a queue of capabilities for MailMessages which have been delivered to it, but not sent yet by the user. MailBoxes maintain 'printable' names which are used to construct the **From**: and **To**: fields when messages are displayed to the owner, and two Eden type stamps: one marking the last MailMessage delivery, and another the last time of picking up and removing a Mail-Message from a MailBox.

The following operations which can be performed on MailBox objects are given in List 14.18.

MailBox.Deliver
> places an incoming MailMessage capability in the queue;

PickUp
> allows the owner to retrieve the oldest MailMessage capability;

Remove
> removes a MailMessage capability from the MailBox;

SetName
> allows calling objects to set the value of the name field;

Show
> retrieves the name, time stamps, and a count of the number of messages in the MailBox.

List 14.18 The operations performed on MailBox objects.

Only the access right **DeliverRts** is needed to deliver a message to a MailBox. Picking up and removing mail requires **PickupRts**, whereas setting the name of a MailBox requires **AdministratorRts**.

Capabilities, as we recall, refer to objects in a location-independent way. Moreover, any object can be invoked by any other, regardless of their physical location. Because of these two issues there is no explicit transport mechanism in Edmas.

The steps performed when a user wishes to send a mail message using Edmas are as follows:

(1)   The text of a mail message is composed using the Emacs editor.

(2)   When the message is complete, it is passed to a MailSendInterface Eject.

(3)   The MailSendInterface performs the folowing tasks:

   (a)   Translation of the string names into capabilities for addressees' MailBoxes (this is accomplished by performing Lookup invocations on a Directory Eject);

   (b)   Creation of a new MailMessage Eject and initialization of the various fields of the MailMessage by a series of invocations. The **From:** field contains a capability of the sender's own MailBox and is used by the Reply facility;

   (c)   When the MailMessage is composed, the MailSendInterface makes a **Deliver** invocation on the MailMessage:

      (i)   the MailMessage becomes frozen, and

      (ii)   the MailMessage delivers itself to the addressees.

(4)   Since the work of the MailSendInterface is completed, it may be deactivated or used to send further messages.

The Eden Appointment Calendar System

The Eden Appointment Calendar System is used to schedule meetings. One of the facilities of the system is to find a time when potential meeting participants are free, and to tentatively schedule a meeting amongst them. The meeting is confirmed only when all participants agree to the proposed time.

The services provided by the facility show that transactions can be used in its implementation, that is, the scheduling of a meeting can be viewed as a transaction. Because the transactions may be longlived, locking the whole of each calendar until a tentative meeting is confirmed or cancelled is unacceptable. Instead the Calendar System uses one Eject to represent each event, and one Eject for each calendar. The Calendar Edentype is basically a list of capabilities for Event Edentypes with hints as to the times of the Events and whether they are tentative or definite. Thus, considering the scheduling of an Event as an transaction, the Event Eject acts as its own commit record.

14.6.9   Lessons learned

Eden is a system for building distributed applications. Through the kernel and Eden Programming Language, it provides high-level support for the sharing of information and processing capacity in a locally distributed system. The designers emphasize that although Eden is built on top of UNIX, it is not an attempt to build a distributed UNIX.

The following lessons can be learned from the Eden project. First, that in some complex computational tasks, a knowledge of location can be useful – location transparency is not always the most natural paradigm. Second, all global system entities can be easily and uniformly named by using capabilities. Third, an object migration facility can be developed to enable load balancing. Fourth, building a system on top of an existing system results in poor performance. This is because there is the high overhead of communication between Ejects and the kernel processes. We do not know if the designers of the Eden system carried out any performance studies of alternative methods and mechanisms.

14.7   LOCUS

LOCUS is a UNIX-compatible, distributed operating system developed by Popek, Walker and their co-workers at the University of California, Los Angeles. This system has been in use for several years. The LOCUS project begun at UCLA in the late 1970s. By early 1981, a prototype system was operational on a small collection of PDP-11s connected by 1 and 10 Mbps ring networks. Next, the system was moved to a set of Vax/ 750s connected by a standard Ethernet. The utility of the LOCUS approach was demonstrated, but the product quality was unsatisfactory. Thus, early in 1983 work began to develop a finished production product at Locus Computing Corporation.

Our presentation of project goals and features of the LOCUS system follows its descriptions in Popek *et al.* (1981), Walker *et al.* (1983), Popek and Walker (1985), Weinstein *et al.* (1985) and Sheltzer and Popek (1986).

LOCUS's general goals include making the development of distributed applications as simple as single machine programming, and realizing the potential that distributed systems with redundancy have for highly reliable, available operation. The LOCUS architecture addresses the goals of:

(1)   **Network transparency** – giving all users the illusion of operating on a single computer. The network is not visible; there is no need to refer to a specific node of a network;

(2)   **High reliability and availability** – introduced for two general reasons. First, many applications demand a high level of reliability

and availability. Second, the distributed environment presents new sources for failure, and recovery mechanisms to deal with them are far more difficult to construct than in centralized computer systems. LOCUS possesses one very important reliability feature, namely, it supports automatic replication of stored data, with the degree of replication indicated by associated reliability profiles; and

(3) **Good performance** – LOCUS achieves two basic performance characteristics desirable in the case of a distributed system:

    (a) Access to local resources in a distributed system should have comparable performance to access to resources in a centralized system, as if mechanisms for remote access were not present. In the case of LOCUS, this means that a program running under LOCUS with all resources residing locally should perform as well as that same program running under UNIX;

    (b) Remote access, of course slower than local access, should be reasonably comparable to local access.

The file system, especially its distributed naming catalog, plays a central role in LOCUS' system structure. The designers motivate this as follows. First, file system activity typically predominates in most operating systems. Second, the generalized name service provided is used by many other parts of LOCUS.

In this context, the designers of the LOCUS system wanted to show that it is feasible, even in a small machine environment, to design and implement a high performance, network-transparent, distributed file system which contains all of the usual functions. In other words, the aim of this project was to design and build a distributed operating system which:

(1) supports a network-wide file system;

(2) permits automatic replication of storage;

(3) supports transparent distributed process execution;

(4) supplies a number of high-reliability functions (for example, nested transactions); and

(5) is upward compatible with UNIX.

LOCUS does not use the server model, which is the basic concept of such systems as V and Amoeba. Instead, it is based on the integrated model of distributed systems, according to which each machine's software is a complete facility, with a general file system, name interpretation mechanisms, etc.

Because of the file system orientation of the LOCUS distributed operating system, and because the generalized name service provided is used by many other parts of this system, we need to begin with a discussion of these basic concepts. Thus, the discussion of LOCUS' research and design issues does not follow the format for previous systems.

14.7.1 Features of the LOCUS architecture

The LOCUS operating system is a distributed version of UNIX. It possesses features to aid in distributed operations and support for transparency, high reliability and availability of the system. LOCUS can also be used on single, stand alone computers.

A LOCUS-based distributed system is built from a collection of workstations and/or mainframes connected by a network, which is invisible to the users and their application programs. Network transparency is provided in such a way that it permits a great deal of system configuration flexibility (including diskless workstations, full duplex I/O to large mainframes, transparently-shared peripherals), with no effect on applications software. It even supports a heterogeneous distributed system.

The LOCUS system allows programs, store data and peripheral devices, to be accessed transparently. In particular, the system provides a high degree of transparency with respect to location of files, and some degree of transparency with respect to the location of process execution. The design philosophy, based on extensive transparency together with UNIX compatibility means that programs which run on a single-machine UNIX system can operate without change in the LOCUS environment, with their resources distributed across several nodes. LOCUS includes a variety of facilities to control the location of data and to determine which users and machines can access data, peripherals, processors and logical resources.

It must be emphasized that for virtually all applications code, LOCUS can provide complete compatibility, at the object code level, with both Berkeley UNIX and System V UNIX. The conversion from UNIX to LOCUS was designed as an automated step of removing the UNIX kernel and associated software, inserting the LOCUS kernel with its supporting system software, and reformatting secondary storage to add the reliability facilities and functional enhancements.

In general, the LOCUS-based distributed system is seen by clients as one large UNIX system, in which each computer can be a client as well as a server, and with UNIX file access, interprocess communication (pipe, signal) and process creation (fork) primitives which are implemented transparently across the network.

14.7.2   Overview of the distributed file system

The functions of the LOCUS distributed file system are:

(1)   creating and removing objects and/or copies of objects,

(2)   supporting access to and modification of those objects,

(3)   implementing atomic file update and synchronization,

(4)   translating pathnames to physical locations, and

(5)   providing support for remote devices and interprocess communication.

Every site in the LOCUS system can be a full function node. However, file system operations can involve more than one host.

The following system calls deal with the file system: **open, create, read, write, commit, close,** and **unlink.**

The LOCUS file system is based on a single tree-structured naming hierarchy, and is an extension of the UNIX naming system. The extensions have been made in the following areas:

(1)   LOCUS' single tree structure covers all objects in the file system on all machines. Names are fully transparent.

(2)   Files can be replicated to varying degrees. It is LOCUS's responsibility to keep all copies up to date, and arrange all accesses to the most recently available version.

(3)   LOCUS provides the standard UNIX, unsynchronized file access policy, and in addition, advisory and enforced locking.

14.7.3   Naming

Naming in the LOCUS system reflects abstraction in the LOCUS file system, which can be viewed as central to the naming facility. There are two levels of names in LOCUS. At the upper level, which is seen by users and application programs, object names look like names in a single, centralized UNIX environment. In other words, almost all objects appear with globally unique names in a single, uniform, hierarchical name space. Thus, each object is known by its path name in a tree. As in UNIX, any user can set a 'working directory' to avoid long path names. The path name does not contain any location-oriented string. This implies that an object can be easily moved or even executed from different sites. Such a hierarchical naming system is shown in Fig. 14.31.

LOCUS' low level names are also globally unique. However, the name space is based on the concept of file groups (it corresponds to UNIX's file system). As in UNIX, each file group is composed of a mass

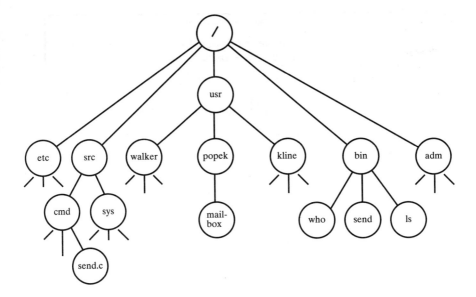

Fig. 14.31 A hierarchical naming system {adapted from Popek and Walker (1985)}.

store. Each location may store any subset of the files in the group. More-over, each file group is divided into two parts:

(1) a small set of file descriptors they serve as a simple low level 'directory', and

(2) a large number of of standard size data blocks.

A file descriptor (inode) contains pointers to the data blocks which form that file. Data blocks can be used as indirect pointer blocks for large files. As a result, a low level file name is a pair <file group number, file descriptor number>. Devices also appear in the file system as leaves in the name structure, and they have global names. A file group structure is illustrated in Fig. 14.32.

LOCUS uses the same method, extended to deal with replication of file groups. A **logical** file group number, and a mapping from logical to physical file group number, are introduced. This mapping is one to many, and is implemented as an extension to **mounting** a file group.

In LOCUS, the application-visible naming hierarchy is imple-mented by having certain low level files serve as high level directories. An entry in such a directory contains an element of a path name and the index of the file descriptor which corresponds to the next directory or data file in the path. Each group is a wholly self-contained subtree of the naming hierarchy, including storage for all files and directories contained

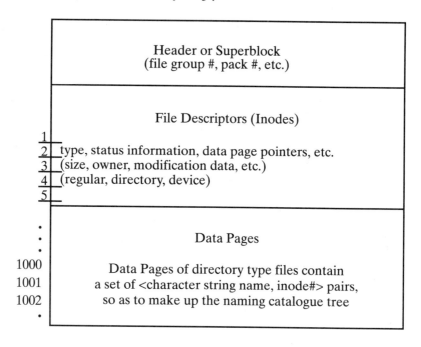

Fig. 14.32   A file group structure {adapted from Popek and Walker (1985)}.

in the subtree. Thus, the set of file groups represents a set of naming trees, which are glued together to form a single, network-wide, naming tree. The gluing operation is done via the **mount** mechanism.

High level names are mapped to low level names as soon as possible. Thus, only low level names are passed within the system, and remapping of names is avoided.

14.7.4   File replication

Storage replication in a distributed file system is provided to increase availability and improve performance. Replication in LOCUS is designed to:

(1)   permit multiple copies at different sites;

(2)   allow a flexible degree of replication and a reasonable freedom to designate where the copies should reside. The system keeps all copies consistent and access, when requested, is made to the most recent version;

(3)   allow the user and application program to be unaware of the replication system if they wish;

(4) support high performance and smooth operation in the face of failures.

LOCUS' file replication is implemented using multiple physical containers for a logical file group. This means that any given logical file group may have a number of corresponding physical containers which reside at various sites around the network. Note that the entire logical file group is not replicated by each physical container as in a 'hot shadow' environment. Instead, any physical container is incomplete – it stores only a subset of the files in the subtree to which it corresponds.

The following advantages of the LOCUS file replication are listed by the designers:

(1) Globally unique low-level names are implemented, so that high-to-low-level name translation need happen only once in a file access. Computer-to-computer communication is based on low-level names.

(2) Physical containers can be of different sizes.

(3) A given file need not be replicated, or may have as many physical copies as there are containers for the file group. A decision to vary the number of copies can be made at any time.

14.7.5 Synchronization

File system operations can involve more than one host. There are three logical functions in a file access, which implies three logical sites:

(1) **Using site** (US) – issues the request to open a file and indicates which pages of the file are to be supplied;

(2) **Storage site** (SS) – stores a copy of the requested file (supplies pages of that file to the using site);

(3) **Current synchronization site** (CSS) – enforces a global access synchronization policy for the file group and selects SSs for each open request.

Since storage in LOCUS may be replicated and there are multiple users, and a consistent file system is to be presented to these users, it is necessary to synchronize access to logical files and their physical counterparts.

The synchronization policy in LOCUS is based on a global 'multiple readers, single writer' policy. This policy provides concurrent read access to replicated copies of data while preventing concurrent update. However, there are three reasons to implement a more sophisticated synchronization policy:

(1) modern operating system environment requires more functionality;

(2)   for reading directories a new type, nolock read, is used; when a file is opened for nolock read, there is no synchronization with other activity on the file; and

(3)   UNIX compatibility; because standard UNIX has few restrictions, normal program behavior sometimes would be blocked by the basic policy.

The designers chose a centralized synchronization protocol with distributed recovery as a synchronization mechanism. A given file group has one site designated as the Current Synchronization Site, which is responsible for coordinating access to the files contained in the file group. All **open** requests (calls) for a file go through the CSS function (except for nolock reads). As a result, the CSS assures that a request gets the most recent version of a file. The CSS does not have to be the site from which data access is obtained, because any site which has a copy of the file can support this **open** request, in particular a Storage Site. The synchronization mechanism will become clear when we look at operations dealing with the file system. First, we must consider services which supply access to remote objects.

14.7.6   Calling remote services

LOCUS is a procedure-based operating system. This means that processes request system service by executing system calls, which trap to the kernel. LOCUS runs as an extension to the process and can sleep on behalf of the process. Because of the requirement for transparency, application programs cannot determine whether a call requires a remote service. If the need for a remote service is identified during execution of the system call, the operating system is responsible for forming a message and sending it to the relevant remote node. After completion of these tasks, the kernel waits for a response message.

The LOCUS call is a special case of a remote procedure call. Operating system procedures are executed on a remote computer as part of the service of a local system call. Processing a system **call** requiring a remote service is illustrated in Fig. 14.33.

14.7.7   Opening and reading files

To read a file, a program on a Using Site (US) issues the **open** system call specifying a file name and indicating that the open is for read. Pathname searching is done within the operating system open call. As a result, the requester's operating system has a <logical filegroup number, inode number> pair for the file to be opened.

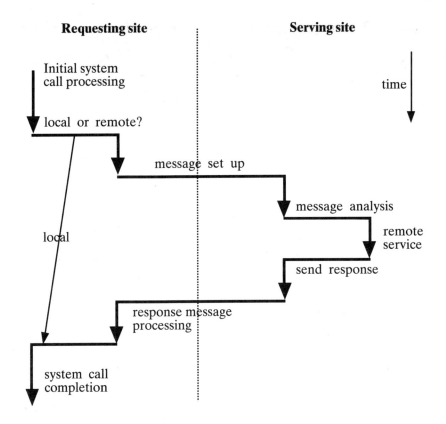

Fig. 14.33 Processing a system call {adapted from Popek and Walker (1985)}.

In the next stage, the CSS is questioned. If the local site is the CSS, only a local procedure call is needed. Otherwise, the CSS is determined by examining the logical mount table, a message is sent to the CSS, the CSS sets up an incore inode for itself, calls the same procedure that would have been called if the US is the CSS, packages the response, and sends it back to the US.

The CSS performs the following tasks:

(1)   enforces synchronization controls, based on state information,

(2)   determines a storage site, based on a copy of the disk inode information and mount table information, and

(3)   determines the most recent version vector.

The most general open protocol, that is, for the case when all logical functions are performed on different physical sites, is given in List 14.19. and illustrated in Fig. 14.34.

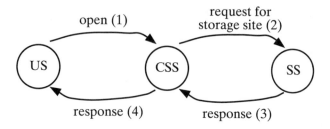

Fig. 14.34   Open protocol {adapted from Popek and Walker (1985)}.

(1)	US → CSS	**open** request
(2)	CSS → SS	request for storage site
(3)	SS → CSS	response to previous message
(4)	CSS → US	response to first message

List 14.19   Steps of the open protocol.

When the file is open, the user process issues **read** calls. These requests are serviced via kernel buffers. If the operation is to be performed locally, data is paged from external storage devices into operating system buffers and then copied from these buffers into the address space of the process.

Requests for data from remote sites, syntactically, operate similarly. There are some semantic differences. The operating system at the US allocates a buffer and queues a request to be sent to the remote SS. The request contains the <logical file group, inode number> pair, the logical page number within the file, and a guess as to where the incore inode information is stored at the SS. Note that the CSS is not involved in the I/O communication.

The request at the SS is treated as follows:

(1)   the incore inode is found using the guess provided,

(2)   the logical page number is translated into a physical disk block number,

(3)   a standard low-level routine is called to allocate a buffer and get the appropriate page from disk,

(4)   a buffer is queued on the network I/O queue for transfer back to the US as a response to a read request.

Steps of the network read protocol are given in List 14.20.

(1)	US → SS	request for page x of file y
(2)	SS → US	response to the above request

List 14.20   The protocol for a network read.

The actions perfomed when the **close** system call is invoked on a remotely stored file depend on how many times the file is concurrently open at a given US. If it is the last **close** of the file, in particular the CSS must be informed to allow it to alter state data which might affect its next synchronization policy decision. The steps of the remote close protocol are presented in List 14.21.

(1)	US → SS	US **close** request
(2)	SS → CSS	SS **close** request
(3)	CSS → SS	response to above message
(4)	SS → US	response to first message

List 14.21 Steps of the close protocol.

14.7.8 File commit

In LOCUS all changes to a given file are handled automically. No changes to a file are permanent until a commit operation is performed. To achieve atomicity, two system calls are provided: **commit** and **abort**; closing a file commits it. LOCUS uses a shadow page mechanism rather than an update logging system, for two reasons. First, the ability to maintain a strict physical relationship amongst data blocks created by logs is not valuable in a UNIX-like system. Second, high-performance shadowing is easier to implement than logging.

Since the US deals with logical pages, the shadow page mechanism is implemented at the SS and is transparent to the US. Accordingly, if a change is made to an existing page of a file, a new physical page is allocated at the SS. Of course, a record is kept of the locations of the old and new pages. The disk inode contains the old page numbers. The incore copy of the disk inode starts with the old pages, but is updated with new page numbers as shadow pages are allocated. Multiple modifications to a given logical file do not need different page allocations. This is because after the first modification the page is marked as being a shadow page and can be reused as such.

The atomic commit operation consists of moving the incore inode information to the disk inode. After this, the file permanently contains the new information. To abort a set of changes rather than commit them, since the old inode and pages are still on disk, it is necessary to discard the incore information. As a result, page frames containing modified pages are freed. In summary one can say that the designers have chosen to deal with file modification by first committing the change to one copy of a file. The centralized synchronization mechanism prevents changes being made to two different copies at the same time and prevents the reading of an old copy while another copy is being modified.

The commit operation contains one special action: the SS sends messages both to all the other SSs of that file and to the CSS. These messages identify the file and contain the new version vector. It is the responsibility of the alternate SSs to bring their versions of the file up to date, either by propagating the entire file or only the changes. The kernel at each site is responsible for propagation.

14.7.9   File support for interprocess communication

In UNIX there is a facility called pipes which allow data to pass between processes. To maintain transparency in LOCUS, it is necessary that pipes between remote processes operate with the same effect as local pipes.

Pipe semantics

A pipe is a one-way communication facility between processes. The output of one or more processes is directed to the input of one or more processes. The pipe is a FIFO stream of bytes. There is no out-of-band or in-band signalling mechanism, nor any data-typing present, except that which might be imposed by a higher level mechanism.

The pipe is a finite length buffer. When a process attempts to read data from an empty pipe, it is blocked. The reading process waits for more data to be written into the pipe. A process which wants to read more data than is in a pipe reads only that portion that is available. An attempt to read data from a pipe after all writers have gone and the pipe has been emptied causes the reader to receive an end-of-file indication.

A process attempting to write an amount of data greater than the capacity of a pipe is blocked. It waits for enough data to be read from the pipe to allow the system call to succeed. An attempt to write data to a pipe after all readers have gone away causes the writing process to receive the SIGPIPE signal. A reader waiting on an empty pipe, or a writer waiting on a full pipe may be interrupted.

A pipe is created in two ways. The first is by using the **pipe** system call. These pipes are called **traditional** or **unnamed**. Note that in the case of these pipes processes use the **write** and **read** system calls to transfer data to or from this pipe, and use the **close** system call when data transfer is completed. Pipes may also be opened using the standard **open** system call. They are called **named** pipes. One or more processes may open the pipe specifying an open mode of **read**, while one or more other processes may open the pipe specifying an open mode of **write**. A named pipe has a name entered in a filesystem directory. A named pipe, once opened, behaves exactly like an unnamed one. However, after all readers and writers have closed the pipe, it remains in the filesystem as an empty pipe ready to be opened by another group of communicating processes.

Pipes in LOCUS

Network transparent pipes in LOCUS use three sites: the current reading site (RS), the current writing site (WS), and the storage site (SS).

The SS is a natural centralized point. It is a site which controls the pipe. For an unnamed pipe, the SS is the site on which the pipe system call was issued. For a named pipe, the SS is the site that stores the file group in which it is named.

Network message exchange for pipes is shown in Fig. 14.35. The WS sends data to the SS and the RS requests data from the SS. These sites use standard LOCUS read and write network messages, respectively. Note that these messages are also used for accessing ordinary files. The SS keeps track of the data which is in the pipe, and controls blocking and unblocking of the reader and writer.

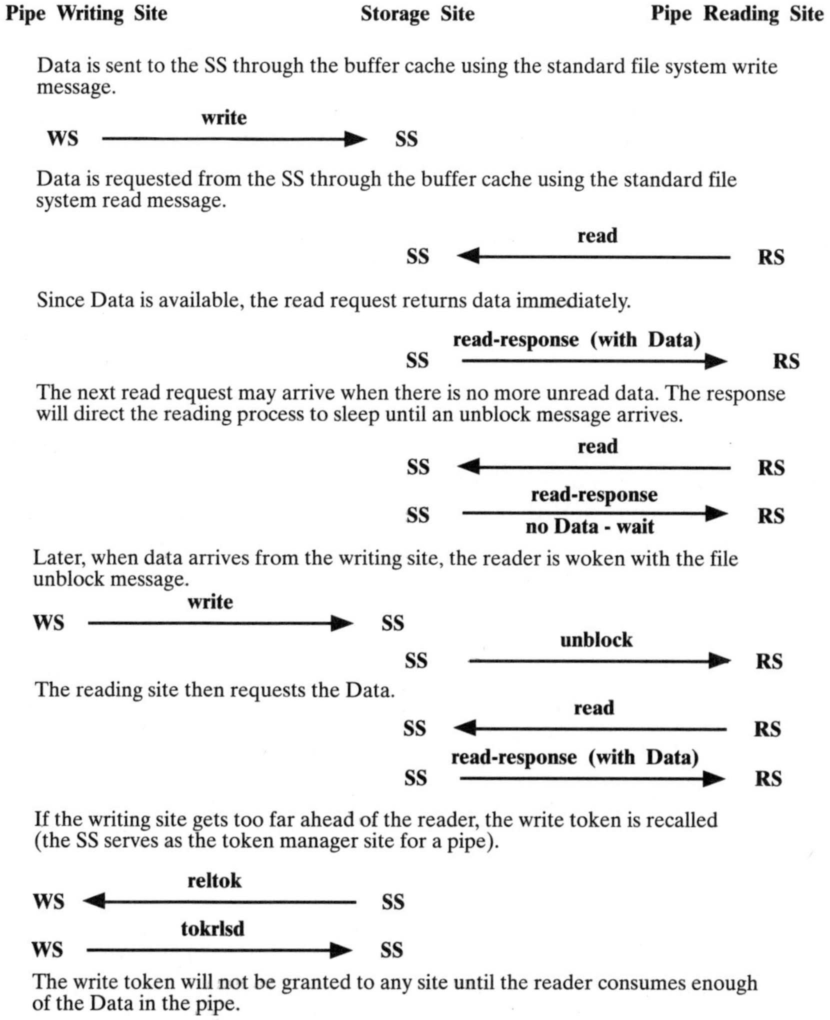

Pipe Writing Site   **Storage Site**   **Pipe Reading Site**

Data is sent to the SS through the buffer cache using the standard file system write message.

write
WS ————————————▶ SS

Data is requested from the SS through the buffer cache using the standard file system read message.

read
SS ◀———————————— RS

Since Data is available, the read request returns data immediately.

read-response (with Data)
SS ————————————▶ RS

The next read request may arrive when there is no more unread data. The response will direct the reading process to sleep until an unblock message arrives.

read
SS ◀———————————— RS
read-response
SS ————————————▶ RS
no Data - wait

Later, when data arrives from the writing site, the reader is woken with the file unblock message.

write
WS ————————————▶ SS
unblock
SS ————————————▶ RS

The reading site then requests the Data.

read
SS ◀———————————— RS
read-response (with Data)
SS ————————————▶ RS

If the writing site gets too far ahead of the reader, the write token is recalled (the SS serves as the token manager site for a pipe).

reltok
WS ◀———————————— SS
tokrlsd
WS ————————————▶ SS

The write token will not be granted to any site until the reader consumes enough of the Data in the pipe.

Fig. 14.35 Network messages for pipes {adapted from Popek and Walker.(1985)}.

Writing sites   Reading sites

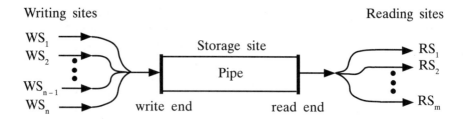

Fig. 14.36 Multiple processes sharing write and read ends of a pipe.

It is important to notice that the LOCUS system allows multiple processes to share the read of a pipe and multiple processes to share the write end of a pipe. This feature is illustrated in Fig. 14.36.

Data written with a single **write** system call are atomic. This means that this data will not be split across separate reads unless the reader requested less data than the writer had written. The sites that play the role of WS or RS may change dynamically while the pipe is open. There are two main reasons for this. First, because there are two or more processes sharing the same end of a pipe. Second, processes can dynamically move from site to site.

14.7.10 Process naming

Processes in LOCUS can run at any site of a network, subject to permission. The site for running a process can be selected either statically, before the process is invoked, or dynamically, when a process is running. The latter choice means that processes in LOCUS can migrate from one site to another, if these sites have the same processor types. Migration is transparent. No load module relinking or any other action is required. This transparency enables remote execution of processes and dynamic load balancing.

Four basic issues must be addressed to achieve such transparency: process naming, performing remote operations on processes, copying or moving processes across the network, and mechanisms for keeping track of which processes exist and where they are located. We will start with process naming.

Section 14.7.3 addressed the naming of files. A different approach is used in LOCUS to name processes. The local process name is extended by some unique identifier to distinguish between different sites. This allows processes to be unambiguously addressed in cross-network references, and ensures that multiple processes are not created with the same process identifier (PID). This LOCUS process naming approach allows each site of the network to autonomously assign names to the processes which originate at that site. The contents of a network process name are shown in Fig. 14.37.

Network process identifier

Site identifier	Local process identifier

Fig. 14.37 Contents of a network process name.

Fig. 14.37 indicates that network-wide process names are made up by combining a UNIX-like local PID with a unique site identifier (SID) to form a network PID. Note that in LOCUS processes can migrate. Thus, the content of the network name does not necessarily indicate the current site of execution. As in UNIX, LOCUS provides for process groups. These are groups of processes which share a common name, the PGRP. Process group names in LOCUS are unique. Uniqueness is also achieved because the groups contain processes originating on the same site, that is, processes containing the same SID.

14.7.11 Remote operations on processes

Remote processes in LOCUS are supported by a facility to create a process on any remote computer, initialize it appropriately, and run it. Remote execution of a process is performed remotely as easily as locally.

Two UNIX system calls, **fork** and **exec**, have been extended and are in use in LOCUS. **fork** causes a new process to be created locally or remotely. The new process runs the same program with the same data as the caller. The UNIX **exec** call, which installs a load module into a process and starts execution, has been extended to allow a process to migrate to another site. The **run** and **migrate** calls have been added. Logically, **run** achieves the effect of the combination of **fork** and **exec**. Thus, it creates a new process and invokes a new program in it immediately. **run** can be used to initiate execution locally or remotely. **migrate** allows a process to change its site of execution while in the midst of execution.

Note that **fork** and **migrate** both copy all of the information about the process. The new process on the destination site executes the same program using the same data. Thus, they can be done only between matching processor types. On the other hand, **exec** and **run** need only copy the process and data structures, so source and destination processors can differ.

It is also possible to have another classification of these four system calls. Table 14.1 sets out remote process system calls.

The decision as to where the new process is to execute is based on information associated with the calling process. It can be set dynamically by a **setxsites** call. This function sets up a list of sites which is used by **fork**, **exec**, **run** and **migrate** to select the execution site. Shell commands to control the execution site are also available.

	old image	new image
move old process to the destination site (the process on the source site is destroyed)	**migrate**	**exec**
create new process (child) on the destination site (the old process continue executing on the source site)	**fork**	**run**

Table 14.1

The decision regarding the site at which a process is to run is influenced by the following factors:

(1) the user may wish to exercise control, either advisory or absolute, over the site, or set of sites, from which the execution choice can be made;

(2) there may be physical constraints on where execution is possible; and

(3) some constraints may be added to assist with administrative control.

14.7.12 Basic aspects of interprocess communication

Since processes are allowed to move, other processes need to know the current location of these migrating processes. A process wanting to send a message to another process knows only its PID. If a destination process is local, it is necessary to search the process table. What if the destination process is remote?

The designers rejected the possibility of using broadcast, with all receivers of a broadcasted message searching locally owned process tables, because of migration – a migrating destination process may receive a message twice or may not receive a message at all.

This problem is solved in LOCUS by using a synchronization site for each process. In Section 14.7.10 we saw that to assure unique network names for processes, the site identifier (SID) is attached to each local PID. The SID specifies the site at which the process was created. Such a

SID, denoted the OSITE (origin site) is used as the synchronization site of the process. If the OSITE is not on the network, then a surrogate origin site is used.

Using this concept, the mechanism for sending a message to a process is as follows. If the destination process is not local, a message is sent to the origin site. If the process is there, the message is delivered to it. The returned value for the message is sent back to the sender. If the process is not at the origin site, then a message containing the current location of the process is sent to the sender. This operation is possible because each site has a list of remote-processes that originated there; with each process entry is associated the current location of this process. Next, the message is transferred to the specified site.

PGRPs, like PIDs, contain a site identifier. Thus, it is possible to track the processes in the group by using a group origin site (GOSITE) as the synchronization site. Note, that the same site which serves as a surrogate OSITE also serves as a surrogate GOSITE. Since each site has a list of PGRPs which originated there and the current locations of these processes, the mechanism for sending a message to all members of a group is nearly identical to the one used for tracking a single process.

It is obvious that the above mechanism requires maintaining a list of remote processes (or PGRPs) along with their current locations. These lists must be updated whenever a process either changes its location (as a result of issuing a **fork**, **exec**, **run**, or **migrate**), that is, a process migrates, or the network is reconfigured.

14.7.13 Accessing remote devices

In LOCUS, devices, like other resources, are accessible remotely in a transparent manner. Since devices are treated as files, their names appear in the single, global naming hierarchy. This means that each device has a globally unique path name.

Transparent remote devices are implemented in two parts. The first is the naming and locating part. It is similar to any other type of entry in the catalog system. It works as follows. First, an inode for the device is found through a pathname search. Second, an internal open is performed. Next, a copy of the inode is placed in memory at the storage site (where the device is located) as well as at the using site (where the request was made).

The second part of remote device operation is the support for the actual operations that are needed. Three types of devices are distinguished:

(1) **buffered block** – device for which the system is responsible, for managing reading and writing of the device in standard sized blocks; operations are performed asynchronously from the caller;

(2) **buffered character** – devices used to transfer characters, e.g., terminals, and

(3) **unbuffered** – device in which data is transferred directly from the process's data image to the device; LOCUS does not support remote unbuffered device access.

14.7.14 Lessons learned

The most interesting lesson learned from this project is that a high performance, network transparent, distributed file system can be designed and implemented, even in a small computer environment. Second, in such a file system, it is very valuable to be able to replicate files in storage. Third, to achieve high performance it is necessary to distinguish between access to local resources and access to remote resources. The code overhead generated by doing so is justified by the increase in performance. And last, balancing the needs of protocol synchronization and failure detection while maintaining good performance presents a considerable challenge.

14.8 Mach

Mach was an attempt to prove that a UNIX kernel could be completely rebuilt to use the concepts developed by the Carnegie–Mellon team under Richard Rashid's leadership, without loss of functionality or of UNIX's trademark – portability. Mach was conceived as an Accent-like operating system adapted to multiprocessors, developed on the basis of a large network of uniprocessor scientific personal computers. Mach was also designed to accommodate successfully the general purpose shared-memory multiprocessors. Such multiprocessors are becoming the successors to traditional general purpose uniprocessor workstations and timesharing systems. It should be noted that work on Mach was sparked also by AI software developed as part of DARPA's Strategic Computing Initiative (SCI).

Mach provides a binary compatible 4.3BSD interface. This is necessary so that Mach would receive wide acceptance in the research and academic communities. Mach also provides a number of new facilities not available in 4.3. Because it handles shared-memory multiprocessor architectures and provides features needed to support the applications and architectures developed as part of the SCI, its design differs from that of Accent. These differences are as follows:

(1) To support multiprocessors, the Accent notion of a process (address space and single program counter) was split into two new concepts:

(a)   a **task**: a basic unit of resource allocation which includes a page address space, protected access to system resources (such as processors, ports, and memory), and

(b)   a **thread**: a basic unit of CPU utilization.

These two give users the ability to execute multiple threads simultaneously within a single task.

(2)   A new virtual memory design. Mach supports large, sparse virtual address-space memory; copy-on-write virtual copy operations, copy-on-write and read/write memory sharing between tasks; memory-mapped files; and user-provided backing store objects and pages.

(3)   To allow finer granularity synchronization than could be achieved with kernel-provided mechanisms, a facility for handling a form of structured sharing of read/write memory between tasks in the same family tree was added.

(4)   The notion of a memory object was generalized to allow general purpose user-state external pager tasks to be built.

(5)   A capability-based interprocess communication facility. The Mach interprocess communication facility was simplified, as a result of using thread mechanisms to handle some forms of asynchrony and error handling (much as was done in the V kernel). The interprocess communication facility is integrated with the virtual memory system and capable of transferring large amounts of data.

(6)   Mach includes a language and compiler for specifying interfaces in a remote procedure call-style between tasks written in C, Pascal, Ada, and Common Lisp.

Note that the basic abstractions of Mach are intended not simply as extensions to normal UNIX facilities but as a new foundation upon which to build further UNIX facilities and develop UNIX-like systems for new architectures. Moreover, it is an attempt to return to the traditional UNIX main features: simplicity, extensibility and abstraction integration.

At the beginning of 1988, Mach ran on over 300 mainframes and workstations in the Department of Computer Science at Carnegie–Mellon, including such multiprocessors and uniprocessors as the VAX 11/780, 784, 785, 8200, 8650, 8800, Micro VAX I and II, IBM RT PC, Encore Multimax, and Sequent Balance 21000. It runs also on the Sun-3 family of workstations: 50, 60, 75, 110, 140, 160, 260, and 280. Work has begun to port it to the Sun-4, Compaq 386 and Apple Macintosh II.

Our presentation of the goals and features of Mach follows its descriptions in Rashid (1986, 1987, 1987a), Jones and Rashid (1986), Accetta *et al.* (1986), Mason (1987), Tevanian (1987), Tevanian and Rashid (1987), Walmer and Thompson (1987), Baron *et al.* (1987), Tevanian *et al.* (1986, 1987), Young *et al.* (1987), Chew and Rashid (1988), Rashid *et al.* (1988), Kirschen (1989) and Black *et al.* (1989).

14.8.1 The Mach architecture

There are two important parts which should be characterized when dealing with the Mach architecture: the Mach computing environment and the kernel.

The Mach computing environment

Mach provides a new foundation for UNIX development that spans networks of uniprocessors and multiprocessors, in particular, large, general purpose multiprocessors, smaller multiprocessor networks, and individual workstations. The Mach computing environment is illustrated in Fig. 14.38.

Mach, as we said earlier, was built as a new foundation upon which UNIX-like facilities can be built and future development of multiprocessor systems for new architectures could continue. Note, however, that in 1987, much of the 4.3 compatibility support for Mach was still implemented using code which executes in kernel-state, that is, in the traditional way. The architects of Mach want to provide a small kernel base upon which UNIX-like environments can be built (for example, Berkeley 4.3. and System V) along with new facilities which may be adapted to new architectures or applications.

An extensible kernel

One of the most important features of Mach is the possibility of a transparent extension of the underlying system to allow user-state processes to provide services which in the past could only be fully integrated into UNIX by adding code to the operating system kernel.

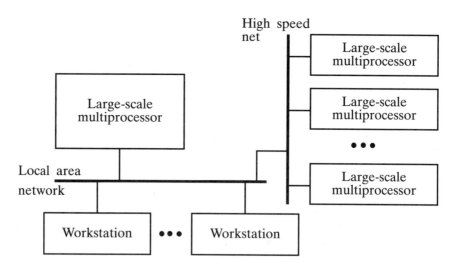

Fig. 14.38   The Mach computing environment {adapted from Accetta *et al.* (1986)}.

Mach extensibility is achieved using an object-oriented approach. Mach provides a small set of primitive functions which have been designed to allow more complex services and resources to be represented as references to objects. Objects can thus be placed in the network without regard to programming details. This results in the Mach kernel abstractions providing a base upon which complete system environments may be built.

Mach is an open system based on a kernel running in each computer, with such services as the file system, network service, and process management outside the kernel. Their relationship is illustrated in Fig. 14.39.

The implementation aspects of basic facilities of the Mach kernel, network- and UNIX-oriented facilities, and the relationship between the Mach kernel and other parts of the Mach distributed operating system are shown in Fig. 14.40.

The Mach kernel treats memory and communication as dual mechanisms. Collections of primitives are defined to provide a programmer with the option of either using shared memory or message communication as the basis for implementing a multithreaded application.

Message based communication can be used to allow one process to provide virtual memory backing storage to another. On the other hand, memory management techniques, for example, copy-on-write memory mapping, can be used to provide efficient implementation of large memory transfers. Note that these primitives are designed in such a way as to allow the implementation of either message passing in terms of memory management or memory sharing in terms of message passing, depending on the kind of multiprocessing or networking environment.

The Mach kernel is responsible for virtual memory management, interprocess communication, multiprocessor scheduling, running low-level

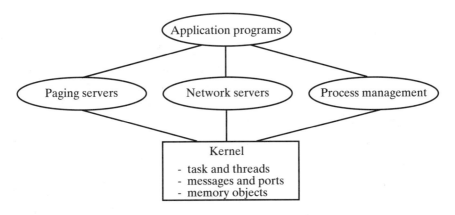

Fig. 14.39 The Mach environment: the kernel and services.

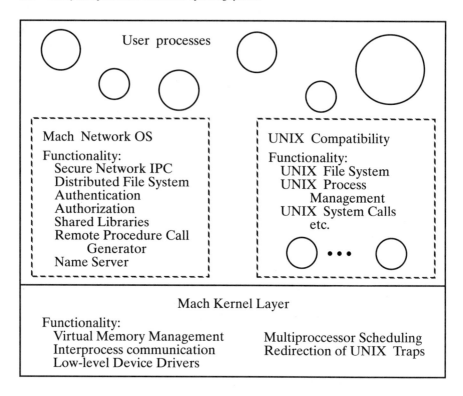

Fig. 14.40 The relationship between the Mach kernel and other parts of the Mach operating system {adapted Accetta *et al.* (1986)}.

device drivers, and redirection of UNIX traps. To carry out these functions, it supports several basic abstractions: task, thread, port, message, and memory object.

14.8.2 Tasks and threads

The UNIX process abstraction does not meet the requirements of modern applications, in particular, shared-memory multiprocessors. To handle shared-memory multiprocessor architecture, the Accent concept of a process was split into two orthogonal abstractions: a task and a thread. Tasks and threads are used in Mach to control program execution.

The basic concepts

A **task** is an execution environment in which threads may run. It is the basic unit of resource allocation. As such, it includes a paged virtual address space and protected access (access rights) to system resources, such as processors, port capabilities and virtual memory. For example, the memory management which controls the resource of memory can be treated as a task. In Mach, a UNIX process is a task with a single thread. Note that tasks perform no computation; they are a framework for running threads. However, tasks are the basic unit of protection.

A **thread** is the basic unit of CPU utilization. It is roughly equivalent to an independent program counter within a task, that is, individual flow of control within a task. As such it has its own private **processor state** (for example, machine registers) and a thread running within a task would then be a process. Threads are the basic unit of scheduling.

The relationship of tasks, threads, and CPUs for multiprocessor systems and distributed systems (networks) are illustrated in Figs. 14.41 and 14.42, respectively, adopted from Mason (1987).

The result of separating the machine state (thread) from the process is that it is possible to have multiple threads per task, with all

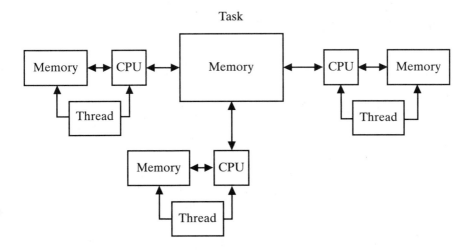

Fig. 14.41 The relationship of tasks, threads and CPUs in a tightly coupled system {adapted from Mason (1987)}.

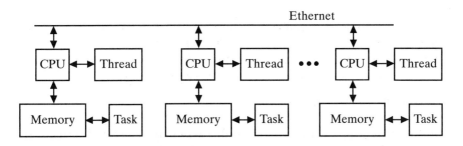

Fig. 14.42 The relationship of tasks, threads and CPUs in a loosely coupled system {adapted from Mason (1987)}.

threads within a task sharing the resources of the task. Moreover, threads can execute in parallel on a multiprocessor. On a uniprocessor, threads execute in pseudo-parallel.

In general, the task is a high-overhead object, much like a process. One can say that a task is a process without the flow of control or register set (hardware state). On the other hand, the thread is the basic unit of computation; it is a lightweight process operating within a task.

Tasks and threads are represented by their ports. When Mach creates a task or a thread, it creates a port, called a task port or thread port respectively. This port is owned by the associated task or thread. Ports provide the mechanism through which Mach lets other tasks and threads manipulate them. Access to a task port indirectly permits access to all threads within that task, but not vice versa. Function requests are directed to the ports. Moreover, each new task is given receive access to two ports: a data port, which may be used by a parent task or by the child task, and a notify port, which may be used by the kernel to send notices of important system events (for example, port destruction).

The Mach kernel can itself be considered a task with multiple threads. The kernel task acts as a server which in turn implements tasks and threads transparently using the communication protocol.

Task and thread states

At any instant, a thread can be in one of three states: running, will-suspend, and suspended.

(1)   A thread that is in **running** state is either executing on some processor, or is eligible for execution on a processor as far as the user is concerned. A thread may be in running state yet blocked for some reason inside the kernel.

(2)   If a thread is in **will-suspend** state, then it can still execute on some processor until a call to **thread_wait** is invoked.

(3)   A thread that is in **suspended** state is not executing on a processor. The thread will not execute on any processor until it returns to **running** state.

A task can also be in **running, will-suspend,** or **suspend** state. It is important to notice that the state of a task affects all threads executing within that task (for example, a thread can be eligible for execution if both it and its task are in the **running** or the **will-suspend** state).

Operations on tasks and threads

Operations on tasks and threads are invoked by sending a message to a port representing the task or a thread. Tasks may be created (effectively forked), destroyed, suspended and resumed. Threads may be created (within a specified task), destroyed, suspended and resumed. Note that when the suspend and resume operations are applied to a task, they affect all threads within that task.

Mach's kernel supported task operations are given in List 14.22.

---

task_create(parent, inherit, child, child_port)
:   creates a new task. If the inherit flag is TRUE the child's address space is created using the parents inheritance values. If the inherit flag is FALSE, the child is created with an empty address space. Access to the child's task and data ports are returned in child and child_port, respectively. The child task initially contains no threads.

task_terminate(task)
:   destroys the specified task, including all port access rights, resources, address space, and threads.

task_suspend(task)
:   places the specified task in will-suspend state. No threads within this task can execute until this task has been resumed.

task_resume(task)
:   places the specified task in running state. Threads within this task that are resumed may then execute.

task_wait(task, wait)
:   places the specified task in suspend state, if it is in will-suspend state; if the wait flag is TRUE then the calling thread will wait for all threads in the task to come to a complete stop.

task_threads(task, list)
:   returns the list of all threads in a task.

task_ports(task, list)
:   returns the list of all ports the specified task has access to.

List 14.22 Task operations supported by the Mach kernel.

Tasks are related to one other in a tree structure by the task creation operation. Regions of memory may be marked as inheritable read-write, copy-on-write or not at all by future child tasks.

Mach's kernel supported thread operations are given in List 14.23.

---

thread_create(task, child, child_data)
> creates a new thread in the specified task. Initially, the new thread is suspended state and its registers contain undefined values.

thread_terminate(thread)
> destroys the specified thread.

thread_suspend(thread)
> places the specified thread in will-suspend state. This indicates to the kernel that the thread is about to become suspended. It becomes suspended after **thread_wait** is invoked.

thread_resume(thread)
> places the specified thread in running state.

thread_wait(thread, wait)
> places the specified thread in suspend state, if it is in will-suspend state; if the wait flag is TRUE and the specified thread will be suspended, then the calling thread will wait (blocked) for the specified thread to come to a complete stop (stop executing).

thread_status(thread, status)
> returns the register state (status) of the specified thread (it consists of necessary processor state, such as processor registers).

thread_mutate(thread, status)
> sets the register state (status) of the specified thread (the status structure is machine dependent as in **thread_status**).

List 14.23   Thread operations supported by the Mach kernel.

Application parallelism in Mach can be achieved in any of the following ways:

(1)   through the creation of a single task with many threads of control executing in a shared address space; shared memory is used for communication and synchronization;

(2)   through the creation of many tasks related by task creation; these tasks share restricted regions of memory; or

(3)   through the creation of many tasks communicating via messages.

User level thread synchronization

The Mach kernel does not enforce a synchronization model. However, it provides basic primitives upon which different models of synchronization may be constructed. One form of synchronization is the Mach interprocess communication facility. On the other hand, if an application desires its own thread-level synchronization, such primitives as **thread_suspend**, **thread_resume** and **thread_wait** can be used.

To perform operations on objects other than messages, it is necessary to send messages to ports which are used to represent the objects. When a task or thread is created, access rights to the port representing the new object are returned. The Mach kernel receives incoming messages on task and thread ports and performs requested operations on the appropriate objects. This allows a thread to suspend a remote thread by sending a suspend message to that thread's **thread port**. Thus, the Mach kernel acts as a server implementing task and thread objects transparently using the communications protocol.

14.8.3 Interprocess communication

Mach's interprocess communication is defined in terms of ports and messages. These two abstractions provide for location independence, security, and data type tagging.

Basic concepts

A **port** is a communication channel, logically a message queue protected by the kernel. A message queue associated with a port has a finite length. Messages may be sent to ports and logically queued there until reception. Ports are the Mach reference objects; ports represent objects. A port may have any number of senders but only one receiver. Access to a port is granted by receiving a message containing a port capability, to either send or receive messages. Note that ports are used like object references are used in object-based systems.

In general, access rights to a port consists of the ability to send to, receive from, or own the port. A task may hold any of these rights or a combination of them. When a new port is created within a task, that task is given all three access rights to that port. A thread within a task may only refer to ports to which that task has been given access.

A task can pass port access rights to another task, using messages. These rights are transferred first from the sending task to the kernel upon message transmission, and then to the receiving task upon message receipt. Passing rights have different semantics depending on the right type. A sender keeps send rights as well as sending them to a receiver. On the other hand, a sender of receive rights and ownership rights loses those rights at the time of the send. A receiver task gets these rights when the receive is issued. In the time period between send and receive, the kernel holds the rights and any message sent to the port is queued awaiting a new task to receive on the port.

Because the message queue associated with a port is of a finite length and may become full, threads are provided with several options for handling problems associated with message transmission to a full queue.

---

msg_send(message, option, timeout)
  sends a message referenced by message from the current task to the destination port specified in the message header. If the destination port is full timeout specifies the maximum wait time. option specifies the failure conditions under which **msg_send** should terminate. The receiving task may use msg_local_port to send a reply to the received message, if the field msg_local_port is not set up to PORT_NULL.

msg_receive(message, option, timeout)
  retrieves the next message from the port specified in the message header, msg_local_port, or the default group of ports. timeout is the maximum time in milliseconds to wait for a message before giving up. option specifies the failure conditions under which **msg_receive** should terminate.

msg_rpc(message, option, rcv_size, send_timeout, receive_timeout)
  sends a message, then receives a reply. Thus, it is a hybrid call which performs a **msg_send** followed by a **msg_receive**, using the same message buffer. message addresses a message buffer which will be used for both **msg_send** and **msg_receive**. msg_remote_port specifies the port to which the message is to be sent, whereas msg_local_port specifies the port on which a message is then to be received. option is a union of the option parameters for the component operations. rcv_size is the maximum size allowed for the received message. send_timeout, receive_timeout are the timeout values to be applied to the component operations.

List 14.24 Primitive message operations.

A **message** is a data object or typed collection of data objects which is used by threads to communicate. Messages may be of any size, but a message header has a fixed size. A header consists of such fields as:

(1)   **msg_size** – the size of a message to be sent, or the maximum size of a message to be received,

(2)   **msg_local_port**, **msg_remote_port** – names of local and remote ports on which a message is to be received or sent, and

(3)   **msg_id** – the meaning of a message to the intended receeipient.

The variable data part of a message may contain data descriptors, pointers and typed capabilities for ports. A single message may transfer up to the entire address space of a task.

Primitive operations
There are two fundamental message operations performed on ports which allow the sending and receiving of messages. They are presented in List 14.24. Note that other than these primitives, all Mach facilities are expressed in terms of remote procedure calls on ports.

At this stage it is worth making two comments relating to transparency and heterogeneity in Mach. First, the indirection provided by message passing allows objects to be arbitrarily placed in the network without regard to programming details. Second, it is possible to run varying system configurations on different classes of computers while providing a consistent interface to all resources.

For efficient communication, Mach's architects designed a set of primitive operations available to manage port rights and control message reception. These primitives are given in List 14.25.

Messages in Mach may be sent and received either synchronously or asynchronously. Note that signals can be used to handle incoming messages outside the flow of control of a normal UNIX-style process. Moreover, a task could create or assign separate threads to handle asynchronous events.

The Mach kernel participates in interprocess communication. However, the Mach kernel itself has no knowledge of a network. From the kernel point of view, messages are always passed between tasks on the same host. Network message servers, as in Accent, are involved in transparent sending of messages between remote tasks, as shown in Fig. 14.43.

Network message servers, besides extending the interprocess communication paradigm to the network, take part in data type conversion and provide secure network transmission. Doing this outside the kernel allows for a flexible choice of data type representation, the amount or type of security to be used on a network, and protocols to use for network transmission.

port_allocate(task, port)

creates a new port, returned in port, for the specified task. The task initially has all three access rights to the port.

port_deallocate(task, port)

relinguishes the target task's, access rights to the specified port. If the task is both the receiver and owner for the port, then the port is destroyed. All tasks with send access are notified of the port's destruction. If the task is the receiver for the port, receive rights are sent to the owner.

port_enable(task, port)

adds this ports to the task's default group of ports for **msg_receive**.

port_disable(task, port)

removes this port from the task's default group of ports for **msg_receive**.

port_messages(task, ports, ports_count)

returns for the specified task an array pointed to by ports which consists of enabled ports on which messages are currently queued (waiting). ports_count is the number of ports returned in the ports array.

port_status(task, port, unrestricted, num_msgs, backlog, receiver, owner)

returns to the task status information about the specified port. num_msgs indicates the number of messages queued on this port. backlog is the number of messages which may be queued to this port without causing the sender to block. receiver and owner are returned true IFF the task has receive rights, and it is the owner to port, respectively.

port_backlog(task, port, backlog)

returns in backlog the number of messages that can be waiting on this port.

List 14.25 Primitive port operations.

In summarizing of interprocess communication in Mach, the following aspects should be emphasized very strongly. The concepts of multiple threads of control within a task and limited sharing between

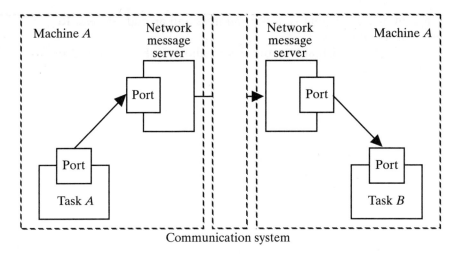

Fig. 14.43 Communication between remote tasks in the Mach system.

tasks allows Mach to provide three levels of synchronization and communication:

(1) **Fine grain communication** – performed on memory shared either within a task or between related tasks. Note that Mach provides a library to support synchronization on shared memory;

(2) **Intra-application interthread communication** – performed using the standard port primitives. However, it can be implemented more efficiently using shared libraries and memory;

(3) **Inter-application interthread communication** – to provide this type of service, the Mach kernel is required to provide protection. Note that as in Accent, rather than using copying, large amounts of data in messages may be mapped copy-on-write from one address to another. Moreover, data forwarded in messages over the network can be transmitted on reference rather than on demand.

14.8.4 Virtual memory management

Mach provides a very interesting virtual memory design and implementation. This design is based on certain basic concepts.

Basic concepts
Every Mach task contains a large, potentially sparse virtual address space within which its threads execute. The sparse virtual address space means that there may be ranges of addresses which are allocated followed by ranges that are not allocated. A task's address space consists of an ordered collection of valid memory regions (virtual memory areas). A region of an address space is that memory associated with a continuous

range of addresses, that is, a start address and an end address. Regions may consist of pages.

The Mach virtual memory design allows tasks to perform the following operations:

(1)   allocate regions of virtual memory,

(2)   deallocate regions of virtual memory,

(3)   set the protections on regions of virtual memory,

(4)   specify the inheritance of regions of virtual memory.

It also allows for both copy-on-write and read/write sharing of memory between tasks. Copy-on-write virtual memory often results in large message transfer or fork operations, while shared memory is created in a controlled fashion via an inheritance mechanism.

Mach allocates virtual memory in blocks referred to as **pages**. The task may allocate memory regions anywhere within the virtual address space defined by the underlying hardware, with the restrictions that region must be aligned on system page boundaries. Note that the system page size is a boot time parameter.

Mach's tasks are able to specify regions of an address space that can be shared by both the parent and the child after a fork operation. Thus a specialized application which wants to improve performance by using shared memory may create a tree of tasks sharing memory.

A task may protect the virtual pages of its address space to allow or prevent access to that memory. Each page has associated with it a protection level and an inheritance level. Memory in Mach is protected on a per-page basis. Each group of pages is associated with two protection values:

(1)   **current protection** – controls actual hardware permissions; in other words, it is used to determine the access rights of an executing thread; and

(2)   **maximum protection** – specifies the largest value the current protection can attain. This protection may never be raised; it may only be lowered. If the maximum protection is lowered below the current protection then the latter is dropped to that level. Thus, in practice, the maximum protection value limits the current protection.

Either protection is a combination of read, write, and execute permissions. Inheritance levels consist of:

(1)   **read/write access** (shared) – in an area of shared memory between the parent and child;

(2)   **copy access** – which copies the region of memory into the child space (copy-on-write can be used for efficiency); and

(3)   **no access** – which means that when no access is allowed, that area is not part of the child address space.

Protection and inheritance is attached to a task's address space, not the physical memory contained in that address space. Note that this protection scheme allows access to a region in shared memory between two or more tasks. The inheritance level sets the access for child tasks, while the protection level controls the access for peer tasks.

Mach's virtual memory is also able to handle page faults and page-out data requests outside the kernel. In order to do this, when virtual memory is created, special paging tasks may be specified to handle paging requests.

Virtual memory implementation

Two basic implementation assumptions were made by the Mach developers. Both are oriented towards separation.

First, Mach's virtual memory implementation should separate

(1)   the machine-dependent portion (contains data structures and algorithms) which has a simple page validate/invalidate/protect interface and has no knowledge of other data structures related to machine independence, from

(2)   the machine-independent portion of the implementation which has full knowledge of all information related to virtual memory. This separation is illustrated in Fig. 14.44.

The advantage of this separation is that 'page size' for different sections of the implementation need not be the same.

Second, the kernel data structures responsible for managing physical resources should be cleanly separated from those managing backing store objects. This assumption was dictated by the complexity of potential sharing relationships between tasks. This separation is shown in Fig. 14.45.

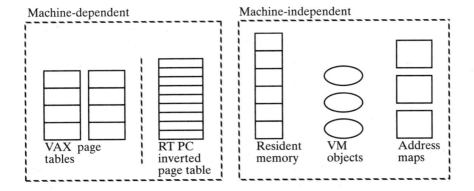

Fig. 14.44 The split between the machine-dependent and machine-independent sections of Mach's virtual memory {adapted from Accetta *et al.* (1986)}.

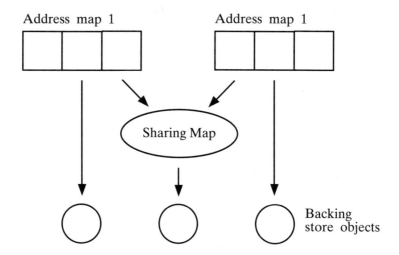

Fig. 14.45 Kernel data structures responsible for management of physical resources must be separated from those that manage backing storage objects
{adapted from Accetta *et al.* (1986)}.

Mach's virtual memory implementation uses the following basic
data structures:

(1)   **address maps** – a doubly linked list of map entries; each entry
describes the properties of a region of virtual memory. There is a
single address map associated with each task.

(2)   **share maps** – a special address map which describes a region of
memory that is shared between tasks. Note that a sharing map
provides a level of indirection from address maps, allowing operations that affect shared memory to affect all maps without back
pointers.

(3)   **VM objects** – a VM object is a unit of backing storage. It specifies
resident pages as well as where to find non-resident pages. These
objects are referenced by address maps. Shadow objects are used
to hold pages that have been copied after a copy-on-write fault.

(4)   **page structures** – specify current attributes for physical pages in
the system.

The virtual memory operations that can be performed on a task are
presented in List 14.26.

Mach's interprocess communication and virtual memory
We mentioned earlier that in Mach interprocess communication and
virtual memory are very closely associated. This association is identical
to the one used in the Accent distributed operating system. Because of
this we will not discuss these aspects further. A message interaction, and

vm_allocate(task, address, size, anywhere)

allocates a region of virtual memory and places it in the specified task's address space. The arguments of this operation are as follows: task specifies the task whose virtual memory is to be affected. address is a starting address; if anywhere option is FALSE, an allocation attempt is made at this virtual address, but if there is not enough space at this address no memory will be allocated; if anywhere option is TRUE, an allocation attempt is made wherever space is available. In either case the address at which memory was allocated is returned in address.

vm_deallocate(task, address, size)

deallocates a region of virtual memory, i.e., relinquishes access to a region of a task's address space and makes it no longer valid. This address range will be available for allocation. task specifies the task whose virtual memory is to be affected. address is a starting address. size is a number of bytes to deallocate.

vm_inherit(task, address, size, inheritance)

specifies how a region of a task's address space is to be passed to child tasks at the time of task creation. task specifies the task whose virtual memory is to be affected. address is a starting address. size is the number of bytes of the region for which inheritance is to change. inheritance specifies how the specified memory is to be inherited in child tasks; there are the following options: VM_INHERIT_SHARE – children will share this memory with the parent; VM_INHERIT_COPY – children will receive a copy of this region; VM_INHERIT_NONE – the region will be absent from child tasks.

vm_protect(task, address, size, set_max, protection)

sets the protection of some pages of allocated memory in a task's address space, where protection is a new protection value for the region: VM_PROT_READ, VM_PROT_WRITE, VM_PROT_EXECUTE. If set_max is set the protection change applies to the maximum protection associated with the address range. Otherwise, the current protection on this range is changed.

vm_read(task, address, size, data, data_count)

allows one task's virtual memory to be read by another task. task specifies the task whose virtual memory is to be read. address is the first address to be read. size is the number of bytes to be read. data is the array of data copied from the given task. data_count is the size of the data array in bytes.

vm_write(task, address, data, data_count)
allows one task's virtual memory to be written by another task. task specifies the task whose virtual memory is to be written. address is the first address to be affected. data is the array of data to be written. data_count is the size of the data array.

vm_copy(task, src_addr, count, dst_addr)
causes the source memory range to be copied to the destination address. task specifies the task whose virtual memory is to be affected. src_addr is the start address of the source range. count is the number of bytes to copy. dst_addr is the start of the destination range in task.

vm_regions(task, address, size, elements, elements_count)
returns a description of the specified region of the task's virtual address space.

vm_statistics(task, vm_stats)
returns statistics about the specified task's use of virtual memory.

List 14.26   Virtual memory operations.

the sending of large messages using memory mapping operations, typical for Mach's communication, can be studied using relevant figures and the description presented in Section 14.8.3.

14.8.5   External memory management

Recall that in Accent secondary storage was based around a kernel-supplied file system. The Mach operating system does not follow this model. It treats secondary storage objects in the same way as other server-provided resources accessible through message passing. This treatment of external memory management allows the advantages of a single level storage to be made available to ordinary user-state servers.

Basic concepts

The interface of external memory management in Mach is based on the abstraction of a Mach memory object. A **memory object** is an abstract object which represents a collection of data on which several operations are defined (for example, read, write). Unlike other Mach objects, the memory object is not provided solely by the Mach kernel, but is provided and managed (created and serviced) by a server, that is, user-level data manager task. Mach's kernel does not make any assumptions about the purpose of the memory object. Each memory object is represented, like other Mach abstract objects, by a port.

Memory object data must be available to tasks in the form of physical memory. To achieve this, the Mach kernel acts as a cache manager for the contents of the memory object. Note that the Mach external memory management interface has been expressed in terms of paging, that is, in terms of kernel activity. This has been done for historical reasons (Young *et al.* 1987). The result is that the term **paging object** is often used to refer to a memory object. Moreover, to describe the data manager task implementing a memory object, the term **pager** is used.

Some implementation aspects

The interface between pagers (data manager tasks) and Mach's kernel can be described in terms of calls made by the three involved parties, that is, an application program, the kernel, and the data manager. These calls, as in other Mach interfaces, are implemented using interprocess communication. In each call, the first argument is the port to which the request is sent. Thus, it represents the object to be affected. The interface consists of three parts.

The first part is represented by calls made by an application program to cause a memory object to be mapped into its address space. These calls are those given in List 14.26 extended by a call presented in List 14.27.

---

vm_allocate_with_pager(task, address, size, anywhere, memory_object, offset)

> allocates (maps) a region of memory specified by address of the application task to the specified offset in the memory_object. The memory object is specified by its port.

List 14.27   Application to kernel interface call.

The second part is represented by calls made by the kernel on the data manager. These calls are presented in List 14.28.

These remote procedure calls are asynchronous. Moreover, the Mach kernel does not wait for acknowledgements.

The third part is represented by calls made by the data manager on Mach's kernel. Their goal is to control the kernel's memory object. These calls are summarized in List 14.29.

pager_init(memory_object, pager_request_port, pager_name)
> initializes a memory object, that is, this call is issued when a memory object is to be mapped for the first time. In this message, pager_request_port is used by the data manager to make cache management requests of the Mach kernel, and pager_name port is used by the kernel to identify this memory object to other tasks.

pager_data_request(memory_object, pager_request_port, offset, length, desired_ access)
> issued in order to process a cache miss (that is, page fault). It requests data from an external data manager. The kernel specifies the range desired and the pager request port to which the data should be returned.

pager_data_write(memory_object, offset, data, data_ count)
> writes a data block to a memory object. This message is issued by the kernel to clean up dirty pages, by specifying the location in the memory object, offset, and including the data to be written.

pager_data_unlock(memory_object, pager_request_port, offset, length, desired_access)
> requests that data be unlocked.

pager_create(old_memory_object, new_memory_object, new_request_ port, new_ name)
> accepts responsibility for a kernel-created memory object.

List 14.28   Kernel to data manager interface calls.

Using memory objects

In Young *et al.* (1987) the utilization of memory objects, in particular two sample data managers and their applications, are presented. The first is a file system with a read/copy-on-write interface. This system uses the minimal subset of the memory management interface. The second is an excerpt from the operation of a consistent network shared memory service.

In this section, we briefly present the second example. This example shows how the memory management interface might be used to implement a region of shared memory between two clients running on different computers. To grasp the basic concepts of this implementa-

pager_data_provided(pager_request_port, offset, data, data_count, lock_value)

    supplies the kernel with the data contents of a region of a memory object. The data manager specifies in this message the location of the data within the memory object, and includes the memory object data. It is usually made in response to **pager_data_request**.

pager_data_lock(pager_request_port, offset, length, lock_value)

    restricts cache access to the specified data. The types of access are specified – can be any combination of read, write, or execute.

pager_flush_request(pager_request_port, offset, length)

    forces cache data to be invalidated.

pager_clean_request(pager_request_port, offset, length)

    forces cached data to be written back to the memory object.

pager_cache(pager_request_port, may_cache_object)

    tells the kernel whether it may retain cached data from the memory object even after all references to it have been removed.

pager_data_unavailable(pager_request_port, offset, size)

    notifies the kernel that no data exists for that region of a memory object.

List 14.29   Data manager to kernel interface calls.

tion it is enough to analyse the message traffic and operations performed by both clients, the kernels of their computers, and a shared memory server.

Sharing a region of memory between two clients running on different computers is performed in three stages:

(1)   clients map the object, call it X, into their address spaces (Fig. 14.46),

(2)   clients read the same 'shared memory' data page (Fig. 14.47), and

(3)   one client writes a page being read on another computer (Fig. 14.48).

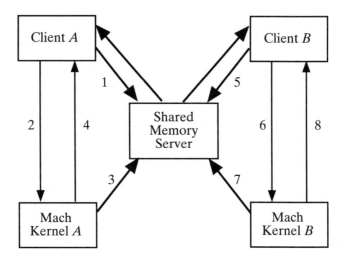

Fig. 14.46   Initialization: Clients map object X into their address spaces {adapted from Young *et al.* (1987)}.

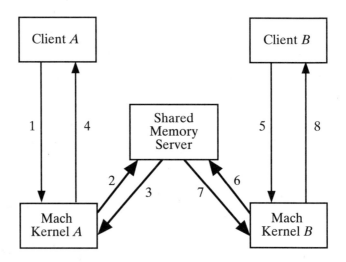

Fig. 14.47   Clients read the same 'shared memory' data page {adapted from Young *et al.* (1987)}.

In the first, initialization stage, the following calls are issued and operations performed:

1   Client A calls Server to acquire memory object X;

2   Client A calls **vm_allocate_with_pager** to map object X into its address space;

3   Kernel A calls **pager_init**(X, request_A, name_A);

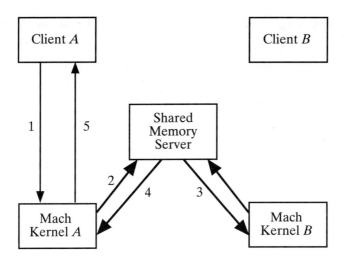

Fig. 14.48 One client writes a page being read on another host {adapted from Young *et al.* (1987)}.

4   Client *A* is resumed;

5   Client *B* calls Server to acquire memory object *X*;

6   Client *B* calls **vm_allocate_with_pager** to map object *X* into its address space;

7   Kernel *B* calls **pager_init**(X, request_B, name_B);

8   Client *B* is resumed.

In the second stage, the following calls are issued and operations performed:

1   Client *A* read faults;

2   Kernel *A* calls **pager_data_request**(X, request_A, offset, page_size, VM_PROT_READ);

3   Server calls **pager_data_provided**(request_A, offset, data, page_size, VM_PROT_WRITE);

4   Client *A* is resumed;

5   Client *B* read faults;

6   Kernel *B* calls **pager_data_request**(X, request_B, offset, page_size, VM_PROT_READ);

7   Server calls **pager_data_provided**(request_B, offset, data, page_size, VM_PROT_WRITE);

8   Client *B* is resumed.

In the third stage, the following calls are issued and operations performed:

1 Client *A* write faults on data being read by *B*;

2 Kernel *A* calls **pager_data_unlock**(X, request_A, offset, page_size, VM_PROT_READ);

3 Server calls **pager_flush_request**(request_B, offset, data, page_size);

4 Server calls **pager_data_lock**(request_A, offset, data, page_size, VM_PROT_NONE);

5 Client *A* is resumed.

14.8.6 Applications

Three applications available in Mach benefit from Mach's primitives: task migration, which relies on network copy-on-reference of process data; transparent remote filesystem; and transaction and database management facilities.

Task migration

As was emphasized in Chapter 8, the real problem of process migration is handling large address spaces. Migration in this case can be performed efficiently using the copy-on-reference technique.

Using Mach's abstraction, task migration can be described in the following way. Each task is associated with a region of its address space. To carry out task migration two fundamental operations must be performed. First, the task migration service creates a memory object to represent a region of the original task's address space. Second, it maps that region into the new task's address space on the remote computer. Note that the kernel which manages the remote computer treats page faults on the newly-migrated task by making paging requests on that memory object. This is done as for other tasks.

Faulting overhead can be reduced by providing the migration manager with some data in advance for tasks with predictable access patterns. Prepaging can proceed while the newly-migrated task begins to run. Another feature of Mach is that since the external memory management is general, there is a wide variety of migration strategies.

Transparent remote filesystem

The remote filesystem available in Mach was originally available in 1982. It was part of CMU's locally maintained version of 4.1.UNIX. Originally, its functions were restricted. At present, its functionality is extended and it supports such UNIX functions as remote current directories and execution of remote files.

The Mach remote filesystem is transparent to the user. However, the system was developed in such a way that the user can receive either 'anonymous' access to the remote filesystem or can effectively log in to it and receive all the normal user privileges. There are two important constructs in Mach's transparent remote filesystem. First, redirection of remote file operations to remote servers is provided transparently by a small number of kernel hooks. Second, links to remote filesystems are created using a special file type. Using these special links allows a machine to connect to an arbitrary number of other machines without the need for mounting all possible remote file systems. As a result, there is no fear of the mount table overflowing.

Database management

A transaction processing system which has been implemented on Mach is called Camelot (Spector [1987], and Eppinger and Spector [1989]). Camelot provides support for distributed transactions on user-defined objects. In this system, servers maintain permanent objects in virtual memory backed by the Camelot disk manager. To implement distributed, permanent, atomic transactions, Camelot uses the write-ahead logging technique. Thus, when the disk manager receives a **pager_flush_request** from the kernel, it verifies that the proper log records have been written before writing the specified pages to disk.

In Mach, the ability to manage memory objects is used efficiently in transaction systems:

(1) Camelot clients can access data easily and quickly by mapping memory objects into their virtual address spaces;

(2) Camelot clients do not have to implement their own page replacement algorithm.

(3) Clients need not reserve fixed size physical memory buffers. Moreover, the amount of physical memory devoted to each client varies dynamically with overall system load.

(4) Recoverable data can be written directly to permanent backing storage without first being written to temporary paging storage.

14.8.7 Matchmaker

Matchmaker was originally developed in the Accent project and is now available with the Mach operating system. Matchmaker is an interface specification language and compiler used in the Mach environment. It provides language support for distributed, object-oriented programming, and in particular:

(1) support for multiple, existing programming languages,

(2) language support for object reference,

(3) language interfaces for object operations,

(4)   language and machine independent operation interface specifications, and

(5)   automated interface code generation from interface specifications.

Matchmaker also possesses additional features. It allows interfaces between cooperating computing entities to be specified and maintained independent of specific languages or machine architectures. Note that its code provides communication, runtime support for type-checking, type conversion, synchronization and exception handling.

Matchmaker is built on top of objects represented by ports and operations invoked by remote procedure call messages. However, these are hidden by Matchmaker from the programmer, allowing services to be defined by a procedural interface.

14.8.8 Lessons learned

The most important lesson learned from this project is that there are many similarities between a distributed operating system and an operating system for a multiprocessor. It seems to us that this system can be treated as a basic example for future work towards the development of operating systems for multiprocessors. Important features of Mach are:

(1)   The task and thread configuration allows Mach to work with a variety of individual architectures, such as tightly coupled multiprocessor machines (for example, such multiprocessors as VAXes and the Encore Multima).

(2)   Mach works well with machines using many closely linked tasks (for example, the BBN Butterfly and the IBM RP3).

(3)   Mach also works with distinct nodes on a network, where there are many nonrelated tasks running on separate CPUs and using network communication (for example, with Sun or MicroVax workstations).

14.9 Summary

In a distributed operating system one can distinguish such fundamental components as a kernel, process, memory, resource, and file management facilities. The following design and research issues must be dealt with to develop these components: interprocess communication; synchronization; process management mechanisms including process migration; resource allocation, particularly, load sharing and/or balancing; deadlock detection and resolution; mechanisms for resource protection; communication security; and authentication.

Distributed operating systems can be developed on the basis of one of the following models: the process model, its submodel the UNIX-like model, and the object model. The major difference between these models is in mechanisms by which the notions of functional entity and synchronization are implemented. Note that at the level of policy these models are equivalent. However, systems based on these models are different at the level of mechanisms.

The most interesting distributed operating systems from the research and application point of view are Accent, V, and Charlotte, representing process model-based systems; Amoeba and Eden, representing object-based systems; and LOCUS and Mach, representing UNIX-like systems.

Our survey of these distributed operating systems shows that though all of them are experimental in nature and oriented towards research, they are very different and not comparable. Each was developed to solve some specific problems in the design of distributed operating systems, but the quality of these solutions cannot be assessed on the basis of common performance indices. Moreover, very little effort was devoted to carrying out performance studies of different problems; comparison is very difficult. The architects of these systems stated different design goals and attacked different problems.

The question arises whether any of these systems can be treated as the basis for standardization? Mach is probably the strongest competitor, as it is strongly supported by the U.S. Department of Defence. However, the result is difficult to predict.

In summary, we can conclude that the research and development of distributed operating systems is still at an early stage.

Bibliography

Accetta M., Baron R., Golub D., Rashid R., Tevanian A. and Young M. (1986). *Mach: A New Kernel Foundation for UNIX Development.* Mach/Camelot, Computer Science Department, Carnegie–Mellon University

Almes G.T., Black A.P., Lazowska E.D. and Noe J.D. (1985). The Eden System: A Technical Review. *IEEE Transactions on Software Engineering,* **SE–11**, 43–59

Almes G.T. and Holman C.L. (1987). Edmas: An Object-Oriented, Locally Distributed Mail System. *IEEE Transactions on Software Engineering,* **SE–13**(9), 1001–9

Artsy Y. and Finkel R. (1989). Designing a Process Migration Facility. The Charlotte Experience. *Computer,* 47–56

Artsy Y., Chang H.-Y. and Finkel R. (1984). *Charlotte: Design and Implementation of a Distributed Kernel.* Technical Report #554, Computer Science Department, University of Wisconsin–Madison

Artsy Y., Chang H.-Y. and Finkel R. (1986). *Processes Migrate in Charlotte.* Technical Report #655, Computer Science Department, University of Wisconsin–Madison

Artsy Y., Chang H.-Y. and Finkel R. (1987). Interprocess Communication in Charlotte. *IEEE Software,* 22–8

Baron R., Black D., Bolosky W., Chew J., Golub D., Rashid R., Tevanian A. and Young M. (1987). *Mach Kernel Interface Manual,* Computer Science Department, Carnegie–Mellon University

Berglund E.J. (1986). An Introduction to the V-System. *IEEE Micro,* 35–52

Black A.P. (1985). Supporting Distributed Applications: Experience with Eden. *Proceedings of the Tenth ACM Symposium on Operating Systems Principles,* Orcas Island, Washington

Black D.L., Rashid R.F., Golub D.B., Hill C.R. and Baron R.V. (1989). Translation Lookaside Buffer Consistency: A Software Approach. *Proceedings of the Third International Conference on Architectural Support for Programming Languages and Operating Systems,* Boston, Massachusetts, 113–22

Cheriton D.R. (1982). *The Thoth System: Multi-Process Structuring and Portability.* New York: American Elsevier

Cheriton D.R. (1984). The V Kernel: A Software Base for Distributed Systems. *IEEE Software,* 19–42

Cheriton D.R. (1986). Request-response and multicast interprocess communication in the V kernel networking in open systems. *Lecture Notes in Computer Science No. 248,* pp. 296–312. New York: Springer-Verlag

Cheriton D.R. (1988). The V Distributed System. *Communications of the ACM,* **31**(3), 314–33

Cheriton D.R. and Deering S.E. (1985). Host Groups: A Multicast Extension for Datagram Internetworks. *9th Data Communication Symposium,* IEEE Computer Society and ACM SIGCOMM

Cheriton D.R. and Lantz K.A. (1986). *V-System 6.0 Reference Manual,* Stanford University, Departments of Computer Science and Electrical Engineering

Cheriton D.R. and Mann T.P. (1986). *A Decentralized Naming Facility.* Technical Report STAN–CS–86–1098, Stanford University, Department of Computer Science

Cheriton D.R. and Mann T.P. (1989). Decentralizing a Global Naming Service for Improved Performance and Fault Tolerance. *ACM Transactions on Computer Systems,* **7**(2), 147–83

Cheriton D.R. and Williamson C.L. (1987). *Network Measurements of the VMTP Request-Response Protocol in the V Distributed System.* Report No. STAN–CS–87–1145, Stanford University, Department of Computer Science.

Cheriton D.R. and Zwaenepoel W. (1983). The Distributed V Kernel and its Performance for Diskless Workstations. *Proceedings of the Ninth ACM Symposium on Operating Systems Principles,* Bretton Woods, New Hampshire, 129–40

Cheriton D. R. and Zwaenepoel W. (1985). Distributed Process Groups in the V Kernel. *ACM Transactions on Computer Systems,* **3**(3)

Cheriton D.R., Malcolm M.A., Melen L.S. and Sager G.R. (1979). Thoth, a Portable Real-Time Operating System. *Communications of the ACM,* **22**(2), 105–15

Chew J.J. and Rashid R.F. (1988). Mach — A Multiprocessor Oriented Operating System and Environment. *README,* **3**(2), 10–1

Eppinger J.L. and Spector A.Z. (1989). A Camelot Perspective. *UNIX Review,* **7**(1), 58–67

Finkel R. and Artsy Y. (1989). The Process Migration Mechanism in Charlotte. *Operating Systems Technical Committee Newsletter,* **3**(1), 11–4

Finkel R., Solomon M., DeWitt D. and Landweber L. (1983). *The Charlotte Distributed Operating System.* Computer Science Technical Report #502, Computer Science Department, University of Wisconsin–Madison

Finkel R. *et al.* (1986). *The Charlotte Distributed Operating System.* Computer Science Technical Report #653, University of Wisconsin–Madison, Computer Science Department

Finkel R., Scott M.L., Kalsow W.K., Artsy Y. and Chang H.-Y. (1989). Experience with Charlotte: Simplicity and Function in a Distributed Operating System. *IEEE Transactions on Software Engineering,* **SE–15**(6), 676–85

Fitzgerald R. and Rashid R.F. (1986). The Integration of Virtual Memory Mangement and Interprocess Communication in Accent. *ACM Transactions on Computer Systems,* **4**(2)

Jessop W.H., Jacobson D.M., Noe J.D., Baer J.-L. and Pu C. (1982). The Eden Transaction Based System. *Proceeding of the 2nd Symposium on Reliability in Distributed Software and Database Systems,* 163–69

Jones M.B. and Rashid R.F. (1986). Mach and Matchmaker: Kernel and Language Support for Object–Oriented Distributed Systems. In *OOPSA'86 Proceedings,* Portland, Oregon, 67–77

Kirschen D. (1989). An Overview of the Mach Operating System. *Operating Systems Technical Committee Newsletter,* **3**(2), 57

Lazowska E.D., Levy H.M., Almes G.T., Fisher M.J., Fowler R.J. and Vestal S.C. (1981). The Architecture of the Eden System. *Proceedings of the Eighth Symposium on Operating Systems Principles,* Pacific Grove, California, 148–59

Mason W.A. (1987). Distributed Processing: The State of the Art. *Byte,* 291–7

Mullender S.J. and Tanenbaum A.S. (1984). Protection and resource control in distributed operating systems. *Computer Networks,* **8**, 421–32

Mullender S.J. and Tanenbaum A.S. (1985). A Distributed File Service Based on Optimistic Concurrency Control. *Proceedings of the 10th Symposium on Operating Systems Principles,* Orcas Island, Washington, 51–62

Mullender S.J. and Tanenbaum A.S. (1986). The Design of a Capability-Based Distributed Operating System. *The Computer Journal,* **29**(4), 289–300

Mullender S.J. and van Renesse R. (1985). Accommodating Heterogeneity in the Amoeba Distributed System. *Proceedings of the SOSP Heterogen-eity Workshop,* Orcas Island, Washington

Mullender S.J. (1987). *Process Management in a Distributed Operating System.* Report CS–R8713, Centrum voor Wiskunde en Informatica, Amsterdam

Popek G. *et al.* (1981). LOCUS: A Network Transparent, High Reliability Distributed System. *Proceedings of the Eighth Symposium on Operating Systems Principles,* Pacific Grove, California, 169–77

Popek G. and Walker B.J. (1985). *The LOCUS Distributed System Architecture,* Cambridge, Mass: The MIT Press

Pu C., Noe J. and Proudfoot A. (1986). Regeneration of Replicated Objects: A Technique and its Eden Implementation. *Proceedings of the 2nd International Conference on Data Engineering,* Los Angeles, California, 175–87

Rashid R.F. (1981). *An Inter-Process Communication Facility for UNIX, Local Networks for Computer Communications*, Springer-Verlag, 319–54

Rashid R.F. (1986). Experiences with the Accent Network Operating System. In *Networking in Open Systems,* (Miller G. and Blanc R.P., eds), *Lecture Notes in Computer Science,* (248), 259–69

Rashid R.F. (1986). Threads of a New System. *UNIX Review,* 37–49

Rashid R.F. (1987). *From RIG to Accent to Mach: The Evolution of a Network Operating System,* Mach/Camelot, Computer Science Department, Carnegie–Mellon University

Rashid R.F. (1987). Mach: A New Foundation for Multiprocessor Systems Development. *COMPCON'87 — Disgest of Papers,* pp. 192–193

Rashid R.F. and Robertson G.G. (1981). Accent: A Communication Oriented Network Operating System Kernel. *Proceedings of the Eighth Symposium on Operating Systems Principles,* Pacific Grove, California, 64–75

Rashid R.F. *et al.* (1988), Machine-Independent Virtual Memory Management for Paged Uniprocessor and Multiprocessor Architectures. *IEEE Transactions on Computers,* **C–37**(8), 896–908

Sheltzer A.B. and Popek G.J. (1986). Internet Locus: Extending Transparency to an Internet Environment. *IEEE Transactions on Software Engineering,* **SE–12**(11), 1067–75

Shizgal I. (1987). *An Amoeba Replicated Service Organization.* Centrum voor Wiskunde en Informatica, Amsterdam, Report CS–R8723

Solomon M.H. and Finkel R.A. (1979). The Roscoe Distributed Operating System. *Proceedings of the Seventh Symposium on Operating Systems Principles,* Pacific Grove, California, 108–114

Spector A.Z. (1987). *Distributed Transaction Processing and the Camelot System, Distributed Operating Systems: Theory and Practice,* Springer-Verlag

Tanenbaum A.S. and Mullender S.J. (1984). The Design of a Capability-Based Distributed Operating System. Rapport Nr. IR–88, *Subfaculteit Wiskunde en Informatica,* Vrije Universiteit Amsterdam

Tanenbaum A.S. and van Renesse R. (1985). Distributed Operating Systems. *Computing Surveys,* **17**(4)

Tanenbaum A.S. and van Renesse R. (1987). Reliability Issues in Distributed Operating Systems. *Proceedings of the 6th Symposium on Reliability of Distributed Software and Database Systems,* Williamson, Virginia, 3–11

Tanenbaum A.S. Mullender S.J. and van Renesse R. (1986). Using Sparse Capabilities in a Distributed Operating System. *Proceedings of the 6th International Conference in Distributed Computing Systems,* 558–63

Tevanian A. (1987). *Architecture-Independent Virtual Memory Management for Parallel and Distributed Environments: The Mach Approach,* CMU–CS–88–106, Carnegie–Mellon University, Department of Computer Science

Tevanian A. and Rashid R. (1987). *Mach: A Basis for Future UNIX Development,* Carnegie–Mellon University, Department of Computer Science

Tevanian A., Rashid R.F., Golub D., Black D., Cooper E. and Young M. (1986). *Mach Threads and the UNIX Kernel: The Battle for Control,* Carnegie–Mellon University, Department of Computer Science

Tevanian A., Rashid R.F., Young M., Golub D., Thompson M.R., Bolosky W. and Sanzi R. (1987). *A UNIX Interface for Shared Memory and Memory Mapped Files Under UNIX,* Carnegie–Mellon University, Department of Computer Science

Theimer M.M., Lantz K.A. and Cheriton D.R. (1985). Pre-emptable Remote Execution Facilities for the V-System. *Proceedings of the Tenth ACM Symposium on Operating Systems Principles,* Orcas Island, Washington, *Operating Systems Review,* **19**(5), 2–12

van Renesse R., van Staveren H. and Tanenbaum A.S. (1988). Performance of the World's Fastest Distributed Operating System. *Operating Systems Review,* **22**(4), 25–34

van Renesse R., van Staveren H. and Tanenbaum A.S. (1989). The Performance of the Amoeba Distributed Operating System. *Software — Practice and Experience,* **19**(3), 223–34

Walker B., Popek G., English R., Kline C. and Thiel G. (1983). The LOCUS Distributed Operating System. *Proceedings of the Ninth ACM Symposium on Operating Systems Principles,* Bretton Woods, New Hampshire, 49–70

Walmer L.R. and Thampson M.R. (1987). *A Mach Tutorial,* Carnegie–Mellon University, Department of Computer Science

Weinstein M.J., Page T.W. Jr., Livezey B.K., and Popek G.J. (1985). Transactions and Synchronization in a Distributed Operating System. *Proceedings of the Tenth ACM Symposium on Operating Systems Principles,* Orcas Island, Washington, *Operating Systems Review,* **19**(5), 115–26

Welch B.B. (1986). *The Sprite Remote Procedure Call System.* Report No. UCB/CSD 86/302, University of California, Computer Science Division (EECS)

Wulf W.A., Levin R. and Harbison S.P. (1981). *HYDRA/C.mmp: An Experimental Computer System,* McGraw-Hill

Young M. *et al.* (1987), Tevanian A., Rashid R., Golub D., Eppinger J., Chew J., Bolosky W., Black D. and Baron R. (1987). *The Duality of Memory and Communication in the Implementation of a Multiprocessor Operating System,* CMU–CS–87–140, Carnegie–Mellon University, Computer Science Department

Index